The Old Christian Right

LEO P. RIBUFFO

The Old Christian Right

THE PROTESTANT FAR RIGHT FROM THE GREAT DEPRESSION TO THE COLD WAR

Temple University Press Philadelphia

Temple University Press

Published 1983
Printed in the United States of America

Library of Congress Cataloging in Publication Data

Ribuffo, Leo P.
The Old Christian Right.

Includes bibliographical references and index.
1. United States—Politics and government—1933–1945.
2. United States—Politics and government—1945–1953.
3. Conservatism—United States—History—20th century.
4. Pelley, William Dudley, 1890–
5. Winrod, Gerald B. (Gerald Burton)
6. Smith, Gerald L. K. (Lyman Kenneth), 1898–
7. Antisemitism—United States—History—20th century.
8. Protestants—United States—Political activity—History—20th century.
9. Protestants—United States—Biography.
I. Title.
E806.R47 1983 973.91 82-19687
ISBN 0-87722-297-5

FOR
MY FATHER AND MOTHER
WHO FIRST TOLD ME ABOUT THE GREAT DEPRESSION

Contents

Acknowledgments

In the course of writing this book, I interviewed far right activists and their aides, lawyers who prosecuted or defended them, jurors who sat in judgment on them, and a senator who warily cooperated with them: Gerald L. K. Smith, Prescott Freese Dennett, Myrtle L. Flowers, O. John Rogge, Joseph W. Burns, James Rowe, Jr., John W. Jackson, Elizabeth R. Young, Leo F. Diegelmann, Frederick A. Raulin, and Burton K. Wheeler. Though generous with their time, hospitality, and anecdotes, most of these men and women hesitated to make available their personal papers (if they had kept them at all). Except for some newspaper clippings, the Gerald L. K. Smith Collection at the University of Michigan was closed to me. The records of the Defenders of the Christian Faith, founded by Gerald B. Winrod in 1925, also remain closed; the founder's son, Rev. Gordon Winrod, never responded to my inquiries. I spoke briefly with William Dudley Pelley's son-in-law, Melford Pearson, but he and other members of the family declined to grant formal interviews, answer questionnaires, or otherwise assist this project. Negotiations with the Justice Department to examine Federal Bureau of Investigation files on Pelley, Winrod, and Smith proved fruitless.

Lacking central caches of material on this book's three central figures, I sought their letters, speeches, and publications in diverse manuscript collections. This search was assisted by funds from the American Council of Learned Societies, National Endowment for the Humanities, and George Washington University Committee on Research. Despite our differences regarding the merits of the free market, the Institute for Humane Studies twice appointed me a summer fellow. Archivists who guided my way are too numerous to list, but Martin Schmitt of the University of Oregon Special Collections and David Crippen of the Ford Archives, Henry Ford Museum deserve special thanks. Candy Hawley of Temple University Press patiently guided the manuscript to publication.

This book has profited beyond measure from criticism by smart friends who read earlier, bulkier drafts: Kenneth Arnold, Justus D. Doenecke, Diana Sylvia Rodriguez, John S. Rosenberg, Robert D. Schulzinger, Michael S. Sherry, Sarah J. Stage, and Daniel J. Singal.

I also gleaned insights and information from Henry D. Abelove, Susanna I. Barrows, Alan Brinkley, Wayne S. Cole, Daniel J. Guttman, Charles J. Herber, Glen Jeansonne, Bruce Kuklick, Linda J. Lear, Leonard Liggio, A. Laurence Moore, Rev. Tom Martin, Sidney C. Rosenzweig, Geoffrey S. Smith, and Leila Zenderland. At an even earlier phase, Sydney E. Ahlstrom served as an astute and patient dissertation advisor. Warren I. Susman, the man most responsible for my becoming a historian, always offered ideas and encouragement.

None of these friends, colleagues, or fellow researchers fully agrees with the interpretation advanced here, and several question it in fundamental ways. Hence I can say with more conviction than usually characterizes a prefatory declaration that I bear final responsibility for what follows.

Introduction

"EXTREMISM" AND EMPATHY

This is a story without a hero. It concentrates on three villains, the opposition they provoked, and the ways in which scholars use their careers to support a general interpretation of American society. The villains, William Dudley Pelley, Gerald B. Winrod, and Gerald L. K. Smith, were strident anti-Semites who charged that sinister Jewish conspirators dominated American politics and world affairs. Pelley, Winrod, and Smith have been selected from a bevy of comparable far right agitators for reasons relating to history, historiography, and convenience. All three attained prominence during the Great Depression, maintained their notoriety during World War II, and currently serve historians as representative "extremists." Emerging from devout Protestant backgrounds, each grounded his politics and prejudice in religious faith. Unlike other Protestants on the far right, however, Pelley, Winrod, and Smith left an extensive legacy of writing that allows the historian to work his way into their minds.

Most accounts of the Depression treat far right agitators in two intertwined ways. These figures provide colorful anecdotes to highlight the presumably precarious state of democracy during the 1930s. In addition, agitators like Pelley, Winrod, and Smith are conscripted to buttress a model of American politics in which far right authoritarians face off against far left zealots and, together, these "extremists" threaten reasonable reform. Frequently scholars carry this framework backward from the Depression at least to the 1890s, and forward through "McCarthyism" to the present. Far right agitators, thus subordinated to "pragmatic" jugglers in the center of the American political ring, rarely appear as complex human beings. Even authors devoting entire books to these villains yearn to reach the last chapter to show how President Franklin D. Roosevelt outwitted them.

Pelley, Winrod, and Smith deserve closer attention. Although similar in some respects, they possessed conflicting temperaments, traveled different paths to neighboring positions on the political spectrum, and disagreed about economics, foreign policy, and what they called the "Jewish question." Their thought was neither admirable nor intellectually compelling, but it could be intricate and occasionally esoteric. Their personalities, too, were more complicated that can be inferred from conventional allusions to "authoritarian personalities" and "paranoid styles." In short, their singular lives reveal more about American society than scholars usually assume.

In this book, the biographical studies of Pelley, Winrod, and Smith illuminate four broader themes. First, their careers show that the "extremism" of the far right often converged with the cultural and political mainstream. These three agitators attracted intermittent support from prominent officials and businessmen, and their political techniques overlapped with those used by "pragmatic" centrists. Most important, their favorite countersubversive, racist, and anti-Semitic motifs had long circulated through American society. Unlike more sophisticated bigots, of course, Pelley, Winrod, and Smith ultimately placed their prejudices within comprehensive conspiracy theories. Yet their conversions to conspiratorial anti-Semitism, traced here in detail, were not inevitable consequences of "authoritarian" personalities, and the turmoil afflicting their lives was widely shared by "normal" Americans.

Second, the "depression decade" is rescued here from its customary chronological isolation. The far right that emerged during the 1930s was not simply an automatic consequence of rising unemployment. For Pelley, Winrod, and Smith—and for the United States generally—the Depression was a cultural as well as an economic crisis. The problems of faith, personal morality, and national purpose that historians typically associate with the 1920s did not evaporate with the Crash. On the contrary, these long-standing concerns affected the ways in which Americans responded to the subsequent economic slump. Across the political spectrum, contemporary interpreters of the Great Depression fell back on familiar phrases, programs, and formulas. Even far right allegations of New Deal subversion look less peculiar when we recall that Franklin D. Roosevelt assumed the presidency only thirteen years after the Red Scare. Catch phrases, programs, and formulas varied according to economic and cultural circumstances. Literary critic Leslie Fiedler postulated "Two Thirties," one experienced by Roosevelt's supporters, the other by his foes. In fact, analysis of different classes, races, or worldviews may reveal a dozen distinguishable "Thirties."[1]

Third, the right-wing political activism begun during the Depression prompted a militant counterattack—what I call the Brown Scare. To a left horrified by Hitler and Mussolini, figures like Pelley, Winrod, and Smith seemed to foreshadow an analogous fascist threat to the United States. Liberals and radicals, often cast as heroes in books about the 1930s, certainly deserve praise for their early opposition to tyranny abroad and bigotry at home. Yet their campaign against what they regarded as native fascism should not be taken at face value. Rather, their tracts warning against incipient dictatorship, no less than publications of the far right, reveal the era's hopes, anxieties, and ambiguities. Even more important, from the mid-1930s through World War II, fear of the far right undermined the left's commitment to civil liberties. Diverse liberals and radicals favored restrictions on the right of native "fascist" agitators to speak, publish, and assemble. In 1944, the Roosevelt administration used the Smith Act to prosecute thirty assorted Nazi propagandists and far right agitators, including Pelley and Winrod. This conspiracy case, *United States* v. *McWilliams*, received almost unanimous approval from the left but, like the Brown Scare in general, set precedents for suppression that liberals and radicals would later regret during the Cold War.

Fourth, I examine the concept of extremism as an aspect of American intellectual history. Pelley, Winrod, and Smith were clearly extreme in the sense that they transgressed the bounds of decency. But the theory segregating far right villainy from the mainstream obscures the sources of indecency. The revisionist complaint that this conflation of "extremes" derived from Cold War fears, though sound as far as it goes, is incomplete. Removing the 1930s from chronological isolation at the latter end, we can see that ideas crystalized during the Depression won general acceptance during the 1950s. Specifically, postwar writers about the "radical right," often veterans of earlier ideological battles, translated Brown Scare motifs and misunderstandings into social science idiom. Indeed, ideological legacies from the 1930s still influence analyses of the "New Christian Right" in the 1980s.

Anyone purporting to explain the behavior of other people makes assumptions about human nature. Most American historians prefer to evade this problem by keeping their notions of personality implicit, unexamined, and vague. Still, leading students of "extremism," even those hostile to "psychohistory" in other contexts, routinely borrow psychoanalytic vocabulary to describe the far right. Since 1950, citing the famous study by Theodor Adorno and associates, they have attributed far right bigotry to authoritarian personalities. In 1963, Richard Hofstadter coined the term "paranoid style" to encompass the "qualities of heated exaggeration, suspiciousness, and conspiratorial fantasy" most often found, he said, on the "extremes." During the last two decades, Hofstadter's phrase has become de rigueur in accounts of the far right.[2]

The concept of extremism was part of a wider trend, begun during the 1930s and triumphant by the 1950s, to enlist psychoanalytical theory in the cause of social order. In so doing, students of the far right, along with most neo-Freudian psychologists, slighted what sociologist Philip Rieff calls the "most universal of Freud's rubrics, ambivalence." Indeed, far right agitators acted as perfect foils in the morality tale about political "pragmatism" and "paranoia" because they seemed incapable of mixed feelings. Nor did scholars of "extremism" sense the implications of a Freudian paradox, noted by Rieff, that it was "possible to become more sound of mind and yet less good—in fact, worse." In some cases, bigots might be well-adjusted to *their* environments (a preeminent neo-Freudian value), and moderates might find the center vital for neurotic reasons.[3]

Flawed application of systematic psychology to the study of the past does not justify a retreat to "common sense," with the accompanying reliance on epithets or crude dichotomies between idealism and realism. Although this book, unlike most concerning the far right, shuns pseudo-psychoanalytical references to the "paranoid style," it is informed both by Freud's insights and by the appreciation of human complexity that marked his best work. Unfortunately, Freud was not always at his best, and his deepest foray into American politics, *Thomas Woodrow Wilson*, shows him at his worst. And the "first psychoanalyst" was not, of course, the last.[4]

Consequently, my interpretations of Pelley, Winrod, and Smith draw on a variety of psychological mentors, including Freud's daughter Anna, his orthodox expositor Otto Fenichel, and his reflective revisionist Erik Erikson. I have also learned from Thomas Szasz's persistent critique of the "myth of mental illness" and from R. D. Laing's attempt to make sense of schizophrenia (though I dissent from Laing's ecstatic insinuation that mad men are the seers of our age). Nor does psychoanalysis in its various forms offer the only valuable perspective on human behavior. Williams James's treatment of religious conversion remains invaluable. In addition, I have been influenced by Erving Goffman's version of role theory and by sociologists of knowledge Karl Mannheim and Peter L. Berger. Such eclecticism, combined with my willingness to borrow Freud's insights without accepting his whole system, will distress some readers, but this approach fits both my own temperament and the evidence left by Pelley, Winrod, and Smith.[5]

With the exception of James's work, specialized studies in the psychology of religion offer surprisingly little help to students of Protestants active in the political right. Freud enjoyed heaping scorn on religion, which he called the "universal obsessional neurosis of humanity." Since World War II, however, there has been a rapprochement between theological liberalism, especially Protestant liberalism, and neo-Freudian psychology. Most neo-Freudians now regard moderate amounts of belief as a sign of mental health, reserving their scorn for fundamentalists and other religious "extremists." Although neither of these attitudes improves upon James's tough-minded empathy, Freud's comprehensive invective is preferable to the neo-Freudian supplement to civil religion. Assailing the "pitiful rearguard actions" of theological liberals and showing grudging respect for "consistent" fundamentalists who tried to ban Darwinism from public schools, Freud at least provides an antidote to psychologists who find neurosis only in the religions of outsiders.[6]

Under the best circumstances, a historian can only metaphorically work his way into the minds of his subjects. Inevitably he constructs rather than finds patterns of thought, belief, and behavior. Despite the claims of history as literary art, he must avoid the temptation to make those patterns too neat. This caveat applies especially to studies of far right agitators, whose seemingly incongruous avowals of tolerance and related deviations from the paranoid style are usually dismissed as face-saving gestures. Often they do reflect conscious duplicity. Sometimes, however, they highlight the difficulties involved in trying to know our own minds. Freud recognized the human tendency to hold "two separate and contradictory convictions" on a subject, and James similarly saw a "hazy penumbra in us all where lying and delusion meet."[7]

Nor do far right ideological delusions readily yield to "reality testing." Even Hofstadter denied that most exemplars of the "paranoid style" were "certifiable lunatics." Smith and Winrod look less like Daniel Paul Schreber, the classic Freudian paranoid, whose belief that mysterious rays were transforming him into a woman led to his incarceration in an asylum, and more like adherents of unconventional faiths who function competently on a day-to-day basis. Indeed, Smith and Winrod's belief in *The Protocols of Zion*, though more vicious than acceptance of *The Book of Mormon* or Mary Baker Eddy's *Science and Health*, was no more remarkable. Pelley, who outdistanced Winrod and Smith in departing from reality, nonetheless built his delusional worldview (as Freud wrote of Schreber) out of the "most general and comprehensible impulses of the human mind."[8]

Anyone purporting to explain leaders of social movements makes assumptions about the relative distribution of power, property, and prestige in society. Most American historians prefer to evade this problem by keeping their notions of social hierarchy implicit, unexamined, and vague. Prominent authorities on "extremism" minimize the problem by maintaining that our citizens share basic values, including the need to divide power among competing groups. According to these "pluralist" social scientists and "consensus" historians, the average citizen identifies with multiple, conflicting interests; pressure groups therefore cut across income levels; mobility blurs boundaries between industrial workers, the bourgeoisie, and the rich; regional and ethnic diversity further obscures clear-cut patterns; and the United States differs from western Europe, where class identification persists.[9]

These warnings about the fallibility of class analysis would be more persuasive if their authors did not themselves fall back on much less precise concepts as surrogates for class. In standard accounts of "extremism," for example, far right sentiments are said to be rooted somewhere in rural America or among the populist mass; elaboration consists largely of allusions to alleged religious, cultural, or regional traits. It is ironic, but unsurprising, that such vague concepts pass muster among scholars who criticize analysts of the "power elite" for failing to differentiate between old millionaires and new ones. Writers using the vocabulary of class are held to higher standards because they usually criticize the existing order as well as describe it. Unfortunately, this prevailing double standard not only underestimates the importance of wealth in American life, but also oversimplifies the religious, cultural, and regional influences that pluralists purport to understand.[10]

Partly because so many scholars dismiss class analysis instead of trying to improve it, our knowledge of American social structure is still "quite crude," as historian Christopher Lasch recently lamented, and this deficiency cannot be remedied in a brief preface. Nonetheless, much as I made explicit the general psychological premises influencing my expositions of Pelley, Winrod, and Smith, I can sketch the social context in which their personalities, theologies, and far right ideologies developed. And class, though sometimes difficult to isolate, remains the essential starting point for comprehending that context.[11]

Pelley, Smith, and to a lesser extent Winrod stressed their rise from poverty to success, but, like countless other "self-made men," they exaggerated their youthful deprivation. None was born into the corporate elite that had begun to dominate the national economy at the turn of the century. Neither did their families belong to the ranks of factory workers or marginal farmers, let alone to the city or country underclass. Though often cited as exemplars of rural ways, all three spent their adolescence in cities; only Smith, whose home town of Viroqua, Wisconsin, was the smallest city, did any agricultural labor (and that only until he left for college at age seventeen). Perhaps most significant, Pelley, Winrod, and Smith's fathers were Protestant preachers *and* independent small businessmen. Illness, bad luck, and poor judgment sometimes brought them hard times. Nonetheless, Pelley, Winrod, and Smith imbibed from their families values that were characteristically if not exclusively bourgeois: piety, propriety, upward mobility, deferred gratification, and hard work. Throughout their lives, they usually affirmed these values, occasionally questioned them, but never escaped their influence. Like their fathers, all three combined preaching of a sort with small business, ultimately the business of far right publishing.[12]

Although an interpretation of the social context of belief and behavior must begin with class, it should not end there. As pluralist students of far right "extremism" insist, opinions and affiliations often cut across class lines. While hailing a society composed of varied groups, however, these scholars underestimate the actual diversity within the United States. Rather, they mistakenly assume that only vestigial "backward-looking" groups rejected the dominant trends toward scientific rationalism, liberal religion, and reformed capitalism. Moreover, according to their framework a moribund fundamentalist remnant typically marches in the vanguard of regression.

Contrary to this pluralist version of the idea of progress, large segments of the population persisted in swimming against the modern mainstream. These groups, whose existence helps to explain why there are many different "Thirties" (or "Twenties" or "Eighties"), frequently constituted what sociologist Peter L. Berger calls "cognitive minorities." Isolated, not always geographically and sometimes willfully from dominant cultural trends, they defended worldviews that conflicted in significant ways with science, liberal religion, or economic rationalization. To be sure, the patterns of rejection and adaptation contained paradoxes; fundamentalists, for instance, used radio (and later television) networks to warn against invisible demons. Unfortunately, most scholars emphasizing conflict in American history share a signal flaw with the consensus scholars whom they criticize: a hesitancy to take seriously groups that retard "progress." Yet an adequate treatment of our past requires investigation of apocalyptic evangelists as well as primitive rebels, far right villains as well as working-class heroes and heroines.[13]

Anyone writing about heroes or villains makes assumptions about right and wrong. Most American historians prefer to evade this problem by purporting to seek objectivity. Still, leading students of "extremism," even those who in other contexts chide revisionists for "present-mindedness," pointedly distance themselves from their far right subjects. I, too, am appalled by Pelley, Winrod, and Smith's bigotry; the anti-Semitic sentiment they fed during the 1930s, we must remember, discouraged the timid Roosevelt administration from admitting anti-Nazi refugees to the United States. In this book, nonetheless, I eschew a persistent tone of outrage. It is not easy to lead readers through alien, obnoxious worldviews, and persistent intrusions highlighting my own opposition to anti-Semitism would only make the task more difficult.[14]

Passage through these alien worldviews may be eased by some stylistic guide posts at the outset. In a concession to stylistic grace, references to American "fascism," "extremism," and the "radical right," terms favored by writers on the far right since the Great Depression, usually appear hereafter unencumbered by quotation marks; even without constant reminders, however, readers should recognize that this book stands as a critique of such problematical labels. Similarly, while explicating the thought of Pelley, Winrod, and Smith, I avoid cluttering the narrative with words like alleged and putative. Messages that Pelley claimed to receive from the spirit world must be regarded as products of his own unconscious, but, since these "psychic receptions" differed from his conscious reflections, they are so marked in the footnotes.

Undoubtedly many prospective readers have no wish to tour the minds and personalities of Pelley, Winrod, or Smith, preferring instead (as philosopher J. Glenn Gray wrote in another context) to see "no quality of the foe except his ideology." Their surviving opponents from the 1930s and 1940s, some of whom I interviewed, lean toward this position; furthermore, these liberals and radicals often continue to believe that restrictions on civil liberties were necessary to fight the native fascist threat. While respecting the flawed heroism of veteran foes of bigotry, and recognizing that haunted memories deserve attention from later generations, I nevertheless distinguish memory from history and insist that accurate reconstruction of and retrospective judgment on the past also make powerful claims.[15]

By presenting Pelley, Winrod, and Smith as complex villains instead of simple ones, we do risk creating sympathy for their prejudices. But the risk is not great. Although bigotry survives in the United States, with anti-Semitism in particular retaining considerable covert favor, no believer in *The Protocols* is likely now to run a serious race for United States senator, as Winrod did in 1938. On the other hand, unrecognized risks accompany the habit of seeing "no quality of the foe except his ideology," the perspective currently characterizing most accounts of the New Christian Right.

With the rediscovery of politicized Protestants by pundits and office seekers, this book, begun as a dissertation more than a decade ago, has acquired unanticipated relevance. By comparing Pelley, Winrod, and Smith to contemporary Protestants on the far right, we can measure continuity and change over the past half century. So far, most commentators have shown little historical perspective. Rather, uncritically appropriating the concept of extremism, itself an ideological legacy from the 1930s, they apply it to the new "new right" of the 1980s less shrewdly than their predecessors applied it to the old "new right" of the 1950s. I address these matters in an epilogue. Here it suffices to agree with historian Peter Stansky that empathic biographies of villains are unusually painful to write, to warn that neither are they comforting to read, and to assert nonetheless that they are very necessary.[16]

The Old Christian Right

1. The Politics of Apocalypse

FROM THE TWENTIES TO THE THIRTIES

The Great Depression as an Intellectual Movement

By the mid-1930s, visions of literal or metaphorical apocalypse had become commonplace. To his friends on the left, the literary critic Edmund Wilson recalled, the stock market Crash of October 1929 had seemed "almost like a rending of the earth in preparation for the Day of Judgment." In 1934, George Soule, Wilson's colleague at the *New Republic,* sketched the "coming American revolution." The Communist John L. Spivak was even more certain that "America faces the barricades." Evangelist Billy Sunday estimated that the Second Coming was closer than ever, and, from a different theological vantage point, Reinhold Niebuhr reflected "on the end of an era" marked by senile capitalism. The social eschatologies varied, of course, but all contained an uneasy mixture of confusion, foreboding, and promise of a bright future.[1]

These commentators were not merely responding to the breakdown of voluntary relief under Herbert Hoover, the banking collapse during the Interregnum of 1933, and the Roosevelt administration's inability to restore full employment. There was ample contrary evidence that the country was more stunned than repentant or revolutionary. Rather, the "Thirties" inherited an apocalyptic disposition from earlier decades, including its much maligned immediate predecessor. When the United States entered the Great Depression, historian Warren Susman has observed, it was already a "culture in crisis, already . . . in search of a satisfactory American Way of Life." Indeed, for diverse social critics, the slump seemed to be the culmination of three generations of economic, social, and moral crises. Attempting to explain it, they appropriated memories, historical analogies, and formulas as familiar as the frontier thesis and the wrath of God.[2]

Among troubled Protestants the 1930s appeared to be another phase in an "ordeal of faith" persisting since the 1870s. Instead of recording a decisive transition in 1929, historian Robert T. Handy estimates that the "American religious depression" began three years before the Crash. The 1920s were marked by declining church attendance, financial difficulties, and the popularity of the lively infidels Sinclair Lewis and H. L. Mencken. In addition, theological liberals had been shaken by World War I and, though institutionally dominant, probably remained a minority within Protestantism.[3]

It is more precise to speak of a mainstream denominational depression. Though attracting fewer headlines after the Scopes trial in 1925, fundamentalism did not evaporate. Proponents of the social gospel still preached reform. Even the popularity of Bruce Barton's *The Man Nobody Knows,* a portrait of Jesus as the "founder of modern business," revealed a continuing desire to Christianize the social order. Above all, declining church membership obscures efforts by Americans to comprehend a society marked by free spending and poverty, increasing divorce and ebbing feminism, paeans to law and widespread defiance of Prohibition. If religion is thus broadly conceived, then the United States in the 1920s was, as the journalist Charles Ferguson wrote, "simply teeming with faith." Unsatisfied by liberal and fundamentalist orthodoxies, distressed Americans turned to cults promising earthly success and rapport with the universe. These movements thrived, Ferguson concluded, by offering "to do something the regular churches make no pretense of doing . . . to solve any problem overnight, and the results are practically guaranteed."[4]

With some modification, all of these tendencies recurred after the Crash. The literature of solace and self-help, from Dale Carnegie's *How to Win Friends and Influence People* to Henry C. Link's *The Return to Religion,* continued to reach the best-seller lists. In significant ways an updated version of the fundamentalist controversy still marked Protestantism during the 1930s. The Great Depression, as contemporary evangelists complained, produced no classic revival. Instead, potential participants joined other sorts of camp meetings. An enlarged band of social Christians embraced or flirted with the New Deal, Socialism, or Communism. Methodist Bishop Francis McConnell and Rev. Harry F. Ward, for example, moved from curiosity about the Soviet Union in the late 1920s to uncritical support in the 1930s. Conversely, wary of the worldly consequences of theological liberalism and skeptical of the social gospel, many fundamentalists regarded the New Deal and Popular Front, now backed by their traditional liberal foes, as the latest forms of infidelity.[5]

The search for infidelity, broadly conceived, was another legacy to the 1930s. Countless Americans had always supposed that republican values were under attack from hidden conspiracies, but the era between World War I and Pearl Harbor was especially hospitable to such allegations. The fear of being deceived into disaster was probably greater than at any time since the Civil War. Modern deceivers, after all, possessed tools unavailable to earlier confidence men. Moreover, Freudian psychology and behaviorism, both popularized during the 1920s, seemed to prove that human rationality was at best a thin veneer. Recalling the "pseudo-environment" created by the Creel Committee during World I, Walter Lippmann lamented in 1922 that the real political world was "out of reach, out of sight, out of mind." Stuart Chase studied semantics in order to combat the "tyranny of words" and the sinister or stupid persons manipulating them. Noting that "more people than ever" were "puzzled, uneasy or vexed by the unknown cunning which seems to have degraded them," the political scientist Harold Lasswell in 1922 began a lifetime study of the phenomenon that "has come to have an ominous clang in many minds—propaganda."[6]

The dominant countersubversive lore since the late nineteenth century guarded against alleged conspiracies on the left. There was some variation, of course. A progressive who damned the Industrial Workers of the World (IWW) might himself be deemed un-American for advocating the income tax. What is most significant, however, is that respectable political, commercial, and religious leaders disseminated images of radicalism later adopted by extremists. Attacks waxed and waned, but by the turn of the century standard descriptions were available for the taking.[7]

As with many attitudes, Theodore Roosevelt expressed countersubversive orthodoxy. To Roosevelt, "radical socialism" embodied everything that Americans should shun: sloth, impiety, and sexual license. Establishment of a "state free-lunch counter," he wrote in 1909, would destroy the family and encourage "free love." American socialists were more circumspect about sex than their European allies, but their newspaper, *Appeal to Reason*, was still an "organ of pornography." In sum, socialism meant the ultimate "annihilation of civilization."[8]

World War I and its offspring, the Red Scare, expanded concern about subversion. Even before the declaration of war, groups like the American Defense Society and National Security League advocated compulsory military training as a vchicle to promote "100% Americanism." Starting in 1917, Woodrow Wilson's administration revoked mailing privileges from pacifist, radical, or merely eccentric periodicals, prosecuted 2,100 persons under vague sedition legislation, and, in the retrospective judgment of George Creel, chairman of the Committee on Public Information (CPI), strove to "saturate the country with truth." Presidential speeches and CPI propaganda insisted that the United States faced a sinister international conspiracy. Legislatures, city councils, and vigilantes supplemented the message. In 1919 the nation slid easily from wartime solidarity into the Red Scare. Not only were Socialists and Wobblies already under attack for opposing the war, but both the Creel Committee and the Senate Judiciary Committee had certified the existence of a "German-Bolshevik conspiracy."[9]

Two aspects of this familiar story deserve emphasis in order to understand the far right that developed during the 1930s. First, campaigns on behalf of "100% Americanism" were led by mainstream political figures, incuding prominent progressives. Mayor Ole Hanson, who crushed the Seattle general strike in 1919, also supported the eight-hour day, workmen's compensation, and the direct primary. Before chairing successive investigations of German brewers and Bolsheviks, Senator Lee Overman (Dem.-N. C.) had championed organized labor and guided the Clayton Act through Congress.[10]

More than anyone else, A. Mitchell Palmer, Wilson's attorney general and organizer of the raids [and deportations] in 1920, personified the Red Scare. According to Palmer's eclectic conception, Communism sought to "overthrow the decencies of private life, to usurp property . . . , to disrupt the present order of life regardless of health, sex, or religious rights." The movement appealed to anarchists, "criminals, moral perverts, [and] hysterical neurasthenic women." While using these countersubversive conventions, Palmer focused on a fresh target, the Soviet Union. Leon Trotsky and his fellow revolutionaries had installed in the Czar's bedroom the "lowest of all types" from the East Side of New York City. Now, fanned from Moscow, "sharp tongues of revolutionary heat" licked at church altars, played in school belfries, crawled "into the sacred corners" of the home, and threatened marriage vows with libertine notions.[11]

Second, dozens of vigilance organizations spawned by World War I and the Red Scare formed, as historian Paul L. Murphy writes, a "new permanent dimension of intolerance." The second Ku Klux Klan, founded in 1915, attracted at least two million members by the mid-1920s and briefly dominated the politics of several states; members were responsible for scores of riots, thousands of beatings, and occasional murders. Muckraker Norman Hapgood recognized in 1927 that many vigilance groups appealed to the "property class" by placing a red taint of "proposals calculated to affect private business."

With the warning, "When you hear a man tryin' to discredit Uncle Sam, that's Bolshevism," the National Security League collected contributions from Henry Clay Frick, J. P. Morgan, and John D. Rockefeller. To Ralph Easley, executive secretary of the National Civic Federation, the "New Unionism" of Sidney Hillman and the Amalgamated Clothing Workers was "nothing less than the 'Old Syndicalism.'"[12]

In short, although Palmer's raids ended in mid-1920, counter-subversive concerns survived. During the 1924 election, the *Wall Street Journal* accused Senator Robert M. LaFollette of "Wisconsin Bolshevism," and President Calvin Coolidge agreed that LaFollette favored a "communistic or socialistic state." Similarly, trade associations paired Communism with the American Federation of Labor. Not only were established vigilance organizations still vigilant, but new ones appeared during the 1920s. The Keymen of America, for instance, tried to enforce a national blacklist of suspicious speakers; after fighting unions for the National Clay Products Industries Association, in 1927 Harry Jung incorporated the National Vigilant Intelligence Federation to combat liberalism, radicalism, and pacifism.[13]

Hence, enemies of the New Deal had ready access to counter-subversive themes crystalized during the late nineteenth century, legitimized during World War I and the Red Scare, and sustained throughout the "tribal twenties": churches, schools, and colleges were dens of radicalism; reds stirred up ignorant blacks, impressionable adolescents, and naive Christians; immigrants were especially troublesome and often deserved deportation. The list of supposed subversives grew longer during the 1930s, but surviving standbys remained near the top: Upton Sinclair, Jane Addams, Charles A. Beard, Scott Nearing, Norman Thomas, and Oswald Garrison Villard among intellectuals; Sidney Hillman within the labor movement; Senator George Norris (Rep.-Neb.) and Representative Fiorello LaGuardia (Rep.-N.Y.) in public office; A. J. Muste, John Haynes Holmes, Harry F. Ward, Rabbi Stephen Wise, and Bishop McConnell among the clergy. The country had been saturated with "truth."[14]

Nor is it remarkable in an overwhelmingly Christian nation that Jews were held responsible for a particularly heinous conspiracy. Mixed feelings about Jews had existed since colonial times. Although Protestant creators of holy commonwealths might identify with Old Testament Hebrews, they also received a tradition blaming Jews for Christ's crucifixion and numerous subsequent crimes. By the mid–nineteenth century, evangelists derided Jewish "rebels against God's purpose," politicians sneered at Judah "Judas Iscariot" Benjamin, the

Confederate secretary of state, and the *New York Times* called financier August Belmont an "agent of foreign Jew Bankers."[15]

As immigrants poured in from eastern Europe after the Civil War, actors, clergy, dime novelists, and serious writers routinely portrayed Jews as libertines, enemies of true religion, and cheats. Some agrarian radicals held the Rothschild family responsible for tight money and unemployment. In *Our Country*, the foremost nativist tract of the 1880s, Rev. Josiah Strong, a theological liberal, urged quick acculturation of Jews and other "new" immigrants from southern and eastern Europe. Some Protestant theological conservatives suffering through an early phase of their "ordeal of faith" expected Jews to return to the Holy Land, possibly in alliance with the Antichrist. Less abstract antagonism ranged from demonstrations against merchants to innuendo in the press about "obnoxious" Jewish traits. Restricted clubs and resorts signaled a deepening concern with the Jewish *parvenu*, an old image put in modern dress.[16]

After twenty-five years of investigation, revision, and rejoinder, scholars still disagree about the extent of anti-Semitism during the late nineteenth century. Tentative conclusions are necessary, however, in order to understand later countersubversive currents. In a nation dedicated to the "Americanization" of immigrants, the literary caricatures were not, as Oscar Handlin contends, devoid of malice. Furthermore, the argument, made most strongly by John Higham, that patricians, radical farmers, and rival immigrants were unusually biased against the Jews probably means that historians have studied these groups more than others. The dominant attitude among Christians, Leonard Dinnerstein correctly concludes, amalgamated "affection, curiosity, suspicion, and rejection." Friends and foes of Jews sometimes used the same stereotypes; when anti-Semites condemned them for sharp trading habits, philo-Semites applauded this kinship with legendary Yankee traders. Finally, comparing the United States and Europe, we can say that American anti-Semitism was relatively less violent, less racist, and less central to the worldviews of those accepting it.[17]

The first two decades of the twentieth century witnessed a shift toward increasing suspicion and rejection. The lynching of Leo Frank in 1915 was only the most dramatic incident in an era that marked, according to historian George M. Fredrickson, the peak of "formalized racism." In the same year, aristocratic Madison Grant published *The Passing of the Great Race*, the foremost nativist tract of the 1910s. Grant denied that the "new immigration" could be assimilated, specifically excluded most Jews from the "white" gene pool, and expected intermarriage to produce "race bastards."[18] Comparable premises were accepted by eminent scientists and prominent progressives. Magazines attacking municipal corruption also worried about the great "Jewish invasion." The issues coalesced for muckraker Burton J. Hendrick, who denounced Jewish theater and liquor "trusts." Although Hendrick, Jacob Riis, and sociologist Edward A. Ross still mixed sympathy with suspicion, they casually claimed that Jews avoided physical labor, manipulated money without engaging in "basic production," valued profit more than life itself, destroyed ethical standards in business, law, and medicine, promoted prostitution among gentile women, intimidated the press, and "overwhelmed" Congress with lies during debates on immigration restriction.[19]

Jews suffered from the general escalation of "100% Americanism" accompanying World War I and the Red Scare. Three years after the armistice, John Spargo sadly noted a "whole library of books" discussing the "Jewish question." Hostility operated in three overlapping areas. First, "polite" anti-Semites further restricted admission to clubs, resorts, universities, and the professions.[20]

Second, often citing wartime intelligence tests, social scientists elaborated and popularizers disseminated the cult of Anglo-Saxon superiority. Madison Grant's disciple, Theodore Lothrop Stoddard, listed most immigrant Jews among the "Asiatic" threats to "Nordic" American civilization. According to novelist Kenneth Roberts, writing in the *Saturday Evening Post*, Jewish "mongoloids" from Russia produced the "mongrelization" of American cities.[21]

Third, writers and officials increasingly associated Jews with radicalism in general and Communism in particular. Speaking for many friends of the Russian monarchy, Samuel Harper in 1918 accused the "Jewish gang in Washington" of softness toward the Soviet Union. Dr. George A. Simons, a self-described 100% American and former director of the Methodist hospital in Petrograd, went even further. In February 1919, he told Senator Lee Overman's subcommittee on Bolshevik propaganda that Communism was "Yiddish." Denying hostility to the "better class" of Jews, Simons shared Attorney General Palmer's opinion that their "apostate" cousins spread Bolshevism in New York City. Simons's allegations particularly interested Senators Knute Nelson (Rep.-Minn.) and Josiah O. Wolcott (Rep.-Del.). They were largely endorsed by subsequent witnesses, including a Northwestern University professor, a Commerce Department agent, two representatives of National City Bank, a YMCA leader and vice-consul in Petrograd, and several Russian émigrés.[22]

References to "Jewish" Communism quickly reached the growing library of anti-Semitic books. The popularity of this motif cannot be explained simply by disproportionate Jewish participation in the Soviet and American Communist parties. Rather, many Americans were already disposed to believe the worst of Jews, and in 1919–20 nothing seemed worse than Communism. Nor were critics inclined to examine the complexity of Jewish affiliation with the left. Grumbling about a "perfect little rat of a Jew" who represented the Soviets, Under Secretary of State William Phillips combined countersubversion and snobbery. Lothrop Stoddard detected connections between Marxism and the Talmud's "dialectical subleties."[23]

The Protocols of the Learned Elders of Zion purported to offer a comprehensive explanation of the "Yiddish" affinity for Bolshevism. In this notorious forgery, created by Russian anti-Semites at the turn of the century, a leader of the secret Jewish world government supposedly explained the plot to destroy Christian civilization. For almost two thousand years, the Elders had been "splitting society by ideas" while manipulating economic and political power. Currently they encouraged alcoholism, spread pornography, discredited Christian clergy, and popularized such subversive doctrines as Darwinism, Marxism, and "Nietzsche-ism." They corrupted governments, at critical moments arranging wars to profit Jews and kill gentiles. Above all, this Jewish "hidden hand" controlled both capitalism and the radical movements pretending to offer an alternative.[24]

Widely distributed among royalist troops during the Russian civil war, *The Protocols* were brought to the United States by émigrés and returning American citizens. Dr. Simons, for example, recommended them to the Overman committee. This monarchist forgery made an incongruous addition to political discourse. But the prevailing fear of subversion, combined with wariness of the "great Jewish invasion," helped readers to overlook the blatant anti-republicanism. Moreover, *The Protocols'* generality left room for elaborations to fit local circumstances. The basic anti-Semitic charges were Americanized under the imprimatur of a national hero, Henry Ford.[25]

On 20 May 1920, Ford's newspaper, the *Dearborn Independent*, published "The International Jew: The World's Problem," the first article in a series destined to continue for almost two years. *Independent* editor William J. Cameron, prodded by Ford himself, wrote most of the articles, and a copy of *The Protocols*, supplied by Russian exiles, provided the central theme. A staff of investigators, led by C. C. Daniels, brother of the Secretary of the Navy, and including several veterans of the Justice Department, provided Ford and Cameron with additional anti-Semitic rumors, clippings, and forged documents. Critics of the anti-Semitic campaign, including former President William Howard Taft, were dismissed by the *Independent* as "gentile fronts" for Jewish conspirators. Most of the series was reissued in four volumes known collectively as *The International Jew.* Without doubt, they were the most influential books in the expanding anti-Semitic library.[26]

According to *The International Jew*, manifestations of the "world's foremost problem" coincided with issues that had unsettled the United States since the Civil War. Both corporate monopoly and government regulation led to steady restrictions on freedom. Moral order was threatened by unravelling family bonds, loosening sexual mores, and "Hollywood lasciviousness." An "endless stream" of immigrants threatened to change the very nature of Americanism. Finally, echoing Walter Lippmann and Harold Lasswell, *The International Jew* protested that man lived in an "era of false labels," ruled "by a whole company of ideas into whose authority he has not inquired at all."

The Protocols offered a "clue to the modern maze." Whether or not an Elder of Zion actually delivered these lectures, the *Dearborn Independent* said, it was clear that Jews, as the document charged, were using ideas to "corrupt Collective Opinion," controlling finance, sponsoring revolution, and exercising power "everywhere." Nor were these activities recently begun. For centuries Jews had used a "pseudo Masonry" and leftist parties to spread radical doctrines, while simultaneously creating such exploitative capitalist mechanisms as stock exchanges, holding companies, and credit. Their slick commercial practices had appeared in North America during the colonial period. The Rothschild family had grown rich providing Hessian mercenaries during the Revolution and soon thereafter had dispatched its first American agent, August Belmont. In the twentieth century, the *Independent* claimed, Jacob Schiff and his henchmen had forced President Taft to abrogate the Russian-American commercial treaty in 1911. Paul Warburg and Eugene Meyer Jr. had created the Federal Reserve Board on behalf of the Semitic banking fraternity, and Jews had formed a "solid ring" around President Wilson. None had exercised greater power than Bernard Baruch, chairman of the War Industries Board and "Jewish high governor of the United States."

Quoting testimony and statistics from the Senate investigation of Bolshevik activities, *The International Jew* went beyond Dr. Simons's denunciations of Yiddish "apostates." Ford's newspaper accused Russian Communists of sacking churches and leaving synagogues "*untouched.*" Furthermore, the "East Sider" Leon Trostky had left a substantial "endowment" to New York City, a large Bolshevik population active in the Wobblies, International Ladies Garment Workers, and Amalgamated Clothing Workers. At bottom, Communism was a "carefully groomed investment" by Jewish financiers who profited from social disorder.

Consistent with *The Protocols'* scheme to "split society by ideas," Jews and their dupes taught "Red" doctrines in the classroom, manipulated the press, and convinced economists that depressions were salutary. These actions paled beside their corruption of gentile morals. The hidden hand's tools included the New York theater, jazz, and related "moron music." Hollywood's "psychic poison" showed that "oriental" Jews had failed to embrace the "Anglo-Saxon, the American view."

Through four volumes of *The International Jew,* Jewish vices appeared as the reverse of any "American view." On the one hand, gentiles represented creative industry, hard work, fair play, purity, and democracy. Jews, on the other hand, stood for exploitative "Finance," indulgence, chicanery, sensuality, and tyranny. And Jews, unlike gentiles who advanced "by individual initiative," took advantage of unprecedented "racial loyalty and solidarity."

To the *Dearborn Independent,* "100% Americanism" was virtually synonymous with Christianity. The amalgamation was easy for the editor, William J. Cameron. An erstwhile preacher, Cameron believed that Anglo-Saxons were descended from Israel's lost tribes and thus rightful heirs to God's blessing. Citing *The Protocols*'s injuction to undermine the clergy, the newspaper blamed Jews for Biblical higher criticism and liberal Protestantism, which reduced Jesus to a "well-meaning but wholly mistaken Jewish prophet." Yet fundamentalists erred, too, when they confused modern Jews with God's chosen people. Zionism fulfilled the "Bolshevist spirit," not the Scripture's promise of Jewish return to Jerusalem. Elsewhere the *Independent* said that neither Jesus nor any disciple—except Judas Iscariot—was Jewish in the modern sense of the term. In the end, then, the "Jewish question" boiled down to a contest between two peoples, each supposing that God was on its side. There was "no idea deeper in Judaism" than belief in divine election. But, the *Independent* protested, the "Anglo-Saxon Celtic race" was the "Ruling People Chosen throughout the centuries to Master the world."

The International Jew's perverse accomplishment was to combine Anglo-Saxon chauvinism, anti-Semitic motifs common during the Progressive era, and the comprehensive conspiracy theory sketched in *The Protocols.* Ford's subordinates distributed several hundred thousand copies of the volumes. At least privately, *The International Jew* won praise from J. P. Morgan, Jr., literary critic John J. Chapman, journalist W. J. Abbot, and C. Mowbray White, chairman of the

National Civic Federation committee on revolutionary movements. To avoid a libel judgment, Ford in 1927 publicly repudiated the series. For Americans susceptible to conspiratorial interpretations of the Depression, however, *The International Jew* contained both a comprehensive "usable past" and additional villains, including Bernard Baruch, Paul Warburg, and Eugene Meyer, Jr., who remained active during the Hoover and Roosevelt administrations.

New Deal and Polarization

The Depression and, to a greater extent, the Roosevelt administration's response to it precipitated the development of a distinctive far right. As Americans weighed rival explanations of the crisis, the country's formerly amorphous ideological spectrum was divided into relatively clear segments. If the 1930s qualifies as an "Age of Roosevelt," it is because the New Deal provided the benchmark for most of these evaluations. In determining their positions, moreover, citizens at least implicitly defined a normative American way of life.

Writers as diverse as Karl Marx and Alexis de Tocqueville, Clinton Rossiter and C. Wright Mills, have stressed that few feudal obstacles blocked American ways. There was no established church, a minimal military establishment, universal white manhood suffrage, and relatively little working-class consciousness. By 1900 the United States was firmly committed to liberal capitalism. To be sure, most Socialists and some Populists not only perceived substantial class conflict but recommended it. Overwhelmingly, however, Democrats and Republicans spoke what Rossiter calls "one political language," thereby affirming private property, individual initiative, and national solidarity across class, regional, and ethnic lines. "It cannot be too often repeated," Theodore Roosevelt said in 1909, again encapsulating the dominant mood, "that in this country, we all of us tend to go up and down together."[27]

Despite its slim prospects, a grassroots socialist alternative in the early 1900s is readily identifiable. Existence of a complementary conservative movement is less certain, especially if the issue is viewed in an international context. Unable to find monarchists, Junkers, or high Anglican Tories, perplexed scholars point to rhetoricians of laissez faire, practitioners of noblesse oblige, and champions of stability amid upheaval. Whereas the western European right resisted capitalism and mass democracy, these "laissez faire conservatives" (to borrow Rossiter's term) used democratic shibboleths to defend their commercial conception of property. Not only was the

American political spectrum narrower than European counterparts, but it was less clearly divided. Seekers after an authentic American right have trouble drawing lines between such designated conservatives as Elihu Root and progressives like Theodore Roosevelt. At most, a hazy conservatism, characterized more by temperamental prudence than by unique beliefs, existed alongside "progressivism" in both major parties before World War I.[28]

An embryonic far right is even harder to discover. In western Europe, nationalist—but hardly conservative—parties advocated a mixture of militant patriotism, mass political participation, opposition to socialism, some economic redistribution, and often anti-Semitism. Making allowances for the twists of history, we can, for example, trace the descent of Nazism from the German *völkisch* parties of the 1880s. During the late nineteenth century in the United States, vigilantes, "white caps," and members of the first Ku Klux Klan broke strikes and lynched blacks in the name of the flag. Yet these groups never congealed into nationwide movements, let alone independent parties.[29]

Following the turbulent 1890s, as suppression and cooptation thwarted Populism and Socialism, differences narrowed between Democrats and Republicans. As late as 1928, despite intense cultural conflict, Herbert Hoover could plausibly conclude: "We are a nation of progressives; we differ as to what is the road to progress." Though he chose the urban ethnic road, Alfred E. Smith still shared Hoover's faith in mildly reformed capitalism, limited government, and Victorian morality. Ellis Hawley discerns a rising "middle-class 'right'" during the 1920s, but, as Hawley's quotation marks suggest, "100% Americans," vigilance organizers, and Ku Klux Klansmen did not yet stand out from the mainstream. Members of the Klan, for instance, adhered to both major parties, and Imperial Wizard Hiram Wesley Evans called on Democrats like William Gibbs McAdoo as well as President Coolidge.[30]

Although the Depression prompted exhilaration on the left and convinced devout anti-Semites that Jewish conspirators had struck again, initially it produced no shift in the nation's ideological axis. Franklin D. Roosevelt and fellow Democrats who criticized Hoover for failing to restore prosperity also denounced his expansion of the federal budget and invasion of states' rights. Almost immediately after Roosevelt's inauguration, however, innovations in style and substance speeded political polarization.[31]

The left looked on with mixed feelings, often applauding the Roosevelt administration's ends while questioning its means. At first condemning the New Deal as a temporary bulwark against inevitable capitalist collapse, the Communist party announced the People's Front in 1935 and thereafter, under the leadership of Earl Browder, gave de facto support to FDR. Socialist leader Norman Thomas astutely criticized the New Deal, but many of his comrades defected to the Democrats. Independent left liberals, ranging from *New Republic* columnists to members of Congress, knew that FDR's program fell short of the cooperative commonwealth, but, failing to organize a third party, they generally supported his reelection in 1936 anyway.[32]

Other veterans of pre–World War I reform accused FDR of doing too much, not too little. Cogently summarizing their case in *The Challenge to Liberty*, Herbert Hoover saw in the New Deal a "new philosophy which must mark the end of liberty." Members of the American Liberty League agreed, adding that depressions were inevitable, even salutary mechanisms serving to cleanse the economy and build character. Liberty League advocates of unadulterated laissez faire differed in many ways from old progressives like Hoover, Governor Alfred M. Landon, and Colonel Frank Knox. Yet the differences must be viewed as variations within a now distinct conservatism, defined not by temperament but by opposition to the New Deal welfare state. Indeed, as battle lines were drawn during the 1930s, foes of the Roosevelt administration joined Hoover in minimizing their earlier advocacy of government intervention and in hailing free enterprise.[33]

Adapting venerable countersubversive themes, conservatives deemed Roosevelt's program un-American as well as unwise. To Senator Carter Glass (Dem.-Va.), the National Industrial Recovery Act attempted to "transplant Hitlerism." His colleague Arthur H. Vandenberg (Rep.-Mich.) called the Agricultural Adjustment Act the "most revolutionary proposal in American history." Representative Joseph W. Martin (Rep.-Mass.) surmised that the Tennessee Valley Authority was "patterned closely after one of the Soviet dreams." By 1934 critics routinely compared the whole New Deal to "Russianized" government.[34]

Lapses into allegedly alien legislation were often blamed on subversive presidential advisors. According to Bainbridge Colby, Wilson's last secretary of state, Roosevelt in 1936 had "gone over hook, line and sinker to the Communists and Socialists by whom he is surrounded." Even the red with "torch in hand" was welcome, Al Smith charged. Another apostate Democrat, William Randolph Hearst, repudiated the "imported, autocratic, Asiatic Socialist party of Karl Marx and Franklin Delano Roosevelt." During the 1936 campaign, Landon accused the administration of moving toward dictatorship; his runningmate Frank Knox speculated that Moscow was the specific destination. Spokesmen for the Republican National Committee called FDR the "Kerensky of the American revolutionary movement" and warned that citizens would soon be required to wear government issue identification tags.[35]

Many "100% Americans" active since the 1910s found in the Roosevelt administration proof that their fears had been justified all along. Freshly energized, they formed the nucleus of a now distinct far right. Moving naturally against the "immigrant crew" on the "New Deal railroad," Harry Jung transformed the American Vigilant Intelligence Federation from a mailing list into a membership organization. George W. Christians, a former Klansman and founder in 1931 of the Crusaders for Economic Liberty, focused his enmity on Washington, D.C. Mrs. Elizabeth Dilling, concerned about Bolshevism since visiting Russia in 1919, published *Roosevelt's Red Record* and *The Red Network*, a "who's who of radicals" including such familiar targets as Jane Addams, Bishop Francis McConnell, Rev. Harry Ward, and Sidney Hillman. Jung, Christians, and Dilling had small constituencies. On the other hand, partly because they attacked economic inequality, Father Charles E. Coughlin and Senator Huey P. Long (Dem.-La.) carried large followings when they moved rightward from the New Deal in 1934–35.[36]

Commentators often had difficulty finding a place on the volatile political spectrum for Long, Coughlin, and other nationalist radicals who advocated some form of sharing the wealth. Their divergence from the left is clear in retrospect. Unlike Norman Thomas or Earl Browder, far right spokesmen criticized individual capitalists but discerned no basic contradictions within capitalism. The National Union for Social Justice, founded by Coughlin in 1934, was typical in affirming the "sanctity of private property." Far right activists rejected internationalism as well as international socialism; at minimum, they concurred in Long's fight against United States membership in the World Court. With the significant exception of Long, they considered wealth sharing much less important than fighting radical and liberal subversion. Dilling and Jung scarcely mentioned economic inequality. Having broadcast against the "Red Fog" as early as 1929, Coughlin ultimately broke with the Roosevelt administration because it cooperated with Communists, sit-down strikers, and the Popular Front regime in Mexico.[37]

Despite their use of overlapping countersubversive conventions, far right spokesmen are distinguishable from conservatives, those disenchanted progressives and proponents of laissez faire who sought primarily to oppose the emerging welfare state. Far right leaders, often inspired by evangelical Protestantism, wanted also to transform—most would have said restore—basic values. Elizabeth Dilling was typical in this respect. In addition to FDR's brain trust, her "red network" contained modernist "Moscow-loving, intellectual" ministers who rewrote the Bible, leaving "faith in little besides the covers." Whereas Frank Knox and Al Smith privately still differentiated between Hyde Park and the Kremlin, far right leaders often took the accusation of New Deal Communism literally. The Liberty Leaguers, though they might have excluded Jews from their clubs or companies, usually avoided lapsing from "polite" to conspiratorial anti-Semitism. By the mid-1930s, however, many if not most far right activists viewed the New Deal conspiracy as part of the broad scheme sketched in *The Protocols* and *The International Jew*.[38]

Ironically, supposed New Deal conspirators were hardly more original than other Americans in their approach to the Depression. Some presidential advisors expressed vague interest in Soviet planning, but most programs had deep American roots. The National Recovery Administration (NRA), for example, drew its inspiration from the War Industries Board. Roosevelt himself was an old Wilsonian, a self-described Christian, Democrat, and believer in balanced budgets.[39]

Why, then, did the Roosevelt administration provoke extraordinary hostility? The New Deal "hit home," William E. Leuchtenburg suggests, because many Americans for the first time directly experienced the federal government. Some practices were new even if they were based on old ideas. On the narrow American spectrum, devoid of serious socialist challenge, such minimal steps toward the welfare state as unemployment insurance, social security, and the National Labor Relation Act bulked large to friends and foes alike. Nonetheless, Leuchtenburg's explanation falls short. Hoover had taken unprecedented steps to combat the Depression but elicited only occasional complaints that he subverted the republic. At a time of cultural as well as economic crisis, the New Deal hit home for reasons of style as well as substance.[40]

Like his progressive predecessors, FDR alternated between denouncing economic royalists and hiring them. Yet he was less likely than Wilson or Theodore Roosevelt to balance these denunciations with reminders that everyone tended to go up and down together. Jouett Shouse, paying greater attention to FDR's words than to his actions, accused him of deliberately "dividing the country into blocs." Few criticisms were more frequent than that Roosevelt abandoned the goal of preserving unity across class lines. In addition, already convinced of his hostility to business and impressed by his working-class backing in 1936, foes exaggerated Roosevelt's aid to the Congress of Industrial Organizations during the sit-down strikes of 1937.[41]

Similarly, magnifying the significance of Roosevelt's symbolic gestures, some conservatives and most far right activists accused FDR of favoring urban minorities. Ethnic tensions and cultural conflicts that historians usually associate with the 1920s survived, somewhat recast, into the Depression. Concern about Prohibition during the 1932 campaign prompted John Dewey to complain that "in the midst of the greatest crisis since the Civil War . . . the only thing the two national parties seem to want to debate is booze." Protestant periodicals took the issue more seriously, and some evangelicals never forgave Roosevelt for joining the wets. In an echo of earlier battles, opponents portrayed New Deal relief agencies as virtual extensions of Tammany Hall. Governor Landon called the Democratic "machine" a threat to "free elections"; Republican National Chairman John Hamilton in 1936 contrasted his own wholesome Kansas origins with the Tammany ties of James A. Farley, his Democratic counterpart.[42]

The returns in 1936 recorded not only disproportionate Roman Catholic votes for the Democrats, a routine occurrence, but also shifts to FDR by blacks and Jews. Earlier, Roosevelt had reconstituted an informal "black cabinet" and admitted more Jews to his inner circle than any previous president. Moreover, unlike Bernand Baruch and Louis D. Brandeis, who had served Wilson, frequently these Jews were children of the "new immigration." Blacks and Jews, like industrial workers, ultimately found Roosevelt to be an inconstant champion; refuge for European exiles from Nazism and legislation against lynching never made his list of priorities. Yet Jewish and black electoral support, combined with prominent appointments, were sufficient to raise suspicion among legatees of nativism.[43]

Roosevelt's manner compounded the strong reaction to his administration. Sympathetic accounts portray a jaunty, puckishly deceptive, cheerfully stubborn man, the first president, according to Arthur M. Schlesinger, Jr., who embodied the "Ivy League convention of casualness." To persons distrustful of the New Deal, however, these traits came across as deviousness, disdain, manipulativeness, and lack of dignity. Aides hoped that Landon's less polished delivery would suggest rugged candor, and at least once in 1936 he was proudly presented as "no radio crooner." Shrewd use of old and new media helped Roosevelt to mobilize his friends, but simultaneously made his obnoxious presence vivid to enemies. In Peter Arno's famous cartoon, economic royalists went "to the Trans-Lux to hiss

Roosevelt." And the President's wife Eleanor, a "new woman" active in the most liberal New Deal causes, provided another well-publicized Roosevelt to hiss.[44]

Politics, of course, is more complex than the ideal types created to interpret it. Rhetorical polarization on the national scene did not necessarily induce sharp partisanship at the local level. Particularly during the 1930s, strange alliances flourished and loyalties changed suddenly. Moved by party loyalty, patronage, or constituent pressure, many congressional conservatives swallowed their doubts and remained loyal to Roosevelt until his attempt to expand the Supreme Court in 1937. The president's coalition even made room for racist Senator Theodore Bilbo (Dem.-Miss.) and red-hunting Representative Martin Dies (Dem.-Tex.), both men with strong affinities for the far right. Throughout the decade, urbane corporate lawyers shuttled between the New Deal and the Liberty League; Communists denounced, wooed, and again denounced Socialists; and rank-and-file Trotskyists coalesced with Coughlinites in the Congress of Industrial Organizations.[45]

Delineation of the far right is especially problematical. Like liberals and radicals, their spokesmen disagreed among themselves, frequently overlooking common interests apparent to later historians. But because scholars pay less attention to these variations than to comparable diversity among liberals or radicals, firm conclusions about the far right must await discussions of Pelley, Winrod, and Smith.

Can It Happen Here?

When surveying the political spectrum during the Depression, liberals and radicals did not speak of a far right, the relatively neutral concept used here. Rather, they usually discerned incipient "fascism" and feared that a version of this European tyranny might triumph in the United States.

Some old progressives had initially viewed Italian Fascism with sympathetic curiosity. They considered the corporate state an experiment in rationalization and compared the strenuous lives of Theodore Roosevelt and Benito Mussolini. By the late 1920s, however, exiles and returning journalists had dampened enthusiasm for Il Duce. Adolf Hitler, whom most authorites regarded as a kind of German Mussolini, was more alarming. "So long as Italy was the chief fascist country, fascism to many people meant castor oil," Raymond Gram Swing of the *Nation* wrote in 1935. "Then Germany increased the vocabulary of repression to include concentration camps, steel whips, and anti-semitism."[46]

Nevertheless, few Americans, aside from radicals or liberals like Swing, condemned the Nazi regime from the outset. The *Saturday Evening Post* praised Hitler for saving Germany from Bolshevism, expected his moderation to restrain Nazi radicals, and applauded the hard-working, refined German people. Many Catholics thought the Führer less menacing than the anti-clerical president of Mexico; many fundamentalists believed Nazi slurs on German priests. Businessmen continued to share profits and patents with the Third Reich.[47]

Even among liberals and radicals, European fascism was easier to denounce than to explain. During the "third period" that ended in 1935, the Communists formulated an influential, if misleading, interpretation. Ignoring sophisticated analysts in their own ranks, party leaders insisted that Mussolini had been a capitalist agent all along. Furthermore, fascists, "social fascists," and liberals differed only in tactics used to serve capital. Expanded to cover Hitler, this theory received classic expression at the Comintern plenary session in December 1933. Fascism, George Dimitrov declared, was the "open terrorist dictatorship of the most reactionary, most chauvinist, and most imperialist elements of finance capital."[48]

Synthesizing the ideas of many anti-Communist left liberals, Alfred Bingham offered an alternate, but not completely antithetical theory. Fascism was "essentially" a revolt by frightened members of the middle classes. They joined Hitler and Mussolini in order to avert "class war," to protect their own property, and to acquire a feeling of "social solidarity." Contrary to Communist belief, Mussolini was a "pragmatic seeker after power" who presided over a bureaucracy dominated by middle-class values and personnel. Because they accepted a free market, Bingham conceded, fascist officials "played into the hands of the profit-makers." Yet he thought economics less important than creation of a "folk movement."[49]

Explanation of European fascism was more than an academic concern. As the Depression deepened, liberals and radicals became increasingly concerned that the horrible system might develop here. George Seldes, a journalist expelled by Mussolini a decade earlier, warned in 1935 that American fascism was already "formidable." It needed "only a Duce, a Fuehrer, an organizer and a loosening of purse strings of those who gain materially by its victory, to become the most powerful force threatening the Republic." "The usual complacent assumption that we cannot become fascist, simply because

America is 'different' or too large," Raymond Gram Swing agreed, "does not bear analysis."[50]

Unfortunately, the left was even more confused about the potential shape of native fascism than about the actual shape of existing regimes in Germany and Italy. In their definition and defense of the American way, conservatives and the far right could fall back on venerable—if often far-fetched—lore which associated socialism with impiety, sensuality, destruction of the family, and economic disaster. Liberal and radical foes of American fascism in the 1930s had to work almost from scratch. Predictably, they detected fascism "in embryo" among their customary foes.[51]

According to the *Nation*, urban bosses like Mayor Frank Hague of Jersey City represented the "most characteristic forms of fascism," the Roman Catholic hierarchy nurtured "potential fascism," and corporations illustrated "our native *Führerprinzip*." Benjamin Stolberg, an independent Marxist, pointed to vigilantes serving the privileged class. Swing wrote that anti-labor violence, legislative curbs on dissent, and escalating nationalism among Elks and American Legionaires fit into a "pattern of fascist action." For Anna Wallace of the *New Republic*, faculty dismissals, censorship, and the "psychological conditioning" of teachers were "unmistakable symptoms" of fascism on campus. The liberal journalist Hamilton Basso warned that "frightened fundamentalists" were vulnerable to "fascist-tending" demagogues. The Communist literary critic Mike Gold called the new humanists "literary blackshirts."[52]

The lists were eclectic but not indiscriminate. Extant or potential fascists usually fell into four sometimes overlapping categories. The first consisted of German nationals and untrustworthy German-Americans. The "invasion of America," Albert Brandt of the *Nation* warned in 1934, included "cells" of foreign students at major universities. George Sylvester Viereck, Kaiser Wilhelm's leading American publicist in 1914–17, was widely regarded as the "brain trust" of Nazi propaganda. Above all, the German-American Bund, organized in 1934, convinced liberal and radical commentators that a "Nazi International" or "Brown Network" extended into the United States.[53]

Second, the fascist label was applied to various far right activists, particularly those whc preached anti-Semitism or cooperated with the Bund. This category usually contained Dilling, Pelley, Winrod, Coughlin, Long, and Gerald L. K. Smith. The underlying premise that native fascism, like the European versions, would flourish among outraged middle classes was also presented with great cogency by Alfred Bingham. In 1935, Bingham concluded, only Senator Long offered a "genuine threat." Less tentative, Swing expressed prevailing left opinion that the Kingfish was "ruthless, ambitious, and indeed plausible enough to Hitlerize America."[54]

Third, retaining from the 1920s a mistaken belief that economic experimentation was the essence of Mussolini's regime, critics of the New Deal, ranging from Herbert Hoover to Norman Thomas, stressed similarities between the Roosevelt administration and expansion of government power in Rome and Berlin. George Soule agreed that the NRA had "really established something much like the 'corporate state.'"[55] Communists played a variation on this theme. During the "third period" they predicted that FDR would join Long and Coughlin in "waving the U.S. swastika." After proclaiming the People's Front in 1935, they continued to define fascism as a reactionary capitalist dictatorship, but detached New Dealers and Socialists from the enemies list. With more or less sophistication, Secretary of Agriculture Henry A. Wallace, Secretary of the Interior Harold L. Ickes, and Norman Thomas stressed connections between big business and prospective American fascism.[56]

Like the two major models attempting to explain Italian and German developments, these kindred theories of native fascism rarely appeared in pure form. More popular than any sophisticated scholarly treatment, Sinclair Lewis's novel *It Can't Happen Here,* published in 1936, reflected both the widespread concern and the analytical uncertainty. At the same time, Lewis's book revealed continuities from the Twenties to the Thirties, not only in the development of the far right, but in interpretations of it.[57] The Depression prompted Lewis, a socialist of sorts, to deepen his political commitment. He began to write *It Can't Happen Here* in the summer of 1935. Much as he had consulted physicians before writing *Arrowsmith* and clergymen before writing *Elmer Gantry,* Lewis consulted experts on native fascism. These authorities included his neighbor George Seldes, Benjamin Stolberg, and Lewis's wife, Dorothy Thompson, a syndicated columnist who had early attacked Hitler and the domestic far right.[58]

It Can't Happen Here opens in 1936 when Berzelius (Buzz) Windrip, Lewis's version of Huey Long, emerges as a presidential contender. Windrip goes beyond the Kingfish by creating a private militia, the Minute Men. The day after his inauguration, he proclaims martial law, arrests one hundred members of Congress, and confines Supreme Court justices to their homes. During the next two years he consolidates the states into eight provinces, disbands all political groups except the American Corporate State and Patriotic party, burns books by Mark Twain and Woodrow Wilson, and centralizes higher education in eight "Corpo Universities." Encouraged by newspapers with "large red headlines and many comic strips," most Americans initially favor the new order. Brutal Minute Men are more convincing still. Nevertheless, within two years the New Underground is functioning in Canada.[59]

Fort Beulah, Vermont, reveals the dictatorship in microcosm. The novel's main character, a country editor named Doremus Jessup, is deprived of his newspaper for attacking Windrip's "pirate gang." His son-in-law is summarily shot after protesting the decision. Doremus, his mistress Lorinda Pike, and his daughter Cissy form the nucleus of the Fort Beulah Underground. In short order Doremus is caught and sentenced to a concentration camp, from which he escapes to Canada. While he languishes, the Corpo regime is transformed for the worse. The head Minute Man seizes power, provokes war with Mexico, and attempts to suppress midwestern rebels. At the close of *It Can't Happen Here,* the American future remains uncertain. During two years of despotism citizens have learned little "except that it was unpleasant to be arrested so often." To teach his fellow countrymen that more than comfort is at stake, Doremus returns from Canada as a New Underground agent.[60]

Aside from corporate trappings, the tyranny in *It Can't Happen Here* is built of American stuff. Corpo race theorist Hector Macgoblin reads Lothrop Stoddard; Minute Men harass poor Jews but allow their wealthy kinsmen to enter any hotel—as long as they pay double rates. Doremus soon abandons his belief that "humor and pioneer independence" would make dictatorship here "absolutely different from anything in Europe." Whips hurt "just as sorely . . . as in the miasmatic fogs of Prussia."[61]

Lewis's portrait of American fascism fit no single theory but borrowed from all of them. At various levels, it consisted of capitalist exploitation, imperialism, militarism, and rule by a band of con men. In the final analysis, however, Lewis had less in common with neo-Marxists like Seldes and Stolberg than with liberal theorists who viewed fascism as middle-class resentiment. Doremus's hired hand joins the Minute Men to avenge insults, and thereafter enjoys the respect of "substantial men of affairs, even dry-goods jobbers."[62]

Lewis certainly did not set out to write a fictional version of Bingham's *Insurgent America.* Rather, he was continuing to ridicule the stock figures he had mocked throughout the 1920s. American fascism was Babbittry writ large. Prudes, prohibitionists, and hypocrites throng to Windrip's banner. Reading about Corpo buffoonery before the national convention of Booster Clubs, Doremus stresses the point: "This is revolution in terms of Rotary." The admirable characters were equally familiar. Cissy Jessup, who preaches sexual freedom and practices espionage, is a version of Carol Kennicott from *Main Street*; Lorinda Pike suggests Carol in spunky middle age.[63]

Although few critics discerned literary excellence, most applauded *It Can't Happen Here* on Lewis's terms, as a "propaganda book." The novel sold 320,000 copies in 1936 and was transferred to the stage by the Federal Theater. Lewis, helping to mold opinion about native "fascism," once again embossed a phrase on the language: "It can't happen here."[64]

2. William Dudley Pelley

SPIRITUALIST IN POLITICS

Innocent Rebellion

In Sinclair Lewis's *It Can't Happen Here*, Buzz Windrip hails William Dudley Pelley's "self-sacrificing" efforts against "sneaking, snaky, sinister, surreptitious" Bolsheviks. The accolade was triply appropriate. By the mid-1930s, native fascism was widely associated with uniformed troopers and abusive anti-Semitism, and Pelley promoted both. In addition, before founding the paramilitary Silver Legion in 1933, he had been, like Doremus Jessup, a rural editor, and, like Sinclair Lewis, a prolific author of fiction, including a novel intended to defend small-town America against Lewis's mockery.[1]

Pelley's earthly existence, which, he insisted after a religious experience in 1928, was only the latest of many, began in Lynn, Massachusetts, on 12 March 1890. His family combined Methodist piety, passion for wealth, and a propensity for financial failure. Coming to Lynn from Canada in 1878, his grandfather had manufactured leather boots until rubber doomed the enterprise. His father, William G. A. Pelley, had attended Boston University Divinity School and alternated between Methodist pastorates and fragile small businesses. In 1894, at age thirty-three, he left a Lynn pulpit to operate a dry goods store and shoe shop in East Templeton; two years afterward he moved to West Gardner, where he sold advertising and wrote for the local newspaper and later opened a shop selling second-hand goods. In 1900 he went to Springfield. There, during the next nine years he was a furniture dealer, writer for the *Springfield Union*, and proprietor of Pelley's Parcel Delivery. There, too, Rev. Pelley's wife, Grace, a woman four years his senior, bore two more children. The family grew larger and moved around, however, without moving upward.[2]

Pelley believed his youth was sacrificed to his father's dream of success. He labored in family enterprises, suffered beatings for slight offenses, and felt "perpetually hungry and shabbily dressed." "Clean" thinking was a typical Victorian counterpart to hard work, but Pelley's parents were so committed to purity that they discouraged all social contact with girls. Three times on Sunday and twice during the week he attended church where a "heavenly Moloch" endorsed striving, chastity, and obedience to parents.[3]

The conflict between father and son took a critical turn during 1907, Pelley's sophomore year at Springfield technical high school. Rev. Pelley's latest stab at success, partnership in the Fulton Toilet Paper Company near Syracuse, New York, took precedence over his son's desire for education. Instead of editing literary magazines and debating, his joys in high school, Pelley had to work six days a week producing "smooth, velvet" tissue that, advertisements said, added "years to your life." Enough customers believed such promotions to bring the Pelleys modest prosperity. The business was soon worth $250,000, Pelley later remembered, claiming credit for the success. Still, he felt "sold to the galleys." His chief recreation was a YMCA lecture series, where he listened to William Jennings Bryan, S.S. McClure, and Senators Henry Cabot Lodge, Robert M. LaFollette, and Albert Beveridge.[4]

Words and ideas helped Pelley to rebel against his father's authority and faith. The angry adolescent "drugged" himself with reading, including Marx's *The Communist Manifesto*, Edward Bellamy's *Looking Backward*, and especially the *Philistine*, a magazine edited by his "idol" Elbert Hubbard. A well-known iconoclast during the "innocent rebellion" before World War I, Hubbard urged lenient child-rearing, advocated divorce for incompatible couples, and mocked all "smug" religions—especially Christianity. These ideas appealed to Pelley partly because they were anathema to his father.[5]

Wanting to produce as well as consume ideas, Pelley in 1909 issued from Fulton, New York, his own "religio-sociological" monthly. As the self-proclaimed youngest publisher in the United States, he asserted that the nation's health was reflected in its "average child-life" and concluded that prevailing child-rearing practices produced self-doubt, guilt, and violence. A baby, born "pure minded, confiding, trusting and gentle," was soon regarded by his parents as an unruly "kid." They inflicted corporal punishment, inculcated distrust for his "wonderful body," and threatened him with damnation because of "some allegorical crime" recounted in Genesis. Raised in this fashion, men naturally gravitated toward theft, murder, and warfare.[6]

Pelley's youthful view that the American future depended on the "environment of our boy life" was reinforced by Progressive era contemporaries who founded juvenile courts, organized the Boy Scouts, and studied "boyology." Yet the *Philosopher* also reflected Pelley's particular ambivalence about his parents. "I have been a child and so have you," he addressed readers, "though perhaps you have forgotton and I have not." Far from honoring his father, as the "heavenly Moloch" required, Pelley made him the butt of a comic article, a figure simultaneously tyrannical and weak: "Pa is great on killing things"—especially his son's aspirations—but he bungles the task of slaughtering chickens for Sunday dinner.[7]

At bottom, the *Philosopher* was a declaration of adulthood. With the bravado and hyperbole that would become his trademarks, Pelley claimed readers in every state. Not only did Pelley claim to be more successful than his father, but he professed to be tougher, even "calloused to the point of not having my feelings hurt." Grateful for living in an age of "strong characters and stronger wills," he called sensitiveness the "worst vice."[8]

This vice tempted him often. In one mawkish story, a blind girl's affliction keeps her pure, generous, and close to God. Indeed, the self-proclaimed youngest American publisher admitted that he was still a "boy" who wondered "why cannot love exist forever." What would become one of Pelley's perennial themes, the special power of maternal love, appeared in the *Philosopher* beside assertions of manly independence. When night comes, he exclaimed, "how like little children we all are . . . crying for the arms that once rocked us to sleep."[9]

Still, Pelley did not simply despise his father and adore his mother. On the one hand, he unconsciously emulated his father while competing with and rebelling against him. In publishing the *Philosopher*, he combined two of Rev. Pelley's occupations, printing and preaching; he, too, sought success through "hustle," and would continue to do so with comparably mixed results. He aspired, moreover, to be as strong as his father pretended to be. On the other hand, Pelley's hymns to maternal nurturing revealed at least as much unfulfilled craving for it and veiled reproach of his mother as nostalgia for the lost serenity of infancy. Grace Pelley, after all, did not protect him from exploitation by her husband. Endorsing a version of the familial "Puritanic code," Pelley defined a great man as someone who made "his body obey his mind." At nineteen, he neither smoked tobacco nor drank alcohol, ate an (unspecified) wholesome diet, and shunned theatrical "lewdery." Violations of "laws of health, chastity, and reason" brought punishment, not in Hell, to be sure, but in ill health and mental anguish. Conversely, human progress required "self-control and purity of heart."[10]

Fear of God, Pelley wrote in the *Philosopher*, was actually fear of parents injected into a young child's "subconscious." Certainly Pelley's conception of Christianity mirrored his conception of his own father, an incarnation of tyranny, weakness, and repression of "emotions and ambitions." Every Sunday, he complained, Protestant clergy hissed the "serpent's hiss of 'sin' 'sin' 'sin'" and told "fairy tales" about groveling souls, who, standing before a great throne, were sentenced to eternal hellfire or blessed with "eternal idleness." Like many theological modernists in the early 1900s, Pelley doubted Jesus's divinity and virgin birth, preferring to consider Him a "Great Teacher."[11]

Adopting popular social gospel themes, Pelley condemned churches—with the notable exception of the Salvation Army—for ignoring poverty and war. Clergy who loafed much, read little, and made an occasional "womanly call" were responsible for this religious "inefficiency." Pelley's wish to replace these "drones" with activists was commonplace, but he wrote with the intensity of someone who considered his father one of the drones. He understood "half-feminized" ministers because he had "lived in their families."[12]

A portion of humanity passing beyond "spiritual childhood," Pelley asserted, was now ready for a nobler faith. The religious order he envisioned resembled Edward Bellamy's social gospel utopia. A unified Christianity, self-supporting, functionally structured, and unimpaired by denominational conflict, would serve God by "helping mankind." The clergy, recruited for their brains, brawn, refinement, and worldly wisdom, would lead a movement to abolish poverty. They would build in each town a beautiful "Guild House" with resources far beyond those of institutional churches in 1909. This would provide meals, day nurseries, and theatre productions devoid of "lewdery," as well as homes and hospitals for anyone who faltered in the "struggle for existence"; charity would be "no disgrace." Perhaps recalling his retreats to YMCA lectures, Pelley dreamed of a "place of laughter" for children from unhappy homes.[13]

Within two generations, Pelley surmised, reformed Christianity might comprise "but one division" of a benevolent army composed of all "great religions." Like Bellamy in *Looking Backward*, however, he paid scant attention to transitional details. Change would come slowly because most Christians retained a childlike faith in theological "fairy tales," but promising trends must be encouraged. Declaring, in effect, an end to his own childhood, Pelley anticipated a career guiding the "thought of my age."[14]

The *Philosopher*, his first experiment in social guidance, fell short of his promise to discuss faith in a "scientific, unsentimental manner." Just as he needed true women and innocent children as antidotes to hustling, Pelley craved the "consolation of sentimental religion" in spite of himself. As he recalled twenty years later, "singing Nature" provided an alternative to his father's theology. Hence, denunciations of orthodoxy coexisted in the *Philosopher* with pantheistic reveries in which Pelley, after teetering on the brink of despair, affirmed that this "world is lovely" and the universe even better.[15]

The loveliness had a decidedly maternal aspect. "Why must I live?" Pelley wondered in one of his stream-of-consciousness ruminations:

> Born of agony only for those who know, sheltered and nurtured for a few brief years, damned by desire and consumed by dread, haunted by the great To Be and in the end only the vague and misty guess, a thousand passions I know not why crying for satisfaction in my breast, filled from birth with the environment of deceit, falsehood, curses, mockery, dishonor, even worse than death.

Then a voice urged him to push upward to the abode of the "Madonna who knows no death and opens for us the gate which keeps the pain and sorrow from existence." There, his worries gone, he could lie by the "river whose seducing waters float away through the clouds" and sleep amid a "lullaby of humming Pans."[16]

Not only did Pelley believe in this heaven, but he expected humanity to commute between mundane existence and the afterlife. Presenting a softened version of his father's predestination, he thought that everyone had an earthly "niche" determined from birth. This world was a "nursery" for the next. Instead of hellfire, death brought a "higher plane" on which humanity received compensation for earthly pain while preparing for another mortal soujourn. Although the mechanics of reincarnation remained vague in the *Philosopher*, Pelley declared that he had "lived before and on this earth."[17]

The higher planes practiced socialism, a system far from Rev. Pelley's McKinley Republicanism and one that his son wanted to install on earth. The *Philosopher* sympathized with the "factory slave," condemned the ostentatious rich, and cited the example of "Comrade Christ," the greatest socialist. Like many other socialists in 1909, however, Pelley was uncertain whether to beat capitalism or to join it; still closer to Bellamy than to Eugene Debs, he presented "Christ the Manufacturer" as well as Christ the militant.[18]

This ambivalence paralleled Pelley's mixed feelings about work and, beneath them, his family conflicts. His dreary youth might have been a blessing, he speculated, because it taught him the importance of "hustling." After slaving in his father's "galleys," he now resented both rich snobs and "lazy" radicals who did no rowing. Sounding like his mentor Elbert Hubbard, who expected quick advancement for the young man who carried a "message to Garcia," Pelley imagined employers "on their knees" in search of hard workers. Yet life's purpose must be more than "getting a good living out of it." Wealth brought neither admission to heaven nor "Love in the hearts of those who stay behind." And, knowing from personal experience that hustling wore out the hustler, he craved a respite somewhere on this side of the "abode of the Madonna who knows no death."[19]

Accordingly, the economic system advocated by the *Philosopher* in 1909 attempted to mesh discipline and release, competition and fellowship. Instead of dismantling giant corporations ("geese which are laying . . . golden eggs"), Pelley, like Bellamy, wanted them administered for the common good by a central "people's business institution." All citizens were entitled to a minimum "fair share" of national wealth. Unlike Bellamy, however, Pelley favored equality of opportunity, not equality of remuneration. Fellow hustlers were assured that the people's trust would "pay you for your ability" and permit considerable affluence.[20]

Revealing another paradox Pelley shared with many eminent Progressive era social critics, the form of government advocated in the *Philosopher* attempted to mesh expertise and grassroots democracy. Voters, informed by "impartial" authorities, would settle controversial questions in weekly national plebiscites; suffrage would be available (and compulsory) for all adults. Despite the complexities of central planning, Pelley considered limited government a "paramount" goal.[21]

Because socialism required a learned, self-disciplined, and "refined" electorate, the *Philosopher* offered a program to meet the need. From another perspective, Pelley's educational utopia promised the happy childhood and formal training he had missed, along with the "common sense" he had supposedly acquired through struggle. Babies, he said, must play together in order to develop altruism and affection. For children aged four to ten, the curriculum should consist of "singing, laughter, joy, and gymnastics." Only then would they be prepared to study reading, writing, arithmetic, and government. Instead of poring over dead languages or developing manners befitting capitalist "parasites," they must learn "TO TAKE CARE OF THEMSELVES." Academic specialization could begin at eighteen. Molded gently by teachers who nurtured their "desire to know," students would emerge at twenty-one as "Herculanean" men and women.[22]

The role of women in Pelley's educational scheme, as in his utopia as a whole, revealed his confusion about them. Undoubtedly recalling his parents' restrictions, he called separation of boys and girls "contrary to the laws of nature." Coeducation produced healthy minds, healthy bodies and, thus, "healthy morals." Socialism, by freeing women from "monotony" and granting "absolute equality," would make relations between the sexes less awkward. Nonetheless, under a kind of socialist cult of true womanhood, women must provide their mates with support, sympathy, and refinement. Every man, the nineteen-year-old publisher concluded, needed a "woman who understands."[23]

Pelley also expected ethnic and racial minorities to benefit from socialism. The *Philosopher*, though marred by paternalism and a single reference to "dagoes," was less ethnocentric than more eminent publications. Indeed, Pelley chided orthodox Christians for failure to teach their children to respect immigrant workers. The blood of ten nationalities, he predicted, would mingle in the United States to create an eleventh, "mightier than them all." Reformed religion spreading abroad could teach "our brown, black and yellow brothers" how to turn earth into heaven.[24]

Similarly, Pelley in 1909 shunned the jingoism that later would characterize the Silver Legion. Patriotism, he said, was an unchristian doctrine "founded on hatred," and war was the "abode of the Devil." Rather than menace civilians with new weapons like the airplane, Pelley believed governments would settle differences in international courts and ultimately build "one world nation."[25]

The path to domestic socialism and international amity, like the complementary religious change, was left murky. Occasionally the *Philosopher* predicted that these movements would be capped by a sort of Second Coming. The "White Christ," a great businessman "schooled by blood sweating experience," would begin a "second age of miracles" and then disappear. More often, however, Pelley stressed that men must make their own utopia.[26]

The *Philosopher* did not survive to guide the transitions. For reasons that remain uncertain—though lack of subscribers seems paramount—the magazine closed after nine issues in November 1909. In 1911, Rev. Pelley lost financial control of the Fulton Tissue Paper Company. Rejecting a job from rival paper suppliers, the younger Pelley turned again to journalism, first as feature writer for the

Springfield Homestead, and then as western Massachusetts correspondent for the *Boston Globe*. To ease suffering caused by his financial problems, he sought a "woman who understands." Marion Harriet Stone, a *Globe* proofreader, provided that understanding. Pelley and Mary Ann, as he called her, were married on 16 December 1911, and a daughter, Harriet, was born the next year.[27]

Domesticity did not quench Pelley's thirst to enlighten humanity. In 1912, encouraged by Mary Ann, a self-reliant and ambitious woman who, he believed, considered him brilliant, Pelley bought the *Chicopee* (Massachusetts) *Journal*. The next year he sold the *Journal* and assumed the mortgage on the *Deerfield Valley Times* in Wilmington, Vermont, his wife's home town. Cushioned by a modest inheritance, he wanted to "revolutionize the country press" while writing stories for national magazines in his spare time.[28]

Everything went wrong. When the *Deerfield Times* failed within a year, Pelley alternately blamed himself and condemned rural New England for rejecting "progress." Mary Ann offered no criticism, but her silence, Pelley recalled in 1918, had been "worse than blistering acid." Indeed, his family situation reached a new low. His mother-in-law nagged him. His father simply disappeared, never to return. His infant daughter Harriet died of meningitis in 1912. In debt, plagued by self-doubt, "almost friendless," Pelley took a job in August 1914 as foreman on the *Bennington* (Vermont) *Banner*. Mary Ann gave birth to a daughter, Adelaide, a month later.[29]

Doggedly Pelley continued to write fiction. Although his first stories, set in a wild west he had never seen, indulged his taste for vicarious adventure, they were virtually unsalable. Inspired by William Allen White's collection of stories, *In Our Town*, he began to write about ordinary people, concluding that stories "grew on bushes" in Vermont. Contrary to the mythology of bucolic bliss, the *Banner* recorded numerous domestic quarrels, grisly accidents, suicides, and murders. Still tempted by what he had called the "vice" of sentimentality, Pelley drew uplifting morals from such sordid events. In "Their Mother," an early experiment with mundane topics, a widow in the imaginary town of Paris, Vermont, struggles to raise six sons.[30]

On a personal level, "Their Mother" represented both Pelley's continued craving for *his* mother and an act of restitution to her. As with issues raised in the *Philosopher*, however, Pelley's ambivalence toward women intersected with broader cultural currents. His young manhood coincided with a rising divorce rate, agitation for women's suffrage, and changing sexual mores. Accusing "new women" of emasculating men and threatening "race suicide," scholars, journalists, and statesmen reaffirmed allegiance to Victorian true women—*their* mothers in fancy if not in fact. While Pelley managed the *Banner*, for example, Congress in 1914 set aside an annual day to honor the American mother, the "greatest source" of national strength.[31]

No one honored mothers more than John Siddall, editor of the *American Magazine*, who printed "Their Mother" in August 1917. A lucrative career had begun for Pelley. During the next decade, he published more than two hundred stories in *Red Book, Collier's*, and the *Saturday Evening Post*, as well as Siddall's *American*. By March 1918 he had accumulated sufficient capital to buy controlling interest in the *St. Johnsbury* (Vermont) *Caledonian*. Despite his success writing fiction, Pelley told prospective subscribers, he could not wean himself from newspaper work.[32]

Deciding in retrospect that his own haughtiness had doomed the *Deerfield Valley Times*, he also promised to keep in step with the local community. Traces of the boy philosopher lingered in occasional columns meditating on the godliness of nature, but usually the young Pelley tried to sound like a crusty country editor who understood human nature, a *persona* he had begun to cultivate at the *Banner*. As he promised in his first editorial, the *Caledonian* recorded the "heartwarming" joys and sorrows of the "town family." In an intermittent column, "Life's Dreary Path," Pelley added epigraphic comment on human "foibles." A country editor's job, he decided, was "profitable"—and "in lots of ways beside money."[33]

Yet it was not profitable enough to prevent Pelley from leaving Vermont for more exotic places four months after buying the *Caledonian*. Impressed by one of his stories in *American Magazine*, Earl S. Taylor, director of the Methodist Centenary Movement, asked Pelley to report on missionary activities in the Far East. Pelley sold partial interest in his newspaper, collected $5,000 from the Centenary Fund, and, with Mary Ann, entrained for San Francisco and steamship connections to the Orient; his travelogues dispatched to the *Caledonian* en route anticipated "real adventure." The Pelleys reached Japan in August 1918, but World War I prevented them from proceding as planned to China and India.[34]

This delay allow Pelley to embark on a real adventure, de facto participation in the Russian Revolution. In July 1918, President Woodrow Wilson had dispatched 7,000 troops to Siberia. The Young Men's Christian Association, which provided amenities to soldiers on all fronts, immediately sought volunteers for Russian duty among Americans in Japan. Pelley, commissioned as a second lieutenant in the YMCA's "Red Triangle" service, arrived at Vladivostok a day after the first United States regiment. From August until mid-November, he traveled more than 8,000 miles in Siberia, often attaching his Red Triangle canteen to troop trains. He doubled as staff correspondent for the American Red Cross, wrote dispatches for the Associated Press, and talked with prominent diplomats as well as American, Czech, and Japanese soldiers. Two thousand miles into Siberia when Germany surrendered in November 1918, he set out for the Pacific coast in a railroad boxcar that he shared with two Foreign Service officers and several hundred thousand rubles belonging to International Harvester.[35]

In Tokyo, where his wife had remained to teach at a Methodist college, Pelley discovered two compelling reasons to abandon the Far Eastern tour. Not only had wartime censors lost important correspondence concerning his finances, but Mary Ann's brother had died suddenly. During the voyage home, Pelley expanded "Their Mother" into his first novel, *The Greater Glory*, which Little, Brown and Co. published in late 1919. Proud of his exciting trip and noted acquaintances, he also lectured Vermonters on the Russian situation and commented on Far Eastern affairs in *Sunset* and *World Outlook*. No other participant in the Great War, he believed, had had a stranger "commission."[36]

Exile's Return

The Siberian expedition was the central event of Pelley's first thirty-eight years. The *St. Johnsbury Caledonian* had edged toward bankruptcy during his absence and he returned too enervated to rescue it. Real adventure, moreover, had heightened his hunger for "something . . . bigger" than rural publishing. Nevertheless, resuming control of the newspaper in December 1918, he tried for seven months to cover the world "at a glance" and provide "breezy" features (including a serialization of *The Greater Glory*).[37]

Pelley's view of the world was broader than that of the typical rural Vermont editor. World War I represented a triumph of "democracy over autocracy," but, he warned in January 1919, decency and self-interest precluded any scheme to "bankrupt Germany" by demanding high reparations. In the Far East, commercial opportunities abounded if Yankees, the world's "most provincial people," learned to treat Orientals respectfully. Similarly, instead of deriding the "heathen," Christian missionaries must see that all people shared a common "yearning after the Infinite."[38]

Yet Pelley himself showed that it was easier to denounce Yankee provincialism than to escape it. He regarded most "Japs" with condescending affection while openly distrusting their Emperor-worshiping rulers. Orientals in general would profit from a dose of "white man's spirituality," a combination of the Declaration of Independence and the Sermon on the Mount.[39]

Trying to mix altruism, empathy, good business, and American superiority, Pelley shared common ground with Woodrow Wilson, whom he greatly admired. A professed Republican, he nonetheless endorsed the League of Nations and, despite counterattacks by fellow Vermont editors, defended Wilson against "childish" senatorial opponents. The League represented "Christianity Militant," an inevitable precursor of the "world-wide get-together movement" that Pelley had predicted in the *Philosopher.*[40]

To be sure, there would be difficulties along the way. Currently, for instance, Bolshevism reduced Russia to "chaos" (a condition, Pelley boasted to *Caledonian* readers, he had seen with his own "naked eye"). No better informed than most of the press, he surmised that the revolution had been "made in Germany," presumed that Communism could "not endure," and reported unfought battles, nonexistent Soviet retreats, and Czar Nicholas' mythical escape. Appalled by Soviet atrocities, he called on the Allies to crush these "hoodlums." Here, too, idealism and national interest seemed to converge. Pelley envisioned a great Russian market and in language reminiscent of Secretary of State John Hay pronounced Siberia a "melon ripe for cutting."[41]

In March 1919, Pelley asked quick action against a domestic "Bolshevik peril of great magnitude." Thereafter, the *Caledonian* paid close attention to IWW agitation, May Day demonstrations, and warnings against subversion issued by the American Defense Society, Attorney General A. Mitchell Palmer, and Lee Overman, chairman of the Senate Subcommittee on Bolshevik Propaganda. In June, Pelley expressed sober second thoughts. Recalling comparable turmoil after the Civil War, the *Caledonian* recommended "keeping cool" while the nation returned to equilibrium. Furthermore, Pelley criticized the United States Supreme Court for overturning child labor legislation, showed interest in the Plumb Plan to nationalize railroads, and supported postwar strikes for higher wages and shorter hours.[42]

One question—the "Jewish question"—was conspicuously absent. According to *The Door to Revelation*, the autobiography Pelley published in 1939, acquaintances in Siberia, including fellow Red Cross agents, had told him that a Jewish conspiracy lay behind Communism. Given the anti-Semitism widespread among White Russians and some of their American patrons, this recollection was plausible and perhaps understated. Judging from the *Caledonian*, however, these Siberian stories had little immediate impact. Pelley's coverage of Senator Overman's investigation, for example, ignored its most striking feature, charges by Russian émigrés and returning American missionaries that Bolshevism was "Yiddish." On the other hand, he routinely reported Jewish as well as Protestant and Roman Catholic activities, and Pelley himself respectfully interviewed a Jewish member of Congress.[43]

In short, Pelley's postwar writings, like his earlier ruminations as the boy philosopher, do not reveal a congenital bigot marching inexorably toward the Silver Shirts. Sympathetic to welfare legislation, labor unions, and Wilsonian foreign policy, he qualified as a low-level participant in the amorphous progressive movement. References to "Huns," "Japs," "Chinamen," and, once, "niggers," show the limit of his commitment to a world devoid of "racial differences." But he was no more—and perhaps less—prejudiced than the typical reformer.[44]

By the spring of 1919, the country's current prospects worried Pelley less than his own. Reduced from Siberian adventurer to a "mere writer of fiction," he consoled himself by recalling that *Uncle Tom's Cabin* had changed history. Apparently his boast of rising *Caledonian* circulation was another exercise in consolation. In June 1919, he relinquished control of the newspaper to rival publishers. A parting editorial, which suggests that he had again fallen out of step with Vermont sentiment, anticipated some gloating over his departure.[45]

Pelley's malaise was reflected in his continued confusion about women in general and heightened, if veiled, hostility to his wife in particular. He endorsed women's suffrage, favored appointment of a "progressive" woman to the St. Johnsbury board of education, and defended feminist leader Carrie Chapman Catt against male jokes. At the same time, he pointedly distinguished between "dignified, lovable" campaigners like Catt and "suffragettes" who preached "'give-us-our-rights-or-we'll-smash-up-something' stuff." Not only must the local school trustee be a "tactful lady," but Pelley's rationale for selecting a woman underscored one of his favorite themes: mothers, possessing superior virtue, should influence their children's education.[46]

According to Pelley's boastful account in *American Magazine*, "Why I Am Glad I Married a Suffragist," Mary Ann joined the women's movement when, having retired from journalism, she felt unfulfilled by household chores. Soon she was also working to replace inept officials, to modernize schools, and to improve conditions at St. Johnsbury factories. These activities rebounded to his advantage, Pelley said, because they rendered Mary Ann an efficient homemaker and more intelligent companion. Beneath surface boasts, however, Pelley was not all that glad he married a suffragist. He approved of Mary Ann's public activities only as long as she remained a true woman who cooked suppers, nurtured children, and acknowledged his status as "boss." Indeed, these provisos, reminiscent of his ambiguous paeans to motherhood in the *Philosopher*, probably signaled his lack of love and respect more than their presence.[47]

Some men proposed to homebodies free from "fads and isms," Pelley told *American Magazine* readers, while others wanted intelligent, self-reliant mates. Pelley's relations with women consisted of repeated efforts to reconcile these conflicting desires. At nineteen, writing in the *Philosopher*, he had oscillated between endorsement of "absolute" equality between the sexes and longing for a deferential "woman who understands." Ten years later, he sought a bright, strong "team-mate" who would subordinate herself in order to catalyze the "elements of his talent into the compound of his triumph." When Mary Ann in 1919 seemed to focus on her own triumphs, he struck back, as he had at his father, by making her the butt of jokes; in "Life's Dreary Path," he portrayed her as a parsimonious nag, criticized her gardening and driving, and asked, "where the fellow who first wrote: 'And they lived happily ever after' got his ideas?"[48]

That same year Pelley became emotionally involved with another woman, a twice divorced Californian designated in his memoirs only as Lillian. Sometime after quitting the *Caledonian*, he traveled alone to San Francisco, vaguely expecting to spread his newly-acquired knowledge of the Orient. Lillian, with whom he had corresponded about his fiction, was a bohemian journalist, artist, and amateur aviator. According to Pelley's recollection, she diagnosed his "infantile fixations" and polished his "provincial" manners. This surrogate mother (whom he called a "wise older sister") also provided the comfort he missed at home. Pelley hungrily accepted her nurture, but, apparently by his choice, their interlude ended without intimacy "in the accepted sense of the word."[49]

Rather, because Mary Ann was again pregnant, Pelley returned east to his "marital stalemate" and growing prominence as an author of local color fiction. Reviewers for the *Boston Transcript, New York Post*, and *Publisher's Weekly* admired the humor in *The Greater Glory*, and subscribers to the *American Magazine* looked forward to new tales of Paris, Vermont. In the fall of 1920, shortly after the birth of his son William Ernest, Pelley began *The Fog*, a rejoinder to Sinclair Lewis's *Main Street*. A collateral career opened at roughly the same time. Jules Brulatour, a movie producer in Fort Lee, New Jersey, wanted to base a film on "White Faith," one of Pelley's unpublished stories. Restless as ever, Pelley agreed to write the script and moved his family to New York City.[50]

Even from the brief remarks in *The Door to Revelation*, it is clear that Pelley's restlessness doomed his marriage. Whereas he viewed life as an adventurous "campaign," Mary Ann wanted a solid "program." The couple had been drifting apart for several years. The final break, which occurred after they moved to New York, was nonetheless "numbing" to Pelley.[51]

The temptation is strong to regard Pelley's private restlessness in the 1920s merely as an inevitable prelude to his public prejudice in the 1930s. Yet his malaise and its immediate catalyst, postwar readjustment, were hardly unique. For Pelley, as for his contemporary Malcolm Cowley, World War I capped the "process of deracination" begun during the previous decade's "innocent rebellion." Observing combat as an ambulance driver Cowley acquired a "spectatorial attitude," while Pelley, a canteen operator, sharpened his editorialist's "bemused toleration." Like Pelley, though with greater erudition, Cowley wrote during the 1920s partly to work out personal problems. Finally, because the war prepared him "only for travel and excitement," Cowley expatriated himself in Paris, France; Pelley, estranged from his wife and hungry for a "Great Thrill," moved to Hollywood where he composed more stories about Paris, Vermont.[52]

Paris, Vermont

Paris, Vermont, the setting for the bulk of the fiction Pelley wrote in the 1910s and 1920s, is a Yoknapatawpha county for sentimentalists. Sam Hod, the "grizzled" owner of the *Paris Daily Telegraph*, frequently hires suffering widows or "hay-barn-scented" lads seeking to rise in the world. The *Telegraph*'s foreman, Bill, tells many of the tales in a voice recalling Pelley's crusty *persona*. When sweethearts meet under "prinkling" stars in Paris, the rural night is likely to grow "increasingly sensuous about them." Villains usually look the part and come from outside the community. Among natives, good fellowship and character count for more than social position; Jim Thorne heads the fish and game club as well as the knitting mill, and his children romp barefoot with offspring of humbler residents.[53]

Yet sentimentality coexisted in Pelley's fiction with a modest, partly conscious revolt against the village. The two decades before 1912, foreman Bill reflected, produced greater changes than any comparable period in American history. The United States became a "nation of speed maniacs." Even Paris increasingly seemed to contain acquaintances instead of friends "whose joys were our joys and failures our failures." Nor did the town escape class conflict. Lapsing from affability, Jim Throne forces the dismissal of Dr. Dodd, the perennial Methodist minister, for demanding higher wages at the knitting mill. But Dodd's successor urges a strike, and scabs turn the strike into a riot.[54]

Pelley often used social change as the backdrop for the travail of "ordinary folks," whose suffering contrasts with the placid image of prinkling stars. Loneliness, disease, and insanity compete with good fellowship in Paris and on surrounding farms. Frustrated men commit suicide, murder their wives, or run off in search of "pagan" satisfactions. Parents in Pelley's fiction, as in his life, pass on bitterness to their children. Teenagers marry early and unwisely to escape isolation. Promising romances are destroyed—or postponed to a bittersweet last page—by poverty, illness, or family responsibility in addition to parental disapproval.[55]

Many of Pelley's characters are financially even less successful than his father had been, and their struggle for fame and fortune compounds personal anguish. They suffer industrial accidents, forge checks and flee, or, sensing failure, take their own lives. Betraying reservations about his own upward striving, as well as jealousy of those who had reached the top, Pelley demanded anguish from Parisians who achieve wealth. For example, Jim Thorne's young grandson dies in the riot provoked by his strikebreakers. Believing that sacrifice is one of life's "great laws," foreman Bill of the *Telegraph* records the sagas of persons who achieve greatness through self-denial. Almost always, these self-denying Vermonters are women possessing more integrity than their weak, narrow-minded mates. They track murderers in order to win reward money, rescue husbands from imminent death, and save their spouses' businesses. Still, like Mary Ann Pelley at her best, no heroine forsakes babies and sweet smiles. On the contrary, women are their finest when they inspire and comfort men. Adapting a favorite image from the *Philosopher,* Pelley has wives cuddling husbands as if they were "small boys." Providing such comfort, Sam Hod says, has been "woman's privilege . . . since the beginin' o' all things created."[56]

The Greater Glory, dedicated to Pelley's mother, Grace, urged "good women everywhere" to continue giving of themselves. We meet Mary Purse, the object of veneration, when, as a teenager in the 1880s, she is rescued from a violent stepfather. Her champion, Herbert (Slug) Truman takes her to Paris where Sam Hod hires her to set type at the *Telegraph.* She marries the newspaper's bookkeeper, Jack Purse, planning to help "step by step as he climbs upward." Their aspirations are doomed by incessant crisis. Mary's stepfather kills her mother and himself, and the family homestead is sold on her wedding day. After fathering six sons, Jack dies suddenly. Penniless and prematurely old, Mary resumes her typesetting job at the *Telegraph.* Nothing matters now but the "successful manhood" of her six sons.[57]

Rejecting the values symbolized by Mary, Mibb Henderson regrets having been born female and compares marriage to slavery. She marries Slug Truman for his money, soon leaving him bankrupt and alcoholic. Thereafter, she pursues an eclectic, exploitative love life and acquires fame as a singer. Occasionally returning to Paris, she mocks Mary's drabness and predicts the end of "fireside and family notions." Mary responds that sacrifice, especially for children, is the "highest sort of service." "And if there's a 'new day dawning' as you seem to think, it's the day when service is going to be glorified and gentleness and self-sacrifice for others considered the things in life really worthwhile."[58]

As Mary's sons become successful teachers, engineers, and journalists, Pelley wrote, she achieves "Greater Glory" than "little minds can conceive." Conversely, Mibb Henderson suffers for her sins. After being beaten by her drunken ex-husband, Slug Truman, she can never sing again. Her psychological punishment is harsher. Missing "damp baby kisses," she proposes to Dick Robinson, a millionaire stunted by an unhappy childhood in Paris and by Mibb's greed. Dick, rejecting the offer, lectures her on the greatness of maternal women. No "fads or isms," he says, can replace a man's veneration "for his mother who was a woman and a wife first, even if it cost her her life and her reason."[59]

Yet even Mary, the blatant symbol of fidelity in a nation of speed maniacs, cannot protect her sons from the consequences of "isms" and ambitions. All of them neglect her, and Tom, the oldest, breaks her heart by refusing to enter the ministry. At the novel's end, however, she hears him address a mass meeting on "Jesus Christ, the King of Nations." Mibb, also moved by Tom's speech, apologizes to Mary for thirty years of taunts. Mary, without bitterness, wraps her in a "mother-heart of eternal sympathy."[60]

The Fog, which appeared in 1921, was intended to answer Sinclair Lewis' "libel" of small-town America. Yet, until "Kismet" unites the hero, Nathan Forge, with his soulmate, Madeleine Theddon, his life in rural Vermont is drearier than Carol Kennicott's existence in Gopher Prarie. Indeed, because Pelley consciously incorporated memories of his own adolescent "fog," and unconsciously revealed misgivings about his postwar existence in St. Johnsbury, dreariness came through despite his customary overwriting.[61]

In this novel, closest to Pelley's autobiography, Nathan Forge grows up a victim of repression, "that worst enemy of the human race." Children who ask about sex, Nathan's mother warns, burn in hell; his father makes him quit school, forbids him to write poetry, and forces him to manage the family cardboard box factory. Nathan looks to the familiar escape—marriage and a home exhibiting "beauty, cheerfulness and peace." At twenty-one, after his first romance collapses, he seeks "Woman—the solacing, maternal spirit," and instead marries crude, greedy Milly Richards.[62]

Madeleine's young adulthood contrasts with Nathan's. Mrs. Theddon, who adopted the girl from an orphanage, refused to restrict her "subconscious mind." Like all of Pelley's idealized women, Madeleine personifies genteel refinement, appreciates sex without practicing it before marriage, and tries above all to help others. Complementing a man, she knows, is the "grandest heritage of true womanhood." Undeterred by academic success and numerous unworthy suitors, she seeks someone "true to himself" despite great suffering. From the opening chapters, it is apparent that Nathan will be the man. Even before their melodramatic encounter, he glimpses Madeleine through the window of a fine restaurant called The Worthy, and she cherishes one of his poems.[63]

Nevertheless, their fated meeting requires two violent deaths plus two trips around the world. Nathan's promising career at the Thorne mills is hampered by his wife Milly, who appears at a company dinner in a "flaming cerise" outfit with manners to match. Conveniently, she dies in an industrial accident soon after an automobile runs over their daughter. Thus liberated in gruesome fashion, Nathan spends seven months in Russia during the Revolution. Escaping from "murderous" Bolsheviks into the Siberian mist, he prays for the first time in years. He emerges simultaneously from a literal and metaphorical fog to see his "Woman of Vague Dreams before him in reality." Madeleine Theddon, clad in the uniform of the Red Cross, the "*Greatest Mother in the World*," urges Nathan to "Lean on me."[64]

Their subsequent marriage affirms traditional sex roles. A "very feminine" woman, Madeleine loves Nathan because he is "rough and crude," hungers for his "iron arms," and abandons medical school to cultivate his creative aspect. In addition to reinforcing his masculinity and providing cultural enrichment, Madeleine responds when

Nathan needs the "mother in her." Predictably, Pelley returned to the image of a man resting in "that soft lap, those cool, gentle hands [stroking] his hair."[65]

Despite this blissful ending, *The Fog* continued Pelley's partial revolt against the village. Even the flawless Madeleine deplores the "plodding" mood in Paris. Pelley differed from his nemesis, Sinclair Lewis, largely in his explicit attempts to mitigate such indictments. Milly and Nathan's father, for instance, appear as victims of circumstance. Expressing Pelley's restlessness, Nathan concludes that provincialism is synonymous with standing still, in a small town or large city, whenever "something inside shreiks . . . to be bigger, better, broader next year than last." Pelley's unsettled attitudes contributed to the uneven prose style noted by several reviewers. Indeed, the critic for the *Literary Review* wondered "how the creator of the better parts" of *The Fog* also could have written the rest of it.[66]

The Greater Glory and *The Fog*, like Pelley's journalism in 1919–20, reveal his oscillation between hatred of sexual repression and fear of liberation. It is hard to discern from his purple prose exactly what is happening when, for example, Nathan's first love lifts a "veil from the vestal treasures of her Inner Shrine. . . ." Still, as foreman Bill warns, we can never mistake "Sex for Ladyhood." In Pelley's fiction, only threatening women, aloof from domestic roles, are physically alluring. Madeleine, anything but sexy despite her "rosebud" lips, never kisses Nathan before the wedding; only the appearance of children suggests closer contact thereafter. She may crave his iron arms but he wants mothering above all else.[67]

Nor could Pelley overcome his perplexity about success. Dick Robinson, Mibb's embittered lover, shows that money isn't everything. It is, however, a necessary prerequisite for the refinement sought by Pelley and his heroes. A product of the working class, Milly Forge lacks "intuitive good taste," reduces dinner parties to chaos, and dismisses Camembert as "smelly cheese." The upwardly mobile Nathan knows enough to envy "poise." Following marriage to Madeleine, he proves his worth by entertaining Thorne executives whom Milly had offended.[68]

This quest for success fits into a larger effort to find meaning. Years after rejecting his father's judgmental religion, Nathan discovers a "divine Order of Merit." According to this scheme, Milly's birth into the working class was a sign of her intuitive lack of taste, not a cause of it. Nathan's "poet soul," on the other hand, was given an opportunity to transcend lowly origins. He reflects:

> The very fact that there's no apparent reason for all our ups and downs convinces me there *is* a reason. . . . There's some

> of us deficient in some attribute or other that only raw dealing and struggle make strong. Others have follies and weaknesses. Sorrow and hard luck burn the dross away or show the whole stuffing of us is dross and not worth the Almighty monkeying with.[69]

These sentiments, attributed by Pelley to a fictional character, would be validated for the author himself during his religious conversion in 1928. In time they would become the basis of the esoteric religious movement he founded in 1930, a movement that served as the overture to the Silver Shirts. In 1921, however, such cosmic ruminations remained safely tucked into *The Fog* as Pelley joined the throng seeking fame and fortune in Hollywood.

Hollywood, California

En route to Japan in 1917, Pelley had thrilled to southern California's "sensuous" foliage and "trumming" ukaleles. This "Land Time Forgot," he had written in the *Caledonian*, was the "only place" outside of Vermont he might choose for home. Five years later, lured by an expanding market for film scripts as well as exotic sights and sounds, Pelley transferred his main residence to greater Los Angeles.[70]

What Pelley later called his "seven year submergence in movies" required an intermediate stop in Fort Lee, New Jersey, where he and producer Jules Brulator transfered his story, "White Faith," to the screen. Pelley's original tale dealt with the appearance in America of the Holy Grail. In the secularized film version, entitled *The Light in the Dark*, a magic goblet restored health to a good woman, transformed a rich cad into a fit husband for her, and attracted the attention of an altruistic thief. According to Pelley, he and Lon Chaney, who played the thief, became close friends; they commuted together from New York City, entertained each other's families, and discussed potential movie properties that ranged upward from Pelley's tales to those by Victor Hugo.[71]

By the time *The Light in the Dark* appeared in February 1922, Pelley was trying to forget the pain of his failed marriage in the "exciting bedlam" of Hollywood. Even in *The Door to Revelation*, written after he had decided that movies served an international Jewish conspiracy, he still boasted of having had "constant entree" into the lives of such stars as Chester Conklin, Dot Reid, Theda Bara, and Lon Chaney. Hollywood also fed his self-confessed "Yankee's weakness . . . for any sort of project that promised a profit." While continuing to publish scores of magazine stories, Pelley, by his own count, wrote or supervised twenty-one movie scripts from 1921 to 1928 at a profit of nearly $100,000.[72]

The most prominent of these films resembled Pelley's sentimental fiction: wealthy wastrels reform under the influence of pure women; a salesgirl traps a rich husband; a young man's bravery wins an inheritance and a worthy wife; and a spunky society girl subdues villains with jujitsu. Still ignorant of the wild west, he contributed two westerns, one of which, *The Sawdust Trail*, starred Hoot Gibson. In 1923, Metro Pictures made a version of *The Fog*. One of his stories did become the basis for *The Shock*, in which prayers for vengeance by a persecuted cripple—played by Lon Chaney—elicit the San Francisco earthquake ("the stupendous climax of a battle between Good and Evil for the soul of a man regenerated by Love," promised the Universal-Jewel trailer). *The Shock* proved so lucrative, Pelley claimed, that Carl Laemmle of Universal Studios permitted Chaney to film *The Hunchback of Notre Dame*.[73]

Yet Hollywood was the worst possible place for someone with Pelley's fears about sex, success, and "refinement." To begin with, more than the foliage was sensual in southern California. Theda Bara, the first cinematic "vamp," achieved stardom in 1915, and was followed by more blatantly sexy successors. Although temptresses never outnumbered screen sweethearts, and vamps typically capitulated to fidelity, Hollywood was a favorite target for defenders of traditional sexual morality. Daliances off screen concerned moralists as much as bare midriffs on it. Wild parties, quick divorces (even by America's sweethearts), and exchanges of sexual favors for choice roles did occur, though their frequency was exaggerated by sensational magazines and hostile moralists.[74]

From the safe distance of Bennington, Pelley had taken Hollywood sexuality in stride. In 1917, he had noted that "Bare Theda" was cross-eyed, and joked that starlets without makeup would look no more "vampish than Mary Ann." Life amid Hollywood temptations, however, compounded his old dilemma, whether to transcend sexual repression or strive for disciplined purity. Pelley's autobiography, though circumspect, reveals that he both "ate of the fleshpots" and felt guilty about doing so.[75]

Hollywood was also a boomtown, where actors with slim skill lived opulently and mediocre writers received unprecedented sums for undistinguished prose. Pelley obviously profited from the situation. Adapting to the prevailing commercialism, he printed scripts at his own press in New York City and published a little magazine, *The Plot*, to keep his name before producers, selling to them "with their own showmanship." On the side, he invested in real estate, fast food restaurants, an advertising agency, and a slick periodical. Even while prospering, however, he adhered to the family tradition of business ineptitude. Never bothering to pay debts to his partners in the *Caledonian*, he had to surrender most of the royalties when his third novel, *Drag*, reached Broadway in 1928.[76]

Worse yet, Pelley felt guilty about having become so much the Yankee profiteer, so little the philosopher above the price system. Hollywood offended his belief that success rightly belonged to persons who worked hardest and suffered most. Small-town innocents who submitted scripts, he remembered, hardly knew that the screenwriter must be "one of the gang." To make matters worse, sensuality was part of Hollywood's currency. The "gang" consisted of "booze-lit and money-drunk" men and women lolling on Santa Monica beaches. Looking back on Hollywood, Pelley used the same image he had created to describe the Fulton Paper Company: he had toiled in the "galleys" and gained "nothing but money."[77]

Pelley wanted respect as much as money. Since screen writers commanded relatively low status, he felt subject to "insolent and depreciative treatment." His chief complaint, a perennial among authors transplanted to Hollywood, was that producers and directors distorted his art. Sometimes they did. The goblet in *The Light in the Dark* had been demoted from the Holy Grail to a magical artifact. On the other hand, Metro's film version of *The Fog* was fairly faithful to the novel. Most often, as Pelley sensed in somber moments, he offered little art to distort.[78]

Although treated no worse than writers with greater talent, Pelley took slights particularly hard. Not only did studio executives disregard creativity, he complained, but they expected high fees to buy "silence against any sort of indignity." In 1925, Pelley contemplated organizing his "brother professional writers" to seek a uniform contract guaranteeing profits and pride—a standard fee "never less than five figures" and "exactly" the same credit for authors as for directors. He especially sought a "showdown" with Adolph Zukor, head of the Famous Players-Lasky Corporation, whose public praise for writers contrasted with his company's disdain for them. Protesting this shabby behavior, he received only an "anemic alibi" from Zukor's assistant who suspected (perhaps correctly) that Pelley was most disturbed by the studio's rejection of his latest novel.[79]

Pelley further objected that movie moguls were crass, "uneducated, and all too frequently illiterate." Certainly he scorned their apparent absence of refinement because he doubted whether he possessed it himself. Yet this criticism of Hollywood was commonplace. The studios were dominated by immigrants and their children, many of them Jewish. Pelley's bête noir, Adolph Zukor, a representative mogul, had moved from fur sales to serious films via penny arcades and nickelodians. According to the Henry Ford-sponsored series, *The International Jew*, movies spearheaded the "Zionist" plot to debase Christian America. But even milder denunciations of Hollywood mores often masked anti-Semitism.[80]

Did Pelley's attack on the "entertainment mongers" mean that by 1925 he had already turned decisively toward Jew-baiting? Contemporary evidence is slim, and his memoirs, in which everything prefigures his twin conversions to spiritualism and anti-Semitism, are inconclusive. Pelley brought to Hollywood an ordinary nativism that had allowed him, in *Sunset* and the *St. Johnsbury Caledonian*, to refer often to "Japs" and, at least once, to "niggers." Similarly, a "little undersized Hebrew" in *The Fog*, published in 1921, calls the heroine a "peach." Still, this passage does not seem remarkable beside F. Scott Fitzgerald's description of Meyer Wolfsheim in *The Great Gatsby*. Furthermore, Pelley in 1925 disliked Adolf Zukor no more than his employee, Cecil B. DeMille, the ostentatiously Christian director whose "cloying" films were typical of Hollywood's "lack of good breeding." While in Hollywood, then, Pelley seems to have remained a conventional nativist, well within the cultural mainstream.[81]

Along with other conventional nativists, however, Pelley developed heightened interest in "racial" issues during the 1920s. He would have received encouragement in ethnocentrism merely by reading the magazines to which he contributed; the *Saturday Evening Post*, for instance, published Kenneth Roberts's warnings against "mongrelization" as well as Pelley's westerns. Nor is there reason to doubt his recollection that friends grumbled about Jewish influence in Hollywood. Then in 1925 an abortive film project brought him to Washington, D.C., where a Justice Department official and a newspaperman repeated what Czechs, White Russians, and Red Cross volunteers had said in 1919—that Communism was Jewish. Though initially skeptical (an illustration of his naiveté, according to *The Door to Revelation*), he retained these Washington contacts, whose repetition of anti-Semitic lore may have reinforced his hostility toward Jewish film-makers. By 1928, he was apparently writing a book to explain the "racial, instead of political" inclinations of mankind (an accomplishment already claimed by Madison Grant in *The Passing of the Great Race*).[82]

But instead of pursuing public issues, either mobilizing screenwriters or attacking Jews, Pelley sank steadily into personal malaise. He felt inessential to his children. His patron at *American Magazine,* John Siddall, died in 1923; his friendship with Chaney ebbed. As Hollywood lost its spell, he suspected again that he was a mere "slinger of sentiment." While listing himself as a Congregationalist in *Who's Who* and filling stories with Christian motifs, he still doubted the existence of God. He may have sought a surrogate faith in psychoanalysis. At least he borrowed a vocabulary from the postwar Freudian vogue, frequently alluding to "inhibitions," "inferiority complexes," and "infantile fixations" (even as a strident anti-Semite during the 1930s, he never attacked Freud). Yet Pelley's automobile seems to have provided more solace than any philosophy. Seven times during the 1920s he drove back and forth across the country in "swashbuckling fashion," sometimes hibernating from Hollywood for long periods at a Greenwich Village apartment.[83]

During one of these eastern soujourns Pelley wrote *Drag,* a comic novel set in Paris, Vermont, which incorporated recent autobiography, heaped symbolic scorn on his mother-in-law, and revealed the latest aspects of his inner "gnawing." Allie Parker, prodded by her dowdy mother, lures David Haskell into marriage, expecting him to support sundry in-laws whom he designates "the Family." David turns himself into a "money-machine" trying to meet her demands. Similar "chivalry" prompts an association with the "sordidly pretty" Lillian Whalen. In rapid succession, David saves Lill from a violent suitor, bails her out of jail, and summons a physician when, pregnant out of wedlock, she begins to give birth. Following this last valiant act, David collapses, worn out at twenty-one by efforts to enrich the Family.[84]

Nursed back to health by the "delectable" but demure Carrie Flynt, David resumes his role as "money machine" until Lill literally flies to the rescue. Now a pioneer pilot, she ascribes her reformation to David's nobility, arranges a New York production of his play based on the Family, and (like Pelley's mentor of the same name) introduces him to urban sophistication. In a final row with his collective "drag," David accuses Allie of marrying "under false pretenses" because "romance" was irrelevant to her choice of mate, and indicts his mother-in-law for failing to inculcate "independence, unselfishness, self-control." Nurse Flynt possesses those qualities in full measure. After a fortuitous airplane crash puts David again under Carrie's care, they finally marry.[85]

Drag, published in 1925, encapsulated Pelley's growing conflicts over work and women. Self-sacrifice, Mary Purse's "greater glory," is nearly David Haskell's fatal flaw. According to Pelley's cult of true manhood, males must seek affluence and acclaim despite the psychological costs. Still, the costs are apparent in David, who remains cynical and "hard" even in triumph.

Expressing a favorite Pelley theme, foreman Bill of the *Paris Telegraph* tells David that "every man's birthright" includes a woman "whose life belongs to her husband inviolate." Throughout *Drag*, however, characters dispute how to acquire this birthright. Representing Pelley's tough and tender sides respectively, Bill says that women, relics from the "stone age," want to be "mastered," while David argues for coddling these sensitive creatures. Although Pelley tends to side with his fictional namesake, the novel's position remains problematical. David's chivalry, after all, inspires Lill's transformation. Of course, true women must mother their men—even Lill develops maternal compassion—but *Drag* comes closer than Pelley's earlier novels to affirming sensuality as well as nurture. Lill, the independent fallen woman, withdraws from the scene, allowing David to marry angelic Carrie Flynt. Yet neither the groom nor the author can muster great enthusiasm. Vapid Carrie pales beside Lill, the most richly drawn woman in Pelley's books.[86]

Life allowed wider latitude than the canons of sentimental fiction. Unable to decide what kind of woman he wanted, Pelley found three to serve different needs. An efficient spinster, identified in *Door to Revelation* only as Beryl, served as secretary and "pivot," managing Pelley's business affairs while he sped across country. Mary Derieux, the fiction editor of *American Magazine*, was a softer surrogate mother, the "literary shepherdess" with whom he also discussed personal problems. Finally, Helen Wilhelmina Hannsman—Mina—was his lover. Her appeal was obvious. She was both a nurse, a profession that to Pelley combined "motherhood incarnate" with the strength of a "soldier," and a fellow veteran of the Siberian intervention, a living reminder of his grand adventure. During the late 1920s, Beryl, Mary, and Mina respectively kept him solvent, polished his prose, and, we may infer, provided "that soft lap, those cool, gentle hands [stroking] his hair." Yet none could quench his thirst for the "Great Thrill."[87]

Conversion: "Seven Minutes in Eternity" and Back

In late 1927, hoping to cure his malaise by withdrawing from Hollywood's "fleshpots" and "galleys," Pelley bought an isolated bungalow in Altadena, California, in the Sierra Madre mountains. There, from October through the following May, he conducted an "accounting with my soul." During the night of 28–29 May 1928, he underwent a mystical experience that altered his life.[88]

According to Pelley's later account, he retired at 10:30 and read himself to sleep as usual. Around 2:00 A.M., he began to cry, "I'm dying! I'm dying!" He whirled through space and landed in a strong pair of arms. Two men dressed in white placed him on a white marble pallet surrounded by alabaster walls and corinthian columns; beyond the portico he saw "magnificent spruces" and "twinkling stars in a sky of deep cyanite." One of the two aides in white (who resembled Bert Boyden, the deceased managing editor of *American Magazine*) reassured him, "We've got you and are here to help you!" Four hours later Pelley had learned that the body was merely an "overcoat" for the spirit that survived after death. The initial passage through the "strange bluish mist" was involuntary, but, after slipping back to earth at 3:30 A.M., Pelley willed himself back for further instruction. Then the oracle resembling Boyden explained that each earthly soujourn fulfilled a preordained, purposeful compact, and promised to reveal more specific information "as you have need in your progressing affairs."[89]

Pelley's experience, whatever it was, in the early morning of 29 May 1928, produced changes associated with many conversions. His physical characteristics altered: lines disappeared from his face; his skin took on a ruddiness; he stood straighter; and his voice lost its nervous edge. His insomnia disappeared and he was able to work twelve hours daily without strain. Old friends noticed the rejuvenation, he said, and, no longer high-strung, he found new ones. Pelley could only conclude, with numberless converts to all kinds of faith, "I had somehow been reborn. . . ."[90]

The rebirth, Pelley wrote, also brought new senses "just as bona fide" as touch or sight. He continued to hear "clairaudient" messages from the other world; heeding a voice reminiscent of "any worried mother," he gave up tobacco—but only temporarily. Within two years of the "Great Release" in May 1928, he took instructions via "automatic writing" and described unseen owners of watches or jewelry. He claimed to have reported events far from his physical presence, as Emmanuel Swedenborg had done two centuries earlier. Pondering Ralph Waldo Emerson's "wonderous essay" on the Oversoul during a trip to New York, he saw a "great shaft of pure whitelight" pour through the roof of his railroad car; he knew then that Jesus was "an actual Personage" and that "all life is whole."[91]

Fearing for his reputation, Pelley hesitated to publish these remarkable providences. Supposedly he yielded to Mary Derieux's request for an article on the advice of an oracle (who helped to compose the memoir in less than two hours). In "My Seven Minutes in Eternity," as *American Magazine* mistitled the account in March 1929, he struggled to prove the otherworldly nature of the experience, pointedly—and inaccurately—denying a personal history of "nerve exhaustion."[92]

Clearly, Pelley had been struggling toward some sort of psychological breakthrough for years. In "My Seven Minutes in Eternity," he admitted to having tried often "to correct my psychology and get back certain religious—not theological—cues that I . . . lost with the passing of boyhood." Indeed, Pelley's experience illustrated what William James called conversion by "self-surrender," in which temporary exhaustion is an essential element. His retreat from Hollywood to Altadena followed the pattern of Jamesian "sick souls" who "drop down, give up, and *don't care* any longer" about their frustrating routine activities. As "egoistic worry" subsides, faith that has been churning on the edges of consciousness takes possession of the mind. The effects, James wrote, were abundant, startling, and sometimes permanent.[93]

Pelley's insistence in *American Magazine* that he had been virtually ignorant of and largely hostile to spiritualism was also inaccurate. His boyhood idol Elbert Hubbard had believed in the human spirit's survival in a "better world"; his political mentor Edward Bellamy had experimented with the occult; and Pelley himself had written in 1909 that he had lived before. Throughout the 1920s, characters in his fiction speak of higher powers, sense kinship from "some far, previous incarnation," and reach matrimony via Kismet. Pelley's sister conducted a seance in his presence, claiming contact with her dead husband. Finally, Mary Derieux, his "literary shepherdess," was chairman of the publications committee of the American Society for Psychical Research; sometime between October 1927 and May 1928 she had prodded him to read a book on reincarnation.[94]

Furthermore, Pelley's conversion narratives were dominated by images and themes that had long affected his living and writing. The realm beyond the "purple passage" was a cosmic version of The Worthy restaurant in *The Fog*. Decor was opulent and diners possessed the poise craved by Pelley no less than by Nathan Forge; only "affable, cultured, gracious" spirits greeted him in the heavenly portico. Prevailing sexual mores contrasted with those of Hollywood "fleshpots." Pelley's familiar distrust of his body appeared in the description of his "return" to it: "Something awful closed about me! It seemed as though a great suit of clammy, cloying armor, a miasma of implacable sinew, had shut around me. It clutched me horridly, an excruciating agony that ended in a click." "Eternity," on the other hand, was "strangely sexless." The oracles recommended a kind of baptism in innocence to put him at ease, and, after emerging from the "most delightful water," he forgot his nakedness.[95]

The conversion applied balm to other fears and painful memories as well. Since boyhood, Pelley had felt like different persons at different times, unable to "tell which one was in command of me." He felt like a "whole crowd of people," the oracles now explained, because he (like everyone else) contained a "whole bundle of personalities"; a spirit acquired a new facet everytime it dwelled in a human overcoat. Despite voracious reading and his protests to the contrary, Pelley worried about his lack of education. Access to a world beyond this one provided knowledge—superior knowledge—unavailable to erudite but earthbound scholars.[96]

Above all, the oracles assured Pelley that no incident was "futile." His father had left home to keep "appointments in life" irrelevant to the family. Pelley and Mary Ann had lost a child and a marriage in order to develop poise, the "gift of peaceful consideration of the universe." From the higher perspective, life was only profitable. Pelley thrilled to the news. His tribulations no longer seemed meaningless and his failures seemed to involve no personal responsibility.[97]

By 1930, Pelley claimed that his clairaudient communications went "far beyond" the established mystical canon. More accurately, fellow psychic investigators introduced him to spiritualist notions which he shaped to fit his own personality. Moving to New York City in 1929, he began to meet weekly with Mary Derieux's spiritualist group, encountered mediums who "confirmed" his visit to the cosmic portico, and contacted an unspecified deceased author who helped him to complete a fourth novel, *Golden Rubbish*. Publication of "My Seven Minutes in Eternity" elicited more than 20,000 letters describing comparable experiences. In January 1930, the *Journal of the American Society for Psychical Research* published a favorable article on Pelley's conversion experience. Thus prodded by associates and anonymous admirers, he surmised that he had been reincarnated to assist a "vast new departure."[98]

Pelley's assertion, which he repeated for the next thirty-five years, that he abandoned a thriving literary career to fulfill this preordained "brevet" was plainly false, but it contained more rationalization than conscious guile. *Drag* had been relatively well-received, even eliciting a trans-Atlantic accolade from the *London Times Literary Supplement*. During the late 1920s, however, Pelley's writing block worsened and rejection slips piled high. His first three novels had contained some wit, fair characterizations, and touching descriptions of adolescence. In *The Blue Lamp*, a mystery published in 1930, even Pelley's eye for local color failed. *Golden Rubbish*, the tale of cynical mortals who discover their true mission, to find archeological evidence of Jesus, was rubbish indeed.[99]

In short, metaphysics grew on Pelley partly because it offered at a critical moment a career as well as a creed. Shortly after moving to New York, he made his clairaudient receptions available as "quasi-religious" programs. Within a year, he asserted, these pamphlets soothed 90,000 "spiritually distressed" recipients. In May 1930, he began to publish the *New Liberator*, a journal of "higher verities" printed in an art nouveau format reminiscent of Elbert Hubbard's *Philistine*. Under this title, or as *Liberation* or *New Liberator Weekly*, the periodical appeared intermittently for three years.[100]

From Practical Mysticism to Prejudiced Politics

Pelley correctly sensed that millions of Americans shared his own "thirst after things of the spirit" and that they were willing to slight established denominations in their search for fulfillment. Large audiences listened to Sir Oliver Lodge, the British spiritualist who lectured in the United States during 1922–23. Also on tour, the theosophist Annie Besant introduced a young Indian whom she pronounced the "World Teacher." Followers of Emile Coué tried to convince themselves, every day in every way, that they were "getting better and better." Kahlil Gibran assured readers of his bestseller, *The Prophet*, that God was "smiling in flowers." Unity, Cosmic Consciousness, the I Am Movement, and disciples of George Gurdjieff all promised—in varying proportions—physical vigor, mental health, and eternal peace. Psychologists, reinvigorating an inquiry that reached back to William James, pursued scientific studies of "paranormal" phenomena. Indeed, their experiments related to the searching 1920s much as James' concern fit into the spiritual crisis of the Gilded Age. Professor J. D. Rhine, the most prominent student of extrasensory perception, wanted to aid a "floundering society." Inevitably, though, mediums, mystics, and popularizers like Upton Sinclair stretched scientific findings to fit their metaphysics.[101]

These latest forms of fidelity joined a long procession of "harmonial" religions. Starting at least with Ralph Waldo Emerson (who looked back to the eighteenth-century mystic Emmanuel Swedenborg), diverse American prophets had promised rewards for right thinking. Harmonial spokesman typically wavered between "pushing to the front" (in Orison Swett Marden's phrase) and what the historian Gail Thain Parker calls the "wonders of letting go." From Emerson to Gibran, the latter wonders were associated with esoteric eastern doctrines.[102]

Having noted Pelley's conflicting inclinations to strive and let go, his "Great Release" of May 1928, and his fondness for Emerson, we need not belabor his place in the harmonial tradition. Most letters about "My Seven Minutes in Eternity" came, in descending order, from Christian Scientists, spiritualists (including Sir Oliver Lodge), and theosophists. Pelley joked that he had joined many sects "without the slightest realization." He urged correspondents to retain their current religious affiliations as long as these supplied "that which you need." He planned neither to join a church nor found one.[103]

Nevertheless, between 1930 and 1933 Pelley built his own eclectic theology from various harmonial components. Spiritualism, Christian Science, and especially theosophy sparkled as facets of "ultimate truth." Pelley found merit in Rosicrucianism, astrology, and collegiate atheism (a "healthy rebellion" against orthodoxy). Along with some theosophists, occasional fundamentalists, and many practitioners of New Thought, he extrapolated the shape of future events from the measurements of the Great Pyramid. Like spiritualists and theosophists, he sought the sanction of science; physicists now know, he said, that solid matter really consisted of moving particles. On the other hand, Pelley still derided orthodox Christians whose God was "particularly interested in private morals . . . or public adulation." Only a "clairaudient adept," who knew better, should lead a congregation.[104]

Liberation described heaven in opulent detail. While a corpse decayed, its "electrical magnetic body" ascended to a higher sphere, where instead of winged angels or divine judges it encountered friendly guides. Except for accident victims and the slaughtered masses of World War I (who had arrived faster than celestial orientation committees could process them), transition involved little difficulty. Returning souls viewed heaven through mental eyes, conversed via telepathy, and learned the true identities of historical figures. Neither heartbreak nor divine wrath marred this "sphere of beauty and poise."[105]

In many respects, however, the afterlife was comfortably familiar. Again following spiritualist premises, Pelley said that "discarnate" beings wore clothes, lived in houses, and retained their basic earthly personalities. Hence there were some snobs, malcontents, and downright vicious souls. Fortunately, heaven was hierarchical, with cosmic troublemakers relegated to the lower "octaves." Each succeeding level required progressively greater manifestations of virtue and admitted progressively smaller populations. The topmost, the Biblical "Seventh-Heaven" and scene of Pelley's "visit" in 1928, contained only Great Souls (or Masters).[106]

Jesus Christ, the greatest Soul, looked in *Liberation* much as he had two decades earlier in the *Philosopher*—a "valiant commander of valiant followers." Psychic investigators who ignored Him, Pelley warned, were prone to lose faith. Furthermore, along with heterodox Christians like Mary Baker Eddy, he argued that an "underlying theme"—in this instance, the doctrine of rebirth—had been suppressed by self-serving clergy. Luckily, Pelley could go straight to the source. Jesus's "mental voice" provided him with "Master Messages," more or less in the diction of the King James Bible, that were then printed in *Liberation*.[107]

According to Pelley's mixture of Darwinism, Genesis, and the occult, "Divine Mind" had created every soul 28 million years earlier. Some had descended to earth in order to develop independence. Encountering a "strictly separate" biological evolution, they had taken the form of cats, birds, whatever was handy. Discarnate superiors, appalled by this lapse into animalism, had required a series of earthly habitations in a single body form (conveniently borrowed from apes) before their fallen brethren could reside permanently in higher octaves. For older (thus wiser) souls who had often taken human form, returns to earth were voluntary. Younger spirits, obliged to make the trip at 500 year intervals, usually looked forward to each round of uplifting adventures. Sounding like Nathan Forge, a clairaudient oracle insisted that "nothing counts in the final summing-up but *Experiencing.*" A cosmic work ethic allocated "refinement, poise, sagacity." Therefore, much as Nathan speculates in *The Fog*, *Liberation* explained that "coarse" humans were spiritually younger than their genteel neighbors. Rough or refined, no one was ever "truly alone." Kindred spirits from earlier lives reappeared as friends or relatives, Masters served as "guardian angels," and mortals could communicate with the discarnate world.[108]

Pelley's views were no more subtle or consistent in 1930 than before his mystical experience, but, now dissolving ambiguities into the premise that "all life was whole," he no longer consciously felt torn by his contradictions. Rather, he cheerfully offered his own answers to others. Despite his denials, Pelley often sounded like a pitchman for a new sect:

> This is a message for you of such self-improvement as you have never encountered in your life. . . .

> Have you spiritual quandaries and questions? Over a period of time you will find them answered in a wealth of learning such as few books contain at the present time.
>
> Have you physical or mental troubles? You will be shown the causes by which they originate, how or why you are living wrongly, and what you should do to bring about a method of meeting life that will sidestep further complications.
>
> Are you poor in this world's goods, while others seemingly enjoy greater affluence? You will learn what true wealth is, where wealth comes from and why some people have it and others do not.[109]

The *Liberation* practicum emphasized problems most troubling to Pelley himself: sex, success, and the meaning of life. As in the *Philosopher*, he inferred divine sanction to abolish prudery. Instead of joining the current cry to liberate the libido, however, he offered an alternative consistent with his May 1928 discovery that sex was relatively unimportant on higher octaves. This view, held by many spiritualists and theosophists since the nineteenth century, certainly enhanced the appeal of both doctrines to Pelley. Subsequent to his conversion, moreover, oracles endorsed a cosmic cult of true womanhood and assuaged guilt about his indulgence in fleshpots and his broken marriage. Because sexuality represented the search for "completion" by altruistic female spirits and their sterner counterparts in male bodies, the voices advised, even casual affairs prepared the heart for "true union." Yet, since most marriages were based on sensuality, greed, or convenience instead of spiritual affinity, they could be terminated without worry.[110]

The oracles also followed Pelley's cult of true manhood in asserting that no man was "truly himself when thwarted financially." Wealth did not automatically follow spirituality but, Pelley said, echoing Elbert Hubbard's "Message to Garcia," anyone could earn a fortune by combining positive thinking and hard work: "Go to your desk tomorrow prepared to do this thing: conserve your energies for one strong development. Give your undivided attention to one group of entities until they have served the purpose that brought them. You will see that you will win beyond your wildest expectations." To facilitate winning, *New Liberator* advertised correspondence schools, promoted manuals, and offered to harness the psychic power of its readers. Persons sending their names to "Silent Contact" were assured that fellow subscribers would, at a mutually agreeable hour, think sympathetically about their afflictions. Participants reported cures of deafness, tuberculosis, and tumors. Inevitably, some malignancies continued to grow, just as many strivers remained poor. Faced with these apparent failures of metaphysics, Pelley countered that suffering was a teaching aid in the "universe of absolute compensation."[111]

Although the oracles helped those who helped themselves, not every inter-octave message came from benevolent Masters. On the contrary, playful or downright malevolent spirits enjoyed confounding mortals. But psychic novices, through diligence, poise, and competent instruction (advertised in *Liberation*), could learn to distinguish clairaudient voices from each other and from their own "pensive thinking."[112]

Whether or not Pelley sought to create a cult, he threw himself into organizational work with his customary chaotic energy. Once again success eluded him, partly because he still could not focus his efforts, and partly because his followers were similarly afflicted. When embezzlement by an associate doomed *Liberation*, Pelley incorporated Galahad Press in February 1931, and sold sufficient stock to resume publication under the title *New Liberator*. The League for the Liberation encompassed groups organized to discuss his clairaudient scripts. In 1932, favored with a large donation, he incorporated the Foundation for Christian Economics in Asheville, North Carolina, and opened Galahad College, a short-lived metaphysical school under the deanship of James Edgerton, president of the New Thought Alliance.[113]

Metaphysical mentorship, though more satisfying than his career as Hollywood writer and promotor, left Pelley unfulfilled. He claimed 10,000 subscribers to *New Liberator* and hundreds of League assemblies, but elsewhere almost admitted that his harmonial conglomerate existed largely on paper. With some warrant, he chided "spiritual vagrants," already veterans of orthodox Christian denominations, New Thought, Unity, theosophy, and spiritualism, who now flirted with his metaphysics but made no commitment.[114]

The deepening Depression renewed Pelley's beat of "big drums." Not only had the oracles in August 1929, anticipated imminent economic collapse, Pelley recalled (conveniently in 1938), but they had predicted that he would lead a mass movement against anti-Christian conspirators and recast the social order. Specifically, he must form a paramilitary organization when an obscure former housepainter assumed the German chancellorship. Pelley, who later made the dubious assertion that he had barely heard of Adolf Hitler in 1929, took the "message" seriously, especially after his favorite medium endorsed it.[115]

Between 1930 and 1933, therefore, *Liberation* emphasized that something special was brewing in the universe. A "Great Time of Troubles" must correct humanity's softness and greed. Many "demon" souls had been reincarnated and one, formerly resident in Ghengis Khan, possibly dwelled now in Joseph Stalin. In this bloodcurdling version of the politics of apocalypse, however, mortals placing themselves in tune with the infinite would encounter "no real suffering." They could look on with poise, knowing that Masters would be "steering" trends from above while "great souls" on earth would handle details. Pelley believed that Jesus, the greatest soul, would return during his lifetime. Indeed, *Liberation* reported sightings of the "materialized Christ" by "responsible persons" and printed recent "photographs" of Him in flowing robes.[116]

While reassuring readers that Depression-era disorder contained both meaning and seeds of a happy ending, Pelley simultaneously moved toward a more "valiant" personal calling. He pronounced himself, by oracular brevet, an officer in the army of reincarnated great souls. To forestall accusations of a "superiority complex" and to relieve his own doubts, Pelley often reviewed his qualifications. Forty years of striving in his current life, he concluded, capped a distinguished record begun during previous earthly visits.[117]

By 1931, Pelley had decided that the worst "demon" spirits inhabited Jewish bodies. For the next two years, however, he spoke with relative circumspection. According to *Liberation*, President Hoover was manipulated by agents of the "International Shylock," the bankers responsible for the Depression in the first place; meanwhile, their covert Communist brethren sought to "emasculate" Christian principles for "racial profit." The Galahad College curriculum in 1932 covered "predatory cliques" in American life, false claims to divine favor by "certain people," and "racial ethics" in the lost world of Atlantis. Finally, when Hitler was appointed Chancellor of Germany on 30 January 1933, Pelley announced formation of the Silver Legion and brought the "work of Christ militant into the open."[118]

From then until World War II, Pelley devoted most of his energy to the Silver Shirts, as the group was called by members and foes alike. Leadership of this uniformed band brought him substantial income, emotional satisfaction, national notoriety, and ultimately, a term in prison. Detecting affinities between Silver Shirts in Asheville and Brownshirts in Berlin, commentators quickly put Pelley on their lists of aspiring *fuehrers*. Pelley himself fueled this speculation. After 1933, he openly praised Hitler, cooperated with the German-American Bund, and fashioned an anti-Semitic program remarkable even by the standards of fellow American bigots. All social issues, he told Silver Shirts, reduced to "one problem"—whether "Christian tenets" could survive assault from the "atheists of Judah."[119]

Only One Problem

The inner dynamics of Pelley's explicitly racial anti-Semitism are harder to trace than the ideological sources. He remembered asking himself before retiring on 28 May 1928, "What Were Races?" He returned from "eternity" believing that they represented gradations of spiritual development. The Master Minds placed least capable souls in black bodies, followed "upward, cycle after cycle by brown, yellow, red, and white men." Thus, Pelley summarized in *The Door to Revelation*, whites had "attained something cosmically which Semitic Asiatics have not attained."[120]

After May 1928, submergence in the occult probably helped to change Pelley from an ordinary nativist into an extraordinary anti-Semite. Many European theosophists inferred that the Aryan "Root Race" was the best race. Although theosophy's founder, Helena Petrova Blavatsky, eschewed anti-Semitism, a Russian associate propagated *The Protocols* and many of her German disciples applauded Hitler. Other German occultists contributed to Nazi ideology, arguing (as Pelley did) that Atlantis had been corrupted by Jews.[121]

In Pelley's circle, to be sure, racist esoterica received considerable earthly support. By 1931, his Washington "connections" included Representative Louis T. McFadden (Rep.-Pa.), who defended *The Protocols* and *The International Jew* in Congress. Most important, Pelley's lover, Wilhelmina Hannsmann, was descended from "purest German stock" and valued "all" that the Third Reich represented.[122]

In his anti-Semitic tracts, Pelley wove together stereotypes common since the turn of the century, lore from *The Protocols* and *The International Jew*, spiritualism, and his deepest personal hopes and fears. His primer, *Forty-five Questions Most Frequently Asked About the Jews*, assumed that readers already distrusted "greedy" Jewish businessmen. Additional "definitive" Jewish traits included lewd dress, vulgarity, and arrogance. Pelley, even more emphatically than Madison Grant, Lothrop Stoddard, and Kenneth Roberts, insisted that Jews were "Oriental." The East European Ashkenazi displayed a "'schnozzle' nose" and manners offensive to "Christian refinement." Sephardic Jews were harder to spot and (Pelley agreed with the muckraker Burton J. Hendrick) sephardic women were strikingly beautiful, but their "Jewish temperament" inevitably surfaced.[123]

Pelley's rejection of orthodox Protestantism facilitated a particularly comprehensive anti-Semitism. Following Madison Grant and William J. Cameron, the compiler of *The International Jew*, he denied that Jesus was Jewish. Rather, the Galilean had descended from emigrant Gauls. Furthermore, because the Bible was not "literally" God's word, no one should confuse the Almighty with Moses's "tribal" deity. In Pelley's paraphrase of Exodus, Jews debased "pure-blooded" Egyptian masters, favored an "ancient version" of the National Recovery Administration, and established the "essence" of Communism in Canaan. Jesus was the "outstanding 'Jew-baiter' of His day," but Jews had corrupted the New Testament to suggest otherwise; His chief target, the Sanhedrin, still led the Jewish campaign for world conquest.[124]

The Silver Shirt version of history since the crucifixion relied heavily on *The International Jew*. According to Pelley, Jewish capitalists and radicals cooperated to destroy Christian civilization. He blamed Adam Weishaupt and the Bavarian Illuminati for the French Revolution (a staple countersubversive motif since the 1790s) and added that the Rothschild family had financed the subversion. Similarly, Jacob Schiff had paid for the Russian Revolution. While citing familiar, inaccurate statistics purporting to show that Jews dominated the Soviet Union, he stressed the suffering Russian mothers he had met in 1918. Turning to the United States, he accused Jews of dominating the slave trade and blamed Judah P. Benjamin for southern secession. While whites, imbued with racial "good sportsmanship," created productive industries during the late nineteenth century, Jews merely manipulated money. By 1913, Pelley charged, they had secured passage of the infamous Federal Reserve Act and almost controlled the entire Wilson administration. War Industries Board Chairman Bernard Baruch, their "uncrowned prince," remained the nation's "real master" in the 1920s.[125]

Pelley showed greater originality in his search for anti-Semitic heroes than in his litany of Jewish villains. He cited "missing" pages in Charles Cotesworth Pinckney's diary to prove that Benjamin Franklin had urged the Constitutional Convention to ban Jewish immigration. Speaking incongruously modern English (as Charles A. Beard noted in a critique of this forgery), Franklin supposedly had warned against "unassimilated" Jewish "vampires" who would "undermine" Christian republicanism within two hundred years.[126]

The New Deal, Pelley insisted, proved Franklin right. Not only did departure from the gold standard enrich Jewish bankers, but Bernard Baruch's "Gentile Front," General Hugh Johnson, led the NRA. Concentrating on the "barucheracy," Pelley initially ignored Franklin D. Roosevelt. In January 1934, however, he surmised that presidential ancestors included "certain Dutch Jews." This Sephardic background explained FDR's many Jewish appointees, his "insane hatred" of Hitler, and his family's commercialization of the presidency. Adolf Berle, Frances Perkins, and Milton Eisenhower (Protestants all) joined Roosevelt on Pelley's roster of "Jewish New Dealers." In their hands, he concluded, *The Protocols* were being fulfilled "flawlessly."[127]

By the mid-1930s, Pelley's list of "judaized" institutions had grown to include the Congress of Industrial Organizations ("a synagogue"), the American Civil Liberties Union, the American Medical Association, the Church of Jesus Christ of Latter Day Saints, and the "*Kosher* League of Nations." *Liberation* chastized "gullible" gentiles who condemned "only a few 'bad' Jews at the top." Even the "little Jew" no longer knew his place.[128]

Urging Christian Americans to awaken from their "jazz-anesthetized" stupor, Pelley participated, from his own weird perspective, in two wider trends, the reaffirmation of the village in the 1930s and the quest for a usable past. Much as his enemy Sinclair Lewis went from mocking rustic smugness in *Main Street* to applauding rustic patriotism in *It Can't Happen Here*, Pelley passed over the bitter memories in *The Fog* to celebrate the "decorous" New England of his youth. He went as far as to declare, in effect, that anti-Semitism was twentieth-century Americanism. While the *Daily Worker* construed the Declaration of Independence as precedent for proletarian revolution, Pelley recast it to condemn a "train of abuses" by "non-Christian tyranny."[129]

Pelley's call for a gentile resurgence was paradoxical because, like everything else, Jewish aggression and Christian acquiescence fit into the cosmic "pattern," of conflict between good and evil. Since destiny *required* their malevolence, he might have absolved Jews of responsibility. Occasionally he did profess clinical detachment from rancor toward "Jews as Jews," a trait unworthy of poised Christians. More typical was his threat in 1936 to punch any "kike" who criticized his silver shirt. The following year he proposed vicious Christmas cards:

> Dear Shylock, in this season
> When we're all bereft of reason,
> As upon my rent you gloat,
> I would like to cut your throat.[130]

Instead of softening his attitude, Pelley's metaphysics allowed a special callousness. There was no need for "lacrimose sentimentality" regarding Jews who required discipline from "parental races." At worst, they would only lose their "present lives."[131]

Nowhere was Pelley harsher than in his description of Hollywood as the epitome of Jewish vices. He took pride, of course, in speaking from experience. Pelley even published film reviews, a rare feature in far right magazines. He agreed with *The International Jew* that motion pictures, like most useful technology, had been invented by gentiles, and noted that some Christians still made admirable movies. (Pelley rehabilitated Cecil B. DeMille to prove the point.) Yet typical Hollywood products were Metro-Goldwyn-Mayer's *House of Rothschild*, which promoted Jewish superiority; *Tobacco Road*, which slandered southern whites; and *A Tale of Two Cities*, which promoted revolution.[132]

Hollywood's greatest threat remained for Pelley what it had been during the 1920s—sex. Enforcement of a stringent production code, starting in 1934, shows that his fears were hardly unique. Nonetheless, the intensity of his feelings reveal the limits of his transformation. Neither the religious conversion of 1928–29, nor love of Mina Hannsmann, whom he married on 4 July 1936, relieved his fear of sexuality or removed from his language calls to "emasculate" the forces of "concupiscence."[133]

To document Hollywood's "moral debauch," Pelley dredged up, manufactured, and exaggerated memories from the 1920s, often presenting them as crude dialect jokes. Lon Chaney's interest in *The Hunchback of Notre Dame* supposedly prompted Carl Laemmle of Universal Studios to proclaim, "What, you should do a football pitcher?" Pelley's attempt in *Torment!* to echo Christ's feeding of the multitudes allegedly provoked another "offensive little Jew":

> Ve ain't makin' it moom-pitchers about your bastard Christ nor his loafs and fishes. Vat ve vant in it moom-pitchers is legs. Understand me? . . . legs! . . . Vimin's legs! Ven ve get done vid you Christians, I guess you find out vy ve got it control of movies and it ain't to preach no sermon in a church. I'm telling you! Better ve should put every goy girl in a whorehouse, and by gott you'll like it!

Pelley cried in retrospect:

> The fleshpots of Hollywood, Oriental custodians of adolescent entertainment. One short word for all of it—JEWS! Do you think me unduly incensed about them? I've seen too many Gentile maidens ravished and been unable to do any-

> thing about it. They have a concupiscent slogan in screendom: "Don't hire till you see the whites of their thighs!"
>
> I know all about Jews.
>
> For six years I toiled in their galleys and got nothing but money.[134]

Pelley's invective served a psychological as well as an organizational purpose. His adaptations of common anti-Semitic theories projected onto Jews traits that he had since adolescence feared in himself. A Yankee profiteer in the mold of his father, Pelley accused Jews of greed, using the same image—"galleys"—to describe movie studios and Rev. Pelley's factory. God, a source of pain and solace, was split into Moses's harsh "tribal" diety, whom Pelley scorned, and the brotherly Jesus, whom he clad in a silver shirt. Perhaps most important, he associated Jews with the sensuality that both attracted and repelled him. Jewish men "ravished" pure Christian women, commanded the Hollywood "fleshpots" Pelley had fled, and, he charged in *Liberation*, disseminated emasculating venereal disease. Marching under the Silver Shirt "snow-white banner," Pelley could see himself as an ascetic enemy of commercialism and a valiant protector of true women; in short, the defender of a recast version of his parents' puritanic code.[135]

Frequent complaints about the shortcomings of anti-Semitic contemporaries highlighted Pelley's intense personal feelings. Paquita de Shishmareff, a Russian émigré who had supplied *The Protocols* to the *Dearborn Independent*, failed to pass muster because her daughter worked for a Jewish movie producer. He warned "Winnie" Winrod, who was "not 'agin'" all Jews, that "straddling . . . does things to your soul." Gerald L. K. Smith, who denied preaching anti-Semitism throughout the 1930s, was even less reliable; according to Pelley, Smith had begun organizing southern branches for the Silver Shirts in 1933 but quit after Jews "put the hit on him."[136]

Although Pelley prized his reputation as the nation's premier anti-Semite, he also had qualms, what might be called a guilty conscience. Indeed, his strongest reservations appeared in psychic receptions that in his model of the mind corresponded to conscience. To be sure, the oracles were hardly philo-Semitic. While chastizing the "emptiness of Israel," however, these unconscious voices absolved modern Jews of responsibility for Christ's crucifixion and emphasized what Pelley noted but passed over—that Jews played "necessary" metahistorical roles. Spiritual children in a world beyond their understanding, they deserved pity as well as punishment. Hence, the oracles advised, wiser souls in gentile bodies should avoid an "overly vicious" response.[137]

We cannot know how much this less cruel, though still anti-Semitic, conscience affected Pelley's private feelings. Clearly, however, it did not halt his public harangues or prevent the Silver Shirts from qualifying, in the American Jewish Committee's judgment, as the country's most vicious anti-Semitic organization.[138]

Silver Legions and the Christian Commonwealth

Creation of the Silver Legion in 1933, Pelley believed, advanced "Liberation" work to the level of "sociological application." From a personal perspective, it marked another attempt to find a satisfying "brevet." Buoyed by a pyramidologist's inference that a "new theocratic state" had been conceived on 31 January 1933, Pelley deduced that his was the embryonic movement, gave fresh emphasis to pyramid prophecy, and looked forward to the predicted day of triumph, 16 September 1936.[139]

As leader of the Silver Shirts, Pelley felt the "Great Thrill" he had craved since leaving Siberia. Once again wearing a uniform, now that of the "Chief," he urged others bred "in the merchandising way" to come forward and be valiant—a word which began to rival poise as his favorite. He pronounced Jesus a Silver Shirt ahead of His time. Jesus clairaudiently accepted the commission and echoed the call to "Stand Forth as Knights." Thus sanctified, Pelley at last considered himself "part of the very essence and fibre of my country's current history."[140]

Pelley was a peculiar-looking chief. He was slightly deaf, stood five feet seven inches tall, weighed only 130 pounds, and sported a goatee that, like his hair and moustache, was turning gray. A pince-nez compounded the unmilitary look. Pelley usually dressed meticulously, but his penchant for large cigars sometimes made him look, as well as sound, like an ideological pitchman. His most striking feature, piercing dark eyes, seemed either inspired or demonic, depending on the observer's politics.[141]

Anyone over eighteen could apply to run with the Chief in the "Great Marathon." Prospective Silver Shirts swore allegiance to Christian principles, submitted a photograph, and listed their "racial extraction," baptismal faith, lodge affiliations, and income. Except for the exclusion of Jews and blacks, standards were lax. Dues, required at the outset, raised negligible sums and were soon abandoned.[142]

Silver Shirts sang an anthem ("The Battle Hymn of the Republic"), honored a coat of arms (the scourge Christ used to drive money-changers from the temple), and wore distinctive paramilitary attire. The "regulation uniform"—whose distribution had been hindered, *Liberation* complained, by "Hebrew clothing monopolists"—consisted of a service hat, blue courduroy trousers, leggings, a tie and a silver shirt. The "great scarlet 'L' emblazened" over the heart signified Love, Loyalty, and Liberation (the letter also decorated the Legion's "snow-white banner.") An impressive-sounding officer corps commanded the rank and file: the Chief, Chamberlain, Quartermaster, Sheriff, and Censor at national headquarters; a Commander, Adjutant, Purser, Bailiff, and Solicitor at state level; and a Chaplain, Scribe, Almoner, Marshall, and Advocate at each local post.[143]

Elaborate regalia and hierarchy gave the Chief a "Great Thrill" while also serving an organizational purpose. Like interwar advertisers and students of propaganda, Pelley, a veteran promoter, understood that ideas hit home only when accompanied by anthems, colors, and gadgets. As early as May 1933, *Liberation* complemented colorful appeals to valor with claims of 50,000 loyal followers. Within a year, national headquarters announced the staffing of regional corps, established a western office in Oklahoma, and divided the movement into five functional departments. Pelley's flair for melodrama did not desert him:

> Men in Little Towns are suddenly galvanized by the piercing tocsins of the Silver Bugles. They crain their necks from ledgers and lathes. . . . Rippling flags go past foggy windows where they've viewed the world with increasing sullenness during this highly successful Jewish Depression. . . . They deploy upon the sidewalks and behold the finest specimens of American manhood DOING something to relive mass resentment. . . . They want to play their parts.[144]

It was all a charade. Pelley's recollection in 1940 that he had signed 25,000 credentials and attracted 75,000 sympathizers was also dubious. According to the historian John Werly, who has made the most detailed study of the Silver Shirts, the group began with 400–800 members in 1933, reached a peak of 15,000 the following year, and declined to 5,000 by 1938. Pelley said that Silver Legion posts functioned in twenty-two states during 1940. Yet noteworthy activity was concentrated in a few areas: Cleveland, Toledo, and Youngstown, Ohio; Minneapolis-St. Paul, Minnesota; San Diego and Los Angeles, California; Seattle, Washington; and Chicago, Illinois. Recruitment appears to have been slight in the Northeast and the South, with the exception of Asheville. Even in his relative strongholds, Pelley's following was ephemeral and meetings rarely attracted more than two hundred persons.[145]

The organization floundered, partly because of Pelley's continuing administrative ineptitude and propensity to trust associates even less reliable than himself. Testifying before Congress in 1940, he betrayed astonishing ignorance of the Legion's finances, regional agents, and local membership. But more important, he encountered the problem that also discouraged Socialists, Communists, and independent liberal—the tendency of middle-class Americans during the Depression to blame themselves for unemployment, to sink into sullenness, or to accept existing authority instead of marching from their lathes and ledgers. Citizens hesitated to criticize their president, Pelley grumbled during the Hoover administration, adding that apathy was "far more dangerous" than Communist machinations. Despite the scarlet Ls emblazoned on their hearts, even some Silver Shirt officers believed that Roosevelt and the "Georgetown Gang. . . . should be 'given a chance.' " Bringing a "New Vision to humankind," Pelley complained in July 1933, was a thankless job.[146]

Evidence is fragmentary concerning the composition of the Silver Legion. Identifying the occupations of 327 members, Werly found them almost evenly divided between the working class (skilled craftsmen and low-level clerks as well as laborers) and the solid middle class (including teachers, clergy, and small businessmen). Few farmers appeared in the sample, but there were ten lawyers, twenty-seven physicians, and eight corporate executives. Post leaders included a Protestant minister, a disabled war veteran, an astrologer, and two engineers. Similarly, identifying 671 Silver Shirts, Werly found that 62 percent of the names were British, 24 percent German, and 9 percent Scandinavian. The presence of no more than 9 percent Irish or French names undermines Pelley's claim, incongruous in view of his recruitment of Ku Klux Klansmen, that Roman Catholics made up half of the Silver Legion.[147]

The Chief was correct, however, in detecting a dualism in the ranks. A fiercely loyal faction, considering the Silver Shirts an extension of metaphysics, expected positive thinking to cure national ills. An equally large group enlisted for "action," anything from assaults on Jewish tailor shops to marches on Washington. When Pelley paid attention to the aspiring thugs, ostensibly to enforce discipline, metaphysicians charged a betrayal of Christ's mandate; if he stressed meditation, "actionist boys" denounced the "old ladies' sewing circle."[148]

The Chief's attitude toward violence combined his venerable capacity for self-deception with a practical desire to stay out of jail. He urged Silver Shirts to obey the law, reminding them that they were too valiant for petty reprisals. No "overt act against any individual Jew" received his sanction, Pelley testified in 1940. Nonetheless, he sympathized with subordinates who chafed under the restraint he formally counseled. He also provided them with a scurrilous portrait of the Jewish "race," including specific images applicable to individual Jews.[149]

Fortunately, the actionist boys, like their Chief, acted less than they talked. In 1934, two United States marines told congressional investigators that San Diego Silver Shirts drilled regularly and built a secret arms cache, but local police ridiculed the testimony. Some of Pelley's followers did harass opponents and destroy private property. In 1934, for example, a Cleveland contingent threatened a professor with "punishment" unless he stopped teaching about Communism. In 1939, five Chicago Silver Shirts, returning from what *Liberation* delicately called a "beer garden," smashed four windows at the empty Goldblatt Brothers department store. Sometimes, though, opponents attacked Silver Shirts. Demonstrators broke up a meeting in Aberdeen, Washington, in 1935. Four years later, well-organized foes disrupted a series of Silver Legion rallies in Chicago. Not quite standing forth like a knight, Field Marshall Roy Zachary, who had been hit on the head, asked police protection. Notably short on valor, Silver Shirts neither instigated nor won most street confrontations.[150]

As might be expected, the tables were turned in their imaginations. Headquarters solicited reports about "every Jew who approaches a Gentile." Pelley especially wanted information about foreclosures, insolence, and white slavery. Eventually, he vowed, every offender would face Silver Shirt court martial. Current Jewish "potentates" would be fortunate to escape with life imprisonment.[151]

A worldwide "wave of anti-Semitism" reinforced Pelley's faith in his ultimate triumph. He applauded the British Imperial Fascist League, the French Croix de Feu, and the Rumanian Christian Nationalists. Pelley never faltered either in his defense of Hitler's "valiant" effort to save Germany from Jewish domination. Rather, he felt complimented by comparisons of himself and the Feuhrer, and promised a similar anti-Semitic program in the United States. Sometime during the late 1930s Pelley met with Fritz Kuhn, leader of the German-American Bund. Though their clashing personalities prevented further contact, Silver Shirts and Bundists often cooperated on the local level.[152]

According to the scenario Pelley sketched in 1935, Jews would replace Roosevelt ("another Kerensky") with somebody worse, thus enjoying ten days of triumph until gentiles rallied behind "a Hitler." During the crisis, Silver Shirts would function as "Lords Protector" of constitutional liberty. Their Chief, presumably the "Hitler" at hand, would quickly destroy Communism by jailing fourteen (unspecified) Jews who financed it. Unhindered by subversives, the nation would pass constitutional amendments creating the Silver Legion's "pièce de résistance," the Christian Commonwealth.[153]

The Commonwealth was essentially the same utopia prescribed by the *Philosopher* in 1909, adapted to fit Pelley's conversions to metaphysics and anti-Semitism and supported with stock notions of the 1930s. Appropriating a popular Turnerian explanation, Pelley said that depression afflicted the United States largely because the frontier had closed and machinery produced more goods than underpaid workers could afford. These structural problems had been exacerbated by Jewish financiers. Happily, a more humane economy not only existed in theory, but had been practiced for thousands of years—in Atlantis.[154]

The Christian Commonwealth, of course, owed less to Atlantis than to Edward Bellamy, whom Pelley continued to admire and now pronounced an "adept psychic." Indeed, he was more faithful to *Looking Backward* in 1935 than he had been twenty-six years earlier. All citizens, he wrote in *No More Hunger*, would belong to a vast civil service and hold shares in the national corporation (which Pelley compared to the War Industries Board, temporarily ignoring his hatred for its chairman, Bernard Baruch). Hence, they would receive "bread to eat as freely" as they breathed air. Improved living conditions would produce clear thinkers, stable citizens, and workers imbued with a "zest for doing." To ensure prosperity in the absence of the expanding frontier, an "Industrial Census" would balance production and demand. Like Bellamy, Pelley envisioned the disappearance of banks, advertising (which manipulated humanity's "inferiority complex"), trade unions (because employees would be happy), money (to be replaced by coded checks), and private legal practices. Still seeking to combine expertise with "true democracy," Pelley anticipated also an automatic end to "slovenly" New Deal bureaucracy and use of referenda to nullify bad laws.[155]

A perverse contribution to the planning vogue of the 1930s that revived interest in Bellamy, the Christian Commonwealth also represented Pelley's latest effort to resolve his nagging personal concerns. The utopia institutionalized, so to speak, his mixed feelings about wealth and the emotional cost of acquiring it. Pelley had never objected to economic inequity per se. Rather, in polemics and fiction, his objection was that wealth was allocated capriciously, without due regard to ability and effort. In the Christ State, therefore, workers would receive luxuries "in the exact degree that . . . effort and talent merit them." The "idealized" civil service would rank citizens from 1-Q (entitling them to $1,000 annually) to 10-Q ($100,000). Once the gospel of success was rendered efficient, ambitious lads like Nathan Forge and David Haskell could not be sidetracked by bad luck or villainy. At the same time, Pelley declined to "penalize" productive businessmen—the Jim Thornes of the future—by confiscating all their wealth. More "selfishly enticing" than any existing system, the Christian Commonwealth would promote unprecedented "personal progress."[156]

Yet financial enticements must be limited. Any salary above $100,000 annually, Pelley wrote, produced "profligate extravagance." Honorary ranks, not money, would reward such valiant persons as Thomas Edison (11-Q), Harriet Beecher Stowe (12-Q), and Abraham Lincoln (13-Q). Moreover, still jealous of "pampered offspring," flesh-and-blood versions of the fops who pursued Madeleine Theddon in *The Fog*, Pelley proscribed virtually all inheritance. Only houses and farms might be deeded to children, because, as Mary Purse might have said in *The Greater Glory*, the "sentiment accruing about an old family residence" was "one of the finest" public assets.[157]

While still disdaining the profligate rich, Pelley made provision for the worthy laggard. Laziness would be rare, he thought, after the Commonwealth liberated humanity's natural zest for doing. Moreover, potential slackers, like their counterparts during World War I, would yield before "social ostracism." Yet Pelley declined to follow Bellamy in punishing recalcitrants with confinement on a meager diet. Having himself alternated between striving and desperate—conscious and unconscious—efforts to relax, Pelley granted dedicated slackers the right to lie on a beach, collecting a basic $1,000 annual grant. Because parents "invited" souls into life without consulting them, he explained, every mortal deserved the "fundamental means to live." Theology aside, he expected this option to help persons like himself—striving artists and sick souls in need of a respite.[158]

The celebration of rural America, an aspect of the Great Depression shared by radicals, New Dealers, and their far right enemies, had special significance for Pelley. Like the heroes of *The Fog* and *Drag*, Pelley had dreamed of—and then enjoyed—metropolitan "refinement" and "poise." After quitting Hollywood "fleshpots," however, he decided that cities "drained" men, rendering them susceptible to demagogues like Franklin D. Roosevelt. To counter this trend, the Christ State would raze tenements, develop suburbs, encourage single family houses on ample plots, and adequately reward farmers, the ultimate producers of wealth from "Nature's storehouse."[159]

Similarly, Pelley repudiated "modernism," his synonym for the "current practice of being flip, superficial, blasé, hard-boiled, contemptuous of moral values, impudent to parents, sympathetic toward concupiscence, and cynically indifferent to old forms of restraint and moderation." Pelley, of course, had indulged in these practices and, as Chief of the Silver Shirts, still claimed to be "hard-boiled." However, under the Commonwealth, as in the nurturing higher octaves, these enticements would evaporate as mankind recognized "its own silliness." Crime, too, would disappear along with the cash necessary to buy illicit goods. Most important, a healthy "oscillation into Puritanism" would follow the reign of concupiscence.[160]

Women perplexed Pelley as much in 1935 as they had in 1909. According to *No More Hunger*, even the poorest woman, guaranteed $1,000 annually, need not "sell her body" or remain with a brutal husband to avoid starvation; at the highest echelon she might qualify for 10-Q appointments, as for Silver Shirt membership, on an "absolutely equal footing." In between, Mibb Hendersons and Allie Parkers could choose mates on the basis of love and "Mutual Interest," the kind of relationship Pelley lauded in fiction and haltingly sought in life. Yet the Commonwealth, like its utopian ancestor in the *Philosopher*, fell short of the "true liberation" it promised. Marriage and motherhood, though no longer coerced by poverty, would still be the things for women to do. In the final analysis, Pelley's tenacious cult of "ladyship" formed the core of the "new status of Womanhood Enobled."[161]

While some residents of the United States could anticipate enoblement under the Commonwealth, others would suffer degradation. Perhaps influenced by the former Klansmen now clad in silver shirts, Pelley in 1935–36 grew increasingly hostile to blacks (whose service during World War I he had praised in the *St. Johnsbury Caledonian*). Characteristically, he suspected them of coveting white women. Adding a metaphysical gloss to a racist convention, he warned that "mongrel" products of racially mixed marriages reverted to lower levels of "spiritual attainment." Since miscegenation was the likely product of black suffrage, all blacks must be made wards of the Commonwealth.[162]

Above all, neither prosperity nor morality was possible until society solved the "one problem." Sometimes Pelley implied that the

Jewish threat, like other evils, would end automatically under the Christ State; after all, Jewish gold would purchase nothing and the hierarchy of talent would be impervious to their machinations. By 1936, however, Pelley, wanted Jews disfranchised and confined to one city per state. In these "Beth Havens," governed by rabbis, their safety would be guaranteed by the Commonwealth. Pelley's practical commitment to male supremacy marked his plan. Jewish women could register to live anywhere with their gentile husbands, but gentile wives must accompany their Jewish spouses to Beth Havens. Relocation would be arranged without "embarassment to any Hebrew" by an "Aryan" Secretary of Jewry.[163]

In the final analysis, Pelley collapsed his anti-Semitic "true democracy" into theocracy. Supposing that a "Christian brotherhood" would govern the Commonwealth much as mystics had ruled Atlantis, he worried little about inconsistencies. Americans would learn the details soon enough, he wrote, because the "Thousand-Year-Reign of the Messiah" was both imminent and inevitable.[164]

Crazy Like a Fox?

While Pelley contemplated an imminent Christian Commonwealth, he struggled with the mundane problems of keeping solvent and warding off opposition. Following the incorporation of Galahad Press in New York during 1931, he discovered that persons who hungered after "things of the spirit" were willing to pay for sustenance. Within a year, he deposited $25,000 in the Galahad Press account. Moving to Washington, D.C., in October 1931, he deposited most of these assets in his own name. After incorporating the Fellowship of Christian Economics in Asheville, North Carolina, during 1932, he opened three accounts there for his various subdivisions and in the March issue of *Liberation* urged readers to purchase Galahad Press stock at ten dollars per share; the stock sale raised $14,000 from two hundred buyers.[165]

Starting in 1933, Pelley juggled funds from all sources to pay for travel as chief of the Silver Shirts. Congressional investigators reported in 1939 that during the previous eight years he had received at least $174,000 from contributions and literature sales. Between September 1937 and July 1939, he cashed money orders worth $30,000 at the Asheville Post Office alone. Several donations from devout spiritualists and small manufacturers amounted to thousands of dollars. Nevertheless, while the chief busied himself with anti-Semitic diatribes, unpaid bills accumulated.[166]

Pelley's chaotic finances made him an easy target for critics. Surveying his paper conglomerate, they often wondered whether he was primarily a subversive or a con artist. Leaning toward the latter interpretation, Arthur Graham of the *New Republic* surmised that he was "crazy like a fox." In 1934, Pelley's activities helped to inspire Nathanael West's novel, *A Cool Million*, the funniest book pertaining to native fascism. Pelley was taken more seriously by creditors, courts, and congressional investigators. Also in 1934, the House of Representatives created a Special Committee on Un-American Activities, which, under the leadership of John McCormack (Dem.-Mass.) and Samuel Dickstein (Dem.-N.Y.), concentrated on the German-American Bund and, to a lesser extent, the Silver Shirts.[167]

Under pressure from creditors, Pelley on 27 January 1934 instructed his treasurer, Harry Seiber, to incorporate the Silver Legion in Delaware and to "clean [all] records clean." Seiber secured the certificate of incorporation and burned the Galahad Press files; in April, the Press filed for bankruptcy. These maneuvers failed to deter Pelley's pursuers. Charles Kramer, a staff member for the House Special Committee on Un-American Activities, arrived in Asheville on 2 May and, cooperating with local authorities, seized Pelley's surviving records. On 23 May, North Carolina indicted Pelley for fraud.[168]

Pelley predictably blamed Jews and their "Gentile satraps" for his problems, but, confined to North Carolina and ordered to suspend *Liberation*, he could not denounce them efficiently. A circular explained to Silver Shirts in June 1934 why they no longer received magazines, answers to letters, and visits from the Chief. After several months of legal wrangling, Pelley was convicted in January 1935, of selling stock unregistered in North Carolina and of advertising Galahad Press, an insolvent company. On the first count, he paid a $1,000 fine; on the second, his lawyer filed a prayer for judgment to continue the case, a rare form of parole allowing Pelley to remain at liberty for five years under court supervision.[169]

The defendant felt guilty of no more than a "technical breach." Galahad stock had been advertised in *Liberation*, a magazine published in North Carolina, but none of it had been sold there. Furthermore, the Press appeared insolvent only because a "biased receivership" undervalued his "beautifully printed" literature. Officials probably were more interested in silencing a local embarassment than in preventing stock fraud. Moreover, Pelley's pathetic insistence on the value of his pamphlets suggests the absence of criminal intent. Even his casual transfer of funds among accounts, though unlawful, reflected Pelley's realistic assessment that Galahad Press, Galahad College, the Foundation for Christian Economics, and various spinoffs depended on himself and his oracles.[170]

Pelley was undone, not by Jews, gentile "satraps," or even by patriotic North Carolinians, but by character traits that persisted after his "Great Release." His self-admitted "Yankee's weakness for . . . any sort of pursuit that promised a profit" remained, redirected toward metaphysical markets. After luring students to Galahad College with false promises of placement in lucrative jobs, for instance, he also tried to sell them nearby bungalows. Cultivating less esoteric markets, he adopted a pseudonym and sold leftover stories to *Liberty* and *Women's Home Companion.* Instead of seeking profit with foxy shrewdness, however, Pelley carried into his post-conversion years the financial ineptitude that was almost a family tradition. The Galahad Press bankruptcy proceedings were simply beyond him. In the absence of a strong woman to organize his fiscal and personal affairs he tended to hire assistants as disorganized as himself.[171]

As Pelley battled legal difficulties during late 1934 and 1935, Silver Shirt activities lay largely in abeyance. In January 1936, however, he declared for the presidency on the Christian party ticket. The campaign existed almost entirely in the pages of *Pelley's Weekly*, a temporary replacement for *Liberation.* He suspected Republican nominee Alfred "Mossman" Landon of Jewish ancestry and chided the Union Party for ignoring the Jewish threat. Praising Robert E. Edmondson, James True, and Eugene N. Sanctuary, all of whom purported to uncover President Roosevelt's Jewish ancestry, Pelley still insisted that his own opposition to Jewish conspiracy was more fervent than theirs.[172]

If Americans preferred useless panaceas to the Silver Legion's unprecedented program, Pelley wrote in October 1936, "What is it to me?" Instead of compromising, he would "withdraw into the seclusion of . . . metaphysical studies." Usually, however, he was not so dour. Until September 16, the great pyramid date, *Pelley's Weekly* predicted with mounting assurance Silver Shirt entrance into the "king's chamber" of victory. Nonetheless, on the ballot only in Washington, he received fewer than 1,600 votes.[173]

When Prophecy Fails

Since neither the pyramid date nor election day installed Pelley in the White House, either as president or as Lord Protector, he faced the classic problem of explaining why his predictions had gone awry. He offered versions of two classic answers. First, prophecy had not failed; the prophets had. Pridefully cherishing one interpretation, they might have misjudged the date. Second, perhaps some significant beginning *had* quietly occurred on 16 September 1936. For example, a victory won by General Francisco Franco's Spanish insurgents might have signaled a "crack" in Communist ramparts. Not surprisingly, Pelley blamed Democratic "skullduggery" for his electoral defeat. Still, the contest was not in vain. Roosevelt's victory hastened the conflict between Light and Dark forces on earth, particularly in the United States.[174]

Pelley expected "pseudo believers" to accuse him of rationalization, and he seems to have had doubts himself. In January 1937, he asked Silver Shirts to "take the status of reservists," subject to recall in event of an outright Communist coup. Forsaking the "minute details" of mass agitation, he planned several solo ventures, including two magazines. *New Liberation*, a successor to *Pelley's Weekly*, would report on the "Red Jew cabal" without reference to metaphysics, a subject considered trite by many Silver Shirts. *Reality* would discuss only "sublimer truths." Not only did Pelley want to spend more time on metaphysics, but he hoped to win back spiritualists disaffected by his politics. In 1937, he published *Behold Life*, a synthesis of his esoteric theology; two years later, *Earth Comes* purported to reconcile science (as Pelley understood it) with his brand of spiritualism.[175]

New Liberation, which became *New Liberation Weekly* for a time and then reverted to *Liberation* in 1938, appeared regularly until 1941. Suspecting a New Deal trend toward mob rule, the magazine de-emphasized Christian "democracy" to stress that the United States was—and should remain—a republic. Similarly, Pelley argued that the rising national debt rendered the nation bankrupt. Using a Hollywood version of their diction, "Chief Pelley of the Tribe of Silver" told American Indians (long admired by theosophists) that he would free them from reservations and put Jews in their place. Solo maneuvers included several suits that failed to reach juries, including one against Secretary of the Interior Harold L. Ickes. Also during the late 1930s, Pelley conferred occasionally with retired general George Van Horne Moseley, an anti-Semite regarded as a likely man-on-horseback by many far right agitators, and published speeches by Representative Jacob Thorkelson (Dem.-Mon.), the most fervent congressional believer in Jewish conspiracy since Louis McFadden's departure.[176]

Still concentrating on the "one problem," Pelley wrote anti-Semitic film reviews, said that the Chrysler corporation, whose hubcaps bore the "Jewish *six-pointed star,*" had been largely spared by the "kosher" CIO, and warned against adopting Irving Berlin's "God Bless America" as a national anthem. In increasingly brutal prose and doggeral, he assailed Roosevelt as a "stooge" for east European "kikes," and criticized Roosevelt's family.[177]

If the president and other "Jews" continued to provoke caucasians, Pelley reflected, their "Great Extermination" might begin in the United States. There were two alternatives to a pogrom: "humanely" performed sterilization and segregation. After prominent Jews perished during spontaneous attacks by furious gentiles, Pelley predicted, their lesser kin would eagerly settle in Beth Havens. Unsqueamish about "Yiddisher gore in the gutters," he opposed extermination for the metaphysical reason that it would breed "pestilence in the souls of the slaughterers."[178]

As memories of the disappointing pyramid date faded, *Liberation* again started to detect signs of imminent victory. Nineteen thirty-eight began a fifteen-year period of "adjustment" destined to end in the collapse of Jewish power, the magazine decided. Supporting evidence ranged from a "tidal wave" of anti-Semitism to numerology, pyramid prophecy, and psychic receptions. Indeed, clairvoyants unaffiliated with the Silver Legion foresaw that Pelley would follow Roosevelt in the White House.[179]

This optimism had less warrant than ever. Pelley's main connection with the White House was irate memoranda issued from the president's desk. When *Liberation,* in October 1938, questioned his family claim to Hyde Park, Roosevelt asked FBI Director J. Edgar Hoover whether Pelley could be prosecuted "for a thing like this." Although Hoover proposed an indictment for criminal libel, the suggestion was not pursued. The next year, Pelley charged Roosevelt, the "lowest form of human worm," with embezzling funds from the Warm Springs Foundation. Attorney General Frank Murphy offered to press charges for criminal libel, but warned that the defense might subpoena Roosevelt. Once again, the matter was dropped.[180]

Congress proved more persistent than the White House. After the House of Representatives established another Special Committee on Un-American Activities in May 1938, Chairman Martin Dies (Dem.-Tex.) oscillated between hunts for New Deal subversives and hearings on the far right. Pelley's opinion of the investigators varied accordingly. As Dies moved toward an attack on the Silver Legion, Pelley denounced the "Jew-lover from Texas." In July 1939, hearing testimony from former Silver Shirts and from Robert Barker, a staff member who had mastered Pelley's finances, the committee informally concluded that the Chief was primarily a "racketeer."[181]

Instead of rushing to Washington in defense of his honor, Pelley took to the road, fearing that testimony might prejudice his parole. When the House voted in August to subpoena him, he was on another marathon drive across country, convinced that he had outwitted "The Probers" (whom he mocked in rhyme). He failed to anticipate, however, that flight could produce as much trouble as anything said under oath. Judge Zebulon Nettles ordered him brought before Buncombe County Court in North Carolina. Pelley, the judge said, had continued to exploit contributors, consorted with "known enemies" of the United States, and now conducted these "nefarious practices from some secret hiding place." North Carolina officials raided Silver Shirt headquarters on 19 October, 1939; Robert Barker arrived the next day to examine the acquisitions.[182]

Pelley surfaced in Washington on 6 February 1940, and asked Dies's secretary for a subpoena. David Mayne, a former committee employee, had forged letters purporting to show that Dies and "Pelly" were secret allies. Pelley planned to perform the "invaluable service" of exposing these forgeries. Appealing to the committee's "chivalry," he would then ask to remain in custody until 18 February, when he was no longer subject to punishment in North Carolina.[183]

On 7, 8, and 10 February, Pelley had an "exceedingly enjoyable time" enlightening the Dies committee about matters mundane and esoteric. Although "very much" anti-Semitic, he disclaimed hatred of individuals, reiterating that confinement of Jews to Beth Havens was a "humane" alternative to sterilization. He hailed Hitler's "excellent" government but denied association with Germany. Nor, Pelley said, did he seek a comparable regime in the United States. Moving to higher octaves, he tried to explain his May 1928 religious experience and subsequent capacity to project himself through space. To the dismay of acting Chairman Joseph Starnes (Dem.-Ala), he reported a "total change of heart" regarding the committee, even offering to disband the Silver Shirts if these "Christian gentlemen" effectively pursued subversives. Deeming Pelley a charlatan who had received $2,000 for every minute in eternity, Representative Joseph Casey (Dem.-Conn.) wondered why he drove 100,000 miles annually to visit followers: "I should think he could project himself."[184]

Immediately after Chairman Starnes adjourned the hearing on 10 February, Pelley was served a warrant from North Carolina and, unable to post bond, jailed for two days. A long battle over extradition began on 10 March. Ultimately, both the United States District Court and Court of Appeals rejected arguments that North Carolina was harassing Pelley. On 21 January 1942 Judge E. Don Phillips ordered him to serve the sentence suspended in 1935. He remained free on bail pending appeal.[185]

While evading the Dies committee and fighting to avoid prison, Pelley also turned his attention to the international crisis. In the mid-1930s, he had supposed that conflicts among nations would dissolve as Christian utopia replaced the "false-prophet system." More conventional analysis followed the great disappointment of 16 September 1936. With condescending affection unchanged twenty years after his visit, Pelley regarded Japan as a quaint land of "children" intimidated by "one lone Yankee's fists." There was ample room in Asia, however, for both Japanese and Yankees to fulfill their respective manifest destinies.[186]

Germany, Pelley said, was the "ideal country." Sometimes drawing on dispatches from the World Service press agency in Erfurt, he dismissed "Jewish atrocity fables," applauded the *Kristallnacht* pogrom of November 1938, and hinted that Hitler might justly "exterminate" European Jewry if the Third Reich faced military defeat. The Nazi-Soviet Pact of 1939, a "truce" with one branch of world Jewry, bought time to beat the other branch. While favoring American neutrality in the subsequent European war, Pelley had no doubt that "Hitler [was] in the right."[187]

By January 1941, the Chief decided to fulfill his promise to the Dies committee to disband the Silver Shirts. The group, he said, was afflicted by "human 'deadwood' " and even the best members needed a "breathing spell." Personally, he wanted to operate on the "plane of mentorship," offering "scouring interpretations" of world events. Undoubtedly, too, Pelley wanted to scour his reputation. Many Americans, he recognized, thought Silver Shirts reprehensible. As part of his transition to an earthly higher octave, Pelley moved in early 1941 from Asheville, North Carolina, to Noblesville, Indiana, a suburb of Indianapolis. In addition, he replaced *Liberation* with the *Galilean*, a metaphysical monthly, and *Roll-Call*, the self-proclaimed "voice of the loyal opposition."[188]

Whether or not other Silver Shirts needed a breather, the Chief needed one badly. The revived optimism of 1938 had faded. Like Pelley's previous careers—small town publisher, sentimental story teller, screenwriter, and full-time metaphysician—his command of the Silver Shirts had lost its "zest." Pelley's attempt to cope with his latest failure seeped through the bravado in *Liberation*. Perhaps he was fated to be a stormy petrel, a "not altogether" happy role. "Noisy courage," a quality often promoted in the magazine, might be "whistling in the dark to bolster up the spirits"; true bravery required quiet poise. Occassionally recognizing that he would never lead valiant knights to victory, Pelley fell back on the belief, present in his fiction and metaphysics, that even failure was "rich in experience."[189]

This latest version of Pelley's persistent tension between striving and acceptance affected his attitude toward American involvement in World War II. On the one hand, he used *Roll-Call* to attack favorite enemies, albeit in slightly softened language. Some arguments did parallel those of the "loyal opposition," that is, reputable congressional isolationists and members of the America First Committee. Pelley accused Roosevelt of usurping power, expected war abroad to destroy freedom at home, predicted British defeat, and judged the United States invulnerable to attack. Unlike most isolationists, however, Pelley continued to hail Hitler. Furthermore, in May 1941, he authorized a Japanese edition of *No More Hunger* as a "friendship" gesture. Nor could he resist blanket diatribes against Jews, including the comedian Ed Wynn, whose "kosher" entertainment supposedly corrupted draftees.[190]

On the other hand, finding solace in metaphysics, Pelley tried to view the world situation with poise. From the spiritual perspective, national leaders were merely "mortal symbols" leading their respective countries through a preordained governmental cycle: monarchies (or dictatorships) evolved into republics; republics sank into mass democracy; democratic inefficiency prompted restoration of autocracy; and the course began again. People profited from the "educating experiences" of living under the diverse systems. The forthcoming "Aquarian Age" would be marked by an international renovation and a version of the "Millenniel Advent" (though Pelley no longer anticipated Jesus's literal return).[191]

If Pelley had restricted himself to general speculation about preordained dictatorships, he might have avoided the penitentiary. Immediately after Japan's attack on Pearl Harbor, he ordered the Silver Shirt remnant to obey military authorities and closed *Roll-Call* before censors could "emasculate" it. But buoyed by Attorney General Francis Biddle's pledge to protect dissent, Pelley soon wrote that the United States, fighting for "Mongolic Judaists," was on the wrong side of the cosmic and profane conflict. According to the *Galilean*, which continued to reach 3,500 subscribers, American diplomacy had "aggressively solicited" the Japanese attack, Pearl Harbor after the raid resembled an "abandoned WPA project in Keokuk," and Christians understandably lacked "slightest enthusiasm" for the war.[192]

Less committed than his attorney general to free speech, President Roosevelt decided in January 1942, that the war provided a "good chance to clean up" some "vile publications." Pelley's was one of the first to go. In March, Pelley suspended the *Galilean* instead of submitting it to the Post Office Department for examination, but he had already done irreparable damage to himself. On 4 April, following specific orders from Attorney General Biddle, FBI agents arrested him in Connecticut. Two months later, a grand jury in Indianapolis charged Pelley, Agnes Marion Henderson (his secretary and latest personal "pivot"), and Fellowship Press Treasurer Lawrence A. Brown with violating the Espionage Act of 1917. According to the indictment, they had disseminated and conspired to disseminate false information with intent to impair the operations of the armed forces. Specifically, Pelley had said that the United States was bankrupt, that the Axis fought for justice, that the Roosevelt administration had baited Japan into war, and that the Pacific fleet lay in ruins.[193]

When the trial began on 28 June 1942, United States Attorney B. Howard Caughran was assisted by Oscar R. Ewing, formerly vice-chairman of the Democratic National Committee. Although his presence as special prosecutor suggested otherwise, Ewing denied in his opening statement that the defendants were on trial for criticizing the Roosevelt administration. On the contrary, he said, they had promoted "defeatism" by spreading untruths "surprisingly consistent" with Axis propaganda. Noting that a copy of the *Galilean* was discovered in a soldier's duffel bag, Ewing promised to show that "many copies" were available to military personnel.[194]

In fact, the prosecution presented no evidence of direct contact—or attempted contact—between the defendants and military personnel. Repeating a pattern established during World War I cases involving the Espionage Act, the government assumed that Pelley's appeals to the general public were dangerous because they reached a handful of soldiers and sailors. A method of content analysis, pioneered by the political scientist Harold Lasswell, provided a modern twist to this "dangerous tendency" test. Experts from the Foreign Broadcast Intelligence Service testified that Pelley's opinions meshed with fourteen Axis propaganda themes; displaying five charts, Lasswell himself pointed to 1,195 specific examples of convergence. In letters, evidence of a more traditional sort, Pelley had boasted of his own "drag" in Japan, looked forward to Hitler's conquest of Moscow, and told General George Van Horn Moseley that his "military" career was really just beginning.[195]

Prosecution ingenuity contrasted with the ineptitude of Pelley's lawyers, Oscar Smith and Floyd Christians. (Christians had unsuccessfully defended D.C. Stephenson, Grand Dragon on the Indiana Ku Klux Klan, against a murder charge.) They denied that Lasswell's content analysis was a "recognized science," but raised few other objections and passed over the government's major weakness, failure to show specific intent to hinder the military. Remarkably, too, they tried to prove that Pelley's expressions were not false as charged, even attempting to call Marriner Eccles of the Federal Reserve Board to show the nation's insolvency. Judge Robert Baltzell refused to subpoena Eccles, other high officials, or a Pearl Harbor salvage crew. Former Representative Jacob Thorkelson did arrive from Montana to ramble about subversion in a thick Norwegian accent. After testifying for twelve minutes about noninterventionist efforts before Pearl Harbor, Charles A. Lindbergh, who had never met Pelley, correctly judged the defense to be "extremely incompetent."[196]

Examined for five hours on 3 August, Pelley, stroking his goatee and looking dazed, called Hitler an "enemy of America," repudiated fantasies of a Silver Shirt protectorate, and accused the prosecution of misinterpreting his "silly little articles." References in *Liberation* to trials before Silver Shirt juries, for example, were as innocent as allusions to "Republican or Democratic juries." Judge Baltzell interposed, "We don't talk about juries that way." In a devastating slip, defense counsel Floyd Christians addressed Pelley as "Mr. Hitler." Prosecutors bothered to cross examine the defendant for fifteen minutes.[197]

In summations delivered on 5 August, Pelley's attorneys compared Silver Legion proposals to conventional political platforms, insisting that they sounded menacing because Lasswell had "lifted" statements from context. Pelley's platform, U.S. Attorney Caughran countered, was the same as Hitler's. Ewing compared the chief defendant to Vidkun Quisling, Benedict Arnold, and Aaron Burr. No murderer, he said, glaring at Pelley, "had a blacker heart than you, who tried to murder the country that nurtured you."[198]

A jury of farmers and small businessmen needed only four hours on 5 August 1942 to convict Pelley on all counts. His codefendants, largely ignored during the trial, were found guilty of conspiracy to circulate seditious literature. Declaring that his "clever mind" made Pelley especially dangerous, Judge Baltzell sentenced him on 12 August to fifteen years in prison. The following month he entered the federal penitentiary at Terre Haute, Indiana, where he would remain until another indictment in 1942 brought him to Washington, D.C.[199]

3. Gerald B. Winrod

PROPHET IN POLITICS

Battering Ram of Righteousness

During the 1930s, Gerald B. Winrod acquired national notoriety as an advocate of alien fascist ideas and as the "Nazi" candidate for United States Senator from Kansas. A decade earlier, however, he was regarded as a leader of a very American movement, the fundamentalist strain within evangelical Protestantism. The Defenders of the Christian Faith, the chief vehicle for his activities until his death in 1957, was created in 1925 to offer the Midwest's first organized challenge to the "forces of evolution" and "Modernism."[1]

In a sense, Winrod was born into the fundamentalist movement. His father, John Wesley Winrod, founded and directed the Healing Tabernacle in Wichita, Kansas—but only after years of intermittent drinking, fighting, and deliverance. The son of poor Missouri farmers, young John was saved for the first time at a Baptist service. After backsliding, however, he provoked a drunken brawl and left Missouri in shame. In Wichita, John's behavior temporarily improved under the influence of Mabel Craig, whom he married in 1899, when he was twenty-six and she was nineteen. Their first child, Gerald Burton, was born on 7 March 1900. Despite family commitments, John continued tending bar and drinking at the "410," an illegal saloon equipped with slot machines. In early 1901, the "410" was destroyed by an irate Kansan, Carry Nation. Inspired by this event, John Winrod recalled later, he quit bartending, resumed church attendance, and found reputable work as a building contractor.[2]

Despite John's turnaround the Winrods remained only nominal Christians until they faced a great crisis in 1910. Mabel developed cancer, lost both breasts to surgery, and became addicted to morphine prescribed to ease her pain. Physicians considered the case terminal, but the family prayed for her recovery. According to John's memoir, God spoke directly to Mabel, warning against further use of morphine. She gripped Him "with a new faith" and was instantly healed of cancer as well as drug addiction.[3]

From that day, when Gerald was ten years old, the Winrods accepted God as savior and healer, refusing even to keep medicine in their home. Shortly thereafter, John believed that he, too, was saved from cancer by divine intervention. Around 1918 John felt called to preach, and by 1925, he and Mabel had established the Wichita Healing Tabernacle; during their subsequent career, he wrote, they often witnessed cure of disease through faith. All in all, John was a "happy ex-bartender."[4]

The elder Winrod's happiness multiplied because the Holy Ghost annointed his son a "battering ram of righteousness." Indeed, young Gerald was even more devout than his parents. "He was so spiritually minded, so serious," Mabel recalled. Spirituality took precedence over education for the younger Winrod, who apparently left school after the fifth grade. He also passed through a conversion experience at age eleven (roughly the same time his mother was "healed") and preached his first sermon a year later. When he was fourteen, the revivalist Newton N. Riddell began guiding his forays into evangelism. Roughly three years later, while working as a bookkeeper in a utilities company, he assumed editorship of a small paper, *Jesus Is Coming Soon.* At twenty-one, he was seeking converts as an evangelist on the chautauqua circuit.[5]

Having established a local reputation, Winrod called a meeting in November 1925 at Salina, Kansas, where thirty ministers and laymen voted unanimously to establish the Defenders of the Christian Faith. They chose "Back to the Bible" as their organizational credo, "Faith of Our Fathers" as their hymn, and Winrod as their executive secretary. Fellowship was preferable to fighting, Winrod said, but fellowship was impossible with theological liberals who, by accepting Darwinism, gave Jesus an "animal ancestry." The fight against them would not be bitter, however, because Defenders of the Christian Faith must be simultaneously "uncompromising" and "sweet." Starting in April 1926, the *Defender,* a monthly magazine owned and edited by Winrod, carried the fight into print.[6]

As Winrod began his long tenure as director of the Defenders, relations between theological liberals and theological conservatives—fundamentalists—were anything but sweet. On the contrary, the contending factions within evangelical Protestantism accused each other of bad judgment and bad faith. Earlier in 1925 their disputes had received international attention when John T. Scopes was prosecuted for teaching evolution at a Dayton, Tennessee, high school. Yet neither acrimony in the churches nor hoopla surrounding the "monkey trial" should obscure the serious issues at stake.[7]

What historians call the fundamentalist controversy of the 1920s represented the culmination of tensions that had unsettled Protestantism since the 1870s. After the Civil War, a growing body of scholarship challenged orthodox understanding of early Christianity and of the Bible itself. Not only did this "higher criticism" threaten the parishioner's sense that his faith was special, but, after the popularization of Darwinism, he might even wonder if mankind differed much from other species. To make matters worse, these disturbing ideas had to be tamed amid social upheaval. Industrial society attracted millions of Roman Catholic and Jewish immigrants, left many native-born Protestants unmoved by traditional religion, and nurtured a prayerful but smug upper class. Responding to both intellectual and social strains, a minority of the clergy formulated a new, liberal theology.[8]

Protestant liberals differed among themselves on Scriptural interpretation, church polity, and definitions of the good society. The label "modernist," applied broadly by opponents like Winrod, fit those who would follow science wherever it led better than those who cherished aspects of orthodoxy. On the whole, however, liberals concurred in a critical, historical approach to Scripture, accepted Darwinism, reduced the sacraments to symbolic observances, defined sin as avoidable error instead of a product of innate depravity, and stressed the "sympathizing Jesus" rather than the divine Christ who died on the Cross. Skeptical of His literal Second Coming and sanguine about human nature, they urged men and women to build God's kingdom themselves. Specifications for this earthly kingdom varied. Theological liberalism did not necessarily entail political liberalism; on the contrary, adherents usually accepted the laissez faire shibboleths of the Gilded Age. Yet a minority of theological liberals, proponents of the social gospel, wanted to revise capitalism or establish socialism.[9]

Although by the turn of the century theological liberals had captured the most prestigious pulpits and seminaries, most Protestants continued to favor less bland religion. Erudite Presbyterians led by Charles Hodge of Princeton Theological Seminary remained certain that the Bible was "inerrant" in the original manuscripts. Diverse outbursts of piety offered alternatives to liberalism more popular than the Prebysterian dialectics of Princeton. Participants in a "holiness" movement that swept through established denominations and inspired several Pentecostal offshoots believed that spiritual rebirth brought special blessings ranging from enhanced purity to healing by faith. In the mid-1870s, Dwight L. Moody waded into the awakening and became its central figure within ten years. Not only did Moody tell urban audiences that Scripture was "true," but the Bible conferences, institutes, and publications he sponsored provided an infrastructure for theological conservatives.[10]

The post–Civil War revival of premillennialism was especially significant for later fundamentalists. Dispensationalism, the premillennial framework winning widest favor, derived from a British sect, the Plymouth Brethren. Dispensationalists on both sides of the Atlantic usually divided history into seven ages, called dispensations, and believed, contrary to liberal optimism, that a corrupt, penultimate age was currently in progress. According to their reading of Scripture, this depraved era would produce the imminent rise of the Antichrist (or Beast) prophesied in Revelation. His restoration of the Roman Empire and the return of the Jews to Jerusalem under his patronage would be followed by Jesus's Second Coming, salvation of the true church, the Beast's defeat at Armageddon, the Millennium (or last dispensation), and the final judgment of all souls.[11]

Some nineteenth-century premillennialists dissented from this particular scheme. Other conservatives, including the Princeton Theological Seminary Calvinists, rejected millennialism altogether. But dispensationalism won a sympathetic hearing from Moody as well as the endorsement of Billy Sunday and many lesser evangelists. More important, revivals and Bible conferences spread this latest form of apocalypticism to a large number of followers.[12]

During the two decades before World War I rival coalitions consisting of theological conservatives and theological liberals eyed each other warily but usually avoided open combat. While the social gospel emerged as a Progressive-era vogue, foes of modernism continued their own organizing in relative obscurity. Some Moody associates, for example, founded the Bible Institute of Los Angeles in 1908. The next year, Rev. C. I. Schofield published a *Reference Bible,* which, annotated from a dispensational perspective, found favor among most premillennialists. Between 1910 and 1915 *The Fundamentals,* a collection of essays by diverse theological conservatives, was widely distributed. Adapting the title of this series, Baptist editor Curtis Lee Laws in 1920 applied the label "fundamentalists" to militant foes of liberal Protestantism.[13]

World War I fostered cohesion as well as militancy among theological conservatives. Trench warfare contrasted sharply with the liberal expectation of progress. Yet because theological liberals expanded their activities instead of confessing their errors, defense of true Christianity seemed more necessary than ever. For instance, while Harvard professors excommunicated German philosophy (personified by Friedrich Nietzsche) from western civilization, theological conservatives went a step further by stressing Nietzsche's debt to Darwinism. Though skeptical that any modern state could be God's country, fundamentalists capitulated to "100% Americanism." The label "made in Germany" was stamped on the bottom of Hell," Billy Sunday declared, but the United States, Baptist John Roach Straton observed, represented the "ark of the covenant of humanity's hopes."[14]

The course of the war held added significance for dispensationalists. The British capture of Jerusalem and Foreign Minister Arthur Balfour's endorsement of a Jewish "national home" in late 1917 showed that the Jews were about to return to Palestine in fulfillment of Bible prophecy. These events added recruits to the dispensationalist camp, heightened their zeal, and inspired a series of prophetic conferences during 1918–1919. Participants in one such meeting in the spring of 1919 founded the World Christian Fundamentals Association (WCFA). This organization, dominated by dispensationalists and led by Baptist William Bell Riley, contained many of the most militant theological conservatives. Almost immediately, Riley began a campaign to bar Darwinism from public schools, a tactic partly inspired by wartime bans on the teaching of German.[15]

It is hard to determine which side fired the first shot in the fundamentalist controversy. As historian George M. Marsden suggests, theological liberals may have been seeking a showdown, and the growth of dispensational sentiment provided an occasion to attack. Mutual sniping was well underway before the war ended. During 1918–1919, the liberal *Christian Century* printed a series of articles assailing fundamentalism. The modernist theologian Shirley Jackson Case suggested in January 1918 that the Central Powers financed American premillennialists. Money for theological conservatives did not come from Germany, replied Reuben A. Torrey of the Bible Institute of Los Angeles, but liberal "higher criticism" did.[16]

The fundamentalist controversy, which persisted in its acute phase until the late 1920s, actually involved two related controversies. First, devout Protestants conducted an intramural struggle concerning the nature of their belief. In particular, the Northern Baptist Convention and the General Assembly of the Northern Presbyterians (Presbyterian Church in the U.S.A.) debated the merits of higher criticism, the acceptability of evolution, the requirements of communion, and the qualifications of missionaries. At the same time, theological conservatives built interdenominational alliances or created non-denominational organizations, such as the World Christian Fundamentals Association or the Defenders of the Christian Faith.[17]

Rival contenders for the faith often resorted to provocative rhetoric. Billy Sunday derided "evolutionary hot air merchants"; Southern Baptist J. Frank Norris introduced a monkey as "kinfolk" of Darwinians; and James M. Gray of the Moody Bible Institute viewed modernism as a prelude to the "red doctrine of the Third International." Liberals were no more temperate. Rev. Leon M. (L. M.) Birkhead of Kansas City, Missouri, a Methodist turned Unitarian, dropped "God out of consideration" from his religion, called Heaven and Hell "fictions," and described the Bible as a "gravely overrated book." According to *Christian Century*, dispensationalism was a pagan, "extremist," and "neurotic" movement allied with "reactionary" capitalists.[18]

Conflict among Protestant believers erupted most frequently in northern churches. Without accepting clichés about the "Bible Belt," however, we must recognize that theologically conservative premises and practices were at least as strong in the South. Indeed, the weak liberal challenge there made for a relative lack of controversy. Many prominent fundamentalists holding northern pulpits were southern-born, and their efforts to defend orthodoxy won approval in the South. Both the Southern Presbyterian General Assembly and the Southern Baptist Convention affirmed the Genesis account of creation. Tennessee, Mississippi, and Arkansas enacted the strictest bans on evolution. The South, Winrod concluded in 1927, "led in the movement against modernism."[19]

Second, division within Protestantism attracted attention from men and women who might be called contenders against the faith. Skeptical intellectuals blamed "puritanism" and its offspring, "fundamentalism," for American provinciality, hypocrisy, and emotional sterility. Neither puritanism nor fundamentalism was defined carefully, but authors writing in several genres presented clergy from several centuries as neurotics, buffoons, and con men. To historian Vernon L. Parrington, Cotton Mather's diary offered a "treasure-trove" for the "abnormal psychologist." H. L. Mencken thought the Scopes trial "better than a circus." According to Upton Sinclair, religion in general and fundamentalism in particular belonged to a "great predatory system" that enriched clergy, stifled thought, and protected greed. In Sinclair Lewis's novel *Elmer Gantry*, a religious demagogue (partly modeled on John Roach Straton) rises from tent evangelist to Methodist bishop. Sometimes, secular debunkers recieved assistance from theological liberals; L. M. Birkhead, for example, befriended Mencken at the Scopes trial and advised Lewis on *Elmer Gantry.*[20]

The debunking of the 1920s permanently affected fundamentalism's reputation. During the 1930s themes previously popularized by Sinclair, Mencken, and Lewis were incorporated into left interpretations of far right Protestants. Furthermore, during the next two generations most scholars and journalists routinely associated fundamentalism with noisiness, rusticity, "anti-intellectualism," and political conservatism. Yet participants in the conservative theological coalition varied significantly in personality, theology, and politics. Certainly there were sensationalists like Sunday, Straton, and Norris, whose antics received ample attention in a decade tempted by sensationalism. On the other hand, James M. Gray and Reuben A. Torrey exuded Victorian propriety; J. Gresham Machen of Princeton Theological Seminary lamented the use of "popular jingles" and "enormous horns" at fundamentalist services. In between, William Bell Riley and Presbyterian spokesman Clarence E. Macartney combined eloquence with dignity.[21]

Nor did shared antipathy to religious liberalism prevent doctrinal disputes within fundamentalism. Rev. J. C. Massee, leader of the fundamentalist caucus at successive Northern Baptist Conventions, hedged on the issue of Biblical inerrancy. Dispensationalism, a powerful force among theological conservatives, was still rejected by many premillennialists. Philip Mauro, a contributor to *The Fundamentals,* recanted his early enthusiasm and in 1927 denounced dispensationalism as a "subtle form of modernism." William Jennings Bryan retained his lifelong democratic optimism in the face of apocalyptic prophecies by friends in the World Christian Fundamentals Association. Dispensational prophets disagreed about the number of dispensations and the timing of the "secret rapture" of the saints. Fundamentalists, Winrod lamented in 1928, agreed "on our name and statement of faith, but beyond that it is bedlam."[22]

Similarly, the connection between fundamentalism and "reactionary" politics was more complex than social gospelers at *Christian Century* supposed. Although premillennialism sometimes fuels reform—or radicalism—its impact in this case was to discourage social activism. Satan wanted to "reform his world a little," dispensationalist Arno C. Gaebelien observed in 1909, in order to promote the "deception that men do not need to be born again." Undoubtedly the prominence of theological liberals in reform movements helped Gaebelein to reach this conclusion. Certainly, too, ebbing social concern by preachers like Riley, who had opposed the Spanish-American War and Straton, who had advocated women's suffrage, reflected the wider postway "farewell to reform." And during the postwar challenge to Victorian sexual mores, exaggerated by proponents and opponents alike, fundamentalists focused worldy energy on continuing the prewar "purity crusade."[23]

Living on this side of the Second Coming, leaders of the fundamentalist coalition inevitably betrayed philosophical inconsistencies, arranged incongruous alliances, and yielded to personal ambitions. Riley, showing greater concern for publicity than theology, could not resist recruiting William Jennings Bryan, a non-dispensationalist, to head a "layman's movement" against evolution; Machen, despite his reservations, preached to jingle singers. Moreover, the fundamentalist subculture could not stand in total isolation from the rest of American society. Suspicious of Roman Catholic doctrines and designs, Straton nonetheless joined Catholics in fighting birth control. The limits of compromise are revealing, too. Fundamentalist spokesmen usually distanced themselves from Pentecostals, the lower-class wing of the holiness rivival.[24]

Contemporary social gospelers and numerous subsequent scholars condenscendingly assumed that rank-and-file fundamentalists simply followed their pastors' marching orders. The 1928 presidential election was often cited to prove the point. Vigorous clerical opposition, which was hardly limited to fundamentalists, did convince many Democrats to desert their party's Roman Catholic nominee, Alfred E. Smith. Yet millions of conservative Protestants still voted for Smith because the shadow of the Pope worried them less than the price of corn or preservation of white supremacy. In short, when fundamentalists applied their beliefs to this world, they, like other humans, were influenced by such factors as social class, geography, gender, and personality.[25]

Within the fundamentalist coalition, Gerald B. Winrod quickly established himself as a significant second-level figure. In 1926, after addressing the World Christian Fundamentals Association, he received a standing ovation and an appointment as extension secretary. WCFA President Riley served on the editorial board of the *Defender*, which also printed contributions from such stalwarts as John Roach Straton and Paul W. Rood of the Bryan Bible League. In 1930, Billy Sunday addressed the Defenders' World-Wide Congress. Prominent fundamentalists invited Winrod to deliver sermons at their churches, and in 1935 the Bible Institute of Los Angeles awarded him an honorary doctorate of divinity for outstanding contributions to preaching, "Biblical Scholarship," and "Christian Journalism."[26]

During the 1920s, too, Winrod established a routine that endured until his death; except for 1930–1931, when he directed an Oklahoma City tabernacle, he used Wichita as a home base. On a typical day, Winrod arrived at Defenders headquarters before dawn, worked until noon, shared lunch and a prayer at his mother's house around the corner, and then resumed writing or editing until 6:30. Though he usually went to sleep by 9:30, he frequently awakened during the night to jot down ideas. Because revivalism was no less important than publishing (and personally more satisfying than a settled pastorate), Winrod spent at least six months annually on the road, preaching on his own or borrowing friendly pulpits. In 1928, for example, he traveled 25,000 miles. A stickler for detail, he tried to supervise the *Defender* from afar, but relied increasingly on secretary Myrtle L. Flowers and his relatives. Indeed, both Winrod's publications and his evangelism looked like family affairs. His wife Frances wrote for the *Defender*, his father's Healing Tabernacle became the Defenders Gospel Tabernacle, and his children Gordon, John Paul, and Geraldine accompanied him on revival tours.[27]

Winrod's sons and daughter were not alone in admiring his performance on the circuit. Women in the audience sometimes compared him to silent film stars, the *Defender* incongruously boasted between denunciations of the movies. Even Winrod's frequent critic William Allen White, publisher of the *Emporia* (Kansas) *Gazette* called him "strapping, handsome, [and] smooth-talking." Such descriptions reflected his stage presence rather than classic good looks. Although Winrod stood six feet, two inches tall and had been blessed with curly black hair, a chunky build and premature baldness made him look anything but dashing. Rather, preaching the Defenders' gospel during the 1920s in a flat, slightly nasal voice, he appeared earnest and older than his years. A small brush moustache and preference for conservative suits added an air of dignity. In demeanor, Winrod more closely resembled his friend William Bell Riley than flamboyant fundamentalists like Straton, Norris, or Billy Sunday.[28]

Presenting a "non-sectarian, interdenominational testimony" to Protestants, even if he had to speak over the heads of their pastors, Winrod built the Defenders of the Christian Faith into a formidable enterprise. In 1927, 1,300 Kansans paid fifty cents to join the organization. By May, 1934, according to the official history, *Defender* subscriptions (equivalent to membership) had reached 60,000. What Winrod liked to call the Defenders "family" also included missions in Africa, Latin America, and Europe, promoted with Spanish, Greek, and Bulgarian editions of the *Defender* as well as a separate *Missionary Messenger*. Winrod was more successful than most in creating his own religious enclave, but this tactic also appealed to many other fundamentalists who agreed that the major denominations had lost their "doctrinal purity."[29]

Although separated by an unbridgable "chasm" from the "heretical" modernists (Winrod's term for all liberal Protestants), he reached out to diverse theological conservatives. He cultivated the large community of Kansas Mennonites, one of whom wrote regularly for the *Defender*. Not only did Winrod refuse to "smite" Pentecostals, but he preached under the auspices of their most colorful woman evangelist, Aimee Semple McPherson. In 1928, he supported Professor C. I. MacInnis of the Bible Institute of Los Angeles, whose orthodoxy had been challenged for opposing legislative bans on evolution. Throughout the 1920s, Winrod warned against consolidation of a dogmatic fundamentalism controlled by "self-appointed custodians of the Truth." Internal bickering made fundamentalists the "butt of ridicule" and allowed liberals to win "decisive victories at every turn," Winrod added. More important, only Jesus Christ was "eligible to occupy the Judgment seat."[30]

Winrod judged modernists, of course, and attempted to roll back their victories by driving Darwinism from the public schools. This strategy still appealed to fundamentalists during the late 1920s, despite the cosmopolitan derision heaped on them during the Scopes trial. In 1926, Winrod sought a ban on evolution in Kansas classrooms and appointed a committee to examine textbooks used locally. "Flying Defenders" also lobbied in California and Minnesota. During early 1927, Winrod himself helped William Bell Riley to draft the bill introduced into the Minnesota legislature. At the World Christian Fundamentals Association convention later that year, he and Riley urged an expanded campaign against Darwinism in southern schools.[31]

Winrod's objections to evolution, summarized in 1932 in his book *Christ Within*, were common to most theological conservatives. He began by disputing this "philosophy's" scientific validity. Charles Darwin's work alone contained more than eight hundred suppositions. For example, when the evolutionist postulated that the earth was once devoid of life, he did "what he condemns the religionist for doing. *He employs faith*." Moreover, if life began by "molecules rushing together," why could not modern chemists repeat the process? Even granting the possibility of spontaneous generation, there was no evidence that man had evolved from lower animals; claims on behalf of missing links were a "burlesque of true science." Each species, Winrod asserted, reproduced "'after his kind' exactly as Genesis indicates." Alluding to the work of scientists Gregor Mendel and Louis Agassiz (who called Darwin's theory a "mere mine of assertions"), Winrod concluded that evolution, like alchemy, astrology, and Ptolemaic astronomy, ultimately would be disproved. Yet evolutionists refused to believe that they might have erred. Rather, as proponents of the "most intolerant cult before the public today," they falsely charged their foes with intolerance, libeled William Jennings Bryan, and mistakenly claimed superior intelligence, even though any twelve-year old could understand their theory. Winrod assured Defenders that their ranks contained many of the best trained minds as well as the most consecrated hearts in Kansas.[32]

Despite these complaints about dogmatic evolutionists, Winrod stressed that Christianity and "true science," as opposed to Darwinian "materialist philosophy," could be best friends. The Bible not only accepted the discoveries of science; it predicted in advance such innovations as genetics and radio. Indeed, the reference in Isaiah 40:22 to the prophet who "sittith upon the circle of the earth" repudiated Ptolemaic astronomy long before scientists did. To underscore the compatibility of science and religion—the "science of things spiritual"—and simultaneously damn his intolerant opponents, Winrod criticized an unspecified professor who urged a young man to keep his microscope but discard his Bible. On the contrary, the boy should use both tools, examining earthly life through the microscope and probing eternal life through Scripture.[33]

Although Winrod believed that a valid natural science, untainted by evolution, complemented religion, he never doubted which sphere contained the more profound knowledge. The fragile learning of mortals dissolved into enigma because "all root causes" proceeded from an invisible spiritual world where the "First Cause" was God. A scholar lacking access to this personal being might merely be an "educated devil." No secular education could substitute for regeneration.[34]

While disputing Darwinism's scientific standing, Winrod moved on another front with even greater determination. This attack was synthesized in an epigram also used by John Roach Straton: "MONKEY MEN MEANS MONKEY MORALS." By denying the divine origin of the Bible, evolutionists allowed mankind to slide into atheism and its companion, gross immorality. Moreover, unlike Christians, who encouraged "progress through love," proponents of natural law maintained that "man advances by force." Winrod used two stock arguments to illustrate the consequences of Social Darwinism: books by Friedrich Nietszche that had fueled German militarism were based on evolution; and the famous murder of Robert Franks by Nathan Leopold and Richard Loeb demonstrated "monkey morals." Echoing Bryan at Dayton, he added that Clarence Darrow had asked mercy for

Leopold and Loeb because their minds had been twisted by Nietzsche's books.[35]

Darwinian ethics were revealed in warfare and homicide, but Winrod was more directly concerned about the depravity that seemed to characterize everyday life. In pamphlets, sermons, and successive issues of the *Defender*, he denounced the American "moral sag," almost always relating the declension to spreading Darwinism: "Billows of immorality are sweeping over land like waves over the ocean. We view it on the stage and the screen, at magazine stands and in the press, in women's dress and modern fashions, in slums and high society—*everywhere, animalism, animalism, animalism*."[36]

Predictable symptoms of the sag also included Sinclair Lewis's novel *Elmer Gantry*, public dances, smoking, gambling, prize fights, and efforts to evade Prohibition. The *Defender* distributed "Keep America Sober" stamps, and Winrod personally recalled that the liquor trade "almost wrecked my boyhood home." In addition, he denounced Christian Science, spiritualism, Annie Besant's "latest messiah," and kindred "anti-Christian agencies" that millions of his contemporaries (including William Dudley Pelley) preferred to orthodox Protestantism. Judging Freud's writings too full of "rank immorality" to quote in the *Defender*, he assured readers that they represented "animalistic psychology" rooted in evolution. Similarly, filmmakers lured "several hundred thousand upturned faces to gaze daily at a screen which smells of filth, lust, vice, crime, and sex." Winrod found Hollywood's technique especially insidious:[37]

> The element of mystery which accompanies the silver screen; the semi-darkness of the theater, the music, the glamor, the quiet atmosphere, the flashes of light off and on the screen—all combine to produce the kind of psychological atmosphere in which a person literally loses himself. One naturally puts everything out of his mind. His attention is focused, one hundred per cent, upon what he is seeing flashing constantly in front of him.
>
> Then, later, these subconscious reactions are bound to come to the surface. And when they do, they produce all manner of abnormal results—results patterned according to the pictures which were photographed into the chemistry of the brain, into the recesses of the soul.[38]

Because the "great American home," built around the marriage sacrament, was the bulwark of civilization, Winrod said, degeneration of family life was the most frightening aspect of the moral sag.

Men and women now regarded their homes as cheap hotels, practiced birth control (thus substituting scientific destruction for God's forethought), and divorced casually—if they bothered to marry at all. Such immoral behavior, and the equally repellent attempt to legitimate it through loose "companionate marriages," recalled for Winrod the wicked world destroyed by the Biblical flood. Yet decay followed "automatically" when children imbibed animalistic attitudes:

> Don't you dare to teach your young people that in every cell of their bodies, in every organ and function of their anatomies; in every department of their minds and emotions; that they are stamped with the image, with the mark of the beast, and expect them to live clean, pure, noble lives and build good, sturdy, dependable homes, with which to preserve the liberties and virtues of true American civilization.[39]

In response to the "new morality" of the 1920s, one which, Winrod said, was as old as Eden, he urged Christians to cultivate pure hearts and center their spiritual lives on family altars. He also advocated more stringent divorce laws. Yet none of these measures would restore the home, let alone save the United States from Darwinism and the wider declension. Short of Jesus Christ's return, a "nationwide revival of old-fashioned Holy Ghost religion" was the only alternative to ruin.[40]

Unfortunately, American Protestantism failed to initiate the revival because it, too, had been weakened by Darwinism and a sort of theological sag. Winrod accurately estimated that modernists controlled most major pulpits, church schools, missionary operations, publishing houses, and denominational offices. Despite their earthly influence, these clergymen were simply pawns in Satan's latest strategy, to undermine the faith by masquerading as an "Angel of Light, . . . an alleged higher intelligence."[41]

Modernists tried to reconcile "exact opposites," Darwinism and Scripture, Winrod said. To become consistent evolutionists, they denied original sin, asserting that mankind "*fell up* through centuries of development." Adhering to natural law, they explained away Biblical miracles as well as Christ's virgin birth, atonement, and resurrection. Instead of a supernatural savior, they portrayed Jesus as a mortal who, along with other men, had "an animal ancestry."[42]

Winrod agreed with William Bell Riley and J. Gresham Machen that the so-called new theology constituted an entirely new religion. Indeed, it shared more basic principles with atheism than with orthodox Protestantism. Liberals undermined sound church polity as well as proper theology. Building grand cathedrals and vast organizations, they forgot that Christianity's great days had not been times of "brick and mortar." Exaggerating the benevolence of sinful humanity, they went "wild" over the social gospel and ultimately aspired to unite all Protestants churches. But this "forced combination of iron and clay" would lack "spiritual power." Even now, though the country desperately needed a revival, the large, prosperous denominations suffered from "soul sleeping sickness."[43]

Old-Fashioned Holy Ghost Religion

In contrast to the "dead" doctrine of modernism, Winrod during the 1920s presented the essentials of "old-fashioned Holy Ghost Religion." The original sin of Adam and Eve, he said, had been transferred to their descendants "under the law of heredity." Although all false religions preached salvation by good works, the "overcoming life" was possible only by the grace of God, whose Son had been crucified to redeem mankind. Seminaries might teach something called comparative religion, but the death and resurrection of Jesus rendered Christianity "unique and incomparable."[44]

Too many ministers failed to cultivate a "secret mystical relationship with the Lord," Winrod wrote, influenced by the holiness strain within fundamentalism. In particular, liberal social gospelers forget that reform was a "mere humanitarian by-product" of spiritual regeneration. The term "church" did not designate an association like the Chamber of Commerce or Red Cross any more than it referred to brick, mortar, and stained glass windows. On the contrary, the church consisted of believers "moved by the supernatural action of the Holy Spirit." No one joined this church; one was reborn into it. While refusing to conjecture about the exact "chemistry of the soul," Winrod knew that the regenerate mortal who turned to Christ became something other than an ordinary sinner "with good intentions plastered over him." Unlike Adamic man, he *wanted* to avoid sin and received extra "strength and grace" during moments of temptation.[45]

Special assistance was essential because converts still faced a world—indeed, a universe—filled with malign forces. Winrod's claim that Satan molded the minds of liberal theologians was no metaphor. On the contrary, the Devil ruled a vast, "perfectly organized" kingdom. Demons, his intelligent agents, spread his power through the earth, the atmosphere, and perhaps the solar system. The murderer, evolutionist, or "flaming youth" were actually victims of these supernatural forces. Committed Christians were special targets of Satan's demonic army.[46]

Like his belief in Satan's omnipresence, Winrod's assertion that religion (meaning conservative Protestantism) was the "science of things spiritual" must be construed literally. As the spiritual "textbook," the Bible met the "needs of every nation, tribe, and tongue." The history, prophecy, and commandments had to be accepted on authority, but other contents could be proved. For example, though the precise workings of atonement remained mysterious, the gift of grace was "experimentally" known by millions. Thus Christians understood that by complying with "immutable spiritual laws," they would "get certain results."[47]

For Winrod, spiritual science encompassed the formulas of dispensationalism. Accordingly, the Old Testament foretold many events later recorded in the New, including the first advent of Jesus. Moreover, as Winrod's claim that Scripture predicted genetics and radio suggests, both Testaments contained "word pictures and types" that illuminated all subsequent history until, quite literally, the end of time. Like most dispensationalists, he divided history into seven periods of time marked by strained relations between God and man. Details varied, but the result was always the same: God offered prosperity in return for obedience; man accepted the covenant yet inevitably failed to fulfill its terms; and the era ended in judgment. Adam and Eve had begun the pattern during the dispensation of Innocence. Noah's descendants, the only survivors of the second dispensation of Conscience, slipped into impiety, built the Tower of Babel, and were scattered about the earth. When Abram's willful sons left the country God had pledged to their father, He cast Israel into bondage, closing the dispensation of Promise. Following the Exodus from Egypt, the Israelites broke the Commandments given to Moses, thus violating the terms of the dispensation of Law, and God used Assyria to destroy their temporal power.[48]

The sixth dispensation, Grace, in which God offered salvation by faith, began with Jesus's crucifixion and continued to the present. But students of Bible prophecy knew what to expect. The ensuing judgment would be the last, and the great "tribulation" preceding it had received extended treatment in Scripture. Satan, the temporary "God of this age," would produce his "masterpiece"—the Antichrist or Beast described in Revelation 13. Even professed Christians would hail this evil man capable of many miracles. He would revive the Roman Empire (the fourth gentile regime predicted in Daniel 7), call down flames from the atmosphere to rout his enemies, and create life itself. Aided by the "false prophet," he would sponsor a degenerate religion that Winrod, like many other fundamentalists, expected to embrace Protestant liberalism and Roman Catholicism (the "whore of Babylon" in Revelation 17–18). Initially, the Beast would help the Jews reclaim Palestine, rebuild their temple at Jerusalem, and resume ancient sacrificial rites. After three years, however, he would turn on them and demand their adulation. Armies preparing to crush Israel, including forces of a "Northern Confederacy" probably led by Russia, would converge on Armageddon.[49]

Only after this decadent era, Winrod and other dispensationalists believed, would Jesus Christ return, cast the Antichrist into a fiery lake, and call for "His bride," the invisible true church. Judging all nations, Jesus would welcome the minority of Jews who had embraced true Christianity. After a thousand years of Christ's rule—the seventh dispensation known as the Millennium—Satan would rally the forces of evil. The final judgment of all souls would follow the Devil's inevitable defeat, and God's eternal kingdom would be at hand.[50]

Although the dispensational framework presented in C. I. Schofield's *Reference Bible* and Gerald B. Winrod's magazine led to a glorious denouement, it was decidedly bleak in the short run. With Satan ascendant, how could one expect anything more promising than the impiety and degeneration reported in the *Defender*? Indeed, unlike some relatively optimistic dispensationalists who anticipated a "secret rapture" of the saints early in the tribulation, Winrod expected them to be tested under the Antichrist's persecution. While confronting pervasive decay and temptation, Christians could at least know that each event, no matter how horrible, contained an understandable higher meaning. It was useless to resist trends predicted in Scripture, Winrod emphasized. Conversely, after determining what the Bible prophesied, believers could make personal decisions "in harmony with divine decrees." As the storm approached, Winrod advised, the "Book of Books" provided a "chart and compass" to navigate the "prophetic seas we are sailing."[51]

Dispensationalism, a source of inspiration to many fundamentalists, contained inherent ironies, contradictions, and problems. This version of premillennialism, which Winrod placed at the center of "old-fashioned holy ghost religion," was scarcely a century old. Claims by adherents to the contrary, neither did it provide a clear-cut approach to Scripture easily accessible to believers; the complementary cosmopolitan assertion that theological conservatives favored biblical "literalism" was similarly misleading. Fundamentalists, like everybody else, had to interpret what they read. Intepretations offered by the dispensationalist wing of fundamentalism often made the Bible seem less like a chart than a puzzle. For instance, a reader unaided by Schofield's footnotes or by Winrod's expositions would not automatically identify the beast envisioned in Daniel 7:23 with the beast rising from the sea in Revelation 13:1, anymore than he was likely to know, unaided by higher criticism, that both passages reflected apocalyptic doctrines from centuries past. Even if he equated the two beasts, he might have plausibly assumed that allusions to Rome meant an empire long gone, not one emerging anew during the 1920s.[52]

Furthermore, eager to see the Second Coming in their own time, dispensationalists yielded to the kind of intellectual sleight-of-hand that they attributed to theological liberals. According to their premillennial reading of Scripture, Jesus would return "seventy weeks" after the rebuilding of Jerusalem had begun, an event said to have occurred in 445 B.C. Dispensationalists doubted, however, that the weeks cited in Daniel 9:24 referred to seven day periods (an option they denied to modernists discussing Genesis), but rather to "weeks of years." Jesus had been crucified, they usually agreed, after sixty-nine of these weeks (that is, 483 years). Why did He not return seven years later? Following the Jewish rejection of Christ, dispensationalists inferred, God had turned His attention to the gentiles and postponed the "seventieth week of Daniel."[53]

Partly because dispensationalist clergy readily mastered such ingenious exegeses of Scripture, serious interpretive issues remained unresolved. Bible students disagreed about how long the current dispensation of Grace would continue. If the last days were at hand after World War I, then who was the Antichrist? Napoleon III, considered the most likely candidate by an earlier premillennialist generation, had fled into exile instead of reviving the Roman Empire. Dispensationalists compounded confusion by slighting the earthly church that might have authorized a definitive system of hermeneutics. In a sense, every person became his own prophet.[54]

The importance of Jews to prophecy raised further complications. The dispensational wing of fundamentalism not only believed that Jews should embrace Jesus, a common Christian presumption, but supposed that some were destined to do so, and that its own version of premillennialism was most likely to win converts. Therefore, dispensationalists pursued missionary work among Jewish immigrants. Arno C. Gaebelein, for example, published a magazine in Yiddish, a language he learned to speak fluently. Most Jews greeted Christian evangelism with indifference or outright hostility. Dispensationalists welcomed the few converts as symbols of approaching

Armageddon, yet remained uncertain whether or not these "Hebrew Christians" must forsake their ethnicity along with their former faith.[55]

Similar ambivalence characterized the dispensationalist attitude toward Zionism. On the one hand, they viewed this "ingathering" of Jews in Palestine as fulfillment of Bible prophecy. Several fundamentalist leaders formed cordial ties with the World Zionist Organization; their cordiality contrasted with complaints by theological liberals at *Christian Century* that Zionist Jews fell short of total Americanism. On the other hand, dispensationalists thought that the Jews, whose ancestors had crucified Jesus, would return to Palestine "in unbelief" and restore Israel in alliance with the Antichrist. In keeping with their premise that dark days must precede the Millennium, they often viewed anti-Semitic persecution, not as a human tragedy, but as a spur to resettle to Holy Land.[56]

In short, dispensationalism incorporated a unique version of the mixed "affection, curiosity, suspicion, and rejection" regarding Jews that historian Leonard Dinnerstein discerns among most Americans at the turn of the century. During the Progressive era and 1920s, these theological conservatives flowed with the mainstream toward increasing suspicion and rejection. Hence, when the *Dearborn Independent* published *The International Jew,* some fundamentalist leaders welcomed the series. The Bible Institute of Los Angeles' magazine, *King's Business,* agreed that the intelligent but tricky "Jewish race" was capable of a vast conspiracy. While dissociating himself from the "evil" of Jewish persecution, James M. Gray of the Moody Bible Institute found the *Independent* articles and *The Protocols of the Learned Elders of Zion* both plausible. To Arno C. Gaebelein, who had earlier denounced anti-Semitism in Germany and the United States, *The International Jew*'s evidence was both "unimpeachable" and consistent with prophecy. "It is predicted in the Word of God," Gaebelein wrote, "that a large part of the Jews will become apostate, along with the Gentile masses.[57]

Although Gerald B. Winrod lacked formal training in theology, he recognized many of the problems latent in dispensationalism. Indeed, he saw a "great deal" of merit in Philip Mauro's complaint that this premillennial system was a "subtle form of modernism." Nevertheless, Mauro's extensive critique, which Winrod reviewed in 1927, failed to shake his faith in a "70th week of Daniel, the Return of the Jews to Palestine, the Translation of the Saints, the Rise of the Antichrist and a Final Period of Tribulation, YET UNFULFILLED." Thus, he continued to accept general dispensational framework and filled in details with his own prophetic readings.[58]

From the prophetic perspective, Winrod maintained, the immoral consequences of materialism and modernism were important signs of the times. Collegians who read *The Interpretation of Dreams* simultaneously yielded to Sigmund Freud's animalistic psychology and fulfilled Jude's prediction that "filthy dreamers" would "defile the flesh." Likewise, when Winrod charged that Darwinism carried the "mark of the beast," he alluded both to evolving animals and to the false messiah of Revelation.[59]

Helping prophecy along during the 1920s, Winrod supported fundamentalist evangelism among Jews. This important work, pursued most effectively by "Hebrew Christians" who understand how to correct "misleading information . . . from Jewish sources," could lead Jews and gentiles to "mutual, common understanding." Prospects for conversions were bright, Winrod surmised, because the literate Jewish community was "so readily reached through the *printed page*."[60]

If Winrod encountered *The Protocols, The International Jew*, or related classics of conspiratorial anti-Semitism during the 1920, they had no discernable impact. His magazine treated Jews as a distinct community unfortunately estranged from Christ, but otherwise avoided negative stereotypes. Indeed, Jews looked much better than Roman Catholics, whom the *Defender* routinely associated with false theology, clerical autocracy, and strong drink. In April 1928, Winrod praised orthodox rabbis for fighting modernism and evolution within Judaism. Later that year, he scorned the "old legend" that Jews sacrificed Christian children in their religious rites and regretted the pogroms it had enflamed. Above all, he regarded the Jewish return to Palestine as prophecy realized "before our eyes today."[61]

The most important event in prophecy, the Second Coming, would be fulfilled, Winrod surmised after surveying well-known expositions of Daniel and Revelation, "on such a date as none of the date-fixers have struck upon." He himself remained convinced through the 1920s that Jesus's return was "quite near." Dividing Grace into seven segments, each corresponding to a stage in Christian church history, he suggested that humanity was passing through the final phase of the last dispensation, represented by the Laodicean church in Revelation 3. In that case, the twentieth verse alluded to Jesus: "Behold, I stand at the door and knock." Accordingly to Winrod's rendering of Daniel, the last days would be a "chain age," marked by consolidation of human thought and action. And the twentieth century produced proliferating "chains of banks, radios, newspapers, stores, churches." Other symptoms of standardization included the League of Nations, the World Bank (a "financial octopus"), Aristide Briand's advocacy of European integration, and liberal endorsement of "One Big Church." Indeed, the Antichrist would synthesize all faiths into a humanist "religious trust."[62]

These signs confirmed the message of the moral sag: the great tribulation approached. Christians must prepare for the struggle, remembering that a "great eternal program is being worked out." In the meantime, only knowledge of Bible prophecy would lend optimism to dark days. For Winrod at least, it was an unfailing guide to religion, morality, and world and domestic politics.[63]

Dispensational Politics

As might be expected of a man who anticipated the early return of Jesus Christ, Winrod did not cultivate an intimate knowledge of practical politics. Yet, constantly seeking to confirm Spriptural forecasts, he was an avid if unconventional student of world affairs. During the 1920s, he, like many articulate Americans, showed special interest in the Soviet Union and Italy, two nations whose "distinctly new governmental systems" seemed ominous. Unlike secular commentators, however, he studied Communism and Fascism through the twin prisms of Darwinism and Bible prophecy.[64]

Because Soviet policy was based on the "same Atheistic-Evolution" that "belched liked poison gas" into Kansas classrooms, Winrod cited Russia as an object lesson. The Bolsheviks attempted to "dethrone God" by persecuting clergymen, abolished representative government, destroyed the free press, and allowed free love to run rampant. The *Defender* paid more attention to impiety and "animalistic marriage standards" than to social planing or assaults or capitalism. Readers had an obligation to feed starving Russians and aid their embattled clergy, but above all they must avoid comparable effects of evolution in the United States.[65]

Mussolini, Like Lenin, bore the stigma of Darwin. As in Winrod's treatment of Kaiser Wilhelm and the Leopold and Loeb case, Friedrich Nietszche was conscripted to be the mediating villain. Mussolini had absorbed Nietzsche's ideas while expatriated in Switzerland; after seizing power in 1922, he based his rule on the "survival of the fittest" and the " 'super man' ideal." Fascism, Winrod summarized in 1927, was "evolution in fearless action." Recognizing the praise accorded to Mussolini by such contemporaries as Thomas Edison, Secretary of State Charles Evans Hughes, and Secretary of the Treasury Andrew Mellon, the *Defender* called him an "intellectual giant." Even so, he was "diabolical," the perpetrator of "some of the most fiendish crimes since Nero burned Christians at the stake.[66]

Furthermore, there could be no doubt that Mussolini's activities were in some sense "phenomenal." Diverse contemporaries considered him a "superior order of being—a *superman.*" In addition to his profane role as master of Darwinian terror, he seemed the best candidate for Antichrist that the world had ever seen. The reference in Revelation to a "Beast with ten Horns" meant, dispensationalists agreed, that ten autocrats would rule nations within the boundaries of the revived Roman Empire. In 1930 Winrod perceived "at least eight such dictators," including Josef Pilsudski of Poland, Paul von Hindenburg of Germany, and King Carol of Rumania. Revelation also prophesied that the most powerful ruler—the Antichrist—would unite these ten nations into a southern league or confederacy. Not only was Mussolini the chief despot, but he spoke openly of restoring Roman glory. Of course, Winrod hedged, he might be only the harbinger, a kind of John the Baptist for Antichrist. In either case, he would "bear watching." And watch him Winrod did. Between 1927 and 1933, the *Defender* devoted more columns to Il Duce than to any other world figure.[67]

Turning from Rome to Washington, the magazine not only eschewed speculation about President Calvin Coolidge's place in prophecy, but it denied having any "political sentiments." In practice, however, Winrod's intense concern with "moral problems" sometimes slipped over into politics. Before a Kansas election in 1928, for example, the *Defender* urged support for candidates "informed" about the dangers of Darwinism and strong drink. Cherishing an important moral premise with political implications, Winrod joined most other fundamentalist leaders in assuming a symbiotic relationship between existing American institutions and the path of the true church. He claimed the Founding Fathers as devout Christians and said that their legacy of majority rule was "invariably a safe guide"; it was also a weapon against the small "intellectual oligarchy" seeking to teach Darwin in the schools. By rejecting Christian counsel in this instance, the nation risked "seething anarchy" as well as moral decay.[68]

Winrod's opposition to Alfred E. Smith during the 1928 presidential race illustrates best his capacity to conflate politics and moral problems. During this campaign, the *Defender* chided William Jennings Bryan's brother Charles for endorsing Smith, hailed J. Frank Norris for speaking against him, and cheerfully noted that Republican candidate Herbert Hoover "doesn't smoke but goes fishing." After Smith discussed his Catholicism before a national meeting of Protestant ministers, Winrod's wife Frances charged him with introducing the religious issue, adding that the Pope still considered himself above the state. Although the Democratic nominee's religion obviously influenced the Winrods, they also disliked his ties to an urban political machine and his opposition to Prohibition. If Smith had been a Protestant, they still would have opposed him, as a *Defender* editorial put it, "because he is a Tammany-Wet."[69]

Except for the contest between Smith and Hoover, the magazine did, for the most part, avoid national politics during the 1920s. Even the Crash in 1929 did not turn Winrod's eyes from the *Schofield Reference Bible* to the *Congressional Record.* In 1930 he reported more or less as usual on the menace of alcohol, the moral sag, and the threat of evolution. Although the *Defender* suffered financially, its editor did not comment specifically on the Depression until December 1930, when he advised that "more religion—rather than more legislation—is the need of the hour."[70]

In the same vein, the first issue of 1931 succinctly posed the national alternatives: "Revival or Ruin." The country had never been "more ripe for revolution" and partisan opposition to President Hoover exacerbated the desperate situation. Yet even Hoover's "constructive measures," thwarted by Congress, would not have restored national well-being. In the final analysis, the Depression was caused by "selfishness, carnality, lust, greed, and human depravity." Still, Winrod typically found optimistic possibilities in a gloomy situation. Applying the axiom that God provided a "revival warning" before every great crisis, he hoped for—and expected—an imminent evangelical upsurge.[71]

The *Defender*'s reaction to the 1932 presidential campaign showed that he did not consider the Depression per se a watershed in American history, but merely another piece of evidence, along with the moral collapse and the rise of Italian Fascism, signalling the approach of Armageddon. Winrod treated the election much as he had discussed the race four years earlier; the bar room, not the breadline, provided the decisive issue. As if to demonstrate his political naiveté, in January he predicted that only a "dry" candidate like former Secretary of the Treasury William G. McAdoo could ever defeat Hoover.[72]

After the Democrats nominated Franklin D. Roosevelt, a "wet," Winrod enlisted his father John to plead from personal experience against the saloon's return. Nothing demonstrated the primacy of Prohibition more clearly than his refusal to endorse Hoover, who had abdicated as "leader of moral righteousness" by accepting a "moist" Republican platform. The *Defender* editor pledged his vote to former Representative William D. Upshaw (Dem.-Ga.). the Prohibition party nominee, with whom he had shared "many prayers." Once again underlining his lack of political sophistication, Winrod predicted that Upshaw might capture enough votes to throw the election into the House of Representatives.[73]

Collectivism and More Moral Sag: The New Deal

Not the Depression itself, but Roosevelt's measures to alleviate it led Winrod to supplement his prophetic and moral vision with more conventional social analysis, to found the *Revealer*, a new magazine emphasizing politics, and ultimately to seek public office. Looking back in 1935, he proudly claimed to have exposed the "cunning" New Deal mind from the first day the Democrats took office. In fact, knowing that Roosevelt opposed Prohibition and fearing that he would recognize the Soviet Union, Winrod had had a well-developed animus even before the inauguration. The president quickly lived up to his worst expectations; disastrous domestic policies accompanied the "fatal deed" of Russian recognition. By May 1933, Winrod was certain that "America will never be the same again."[74]

In the *Defender* and especially in the *Revealer*, published between November 1934 and January 1937, the recently "politicized" minister attacked the Roosevelt administration's programs and personalities. From the outset, Winrod most feared the expansion of federal authority. The bank holiday exposed Americans to the dictatorial lash that already afflicted Fascist Italy and Nazi Germany, the Civilian Conservation Corps prepared young men "to take up arms overnight," and the National Industrial Recovery Act placed the whole nation "under military discipline."[75]

The *Revealer*, stressing state and local issues, warned midwestern farmers that New Deal agricultural policy was ineffective and insidious. In 1935, Winrod compared Secretary of Agriculture Henry A. Wallace, the least practical of Roosevelt's "visionaries," to Joseph, son of Jacob, and the "most amazing secretary of agriculture of ancient times." Whereas Joseph prepared for famine by storing crops, Wallace destroyed food instead of distributing it to starving citizens. The "alleged *over-production*" was a myth, Winrod said, as long as a single stomach was empty. Moreover, using subsidies to "to BUY THEIR WAY into the freedom" of farmers, Roosevelt and his fellow "conspirators" followed the pattern of other tyrants who controlled populations by manipulating food supply. Winrod asserted that if the United States Supreme Court had not overturned the Agricultural

Adjustment Act in 1935, Kansas farmers ultimately would have lost their property to government confiscation.[76]

The New Deal's shifting fiscal policy was even less satisfactory to Winrod than its agricultural program. Roosevelt asked Congress to raise taxes on large incomes in 1935, but the new revenue would go to bureaucrats and government officials, not to ordinary citizens. Indeed, the president himself grew richer instead of offering to share his own fortune. This apparent hypocrisy annoyed Winrod, but less so than FDR's failure to confront the "international banking fraternity."[77]

According to the *Defender*, the economic and political—as opposed to the moral and theological—causes of the Depression, were relatively simple. An economic as well as political novice, Winrod adapted anti-banking notions that had accumulated at least since the Civil War, perhaps since Alexander Hamilton presented his financial program. The Founding Fathers, he said, had warned against the world-wide financial "spider web." By passing the National Banking Act of 1863, however, Congress had surrendered power over the national money supply to private interests. The Federal Reserve Act of 1913 had consummated the "diabolical scheme" that allowed bankers to "enslave" millions of citizens. They quickly used this power to precipitate the Depression. Roosevelt not only failed to restore congressional control of money, but he supported legislation (unspecified by Winrod, but probably revisions of the Federal Reserve Act) to strengthen the bankers' grip.[78]

A successful magazine publisher, Winrod was a small businessman as well as a prophet in politics. Indeed, his social views in their secular aspect were largely congruent with those of other small businessmen opposing the New Deal. Although convinced that the Depression was somehow related to maldistribution of wealth, he proposed neither a comprehensive program nor piecemeal reforms to redistribute the nation's bounty. Unlike Pelley, he never doubted the gospel of success, concluding in 1935: "Any man who will live a good life, work hard, develop his mental faculties and take advantage of his opportunities for self-advancement, can climb without restraint to the topmost rung of human achievement, under the American system of government." Predictably, then, Winrod applauded Roosevelt's conservative detractors instead of those critics who complained that the president's program was too limited. For example, the *Defender* dismissed Senators Huey Long and Robert La Follete, Jr., as radical demagogues; Senator William E. Borah forfeited Christian support by supporting Soviet recognition. On the other hand,

Winrod continued to praise Herbert Hoover, a "true American" who did not go "to Moscow, Rome, or Berlin" to discover how to govern the United States. He even hailed Al Smith for aiding the Liberty League.[79]

Winrod's willingness to praise his old enemy Smith underscored his deep concern about the "almost unbelievable" changes wrought by the New Deal. Discerning the "sinister" shadow of dictatorship over Washington, he found Tammany Hall and Vatican City relatively less menancing. Yet Winrod was initially unsure what form of autocracy FDR intended. The Roosevelt coalition ranged from "wet radicals" to utopian dreamers; administration measures included the "socialistic" Tennessee Valley Authority as well as the National Recovery Administration, a "first taste" of American fascism. By 1935, Winrod decided that the New Deal was primarily a "red program" that, if carried to its "logical end," would establish Communism. As in Russia, free speech, an independent press, private property, and the right to vote would be extinguished.[80]

Skeptics who doubted this thesis needed only investigate the "so called super-intellectuals" surrounding the president. Drawing information and invective from the *Chicago Tribune* and Representative Hamilton Fish (Congress's "foremost authority" on Communism), Winrod arraigned Rexford Tugwell for editing the *New Republic*, claimed that Secretary Wallace's advisor Mordecai Ezekiel made agricultural policy according to the "basic features" of a Soviet five-year plan, and noted that William Bullitt, ambassador to the Soviet Union, had married the widow of the infamous radical John Reed. With such backgrounds, these advisors, along with Raymond Moley, Bernard Baruch, and James P. Warburg, were susceptible to Communism's "filthy odor." Hence the time had come in 1933 for Christians to vote against any official smelling of "Red taint."[81]

This explicit call to the polls represented not the exhortation of a politician, but the invocation of a revivalist who continued to believe that the nation's "supreme need" was the "expression of aroused Christian opinion." Although Winrod began to borrow heavily from partisan sources, his analysis of 1930s social issues elaborated rather than repudiated what he had written in the previous decade. Using the same forceful language and some of the same allusions, he persisted in denouncing symptoms of moral breakdown: "organized demon intelligences" encouraged drinking, gambling, smoking, immodest dress, sensual dances, birth control, sexual promiscuity, divorce, suggestive films, nudism, disrespect for the Sabbath, and even murder.[82]

Indeed, Winrod continued to believe that repudiation of God's will was the deeper cause behind the superficial financial and political causes of the Great Depression and New Deal. The slump was "first spiritual, then moral, then economic." After modernists undermined Christianity, morality necessarily decayed and the economy collapsed "in logical order." Finally, the country's political order was "cracking up." The "idea of liberalism," which by the mid-1930s Winrod considered a secular as well as a theological phenomenon, played a critical role in the declension. The varying manifestations of this child of Darwinism shared a common principle: "*that whatever is, is wrong, and must be changed.*" There was also a style common to liberals, a "smart-alecky" arrogance that characterized modernists who mocked fundamentalism in the 1920s and Brain Trusters who later threatened "fundamentals of democratic government."[83]

Noting other affinities between the New Deal and the continuing moral sag, Winrod attacked Works Progress Administration (WPA) director Harry Hopkins for using "gutter language" ("damn") and pictured Raymond Moley surrounded by attractive women secretaries, leaving the rest to the reader's imagination. He persistently reminded readers that the Roosevelt administration had repealed Prohibition. In 1936, after a drunk driver struck Winrod's car, he telegraphed the White House and, holding Roosevelt "PERSONALLY RESPONSIBLE" for the return of the saloon, requested $100 for repairs. With uncharacteristic humor, he suggested that Democratic National Chairman James A. Farley might split the expense.[84]

Ultimately, both the American spiritual crisis and the political debacle accompanying it had to be seen as part of a broader "catastrophic period in world history." Hence, like Rexford Tugwell or Herbert Hoover (but from a perspective strange to both men), Winrod during the 1930s scrutinized European affairs with heightened earnestness, hunting for clues to future trends in the United States. Except that the *Defender*'s accounts of Soviet life were now longer, more frequent, and more lurid, they differed little from the earlier versions: Communist leaders still encouraged drinking, promoted public fornication, and treated Christians like "cattle."[85]

Denying the uniqueness of Soviet economics, Winrod promoted a crude version of the contemporary thesis that Communist and Fascist "collectivism" had much in common. The twin tyrannies regimented small businesses, denied the right to strike, and generally "told people what to do and how to do it." Russian commissars tried especially hard to "FORCE ATHEISM" onto their subjects, but no autocracy respected God. Lenin, Mussolini, and Hitler shared a critical trait. Like Franklin Roosevelt, each had begun his intellectual development with the liberal premise: "whatever is, is wrong."[86]

Because they proved that collectivism was the "spirit of the age," European trends heightened Winrod's apprehension about the New Deal and gave urgency to the "constantly" posed questions: "Which way will America turn? To the Right or to the Left? How long before Constitutional government will be replaced by some sort of fascist or socialist dictatorship?" Unless citizens manifested more character, Winrod answered, full-blown dictatorship would soon cross the Atlantic. Yet it was possible to guide the country back to the "main highway" of constitutional government because Americans *did* have more character than benighted Europeans.[87]

After the Crash, Winrod vigorously asserted a conception of unique American virtue that had always been implicit in his writing. His countrymen were neither so "docile" as Germans and Italians nor so "ignorant" as Russians had been when dictatorship conquered their respective nations. Indeed, if a tyrant took control of the United States, Winrod predicted, a "rugged individualist will probably kill him." As of 1934, citizens were not awake to the danger, but they would leap from "lethargy with a start, when the coils of dictatorship start to pinch."[88]

World Powers in Prophecy

Far from forsaking dispensationalism for politics in the 1930s, Winrod merely delineated a political and economic analysis to fit within the more important theological framework. The final disposition of American and world destiny lay with the Almighty, who guided events toward His final conflict with Satan. As much as Darwinism or Freudian psychology, the collectivizing trend was a "clean-cut fulfillment" of prophecy. For example, in its very construction the National Recovery Administration emblem recalled the monster rising from the sea in Revelation 13:1. That portrait of the Beast had seven heads and ten horns, and the NRA's "ferocious" blue eagle, Winrod noted ominously, bore seven feathers on one wing and ten on the other.[89]

Hence the Bible remained a chart and compass as mankind approached the last days. More than ever, Winrod felt in 1933 that Jews, always important to dispensationalism, were the hub of prophesy. According to his rendering of Ezekiel, while eastern countries united under Gog and most of the West followed the Antichrist, the Jews, carrying most of the world's gold, would return to Palestine. Still steeped in "spiritual darkneness," they would select their own king, known as the False Prophet. Attracted by the gold supply, Gog's forces would attack Palestine, forcing the Jewish ruler into a fatal alliance with the Antichrist. This pact would begin the period of "*great tribulation* for the entire world until the return of Christ."[90]

After defeating Gog's armies in an epic battle described in Daniel 11, the Antichrist would begin his dominion over mankind. Always convinced that the Beast would be an extraordinary man, capable of "many mighty miracles," Winrod explored some of his specific traits as Armageddon seemed to draw closer during the 1930s. Using Satan's power, this monster would awe mankind by creating an arsenal of mysterious weapons, forcing adherence to a "humanized religious system," and establishing a world government, a "world-wide *recovery program*," and a world bank. The bank's currency would dominate the international economy, and "no man might buy or sell, save he had the mark, or the name of the beast, or the number of his name."[91]

By 1935, departing from standard dispensationalist expectations, Winrod determined that the Antichrist himself would be a Jew. John 5:43 removed "all doubt"; if he were to be a gentile, an "entirely different Greek word" would have appeared in the original text. Even before reaching this conclusion, however, Winrod emphasized that an intimate bond would develop between regathered Israel and the Beast. One of his first acts would be the restoration of their formal title to Palestine. Yet the Antichrist would eventually turn against Israel in the worst pogrom in history. Then, seven years after the Antichrist's victory over Gog, in the midst of the worst of all wars, Jesus would "return to this planet exactly as he went away."[92]

In the interim, Scripture helped Christians to understand specific national policies through the most prominent statesmen whose deeds were "cast into prophetic molds: Roosevelt, Hitler, Mussolini, and Stalin." As late as 1933, Winrod saw a "*strong possibility*" that Mussolini would mature into the Beast. Supplementing his earlier analysis, Winrod noted Mussolini's enthusiasm for *The Prince* by Nicolo Machiavelli, the "pivot" of modern liberalism, as well as his congenial relations with world Jewry. Indeed, Il Duce's development into the Antichrist would confirm rumors of his own Jewish ancestry. If Mussolini did assume this prophetic role, moreover, his chief enemy would be his current ideological bête noir, the Soviet Union.[93]

The Communists may have taken the Bible out of Russia, Winrod declared, but they could not take Russia out of the Bible. Russia was intended to be Magog, the homeland of Gog cited in Ezekiel 38. The mention of Meshech in verse two referred to Moscow, Winrod said, and the word *Rusch* (or *Rosh*) in the original text, meaning "from the north," had been the root-word for Russia. God instructed the prophet Ezekiel to speak against Gog, thereby signalling animosity between the Almighty and the nation that would try to tear religion out of the heart of the world. No modern state, Winrod reminded his readers, had persecuted Christians so horribly as the Soviet Union.[94]

Germany under Adolf Hitler did not quite fit into the dispensational framework. Gomer, the country's Biblical symbol, first appeared in Genesis 10; he could be identified by the name of his son, *Ashkanaz*, the word for Germany, Winrod said, "in the Jewish tongue." Significantly, Gomer appeared in conjunction with Gog, his future ally in Ezekiel 38:6. Winrod emphatically maintained, therefore, that Germany's future lay "with Russia and not central Europe."[95]

Admitting that this reading of Scripture conflicted with the state of world politics in 1933, Winrod tried to distinguish Hitler's anti-Semitic fascism from Mussolini's pro-Semitic version. Germany and Russia both felt "down trodden." Comparing Nazi anti-Semitism with Russia's long tradition of pogroms, Winrod added that the two countries shared an "identical" attitude toward the Jew, the "tap-root of prophecy." Still, he recognized that Nazi antipathy to Communism undermined his prediction of a German-Soviet alliance. As late as January 1934, he left open the possibility that Hitler was a "prophetic misfit" who would "likely pass off the scene" or radically change policies.[96]

During the inevitable warfare between God and Antichrist, the bloody years of tribulation, the return of Jesus, and the final battle at Armageddon, no nation would escape God's punishment. Yet, expounding a theological exceptionalism parallel to his notion of special American character, Winrod "dared to hope and believe" that the United States would escape "much of the hell and horror." Saluted in Isaiah 18 as a "land shadowing with wings"—a reference to the American eagle—it possessed many prophetic as well as geographic and economic advantages. In 1492, a miraculous wind had changed the direction of Columbus's ships, thus saving the United States from "papal sorceries."[97]

Having received such special grace in the past, the United States might mitigate holy wrath if her citizens now gave "God a chance." After all of his political arguments, Winrod reaffirmed the familiar answer: "Let revival fires be lighted across the continent. . . . Then, and not until then, every problem, whether it be political or economic, a blight of socialism or a curse of Communism, will have a rational and permanent solution.[98]

The Protocols as Prophecy

In his inexorable campaign to establish the Beast's empire, Satan moved in characteristically deceptive fashion. Like God, he typically worked through personalities, using demons to infiltrate human souls or "counterfeit light" to distort mortal minds. Despite these perils, Winrod lamented, most persons lived "on the surface," neither knowing nor caring about the "hidden evils which may be lurking in the shadows." Christians used Scripture to pry beneath superficial meanings, but even experienced Bible students had more difficulty identifying Satan's deputies than determining the Almighty's visible saints. For over twenty years Winrod had known that the Antichrist would dominate the world, he wrote in 1932, but only recently had he "learned of a HIDDEN HAND consciously preparing the way" for the Beast. The key to the sinister forces behind the "hidden-hand"—as well as the phrase itself—lay in *The Protocols of the Learned Elders of Zion.*[99]

Although Winrod liked *The Protocols* partly for the liberal enemies they had made, he approached this notorious document with some skepticism. It remains unclear when he first encountered the notion of an international Zionist plot. If he was influenced during the early 1920s by discussion of *The International Jew* in fundamentalist magazines, no record survives; both Winrod's writings in the late 1920s and his allusion in 1932 to his "recent" discovery of the "hidden hand" suggest otherwise. In June 1932, the *Defender* recommended *Tainted Contacts,* an attack on the Federal Council of Churches by Eugene N. Sanctuary, a retired army officer and active anti-Semite. Not until February 1933, however, did Winrod's magazine explicitly discuss the Jewish "World Conspiracy."[100]

Since *The Protocols* seemed "somewhat questionable," Winrod considered the objection that Russian royalists had concocted them from aged anti-Semitic tracts. Their resemblance to earlier documents, he concluded, tended to confirm the existence of a venerable "subterranean unnamed occult organization." Visiting Paris in 1935, he was assured by Philip Stepanov, whose father had "discovered" *The Protocols,* that Sergey Nilus, their "translator," had not been an immoral monk, as Winrod feared, but a family man and firm believer in Bible prophecy.[101]

Winrod never vouched for the "absolute historicity" of *The Protocols,* yet his writings after 1935 depended on de facto acceptance of their accuracy. Accordingly, he saw the "hidden hand" of the Elders of Zion behind the New Deal, and praised Hitler's suppression of alleged Jewish subversives in Germany. Furthermore, without identifying any individual Elder, he surmised that the group overlapped with some of the "sinister" leaders of the World Zionist Organization, "wise men" whose records might be named "protocols." It was not strange that such documents were prepared, Winrod said, but that they had leaked to the public.[102]

The Protocols appealed to Winrod's desire to view the world in orderly terms. He possessed the frame of mind that he ascribed to his opponents, "consistent evolutionists" and "logical modernists" who moved inevitably down a slippery slope from liberalism to atheism, nudism, and Communism. He had always been disposed, via his theological framework, to see concealed forces behind cursory explanations and inclined, according to dispensational hermeneutics, to think Jews extraordinarily influential in the determination of events. He was also suspicious of a "world-wide conspiracy . . . to dethrone God." *The Protocols* provided symmetrical balance to his system. Following their lead, he cast Jews as both symbols and historical actors, Satan's identifiable, semi-autonomous deputies arrayed against God's semi-autonomous prophets.[103]

Impressed by the symmetry if not the acuity of Winrod's thought, students of his career have been susceptible to a kind of theological determinism. His conversion to conspiratorial anti-Semitism, however, was not an inevitable consequence of the "essentially Manichean worldview" that Richard Hofstadter, for example, attributes to fundamentalists. Even dispensational theology left room to maneuver. Other fundamentalists, equally convinced that God and Satan approached Armageddon, did not slide from the *Schofield Reference Bible* to *The Protocols of the Learned Elders of Zion*. Arno C. Gaebelein, despite his flirtation with *The International Jew* in 1922, continued to support Zionism and later condemned Nazi persecution of German Jews. Billy Sunday said that his blood boiled whenever he heard Jews called "Sheenies" or "Christ-killers."[104]

In a sense, Winrod's anti-Semitism is harder to explain than Pelley or Smith's. Pelley, as we have seen, was a bundle of resentments in search of a target, and his bitterness extended to Jews he had known in Hollywood; Smith, as we shall see, resolved mounting fears of isolation and obscurity by believing that Jewish plotters menaced the United States as well as himself. In this context, both the ease with which Winrod accepted *The Protocols* and the relative absence of rancor accompanying this decision present special problems for the historian. Winrod shared with other fundamentalists a chronic sense of embattlement, yet he suffered no acute personal crisis during the early 1930s. Therefore, while Pelley and Smith's inner turmoil overflowed in their prose, Winrod's writings offer few blatant psychological clues.[105]

Interpretive problems can be mitigated, though not entirely resolved, by considering Winrod's "Manichean" theology in conjunction with his social and geographical position. His acceptance of *The Protocols* coincided not with a psychological crisis, but with his growing belief that the New Deal threatened values that Winrod, an independent small businessman as well as godly man, held dear. Hence, more inclined to public combat than fundamentalists with strong institutional ties who spent the 1930s building bible institutes and publishing houses, he was also more vulnerable to a conspiracy theory that united his public enemies. Furthermore, unlike Gaebelein, who developed sympathy for Jews while trying to convert them in New York City, Winrod had no direct experience in an ethnic ghetto, knew few if any Jews aside from Hebrew Christians, and thus could view them primarily as symbols instead of human beings. On the other hand, he did have close ties with German-American Mennonites in Kansas, some of whom applauded Hitler's anti-Semitism. Indeed, one of Winrod's Mennonite associates returned to Nazi Germany on the eve of World War II.[106]

Although dispensational theology alone did not make Winrod an anti-Semite, it decisively influenced the kind of anti-Semitism he preached. From the outset, he read *The Protocols* almost as if they were a newly discovered Bible scroll, supplementing Daniel, Ezekiel, and Revelation. Their disclosures were not only "in keeping" with Scriptural predictions that Jews would return to Palestine in unbelief, but they contained "prophecy" of their own whose fulfillment was "too glaring to be ignored." Moreover, the deplorable events coming to pass were part of a conspiracy decidedly "NOT of recent origin." Swinging from King Solomon to Armageddon, Winrod combined familiar anti-Semitic lore and conservative theology to produce an exraordinarily coherent theory of subversion by a "certain element of apostate Jewry."[107]

The two Testaments showed that Jews had always been a disobedient people. An especially rebellious elite, spiritual ancestors of the modern Elders of Zion, began to consolidate power under Solomon and soon wielded "Satanic influence" over the whole nation. Known as the Pharisees in Jesus's time, these occult operators engineered His illegal trial, executed the Son of God like a common criminal and, using an early "Gentile front," managed Roman persecution of the infant Christian church. After the Pharisees led an unsuccessful revolt in 135 A.D., Emperor Hadrian drove the Jews from Palestine.[108]

Undaunted by this setback, the early Elders reaffirmed the "false Messianic ideal" that Israel deserved to dominate the world and composed the Talmud, a "horrible" code prefiguring *The Protocols*. The disapora intensified the Jewish elite's power by broadening the sphere of operation. From the Dark Ages to the Reformation, Winrod wrote, their anti-Christian ideas infected such groups as the Gnostics, Swedenborgians, Rosecrucians, and Jesuits; Mussolini's favorite book, *The Prince*, could be called the *"Fifteenth-Century Protocols."* During the 1700s, the apostate Jews found a peculiarly effective weapon—the Illuminati—the secret organization founded by Adam Weishaupt.[109]

Whereas Pelley merely mentioned the Illuminati, a favorite target of Protestant countersubversives since the 1790s, Winrod placed them at the center of his argument. Weishaupt, a some-time Jesuit and full-time "human devil," practiced virtually everything that Defenders opposed, from abortion to radicalism. After studying with "Cabalistic Jews from Egypt" and surrounding himself with Jewish lieutenants, he infiltrated agents into European Masonry. Not the economic deprivation of the poor and middle classes, but the machinations of these "illuminized" lodges, whose members included Marat, Robespierre, and Danton, produced the French Revolution.[110]

Winrod maintained that Marx had "edited his teachings" out of Weishaput's oeuvre. Thus the Russian Revolution began where the French left off. Bolshevism also was the "lineal descendant" of Illuminism because apostate Jews controlled both eighteenth-century subversion and the Soviet Union. Winrod surmised that Lenin and Trotsky had attended early Zionist conferences where *The Protocols* were probably discussed, and he invoked shifting statistics to show that Jews, including "many" from the East Side of New York, controlled Russia. Stalin himself was merely the "Gentile front" for politburo member Lazar Kaganovich, a descendant of Jewish kings.[111]

Although no "informed person" could doubt Communism's "Jewish character," that supposition presented special problems for Winrod. If Scripture predicted an anti-Semitic coalition between Germany and Russia, how could one partner be ruled by Jews? And why would Jewish Communists attack their brethern in the Middle East? Sometimes Winrod suggested that Russian destiny was not determined by her "foreign" rulers, but by the natives who seethed with hatred for Jews. He further surmised that the Kremlin dictatorship represented a different stratum of Jewry from the settlers of Palestine. Prophecy had made provision for the situation in Zechariah 14:14: "And Judah shall also fight at Jerusalem."[112]

Sketching these possibilities with less than his usual confidence in the biblical chart and compass, Winrod never resolved the implied "paradoxes" to his own satisfaction. Yet, for someone seeking a venerable subversive tradition, the concept of "Jewish-Communism" carried benefits outweighing the exegetic difficulties. It made absolutely clear why Bolsheviks persecuted Christians: "Behind the Red Menace in its modern form is the same *Jewish impulse* which killed Jesus Christ." Moreover, the theory allowed Winrod, along with Pelley and countless other anti-Semites, to perceive a common enemy behind two diverse forces, international banking and revolutionary agitation.[113]

Drawing on familiar anti-Semitic lore and taking a position congenial to a small businessman suspicious of corporate power, Winrod traced a "mortgage" on all countries from the invention of interest by "tricky" Jewish goldsmiths through passage of the National Baking Act of 1863 and enforcement of the gold standard to the Depression. He claimed that few Jews lost money in the Crash. On the contrary, the speculation of the 1920s had been a tactical suggestion of the sixth *Protocol.* Of course *The Protocols* further explained that financiers and international Communists, though seemingly locked in mortal combat, were cooperative cousins under the skin.[114]

Echoing *The International Jew,* Winrod accused Jacob Schiff of financing the Russian Revolution. Despite Communist appeals to the proletariat, Russia was governed by Jewish capitalists who privately despised the masses. Similarly, American gentiles who embraced Communism merely fell for insincere "soap-box oratory." The two-pronged attack on Christian civilization virtually assured a Jewish victory—albeit a short-lived one. If the false revolutionaries failed to agitate their way into office, they still forced governments to seek relief from the Jewish profiteers who had arranged the economic collapse in 1929.[115]

As early as 1933, aware that *The Protocols* instructed conspirators to infect society with the "poison of Liberalism," Winrod held Jews responsible for the New Deal. FDR's "very large percent" of Jewish advisors included Bernard Baruch and James P. Warburg, whose father Felix had created the Federal Reserve System. In 1936, three years after Pelley, Winrod claimed to have uncovered Roosevelt's Jewish ancestry. While hesitating to condemn the president and his associates simply on the basis of their ethnic origin, the evangelist nevertheless warned that the "Semitic mind," unable to assimilate "Christian and American viewpoints," could not be trusted with the nation's fate.[116]

From the crucifixion of Christ to the torture of Russian Christians and the plowing under of Kansas wheat in a hungry nation, Winrod said that a Jewish elite had played satanic roles in a divinely directed drama now drawing to a close. The modern version of this plot provided an "exact parallel" to Bible prophecies about the last days. The Elders of Zion did not know it, but the Beast would ultimately usurp their gold as well as the idolatrous church proposed in the seventeenth *Protocol.* As Winrod saw it, almost every page of *The Protocols* breathed the "Antichrist atmosphere."[117]

Even though Winrod regarded apostate Jews as Satan's pawns, he held them responsible for generations of human suffering; preachers who excused them because they were God's chosen people were preaching "sentimental gush." A "loving and sympathetic attitude" was commendable, Winrod said, alluding to fundamentalists who still sympathized with Zionism, but it must not "over-balance the plain teachings" of prophets who knew in advance that Jewish leaders would oppress millions of gentiles. Analyzing these prophecies no more indicated hatred of Jews than explicating Ezekiel to chart the future of the United States showed hostility to Americans. The flyleaf of Winrod's pamphlet, *The Truth About the Protocols,* explicitly rejected opposition to Jews "as a race or religion."[118]

These assertions of tolerance cannot be accepted at face value. Although Winrod did not classify Judaism with "heathen" corruptions like Hinduism or Islam, he joined other dispensationalists in anticipating salvation only for those Jews who embraced Jesus before Armageddon. Furthermore, he obviously came to accept hoary stereotypes that circulated in the dominant culture: Jews were tricky, egotistical, greedy, prone to immorality, and more dangerous than "people of lower capacities." Occasionally Winrod supposed that the destructive traits were passed through the genes. For example, because their ancestors had crucified Jesus, Jewish commissars carried hatred of Christianity *"in their blood."*[119]

Nonetheless, Winrod's denial of ethnic animosity does show the limits of his anti-Semitism. Unlike Pelley, he never wrote long disquisitions on racial inferiority, never mocked the accents of immigrants, and never proposed stripping Jews of constitutional rights. Furthermore, Winrod's stereotypical portraits of Jews, like his social and economic views, were subordinated to an overriding theological system. On the one hand, by disposing him to seek orderly explanations and to read documents in typological fashion, Winrod's religion contributed to his belief in *The Protocols.* On the other hand, firm adherence to doctrine softened his anti-Semitism. He admitted that Zionist Elders were fulfilling a "predestined purpose," recalled that Jesus had appeared on earth "in the garb of a Jew," and continued to insist that a "faithful remnant" of Israel would someday enjoy divine grace. In the meantime, he urged Bible students to hold a "high attitude" as they observed the world scene:

> Let no defender of the faith allow his heart to be filled with hatred for the Jews. Your attitude should not be so much a matter of trying to determine what is right or wrong! You should be interested rather in interpreting these strange events in the light of fulfilled prophecy.[120]

Winrod personally applied the distinction between good and bad Jews to politics as well as theology. Because Henry Ford failed to understand the "prophetic element" in *The Protocols*, the supplemental text that he sponsored, *The International Jew*, appeared to attack an entire people. Winrod believed that the "great rank and file" remained ignorant of the conspiracy. Perhaps no more than three hundred Elders were "in the know," and they would sacrifice their coreligionists in a profitable war. This cabal sponsored Communism, but it would be "absurd" to consider all Jews Communists and "horrible" to punish innocent individuals for the crimes of "apostate" Jewish conspirators. In 1936, Winrod vowed "to defend the religious liberties of good Jews with the same zeal that I would defend my own." The best Jews, of course, became Hebrew Christians.[121]

Without any sense of inconsistency, he simultaneously denounced Elders and continued to promote the "great task" of Jewish evangelism. The refusal of some Hebrew Christians to understand that he bore no ill will to their ethnic group puzzled Winrod because, as he tried to convince skeptical converts in 1933, he merely presented "true, prophetic facts."[122]

Yet the absence of an infallible method of separating virtuous from ignoble Jews disturbed Winrod himself. As a step toward accurate classification, he proposed in 1936 that the "DANGEROUS 'JEWS'" had descended from Dan, son of Jacob. This power-hungry clan had swept over the world, leaving its mark on the "Dan-ube and Mace-Don-ia" as well as the "DON" in Russia. Significantly, Genesis 30:6 described Dan as a serpent, and the Elders chose as their symbol a snake crawling among nations. Unfortunately, no mortal could discover the tribal origins of any modern Jew, but Winrod believed that "destiny will finally put each in his own place." He suspected that Mussolini and Roosevelt shared this bloodline and, like Thomas Aquinas and other medieval theologians, expected the Antichrist to be a Danite.[123]

Philip Dru and Adolf Hitler

Winrod's interpretation of religion, domestic politics, and world affairs changed little between publication of *Antichrist and the Tribe of Dan* in 1936 and American entry into World War II. The *Defender* and the *Revealer*, until the latter's demise in January 1937, continued to affirm that the Beast was "UNDOUBTEDLY IN THE FLESH AT THE PRESENT HOUR," that the Bible provided the best guide to the unfolding of history, and that Winrod marched with the "winning side of a great moral, spiritual, and prophetic trend." Playing slight variations on favorite themes, the editor found fresh evidence of God's special concern for the United States, continued to deride liberal theologians and Russian Communists, noted fresh subversive movements (including the CIO's effort to create a "Soviet America"), and concluded in 1939 that Jews dominated the United States "more completely" than any country except the Soviet Union.[124]

Although many *Defender* articles in the late 1930s simply repeated what Winrod had previously written, sometimes reprinting whole paragraphs verbatim, there were three important shifts in emphasis. First, he muted his antipathy to Catholicism. As late as 1936, Winrod had written that the Roman Catholic Church, though superficially Christian, actually preserved the "paganism of Old Babylon" in such practices as the use of rosaries and holy water. Along with most dispensationalists, he expected the Catholic Church to become a bulwark of the Beast's false religion, represented by the scarlet woman in Revelation 17:3. This scriptural exegesis fueled his campaign against Alfred E. Smith in 1928, his suspicion of Father Coughlin, and his assertion in 1935 that Jews and Catholics often collaborated against Protestants. Without repudiating this theological position, Winrod, in search of anti-Communist allies and Kansas votes, mentioned it with decreasing frequency after 1934. By 1939, he was protesting the persecution of priests by the Spanish Republic, favorably quoting Father Coughlin, and urging Catholics and Protestants to cooperate in "patriotic Americanism."[125]

Second, about 1938 Winrod discovered another contemporary text that, along with *The Protocols* and Scripture itself, seemed to foretell important events. The New Deal was not new to occultists who understood the "Delphic language" of Colonel Edward M. House's "prophetic novel," *Philip Dru: Administrator.*[126]

In House's book, published in 1912, an ambitious senator and a billionaire resembling J. P. Morgan collect funds from one thousand capitalists to elect a pliable congress and puppet president. Discovery of this plot precipitates civil war. Philip Dru, a reform-minded West

Point graduate, leads a volunteer militia to victory over the pro-capitalist regular army and proclaims himself "administrator of the republic." His administration fulfills House's Progressive-era fantasies. Dru negotiates reciprocal trade treaties, rescues Mexico from its landed aristocracy, establishes various welfare programs, and appoints expert commissions to rationalize American institutions. After proposing a new constitution, Dru retires to tour the world with the sentimental novel's heroine.[127]

Both the story and its author's biography offered much grist for Winrod's typological mill. Indulging his propensity to find conspiratorial continuity, he supposed that House's father must have known of the planter plot to establish a "slave empire." Colonel House himself had maneuvered the Federal Reserve Act through Congress, exercised "well nigh hypnotic" influence over President Wilson, and later advised Roosevelt. The novel, which may have been the Brain Trust's "textbook," foreshadowed FDR's assault on the Supreme Court and denunciations of businessmen as "human devils." Fittingly, too, the fictional hero of *Philip Dru* formulated his program while living with Polish Jews on the East Side of New York.[128]

Winrod's third and most important shift provided much of the basis for his notoriety: after 1934 he grew increasingly sympathetic to the Nazi regime. In 1932, the *Defender* had recommended Dorothy Thompson's highly critical book, *I Saw Hitler* (while lamenting the author's marriage to Sinclar Lewis). The next year, Winrod had called Hitler a "wild beast" as well as a potential "prophetic misfit," adding that his subordination of German Christianity to Teutonic mysticism was a "foretaste" of the Beast's program. In 1933, along with such dispensational magazines as the *King's Business* and the *Moody Bible Institute Monthly*, the *Defender* had viewed Nazi anti-Semitism primarily as an incentive for Jews to move to Palestine, thus fulfilling prophecy. Even then, however, Winrod had urged readers "in fairness" to recall that Hitler faced two hundred thousand "Communistic Jews." Within two years, he was praising Germany as the single nation brave enough to defy Jewish occultism, Communism, and finance.[129]

Terrified of Communism and hostile to a putative Jewish conspiracy, Winrod after 1934 uncritically accepted Nazi justifications for their anti-Semitic policies. In short, the Nazis acted to save Germany from Jewish radicalism, economic exploitation, and "spasms of racial lust" worse than those on the American stage and screen. Winrod went on to absolve them of bias against the Jewish religion and claimed that they protected good Jews "from fanatics."[130]

Deciding that he had been deceived by propaganda about Hitler's religion, Winrod in 1935 called him a devout Catholic who shunned pagan Teutonic cultists. Furthermore, German churches were "packed" and higher criticism of Scripture, an invention of Jews who pretended to accept Christianity, was disappearing. The *Defender* was especially encouraged by growth of the German Free Church, a coalition of four million non-Lutheran Protestants including Baptists, Methodists, and Mennonites. Winrod entertained German Methodist Bishop F. H. Otto Melle, former president of the Free Church Confederation, during his 1939 visit to the United States, and published three of his sermons in the *Defender*.[131]

This show of hospitality highlights Winrod's willingness to believe the best of Hitler's regime. Despite claims to the contrary by Winrod and Melle himself, the bishop had not stood aloof from politics, but had conciliated the Nazis more than the typical German clergyman. During a conference at Oxford in 1937, for example, Melle had dissociated himself from a statement obliquely criticizing Nazi harassment of the churches and praised the German "resurrection" under National Socialism. Whether Winrod admitted it or not, the Free Churches prospered partly because Hitler appreciated their propaganda.[132]

Then too, Winrod invariably reacted to appeals on behalf of German Jewry by contrasting the Third Reich with the Soviet Union. *The Revealer* doubted, for example, that the 1936 Olympic games could have been held in Moscow instead of Berlin. Two years later, when President Roosevelt condemned the *Kristallnacht* pogrom in which Nazis burned 300 synagogues, looted hundreds of stores, and arrested 25,000 Jews, the *Defender* asked why he denounced the smashing of "Jewish shop windows" while showing "no concern" for Russian Christians.[133]

These remarks, like Winrod's hospitality for Bishop Melle, revealed a highly selective sensitivity to human suffering. Callous and naive as they were, however, they did not prove what many of Winrod's contemporaries took for granted—that he sought a Nazi dictatorship in the United States. His commitment to American exceptionalism saved him from that folly. The kind of autocracy appropriate—perhaps necessary—to govern Europeans would never fit the United States. Claiming to oppose dictatorships "regardless of the color of their shirts," Winrod unconvincingly maintained that his discussion of German Protestantism was "in no sense a defense" of the Nazi regime. With greater accuracy he declared that "Christians in this part of the world are ready to support but one *ism*—Americanism."[134]

Gerald B. Winrod for Senator

In 1938 Winrod entered the Republican primary for United States Senator from Kansas, hoping to use the office as a "sounding board for the gospel of Jesus Christ." Despite this unusual conception of congressional responsibilities, his candidacy was not a symbolic gesture like Pelley's campaign for president in 1936. Nor did he have to rely on a paper organization like the Silver Shirts to support his effort; by 1938, the *Defender* reached 110,000 subscribers. Assured of contributions from a national network of theologically conservative Protestants, certain of votes from thousands of local fundamentalists, and able to draw on two decades of experience as a public speaker, he seemed a plausible winner in a state known for eccentric political candidates.[135]

Winrod could hardly have found a better base—first as an evangelist and then as an office-seeker—than Kansas. Most residents emphatically agreed with the Defenders about the merits of Prohibition. A smaller but considerable number of them shared Winrod's distrust of Roman Catholics and Jews. During the mid-1920s, at least 40,000 and perhaps as many as 100,000 Kansans had joined the Ku Klux Klan. Although scholarly estimates of membership vary, there is no doubt that Klansmen intimidated many law-abiding citizens, physically assaulted others (including Catholic officials), and exerted substantial political power. In 1924, when both the incumbent Democratic governor and his Republican opponent courted the Klan, *Emporia Gazette* publisher William Allen White attracted almost 150,000 votes as an independent candidate opposed to the "shirt tail knights." The Klan's influence, which ebbed in the late 1920s, showed at least that some Kansans wold not automatically reject a candidate who attacked Jews and Catholics. For his part, Winrod denied belonging to the Klan "or any other secret organization," but, according to his secretary, M. L. Flowers, neither did he oppose the group.[136]

Although Republicans customarily won the major elections in Kansas, the Depression had upset the political order. Many farmers approved of Roosevelt's agricultural program and voted for New Dealers; even Governor Alfred M. Landon failed to carry the state against FDR in 1936. When Winrod entered the 1938 Republican primary, Democrats held both the governorship and the Senate seat he coveted.[137]

Not victories by Democrats, but unsuccessful races by John R. Brinkley did most to unsettle Kansas politics. Brinkley, a diploma mill physician, claimed to restore human sexual prowess by transplanting goat glands, made a fortune lecturing on health, and reached a wide audience through his own radio station, KFKB. He first ran for governor in 1930 after medical examiners had revoked his license. Touring in his own limousine, he recruited Protestant ministers to open campaign rallies with prayer and piously declined to "talk politics on Sunday." A quack, opportunist, and nativist, Brinkley nonetheless sympathized with the economic plight of the poorest Kansans. His inconsistent platform, like many others pledging to redistribute wealth, promised frugal, limited government as well as publicly financed pensions and medical care (including a state hospital for blacks), conservation (along with a lake in every country), 7,000 miles of new roads, and inexpensive automobile licenses. In 1930, he received 183,000 write-in votes—27,000 short of victory—but claimed with some warrant to have been counted out. On the ballot as an independent two years later he ran a close third. Brinkley's constituency, as incongruous as his platform, included ex-Klansmen, Catholics, and blacks, many of whom had never voted before.[138]

Impressed by Brinkley's ostentatious godliness, Winrod wished him "every spiritual blessing" in his "stand for the highest religious and moral interests." This endorsement, printed in Brinkley's magazine *Publicity* during the 1932 campaign, demonstrated Winrod's deepening interest in state and local affairs. In the mid-1930s, the *Revealer* attacked Wichita educators for allowing children "flagrantly" to expose their flesh in gym classes, congratulated Kansas for retaining Prohibition, and criticized Republican Senator Arthur Capper for occasionally cooperating with the Roosevelt administration. Winrod was even less pleased with Governor Landon, an alleged friend of Jewish radicals, but grudgingly supported him against FDR in 1936.[139]

Winrod demonstrated his capacity to mobilize a formidable following in a February 1937 special mailing that urged Defenders to pray and protest against Roosevelt's plan to render the Supreme Court "impotent." He later claimed that Congress received one million Defenders petitions demanding "Hands off the Supreme Court!" Winrod probably exaggerated, but the effort was sufficiently impressive to provoke a counterattack by Senator Joseph Robinson (Dem.-Ark.), manager of the administration bill. When Robinson accused him of reviving Ku Klux Klan methods, Winrod replied that he was just an ordinary minister with many friends.[140]

Mobilizing his friends again in 1938, Winrod faced three opponents in the Republican senatorial primary. Next to Winrod himself, former State Senator Dallas Knapp, a member of the party old guard, was most hostile to the New Deal. Former Governor Clyde M. Reed, an anti-Klan publisher in the 1920s, presented the generally balanced critique of the Roosevelt administration characteristic of Republican moderates like Landon and William Allen White. Jesse Fisher, a Methodist minister and southwest Kansas favorite son, staked out a position between Reed and Knapp.[141]

This primary, a *Topeka State Journal* pundit observed, created the "biggest political puzzle" Kansas had faced in thirty years. Interest extended far beyond the state. In June, President Roosevelt asked White to explain rumors that an "openly" fascist "man named Winrod" whom he had never heard of was the likely Republican nominee. The *Philadelphia Record* devoted a long article to the evangelist's allegedly Nazi beliefs. Detecting an affinity between Winrod and Brinkley, *Time* compared Kansas to a "family whose freak son is the only one who could ever get his picture into the papers."[142]

The frequent comparison of Winrod to Brinkley was misleading. Outsiders spurned by the press as well as the regular Republican organization, they both mounted colorful campaigns, relied on private networks of followers, and cultivated radio audiences. The evangelist, for example, barnstormed in a sedan that one reporter likened to a circus wagon, had Defenders distribute 100,000 invitations to "Winrod Radio Party," and transcribed many of his broadcasts for circulation. Personally, however, Winrod was less flashy than Brinkley, who wore ostentatious jewelry and otherwise enjoyed displaying his affluence. Indeologically, Winrod's conspiratorial anti-Semitism exceded the goat gland doctor's commonplace nativism. Perhaps most important for winning votes, Winrod's small businessman's platform lacked Brinkley's promise of economic spoils.[143]

On the whole, Winrod's campaign oratory was consistent with his writing in the *Defender*, but more subdued. He still asserted that the country's tribulation derived from a "moral and spiritual sag," and demanded a return to God, who patiently wanted to help the United States as He had by guiding the Constitutional Convention in 1787. Less blessed Europeans simply reverted "to type" when they embraced Fascism or Communism. But these "alien isms" also found support among deluded or malevolent Americans, particularly residents of coastal cities. A "strange feeling" overcame Winrod in these places:

> The names appearing on the places of business, the condition of the shop windows, the babble of foreign tongues, the language used on the signs in public places, the filth of the

> streets, the greasy lives of the people, the utter disregard for American standards of morality, the flagrant violation of the Christian Sabbath . . . the whole atmosphere of these great unassimilated sections of foreign population causes the visitor from these middle states to feel that he has moved out of one world into another. They don't speak our language. They don't breathe our air.

Playing a local variation on the theme of American exceptionalism, Winrod was glad to live in an "entirely different atmosphere"; Kansas air had invigorated abolitionism, temperance, and women's suffrage. Yet Communists now operated close to home, in Fort Scott and Topeka, as well as New York and San Francisco.[144]

The ineffective, alien, and tyrannical New Deal was the foremost threat to republican virtue. Speaking regularly over radio stations WIBW and KCKN, Winrod depicted the anguish of unemployment, blamed FDR for the 1938 recession, and claimed that "wild" pump priming merely enriched international bankers. His esteem for businessmen reached a peak during the campaign. He stressed that he was one of them, a victim of "class legislation" comparable to Communist persecution of the kulaks. Making a special appeal to farmers, he promised an "honest money system" instead of the AAA's "crazy" destruction of God-given bounty. Finally, he reiterated that the administration's "occult pattern" was revealed in *Philip Dru: Administrator.*[145]

The reference to House's novel was vintage Winrod, but the omissions from Winrod's addresses were more revealing than the content. Deciding that a senate seat was well worth verbal discretion, he passed over some favorite themes and approached others circumspectly. After spending five years tracing an intricate, two-thousand-year-old Jewish conspiracy, he never mentioned it in the campaign, even though Payne Ratner, a gubernatorial aspirant with a Jewish father, provided an obvious target. His denunciations of Communism eschewed the usual statistics on the ethnic background of commissars. While indicting the "mysterious invisible government" in Washington, he did not discuss the religion of Brain Trusters or Roosevelt's family tree. Suggesting with more hesitation than usual that FDR deliberately prolonged the Depression, he made no connection to the twentieth *Protocol.* In short, worldly ambition moved Winrod to deemphasize his anti-Semitism but not his economic conservatism.[146]

Preaching this softened version of his views, Winrod dominated the early phase of the campaign. In June, William Allen White told President Roosevelt that this "Fascist, raw and unashamed," stood a "fairly good chance of going to the Senate. White, whom the *Defender* had called a "clownish editor," produced a steady stream of editorials in the *Emporia Gazette* urging Republicans to unite behind Clyde Reed. Winrod was personally honest and courageous in his ignorance, White said, but his "Nazi" views insulted the "rather high I.Q. of this state."[147]

Nor was White alone in recalling a less subdued Winrod. The Wichita Printing and Trades Council rallied organized labor against him. The Kansas City, Kansas, NAACP recalled his "prejudice against other races and religions." Republican National Chairman John D. Hamilton, a Kansan, repudiated him, and former Governor Landon worked discretely but effectively for Clyde Reed. Vowing that the "SWASTIKA MUST NOT FLY OVER KANSAS," nine Protestant ministers reprinted excerpts from Winrod's magazines showing that he accepted Nazi justifications for anti-Semitism. Moreover, building a chain of guilt by association almost worthy of the *Defender*, they inferred that Winrod cooperated with the German government because both circulated *The Protocols*.[148]

No one fought Winrod harder than Rev. L. M. Birkhead, the modernist Unitarian from Kansas City, Missouri. The two had feuded across state lines since the late 1920s, when Birkhead had regularly denounced fundamentalists and Winrod had heckled him from the audience. The 1930s pushed Birkhead, along with countless contemporaries, from wry social comment to vigorous commitment. Visiting Germany in 1935, he saw a nation "poisoned" by anti-Semitism. As he later recalled, an assistant to Nazi propagandist Julius Streicher had revealed a list of Americans who would help Germany "when *Der Tag* came." He determined to fight such native fascists and on 1 November 1937 founded Friends of Democracy (a name his acquaintance Sinclair Lewis helped to choose). Birkhead's politicization, like Winrod's, involved no total transformation. As executive director of Friends of Democracy, the *New Yorker* reported, he retained the "singleness of purpose . . . of a religious crusader."[149]

Making Winrod one of his first targets, Birkhead contributed information about the Defenders to columnist Dorothy Thompson and the American Civil Liberties Union. Winrod responded by calling Birkhead a "professional snooper" and traitor to Christ. Retaking the offensive in 1938, Birkhead charged candidate Winrod with representing a "formidable Hitler party," and implied that his funds as well as his opinions could be traced to Berlin.[150]

In a radio broadcast on 14 July, Winrod responded to what he called "fantastic rumors and half-truths." Many of the magazine articles quoted against him had been written by others, he said, disingenuously adding that he could not approve everything in the *Defender* while on the road. Claiming that his pamphlets had been misconstrued, he distinguished between "illuminized" European masons and the fine Kansas lodges, applauded local chapters of the "questionable" Federal Council of Churches, and, denying that he was anti-Catholic despite deep theological disagreements, reiterated the need for a religious united front against Communism.[151]

While promising to oppose the "apostate, atheistic Communist Jew," Winrod also professed "utmost respect" for devout Jews, whose constitutional rights he would defend. He insisted that neither his funds nor his beliefs came from Nazi of Fascist sources. Until Birkhead accused him of collaborating with Nazi leader Julius Streicher, Winrod did not "know there was such a man on earth." His four-day visit to Germany in 1935 had been spent largely in religious study at Wittenberg. Indeed, the tour of eight European countries strengthened his opposition to "every ism except Americanism." He had been arrested, subjected to "every indignity" except violence, and barred from Italy for criticizing Mussolini.[152]

Insisting that he had not mentioned racial or religious issues in any of three hundred speeches, Winrod accused his foes of introducing these matters into the campaign. He would cooperate "in every way" with an investigation of his finances by the House Committee on Un-American Activities, but the panel should also probe eastern interests that had spent a million dollars to defeat him. At the campaign's close, his literature said that powerful Jewish organizations had bankrolled "Gentile fronts" to defeat him.[153]

By the time Republicans voted on 3 August, the *Topeka State Journal* noted, eclectic opposition had "devalued Gerald Winrod in a most impressive manner." He received 53,149 votes, finishing third behind Clyde Reed and Dallas Knapp. His strongest support came from Mennonite communities and from counties where the Ku Klux Klan had thrived. Winrod's devaluation stemmed partly from the unsubstantiated charges that he received funds from Nazi Germany. In addition, his economic conservatism hardly appealed to the many Brinkeyites who wanted to redistribute wealth. No longer subdued in defeat, Winrod blamed "JEWISH FINANCIAL INTERESTS" for defaming him and refused to support Republican gubernatorial nominee Payne Ratner. Still seeking to undermine the New Deal, however, he endorsed Reed, who was elected in November.[154]

Prophet Indicted

The Senate race was a harbinger of Winrod's future troubles. Because this campaign spread his reputation as a native Nazi, he spent increasing time and type defending himself against such diverse critics as Friends of Democracy, the *Saturday Evening Post*, and the national commander of Disabled War Veterans; his almost ritualistic response charged foes with "fronting" for powerful Jews. As Winrod's notoriety grew, his official biographer recalled, old friends "fell silent, and then drifted away." According to L. M. Birkhead, the House Committee on Un-American Activities planned to investigate Winrod until a mutual friend interceded with Chairman Martin Dies. Then, in June 1940, Frances Winrod sued for divorce, claiming that her husband aspired to be "nominal head of the country when the revolution comes." Thirty-three years later, Winrod's secretary said that Frances had been sick when she made this allegation. She repudiated it shortly thereafter and remarried her ex-husband.[155]

Despite personal difficulties, Winrod "intensified" his study of the deteriorating world situation. His exultant response to the Nazi-Soviet Pact of August 1939 highlighted his faith in Scripture as "history written in advance." The treaty shocked diplomats and reporters alike, but a "special prophetic edition" of the *Defender* reminded readers that Winrod had foreseen this alliance as early as 1934. In the late 1930s, he explained, a reaction against the Jewish autocracy had spread among ordinary, oppressed Russians. Taking advantage of this situation, Stalin eliminated Jewish rivals in the purges, permitted "somewhat better treatment of Christians," and arranged the pact with Germany.[156]

Winrod expected (and soon perceived) the "Nazification" of Russian opinion. The outbreak of World War II also fit into the dispensational scheme. Winrod suggested, for instance, that the Maginot line divided the Northern Confederacy from the Beast's Roman imperium. Still convinced that Mussolini would play a critical role in the divine plan, he supposed that the Rome-Berlin Axis, a prophetic incongruity, would not survive. The war, of course, signaled impending apocalypse. Whole countries would be excluded from the coming kingdom because they persecuted Christians. After a period of purification, however, the United States would be "singled out for special duty and holy service." In the meantime, Winrod concluded in 1939, it must adopt a policy of "rigid neutrality."[157]

To counteract prowar sentiment in the United States, Winrod sponsored a drive in September 1939 similar to his mobilization against the Roosevelt Supreme Court plan. Defenders petitioned Congress to reject "every proposal that might ultimately cause American blood to flow on foreign soil." More than Pelley, Smith, and most other far right agitators, Winrod respected the pacifist refusal to fight in any war. Accordingly, the *Defender* praised Quakers and Mennonites, depicted the horror of combat, and emphasized that this destructiveness was rooted in human depravity.[158]

Yet, from 1939 to 1941 Winrod's case against American participation in World War II consisted primarily of crude adaptations of familiar isolationist—not pacifist—arguments. Capitalist profiteers and sinister molders of opinion who had nudged the United States into World War I were repeating their "Satanic symphony." As an anti-Semitic non-interventionist, Winrod added that Jews had surrounded President Wilson in 1917 and now manipulated debate on foreign policy. Citizens must quickly decide if bloodshed was warranted because New Dealers wished to save German Jewry from Nazism.[159]

Although Wilson had wanted to make the world safe for democracy, Winrod said, World War I left "little or no actual democracy" in its wake. Not only was the Soviet Union a monstrous tyranny, but China, another prospective American ally, was less democratic than Japan. Both Great Britain and France were curtailing freedom. If the United States went to war, Winrod inferred, the "coils of dictatorship" would be tightened here, too. By choosing peace, the nation could remain economically self-sufficient, separated from combat by two oceans, and uncontaminated by Europeans who had "made practically no changes for the better during the last 150 years." This country needed an army strong enough to smash invaders, but the Commander-in-Chief must recognize that "our frontier, most emphatically, is not the river Rhine."[160]

Winrod learned of the Japanese raid at Pearl Harbor while delivering a Sunday sermon in Pontiac, Michigan. At the close of the service, he knelt in prayer, "knowing that our Country faced rough roads in the months ahead." For the duration of the war, Winrod decided, differences over foreign and domestic policy must be submerged in common concern for American survival. Because "persistent, cumulative, nation-wide prayer" was necessary to bring the United States safely through the struggle, the Defenders organized a Prayer Chain whose members pledged to pray fifteen to thirty minutes daily for the United States.[161]

Although the *Defender* still attacked both the Roosevelt administration and Winrod's journalistic detractors, it was not so violently partisan in wartime as it had been during the 1930s. Rather, the magazine reviewed inspirational biographies of Generals Douglas MacArthur, Dwight David Eisenhower, and other heroes, and boosted Rev. Sam Swain's National Spiritual Defense Crusade, a systematic—and possibly lucrative—effort to organize prayer power for men in combat. Winrod mourned Kaj Monk, a Danish theologian killed by the Gestapo. He insisted that the "melee of events" still portended the imminent division of Europe into Northern and Southern Confederacies. More convinced than ever that his own country's fate lay beyond mortal hands, he delineated God's miraculous intervention on behalf of American troops and, citing Isaiah 19, insisted that the United States "WILL NEVER COME UNDER THE HEEL OF A FOREIGN FOE."[162]

Yet neither the softened tone of the *Defender* nor the Prayer Chain's daily drive "to release 500,000 hours of unified spiritual effort" convinced the federal government of Winrod's patriotism. Six months before Pearl Harbor, the FBI had included him among persons "to be considered for custodial detention" in event of a national emergency. After the United States declared war, he became a target of the Roosevelt administration's effort to silence native fascists. In May 1942, a grand jury empaneled in the District of Columbia to investigate sedition called Winrod to testify; on 24 July, his name headed the list of twenty-eight men and women indicted for conspiracy to cause insubordination in the armed forces. This mass conspiracy case, initially called *United States* v. *Winrod*, would disrupt his affairs for the next five years.[163]

To avoid the disgrace of arrest, Winrod paid his own way to Washington, D.C., where he surrendered to federal marshals on 28 July 1942. As he was arraigned, finger-printed, and released on $5,000 bail, he may have found solace in his belief that all prophets, "thorns in the flesh [of] wicked leadership," suffered persecution.[164]

4. Gerald L. K. Smith

DRAMATIST IN POLITICS

"Completely Dedicated"—and Highly Ambitious

Gerald L. K. Smith agreed with Gerald B. Winrod that struggling individuals and sovereign nations must put "Christ First." The shared perspective was neither accidental nor surprising because Smith, like Winrod, had been a Protestant minister before entering politics. Yet they were not, as historian Ralph Lord Roy suggests, twin "apostles of discord." Though ultimately settling near each other on the political spectrum, Smith and Winrod followed different personal and theological paths to the far right.[1]

Gerald Lyman Kenneth Smith's childhood was marked by hard times and high ambitions. He was born in Pardeeville, Wisconsin, a small town thirty-five miles north of Madison, on 27 February 1898, the second child and only son of Lyman Z. Smith and Sarah Henthorn Smith. Sarah's father had served in the Union army before coming to Wisconsin. On the Smith side, Gerald's father, grandfather, and great-grandfather were farmers and small businessmen who doubled as clergy in the Christian Church (or Disciples of Christ). His paternal grandfather, Zachariah Smith, a pioneer in south central Wisconsin, had arrived with $500 in gold, established a ranch, and sold horses to wealthy midwesterners, including railroad entrepreneur James J. Hill. Lyman Smith earned his living selling spices and spice extracts and, in keeping with usual Disciples practice, preached without pay.[2]

When Gerald was two, however, his father came down with a debilitating disease thought to be pernicious anemia. Unable to continue as a traveling salesman—sometimes barely able to walk—Lyman retreated with his wife, son, and ten-year-old daughter to a small farm in Sylvan township, forty miles southeast of LaCrosse.

Gerald helped with the chores as soon as he was able. Impoverished by his father's illness, he recalled, the family "eked out a livelihood" for ten years.[3]

But their poverty was of a special sort. The Smiths owned a farm with some livestock (including the five cows Gerald milked each day) and managed to hire a handyman when Lyman was completely disabled. More important, the Smiths never forgot, and never let their son forget, that the family had seen better days. Years later, Smith repeatedly recalled that this "proud" couple rejected charity from relatives and friends. Nor did his "sophisticated" and "high-toned" parents have anything in common with the illiterate Kickapoo Mountain "hillbillies" among whom they temporarily lived. Still, though the Smiths were neither dirt poor nor broken in spirit, their lives were undeniably difficult. Isolation was as great a burden as economic deprivation. The Smith farm was certainly off the beaten track, which may explain why they were missed by the 1900 census. More than two miles from the nearest store, they were served by stage coach before the introduction of Rural Free Delivery. Until he was eleven, Smith attended a one-room schoolhouse in the woods.[4]

Rural isolation, combined with a sense that his family differed from the surrounding hillbillies, permanently affected Smith. Throughout his life, and particularly during crises, he expressed feelings of loneliness; the theme recurs often in his autobiography, *Besieged Patriot*. At age eleven, a desire for companship may have contributed to Smith's decision to attend a larger school in Viola. Undoubtedly he was also moved by dissatisfaction with the local schoolhouse and by ambition remarkable in a child. The boy's choice demanded self-discipline. Smith rose before dawn, completed his barnyard rounds, and then rode horseback seven miles to Viola; during the noon break, he pitched hay to pay for his horse's feed.[5]

Despite such rigors, Smith looked back on his childhood with nostalgia typical of a self-made man. *Besieged Patriot* contained none of the bitterness characteristic of Pelley's memoirs; if Smith suffered corporal punishment at home, he made no mention of it. Sarah Smith apparently dispensed discipline during acute phases of her husband's illness. Though she wasted "no sentimental pity" on him, Smith recalled, his mother was not unusually harsh. His recollections emphasized her piety, gentility, and tolerance. Smith's father stands out, both in *Beseiged Patriot* and in oral reminiscences, as the "best Christian man" he ever knew. Lyman's illness "was my fortune," he said, because it allowed them to spend much time together. Perhaps the most important lesson was Lyman's admonition to "think everything out for myself."[6]

The Smith family ethic of independence meshed with the principles and practices of the Christian Church. One of the founders, Thomas Campbell, had declared that "every man must be allowed to judge for himself, as every man must bear his own judgment," and for over a century this precept was the basis for denominational action or inaction. Disciples generally opposed a "settled clergy," discouraged the title "reverend," and urged ministers like the Smiths to earn their livings outside the pulpit. Seeking to restore a pure apostolic Christianity purged of human additions, the Church was loosely structured, required few credal obligations, and contained diverse views of God and man. Members distinguished between belief in Jesus Christ, a requirement of faith, and political views, which were matters of "opinion."[7]

Objecting to denominational missionary societies, the "one man system" that allowed pastors to settle permanently, and the use of instrumental music in services, some theological conservatives seceded at the turn of the century to form the Churches of Christ. Most of the secessionists, poor and border-state Disciples, also resented the social pretensions of their "organ grinding" brethen. His own family, Smith recalled, stayed with the group that used the organ because Lyman considered eight notes no more sinful than one note on a tuning fork. This decision to remain with the theological moderates hardly denoted a decline in familial piety. On the contrary, every night the Smiths gathered in prayer around their family altar. When physically able, Lyman worshiped at the Sugar Grove Christian Church in nearby Soldier's Grove. Before turning twelve, Gerald publicly confessed his faith in Jesus, delivered a small sermon to his parents, and, much to their delight, directed his ambition toward becoming a minister.[8]

After a decade on the farm, Lyman Smith recovered sufficiently to resume selling spices and moved his family to a comfortable home in Viroqua, the seat of Vernon county. Gerald still worked hard, planting tobacco and hawking patent medicine to save money for college, but extra-curricular activities at Viroqua high school provided relief from rural isolation. He edited the yearbook, participated in sports, and debated, winning an oratory contest with a rendition of William Jennings Bryan's "Cross of Gold" speech. He promised his parents, however, never to use his eloquence, a gift from God, to make money or win public office. In retrospect, Smith characterized himself as a "naive, innocent, completely dedicated young Christian."[9]

In 1915, Smith entered Valparaiso University in Indiana. Attracting national attention as the "poor man's Harvard." Valparaiso catered to upwardly mobile midwesterners who needed to hold jobs while attending college. Smith maintained an A-minus average, specializing in public speaking and dramatics supplemented with strong doses of classics, psychology, and English literature. Outside of class, he acted in several plays, chaired the social committee, and was vice president of the YMCA. To pay for board and room—initially a closet—he washed dishes, swept floors, and waited tables. Luckily, Smith's tutor in theology, Rev. Claude Hill of the Valparaiso First Christian Church, arranged for him to serve a small congregation at Deep River, Indiana. In return for $25 monthly, the young pastor organized revivals, baptised adults, and supervised conversions; on alternate weekends, he performed the same duties at a church in Gary. Thus, he was able to graduate in less than three years with money to spare. " 'Billy Sunday' is our real evangelist," the class yearbook wrote of Smith, "Straightforward, clean, wholesome and energetic, he has the confidence of all."[10]

The five years after Smith received his Bachelor of Oratory degree in August 1917 brought increased prosperity, restless ambition, sickness, and love. His plans to attend graduate school at the University of Illinois were ruined by an attack of nephritis. After recuperating at the family farm, he began preaching (for $100 per month) in nearby Soldier's Grove, where he revitalized a weak Disciples congregation. By early 1920, he had moved to the larger Christian Church in Footville, Wisconsin. A flyer he issued promising activities "for all" revealed more self-promotion than naive dedication but it was close to the mark. He organized a vacation Bible school, a Christ Athletic Association, and a transportation network to bring farmers to services. Impressed by Smith's example, several young men decided to enter the ministry.[11]

Smith took seriously the Christian Church's mission to restore simple "New Testament" religion, and he thought prospects were bright in the early 1920s. What Disciples called "denominational churches" not only erred theologically by adopting "man-made" creeds, Smith said, but they left parishioners without "soul-satisfying" faith. These men and women, members of the Christian Church without knowing it, could be brought formally into the fold. During his first year at Footville, Smith won 125 converts, half of them from competing Protestant congregations. Furthermore, most ministers forgot that Jesus was the Savior of outsiders. Pool rooms, lodge halls, and street corners were "filled with good folks who are going to hell," Smith exclaimed in 1922. The Christian Church must bring its unique "plea" to all lost souls, including drunks, skeptics, and prostitutes.[12]

The ambitious young minister also tried to convince leading Disciples that Wisconsin offered the "Restoration movement its greatest home mission opportunity." Certainly it offered Smith a chance to develop a dramatic style and to make a name for himself. Rival clergy might be "real nice and courteous" where Disciples were strong, Smith told a church congress in 1922, "but you just try to plant a New Testament Church sometime and they'll ride you until you'll think you are a second 'man of war.'" In Wisconsin, which contained fewer than twenty-five Disciples congregations, Smith felt that he was in a "fight" requiring unconventional tactics. He not only spoke in pool rooms but leaped upon a pool table to preach the gospel. As chairman of the state Committee on Missionary Evangelism, he publicized his activities in a major Disciples publication, *Christian Standard.* In 1922, the magazine praised him for creating at Footville "one of the livest [sic] rural churches in America."[13]

While Smith was at Footville, he met Elna Sorenson, a Methodist member of a visiting singing group, whom he subsequently courted in his new Model T. On 21 June 1922, they were married in the Beloit Christian Church, where the groom had been appointed pastor in February. A sturdy woman beneath her genteel beauty, Elna was a source of emotional support throughout Smith's life. When he later emerged as a far right agitator, she also managed his finances, rebutted his critics, and accompanied him through picket lines. Their first crisis came soon after the wedding. Falling ill, apparently from exhaustion, Smith had to resign his Beloit pulpit.[14]

The illness caused only a brief delay in Smith's professional climb. He soon accepted a pulpit in the town of Kansas, Illinois, and then in December 1923 was called to the Seventh Christian Church in Indianapolis, Indiana. Disciples were strong in the region, but this largely working class church was divided and dispirited. Within two years, Smith restored morale, attracted 1,150 new members, and began raising funds for a larger building. The liberal Disciples magazine *Christian-Evangelist* noted that he became immediately an "acknowledged figure in Hoosier Discipledom," serving as president of the Marion County Sunday School Union and chairman of the General Work Committee of the Indianapolis Christian Church Union. In 1926, Smith moved to another troubled Indianapolis congregation, the University Place Christian Church near the campus of Butler University. His stirring evangelical campaigns caused membership to triple. After one such revival in 1928, a church officer declared the congregation's "love" for their remarkable pastor. Similarly impressed, Dean Frederick D. Kershner of the Butler University School of Religion served on the University Place board of elders, befriended

Smith, and praised him as the pastor who "never takes a regular vacation."[15]

While Smith moved upward professionally, the Christian Church, like evangelical Protestantism generally, was torn between theological liberals and conservatives. The unique fundamentalist controversy among Disciples centered on the question of "open membership," the conservative charge that liberals did not require baptism as a condition for church membership. Without formally seceding, most of the conservatives eventually built their own colleges, missionary societies, and assembly, the North American Christian Convention (often called the Disciples of Christ Number Two).[16]

According to Smith's subsequent recollections, he did not agree fully with either the theological liberals or conservatives during the 1920s. In 1922, he condemned the "awful" modernist assertion that Jesus was the "illegitimate son of an adulterous Mary," and throughout the decade joined most Disciples in rejecting open membership. On the other hand, he declined the label "fundamentalist" because it denoted a "dogmatic codification of belief" contrary to the Disciples' affirmation of simple, apostolic Christianity. Unlike Winrod, he remained aloof from the World Christian Fundamentals Association, considered both sides in the Scopes trial too rigid, and showed no interest in dispensationalism. This moderate stance may have reflected the teaching of Smith's mentor, Rev. Claude Hill, who deprecated controversy over higher criticism and evolution, listed social gospel novelist Charles M. Sheldon among his friends, and approvingly quoted Disciples modernist Shailer Matthews. Late in life, Smith recalled that he himself had "toyed with modernism." Apparently he was moving in a liberal direction by the late 1920s. Perhaps influenced by his friend Frederick Kershner, a *Christian-Evangelist* editor, he wrote for that magazine instead of the conservative *Christian Standard.* In 1928, Smith even told readers not to worry if their children returned from college temporarily alienated from religion.[17]

Throughout the 1920s, work in the world—and the recognition accompanying it—attracted Smith more than theological disputation. If he did consider the social gospel a theological "fad," as he recalled in 1969, he nonetheless agreed with Rev. Hill that Christians must not be "speculative, philosophic unlookers." While in Indiana, Smith sponsored charity drives, advised youth groups, and traveled widely on behalf of the National Recreation Association, urging cities to set aside land for parks and playgrounds. He also exposed miserable working conditions in factories and organized locals for the American Federation of Labor. In 1928, he preached against Alfred E. Smith's presidential candidacy. Yet he opposed the powerful Indiana Ku Klux Klan, Smith claimed years later, because his father had taught that "anything good enough to help humanity is not a secret."[18]

Despite Smith's apparent popularity and influence, he left Indianapolis in 1929 for the Kings Highway Christian Church in Shreveport, Louisiana. His subsequent explanation, that his wife had developed tuberculosis and needed a warmer climate, was plausible. Yet thwarted ambition may have played a part. Not everyone at the University Place Christian Church loved him. Rumors spread that he worked with, not against, the Klan. Some parishioners apparently resented paying for a tabernacle that Smith had built but failed to fill with his oratory. A former boarder at the Smiths, interviewed by the B'nai B'rith Anti-Defamation League in 1942, charged that the ambitious young minister had been "greedy for power and money"; other members of the congregation accused him of having vindictively damaged the parsonage before leaving.[19]

Initially, Smith was welcomed by his affluent new congregation in Louisiana. Always vulnerable to flattery from persons he considered "high toned," he enjoyed the attention of Shreveport's elite, joined two country clubs, and accepted the prevailing opinion among his parishioners that Governor Huey P. Long was a dangerous boor. Business groups, community boosters, and fellow clergymen sought his services as an orator. In 1932, he addressed both the state bankers' association and the state Federation of Labor, an organization he served as chaplain. That same year, he represented the National Recreation Association at the Olympic Games in Los Angeles. At home he often preached on radio and joined Disciples revivals throughout Louisiana. Consistent with his memories of a modernist flirtation, his ministry revealed an ecumenical aspect that would have distressed Winrod. During 1930, for example, he exchanged pulpits with Rabbi Abraham Brill at the B'nai Zion Temple, who gave a Bible to his "dear brother" Gerald L. K. Smith.[20]

Smith's self-promotion and social activism soon divided the Kings Highway Church. Some parishioners condemned his frequent absences. More important, Smith's colorful denunciations of irresponsible wealth appalled many "high-toned" men who had cultivated him; Smith, in turn, repudiated the "silk stocking crowd." While raising $200,000 for the Community Chest in 1931, he demanded that owners of three-quarters of Shreveport's wealth give three-quarters of the donations. He opposed an open shop campaign by the "throat-choking" Chamber of Commerce. Although they had been nailed to the cross, Smith told delegates to the Louisiana Federation of Labor convention in 1931, resurrection would following crucifixion. His denunciations of "coal mining peonage" reached ten million listeners over KWKH, Smith claimed, until Standard Oil interests bought the radio station. He had less patience than ever with theological disputes. When a letter to *Christian-Evangelist* chided him for calling Mary the "Bride of God," Smith asked why the magazine indulged in such "hair-splitting" instead of joining his crusade against economic exploitation. In response, Frederick Kershner belatedly praised his friend's "excellent" radio series. Also impressed, *Christian Century* applauded Smith for fighting Kings Highway conservatives to preach an "impassioned gospel of social justice."[21]

Facing strong opposition himself, Smith began to change his opinion of Huey Long. Long, he decided, needed tough tactics to challenge the "feudal lords" who ruled Louisiana from plantations or New Orleans townhouses. Indeed, Smith detected affinities between Long and the "progressive impulses" of his own father, a "Bob LaFollete man" in Wisconsin. In later years, Smith's story of his change of heart centered on Long's intervention in 1933 to prevent three rich members of the Kings Highway congregation from foreclosing mortgages on homes and the church building itself. This stylized account, reminiscent of Progressive-era autobiographies in which middle-class reformers suddenly discover the poor, should not be taken at face value. For a year, Smith tried both to applaud Long and to hold his pulpit.[22]

Kings Highway Church to Kingfish

Smith's view of Louisiana as an impoverished "feudal" barony had merit, but his comparison of Huey P. Long and Robert M. LaFollette was misleading. Long had risen rapidly to the governorship in 1928 and the United States Senate in 1932. At the same time, he transformed Louisiana politics by focusing—and sometimes relieving—the resentment and economic distress of his poor, largely rural constituency. Unlike Wisconsin under LaFollette, however, the new roads, free school books, and expanded services were not without substantial cost in liberty. Long packed commissions and courts, virtually nullified the divisions among branches of state government, built a militia larger than any other state's and used it to occupy New Orleans during the 1934 election.[23]

Along with figures as diverse as John Maynard Keynes, Alfred M.

Landon, and William Dudley Pelley, Long understood the great irony of the Depression, the spread of poverty and unemployment in the midst of abundance. Expecting Franklin D. Roosevelt to end the irony by redistributing wealth, he supported the Democratic ticket in 1932. By February 1934, however, convinced that Roosevelt had no intention of seizing the "pompous fortunes" of the rich, Long formed the Share Our Wealth Society to advance his own plan for redistribution and, ultimately, his own presidential candidacy. Furthermore, believing that Roosevelt had lied to him about economic goals, Long turned on the administration what political scientist Alan Sindler calls his "intense personalization of politics." He mocked Secretary of the Interior Harold L. Ickes (the "chinch bug of Chicago"), Secretary of Agriculture Henry A. Wallace (the "ignoramus of Iowa") and other vassals at "Prince Franklin's" court. This clowning was necessary, the self-designated "Kingfish" believed, to make politics meaningful to his poorly educated, skeptical following. Long professed to "put the truth into what I say and then . . . embellish it." His tactics outraged opponents across the political spectrum, with the left generally concurring in Raymond Gram Swing's opinion that Long was "ruthless, ambitious, and indeed plausible enough to Hitlerize America."[24]

When Gerald L. K. Smith first entered his orbit, Long had not yet broken irrevocably with the Roosevelt administration. Hence, while Pelley and Winrod were condemning the New Deal as a Jewish plot, Smith served on the parish and state Civil Works Administration committees. Suspecting that the CWA planned to cut thousands of jobs in Louisiana, Smith visited Washington in January 1934 to lobby with Harry Hopkins, head of the Federal Emergency Relief Administration, and Frances Perkins, whom he called FDR's "noble" Secretary of Labor. Long allowed Smith to use his hotel suite as a base of operation. The visiting minister joined Long in a meeting with comedian Will Rogers, a telephone conversation with Father Charles E. Coughlin, and ad hoc jaunts around the capital. After a month with the Kingfish, Smith was transformed from a mere supporter into a self-designated "hero-worshiper."[25]

Hostile publicity about Smith's trip to Washington finally prodded him from the pulpit in February 1934, but he seems to have had a job lined up with Long beforehand. The *Shreveport Times* criticized him for accompanying the senator, the *Washington Herald*, identified him as a bodyguard, and the *Shreveport Journal*, reporting one of the Kingfish's scuffles, accused Smith of participating in a "riot." Thus Smith returned to a Kings Highway congregation increasingly concerned about their church's reputation. His resignation, though conveniently timed, was nonetheless consistent with Disciples anticlericalism. Now, like Savanarola of Florence, he told a Long rally, he had left the "formal ministry" to carry on a "ministry of truth to the people" as organizer of the Share Our Wealth campaign.[26]

Smith was at least as attracted by Long's political style as by his legislative record and economic program. Long, he wrote in the *New Republic* in February 1935, was a "superman" capable of accomplishing as much as any ten men on a typical day. The Kingfish's domination of the legislature resembled the "dictatorship of the surgical theatre," where subordinates obeyed a great physician to serve the patient. Nor was he a demagogue, despite his "surface similarities." To be sure, Long "dramatized" his actions in order to win elections, but unlike mere demagogues, kept his promises afterward and governed as a statesman.[27]

This hero-worship, which involved ritual as well as the written word, outlived the hero by more than forty years. Smith liked to be seen with Long and wore his castoff suits. Opponents said that he even slept on the floor at the foot of Long's bed at night. Smith denied the allegation but, so deep was his devotion, that it was conceivable if unlikely. Until his own death, Smith praised the Kingfish as the "man I loved" more than any other.[28]

While taking no credit for bills passed in Baton Rouge or Washington, Smith, significantly, claimed a role in molding Long's dramatic style. Certainly both men, raised in solid middle-class families, shared a common approach to their "hillbilly" constituency. They spoke for poor whites and pretended to speak like them, but never in their own minds identified with them. Because the "child-minded" majority rarely understood issues, Smith explained years later, they could be mobilized only by dramatizing issues and rewarding loyalty. Accordingly, Share Our Wealth was the "red bicycle in front of the Christmas tree."[29]

The Share Our Wealth plan centered around a guaranteed annual income. Every family would receive a "homestead allowance . . . of not less than one-third the average family wealth of the country." No personal estate could exceed 100 to 300 times the average family stake (an estimated $1.5 to $5 million), and the federal government would expropriate all income above $1 million per year. These levies would also support veterans' bonuses, college educations for capable students, and "adequate" pensions for citizens over sixty. (The word "adequate" aided recruitment, Smith explained, because every aged person imagined his own figure.) In the shorter run, a would-be wealth sharer received a copy of Long's autobiography, *Every Man a King*, a subscription to his newspaper, *American Progress*, and directions for forming a local chapter.[30]

New Dealers, Liberty Leaguers, Socialists, and Communists agreed that Share Our Wealth was infeasible, even absurd. Yet, as Raymond Gram Swing observed, simplicity was one secret of its success. Long neither used sinister-sounding socialist concepts nor planned complex alphabetical agencies. Quoting Thomas Jefferson, Abraham Lincoln, Robert E. Lee, and the Bible, he emphasized that Share Our Wealth was consistent with (indeed, demanded by) the "law of God" and the best American traditions.[31]

A complementary factor in the Share Our Wealth movement's spread was Smith's work as national organizer. Almost six feet tall with wavy reddish-brown hair, a large beak nose, blue eyes, and a powerful voice, he boasted that his "210 pounds of fighting Louisiana flesh" cut an impressive figure on the stump. Privately, and particularly among reporters, he could be engaging. Only Swing went so far as to call him "kindly," but even H. L. Mencken and F. Raymond Daniell of the *New York Times* were charmed by Smith's roguish admission that his platform histronics constituted a studied performance. A favorite technique was to ask who in the audience owned four "good suits of clothes, coats and pants to match," or two pairs of shoes, or three sets of underwear with "all the buttons on." Whatever the item, few hands rose to confirm ownership. Then Smith preached on this "text": J. P. Morgan possessed copious apparel, including shoes and underwear, but poor men were "broke, busted," and crushed beneath the "heel of capital and vested interests." Indeed, such "contemptible hoarders" as Morgan, Andrew Mellon, and Bernard Baruch allowed the Depression to continue. Vigorous gestures accompanied the performance. Smith took pride in his muscles and his willingness to use them. Favoring sexual allusions to underscore his masculinity, he derided "caponized" clergy and "pimps" in the press corps. Also stressing his "he-man" qualities, Smith told crowds that organizing Share Our Wealth clubs was dangerous business. Yet he carried no gun. "Here is my 'gat,'" he added, holding up a Bible. "They could shoot me down on this platform tonight."[32]

The danger was not entirely fanciful. In upstate Louisiana, Smith wrestled a gun away from a potential assassin. On another occasion, an anti-Long mob prevented his appearance in Baton Rouge. Elsewhere, he dispersed angry Georgians by asking who dared to touch a "man of God." Customarily surrounded by supporters, however, he turned heckling to advantage. At least once Smith grabbed a critic's collar, and held him, shaking him at appropriate moments during the speech. Until his late middle age, Smith intermittently used his physical presence to intimidate opponents.[33]

Starting with Share Our Wealth's organizational meeting at Shreveport in March 1934, *American Progress* regularly reported that "Dr. Smith" was drawing overflow crowds. Within a year, the newspaper claimed 4,600,000 Share Our Wealth members. The figure was exaggerated and affiliation required little more than a desire to share somebody else's wealth, but the group's political potential was clear, both to Long and President Roosevelt.[34]

Despite his strong efforts on behalf of Share Our Wealth, both Smith's relationship with Long and his influence within the Louisiana hierarchy remained uncertain. Smith always maintained that Long respected him alone and predicted that other aides would probably go to prison. Yet Smith, like most of Long's subordinates, was obliged to run trivial errands, including trips to the laundry with dirty shirts. According to the recollections of his rivals, Long considered firing Smith in 1935. Certainly Robert Maestri and Seymour Weiss, two of Long's most important financial backers, hoped that he would be sent packing.[35]

Such internecine conflicts strained but never split the organization while the Kingfish could return from Washington to set matters straight. During one of these trips, he was shot by Dr. Carl Austin Weiss and died two days later, on 10 September 1935. The next day, at the request of Long's father and widow, Smith preached to one-hundred-fifty-thousand mourners at the open air funeral in Baton Rouge. Thus he received extensive publicity as a national figure in his own right, the probable heir to the Share Our Wealth following. Until his last days, Smith distributed copies of his eulogy to document—and dramatize—his connection with Long.[36]

Although Smith's eulogy was not quite the "political speech for himself" that Long's son Russell recalled, it did combine prayer for the deceased with exhortations to continue the martyr's program. Long, Smith said, had felt for the poor an affection "as everlasting as the soul." This humanitarianism was combined with political genius. "Drama was his natural art," Smith said, stressing a favorite theme, and Long had become a "symbol of the mass mind." Perhaps God had permitted his "dramatic" death to light the way for further reform. Indeed, his spirit would not rest "as long as hungry bodies cry for food, as long as lean human frames stand naked, as long as homeless wretches haunt this land of plenty." Disclaiming political ambitions, Smith charged the mourners to "Take up the torch, complete the task, subdue selfish ambition, sacrifice for the sake of victory."[37]

Smith took up the torch in order to advance both his own career and the Share Our Wealth program. He began by attributing Long's "mysterious death" to the "most subtle plot in American history." In rapid succession during September 1935, he urged Speaker of the House James F. Byrnes to begin an investigation, refused to testify at a Louisiana inquest (because, he said, the district attorney had been one of the "co-plotters"), accused federal appointees of participating in the conspiracy, and concluded that President Roosevelt had at least acquiesced in Long's assassination. Shoring up his constituency while making headlines, Smith circularized Share Our Wealth members in Louisiana, assuring them that state officials stood "together as one man" behind Long's policies.[38]

At the same time, Smith knew that Long's political heirs were standing apart as three factions. Virtually a faction unto himself, Smith continued to oppose the New Deal. Robert Maestri and Seymour Weiss, under investigation for tax evasion by the Internal Revenue Service, wanted to make peace with the Roosevelt administration. Finally, upcountry Longites looked to Governor O. K. Allen, Long's docile successor in Baton Rouge, and State Senator James Noe, both of whom sympathized with Share Our Wealth.[39]

In late 1935, Smith's claim to leadership was literally based on paper—the Share Our Wealth membership lists—but he neither possessed them nor knew where they were. Nevertheless, with bravado worthy of Long, Smith endorsed Noe for governor and Public Service Commissioner Wade O. Martin, Sr., for United States senator, having convinced Martin that he would make a fine administrative assistant. When Maestri, Weiss, and Allen designated a rival slate, Smith capitulated, he said, in order to save the Long organization's "life." Noe believed, however, that the Share Our Wealth director switched sides in order to protect his $600 weekly salary. In November, the factions compromised on a slate headed by Judge Richard W. Leche for governor and Allen J. Ellender, Speaker of the Louisiana House of Representatives, for senator. Smith pronounced this ticket "in the spirit" of the Kingfish and Share Our Wealh, but was allowed small part in the successful primary campaign. By early 1936, Leche had arranged a détente with the White House, and Smith, cut from the payroll, was obliged to exercise his talents elsewhere."[40]

Applying Long's Lessons: 1936–1941

Smith's talents were considerable. Unlike Winrod, who remained a political innocent to the day he died, Smith had learned "some of the most valuable lessons of life" from Huey Long, one of the greatest modern campaigners. The most obvious inheritance was a heightened sense of showmanship. Smith let a shock of hair fall over his forehead as his mentor had done. He, too, invented nicknames for such opponents as Harold Ickes ("the itch") and Henry Wallace ("secretary of swine assassination."). And both men embellished issues to make them vivid, to "dramatize" them, as Smith liked to say.[41]

Second, the Long years affected Smith's perspective on issues, though the nature of that influence is harder to isolate. With the crucial exception of public attacks on "organized Jewry" that began to appear during World War II, the major motifs of his career surfaced before Smith left Louisiana. As Share Our Wealth organizer, he attacked concentrated wealth, concurred in Long's view that bankers were "our constant rulers," and typically chided the same villains: Mellon, Baruch, and Morgan. Perhaps more than Long, he believed that financiers operated a conscious conspiracy. Smith's view of Long's assassination clearly revealed his affinity for conspiratorial interpretations, which would grow in fits and starts during the next four decades.[42]

For Long and Smith, the New Deal constituted an un-American autocracy. The Kingfish compared New Deal tickets to "other tickets in Moscow," and his newspaper, *American Progress*, accused the president of building a form of Communism worse than the Soviet version because a "handful of Roosevelts, Astors, Rockefellers, and Morgans" remained in control. Smith not only agreed with these sentiments but further embellished them. During the previous four years, he recalled to H. L. Mencken in 1939, there had not been a

> single day that I have not done my good deed; namely, make a speech, write a letter, or in some form or other expose, reveal, or attack the Roosevelt New Deal conspiracy. This obsession (if that is what some people would choose to call it) has kept burning in my heart a consistent and never fading enthusiasm.[43]

Third, affected by Long's "intense personalization of politics" (to recall Alan Sindler's phrase), Smith viewed his conflict with Roosevelt in personal terms. The Kingfish disliked FDR because "he lied to me" about redistributing wealth. Smith, regarding the president as a silent partner in Long's murder, could hardly contain his anger when discussing that man; on one such occasion, the *New York Times* reported, he paced the room, chewing matches, striking them, and throwing the burnt sticks at an ashtray.[44]

Between 1936 and 1941 Smith's strategy was molded by these legacies from the Kingfish, by his failure to hold a base in Louisiana, and by his feeling that, after Long's death, he was "alone in the world . . . alone in capital letters." Unwilling to drop back into obscurity, Smith explained later, he had "opportunized on all forums available." The first forum, a "grassroots" convention in January 1936, sponsored by Georgia Governor Eugene Talmadge, suggested how far from Share Our Wealth Smith's opportunizing might lead. He endorsed Talmadge, a racist fiscal conservative, in the Georgia presidential primary and pledged to "drive that cripple from the White House." Talmadge quickly lost both the primary and his tolerance for Smith.[45]

Dr. Francis Townsend proved a firmer ally. Townsend's organization, the Old Age Revolving Pension Plan, Ltd. (OARP), advocated a $200 monthly grant to everyone over sixty. The claim of four million adherents was exaggerated, but Townsend's following was large enough to worry legislators from both parties as well as the Roosevelt administration. An investigation begun by the House of Representatives in March 1936 revealed inconsistency, ineptitude, and economic ignorance within OARP, but no gross mismanagement or corruption. Nonetheless, the investigators badgered Townsend and cast unwarranted doubt on his honesty.[46]

Smith, seated in the audience, decided that a "fine old man" was being persecuted by "shysters." He had met Townsend previously, mistakenly believing that OARP had acquired the Share Our Wealth membership lists. Now he promised both ideological and physical support. When Townsend abruptly walked out of the "inquisition" on 21 May 1936, Smith let out a yell, moved to his side, and pushed him through the crowd to an exit. In the process, as Townsend later recalled, Smith grinned at the congressional committee "with joyous malevolence."[47]

The frail, sixty-nine-year-old physician and the husky, thirty-eight-year-old minister made an odd-looking pair, but they had much in common. Townsend, too, hated Roosevelt, feared New Deal "bureaucracy," and wanted to redistribute wealth without restructuring capitalism. And he valued showmanship, having endorsed a $200 monthly pension because that figure "had drama." Soon Smith was calling Townsend a second Moses. In turn, Townsend suggested Smith as a presidential possibility, appointed him to the OARP board of directors, and joined him in seeking a "bloodless revolution . . . expressed in ballots" to rescue the United States from Roosevelt's "tyranny." During the spring and summer of 1936, they toured together from Maine to the Rose Bowl. Responding partly to Smith's suggestion that his movement needed a jauntier image, Townsend encouraged him to create a young people's auxiliary and changed OARP's name to the more ecumenical Townsend National Recovery Plan (TNRP). Much of Smith's appeal for Townsend was his youthful willingness to "lick" enemies of the American way. Townsend also mistakenly believed that the erstwhile Share Our Wealth organizer represented a large constituency, an impression Smith cultivated. Yet scholars who write that Smith virtually mesmerized a feeble old man yield to stereotypes about age that the TNRP founder, to his credit, tried to dispel. To similar allegations in 1936, Townsend replied that he had been following "my own advice for a good many years."[48]

Smith and Townsend used each other, and both cautiously made common cause with Father Charles E. Coughlin, who also wanted to defeat Roosevelt in 1936. Their Union Party, Coughlin's instrument in fact, then used Representative William Lemke (Rep.-N.D.) as a presidential candidate.[49]

The familiar story of this tenuous coalition requires no repetition here, but Smith's role needs reconsideration. As the disciple of Long, a practical politician who "liked to win," Smith doubted the value of symbolic protests. When his first choice, Senator William E. Borah (Rep.-Id.) declined to run for president, he considered Lemke a colorless substitute. Therefore Smith, like Long, looked beyond 1936. Either a Roosevelt or Landon administration would end in chaos, Smith predicted, and he had a strategy for the crisis: "I want to get as many people as I can now so that when chaos comes, I'll be a leader."[50]

Meanwhile, Smith opportunized on Townsendite and Union Party forums. On 15 July, opening day of the TNRP national convention in Cleveland, he told 11,000 delegates that the United States faced a choice between the New Deal "red flag or the stars and stripes." Describing an alleged plot by eight hundred "plants" to disrupt the session, he asked who would fight to hang the troublemakers; every hand went up. Seated in the press gallery, his mouth open and glasses slipping from his nose, H. L. Mencken concluded that he was watching the "damnest orator ever heard on this or any other earth." Smith cited the accolade for the next forty years, and Mencken affirmed it until his own death.[51]

Other witnesses were appalled. The delegates, prodded by New Dealers in the ranks, barred formal endorsement of any presidential candidate and issued invitations to all of them except Communist Earl Browder. Socialist Norman Thomas braved their wrath to say that the Townsend plan could no more end the Depression than cough drops cured tuberculosis. Representative Lemke, a lukewarm supporter of the scheme, arrived to receive personal—as opposed to institutional—endorsements from Townsend and Smith.[52]

Division among Townsendites did not deter Smith from a second virtuoso performance at the final convention session on July 19. After delegates rejected his feigned offer to "soft pedal," he led them through a full range of emotions. How could the United States be a "land of too much," he asked, dramatizing the Depression's irony, when hundreds of thousands of children never tasted milk? When New Dealers dumped "milk in the sewer, they plow under your babies." Yet Alfred M. Landon, the Republican nominee dominated by Wall Street and William Randolph Hearst, was no better. As America faced a choice between Scripture and "brain trust cake . . . baked in Moscow," Smith felt honored to vote for William Lemke, the "only real Democrat" running for president. Toward the end, Smith noted a newspaper story comparing Norman Thomas before the Townsendites to an enemy of Santa Claus among children. The United States, he insisted, must continue to believe in "Santa Claus, Christmas trees, Easter bunny, the Holy Bible, and the Townsend plan." The audience, already standing, cheered and waved. Smith calmed them with the Lord's Prayer.[53]

This performance, probably the oratorical peak of Smith's career, was followed by steady deterioration of the Union Party alliance. Speaking with Father Coughlin's reluctant permission at the National Union for Social Justice convention in August, Smith candidly admitted that the "election to me is only an incident." As if to underscore the point, he disdained the Union Party presidential nominee. Even while offering his endorsement in Cleveland, he had vowed to chop off Lemke's "dad-gum head" if he deviated "one-eighth of an inch" from the Townsend platform. Thereafter, they appeared together at best politely; at worst, Smith interrupted Lemke to offer advice on platform technique.[54]

Touring solo during the fall, Smith promoted economic redistribution, attacked presidential candidates, demanded national regeneration, cultivated newspapermen, and appeared constantly on the front pages. The United States must "democratize wealth without destroying the capitalist system." Landon and Roosevelt were weak as well as unwise, tools respectively of Wall Street and "Reds." Indeed, the whole country was "flabby." To reconstitute American vigor, Smith proposed free universities for students who passed physical as well as mental tests, and claimed that he was already organizing Union Party youth batallions filled with sturdy "green boys"; no "parlor pinks," "campus intellectuals," or "sophisticates" need apply. No Disciple of Christ had received as much publicity as Smith since the days of James A. Garfield and Champ Clark, commented Frederick Kershner in *Christian-Evangelist.*[55]

At the same time, Smith continued to distinguish himself from the unsophisticated masses whom he mobilized. Addressing the Townsend convention, he had demanded applause or silence on cue because "I'm running this proposition." During other harangues, as if to underscore that his dramatizations were not to be taken literally by worldly men, he winked at journalists and asked, "How am I doing?" Smith's life-long pride in his brief connection with Mencken, an association unimaginable for Winrod, highlighted his fascination with worldliness.[56]

The 1936 campaign trail ended inauspiciously in Smith's "adopted city" of New Orleans, where the state Democratic organization, now loyal to Roosevelt, falsely accused him of changing his name from Schmidt and plagarizing Huey Long's funeral oration, while also saying, with greater plausibility, that he had flirted with the Silver Shirts and tried to profit from Share Our Wealth. On election eve, he roused an audience of 70,000 by denouncing the "Second Louisiana Purchase" (a term borrowed from columnist Westbrook Pegler to describe the rapprochement between the Leche and Roosevelt administrations). This address, broadcast statewide at Smith's expense, led to his arrest for disturbing the peace. Blaming his predicament on New Orleans Mayor Robert Maestri, he refused bail and spent two days in jail before charges were dropped.[57]

Incarceration, though embarrassing, was less damaging to Smith's reputation than the growing suspicion that he was an anti-Semitic native fascist. His demagoguery, Herbert Harris wrote, gave "to Sinclair Lewis's *It Can Happen Here* a note of terrible and authentic prophecy." According to journalists Harris, Heywood Broun, and Harnett Kane, Smith had cast slurs on Jews and favored a boycott of Jewish merchants in New Orleans.[58]

Smith fueled these suspicions by announcing on 20 October 1936 that he planned a "vigorously nationalistic" organization opposed to collectivism. Rev. Clinton Wunder, a deposed Townsend advisor who chaired the National Pension Committee for Roosevelt, asked, "Has he made a deal with Hitler?" Dr. Townsend himself announced that Smith, earlier dropped from the TNRP board, now had "no connection whatsoever with our organization." Smith responded that he could not be fired because he had already quit, reiterated his support for old-fashioned Americanism, and denounced the "libel" that he was a fascist.[59]

"The 'Lunatic Fringe,'" a *March of Time* newsreel focusing on

Smith during late 1936, permanently damaged his reputation. In a striking sequence, he stands before a mirror and (as narrator Westbrook Van Voorhis portentiously announces) "schools his booming voice in the gospel of discontent." Convinced by director Jack Glenn to exhort while cameras rolled, Smith appears repeating his favorite lines, including "I see chaos approaching" and "God, let me be a rabble-rouser." The *March of Time* kept open the possibility that Smith was merely a "political windbag" who grew rich from Share Our Wealth, orated in the shower, and interrupted exhortations to ask reporters, "Wasn't that a good one?" Yet the dominant mood was sinister. The newsreel intersperses clips of Hitler and Mussolini with Smith nervously striking matches and staring into the flames. Later, as his audience raises hands high, Smith is credited with inspiring the first appearance in America of the fascist salute. "In Gerald Smith's sweating, bombastic oratory," Van Voorhis declares, "serious commentators see the making of a fascist dictator."[60]

Smith watched "The 'Lunatic Fringe'" at Radio City Music Hall, where a fellow viewer, meeting him in the lobby afterward, screamed with horror. His reputation as a fascist continued to spread across the country, some speaking engagements were cancelled, and the German-American Bund and native anti-Semites sought him out. Smith had been undone by his own vanity as well as by *March of Time*'s customary sensationalism. In 1939, however, he belatedly filed a $5 million libel judgment against Time, Incorporated, and others responsible for "The 'Lunatic Fringe.'" Not only did this film make him look like a "crackpot" and "Jew-baiter," his suit argued, but it subjected him to unsolicited approaches from "sponsors of Hitlerism and Jew-baiting." Aware that *March of Time* "news" footage was often staged, Smith's lawyers, one of whom was Jewish, said that the supposed first fascist salute in America was probably a response to the production crew's question, "How many of you want coffee?" The suit was settled out of court for one dollar, but this symbolic victory hardly dented Smith's image as a native fascist and anti-Semite.[61]

Although Smith qualified as an accomplished demagogue by the mid-1930s, it is difficult to determine how bigoted he was. Proud that "God made me a rabble-rouser," he nonetheless considered himself devoid of racial or religious prejudice. In February 1934, for instance, he called the allegation of anti-Semitism the "dirtiest" charge ever leveled against a "friend" of Jews. Denying that he had supported the Ku Klux Klan, Smith took partial credit for Huey Long's attack on Imperial Wizard Hiram Wesley Evans. Smith explained his brief association with the Silver Shirts by saying that Pelley, attempting to exploit his reputation, had sent an unsolicited membership card; after encouraging Pelley to "reveal his full hand," he had repudiated the group in a hand-written letter. During 1936, rumors of Smith's anti-Semitism reached the B'nai B'rith Anti-Defamation League, but an observer dispatched by Midwestern Director Richard Gutstadt gave him a clean bill of health.[62]

Nevertheless, the journalistic reports that Smith privately denigrated Jews are plausible, especially in light of his other attitudes. While professing friendship for hungry blacks, he also told dialect stories about "Mistah Bones," segregated "niggahs" from "white folk" at southern Share Our Wealth rallies, and cooperated with the racist Eugene Talmadge. He admitted having shared the anti-Catholic bias "characteristic of Protestants" during the 1920s, when he preached against Alfred E. Smith. It would have been almost impossible, therefore, for him to escape totally the anti-Jewish prejudice widespread among Americans from urban slums to the State Department. At a Christian Church congress in 1922, Smith told a joke about "Abie" and "Isaac" which, though devoid of malice, still stereotyped Jews as financial operators. In short, even if the evidence is fragmentary and mostly hearsay, we can infer that Smith during the mid-1930s accepted some sort of "polite" anti-Semitism, a foundation on which he later built sweeping indictments of the "international Jew."[63]

On 30 April 1937, four months after Lemke received less than five percent of the vote, Smith launched his nationalist organization, the Committee of One Million. The Committee, according to its letterhead and its founder's declarations, was "non-partisan," "non-racial," and "non-sectarian." In October, he arranged to deliver twenty-six Sunday radio talks over a forty-eight station network originally assembled by Father Coughlin. Although the cost was substantial ($96,000), Smith boasted that four hundred business leaders had pledged one percent of their income to his cause.[64]

Data on Smith's finances are skimpy, but because he was closer than Pelley and Winrod to the political mainstream during the late 1930s he did receive notable support from big businessmen. The Committee of One Million, he recalled, received donations from J. Howard Pew, Lewis H. Brown, and Axtel Biles, presidents respectively of Sun Oil, Johns-Manville, and the American Petroleum Institute. American Civil Liberties Union General Counsel Morris L. Ernst, who informally monitored the far right for President Roosevelt, reported to the White House that Smith's contributors also included the heads of several middle-size oil companies, including Quaker State, Penzoil, and Kendall Refining. At least one supporter bore an impressive pedigree: John Vernon Bouvier, honorary president of the Sons of the American Revolution, invited Smith to address socially prominent New Yorkers at Southampton, Long Island. These affluent angels had no desire to share their own wealth, Smith recalled, but they needed someone to keep "in tow" the "wild bunch of people" unsettled by the Depression. Smith "opportunized" on the situation; undoubtedly, too, he enjoyed the attention of affluent executives and socialites.[65]

This alliance lasted no longer than its predecessors. While Smith wanted big businessmen to subsidize his barnstorming, they wanted to build a national organization. In late 1937, Patrick Powers, New York organizer of the Committee of One Million, sued for a portion of the $11,000 treasury and threatened to release the names of contributors. The "shortsighted . . . magnates," as Smith characterized his backers, withdrew their support to avoid publicity. In retrospect, he said that Powers's "providential" act of blackmail had saved him from the "political brothel" run by the New York Republican establishment.[66]

At the time, however, Smith again felt alone, barred from doors "ordinarily open to the conventional moron." Once again, eloquence served as defense against isolation. If he failed to "get" his audience within five minutes, Smith explained to Mencken, "they might get me in the next five." He spoke to local clubs and veterans organizations, trying to win over "the people," a "much more reliable" source of funds than the business elite had been. Some prestigious doors remained open, however. In January 1939 Smith addressed the New York Advertising Club, where radio commentator Lowell Thomas introduced him as the "most fearless and dynamic orator in America." There he met Merwin K. Hart, head of both Utica Mutual Life Insurance and the New York Economic Council, a conservative lobby, who subsequently supported his activities.[67]

Soon Smith got his audience. Lured by midwestern hostility to Roosevelt, by the prospect of inheriting Father Coughlin's constituency, and by WJR, a powerful radio station owned by an enemy of the New Deal, he had settled in Detroit by 1939. In January of that year one of his rallies filled all 23,000 seats in Detroit's Olympic Stadium. A stream of contributions, usually small sums sent by mail or collected after speeches, paid the salaries of Smith ($6,500 in 1944); Elna, who doubled as his secretary; and a staff exceding twenty in 1942. Help still came from some "magnates," including automakers Horace and John Dodge, W. C. Durant, and Ransom E. Olds. In addition to salaries, donations covered a suite of offices and radio time over WJR. At roughly $400 per broadcast, Smith spoke one, twice, or three times weekly between 1939 and 1942.[68]

From 1939 to 1941, Smith applauded from afar as several Louisiana enemies, including Governor Richard Leche, were sentenced to federal prison for graft; Assistant Attorney General O. John Rogge, who supervised the investigation, found no evidence that Smith had joined in the corruption. In 1940, the erstwhile Share Our Wealth organizer campaigned for Huey Long's brother Earl, an unsuccessful candidate for governor, and was rewarded, he remembered, with the page from New Orleans police files recording his arrest four years earlier.[69]

Secure in Michigan, Smith claimed two million followers and the "balance of power" in the Midwest. The exaggeration was typical. Nevertheless, until the middle of World War II, his supporters were sufficiently numerous to give Smith some political influence as well as a secure income.[70]

Dangerous Enemies and Prominent Friends

Smith's critics, noting his easy transitions from ally to ally and his theatrical efforts to capture an audience, often doubted his commitment to anything beyond self-aggrandizement. Discounting his indignant response—that there was not "one cynical corpuscle" in his body—it must be recognized that Smith's self-confessed "opportunizing" promoted a cause as well as a career. Interwoven with his showmanship was a core of belief that, with some shifts in emphasis, remained constant from the mid-1930s until the mid-1940s. Franklin D. Roosevelt headed his list of the country's "dangerous enemies," and his arguments against the New Deal, if not his style of presentation, were commonplace, largely consisting of gleanings from Roosevelt's prominent foes, including Alfred E. Smith, Martin Dies, Hugh Johnson (after he left the NRA), and Thomas E. Dewey (before he yielded to internationalism).[71]

Until the mid-1940s, Smith considered the Depression neither a product of President Hoover's ineptitude nor, as Pelley and Winrod supposed, the result of Jewish machinations. Rather, it was a "natural reaction" to the waste of World War I and the excesses of the 1920s. The Democrats had seemed to offer a way out in 1932, but in forsaking his party platform Roosevelt adopted measures "more extreme" than those proposed by the Socialists. Moreover, to create a personal constitutency in the "emotionally frustrated" nation, FDR "crooned" on the radio more skillfully than Bing Crosby. This crooning concealed FDR's politicization of relief, reliance on "pinks," and support of bosses like Governor Richard Leche.[72]

Smith related his specific charges to a central theme: Roosevelt was making an unprecedented bid for "dictatorial power." FDR tried to appoint a "rubber stamp" Supreme Court in 1937 and attempted to purge "eminent" members of Congress one year later. To dramatize the "cancerous" paralysis of the New Deal planned economy, Smith portrayed the farmer "managed" by bureaucrats and the tailor arrested for charging less to press pants than the NRA code allowed. Distorting FDR's fitful support of national health care, Smith envisioned incipient "medical regimentation"; Democratic appointees would replace distinguished physicians, play politics with "anesthetics, the birth of our little children, the physical ailments of our mothers and fathers," and feed community gossip with "intimate details" from private records. If the New Dealers regimented doctors, Smith warned, they could also imprison Christian clergy.[73]

Like most hostile and many friendly commentators, Smith saw affinities between the New Deal and concurrent developments in Europe. Despite a spreading reputation as an extremist, he defined himself as a true liberal embattled by alien forces on the fringes. While Pelley and Winrod respectively rooted Communism in racial instincts and religious heresy, Smith, a veteran of rough-and-tumble politics in Louisiana, stressed the influence of greed and ambition. Marxism, which purported to unmask ideological rationalizations by a ruling class, was itself a cover for racketeering. Smith's Marx thought

> that if you could not believe in God, then overthrow God; that if you could not obey the Church, then overthrow the Church; that if you could not make money, then slaughter those who have made money. . . . Establish a society that not only consents to inferiority, but makes the inferior dictator.

Nazism was "practically the same thing" as Communism, Smith said, propounding a simplistic version of the theory of totalitarianism circulating during the 1930s. Adolf Hitler rose to power by promising a better collectivism than the Russian brand. Not surprisingly, therefore, Hitler and Stalin jointly invaded Poland in 1939. While Soviet armies "liquidated" Christians, Nazi troops "hounded" Polish Jews.[74]

Even before World War II made dissociation prudent, Smith condemned the "crazy butcher Hitler" and his followers in the German-American Bund. The Bund meeting at Madison Square Garden in 1939 to mark George Washington's birthday was a "crime." But Americans were not deceived. They knew that "Hitlerism," instead of implementing Washington's ideals, afflicted Germany with "Christian persecution, Jewish persecution, and paganistic tyranny."[75]

Unlike Nazi Germany, the Soviet Union, and other European nations, the United States was the "greatest place . . . outside of heaven itself," Smith exclaimed. In return for "faithful adoration," God had blessed Americans with freedom, abundance, and a "class-less society" which allowed immigrants to become "giants." Yet, for twenty-five years the nation had been menaced by subversives whose ideas "originated in the very lands . . . our fathers sought to escape." By the late 1930s, Smith estimated, one million propagandists used alien words like "proletariat" and "bourgeoisie" to promote civil war. Both Communist and Nazi sympathizers wanted to replace "rugged individuality" with "efficient regimentation."[76]

The New Deal, Smith said, borrowed Nazi techniques and Communist ideology. While accusing Roosevelt of trying to absorb opposition in "true Hitlerian fashion," he was much more concerned with the administration's opening to the left. More circumspect during the late 1930s than he had been at the Townsend convention in 1936, Smith claimed to restrict the label Communist to party members. Yet it was his prerogative to "interpret the associations" of fellow travelers, and Roosevelt's associations were damning. The president recognized Russia, hired brain trusters favorable to Soviet planning, allowed the Department of Labor to work in "close harmony" with Communists, and supported legislation, including the Agricultural Adjustment Act, based on Marxist theories. Eleanor Roosevelt entertained unspecified "known communist organizers" at the White House, and Attorney General Robert H. Jackson belonged to a party front, the National Lawyers Guild. Borrowing statistics from Representative Dies and the House Committee on Un-American Activities, Smith added that 2,500 fellow travelers inhabited the Washington bureaucracy. Roosevelt and his advisors were not Communists, he summarized, but radicalism in general and Communism in particular prospered under their patronage.[77]

In addition to infiltrating the government, Communists organized fronts and named them, Smith complained, after "everybody from Jesus Christ to Abraham Lincoln." His accounts of "fronts," sometimes lurid and always sweeping, ranged from Communist dominated groups, including the American League for Peace and Democracy, to organizations like the American Civil Liberties Union, in which Communists exerted little influence. Ever fond of sexual innuendo, Smith played up the venerable theme associating Communism with loose living. Party leaders, he said, used women to lure soldiers into front groups. Nor was Smith's wrath confined to Stalinists. In 1937 he said that John Dewey, then investigating the Moscow purges, was "Trotsky's main man up here."[78]

The effort by the Congress of Industrial Organizations to "capture" the nation's basic industries worried Smith especially. He thought that the CIO had begun as a "sincere attempt" to organize workers and admired CIO President John L. Lewis. Yet he could not forgive Lewis, whose capacity to "opportunize" exceeded his own, for cooperating with Communists. Smith's list of "reds" operating "right at the top" of the CIO was typically indiscriminate, including anti-Communist liberals and socialists as well as Communist party members and fellow travelers. In his litany, for example, Sidney Hillman, the pro–New Deal president of the Amalgamated Clothing Workers, appeared as an "intimate" of Lenin. Borrowing an allegation from AFL President William Green, Smith accused Lewis of decorating his study with Stalin's picture.[79]

While Pelley and Winrod fulminated against the CIO from afar, Smith began a campaign in 1937 to "beat Lewis and his radical crowd in a headon fight." His sometime sponsors among the "magnates" usually got their money's worth. In April 1938, for example, after he addressed Johns-Manville employees on behalf of the company union, they not only repudiated the CIO in a National Labor Relations Board election, but destroyed the local CIO headquarters. Four months later, he attacked the CIO before an audience of 20,000 in Akron, Ohio; if he had arrived two years earlier, he boasted to Mencken, John L. Lewis "couldn't have gotten inside the town." Instead of apologizing for tough tactics, Smith bragged that "soft-gloved boys" must "realize that when the cattle stampede it takes cowboys not pansies to turn the herd."[80]

A Michigan resident, Smith particularly disliked the United Auto Workers. He surmised that their sit-down strikes in 1937 had been directed from the Kremlin, perhaps by Stalin himself. Certainly the UAW leaders included Communists, but Smith exaggerated their influence, underestimated grassroots militancy, and misconstrued divisions within the union. During the complex struggle for control in 1938–39, he became the de facto ally of UAW President Homer Martin, a former Baptist preacher whose incongruous supporters also included Coughlinites and Lovestoneite Communists. There was no "extended intimacy" with Martin, Smith later recalled, because he was not "bright enough to collaborate with anybody on anything important." Nevertheless, Smith repeated the familiar charge that

Martin's smarter rival, Walter Reuther, had studied "radical organization" in Moscow.[81]

In Smith's own mind, there was no conflict between organizing for the AFL (thereby enraging the "country club set") during the early 1930s and riding herd on the CIO (thereby serving magnates) later in the decade. He still asked God to bless both collective bargaining and the worker's right "to be paid well under good working conditions." Yet fear of "CIO Communism" drove him to repudiate these prerogatives in practice while honoring them rhetorically. The platform Smith prepared to guide his followers during the 1940 presidential campaign proposed barring aliens from union offices, removing "radicals" from the National Labor Relations Board, and developing procedures to prevent "riots, strikes, bloodshed, and prolonged idleness."[82]

This platform, shrewder and more specific than any composed by Pelley or Winrod, also demanded lower taxes, reduction of the national debt, limitation of federal power, and restoration of authority to states and local communities. Economic relief, though necessary, must not be administered by a "political bureaucracy." Government at all levels should be free from subversion. Accordingly, the president elected in 1940 must fire every "red" and "pink," Congress must continue the Committee on Un-American Activities under its courageous chairman, Martin Dies, and police departments must observe Communists and "Hitlerites" on the local level. In addition, Smith demanded loyalty oaths for teachers and, notwithstanding "technical rules," summary dismissal of Communists employed in industry.[83]

Despite his impatience with "technical rules," Smith did not consider himself an enemy of civil liberties. Sometimes, confident that he represented majority opinion, he favored "full" exercise of free speech by rival agitators, as long as their clandestine goals were exposed. More often, he said that the First Amendment guaranteed "free speech to all good Americans"; it did not permit the Communist Earl Browder or *Bundesleiter* Fritz Kuhn to advocate destruction of republican government. Smith wanted to replicate on a larger scale the deportations of 1919–20. This program would make available two million jobs to native-born citizens and those immigrants who loved the American flag instead of the swastika or hammer and sickle.[84]

Significantly, Smith's platform for 1940 also demanded the release of business from the New Deal "chamber of torture." Thus, freed from bureaucratic regulation, creative industrialists would restore prosperity. Smith's alliance with big business, conceived in opportunism and vanity, helped to erode the anti-capitalist features of his program. While he continued after 1936 to condemn monopoly and lament the demise of Share Our Wealth, his emphasis shifted. Instead of a passionate advocate of redistributed income, by 1940 he was primarily a foe of subversion.[85]

This shift facilitated alliances with Republicans and conservative Democrats who shared Smith's low opinion of Roosevelt. In 1938, he supported Governor Martin Davey of Ohio, an anti–New Deal Democrat who had used the national guard against steel strikers. After Davey lost the Democratic primary, Smith shifted his allegiance to Republican gubernatorial nominee John Bricker, the winner in November. For his services on the stump, Morris Ernst reported to the White House, Smith received $12,000 and $8,000 respectively from the Democratic and Republican state committees. Also respecting Smith's influence, Representative Roy O. Woodruff (Rep.-Mich.), placed his speeches in the *Congressional Record.* So did Representative Clare Hoffman (Rep.-Mich.), a bitter critic of Dr. Townsend whom Smith had scorned in 1936 as a "fog horn blown by someone else." During 1938, Smith solicited funds from the Dodge family for and campaigned on behalf of Senator Arthur Vandenberg; two years later Vandenberg gratefully told Congress of his "inspiring leadership." In short, although Smith's denunciations of "dangerous enemies" reinforced opinions on the left that he was surely a demagogue and probably a fascist, they also attracted prominent friends.[86]

Henry Ford and *The International Jew*

Henry Ford was Smith's most prominent friend. The origin of the tie with Ford and his staff remains obscure. Harry Bennett, chief of the Ford Motor Company service department, the tough unit charged with preventing unionization, remembered that "some big businessmen" had encouraged support of Smith in 1939; Bennett donated at least $2,000 for radio time but "quickly became disillusioned." Smith's recollection that Ford's secretary Ernest Liebold had insisted on introducing him to Ford is also plausible. Liebold and Smith became mutually respectful acquaintances between 1940 and 1944. Liebold admired Smith's speaking style, requested copies of his radio talks, and provided information about CIO activities. Smith, in turn, sent his unlisted telephone number to Liebold and gave advice about fellow "nationalists."[87]

There was some basis for Smith's claim that Ford was one of his "staunchest admirers." Ford told subordinates that Smith was a "nice fellow" whom he backed "100 per cent." The reclusive automaker invited Smith to his home, instructed Liebold to admit him whenever he called at the office, and may have urged him to run for president. Moreover, he asked friends to contribute to the Committee of One Million and probably gave money himself, though Smith ruefully recalled that rich men were "never as helpful as people think." It appears that Ford wanted to assist Smith substantially until Bennett dissuaded him. Indeed, Bennett threatened to run Smith "right out of Detroit" unless he stopped badgering the service department. Liebold was more cordial, yet he looked first to his chief assignment, protection of Ford's reputation. He declined to intervene, for example, when the Detroit Arts Commission barred Smith from its auditorium in 1941.[88]

Whether or not Smith sensed that Ford was never a very staunch supporter of anyone, he was able for the first time since Long's death to bask in the reflected glory of a famous man. He later recalled his relationship with Ford almost as enthusiastically as his tenure with Long; it was "even better than a Congressional medal." Hence he zealously defended Ford during the CIO's successful attempt to organize the motor company in 1941. Not since Lincoln's time, Smith told listeners over WJR, had a great man been "so universally persecuted by the forces of destruction and evil." In addition to New Dealers and UAW radicals, the conspiracy against Ford included jealous capitalists who "lived by their wits." Ford was different—a sage, a benefactor of labor, and a "symbol of the American opportunity" to rise through creative hard work.[89]

To other Americans, Ford symbolized prejudice instead of industrial statesmanship. Even after his public repudiation of *The International Jew* in 1927, he continued to believe its major premises. In 1940, for example, he held Jewish bankers responsible for World War II. At roughly the same time, Ford urged on Smith the theme that ultimately superseded the New Deal as his major concern: the "Jewish question."[90]

On the eve of World War II Smith still insisted that he had "NEVER MADE AN ATTACK ON ANY RELIGIOUS OR RACIAL MINORITY." Rather, "certain bigots" had attacked him and Long for associating with Negroes, Catholics, and Jews. After moving to Detroit, Smith convinced Leo Butzel, a prominent Jewish attorney, that he eschewed anti-Semitism and thereafter used Butzel's reputation to bolster his own. Similarly, following a personal meeting with Smith in 1937 or 1938, Richard E. Gutstadt, Midwest director of the B'nai B'rith Anti-Defamation League, answered numerous inquiries by defending him against charges of prejudice.[91]

In December 1940, however, Gutstadt heard a disturbing rumor that advertisements for an anti-Semitic novel, *T and T* by Father Michael De Sanctis Caralt, had been distributed at one of Smith's meetings. After pleading ignorance of *T and T* and noting that the priest had made no statements derogatory to Jews during their encounter, Smith launched into an elaborate apologia. Regretting his anti-Catholic bias "characteristic of Protestants" during the 1920's, he now regarded the Church with "great respect." As for Gutstadt's special concern, Smith insisted that none of his speeches or writings contained one word that "could be even mildly construed as anti-Semitic."[92]

To underscore his tolerance, Smith emphasized to Gutstadt that he regularly resisted the entreaties of bigots. Although flooded with correspondence urging him to denounce Long's assassin as a Jew, he had refused to discuss the subject. When the *March of Time*'s "The 'Lunatic Fringe' " appeared he was approached "by practically all the 'crack pots' and hate mongers." While Jews opposed him because they believed the newsreel, anti-Semites "fought me because I refused to perform as the film suggested I might." Currently, many unsolicited letters condemned him for lacking courage to point out what they called the "real problem."[93]

Asserting that he was aware of past Jewish suffering, Smith added that he was particularly "sensitive to the psychology of the hour and the panic of the Jewish people." Thus he tried to accept "philosophically" their mistaken belief that he was an anti-Semite. He followed a strict rule never to attack rabbis who condemned him: "Perhaps I love self-respect more than self-defense." Yet widespread hostility from Jews made him shudder. He told Gutstadt, a spokesman for the "most highly respected organization within your race," of his wish to confer with a "far-sighted" Jewish leader in order to "develop understanding . . . especially in view of the world crisis." Apparently the two men never arranged a second meeting, but Gutstadt said that he would continue his unpopular defense of Smith.[94]

Gutstadt's appraisal was generous. To be sure, Smith neither attacked Jews in speeches, an act which would have imperiled his connection with presidential contender Arthur Vandenberg, nor agreed with Pelley and Winrod that there existed a worldwide Zionist conspiracy. Nevertheless, his personal feelings in the late 1930s and early 1940s were more complex and less tolerant than his avowals implied, probably more complex and less tolerant than he admitted to himself. The "Jewish question," though not yet *the* central issue for Smith, as it was for Pelley and Winrod, was nonetheless an important issue. He apparently believed that Long's Catholic assassin *was* Jewish. Moreover, he did not work hard to distance himself from the anti-Semitic activists who, by his own admission, flooded his office with letters. Gutstadt's plea did not move him to investigate *T and T* or repudiate Father Caralt. Personally estranged from Coughlin, who had published *The Protocols* in 1938, Smith nonetheless praised the radio priest in an effort to win his following. Smith avoided Jew-baiting, L. M. Birkhead of Friends of Democracy observed in 1942, but some of his best friends were anti-Semites.[95]

The most influential of these friends worked at the Ford Motor Company. Smith admired Ford's publicity agent, William J. Cameron, who had written most of *The International Jew*, and collaborated with Liebold, who gave him a bound file of the *Dearborn Independent* which contained the series. Indeed, in September 1940, three months before assuring Gutstadt that nothing he said could "be even mildly construed as anti-Semitic," Smith told Liebold that Wendell Willkie's appointment to the board of Lehman Brothers, was "very interesting." Above all, sometime between 1939 and 1944, Ford himself inspired Smith to give a "good solid reading" to *The International Jew*.[96]

Although vague about the date, Smith's recollection of the event leaves no doubt about his susceptibility to anti-Semitic motifs and awe of Ford. While issuing his familiar denunciations of leftist agitators, without trying "to screen names" on the basis of ethnicity, Smith heard a "very unavoidable question" from a "very unavoidable man." Ford, who had succeeded Long as Smith's living hero, related that Jews *did* play a crucial role in national and worldwide subversion. Adding that he repudiated *The International Jew* under duress, Ford hoped that Smith would someday reissue the volumes.[97]

Still, Smith did not immediately embrace *The International Jew* as Winrod had seized on *The Protocols*. Rather, Smith later recalled melodramatically, he wavered for two years, "struggling with my soul and frustrating my spirit." We cannot know exactly when he first gave a "solid" reading to *The International Jew*, but his struggle apparently lasted longer than he remembered. Throughout World War II, Smith felt and expressed mixed feelings about the "Jewish question."[98]

War Promoters and War

Differing from Pelley, Winrod, and Henry Ford between 1939 and 1941, Smith did not hold Jewish intrigue responsible for World War II. Rather, he combined commonplace suspicion of "merchants of death" with stock arguments against American intervention. Although sympathetic to individual conscientious objectors, one of whom, Don Lohbeck, was his chief aide during the early 1940s, Smith was emphatically no pacifist. On the contrary, he complained that Roosevelt had squandered appropriations on New Deal boondoggles instead of building an adequate defense. Americans would sacrifice their lives and fortunes to protect the United States against Nazi tyranny, Smith declared, but national security required no intervention in the European conflict. Only "enigmatic financiers" who profited from overseas loans or munitions sales and "war promoters" in government wanted to abandon neutrality. President Roosevelt, eager to expand his own authority, stood out among these war promoters. Smith agreed with noninterventionists as diverse as Norman Thomas and Senator Robert A. Taft (Rep.-Ohio) that war against dictatorship abroad would produce dictatorship at home.[99]

Smith did not belong to the foremost noninterventionist group, the America First Committee—and could not have joined if he had tried. Wary of notoriety, the organization's leaders warned several chapters against cooperating with his Committee of One Million. Undoubtedly, however, there was some overlap of membership, especially in Michigan. In 1941, Smith himself had occasional contacts with Senator Gerald P. Nye, an America First Committee advisor, and Charles A. Lindbergh, the group's most prominent spokesman. He sponsored at least one speech by Nye (who in 1942 contributed an article to his magazine) and met with Lindbergh (who contributed money to Smith's Senate campaign, also in 1942).[100]

Operating on his own, Smith launched a petition drive in 1940 demanding neutrality, military preparedness, and suppression of un-American activities. In July, tokens of the purported one million signatures collected by his followers were presented to Congress by Senator Arthur H. Vandenberg. The next year, Representative Hamilton Fish asked Smith to testify against the Lend-Lease bill. When Sol Bloom, chairman of the House Committee of Foreign Affairs, doubted his credentials, Smith replied that Senator Vandenberg and Representative Joseph W. Martin, the Republican floor leader, would vouch for his "stability and integrity." He appeared before Bloom's Committee in January 1941, and a month later addressed the Senate Foreign Relations Committee.[101]

In both appearances, Smith showed that he, like his mentor Huey Long, could make restrained, cogent arguments when he wished. A self-appointed spokesman for the inarticulate, he offered an unexaggerated, sincere distillation of letters so numerous that forty employees were needed to count them. This correspondence revealed a fear that a definite plan to enter the war lay behind Lend-Lease. His followers endorsed humanitarian aid to Great Britain, and Smith personally thought that her defeat would be "super-tragic." Yet assistance must stop short of war. Lend-Lease would tempt Britain's enemies to fight the United States. In addition, it would violate neutrality legislation, undermine the Monroe Doctrine, and make Roosevelt "economic dictator."[102]

To underscore the danger of executive power, and to show that he was a patriot as well as a polemicist, Smith offered a "sacrifice": his first public criticism of Huey Long. When Long was abusing power, Smith told the Senate Foreign Relations Committee, he had remained silent because he had loved the Kingfish "for his courage and dramatic and intellectual ability, just as many of you love the President." Now, having seen Richard Leche abuse the strong governorship created by Long, Smith asked the senators to contemplate a comparable development, Vice-President Henry A. Wallace's accession to the presidency.[103]

Unlike Pelley, who spent the war in jail, and Winrod, who commuted between the collapsing Defenders in Wichita and United States District Court in Washington, Smith continued after Pearl Harbor to influence some conservative officials and a substantial midwestern constituency. His annual publication and radio budget, Smith said in April 1943, was $75,000. During 1942, he founded a monthly magazine, the *Cross and the Flag,* and ran a strong race for the Republican Senate nomination from Michigan (after his parents released him from his childhood pledge never to seek office).[104]

Along with most of his countrymen, Smith did not forsake prewar concerns but reshaped them to fit the wartime context. It was essential, for example, to preserve private enterprise, to give defense contracts to small business as well as large corporations, and to prevent bankers from making excess profits. Members of the armed forces deserved pay raises and postwar bonuses. By dismantling the New Deal, Americans could simultaneously reclaim lost liberties and protect troops who might be "slaughtered" due to "political racketeering." The Roosevelt administration's enemies remained Smith's friends, at least rhetorically. No longer in contact with Dr. Townsend or Father Coughlin, he nonetheless supported a fair hearing for the Townsend Plan and "free speech" for the radio priest, who had been silenced by the Roman Catholic hierarchy. Responding to social dislocation on the home front, Smith reminded adolescents to respect their parents, recommended family altars as antidotes to divorce, and demanded a return to the religious faith that had made the United States "strong, virile, courageous." He grudgingly accepted military cooperation with Britain and the Soviet Union, still insisting, however, that any "victory which does not put America first is not a victory."[105]

After promising to infuse the Senate with "guts," Smith in 1942 offered voters a sample of his visceral politics. He toured Michigan, often speaking eight hours a day, always opening meetings with prayer and stressing his audience's "home problems." Smith's favorite home problem was the prospect of gasoline rationing imposed by Washington to save rubber tires. Rationing, he predicted, would impoverish autoworkers, reduce farmers to "hitch hiking bondage," imprison suburbanites, and destroy the rural church. Yet only inept New Dealers and foreign rubber monopolies prevented production of "tires for everybody" (a phrase that became an effective campaign slogan). If Henry Ford, the quintessential American entrepreneur, were placed in charge, Smith declared in May 1942, enough tires could be produced by the next spring without hurting the war effort.[106]

Smith's assertion that rubber supply had been horribly bungled came close to the mark. A synthetic substitute could be made, as he reminded rural audiences, from "practically anything" grown on farms. Yet the rubber industry had shown little interest in this alternative and Roosevelt had vetoed a plan to use it. Instead, a presidential panel headed by Bernard Baruch favored petroleum as the base for synthetic rubber and endorsed gasoline rationing, which the administration imposed after the 1942 elections. Meanwhile, Smith mocked Washington's vacillation, compared Baruch's committee to Satan investigating hell, and said that as senator he would have "dramatized" the importance of a sound transportation system.[107]

To support his claim that American ingenuity could provide "tires for everybody," Smith consulted chemists at the Ford Motor and Dow Chemical companies, and then "reduced their scientific findings to popular appeal." A synthetic tire made by Ford was his favorite campaign prop. In the midst of his discourses on boondoggling bureaucracy and international finance, the tire was unveiled. The audience, Smith reported to Mencken,

> looked at it about as they might review the remains at a funeral. In fact, as the people anticipated the thought of no tires and no automobile transportation, they were just about as sad as people get at funerals. In fact, I have seen many a man look happier at the funeral of his wife than these people looked when they reviewed the prospect of no tires. . . . I have seen people stamped in public gatherings, rush for free barbe-

cue, etc., but I have never seen an audience of people as anxious to see anything since Lindbergh flew the Atlantic.[108]

Such dramatizations were anathema to Judge Homer E. Ferguson, whom Republican leaders, searching for a strong senatorial candidate, had drafted from the bench. Although Ferguson shared Smith's antipathy to the New Deal, he ran primarily on his reputation as the scourge of corruption in Detroit. A third contender, Elton R. Eaton, publisher of the *Plymouth Mail*, called himself the one man brave enough to "unmask" Smith's demagoguery. Smith professed high regard for both opponents but insisted that he alone raised basic issues.[109]

An issue that he did not raise was the "Jewish question." Yet this issue remained very much in mind, still coexisting with Smith's sense that he was a tolerant man. For example, without blaming World War II on Zionist conspirators, he had concluded during his battle against intervention that many American Jews were war promoters. Furthermore, he complained to Leo Butzel in October 1941, they had mistakenly applied the "tar brush" to major noninterventionists, including himself, none of whom was anti-Semitic. If responsible figures like Butzel did not want Jews "to take their share of the blame for prowar propaganda," Smith added angrily, then they "should devise ways and means of disowning, criticizing or to make it plain,—for shutting up such agitators, as are constantly being elevated to high position of authority where they pose as spokemen for American Jewry."[110]

While privately trying to sort out his mixed feelings about Jews, in 1942 Smith sought votes from citizens who were unambiguously hostile to them. Specifically, he directed appeals to Father Coughlin's "abused" constituency. The journalist William Bradford Huie captured Smith's ambiguity. On the one hand, Huie noted, because Smith shunned public anti-Semitism, he was more potent politically than Pelley, Winrod, and other devotees of the "*Protocols of Zion* insanities." On the other hand, despite his strong doubt that Smith was "for the racial hate-mongers," Huie had "no doubt whatever that the racial hate-mongers are for Smith."[111]

Notwithstanding Coughlinite support, Senator Vandenberg's neutrality, and a campaign budget $4,500 larger than Ferguson's, Smith lost the September 12 primary by a margin of two to one. Finding solace in his "sensationally large" total of 120,000 votes, he conceded graciously. This graciousness evaporated when Ferguson refused to confer with him, and the Republican state chairman, unwilling to inflame "group hatreds," prevented him from address-the party convention. In late September, therefore, Smith entered the general election as an "Independent Republican," planning to dramatize "tires for everybody" by driving above the speed limit. Such stunts no longer attracted much attention. Although Smith received 32,173 votes, Ferguson defeated Democratic Senator Prentiss Brown, 589,652 to 561,595.[112]

Ironically, Smith's candidacy, like Winrod's in 1938, damaged his reputation by heightening his visibility. Major Michigan newspapers urged defeat of this "fascist" aspirant to the Senate. Outside the state, he led radio broadcaster Walter Winchell's list of "Americans We Could Do Without." Books and magazines exposing "fifth columnists" invariably counted him among "would-be *fuehrers*." These descriptions, issued in wartime to a nation suspicious of alien dangers, increasingly placed Smith beyond the bounds of respectability. News vendors refused to carry the *Cross and the Flag*, and Senator Nye made excuses for contributing to it. Senator Vandenberg wrote his last letter to "My dear Gerald" in August 1943. Ford cut his ties six months later; soothing Smith's pride, Ernest Lieboeld said that the company had yielded to pressure from the Roosevelt administration. By April 1944, Smith's staff had shrunk from twenty to a half dozen.[113]

In addition to alienating obscure and prominent friends, Smith's activities prompted counterattacks from his most "dangerous enemy," President Roosevelt. *United States* v. *Winrod*, the mass sedition indictment Roosevelt had pushed in 1942, named the *Cross and the Flag* as a source of subversion, though Smith himself escaped indictment. During March 1943, encountering an article about Smith in the *Hour*, a newsletter dedicated to exposing far right agitators, FDR asked J. Edgar Hoover, "Is anything being done about this?" Hoover replied that the FBI had been investigating Smith for more than a year.[114]

Three months later, the president telephoned Attorney General Francis Biddle about a rumor that Smith was counseling tax evasion. The Treasury Department was investigating his returns from 1938 to 1940, Biddle reported, but found no evidence that Smith himself evaded taxes or encouraged others to do so. Furthermore, he was "careful to profess loyalty to the war effort." Biddle enclosed an FBI summary of Smith's career, including speculation about "associations with women other than his wife." In September 1943, Hoover reported to the White House Smith's recent contact with Senator Burton K. Wheeler, Senator Robert R. Reynolds (Dem.-N.C.), and Henry Ford.[115]

Smith's waning legitimacy may be gauged by the shrinking availability of public forums, the acrimonious debates on his right to speak, and the thousands of pickets he eluded to reach the various podiums. As early as 1941, both the Detroit Arts Commission and Masonic Order denied him their meeting halls. In June 1942, Mayor Frank Lausche rejected his application to use the Cleveland municipal auditorium. He made a lucid if unavailing appeal to the City Council; less restrained, several hundred supporters created a disturbance in chambers, with one woman trying to punch Councilman Joseph Kirzek, leader of the anti-Smith forces.[116]

Under more sedate circumstances, Buffalo, New York, in 1943 and Minneapolis, Minnesota, in 1944 rejected Smith's requests to use municipal facilities. In Minneapolis, Smith again appealed personally to the City Council, aided by the American Civil Liberties Union and Mrs. Ernest Lundeen, widow of the isolationist senator. His most articulate foe, Hubert H. Humphrey, would have allowed Smith to express his views in a rented hall, but denied his right to a public building. Although Smith offered to debate the "sincere but misinformed" Humphrey if he paid half the rent on a hall, the encounter never occurred.[117]

In 1945 this pattern was repeated in California, where Smith spoke under the auspices of the Payroll Guarantee Association, a Townsendite offshoot better known as the Ham and Eggers. The San Jose City Council, San Francisco Odd Fellows, and Scottish Rite Masons refused to rent him meeting rooms. Following an angry hearing, the San Francisco Board of Education barred him from city schools, a decision later reversed by the California Supreme Court.[118]

The most volatile confrontations took place in Los Angeles. Pleased by an overflow crowd at the Embassy Auditorium on 31 May 1945, he scheduled a second speech at the larger Los Angeles Philharmonic Auditorium. The nervous management tried to cancel this reservation and then required Smith to forfeit $1000 if he digressed from a prepared text. Predicably preferring drama to cash, he spoke extemporaneously, assuring another packed house that he would not sell free speech for one million dollars. California opponents, appalled by Smith's success, began a systematic counterattack. The Los Angeles Council for Civic Unity picketed his meetings, warning the unwary that he "consistently followed the Nazi line." A Council counter-rally that attracted twelve thousand persons on 10 July featured California Attorney General Robert Kenny, as well as actors Orson Welles and Gregory Peck. Smith, always fascinated by fame, delighted in opposition from Hollywood "Muscovites," including, the *Cross and the Flag* noted, the "sexy and glamorous" actress Olivia de Havilland.[119]

To secure his Pacific "beachhead," Smith applied through the Ham and Eggers to appear at Francis Polytechnic High School in late 1945. Seeing no legal alternative, the Los Angeles Board of Education reluctantly granted permission. Carey McWilliams, formerly California Commissioner of Immigration and Housing, urged the Board to reconsider. Representing Mobilization for Democracy, a state coalition against "home-grown Fascism," McWilliams called Smith a student of *Mein Kampf* and, echoing Hubert Humphrey in Minneapolis, denied that the First Amendment was central to the issue at hand. Free speech depended on social stability that was currently threatened by a "dangerously large" population of potential fascists. Hence McWilliams, invoking Justice Oliver Wendell Holmes, viewed Smith as a walking "clear and present danger [to] democracy itself." Finally, he envisioned the falling dominoes of authoritarianism:

> Today you are asked to permit Smith to speak, presumably on the subject of a fantastic pension scheme . . . but tomorrow you will be asked to permit the KKK to hold a meeting in the schools; and the day after tomorrow you will be asked to permit someone to speak on the subject of organizing a boycott against Jewish merchants.[120]

Despite McWilliams's eloquence, Smith met his followers at Francis High School on October 17. But he had to enter through a side door in order to evade 10,000 demonstrators. Two weeks later, 500 students from the school picketed the Board of Education, unsuccessfully demanding cancellation of Smith's next rally. When he spoke at Francis High School on 3 November, 7,500 protesters appeared. The demonstration degenerated into an "uproar," the *Los Angeles Times* reported, leaving fifty-seven protestors under arrest and several treated for injuries.[121]

Undaunted by vigorous opposition, Smith continued to address wartime issues. The prospect of compulsory national service, tentatively endorsed by Roosevelt in 1944, prompted another round of testimony before Congress. This time he was more colorful than cogent, picturing husbands separated from the refined influence of their wives, wives lost without the steady minds of their husbands, and young women embarassed on the job by "vulgar talk." Nor was preservation of traditional sex roles the only issue at stake. The labor draft also threatened individualism, the "acme" of American and Christian values.[122]

More seriously, the *Cross and the Flag* discussed the Detroit race riot that left thirty-five persons dead in June 1943. Liberals and radicals correctly blamed far right agitators like Smith for having spread prejudice in the city. Smith, on the defensive, compared the "uncivilized" riot to "pagan" Nazi assaults on Jews, and simultaneously tried to present himself as a moderate. He neither agreed with some southern sheriffs who blamed blacks for all disorders nor joined northern demagogues who "over-encouraged them."[123]

In fact, Smith was a paternalistic segregationist wary of black emigrants from southern "discipline." In looser northern cities, he surmised, hundreds of white women were raped by blacks and a like number of black women were "seduced" by whites. Although Smith automatically ascribed the more brutal offense to blacks, he did not "blame" them. Indeed, "vile" films and magazines undermined morality among both races, scantily clad women tempted "undisciplined men beyond the borders of self control," and ambitious politicians, especially Communists, endorsed social integration and even intermarriage.[124]

To combat the "mongrelizers," Smith denounced "promiscuous mixture" in hotels, restaurants, and residential neighborhoods. Nor should black men "crowd" white women on buses. The "natural" tendency toward segregation did not mean that either race was superior in the sight of God. Smith repudiated "all forms of bigotry," including the Ku Klux Klan, and claimed many black friends (though he named none). Urging blacks to pursue economic advancement, he nonetheless opposed the Roosevelt administration's weak Fair Employment Practices Commission because forced hiring, like intermarriage, produced "bad racial feeling." Blacks should rise through individual effort, following the example of Booker T. Washington. Ultimately, Smith believed, racial conflicts could be solved only through "Christian statesmanship."[125]

Such segregationist sentiments and complementary sexual fears were common in the North as well as the South, but Smith's "Abraham Lincoln Plan," proposed a year after the Detroit riot, was extraordinary. According to this scheme, the United States would provide land, transportation, and $5,000 to any black who voluntarily emigrated to Africa, there to govern territory acquired from Britain and France in lieu of war debts. Because Negroes comprised ten percent of the population, Smith concluded, the United States could appropriate one-tenth of its wealth to solve a "problem which [they] did not create." Unlike Pelley, who would have reduced blacks to the status of federal wards, Smith wanted the "negro problem" literally to go away.[126]

Along with commentators across the political spectrum, Smith anticipated a postwar depression that would make "1932 look like a boom." The left expected mass unemployment to provide recruits for the far right, and so did Smith. Eager to expand the shrinking Committee of One Million, he gave greater emphasis to sharing the wealth in 1945 than at any time since 1936. A properly apportioned gross national product, he declared, could provide a $2,500 minimum annual income to every family, early retirement, veterans' bonuses, and expanded unemployment compensation.[127]

Misgivings about the postwar economy fueled Smith's already formidable nationalism during 1944–45. Immigration must cease, he wrote, as long as a single citizen lacked work. Pointedly refusing to flatter military allies, the *Cross and the Flag* chided Britain for suppressing Indian independence and placed the Soviet Union in the "vanguard of the anti-Christ." As one of the victors, Stalin inevitably would "get some loot," but American military strategy must not advance Communism in Europe. A month after Germany's capitulation, Smith called the Soviet Union a "military threat to the world."[128]

A self-proclaimed isolationist, Smith associated this label with his conception of individualism. The phrase "my nation," like "my home," fostered pride and enterprise. The United States was separate from other nations just as a house stood apart from others on the same street. Smith endorsed international trade, philanthropy, and evangelism, yet emphasized the limits of neighborly goodwill. Accordingly, he scorned Union Now "bunk," Henry R. Luce's prophecy of an "American Century," the Bretton Woods financial "conspiracy," and "anything that even smells like a League of Nations." He especially liked to scorn these proposals in face-to-face encounters. If they could not convince a "narrow-minded provincial isolationist" like himself, Smith teased the few internationalists who consented to debate, how were they going to persuade millions "less intelligent than I am?"[129]

Smith attended the United Nations organizational conference in April 1945, but received neither press credentials nor accomodations through the State Department. This frigid reception in San Francisco, the "temporary capital of the world intrigue," symbolized to him the prevailing disregard for "America First." Smith urged President Harry S. Truman to make an appearance, believing that his "obvious integrity" would save the United States from betrayal. When Truman failed to appear, he mistakenly hoped that Senator Vandenberg would rally the Senate against the UN charter.[130]

Although Smith underestimated the breadth of support for postwar international cooperation, many of his views still coincided with those of congressional conservatives. After his Senate campaign, however, Smith began to ruminate publicly, as well as reflect privately, on the "Jewish question," the issue that would subsume all others and carry him far from the political mainstream.

Making the "Dean of American Anti-Semitism"

When the journalist William Bradford Huie doubted in 1942 that Smith was "for the racial hate-mongers," he also issued a warning. Unless Smith explicitly rejected such associations, he could "expect from sober-minded Americans only the verdict that he is a dangerous demagogue, willing to exploit the lowest prejudices to his own advantage." Instead of rejecting bigots and bigotry, however, Smith embarked during the war on a course that ultimately made him, in Seymour Martin Lipset and Earl Raab's phrase, the "dean of American anti-Semitism." Loss of reputable allies (along with their moderating influence), growing opposition, fear of isolation, and the need to resolve persisting ambivalence combined to alter Smith's worldview and personality. But his transition, marked by conflicting words and deeds, was not simple.[131]

Smith both lashed out at detractors with typical overkill and denied—almost ingenuously—that he was a traitor or bigot. He noted often that his adopted son, Gerry, had been wounded while serving with the army. Even more frequently, Smith recalled his mother's early instruction that racial and religious hatred were sinful. On several occasions during the early 1940s, he offered to quit public life if anyone could show that he had made racial or religious slurs.[132]

While affirming his own tolerance, however, Smith allowed ethnic slurs by followers to pass without reprimand. In 1942, after Smith had told the Cleveland City Council that he would rather retire than promote bigotry, his supporters shouted at Councilman Joseph Kirzek, a Roman Catholic, "Go back to the kikes, you kike!" Similarly, Smith drew closer to men and women whose reputations as bigots were—deservedly—even firmer than his own. Elizabeth Dilling, the anti-Semitic author of *The Red Network*, looked to him like the "Frances Willard of Nationalism." Winrod helped Smith to start the *Cross and the Flag* in 1942, an FBI informant reported to J. Edgar Hoover; whether or not this report was reliable, Smith praised Winrod the next year as a "sincere patriotic Christian American."[133]

Although Smith still refrained from calling himself a fundamentalist, a decade of far right activism led him to a more conservative theology (unlike Winrod, whose theological conservatism led to far right politics). Whereas modernist skepticism had "fertilized the world" for Nazism and Communism, he wrote in 1944, "old-fashioned Gospel preachers" agreed with the spirit of the *Cross and the Flag*. And many of them did agree. The California Pastors Association, consisting of one thousand theological conservatives, helped Smith to secure auditoriums during his volatile western tour in 1945. Without becoming a dispensationalist, Smith alluded occasionally to Biblical prophecy, suggesting, for example, that the proposed labor draft—Senate bill 666—might relate to the Beast bearing the same number in Revelation.[134]

Certainly Smith was searching harder than ever for hidden meanings and hidden actors behind events. To be sure, he had detected conspiracies among dangerous enemies at least since practicing the "personalization of politics" under Huey Long. Yet he had continued during the 1930s to recognize the power of abstract forces, such as economic trends causing the Depression. By the early 1940s, the Depression began to look like the deliberate creation of international bankers. Still eschewing anything like Winrod's comprehensive framework, which related figures as diverse as Colonel House and Pontius Pilate, Smith was nonetheless dissatisfied with ordinary notions of historical causation. President Roosevelt's death in 1945 seemed to him a "super mystery," possibly a secret assassination or suicide. At the very least, Smith believed, FDR's physical deterioration was hastened by his guilty memories of complicity in Pearl Harbor and concessions to Stalin.[135]

Complementing this heightened interest in mysterious explanations, particularly regarding the deaths of contemporaries, Smith expressed growing concern for his own safety. During the mid-1930s he had said, largely for platform effect, that his advocacy of Share Our Wealth or the Townsend Plan involved great risk. Rather than see him in the Senate, Smith told voters in 1942, some enemies would "CUT MY THROAT." If Smith convinced no one else of the danger, he ultimately convinced himself. The prospect of joining Huey Long in martyrdom may have seemed more appealing than the probable alternative—isolation, obscurity, and lost self-esteem. Facing angry demonstrators, Smith was almost exultant, "perfectly willing to burn that the bonfire of my bones may light the way." Beneath this showmanship, he suffered from his growing notoriety during World War II. He particularly missed association with prominent, "high-toned" men. After Ford joined the war effort, Lindbergh shunned controversy, and Father Coughlin fell silent, Smith felt that he "stood alone."[136]

The changes in worldview and personality that accompanied Smith's waning prospects accumulated gradually. Borrowing from sociologist Erving Goffman, we can say that between the late 1930s and 1946 he was an outsider experimenting with "recipes for an appropriate attitude regarding the self." The signal event in self-definition was his decision, made finally in 1946, that *Jewish* conspirators were responsible for his beleaguered situation.[137]

Smith's recollection that he struggled with his soul before embracing *The International Jew* and *The Protocols* was typically melodramatic but not without foundation. Considerable hesitation preceded his conversion to conspiratorial anti-Semitism. Correspondence with Richard Gutstadt of the Anti-Defamation League revealed the early phase of his internal struggle. Writing in 1940 that he knew "how Jews must feel in Berlin because I know how I felt in New York," he declared: "Still I am strong, Still I am open-minded. Still I have taken the lash; I have not struck back." For four years after its founding in 1942, Smith used the *Cross and the Flag* to convince the public—and himself—that his view of the "anti-Semitic problem" was balanced, sensible, and fair.[138]

As late as 1945, Smith admitted that Jews had "suffered as perhaps no people had suffered," with the possible exception of Russian Christians under Communism. Thus their resistance to anti-Semitism was justifiable. They erred, however, by including him among their foes because he disagreed with "certain Jewish organizations" about Lend-Lease or the New Deal. It was his privilege to disagree. He also criticized members of "every other race or religion, including my own." He simply did not want his country ruled "by any clique, whether it be a clique of specially favored Irishmen, or specially favored Baptist preachers, or specially favored Jews." Moreover, he recognized that misdeeds by "certain Jews" neither implicated all of them nor justified "physical outbreaks."[139]

Similarly, Smith assured Leo Butzel in 1941 that he tried always to act "in the spirit of the Man of Galilee and not in the spirit of the New York householder advertising for a non-Jewish cook." Throughout the war years he denied "any desire whatsoever" to injure any group. Sometimes, he tried to sound like an unbiased investigator. Accurately perceiving a rising tide of anti-Semitism among Americans in 1945, he pondered:

> If a general dislike of Jews develops among Gentiles, the question can be raised, What developed it? What started it? If it is assumed that certain Jews were to blame, the next ques-

> tion is, what have they done to inspire the antipathy? If certain Gentiles are to blame, the question can be raised, why do they insist on hating the entire race without examining the numbers . . . one at the time and allowing each one to stand or fall on his own merits in this estimation?

Elsewhere, echoing the ethic of independence cherished by the Smith family and the Christian Church, Smith urged "good Americans" to leave "matters of faith and religion . . . to every individual, according to his conscience and enlightenment."

> If Americanism means anything, it means that the Protestant has the right to be a Protestant, the Catholic has the right to be Catholic, and the Jew has the right to be a Jew. Yes, as far as this world is concerned, the unbeliever, if he is willing to face his God with his unbelief, has a legal right to be an atheist.[140]

Smith's professions of tolerance and objectivity were undercut, however, by his opportunitism, suspicion, and condescension. As the son of tolerant Sarah Smith, he told Richard Gutstadt of his understanding of Jewish "panic"; as the dramatic disciple of Huey Long, he willingly profited from a "certain type of 'forbiden fruit' psychology, a sort of 'Police Gazette' patriotism." Smith reported to Mencken in 1943 that he drew unusually large crowds because "the Jews always advertise me as the most dangerous man in America."[141]

These conflicting pronouncements suggest that Smith's attitude toward Jews intertwined self-deception, need for a scapegoat in a period of personal crisis, some disingenuousness, and an earnest desire, within the limits of his definition of the word, to be tolerant. In the same article or letter, often in the same paragraph, he invoked the sweet love of Jesus and, using sterner language, instructed Jews like Leo Butzel to "shut up" their trouble-makers. Almost certainly he would have been unable to unravel his own amalgam of beliefs. Rather, Smith provided a classic illustration of a mind where (to recall William James's phrase) "lying and delusion meet."[142]

In retrospect, Smith's expressions during the early 1940s involved less conscious duplicity to salvage a damaged reputation than insensitivity and incapacity to see that "good Americans" held values different from his own. The *Cross and the Flag* was founded "on the principle that Christian character is the basis of all real Americanism." This venerable premise—more accurately rendered as white Christian character—also dominated Smith's social philosophy and political organizations. He assumed that Christians had been nurtured in partriotism unless they betrayed unworthiness. Jewish Americanism, by definition, was less real. A Jew might qualify for the accolade, but he bore the burden of proof.[143]

While adamantly asserting and halfway believing that he considered Jews no different from anybody else, Smith routinely treated them as a special case. He regularly associated them with wrong positions on critical issues. More than 500,000 "Jews and other immigrants" received sanctuary after Hitler seized power, Smith wrote, and Rabbi Stephen Wise wanted to open the gates wider. During the Detroit riot, looting by blacks "wasn't anti-white. It was anti-Jewish." A "general belief" prevailed in 1944 that Jewish spokesmen had "needled" the Roosevelt administration to indict Pelley, Winrod, and other far right agitators accused of sedition.[144]

Like his followers who yelled "kike" at a Roman Catholic councilman in Cleveland, Smith was quick to infer that Jews spearheaded opposition to his own efforts. Indeed, although Smith's most prominent adversaries were Christians like Hubert Humphrey, Robert Kenny, and Carey McWilliams, he was particularly incensed by editorials in local Jewish newspapers. On several occasions in 1945–46, he confidently estimated that thousands of pickets were "mostly young Jews" or "ninety-eight percent Jewish."[145]

Smith may have criticized members of "every other race and religion," as he wrote in the *Cross and the Flag*, but attacks on James A. Farley, for example, never noted the Postmaster General's Irish Catholic background. On the other hand, he indentified CIO leader Sidney Hillman as a former rabbinical student. He denounced politicians who happened to be Baptists or Methodists, but never conceptualized a "Methodist problem" or a "Baptist problem." In his speeches and writing, Jews appeared less like Baptists or Methodists, members of different denominations within the umbrella of "Americanism," than like blacks, a potentially disruptive part of the population. During the early 1940s, he had difficulty deciding what, in addition to the spirit of Jesus, was needed to solve the "Jewish problem." Significantly, however, he used the language of social control, not acceptance. "If someone will figure out the best way to *handle* the Jews," Smith wrote in 1944, "he will go down in history as the wisest person in all the centuries."[146]

Conceding that blacks and Jews must be judged as individuals, Smith approved the same trait in worthy members of both groups—submissiveness. The best Negro preachers did not question white dominance of a segregated nation. "Responsible" Jews acquiesed in the amalgamation of Christianity and true Americanism that Smith took for granted. Only "bouncy and twitchy" Protestant ministers excluded Jesus from their invocations "in order to please the Jews." Even "responsible" Jews—that is, those who did not protest nationalist enterprises—must not be too obtrusive. While some authorities claimed that Jews controlled the Soviet Union, Smith wrote in May 1945, others said that Stalin was liquidating them. Without choosing between the two opinions, he inferred a lesson relevant to the United States: it was dangerous for "aggressive members of the race to obtain too much power in government. The reaction is usually intemperate."[147]

Because an anti-Semitic tide had already risen among Americans, Smith recommended in 1944 that Jews "yell 'America First' so loud" that they could be heard "from the Atlantic to the Pacific." Despite earnest protests that he was not part of the tide, Smith's practical conception of tolerance carried connotations of grudging forebearance instead of willing approval. Placing Jews and blacks on *his* list of outsiders, he offered a version of the familiar social bargain that Erving Goffman has described in another context: "The stigmatized are tactfully expected to be gentlemanly and not to press their luck; they should not test the limits of the acceptance shown them, nor make it the basis of still further demands."[148]

If Jews did not know their place, Smith offered copious advice about where to find it. Never had a people been "so short of public relations counsels and messengers of goodwill." Formally acknowledging the right to combat anti-Semitism as part of nature's "law of self-defense," he honored that prerogative in the 1940s, like labor's right to unionize during the 1930s, in theory instead of practice. By 1944, he listed the B'nai B'rith Anti-Defamation League among the "Gestapo organizations." Three forces—Communists, certain "extreme" Jewish groups like the ADL, and the "Jew Walter Winchell"—promoted more anti-Semitism "than all the Jew baiters combined." New Dealers and internationalist Republicans, whose propaganda indirectly prompted a backlash against Jews, also qualified as the "real anti-semites." Instead of creating animosity themselves or with these allies, Jews should "master the art of making friends, even among those with whom they are not always in agreement." More than anything else in 1943, they needed leaders "with some common sense."[149]

To Smith, this kind of advice did not seem patronizing and offensive. Nor did it seem to clash with his refusal "to fight the Jews or the Negroes or anybody else because of their race and their religion." Hence he was genuinely baffled by his spreading reputation as an anti-Semite. "For the life of me," he wrote in 1944, "I cannot understand why it is that most of the articulate Jewish organizations are so sensitive to criticism." Nor could he appreciate that his definition of patriotism relegated Jews to inferior status or that he was insensitive to their unique predicament. In 1941, Smith compared Hitler's genocide to the Soviet liquidation of Christians. Yet he *felt* sympathy for Stalin's victims, with whom he identified, and almost none for Hitler's. Referring casually—almost callously—in 1939 to "Hitler scared Jews" in the United States, he made no connection between that fear and their suspicion of his associations and rhetoric. Indeed, Smith failed to see that almost all Americans, while involved in a war against Nazism, found little reassurance in his less-than-fastidious selection for censure of "certain Jews," "atheistic Jews," or "Communistic Jews."[150]

Ironically, Smith continued to complain throughout the war, as he had in his earlier correspondence with Gutstadt, that Jews made no attempt to understand him, that they did not comprehend "'Bible Belt' psychology." Struggling with his soul, Smith saw himself, not as a bigot dedicated to a narrow conception of "real Americanism," but as a man showing extraordinary forebearance in the face of his lifelong fear—isolation. In 1941, he had described the "awful psychology" created among nationalists who received an "editorial lambasting" from Jewish organizations: "It makes the individual feel like a lonely person walking through the woods." Despite his own sense of isolation, Smith noted his fairness and patience, repeating the self-justification that he had fashioned from his individualist ethic. He wrote in 1945:

> Although I have been persecuted, smeared and threatened by numerous Jewish organizations, I try never to say *the Jews.* Whenever I answer my critics among this race, I refer to them as *certain Jews.* Even though one million Jews might hate me and desire my destruction, I am going to assume, until God gives me wisdom to do otherwise, that no race, no group of human beings on earth should be dealt with in mass. If one million people of a certain group are bad and out of that one million, there is one good person, then as a Christian I must recognize that goodness and support justice.[151]

Smith's role in the 1944 presidential campaign highlighted both his sinking reputation and his mixed feelings about Jews. An imbroglio with Wendell Willkie attracted national attention in March. Disdaining Willkie as an apostle of internationalism, Smith urged his Wisconsin followers to support any other candidate in the Republican primary. Willkie, picking up the challenge, responded that no Republican could win the presidency without repudiating Smith. After

Willkie lost the primary and withdrew from the race, Smith warned other aspirants that attacks on him would cost votes.[152]

Governor Thomas E. Dewey of New York refused to listen. On the contrary, speaking to the United Jewish Appeal on March 31, Dewey declared that "rodents" like Smith must not be "permitted to pollute the stream of American life." Smith responded cautiously that Dewey had been "misinformed" about his beliefs; he, too, had learned as a child to shun prejudice. Adding that Dewey's "dear mother" attended Committee of One Million meetings in Michigan (an assertion Dewey denied), Smith hoped that he would come to share her "faith." By the time Dewey won the Republican nomination, Smith decided that he belonged "body and soul" to British Prime Minister Winston Churchill. The only good news was the refusal of Dewey's running mate, Governor John Bricker, to repudiate Smith.[153]

Refusing to choose between Roosevelt and Dewey, Smith inflated his own "spare tire party," baptized the American First Party despite protest from leaders of the defunct American First Committee. Charles A. Lindbergh, Senator Gerald P. Nye, and Senator Robert R. Reynolds declined his offer to run for president. In effect nominating himself, Smith made another round of front page headlines by seeking Dewey's running mate, John Bricker, as his own. Dewey immediately issued a statement comparing Smith to Adolf Hitler. Perhaps wary of Smith's residual support in Ohio, Bricker followed with a vague denunciation of all bigotry.[154]

The America First Party national convention, a collection of 175 delegates, mostly elderly women, endorsed Smith's candidacy on August 30; in lieu of Bricker, an obscure Ohio Coughlinite joined the ticket. Placing Smith in nomination, his friend and pastor Leland Marion asserted, "We do not have to have the OK of 3,000,000 Jews to elect a President of the United States." Marion's views were shared by others at the session. Homer Maertz, an erstwhile Silver Shirt arrested in 1938 for smashing store windows in Chicago, now wanted to deport all Jews who failed to leave the country within five years; any who insisted on remaining would be sterilized.[155]

Maertz's proposal, the *Detroit Free Press* reported, prompted anti-Semitic denunciations from a half-dozen delegates. Saying that this outburst represented "personal opinions, not the findings of the convention," Smith buried the resolution in committee. Personally, he opposed Maertz's "materialistic solution." "Let's deal with this problem in the manner of the Man of Galilee," he advised, "not with the paganism of Hitler, the atheism of Stalin nor [sic] the imperialism of the Bank of England."[156]

The convention adopted Smith's plank, noting a "Jewish problem" and demanding its solution "honestly, realistically, and courageously." Estimating on the basis of a University of Denver poll that two-thirds of all Americans were "'anti-Semitic,'" the platform proclaimed opposition to all prejudice but encouraged the research necessary to meet the "world's most unsolved question." It posed seven specific inquiries including: Did "apostate Jews" constitute ninety-five percent of the founders of Communism? Were the media largely in the hands of "certain Jews?" Was the New Deal "heavily staffed with a certain type of Jewish bureaucrat?" Had Palestine been awarded to Jews because they had helped to lure the United States into World War I? After raising these questions, laden with innuendo, the convention took no stand beyond calling for "unimpeachable facts" to determine whether they should be answered affirmatively, or rejected as the product of "superficial and prejudiced thinkers."[157]

The America First Party failed even to reach the stature of a well-publicized political sect. The Office of Price Administration refused to authorize gasoline for Smith's national tour. The Department of Interior turned down his request for a buffalo to serve as party mascot. Secretary Harold L. Ickes, while lamenting that he could not introduce Smith to "one of our loudest-mouthed bull buffaloes," refused to "play politics" with national parks. On election day, Smith received 1,530 votes in Michigan and 251 in Texas. Looking on the bright side, he expected the Republicans, defeated again by Roosevelt, to learn the liabilities of internationism.[158]

Yet the 1944 election was more important for Smith than he realized. He had moved a considerable distance from the political mainstream. Never again would national officials or news media consider him a serious force. At best, metropolitan newspapers might devote a filler to the colorful crank who tried to borrow a buffalo from Secretary Ickes. More often, they joined Dewey in condemning him as a native fascist. Significantly, Smith no longer appeared before Congress as a popular spokesman whose opinions deserved attention. Instead, the House Committee to Investigate Campaign Expenditures summoned him in October 1944 to explain his finances. Two years later, when the House Committee on Un-American Activities investigated his record, even members renowned for their red hunting balked at Smith's attempt to associate himself with their efforts.[159]

By 1946, Smith had decided that the hostile questions about "certain Jews" in the American First Party platform could be transformed into declarations. In January, for example, he told the House Committee on Un-American Activities that Jews running Hollywood used movies to spread Communism. Nor did he see how the major parties could avoid the "Jewish problem" in 1948. Smith himself had no intention of avoiding it. On the contrary, taking the decisive step of combining his anti-Semitic innuendo with a comprehensive conspiracy theory, he announced plans in September 1946 to distribute Henry Ford's "forbidden manuscript," *The International Jew*.[160]

During the next two years, the *Cross and the Flag* displayed Smith's familiarity with the anti-Semitic lore that had circulated since the 1920s. *The International Jew* provided the central theme: Jewish Communists (including Lenin, Smith said) conspired with Jewish capitalists to exercise world power. Smith did not formally abandon the distinction between Jewish conspirators and innocent bystanders attending synagogues. Yet his tone toughened as his beliefs hardened. Criticism of "certain Jews," a locution that had never reassured his foes, was largely superseded during the late 1940s by sweeping condemnations of Jews.[161]

Seeking a usable past to legitimate his position, Smith in 1948 resurrected Martin Luther's *Against the Jews and Their Lies* as well as assorted anti-Jewish statements issued from the papacy. Then he appealed to the highest authority, the Savior crucified by Jews. Twenty "choice texts" from the New Testament proved that "conflict between Jesus and the Jews" was not invented by modern bigots. Then, like Luther, who "suffered greatly" from Jewish persecution, Smith took his stand:

> The issue for the next five years and as long as man inhabits earth will be: "Who shall control the destiny of our people, Jesus Christ or the Jews?" That sounds like a ruthless and pointed statement. It is no more ruthless than truth itself. It is no more pointed than the words of Jesus Christ, our beloved Lord.
>
> The challenge of the Christian is not to hate the Jew, but the challenge of the Christian is to love the name of Jesus Christ and to make no compromise with that name in order to please the Jews. But whenever the Christian has to make a decision between the authority of Jesus Christ and the will and the authority of the Jew, he must always have the courage and the will and the determination to obey the authority of Jesus Christ. It is not sinful to criticize a Jew. It is no disgrace to be condemned by a Jew. It should not be a matter of shame for a person to be attacked or criticized or cursed by a Jew. When I am hated by a Jew, when a Jew seeks to kill me, or smear me, or brand me an evil force, then I have fellowship with Jesus Christ.[162]

Smith's conversion to conspiratorial anti-Semitism, virtually complete by 1948, had been, in William James's terminology, of the volitional type—usually gradual, "with a building up, piece by piece, of a new set of moral and spiritual habits," though including "critical points . . . at which the movement forward seems much more rapid." Smith no longer felt like a "lonely person walking through the woods," as he had written to Leo Butzel in 1941. Rather, like James's volitional convert, he felt "unified and consciously right, superior and happy." Following years of ambivalence and, in his own mind, patience, he settled on a personally satisfying recipe for identity. He would be the besieged patriot, the persecuted crusader against the International Jew, and the dean of American anti-Semitism.[163]

5. Brown Scare

Subversion, Celebration, Intervention, and Freedom of Expression

Diverse Americans, fearing that fascism could, indeed, "happen here," mounted counterattacks that led to Pelley's imprisonment, Winrod's indictment, and Smith's ostracism. These attacks on native fascist agitators during the 1930s and 1940s were part of a broader effort to erase racial and ethnic prejudice. While pursuing these worthy goals, however, foes of the far right often exaggerated both its power and its Axis connections. In addition, the campaign against domestic fascism—the Brown Scare—distorted the debate over American entry into World War II, set precedents for Cold War suppression, and spread misleading notions that would ultimately mold the postwar theory of extremism.

Like "100% Americans" during the Red Scare of 1919–20, liberals and radicals during the 1930s founded or redirected organizations specifically to combat subversion—in this instance, far right subversion. Many of these groups were ephemeral, but several attracted prominent backers and mobilized substantial constituencies. The Non-Sectarian Anti-Nazi League (initially created to boycott German imports) and the Mobilization for Democracy (Smith's potent adversary in California) sponsored forums, issued newsletters, and mustered demonstrators against those whom they considered native fascists. So did the Council for Democracy and the American Council Against Nazi Propaganda, led respectively by journalist Raymond Gram Swing and William E. Dodd, ambassador to Germany from 1933 to 1938. The Council Against Intolerance, headed by James Waterman Wise, specialized in combating bigotry in the schools.[1]

Friends of Democracy, the foremost of these new organizations, was founded in Kansas City, Missouri, in 1937 by Winrod's bête noire, Rev. L. M. Birkhead. The Friends' distinguished advisory board came to include John Dewey, Thomas Mann, Paul Douglas, and Van Wyck Brooks; starting in 1942, the mystery novelist Rex Stout served as president. Yet Birkhead was usually given a free hand. By 1939, when he opened a second office in New York City, he had compiled dossiers on 800 "pro-Nazi and Fascist" groups. Friends of Democracy fought the far right with what Birkhead liked to call "pitiless publicity," a technique first used effectively against Winrod during his 1938 Senate race.[2]

The numerous exposés of native fascism issued by established radical parties and Jewish self-defense organizations, as well as by specialized groups like Friends of Democracy, are usually accepted at face value by historians. Yet these tracts, like those produced by Pelley, Winrod, and Smith, constitute a countersubversive canon illustrative of the cultural tensions of the 1930s and 1940s. Although Birkhead's pitiless publicity was never so vicious or irresponsible as *Liberation*, the *Defender*, and the *Cross and the Flag*, both far right agitators and their foes drew on common intellectual currents and, to some extent, still spoke what Clinton Rossiter calls our shared political language. Both sides, moreover, spoke in idioms developed during the cultural crisis of the 1920s.[3]

For instance, far right activists and their opponents were influenced by the fear of deception that characterized the whole interwar period. "When the United States gets fascism," Huey Long was supposed to have said, "it will call it anti-fascism." The remark was apocryphal, but the underlying premise, that fascism would triumph in disguise, was shared by socialists and centrist liberals, Communist theoreticians and the editors of *Life*. Americans might fall for someone like Buzz Windrip, Sinclair Lewis suggested in *It Can't Happen Here*, because they were accustomed to being duped by con men and ad men. Appropriately, students of deceptive language and the emotional power of symbols (significant intellectual enterprises during the Depression) paid close attention to native fascism. The Institute for Propaganda Analysis (IPA), established at Columbia University in 1937, published copious material on the far right, with IPA editorial director Harold Lavine contributing the wittiest exposé, *The Fifth Column in America*. And Professor Harold Lasswell, who had debunked democracy during the 1920's, defended it during the 1930s by developing a method of content analysis to dig beneath false professions of patriotism (the method used to convict Pelley in 1942).[4]

When far right activists and their opponents called each other un-American, both sides were participating in a national celebration begun during the Depression that would have long-range consequences. On one side, Pelley, Winrod, Smith, and their fellows took comfort in the belief that government bureaucracy, sexual freedom, and modernist theology were products of "red infiltration." But otherwise sophisticated liberals and radicals who exaggerated the far right's tie to Berlin and supposed that only disguised fascism could happen here were also affirming American virtue.[5]

Frequent, if anxiety-laden, paeans to "the people" characterized the American celebration. The "people's" deeds, feelings, and memories filled Federal Writers Project notebooks, *New Masses* columns, and documentary travelogues by distinguished authors. The next century, Vice-President Henry A. Wallace predicted in 1942, would belong to the "common man." Yet many commentators, while hailing the common man, wondered what he would do with his century. After all, only a decade before their transitions to national celebration, social science skeptics like Harold Lasswell and rebels against the village like Sinclair Lewis had portrayed the irrationality, pettiness, and provincialism of ordinary Americans. Such doubts persisted, for instance, in *Life*'s warning in 1939 that small-town simple folk were "easy meat" for demagogues. Until the post-World War II era, however, these qualms were usually subordinated to cries of "The People, Yes."[6]

Themes from the fundamentalist controversy were also incorporated into the Brown Scare. Many secular commentators, such as Heinz H. F. Eulau of the *New Republic*, believed that "authoritarian fundamentalists" comprised the largest segment of "potential fascists" in the United States, but, like the debunkers of the 1920s, they seldom bothered to analyze the religious issues at stake. For example, still considering "fundamentalist" more or less synonymous with loud, commentators routinely mischaracterized Gerald Smith as an "old-fashioned" fundamentalist in the mold of Billy Sunday. Greater theological precision seemed unnecessary to secular writers who considered appeals to Scripture another means to deceive the multitudes; much as Sinclair Lewis in 1922 had presented Elmer Gantry's "faith" as a cover for careerism, Eulau suspected that Smith and Winrod's "Fascist-oriented fundamentalism" really had "little to do with religion."[7]

Meanwhile, faithful Protestants continued the fundamentalist conflict from another angle. While Winrod charged that his traditional enemies, theologically liberal social gospelers, capitulated to Moscow, they accused him of serving Berlin. They, too, built on earlier acrimony, such as *Christian Century*'s description of post–World War I dispensationalists as servants of capitalist reaction. No one better illustrates this continuity from the 1920s to the Brown

Scare than L. M. Birkhead. As modernist pastor of All Souls Unitarian Church in Kansas City, Birkhead had not only befriended Sinclair Lewis and H. L. Mencken, but also chided fundamentalists in pamphlets, radio programs, and debates (including a confrontation on evolution with William Bell Riley of the World Christian Fundamentals Association). Orthodoxy stirred "hatreds," he said, and small-town preachers especially spread "narrowness, prejudice, [and] littleness." Both Birkhead's conception of his fundamentalist foes and his flair for sweeping assertion survived in Friends of Democracy's "pitiless publicity."[8]

Of course, many rural and urban fundamentalist pastors did stir hatred, with some becoming, like Winrod, far right activists or, like Riley, far right fellow travelers. Yet there was no necessary connection between conservative theology and far right activism. Many fundamentalist leaders, largely oblivious to politics, spent the 1930s building seminaries, missionary societies, and publishing houses. And a majority of devout fundamentalists, because they were poor, southern, or both, voted for Roosevelt. Nevertheless, the convention associating fundamentalism with bigotry and reaction, created during the 1920s, was widely disseminated during the Brown Scare. Following World War II, this convention, combined with surfacing suspicion of "simple folk," would decisively influence interpretations of the far right.[9]

Efforts begun during the Depression to sort out political allies and enemies also bestowed a legacy to postwar theories of extremism. What Max Lerner called the "burning question" of fascism moved many political liberals to ally with the Communist Party against the far right. Others refused to support this Popular Front, insisting that Germany and the Soviet Union were equally "totalitarian." For these liberals, a crucial domestic corollary held that Americans tolerant of totalitarian regimes abroad were suspect themselves. Thus, as L. M. Birkhead insisted, sound domestic politics lay between the "extremists of the Right and the Left." Amid the shifting alliances of the 1930s, it remained difficult to fix exact boundaries of reputability, especially since Communists often converted to the ranks of conservatism or anti-Communist liberalism. Nevertheless, the militant centrism that would dominate the 1950s already existed in embryo.[10]

Powerful media, often using new formats, helped to spread the Brown Scare beyond politicized liberals and radicals to the simple folk whom *Life* wanted to inoculate against native fascism. Far right agitators glared menacingly from *Life*'s photoessays and, accompanied by portentious narration, from *March of Time* newsreels. Newspaper columns by Washington insider Drew Pearson, who purported to show the real story beneath surface deception, regularly scored the far right. Walter Winchell, the most popular if not the most eminent radio newscaster, emphasized the domestic fascist menace. In 1936, Warner Brothers released Hollywood's chief treatment of native fascism, *Black Legion*, in which a common man (Humphrey Bogart) is duped into joining a paramilitary band.[11]

Some of the most influential attacks were cast in a popular genre of the 1930s and 1940s—the documentary. To a nation wary of propagandists and deceivers, documentary books, films, and broadcasts seemed to provide reliable information, invulnerable to falsification. The exposure of the far right, Richard Rollins wrote in *I Find Treason*, must be "based entirely upon documentary evidence that would leave the subverts powerless to defend or deny." Paradoxically, the documentary's apparent factuality enhanced its power to affect emotions. Birkhead's lists of native fascists made tiny far right sects seem potent; Rollins's repeated accounts of casual encounters among local agitators seemed to signal an imminent coup. Indeed, Rollins's *I Find Treason* and Elizabeth Dilling's *The Red Network* were stylistic cousins under their bindings.[12]

During the Brown Scare, as in the Red Scare of 1919–20, official action ultimately overshadowed private polemics. The careers of Pelley and Smith underscore the efforts of successive committees created by the United States House of Representatives to investigate Un-American Activities. Parallel committees were established by several legislatures; some states also required registration of subversive organizations, tried to ban public display of masks and paramilitary regalia, and attempted to outlaw the libel of racial, religious, and ethnic groups. These laws, though subject to constitutional challenge, were nonetheless useful to prosecutors and police. In 1938, for example, six members of the German-American Bund on Long Island were convicted of failing to register as members of an oath-bound organization. Lacking special legislation, local officials often used ordinances forbidding breach of the peace to restrain far right activities.[13]

Throughout the 1930s, the Brown Scare proceeded simultaneously with a muted Red Scare that, though pursued avidly by conservatives and far right agitators, found only intermittent support in the White House. Some probers of native fascism were already veteran countersubversives now in search of fresh subversives to counter. For example, Martin Dies, chairman of the House Committee on Un-American Activities from 1938 until 1945, had long suspected Communist infiltration of the New Deal and considered Gerald L. K. Smith a competent authority on the subject. Nevertheless, eager for publicity and pressed by liberal colleagues, he held hearings on the Silver Legion and the German-American Bund as well as the CIO and the Federal Theatre Project. Dies staked his own peculiar claim to the center in 1940, claiming that the United States must suppress two "fifth columns," because Stalin and Hitler both used "trojan horse methods of conquest."[14]

Among liberals and radicals, less experienced than Dies in techniques of suppression, the Brown Scare prompted a reexamination of the meaning of freedom in general and a willingness to curb the liberty of native fascists in particular. Many congressional liberals voted to recharter the House Committee on Un-American Activities in 1938 because they wanted to investigage Silver Shirts and Bundists. Representative Jerry Voorhis (Dem.-Cal.), who pressed Dies to subpoena Pelley, believed that the hearings in 1940 revealed an "attempt to form a united fascist movement." That same year, liberals acquiesced in passage of the Smith Act, which, Representative Samuel Dickstein (Dem.-N.Y.) hoped, would be used to indict far right agitators.[15]

Risks as well as irony accompanied these tactics. During the previous two decades, the left had been disrupted and in some instances disseminated by investigations, censorship, and cancellation of ings in the name of public order. Left spokesmen applying such measures against the far right, the *Nation* warned in 1939, would bear the brunt of future enforcement. Roger N. Baldwin, executive director of the American Civil Liberties Union, warned that "any restrictions on freedom of speech, press or assembly, regardless of whom they affect, lay down the precedents by which those rights are generally injured."[16]

Still, there was much support for the position that Baldwin in 1938 called "'Liberty for Our Side' only." Writing in the *Nation*, Ludwig Lore presented the case as early as 1933. By allowing "untrammeled self-sepression," Lore believed, the European left had inadvertently aided the Fascist and Nazi triumphs. The columnist Heywood Broun, backed by his editors at the *New Republic*, also derided a "policy of fair play" for anyone "whether or not he has anything to say." Rather, Broun urged, civil libertarians should defend the "underdog" instead of running "to every fire."[17]

Left intellectuals often justified restrictions on freedom of expression by stressing again the impact of propaganda on the unconscious. Adherents to the "clear and present danger" test, wrote legal realist Karl Lowenstein, were "innocent dupes" of totalitarians who could prepare "internal revolution by remote control." According to L. M. Birkhead, agitators exploiting prejudice to seek power forfeited their constitutional right to talk nonsense. Although Max Lerner granted fascists the right to speak and publish, he sought to protect the public against deception. Under Lerner's proposed Truth in Opinion Act, a board analogous to the Securities and Exchange Commission would reveal the financial and ideological sources of "underground" publications, guarantee equal time to answer "inflammatory" radio programs, and possibly ban "poisonous" material. Standing even farther from what he called the ACLU's "crazy ethical absolutism," Lewis Mumford not only wanted to bar "pro-fascist" material from the mail, but recommended exile or jail for the "ringleaders."[18]

The most powerful liberal, President Franklin D. Roosevelt, also wanted to fight native fascism. Actions previously discussed—surveillance of Smith, indictment of Winrod, and successful prosecution of Pelley—fitted into an extensive campaign against the far right. As early as 1935, Roosevelt authorized a Federal Bureau of Investigation survey of pro-Nazi groups. During the next two years, he and White House aides requested special reports on several far right agitators, and Attorney General Homer Cummings considered indicting one of them, George Christians of the Crusader White Shirts.[19]

The president's mobilization of the FBI against the far right, a step in the agency's politicization, was probably the most consequential decision of the Brown Scare. When Roosevelt took office, the FBI had spent almost a decade in what journalist Sanford Ungar calls "benign obscurity." In 1924, Attorney General Harlan Fiske Stone had forbidden political surveillance and charged the new director, J. Edgar Hoover, with creating an honest, efficient agency. Hoover had done so. In addition, he had begun to build a national constituency by advertising FBI pursuit of colorful criminals. After initial hesitation, the Roosevelt administration had embraced Hoover's conception of crime control, extended FBI jurisdiction, and authorized agents to make arrests. Most important, the president and the director grew to like and respect each other.[20]

In late 1936, Roosevelt ordered a comprehensive investigation by the FBI and military intelligence of "subversive activities in the United States, particularly Fascism and Communism." After meeting with FDR, Hoover concluded that the administration sought a "broad picture" of subversion, sanctioned use of "all possible sources," and wanted the probe hidden from Congress. The director immediately informed FBI field offices of the new policy. Two years later, he reconstituted the General Intelligence Division, which, under his supervision during the Red Scare, had compiled dossiers on at least 100,000 dissidents. The FBI quickly compiled extensive files on "radical," "fascist," and "nationalist" groups. On the far right, these included the Silver Shirts, George Deatherage's Knights of the White Camelia, the Coughlinite Christian Front, and Joseph E. McWilliams's various enterprises. By late 1939, Hoover had outflanked military and naval intelligence to become the administration's premier investigator.[21]

The outbreak of the European war in September 1939 began a new phase of the Brown Scare, a phase marked by acrimonious debate over intervention abroad, by further shifts in political coalitions at home, and by heightened anxiety about subversion. On the one hand, many conservative Democrats and Republicans who were still critical of the New Deal favored Roosevelt's steady expansion of aid to the Allies during 1939–41. On the other hand, many liberals and socialists who shared FDR's commitment to the welfare state now worked with isolationist conservatives to prevent American belligerency. The Communist party, sui generis, favored neutrality until Germany attacked the Soviet Union in June 1941.[22]

Rivals in this foreign policy debate conjured up specters of native fascism. War against fascism abroad, isolationists predicted, would establish it at home. With greater effect, interventionists portrayed domestic fascists already on the march—in the ranks of the administration's isolationist critics. This "Trojan Horse" threatened the United States, Roosevelt told radio listeners in May 1940; members of the America First Committee, he said on another occasion, were "unwitting aids of the agents of Nazism." According to Secretary of the Interior Harold L. Ickes, the Committee consisted of appeasers, anti-Semites, and enemies of democracy. Encouraged by the White House and privy to information from J. Edgar Hoover, Walter Winchell assailed the "Hitler First-America Last-Committee" and portrayed Pelley, Winrod, and Smith as typical "assolationists."[23]

Although America First Committee leaders repudiated native fascists, their noninterventionist premises, standard fare for two decades, inevitably overlapped with those of the far right. As noted earlier, congressional isolationists sometimes cooperated with agitators like Smith, and the America First Committee's most popular speaker, Charles A. Lindbergh, in September 1941, listed "the Jews" among the three most powerful forces promoting the war. Lindbergh's brand of anti-Semitism (a "gentle" form, Pelley lamented) probably characterized as many interventionists as isolationists. To Americans accustomed to Brown Scare motifs, however, it sounded like an echo of Hitler.[24]

Organized isolationism was undone less by its own lapses into bigotry than by an opposition campaign portraying those lapses as evidence of subversion. There was no conspiracy among liberals, radicals, anglophiles, and Jews, as the far right believed, but interventionist groups did work together to discredit isolationists. L. M. Birkhead's Friends of Democracy was especially zealous and, acting in tandem with the Fight for Freedom Committee, especially effective. A Friends of Democracy pamphlet issued in March 1941, presented the America First Committee as a "Nazi front" hospitable to native fascists. In September, another Friends of Democracy pamphlet, distributed by Fight for Freedom, asked rhetorically *Is Lindbergh a Nazi*? And Birkhead, estimating that the United States contained fifteen million Nazi sympathizers, asked the federal government to observe the America First Committee officially.[25]

Birkhead had no reason to fear that the America First Committee would escape observation. Government surveillance escalated along with administration rhetoric. In November 1939, Roosevelt urged local police to give the FBI "any information relating to espionage, counterespionage, sabotage, subversive activities, and violations of neutrality law." At the same time, the agency began compiling a "custodial detention" index of persons with "strong" Nazi or Communist "tendencies" whose "presence at liberty in time of war or national emergency would constitute a menace." Director Hoover defined subversive activities with customary broadness and continued to monitor them via "all possible sources." Agents attended anti-war demonstrations, examined education and employment records, opened first-class mail and, began electronic surveillance after receiving Roosevelt's authorization in May 1940.[26]

Starting in November 1939, Hoover sent to the White House regular summaries of news from the field. As many as four memoranda arrived daily by messenger. Some simply revealed that FBI agents knew how to paraphrase newspapers; other contained factual errors, unsubstantiated rumors, or juicy gossip (such as suspicion of Gerald L. K. Smith's marital infidelity). Hoover knew how to make trivia sound lurid, if only by marking reports "personal and confidential." Occasionally, too, he massaged Roosevelt's vanity, noting, for example, that Van Buren, Arkansas, planned to commemorate the visit to a local tree by the presidential dog, Fala. Undoubtedly most of this material never reached Roosevelt's desk. Nor did FBI memoranda convince him that Senator George Norris (Rep.-Neb.) or labor leader Walter Reuther was dangerous. Nevertheless, FDR was genuinely grateful to Hoover for doing a "wonderful job" and supplying many "valuable reports."[27]

Roosevelt's concern about American Communism, which may have been greater than his concern about the far right when he first authorized Hoover to investigate subversion, ebbed after the Soviet

Union entered World War II, while his wariness of native fascism expanded throughout the battle against the isolationists. Sometimes responding to complaints by supporters (including Walter Winchell) or relatives (including his wife, Eleanor), the president in 1940–41 sought FBI reports on James True, Joseph E. McWilliams, Lawrence Dennis, and Robert Edmondson. In addition, he passed on to the director or the attorney general periodicals that appeared "scurrilous." Hoover dutifully responded with digests from FBI files.[28]

Just as Hoover's investigations of alleged subversion on the left slid from Earl Browder to Walter Reuther, so they moved easily on the right from Pelley, Winrod, and Smith to conservatives and reputable isolationists. Throughout 1940–41, for example, the FBI followed the activities of former ambassador Joseph P. Kennedy, Senator Gerald P. Nye, Senator Burton K. Wheeler, Charles A. Lindbergh, and the America First Committee.[29]

Not only did a high proportion of these reports reach the president, but he showed active interest in political surveillance. Presidential assistants routinely sent Hoover constituent mail protesting Roosevelt's speeches. Press Secretary Stephen Early wanted an agent to visit one letter writer who had questioned the president's health, an act "closely akin" to Fifth Column behavior. Roosevelt himself asked the FBI to pursue rumors that Representative Hamilton Fish had spent several hundred thousand dollars on subversive activities. Indeed, Roosevelt sometimes considered the FBI soft on subversion. Dissatisfied with Hoover's report that the America First Committee received no illicit money, FDR urged Attorney General Francis Biddle in December 1940 to bring the issue to a grand jury.[30]

Biddle, widely regarded as a civil libertarian, sometimes acted as a brake on Roosevelt. In early 1941, however, he assigned a special assistant, William Power Maloney, to investigate connections among prominent isolationists, far right agitators, and the Axis. The choice of Maloney, who operated with minimum concern for due process and maximum concern for publicity, could hardly have been less appropriate for this sensitive job; while an assistant United States attorney in New York, he had indicted three nonexistent persons. In July 1941, Maloney empaneled a grand jury in the District of Columbia. Three months later, he secured the indictment of pro-Nazi publicist George Sylvester Viereck for filing improperly under the Foreign Agents Registration Act. Furthermore, purporting to have discovered a conspiracy involving isolationists and far right agitators, he leaked grand jury testimony to columnists Drew Pearson, Walter Winchell, and Dillard Stokes of the *Washington Post*.[31]

American entry into the war made further indictments virtually inevitable, but Biddle wanted to avoid repeating the "extravagant abuses" of 1917–18. Consequently, he dropped three sedition indictments brought by United States attorneys immediately after Pearl Harbor and forbade FBI agents to make arrests for disloyalty without approval from Washington. Investigations proceeded in various jurisdictions, however, supervised by Assistant Attorney General Wendell Berge. In early 1942, these probes produced indictments under the Espionage Act of 1917 of Pelley, George W. Christians of the Crusader White Shirts, and Ellis O. Jones and Robert Noble (whose organization, Friends of Progress, had conducted a grotesque "impeachment of Roosevelt); all were convicted. Pressured by the Justice Department, Archbishop Edward Mooney on 1 May forced Coughlin to retire from politics. By early summer, ranking German-American Bundists faced denaturalization hearings or prosecution.[32]

The Attorney General's caution conflicted with Roosevelt's view that the war offered an opportunity to "clean up . . . vile publications." Roosevelt grumbled to other cabinet members that far right activists remained at large, and in 1942 instructed the FBI to circumvent Biddle's order that no arrests be made for sedition without specific authorizations. Furthermore, because representatives possessed "no valid" immunity from investigation, FDR ordered a probe of Martin Dies whom he suspected (on the basis of speculation by ACLU General Counsel Morris Ernst) of accepting $20,000 from German agents. In addition to bombarding Biddle with memoranda, Roosevelt gruffly asked him at cabinet meetings, "When are you going to indict the seditionists?" The president, Biddle recalled with his customary patrician understatement, "was not much interested . . . in the constitutional right to criticize the government in wartime."[33]

Neither was Special Prosecutor Maloney. Extending the term of his District of Columbia grand jury into 1942, he called more than one hundred witnesses, including Representatives Clare Hoffman and Hamilton Fish; he also secured perjury indictments against Fish's aide George Hill, as well as Winrod's secretary, Myrtle Flowers, and threatened other witnesses with the same fate. Playing for headlines, Maloney speculated about indicting Fish, warned that German submariners would probably try to rescue Viereck, and continued leaking testimony to the press.[34]

Finally, on 21 July 1942, the grand jury charged twenty-eight German agents, Bundists, and native far right agitators—including Pelley and Winrod—with conspiring to cause insubordination in the armed forces. This indictment, known as *United States* v. *Winrod*, set in motion the major prosecution of the Brown Scare. At the next cabinet meeting, his gruffness gone, President Roosevelt congratulated Attorney General Biddle on the grand jury's "true bill." But the mass sedition case, hampered by Maloney's ineptitude, would not come to trial until 1944. Then, expanded to thirty defendants and retitled *United States* v. *McWilliams*, it would end in tragedy and farce.[35]

Under Cover and Under Indictment

While eagerly awaiting the Justice Department's mass sedition prosecution, many Americans expanded their private fight against native fascism. Friends of Democracy prospered during World War II, received accolades from Eleanor Roosevelt, and added to its advisory board such distinguished figures as Philip Murray, Frank P. Graham, and Mary McLeod Bethune; in January 1943, the organization began a newsletter, *Propaganda Battlefront. Life* published fresh photoessays on far right agitators, and the *New Republic* devoted a regular feature to "enemies at home." Notable book-length exposés appeared by George Seldes, Albert E. Kahn of the American Council Against Nazi Propaganda, and Henry Hoke, a mail order specialist, who regarded magazines like the *Defender* and the *Cross and the Flag* as the "*blackest* mail fraud of all times." Walter Winchell continued both to pound "Americans we could do without" and to publicize exposés written by others.[36]

Familiar themes were adapted to fit the dominant mood favoring wartime unity and postwar international cooperation. Both goals were threatened, Friends of Democracy director L. M. Birkhead warned, by fascists who now hid under the cover of "supernationalism." Indeed, those whom Kahn and Michael Sayers called "Axis psychological saboteurs" were sometimes considered as dangerous as enemy soldiers. Once again, "Axis" was broadly defined to encompass many conservatives and isolationists. Writing from a Popular Front perspective, Seldes included within the "Fascist International" not only the "lunatic fringes" mobilized by Pelley, Smith, and Winrod, but also the National Association of Manufacturers, the American Legion, and *Reader's Digest.* Kahn and Sayers remembered the America First Committee as a "vehicle for German political conspiracy." Similarly, Birkhead held "Nazi and Fascist forces" responsible for a wartime isolationist revival. Unless voters defeated Robert A. Taft and other senators "very closely" tied to the Axis line, Birkhead added, postwar cooperation might suffer the same fate as the Versailles Treaty.[37]

In July 1943, E. P. Dutton published the most comprehensive, frightening, and widely-read exposé of native fascism—*Under Cover* by Avedis Derounian. Derounian, an Armenian immigrant whose family had come to the United States when he was twelve, considered his adopted country a refuge; as a young journalist, he participated in the American celebration of the 1930s. Appalled by the far right he had encountered in New York City, Derounian became an "independent under-cover man" in 1939. Assuming various aliases, but usually posing as an Italian-American bigot named George Pagnanelli, Derounian attended hundreds of rallies, met scores of far right activists, and sought out dozens of isolationist politicians. To improve his credibility among native fascists, he briefly published his own anti-Semitic paper. After Pearl Harbor, convinced that far right subversives disguised as patriots planned another sneak attack "on the psychological front," Derounian continued his secret investigation.[38]

At the same time, unknown to his far right "friends," Derounian attacked native fascism in the *American Mercury* (using the pseudonym John Roy Carlson), advised *Life* on "Our Fascist Enemies Within," and after 1940 consulted almost daily with Friends of Democracy. He also reported his activities to the New York police, the FBI, and eleven other federal agencies. *Under Cover*, his final report on four years in the "Nazi underworld of America," was accepted by E. P. Dutton after nineteen publishers, wary of low sales and libel suits, had rejected it. Sharing the prevailing opinion that native fascists would triumph in disguise, Derounian had undertaken "to live, then to write" the book in order to teach Americans to recognize fascists no matter "how subtle" their approach. He finished the last chapters at a "hideout" and again adopted the pseudonym John Roy Carlson.[39]

Under Cover, which led nonfiction best-sellers in 1944, was frequently exciting and sometimes informative. Derounian showed that far right activists exchanged cordial letters, read each other's magazines, and often collaborated to spread prejudice. Moreover, some of those still clinging to reputability were, like Gerald L. K. Smith, willing to accept quiet support from overt anti-Semites. The standard roster of native fascists dominated the book: Joseph E. McWilliams, Elizabeth Dilling, Lawrence Dennis, and assorted Bundists. With an eye for detail, Derounian captured Smith's incessant energy and Pelley's otherworldly vagueness. According to *Under Cover*, Winrod changed "completely" after visiting Germany in 1935, made a second trip there in 1936, and later spent several hours at the German embassy. To bolster his exposé, Derounian, even more than Richard Rollins in *I Find Treason*, used the documentary technique popularized during the Depression. *Under Cover,* he boasted, contained "66 documents, photographs, and photographic reproductions."[40]

Yet *Under Cover's* failings outweighed its virtues. As with many documentaries composed during the 1930s and 1940s, the air of accuracy was unwarranted. Sometimes Derounian's facts were wrong. Winrod, for example, visited Germany only once—in 1934, *after* his conversion to anti-Semitism. Long conversations that Derounian could not have recalled verbatim nonetheless appeared in quotation marks. A remarkably large number of these conversations were said to have occurred in dark corners, accompanied by sordid leers. Most important, along with many others who envisioned a conspiracy stretching from Berlin to the United States Senate, Derounian presumed guilt on the basis of slender association. Throughout *Under Cover,* casual encounters were presented as sturdy alliances, while occasional cooperation was transformed into warm friendship. Smith and Governor Eugene Talmadge, for instance, appeared as current "friends" even though they had parted on bad terms in 1936. Derounian's documentary evidence included commonplace congressional responses to inquiries from far right constitutents. But neither personal acquaintenance, however slight, nor correspondence, however routine, was necessary to link someone to the "Nazi Underworld." It was sufficient to be quoted favorably by far right agitators or Bundists.[41]

Derounian's main targets were prewar isolationists, particularly those continuing to serve in Congress after Pearl Harbor. The America First Committee had begun as a respectable organization, he conceded, but was captured by an "overwhelming majority of fascist party-liners." *Under Cover's* chief value, Derounian commented after publication, was to show the "tie-in" among far right agitators, ten Representatives (including Fish and Hoffman) and fourteen Senators (including Wheeler, Nye, and Taft).[42]

Partly in spite of its flaws and partly because of them, *Under Cover* hit a nerve of wartime patriotism and anxiety. More than one million copies were sold. Walter Winchell called it the "most sensational book in the last ten years," Rex Stout's fictional hero Nero Wolfe read it, and Max Lerner hailed Derounian as a "guerilla warrior in enemy territory." Their predictable enthusiasm was shared by figures as diverse as Clifton Fadiman, Bennett Cerf, Kate Smith, and Mary Margaret McBride. *Under Cover* ran serially in the Republican *New York Herald-Tribune* as well as liberal Democratic *New York Post.* Pronouncing Derounian's evidence authentic, the Council on Books in Wartime produced a film version of *Under Cover.*[43]

Condemnations were as spirited as endorsements. Virtually alone on the left, Norman Thomas (described in *Under Cover* as a "zealot" who had cooperated with Communists and fascists to "sabotage national defense") accused Derounian of distorting the nature of anti-war sentiment in 1940–41. Hostile reaction was unanimous among far right agitators, conservatives, and isolationists—especially those derided in the book. Gerald L. K. Smith, in one of his resorts to physical intimidation, ejected Derounian, a much smaller man, from a Committee of One Million rally. More decorous, conservative newspaperman Frank Gannett threatened legal action. Derounian or E. P. Dutton were sued by three minor subjects charged in *Under Cover* with anti-Semitism or Axis ties; all won favorable verdicts or apologies. Representative Hamilton Fish dismissed *Under Cover* as "left wing New Deal and Communist front propaganda," Senator Gerald P. Nye felt maligned by "clever editing," and Representative Clare Hoffman suspected that the book was being used to indoctrinate soldiers. Senator Burton K. Wheeler wondered why the thirty-four-year-old author was exempt from the draft (he was deferred, the Selective Service responded, as a pre-Pearl Harbor father). In November 1944, Wheeler proposed a Senate investigation of Derounian.[44]

After the Senate refused in March 1945 to fund this probe, Wheeler's friend John T. Flynn led an unofficial assault on *Under Cover.* Flynn, who had chaired the New York chapter of the America First Committee, argued in the *Chicago Tribune, Washington Times-Herald,* and comparable conservative publications that Derounian's book spearheaded a "conspiracy" to discredit all isolationists. Chief conspirators included the Communist party and several "private gestapos": the B'nai B'rith Anti-Defamation League, the Non-Sectarian Anti-Nazi League, and Friends of Democracy. According to Flynn, they had developed a "new technique in character assassination," using "innuendo" falsely to associate patriots like Wheeler, Nye, and himself with Bundists and Silver Shirts.[45]

Flynn's denunciation of the "smear terror" contained a mixture of blind anger, bad judgment, insight, and irony. He overstated the unity of his foes while also exaggerating Jewish and Communist influence among them. Beneath his exaggerated charge of conspiracy, however, Flynn correctly sensed that internationalists continued to work together after Pearl Harbor in spreading the notion that unrepentant isolationists were Axis sympathizers. A case in point was the Fight for Freedom Committee, transformed into Freedom House in 1942, which promoted *Under Cover* and provided radio time for L. M. Birkhead to answer Wheeler's attack on the book. Perhaps more than Flynn realized, Friends of Democracy was by 1943 the foremost source of information about native fascists and their putative isolationist allies. Even Flynn's obsession (which he shared with Winrod and Smith) that Walter Winchell was the Roosevelt administration's radio hatchet man had some basis in Winchell's large audience, friendship with J. Edgar Hoover, and access to the White House.[46]

Ironically, *Smear Terror*, Flynn's pamphlet complaining that respectable isolationists had been unfairly linked to far right agitators, was itself distributed by far right agitators. Moreover, while condemning the internationalist "smear bund" for relying on flimsy evidence, innuendo, and guilt-by-association, Flynn used these techniques himself. His quotations from Birkhead's early writings made modernist religion sound lurid. Conflating centrist and Popular Front liberals, he noted that Friends of Democracy President Rex Stout had contributed to the *New Masses*, and treated Derounian (a Willkie Republican who repudiated the "extreme Left" in *Under Cover*) as a fellow traveler. Nor did Flynn's disdain for "gestapos" prevent his use of material supplied secretly by the Dies committee. Stung by internationalist allegations of disloyalty, he was by 1944 already in transit from liberal isolationism to postwar conservation.[47]

Such transitions occurred often, but their connection to the Brown Scare deserves emphasis. The more internationalists tried "to smear people now," Senator Wheeler wrote to Flynn in 1943, "the more it is going to react against them when this war is over." For many unreconstructed isolationists, the left's vulnerability during the Cold War would provide such an opportunity to settle old scores.[48]

Before this reversal, however, criticism of *Under Cover* coverged with the larger controversy surrounding the mass sedition case. *United States* v. *Winrod*, the indictment returned in July 1942, was more a product of Special Prosecutor William Power Maloney's showmanship than a result of legal craftsmanship. The government charged that twenty-six men and women had violated the Espionage Act of 1917 and the Smith Act by conspiring to cause insubordination in the armed forces. Specifically, they had urged Roosevelt's impeachment, blamed his administration for fostering miscegenation, and endorsed Axis foreign policy. To disseminate this propaganda, the accused had organized or used groups as varied as the Silver Shirts and the America First Committee. On 4 January 1943, Maloney with his usual flair for publicity, announced a second, presumably stronger indictment, also called *United States* v. *Winrod*, which added six defendants, traced the conspiracy back to Hitler's triumph in 1933, and named as coconspirator the publisher of *World Service*, a German propaganda sheet.[49]

The charge of conspiracy had several advantages for the prosecution. It allowed Maloney to bring scattered defendants to trial in the jurisdiction of his choice. Using two aliases, the special prosecutor's journalistic ally, Dillard Stokes of the *Washington Post,* had solicited letters from the accused and these were used to establish venue in the District of Columbia. Prevailing practice also allowed juries to find a conspiracy among persons who had never met or reached formal agreement. In order to show intent to conspire, prosecutors customarily introduced—and courts customarily admitted—circumstantial evidence. Convictions were possible even if the plan had misfired. Federal procedure demanded an overt act in furtherance of the conspiracy, but this act might be something as trivial as sending letters to Dillard Stokes. If jurors decided that defendants had conspired, each conspirator was held responsible for the words and deeds of the others. Under these lax rules, the American Civil Liberties Union noted, juries were "more likely to convict for conspiracy" than for substantive offenses.[50]

The sedition indictments divided prominent civil libertarians. Zechariah Chafee, Jr., the premier authority on freedom of speech, called them "indefensible." Roger N. Baldwin, executive director of the ACLU, considered the case "monstrous," and ACLU General Counsel Arthur Garfield Hays drafted a protest against this "sort of attack on free speech, once removed." On the other hand, ACLU General Counsel Morris L. Ernst, who had persistently urged President Roosevelt to take action against the far right, refused to sign Hays's statement. After months of wavering, the ACLU decided in early 1943 to stand aside, a majority of directors believing that the accused "were cooperating with or acting on behalf of" the enemy.[51]

Except for occasional Socialists like Norman Thomas and the Socialist Workers Party, itself a victim of the Smith Act in 1942, the left expressed few doubts about the sedition case. On the contrary, newspapers from the *Washington Post* leftward to the *New York Daily Worker* applauded Special Prosecutor Maloney's efforts, often urging him to pursue Representative Fish and Senator Nye as well as Pelley and Winrod. L. M. Birkhead, Avedis Derounian, George Seldes, Albert Kahn, and Michael Sayers all looked forward to the trial in their exposés of the far right. In *Under Cover,* Derounian particularly stressed connections between congressional isolationists and the defendants in *United States* v. *Winrod.*[52]

This enthusiasm on the left helped to convince conservatives and isolationists that the sedition prosecution, like the publication of *Under Cover,* was intended to discredit reputable critics of the Roosevelt administration. Nor was this suspicion groundless. The *Chicago Tribune* justifiably complained that indictments lumping the America First Committee with "crackpots" unfairly denigrated all prewar isolationists. Similarly, Senator Traft assailed "witch hunting" reminiscent of World War I, Representative Fish proposed an amendment to the Smith Act requiring direct contact with the armed forces in any case alleging conspiracy to cause insubordination, and Senator Nye pronounced the second list of defendants "no more guilty of conspiracy than I am" (an inadvertent confession, according to the *Daily Worker*). Senator Wheeler, who had been deeply affected by the excesses of 1917–18, when he served as United States attorney in Montana, denounced the "entrapment" practiced by Special Prosecutor Maloney and his "stooge" Dillard Stokes.[53]

Maloney was undone—and the sedition trial delayed—by his own irresponsibility, by superiors skeptical of his competence, and by Senator Wheeler's persistence. The special prosecutor's weak case and flamboyant behavior disturbed Assistant Attorney General Wendell Berge and James Rowe, Jr., an aide to Attorney General Biddle. Nevertheless, Maloney continued to leak grand jury testimony in late 1942 and hinted of plans to indict Wheeler. Wheeler defied Maloney to charge him, released to the press Zechariah Chafee's criticism of *United States* v. *Winrod*, and sought a Senate probe of the Justice Department. Many of the accused were "reprehensible," he said, but their activities must be examined in a responsible way. Afraid of Wheeler, the special prosecutor looked for an escape in January 1943. Biddle moved Maloney out of the way by promoting him to head the Trial section.[54]

Along with leading liberal newspapers, President Roosevelt worried that this kick upstairs signaled "appeasement" of isolationists. Rowe assured him that Maloney's successor, O. John Rogge, was "equally tough." The youngest man ever to receive a Harvard law degree, Rogge went on to prosecute Governor Richard Leche's corrupt Louisiana machine and to serve as assistant attorney general. Serious and incorruptible, he was ambivalent about the sedition case. Believing that the far right spread prejudice and aided the Nazi cause, he had declined to sign Arthur Garfield Hays's aborted protest letter to Biddle. Yet, impressed by Chafee's recently published *Free Speech in the United States*, he disliked conspiracy trials. If the original decision had been his, Rogge reflected thirty-six years later, he might not have initiated the sedition prosecution. Entering in mid-battle on 7 February 1943, he was determined to win. Joseph W. Burns, one of the best trial lawyers at the Justic Department, assisted him.[55]

Their skill was soon tested. In March, U.S. District Judge Jesse C. Adkins dismissed one count of the second indictment because it held the accused responsible for activities between 1933 and passage of the

Smith Act in 1940. Immediately Rogge extended the life of the District of Columbia grand jury and attempted to strengthen the case. He deliberately shunned those provisions of the Smith Act forbidding advocacy of violent revolution, and focused on thirty persons whom he suspected of direct ties to the Nazis. Even circumstantial evidence, however, suggested that no more than three or four of them had received money from Germany. Nor was there sufficient proof to try the thirty individually for the substantive offenses of urging military insurbordination or failing to register as foreign agents. Therefore, Rogge the civil libertarian, like Maloney the showman, took advantage of conspiracy law.[56]

Unlike the two previous indictments, *United States* v. *McWilliams*, returned on 3 January 1944, postulated an *international* Nazi conspiracy dedicated to Hitler's "publicly announced" program to destroy democracy and establish "national socialist or fascist" governments in the United States and elsewhere. To further these ends, the thirty defendants allegedly had conspired with each other and with Nazi Germany. Moreover, they had maintained that fascism was superior to democracy, that the Roosevelt administration was dominated by plutocrats, radicals, and Jews, and that the Axis justly battled the combined threats of Communism and Judaism. By cooperating to disseminate this "systematic propaganda" with intent to impair the loyalty of the armed forces, they had violated the Smith Act.[57]

The final list of thirty defendants fell roughly into four categories. The first, leaders of far right organizations, included Winrod, Pelley and his lawyer Howard Victor Broenstrupp, Joseph E. McWilliams, George E. Deatherage, and Edward James Smythe, as well as Ellis O. Jones, Robert Noble, and Franz K. Ferenz of the Friends of Progress, Lois de Lafayette Washburn and Frank W. Clark of the National Liberty Party, and E. J. Parker Sage, William R. Lyman, and Garland L. Alderman of the National Workers League. The second group, writers and small publishers, included Elmer Frederik Elmhurst, Robert E. Edmondson, James True, Charles B. Hudson, Elmer J. Garner, David Baxter, Peter Stahrenberg, Elizabeth Dilling, Lawrence Dennis, and retired Colonel Eugene Nelson Sanctuary. Third, Nazi Germany's public relations specialist George Sylvester Viereck was joined by Prescott Freese Dennett, his associate in the Make Europe Pay Debts Committee. Finally, the grand jury indicted four former leaders of the German-American Bund: Gerhard Wilhelm Kunze, August Klapprott, Herman Max Schwinn, and Hans Diebel (who also ran the Aryan Bookstore in Los Angeles). Two far right fixtures were conspicuous in their absence: Father Charles E. Coughlin, who had been silenced by the Roman Catholic hierarchy in May 1942, and Gerald L. K. Smith, who remained at large and agitating (as Attorney Gerald Biddle told a disgruntled President Roosevelt in 1943) because Treasury and Justice Department investigations had discovered no illegalities.[58]

The defendants were an odd lot. They varied from vigorous agitators in their prime to men beyond seventy enfeebled by ill health. Most were poorly educated, but Dennis, Jones, and Dilling had attended respectively Harvard, Yale, and the University of Chicago. Winrod, who had received 53,000 votes in his race for senator, probably possessed the largest constituency; on the other hand, Sage, Lyman and Alderman were, according to FBI estimates, the only members of their National Workers League. All of the accused were isolationists during 1939–41, yet a handful had earlier supported FDR. Pelley, Jones, Noble, Ferenz, Viereck, and Kunze were already serving sentences for sedition or impeding the draft; Schwinn and Diebel were in custody as enemy aliens. Except for Dennis, Viereck, and Dennett, all were overt anti-Semites. Still, opinions spanned a bizarre spectrum, from Clark and Washburn, who endorsed genocide, through Pelley, who favored restriction of Jews to one city per state, to Winrod, who simultaneously denounced "bad" Jews and tried to convert "good" ones. Several defendants possessed erratic temperaments as well as vicious beliefs. Three, McWilliams, Dennett and Smythe, had been involuntarily committed for psychiatric examinations.[59]

Some of the defense attorneys were as peculiar as their clients. Sanctuary hired Henry Klein, an anti-Semitic Jew, and Albert W. Dilling, Elizabeth's lawyer and ex-husband, still shared her countersubversive views if not her domicile. But most counsel were competent professionals, two-thirds of whom had been appointed by the court without pay to serve indigent defendants; for example, William A. Gallagher taught criminal law, Joseph H. Bilbrey had been a United States attorney, and E. Hilton Jackson and John W. Jackson, Winrod's local counsel, had effectively challenged the second indictment. Selected largely from the civil bar, however, most had scant experience in criminal trials. Like Rogge, they pored over Chafee's *Free Speech* in an effort to master the complexities of sedition.[60]

Although untrained in law, Lawrence Dennis probably held the clearest conception of the trial issues at the outset. Author of *The Coming American Fascism*, Dennis defined fascism as a mixture of nationalism and corporate rationalization, predicted that the United States was moving toward some form of the system, and claimed to favor a "nice" version. A former Foreign Service officer, Dennis was more likely to be found debating social critic Alfred Bingham at the Harvard Club than to be seen with Pelley or Winrod on the hustings. Fascinated by far right agitators, however, he acquired a reputation as the one man "brain trust" of native fascism, and this reputation, combined with his uncompromising noninterventionism, led to his indictment in *McWilliams.* Special Prosecutor Rogge, impressed by Dennis's intelligence, outlined the government case to him in October 1943. It would be fatal, Dennis concluded thereafter, to concede the existence of an international Nazi movement because wartime jurors would likely assume that anyone indicted had belonged to it.[61]

Perhaps persuaded by Rogge, Chief Justice Edward C. Eicher of the United States District Court for the District of Columbia placed *McWilliams* on his own docket. A self-described "Andy Jackson Dimmycrat" who had been representative from Iowa and chairman of the Securities and Exchange Commission, Eicher was appointed to the bench in 1942. Admitting to Roosevelt that he felt "sort of silly" in judicial robes, he nonetheless vowed to preserve the "essential respect" due the courts. Eicher's ties to the administration convinced the most suspicious *McWilliams* defendants that he planned in advance to convict them. This supposition was groundless and inconsistent with his Mennonite probity. But pretrial hearings begun in January 1944 showed that he had few qualms about conspiracy cases. Eicher considered the charges in *McWilliams* adequately specific, sanctioned removal of all defendants to the District of Columbia because one of them might have committed an overt act there, and noted that "wrongful intent" was sufficient for convinction even if propaganda never reached the armed forces. Furthermore, activities antedating the Smith Act were pertinent to show intent and origins of the conspiracy.[62]

Pretrial hearings also suggested that respect for the judicial system would be at a premium. Defense lawyers denied the indictment's validity because nine government employees sat on the grand jury, questioned the Court's jurisdiction, and called the bill of particulars inflammatory as well as vague. At one point, Eicher ejected Sanctuary's contentious counsel, Henry Klein, for giving a "political speech." It was the first of many to be heard in District Court.[63]

Brown Scare at the Bar: *United States* v. *McWilliams*

The prelude to *United States* v. *McWilliams,* which finally came to trial on 17 April 1944, was hardly propitious. One defendant, Edward James Smythe, did not appear. Another, Lois de LaFayette Washburn, thumbed her nose at the courthouse and give a Nazi salute from its steps. Surveying the accused, James Wechsler of *PM* observed, "Seldom have so many wild-eyed, jumpy lunatic fringe characters been assembled in one spot, within speaking, winking, and whispering distance of one another."[64]

Chief Justice Eicher, following a week of rest beforehand, presided at the opening with a mixture of earnestness and affability. Within five minutes, Eugene Sanctuary's lawyer Henry Klein moved for postponement until he could secure testimony from President Roosevelt, Attorney General Biddle, and Secretary of State Cordell Hull; Prime Minister Winston Churchill and Nazi leader Rudolf Hess would be helpful too. During the arraignment, Lois de Lafayette Washburn addressed her namesake, "Lafeyette, we are here to defend what you gave us, freedom from tyranny." At day's end, Eicher must have known that rest would be rare and affability hard to maintain in the coming weeks.[65]

Smythe, who was apprehended near the Canadian border on 18 April, quickly established himself as court clown. Amid raucous laughter he testified the next day that he was vacationing in upstate New York because FBI "hounding" had left him a nervous wreck. His attorney James J. Laughlin insisted that government tampering with the mail had prevented Smythe from learning the trial date. Understandably skeptical, Eicher confiscated Smythe's bond.[66]

A month-long wrangle over jury selection began on 19 April. Within a week Eicher discharged a portion of the first venire because Rogge inadvertently mentioned the earlier indictments. The persistent illness of James True produced further delays. More important, adhering to a "plain reading of the statute," Eicher limited the thirty defendants to a total of ten peremptory challenges. Fearing that cooperation in legal matters might signal agreement among their clients, counsel proceeded under protest. Ira Chase Koehne, the aged attorney for Broenstrupp and Baxter, was fined $50 for his sarcastic challenge to the "upper portion" of three prospective jurors. Defendants submitted five hundred sensible and silly questions for the venire. Eicher boiled them down to sixty-one that he posed from the bench. Thus Washburn was unable to discover veniremen who thought that Jesus Christ was Jewish. But Eicher went far—too far—to protect bigoted defendants from a hostile jury. He asked, for instance, whether prospects were Jews, had Jewish relatives, or read Jewish publications. Several lawyers rejected jurors on the basis of this information. Only Dennis, Viereck, and Dennett dissociated themselves from challenges founded "on race."[67]

Maneuvers in and out of court accompanied jury selection. During recesses, Klein distributed literature calling for Roosevelt's impeachment. Albert Dilling tried and failed to convince the Senate Judiciary Committee to monitor the trial. Dennis requested mental tests for all defendants and sought severance because Smythe, Dennett, and Washburn were unbalanced. Sixteen lawyers, led by Laughlin, asked Eicher to disqualify himself for bias.[68]

A veteran of more than 2,000 trials, Laughlin liked to play to the press. Smythe and Noble, whom Laughlin had met through isolationist Senator William Langer, encouraged his flamboyance. At the end of April, Laughlin twice asked the United States Court of Appeals to halt the trial, moved to impound records of the Communist Party and the B'nai B'rith Anti-Defamation League (groups he held responsible for the case), and asked to subpoena Henry Ford and Charles A. Lindbergh. Encouraged by Albert Dilling, he filed an affidavit alleging that FDR planned to promote Eicher, perhaps to the United States Supreme Court, if the prosecution were "successful." Rogge retaliated by accusing Laughlin of making untimely, irrelevant, and deliberately disruptive motions. Despite a typically vigorous and voluble self-defense, Judge Jennings Bailey found Laughlin guilty of contempt on May 10.[69]

While *McWilliams* recessed for nine days during this collateral hearing, death claimed Elmer Garner, at eighty the oldest defendant. More important for the case, jury selection had to begin for a third time because the April venire expired on May 2. Another week was necessary to choose ten men and two women. The panel reflected both the skill of defense counsel and the preconceptions of most defendants. It contained at least three German-Americans but no blacks or Jews. Revelations of anti-Semitism, Dennis reflected, would not perturb this "southern town" jury.[70]

Outlining his case on 17 May, Rogge recalled that the "conspirator" Hitler had forced his appointment as German chancellor by subverting civil government and the armed forces. The triumphant Nazis quickly established branches abroad, including the German-American Bund, their "spearhead" in the United States. The defendants joined this "worldwide Nazi conspiracy" and schemed to create here the "same form of government" that existed in the Third Reich. Operating under a patriotic "smokescreen," they abused democratic freedoms in order to attack democracy, stirred anti-Semitism, and tried to undermine the military, a violation of Section I of Title I of the Alien Registration Act. Just as the "most stringent protection of free speech" proscribed a false cry of "Fire!" in a crowded theatre, Rogge said, paraphrasing Oliver Wendell Holmes, neither could it be construed to allow conspirators to impair the "loyalty of our armed forces."[71]

Rogge's opening statement required three hours, partly because he was interrupted throughout. Jones, representing himself, denounced the conspiracy between Biddle and the special prosecutor to persecute "reputable" Americans. Hearing that he had sponsored a joint meeting of the Ku Klux Klan and the German-American Bund, Smythe interjected, "Three cheers." Rogge's description of Dennis as the American "Alfred Rosenberg" elicited laughter from the defendants. To his remark that they had already chosen a *fuehrer,* some chanted, "Who? Who?" Counsel were more discrete in their skepticism. They objected to "inflammatory" allusions to Germany, suggested that literature deemed subversive by Rogge was available at the Library of Congress, and moved to strike the entire opening. The jury sat stunned.[72]

Starting on 19 May, defense attorneys affirmed the patriotism of their respective clients and stressed that the putative conspirators had little if any contact with each other. Some openings also stressed favorite political motifs. By arrangement with his fellows, Dennis spoke first and at greatest length. He both ridiculed the notion of a worldwide Nazi conspiracy and attacked "Vishinsky Rogge" for concocting a "political trial." The comparison drew applause from the accused, but Dennis later apologized to the Soviet prosecutor, whom he credited with greater ability.[73]

Dennis's ad hominem attack was part of a general decline in courtroom decorum. On 19 May, Klein persistently protested the thirty minute limit on defense openings; Jones followed with a soliloquy on his "persecution." Seeking to halt the trend toward incivility, Eicher cited both for contempt and threatened disruptive defendants with jail. The $200 fine did not prevent Klein from making a spirited opening in which he listed Felix Frankfurter among Jewish Communists and accused FDR of submission to Stalin. Similarly, Albert Dilling announced plans to show that "Jewish International Bankers" had financed the Russian Revolution.[74]

To prove the existence of a "worldwide Nazi movement," Rogge submitted histories of Germany, Nazi newspapers, speeches by Hitler and his subordinates, copies of *Mein Kampf,* and a flag bearing a swastika. Documents produced prior to the Smith Act were necessary, he explained, to show the conspiracy's beginnings. Defense lawyers objected to everything. The exhibits, they argued, were intended to develop the jury's taste for a "Nazi flavor" (or "sauerkraut flavor," as Dilling said privately). If the Constitution allowed Rogge to open a "historical debate," Dennis warned, then defendants and lawyers would be "entitled to discuss history until we are all old men." But Eicher believed that such material was relevant to the Smith Act. He "provisionally" admitted all government exhibits, expecting them to be "connected up" before Rogge rested his case. Hence, starting in late May, customs officials, postal clerks, and employees of the Library of Congress took the stand to identify books, articles, and pamphlets dealing with the Third Reich. Furthermore, a Foreign Service officer and two émigré scholars supported the prosecution interpretation of Nazi means and ends.[75]

The government pursued three lines of argument to show that defendants had joined the "worldwide Nazi movement." First, Rogge magnified a few direct contacts with Germany, such as Winrod's brief visit in 1935. The German press had praised several of the far right anti-Semites, and they in turn had received Nazi publications.[76]

Second, the prosecution portrayed the German-American Bund as the decisive link between Berlin and the native far right. Peter Gissibl, an erstwhile Bund leader and Rogge's first witness, testified on 23 May that his organization had cultivated some defendants "because we thought they would create a favorable atmosphere towards Germany." Gissibl, William Luedtke, who had sat on the national executive committee, and four lesser Bundists recalled contacts with Deatherage, McWilliams, and Pelley. Moreover, relying on records seized from the *Deutsches Haus* and the Aryan Bookstore in Los Angeles, Rogge demonstrated that the Bundists had bought, distributed, and occasionally read tracts by Pelley, Winrod, Dilling, and Edmondson.[77]

Third, the defendants' expressions of opinion resembled Nazi doctrines and thus furthered Nazi ends. They served, Rogge said, "to destroy the faith of all of us and have our soldiers not believe in our leaders, in order that we remain weak so that the Axis nations . . . could accomplish their objective." Testimony by FBI and Naval Intelligence agents, amateur investigators, and former followers showed that the defendants did indeed hold vile views. Schwinn, for instance, had compared Hitler to Jesus, Noble considered the *Fuehrer* a "brother." Pelley regarded himself as the "American Hitler," at least with reference to Jews. Deatherage also destested "kikes." True once offered a gun to a woman with the recommendation that she kill six Jews. Clark favored baseball bats for the same purpose and expected all Jews to "be buried here" when the "masses wake up." Nor was anti-Semitism the only manifestation of viciousness. According to Jones, infantile paralysis had destroyed Roosevelt's mind. True and Winrod allegedly regretted that no one had killed the president.[78]

The government accused the defendants of sharing their grotesque ideas with each other and cooperating to spread them to a wider audience. Reading publications or confiscated correspondence into the record, presenting bills of sale, and calling postal clerks to testify, Rogge and Burns showed that the home-grown far right often received or recommended each other's magazines, occasionally exchanged flattering letters, and intermittently borrowed bits of anti-Semitic lore. Winrod, for instance, not only subscribed to publications by Pelley, True, Deatherage, Edmondson, and Dilling, but assimilated Edmondson's notion that FDR had Jewish ancestors. Witnesses ranging from True's landlady to former employees of Pelley and Winrod testified that some defendants had conferred.[79]

Defense counsel, following typical tactics in conspiracy cases, responded by stressing disparities among the accused. Pelley's lawyer, William Powers, said that his client and Winrod were "not on speaking terms." Professing total ignorance of writings by Winrod and Pelley, Dennis wanted a continuance to remedy the situation at the rate of thirty-five pages per hour; he also repeatedly asked sanity tests for everyone. Except for former members of the organization, who had no choice in the matter, the accused especially wanted to stand apart from the Bund. After meeting *Bundesleiter* Fritz Kuhn, Powers noted, Pelley was not on "speaking terms" with him either. But the government, following typical prosecution tactics in conspiracy trials, countered that none of these personal quarrels mattered. It needed only to show that there had been a "loose-knit movement of many organizations" whose leaders were not necessarily "agreed on all details."[80]

Resurrecting a theme from pretrial motions, defense attorneys noted that most of the accused had never expressed their opinions, however eccentric, within the District of Columbia. Consequently, as John Jackson urged, there was no "plausible reason" to try them there. Again using conventional tactics, Rogge cited minor overt acts by a handful of the accused in order to establish venue. Pelley's magazines had been mailed to Washington. Winrod and True had eaten together at a downtown restaurant. According to Representative Hamilton Fish's aide George Hill, Viereck planned to distribute isolationist appeals under congressional frank. There could be "no better evidence of an overt act in this district," Rogge claimed, than this tract conceived and printed in Washington.[81]

Although Rogge pronounced military insubordination the "important element in this case," he slighted the issue during direct examination. Witnesses occasionally recalled seeing stray soldiers or sailors at meetings sponsored by the Bund or Silver Shirts. The recollections were hardly impressive. The vaguely remembered men in uniform, Powers suggested to a witness, might have been Sea Scouts. On the other hand, Gissibl and his fellow Bundists admitted during cross examination that they had never been ordered to undermine the military. Lacking evidence of specific appeals, Rogge argued that the Smith Act did not require propaganda to reach a single member of the armed forces. There was "no question," for example, about the guilt of someone who urged mothers to keep their sons out of service.[82]

Despite protests by Dennis and Ben Lindas, Viereck's able attorney, Jews were discussed much more than the military. The government opened the question by using anti-Semitism as evidence of Nazi connections. Jones, Klein, and Albert Dilling responded that opposition to the international Zionist conspiracy was not Nazism but good sense. To prove the point, Dilling tried unsuccessfully to introduce *The Protocols of the Learned Elders of Zion,* which he deemed "genuine," as a defense exhibit. But similar views were not confined to lawyers long associated with the far right. On the contrary, the behavior of several attorneys shows that anti-Semitism was common among the bar. Ethelbert Frey, appointed by the court to represent Edmondson, also endorsed *The Protocols* and denounced "Jewish Marxism." A half-dozen colleagues blamed the Anti-Defamation League for the trial or asked witnesses if they had Jewish relatives.[83]

Much of the record, however, was devoid of exciting exchanges about Nazis or Jews. Instead, it contained technical objections to virtually every prosecution witness and exhibit. A list of German periodicals mailed to the accused provoked typical reactions. Counsel said that unauthorized personnel had opened the magazines. They speculated about government "entrapment," and noted that periodicals often arrived unsolicited. Then too, they chided the government for introducing photocopies instead of original documents and for attributing letters to defendants without expert verification of signatures. They complained that exhibits from Pelley's headquarters and the *Deutsches Haus* had been seized illegally; they spent hours disputing Rogge's contention that the *Haus* and Diebel's bookstore within were both "Bund enterprises."[84]

Government presentation of evidence seemed no more satisfactory than the mode of acquisition. Defense lawyers complained, with some justification, that Rogge read statements out of context, moved exhibits quickly past the jury, and failed to supply copies for everyone. They objected that evidence in German was incomprehensible to most counsel and clients, adding that government translators were biased and incompetent. Fluent in German, Rogge responded that he had "never seen better translations."[85]

For more than seven months, Chief Justice Eicher strove to be fair in the face of "historical debates," anti-Semitic harrangues, and legal jousts. He reprimanded Rogge for discussing the case with *PM* and the *Daily Worker*. Courteous to defendants in court and in chambers, he even granted "Dr. Winrod" the benefit of his honorary degree from the Bible Institute of Los Angeles. He made allowances for Dennis and Jones because they lacked legal training. Nonetheless, Eicher's major rulings favored the government from the outset. His decision to admit provisionally very general evidence about Nazism was crucial. He stuck to it despite astute pleas to reconsider from Bilbrey, John Jackson, and McWilliams's lawyer, Maximilian St.-George. It was necessary, Eicher said, to see the "entire picture" before determining whether the Smith Act had been violated. Again without conscious bias, he also gave wider latitude to the prosecution in its effort to prove the existence of a "worldwide Nazi movement" than to defense lawyers determined to demonstrate the contrary.[86]

Accordingly, the defense played to the jury, which was likely to remember skeptical questions or sarcastic asides even though they were ruled out of order. Shrewd questioning undermined the credibility of several prosecution witnesses. A woman presented as an authority on subversion was confused without notes and unaware that Father Coughlin sponsored *Social Justice*. A Naval Intelligence agent recalled seeing "Dillinger's" literature at the Aryan Bookstore. Gissibl admitted appearing for the government in seventeen trials and Luedtke had a comparable record. Another Bundist had been convicted of impairing the morals of a minor and indecent exposure.[87]

Since Eicher rarely sustained defense objections, a pattern developed in May that persisted until the trial's end. After Rogge or Burns introduced an exhibit, called a witness, or posed a question, attorneys rose in turn to object, to be overruled, and to note an "exception" for purposes of appeal. Eicher permitted an initial objection to count for all defendants and asked "reasonable cooperation" in avoiding repetition. Yet, always afraid that procedural agreement would signal conspiracy among their clients, a half-dozen counsel often sought recognition to make—and to argue—the same point. Later they might rise again, moving to strike testimony and arguing that point. Furthermore, Eicher faced hundreds of motions to disqualify himself, to direct verdicts of innocent, or to declare a mistrial.[88]

During mid-June, the Supreme Court decision in *United States* v. *Hartzel* prompted the sturdiest defense challenge. An anti-Semite as vicious as any in *McWilliams*, Elmer Hartzel in 1942 had urged internal race war and foreign occupation of the United States. He was indicted under the Espionage Act of 1917 and found guilty of impairing the morale of the armed forces. By a five to four vote, the Supreme Court overturned the conviction. Although some of Hartzel's writings had reached army officers and men eligible for the draft, there was not "sufficient" evidence for the jury to find that he had "intended specifically to cause insubordination."[89]

Rogge found "no new principle of law" in the decision, but consented to argue the issue because opposing counsel disputed his view with such "vehemence." Leading the defense presentation on June 19, E. Hilton Jackson called *Hartzel* a constitutional landmark comparable to *Marbury* v. *Madison*. The Supreme Court, he said, had created a "material categorical definition of reasonable doubt" that applied to *McWilliams*. The Espionage Act of 1917 was "strikingly similar" to Title I, Section I of the Smith Act. Yet Hartzel had been set free even though his writings were more vitriolic than any distributed by the defendants. For three months, moreover, the government had offered evidence in *McWilliams* without approaching the Supreme Court's reasonable standard of proof. Jackson closed with a ringing plea for free speech.[90]

Less impassioned, Rogge drew a "plain line of distinction" between the two cases. In a "significant sentence," he said, the Supreme Court absolved Elmer Hartzel of foreign connections; the *McWilliams* defendants, on the other hand, belonged to a "worldwide Nazi movement." Furthermore, the special prosecutor used *Hartzel* to justify his potpourri of international exhibits. In evaluating a pamphleteers' aims, a majority of justices held, jurors must consider "not only the language actually used" but the "circumstances surrounding their preparation." Therefore, Rogge maintained, the same words might be innocent in one context and seditious in another if, for example, the speaker were "connected with a Nazi organization." Unlike the government in *Hartzel*, he had much evidence of "specific intent" to subvert the armed forces.[91]

These illustrations of intent were closer to Elmer Hartzel's harangues than Rogge admitted, yet his skillful performance left a contrary impression. Eicher listened carefully to both sides, complimented Jackson on his presentation, and heard defense rebuttals. He concluded that *Hartzel* differed from *McWilliams* because it turned "entirely" on the sufficiency of evidence regarding a "sole defendant" charged with a "substantive offense." Refusing a mistrial, he implicitly reaffirmed his faith that government testimony and exhibits would be linked to the Smith Act.[92]

Ironically, Eicher's rulings against the defense provided occasions for undermining the judicial dignity that he valued. The 22 May crackdown on Klein and Jones, while eliciting a letter of commendation from Secretary of the Interior Harold L. Ickes, failed to reverse the tide of incivility. By mid-June, Eicher had levied fines for contempt against Klein, Jones, Laughlin, Albert Dilling, St.-George, and Koehne. Their responses varied from vindictiveness to petulance. On 1 July, Laughlin urged the House of Representatives to impeach Eicher for "abusive, arbitrary, and tyrannical" conduct. At roughly the same time, Dilling formed a "contempt club" whose members received badges bearing the chief justice's initials.[93]

On 5 July, Eicher asked members of the "club, as they see fit to call it," to explain why its formation was not another act of contempt. Rogge volunteered that St.-George and Dilling had worn their badges in court. Denying disrespect for the chief justice, Dilling said that he had formed the group to rebuild defense "morale" shattered by citations from the bench. Eicher tolerantly accepted the disingenuous explanation. During the inquiry, however, he learned of the impeachment petition. Lacking Dilling's minimal tact, Laughlin contended that the chief justice had "no power" to inquire into his actions outside the courtroom. Eicher immediately dismissed him from the case and, the next day, barred him from the room. Henry Klein, on the other hand, departed voluntarily. Also on July 5, Sanctuary announced that his attorney, fearing for his life, had returned to New York City.[94]

Although disputes erupted almost daily, there was no concerted effort to destroy Eicher's authority. Rather, even the "vast majority" of defense lawyers whom he credited with good behavior grew grouchy as the trial dragged on. Loss of income undoubtedly contributed to the mood (though the Chief Justice eased the burden by assigning remunerative civil cases). Above all, counsel were aggravated by Eicher's failure to agree that the government case was flimsy. When they told him so, he occasionally lost his temper. For the most part, he was remarkably patient, even passing over Koehne's assertion that dismissal of Laughlin was itself an impeachable offense.[95]

Whereas defense relations with Eicher declined from civility, defense relations with the prosecution began poorly and got worse. Each side wasted time and each blamed the other for delays. Each side interrupted the proceedings and each chided the other for interruptions. Insults sometimes broke through the veil of formality; Albert Dilling went so far as to call Rogge an "old-time Communist fellow traveler." In addition, competing strategies divided prudent defense counsel, who considered the hearing fair if unorthodox, from colleagues favoring a political attack on a "political trial." Some defendents operated in legal limbo. Sanctuary refused to cooperate with the court-appointed substitute for Klein. Noble, who noisily rejected a replacement for Laughlin, was finally severed from the case. Eicher sensibly denied Smythe's belated request to represent himself; nonetheless, Smythe occasionally intruded on events, if only, after too many drinks, to designate "rats" among counsel and the accused.[96]

Following initial mutual suspicion, most defendants got along famously. Elizabeth and Albert Dilling brought lunch to the men previously convicted who missed their main meal at the District jail. Observing the Dillings in tandem, *PM* wondered if the trial would reconcile the foremost far right couple. It did not, but other, stranger bonds were forged. Winrod tried to convince Viereck, formerly notorious as the "poet of passion," that the Antichrist stalked the land. Even Dennis developed condescending affection for the "crackpots." Far right activists who had never met now planned to cooperate in future ventures.[97]

At first, more than two dozen reporters crowded into the courtroom. With unmatched enthusiasm, the *Daily Worker* urged public meetings to discuss *McWilliams* and the "real powers" behind American fascism. Interest waned, however, as hearings dragged through the summer. Except for earnest writers from the *Worker*, the few remaining reporters filed stories smacking of surrealism. In June the *Washington Post* ridiculed the "courtroom farce." Similarly, Executive Director Roger N. Baldwin of the American Civil Liberties Union concluded in July that the government had "nothing substantial" linking the defendants to the Axis. Although the ACLU remained aloof, General Counsel Arthur Garfield Hays declared himself "personally . . . unreservedly opposed" to the trial. Renewing the senatorial attack on 8 September, William Langer said that the defendants possessed large imaginations and paper organizations but no "underground armies, fleets, or battleships." Winrod's Defenders promptly distributed thousands of copies of the speech.[98]

The unexpected length of the trial forced modifications in courtroom routine. Chief Justice Eicher granted severance to True, whose poor health had caused several postponements, and Baxter, who was too deaf to hear testimony. He allowed other defendants voluntarily to absent themselves: Elizabeth Dilling stumped Ohio with Gerald L. K. Smith; Washburn taught stenography; and McWilliams took a factory job in Chicago. Morning sessions ceased in late summer. Despite disruptions and delays, the special prosecutor vowed to present nearly one hundred witnesses and 9,000 exhibits "if it takes forever." In one of Rogge's dreams, however, Eicher simply walked off the bench. Members of the prosecution staff apparently sided with his unconscious; when Eicher declared a two week recess in August, one of them quipped, "Will we have a vacation every summer?"[99]

The "annual summer vacation," as Dennis called the recess, had no lasting effect on worn nerves. Claiming that a shot had been fired at St.-George and himself, W. Hobart Little, counsel for Elmhurst, asked the court for protection. A radio broadcast in which President Roosevelt attacked "fear propaganda" by Hitler, Mussolini, "silver shirts and others on the lunatic fringe" induced a courtroom controversy on 9 October. Powers attributed to FDR a "personal animus" against Pelley, an inference that was accurate but irrelevant. Conceding Roosevelt's integrity, John Jackson still feared that jurors had been influenced by an eminent "star witness." Eicher neither polled the jurors nor declared a mistrial.[100]

Two days later, Hermann Rauschning, the government's leading expert on the Third Reich, took the stand. A former intimate of Hitler who left Germany in 1939, Rauschning had written several popular, critical accounts of Nazism. In an accent perplexing to court and counsel, he recalled Hitler's dissemination of propaganda among Weimar Republic troops and defined Nazism as a "world revolution" against all "established values and established orders." Furthermore, Hitler told him of aspirations to undermine the United States by subverting the military and supporting every cooperative group.[101]

Defense lawyers continued to object for the record that discussions of Nazism were irrelevant. Obliged to discuss the subject, however, most came around to refuting the government's specific interpretation. By presenting a "clear picture" of the German situation, Dennis said, he could show that the accused differed from their alleged coconspirators in Berlin. Fellow counsel chose Dennis to lead the cross examination of Rauschning. The émigré betrayed as much arrogance as erudition during their eight hours of fencing. More important, mixing impressive knowledge of current affairs with falsely naive questions, Dennis led Rauschning to admit that the Nazis had achieved power "legally." Indeed, the witness had joined them with no intention of backing a coup d'etat. Rauschning, whom Dennis pointedly called an "ex-Nazi," also conceded that German subversion had produced neither the far right movements in Rumania and Hungary nor the French collapse in 1940.[102]

Rogge insisted that Dennis's questions, similar to many asked on direct examination, were misleading, immaterial, and repetitious. Dennis demanded the right to show that "there was no Nazi world conspiracy of ideas." Overruling Rogge in several instances, the court let Dennis bear down. If Hitler did not say whom he supported, how did Rauschning determine which organizations followed a Nazi "line?" Would a hypothetical American National Socialist be guilty of using the "Nazi technique of soliciting mutiny" if he asked soldiers for their votes. It was necessary, Rauschning replied, to consider the purposes for which he sought support. Dennis still doubted that a propagandist's "future intentions" could be inferred from words. Rauschning recommended a close study of "these personalties" and judgments based on their general "political life."[103]

The trial reverted to three weeks of ordinary contentiousness after Rauschning departed on 18 October. Rogge introduced another batch of German documents; defense lawyers offered what John Jackson now called the "usual objection" that the exhibits were "remote" and irrelevant. For most of three days in late October they cross examined Robert M. Kempner, an émigré jurist at the University of Pennsylvania, on the accuracy of his translations, the merits of competing German-English dictionaries, and the political connotations of "*völkisch.*" Thereafter they covered familiar ground by questioning Kempner's version of recent German history. Fresh rounds of recrimination relieved the tedium.[104]

Sixty-five-year-old Henry D. Allen, the former Silver Shirt leader in San Diego, was sworn in on 9 November. Allen identified letters from some of the accused and described Deatherage's effort to create a "national hook-up," the American Nationalist Confederation. Rogge pursued connections among the defendants. In 1938 the witness had called on Winrod, conferred with Edmondson, dropped in at Dilling's headquarters (where he met Albert, not Elizabeth), visited James True, and talked "very briefly" to someone at the German embassy. Finally, he had heard some of the accused "say that Hitler had done a fine job in getting rid of the Jews."[105]

To no avail defense attorneys complained that the letters to Allen had not been authenticated, that the American Nationalist Confederation was a political party instead of a conspiracy, and that exhibits at hand went beyond the bill of particulars. When Allen recalled meeting him, Dilling asked "whether my name is being included as a coconspirator?" "Not yet," said Burns.[106]

Dilling had no reason to worry. Allen proved to be remarkably helpful to the defendants. Perhaps, as St.-George and Dennis surmised, he wanted to retaliate against the government for excluding him from California as a military threat. Under cross examination he pronounced "essentially pro-American" the agitators and pamphleteers whom he knew. Instead of conspiring, moreover, each "wanted to go his own individual way"; the American Nationalist

Confederation was merely a "letterhead set-up." While a Silver Shirt, he had never received arms or plotted insurrection.[107]

Most important, true to his Silver Shirt heritage, Allen was as bigoted as most of the accused. The letters before the court, he asserted, had been stolen from him by "the Jews" and their minions in San Diego law enforcement agencies. A transparently sincere bigot, he needed little encouragement to endorse *The Protocols*, complain of Anti-Defamation League "persecution," and recall a 1935 attack on himself and his son, allegedly by Jews, in a "Sheeny" clothing store. Allen received encouragement nonetheless, especially from Dilling and Frey, who shared his opinion that Communism was "essentially Jewish."[108]

Even counsel unencumbered by this delusion considered Allen a prize. This major prosecution witness, after all, held anti-Semitic views that the indictment called evidence of conspiracy. Playing to the jury, St.-George asked Allen to elaborate on the clothing shop fight. He got more of a show than he expected. Describing the incident, which cost his son's left eye, Allen burst into tears, and his two teenage daughters rushed forward to comfort him.[109]

After a recess Rogge protested that St.-George was trying to "stir up" Allen's emotions. Aided by friendly rulings from the bench, he managed to limit damage to the prosecution. Eicher sustained objections to questions about the "world-wide movement to destroy democracy" and struck Allen's surmise that Deatherage was no "Nazi agent." On redirect examination, Rogge introduced grand jury records to refresh Allen's memory. Although defense lawyers repeatedly accused the prosecutor of impeaching his own witness, they were pleased by the sum of Allen's testimony. Before Allen left the stand on 27 November, E. Hilton Jackson pronounced the government case "dead."[110]

The trial was closer to abrupt termination than anyone supposed. Eicher died of a heart attack during the night of 29 November. Winrod and Henry Allen detected the punishing hand of God. Senator Langer was more generous: "Solomon himself could not have survived the trial." On 7 December, after no defendant except Dennett agreed to continue hearings with a new judge, Justice James M. Proctor declared a mistrial.[111]

The case lingered until 1947. The Popular Front left demanded quick reprosecution, but few potential participants shared their enthusiasm. Between December 1944 and the following March, largely as a tactic to have the indictment dropped, some defendents moved for trial. Rogge dutifully announced the government's readiness to proceed. The District Court, overwhelmed by criminal cases and dreading another sedition marathon, declined to schedule *McWilliams* in 1945. Meanwhile the Supreme Court decision in *United States* v. *Keegan*, handed down 12 June, convinced Rogge that sedition convictions would be reversed on appeal. He candidly raised the issue in early 1946 with Eicher's successor, Chief Justice Bolitha Laws; after gathering fresh evidence in Germany during the spring, Rogge reiterated his doubts.[112]

Keegan and its companion, *United States* v. *Kunze*, involved Bundists convicted of urging draft evasion. These two cases had much in common with *McWilliams*, including witnesses, defendants, and transcripts filled with data about the Bund. Overturning the convictions, the Supreme Court noted that introduction of copious "background material" bordered on "abuse." Neither "Bund commands" nor testimony by the ubiquitous William Luedtke showed a "nationwide conspiracy" against selective service. Essentially the government had tried to prove "sinister and undisclosed intent" by citing "so-called un-American sentiments."[113]

Yet the denouement of *McWilliams* had less to do with Supreme Court precedents than with the temper of the Truman administration. Rogge had no wish to retry the case himself and thought that no prosecutor could win in the long run, but he still wanted to warn the nation about international fascism as he had "come to know it." Specifically, he expected to publicize evidence from Germany that proved prominent isolationists had been conscious or unwitting Nazi agents. According to Rogge, Attorney General Tom Clark, who had succeeded Biddle in May 1945, refused to release this "official German report" because it implicated the president's friend Burton K. Wheeler. The special prosecutor felt free, however, to discuss his findings. Lecturing at Swarthmore College on 22 October 1946, Rogge stressed Nazi plans to organize Senator Wheeler and other isolationists during 1939–41. Three days later, after Wheeler had visited Truman at the White House, Clark fired Rogge for drawing on the restricted report.[114]

With Rogge's dismissal, the sedition case again became front-page news after two years in legal limbo. Many liberals, radicals, and Brown Scare sensationalists were outraged. Walter Winchell favored impeaching the attorney general. Noting that Clark had been "busy as a beaver" stirring anti-Communist sentiment, the *Daily Worker* viewed his removal of Rogge as a complementary "victory for every American fascist—and for J. Edgar Hoover." *PM* Washington correspondent I. F. Stone lamented that the Justice Department's pursuit of the far right had always been "half-hearted."[115]

Just as earlier phases of the Brown Scare had reflected the cultural nationalism of the Depression and the heightened fears of World War II, the controversy surrounding Rogge highlighted postwar tensions. To diverse liberals, his dismissal, apparently at the behest of Senator Wheeler, was fresh evidence of Truman's chronic cronyism. To Communists and Popular Front liberals, it also represented another in a series of rightward moves by the administration. In one sense they were mistaken; the Justice Department was *more* willing than Rogge to prosecute native fascists—as long as the category excluded the President's friends. Nevertheless, his removal did relate to the Cold War, if not so directly as the *Daily Worker* supposed. Rogge, a Popular Front hero, was an incongruous figure at the Justice Department in October 1946, a month after Henry A. Wallace had been removed as Secretary of Commerce for publicly urging compromise with the Soviet Union. After his own dismissal (also for giving a speech that he believed to have been cleared), Rogge became a major figure in Wallace's Progressive Party and detected "incipient fascism" in Cold War attacks on American radicals.[116]

Although Rogge was absent from the last act of *McWilliams*, in District Court on 22 November 1946, his "official German report" was there. Honoring objections from defense counsel, however, Chief Justice Bolitha Laws refused to admit it as evidence. Moreover, noting Rogge's reservations about continued prosecution, Laws granted motions to dismiss the indictments because defendants had been denied a speedy trial. Lack of "clear" proof of guilt after five years of "intensive investigation" raised "serious doubt" about the validity of *McWilliams*, and another long trial would be a "travesty on justice." The Court of Appeals upheld Laws's ruling by a two to one vote on 30 June 1947.[117]

The question persists: how would *McWilliams* have fared if Chief Justice Eicher had lived? The basis for speculation is a record far from finished. After seven months, the government had called thirty-nine of one hundred witnesses. Courthouse handicappers anticipated appearances by Avedis Derounian, L. M. Birkhead, and Professor Harold Lasswell, whose comparison of Nazi and Silver Shirt propaganda themes had helped to imprison Pelley. Yet neither press speculation, government motions in 1945–46, Rogge's suppressed report, nor the postwar account by St.-George and Dennis point to major shifts in the nature, or quality, of evidence or argument.[118]

Withal the government case was more ingenious than convincing. It did not show—and could not have shown—that the accused belonged to a "worldwide Nazi movement" extending from Berlin to the District of Columbia. Indeed, the Bund, the alleged "spearhead," was virtually disowned by the German government two years before

Congress passed the Smith Act. Connections among the accused were tenuous. Because few if any of them appealed directly to the army or navy, Rogge inferred specific intent to promote insubordination from their putative Nazi ties and general malevolence. While he ritualistically invoked Holmes's "clear and present danger" doctrine from *Schenck* v. *United States*, his arguments more closely resembled the looser "bad tendency test" enunciated in *Gitlow* v. *New York*. That is, obnoxious words addressed to the general public might have reached the armed forces and thus damaged morale.[119]

Still, Lawrence Dennis might have been too optimistic in August 1944 when he predicted acquittal of all or most defendants. Certainly flimsier cases had sent more admirable men and women to prison during World War I. Rogge had the advantage of a conspiracy indictment that included persons already serving sentences for comparable crimes. Although Pelley never appealed specifically to the military, a jury needed only three hours to convict him of urging insubordination. The *McWilliams* jurors were serious, confused, bored, and appreciative of legal disputes that allowed them to leave the courtroom for refreshments. When the trial ended abruptly in November 1944, they were apparently split, with some favoring conviction of all defendants and others totally unconvinced by the prosecution. Under the circumstances, they might have compromised by convicting the most prominent or obnoxious figures.[120]

Most accounts of *McWilliams* blame irascible defendants and their lawyers for making the trial a farce. Clearly Symthe, Jones, Laughlin, and Albert Dilling were often insufferable and some of their peers were intermittently troublesome. Yet their antics should not obscure the weakness of the government case. Lacking convincing evidence of a "worldwide Nazi movement" to subvert the armed forces, Rogge substituted quantity for quality. In the long run, Chief Justice Eicher's failure to maintain order was less harmful to the trial than his lax standard of evidence. Wisdom as well as wit lay in counsel William A. Gallagher's remark that Rogge was prosecuting a "conspiracy to import German literature."[121]

Rogge was probably correct to expect an appellate reversal of *McWilliams*, but the question would have been close. In 1942, the Court of Appeals for the Seventh Circuit upheld *United States* v. *Pelley* and the Supreme Court declined to review the case. Elmer Hartzel, a comparable bigot, very likely escaped Pelley's fate because victory over the Axis seemed certain two years later. Nevertheless, while a majority of the Supreme Court said in *Hartzel* that restrictions on speech must be narrowly construed, four justices dissented, warning of subtle attempts to create military disaffection. As late as June 1945, the four dissenters in *Keegan* were impressed by the Bund's "consistent purpose" to promote German interests, which included obstruction of the American war effort.[122]

Quite possibly, then, Special Prosecutor Maloney's incompetence, which delayed *McWilliams* in 1942, saved Pelley, Winrod, and their fellow far right activists from prison. Even though the case ended in mistrial, Attorney General Biddle observed later, it served President Roosevelt's prime purpose by curtailing far right propaganda. Furthermore, by forcing the accused to move to Washington, to hire lawyers, and to raise bail or languish in jail, the government punished them without convicting them.[123]

These difficulties hardly bulk large amid the horrors of World War II, especially since many of the defendants approved both the war's worst atrocities and the Smith Act under which they were tried. Nonetheless, as the legal culmination of the Brown Scare, *McWilliams* retains retrospective significance for two related reasons. First, it illuminates the Roosevelt administration's mixed record on civil liberties. As is often the case concerning his administration, the president's scholarly advocates give him undue credit for the better judgment of subordinates who, in this instance, warned against prewar bans on "scurrilous" pamphlets and grand jury probes of the America First Committee. After Pearl Harbor, Roosevelt personally intervened to curtail far right expressions that were only distantly dangerous or merely obnoxious. In addition, his enthusiasm for Special Prosecutor Maloney in 1943 suggests that he expected the sedition trial to discredit reputable critics of New Deal foreign policy as well as far right agitators (the charge made by Senators Wheeler, Taft, and Langer at the time). In this context, Roosevelt's cooperation with the Dies Committee and his decision to relocate 110,000 Japanese-Americans in 1942 look less like incongruous blots on a civil libertarian record, as his proponents maintain, than like routine decisions by a president little concerned about civil liberties.[124]

Second, much as Roosevelt deserves credit for helping to create the welfare state, he bears responsibility for helping to create the national security state. The FBI, politicized during the 1930s, would serve subsequent presidents determined to root out subversion, variously defined. And though *United States* v. *McWilliams* left no legal precedents, the case did set an important political precedent for prosecuting unpopular dissidents and thus foreshadowed Smith Act cases of the Cold War era.[125]

From Brown Scare to Second Red Scare: Gerald L. K. Smith, the Constitution, and *Terminiello* v. *Chicago*

Gerald L. K. Smith avoided indictment in *United States* v. *McWilliams*, but his determination to hold meetings in Chicago, where his opposition was especially strong, involved him in *Terminiello* v. *Chicago*, a landmark test of the First Amendment. This case, decided in 1949 by a sharply divided United States Supreme Court, revealed the left's continuing perplexity about civil liberties as the Brown Scare merged with the second Red Scare.[126]

Smith's initial sorties into Chicago during 1945 provoked the familiar picket lines, low-level street violence, and protests against native fascism. Nevertheless, he scheduled speeches by himself and a new associate, Father Arthur Terminiello, at the West Side Women's Club on 7 February 1946. Terminiello, a thirty-eight year old priest from Birmingham, Alabama and leader of the Union of Christian Crusaders, was the "best if not the only" substitute for Father Coughlin. Elizabeth Dilling and Frederick Kister of the Christian War Veterans, a Smith spinoff, also planned to participate.[127]

Protestors turned out in force from the Socialist and Socialist Workers parties, the University of Chicago, and the Chicago Civil Liberties Committee, a Popular Front group currently estranged from the American Civil Liberties Union. Before the meeting started at 8:15 on 7 February, the picket line degenerated into a mob. Some of the 1,500 demonstrators shoved Smith's followers, broke twenty-eight windows in the Women's Club, and threw rocks, bottles, and stench bombs, occasionally hitting some of the 300 police on duty; more than a dozen of the protestors were arrested. Police also ejected from the Women's Club a man who shouted at Smith, "You're a God-damned liar."[128]

Father Terminiello sank to the occasion. After making a pro forma distinction between decent American Jews and "Communistic Zionist Jews," he assailed the "scum" on the picket line and asked, "Do you wonder why they were persecuted in other countries of the world?" Following this speech, it took police an hour to escort Terminiello, along with Gerald and Elna Smith, through the angry crowd outside. The next day, acting on a complaint by the executive director of the Chicago Civil Liberties Committee, Ira Latimer, the city charged Smith, Termininiello, and Kister with creating a "diversion tending to a breach of the peace."[129]

Although the accused rejected Chicago's offer to plead guilty to the lesser offense of disorderly conduct, only Terminiello came to trial. In proceedings begun on 27 March, prosecution witnesses, including Ira Latimer, testified that Terminiello's speech had moved listeners to demand death for Jews and "niggers." Defense witnesses, including Elizabeth Dilling, had heard no such comments. Defense counsel Albert Dilling and Maximilian St.-George, both veterans of *McWilliams*, asserted that radicals had stirred the demonstrators to violence. On 28 May, Smith tried to steal the show and almost succeeded. Assailing Chicago for cooperating with the "Communist stooge" Latimer, he was found guilty of contempt by trial Judge John V. McCormick and sentenced to sixty days in jail (where, the *Cross and the Flag* speculated, his assassination might be arranged). Smith both reiterated his readiness for martyrdom and successfully appealed the contempt citation. Father Terminiello, his case almost lost in this scuffle, was convicted on 3 April and fined $100.[130]

In the series of appeals that followed, attorneys Dilling and St.-George persistently maintained that freedom of speech was the "one and only issue" in the Terminiello case. Even if jurists agreed with that premise—and most did not—application of the Bill of Rights to the priest's situation was problematical. During the previous two decades, the United States Supreme Court had struck down ordinances forbidding picketing, distribution of leaflets, and displays of red flags, ruled in favor of labor organizers and evangelists who refused to register with authorities, and generally required restrictions on expression to be specific and narrowly construed. Some justices believed that the First Amendment had a "preferred" position within the Constitution, but none questioned the legality of punishing incitement to violence.[131]

Two decisions concerning Jehovah's Witnesses, *Cantwell* v. *Connecticut* and *Chaplinsky* v. *New Hampshire*, were especially pertinent to *Terminiello*. Jesse Cantwell, who in the course of seeking converts had played a record attacking the Roman Catholic Church, was convicted of breach of the peace. The United States Supreme Court voted unanimously in 1940 to overturn the conviction. Cantwell had aroused animosity, Justice Owen Roberts wrote, but he had created no "clear and present danger to public peace." Two years later, however, the court unanimously ruled against Walter Chaplinsky, who had called a policeman a "damned Fascist." According to Justice Frank Murphy's opinion, Chaplinsky had uttered "insulting or 'fighting' words—those which by their very utterance inflict injury or tend to incite an immediate breach of the peace."[132]

In June 1947, the Appellate Court for the First District of Illinois decided, with one dissent, that Terminiello had gone beyond the limits set in *Cantwell.* The jury had grounds to believe that Terminiello was encouraging mob violence, and he must have known that Smith's "very presence" would promote disorder, the majority opinion concluded. On 18 March 1948 the Illinois Supreme Court unanimously affirmed the conviction, noting that Terminiello had plainly uttered "fighting words" unprotected under *Chaplinsky.*[133]

The case might have died there for lack of funds, but Smith apparently helped to finance an appeal to the United States Supreme Court (despite his ebbing enthusiasm for Terminiello, whom he later called a "very ordinary little fellow . . . with no native eloquence"). In 1948, too, the American Civil Liberties Union belatedly entered the case. The timing of this action reflected the ACLU's ambivalence about defending far right agitators, an ambivalence connected to broader problems worrying left civil libertarians.[134]

During and immediately after World War II, many liberals and radicals continued to favor what Roger Baldwin in 1938 had called derisively "'Liberty for Our Side' only." The Communist party would have jailed Gerald L. K. Smith for sedition instead of allowing him to sponsor meetings, and almost all proponents of the Popular Front, along with many centrist liberals, would have denied his access to public auditoriums. The centrist Council for Democracy opposed peacetime bans on rallies by "anti-democratic groups," yet endorsed restrictions on "political uniforms." Law Professor David Riesman recommended libel suits against native fascist defamers of minority groups. Nonetheless, after brilliantly surveying the issue of "democracy and defamation," Riesman correctly concluded in 1942 that the "legislative and administrative complexities" involved were "all but overwhelming."[135]

In April 1939, under increasing pressure from friends and critics to stop defending the constitutional rights of "anti-democratic" forces, the American Civil Liberties Union board of directors reaffirmed its commitment to "free speech for Nazis, Fascists, and Communists." Specifically, the board opposed prosecutions for group libel, suppression of publications, and restrictions on public meetings (like Smith and Terminiello's) likely to disturb the peace. These principles were difficult to apply, however, particularly because the ACLU itself was divided on their meaning.[136]

On the eve of World War II, the ACLU directors included advocates of the Popular Front, centrist liberals, Socialists, and one Communist, Elizabeth Gurley Flynn. Rev. Harry F. Ward, chairman until 1940, also headed the foremost Popular Front group, the American League

Against War and Fascism (renamed the American League for Peace and Democracy in 1939). Ward wanted the ACLU to aid labor and minorities at the expense of conservatives and native fascists. Executive Director Roger Baldwin, despite his criticism of "'Liberty for Our Side' only" also viewed constitutional freedoms as "tools for social change." General Counsel Morris L. Ernst, the most militant centrist at the national office, urged President Roosevelt to attack the far right, even if he had to bend the First Amendment, and believed that the ACLU leaned too far to the left. A more consistent civil libertarian than Ernst, Norman Thomas also perceived undue Communist influence within the organization. Some ACLU leaders, notably General Counsel Osmond K. Fraenkel, strived for an even-handed application of the Bill of Rights.[137]

The Nazi-Soviet Pact of August 1939 precipitated a crisis within the ACLU that affected subsequent treatment of the far left and far right. In February 1940, a majority of directors resolved that it was "inappropriate" for anyone to serve on ACLU governing committees who belonged to "any political organization which supports totalitarian dictatorships in any country, or who by his public declarations and connections indicates his support for such principles." The proscription encompassed groups favorable to Nazi Germany, Fascist Italy, and the Soviet Union, as well as "native organizations with obvious anti-democratic objectives."[138]

This policy quickly exacerbated ACLU factionalism. Roger Baldwin, trading the Popular Front for sturdy anti-Communism following the Nazi-Soviet Pact, inaccurately maintained that the directors merely restated traditional policy. Believing otherwise, Rev. Ward resigned from the ACLU on 26 February. Seventeen prominent liberals, including Carey McWilliams, I. F. Stone, and James Wechsler, urged reconsideration of the "purge resolution" which made views on foreign affairs a test for office; the board's reference to "native organizations" obscured the anti-Communist intent, they added, because Silver Shirts would no more join the ACLU than the B'nai B'rith. Acting in accordance with the new policy, however, a majority of directors voted to remove Elizabeth Gurley Flynn from the board on 7 May 1940.[139]

The ACLU's embrace of the anti-"totalitarian" center produced short-term gains that masked long-term problems. The organization attracted new members and arranged a truce with Chairman Martin Dies of the House Committee on Un-American Activities. Yet supporters of the Popular Front retained a significant presence on the board of directors and comprised a larger proportion of the general membership. One of many issues still creating disharmony was the prospect of defending native fascists during World War II. Except for the most staunch civil libertarians, notably General Counsel Arthur Garfield Hays and Osmond Fraenkel, all factions wanted to sidestep *United States* v. *McWilliams*. In addition, the Popular Front contingent opposed ACLU aid to fascists who remained at large. As Morris Ernst's advice to the White House showed, some centrists concurred in this view. But others, including Baldwin, believed that preserving basic liberties for far right agitators was both correct in principle and good public relations. Among those who disagreed, Popular Front liberals Freda Kirchway of the *Nation* and Rev. William B. Spofford quit the ACLU during the early 1940s.[140]

The liberty to assemble peaceably raised special problems. The common man's vulnerability to "emotions, fallacies [and] prejudices" expanded in group settings where demagogues exploited them, the Council for Democracy warned in 1943. Such suspicions, latent beneath celebrations of "the people" during the 1930s, surfaced among commentators contemplating twelve million common men marching home to postwar unemployment. As the young social critic Daniel Bell speculated in 1944, returning soldiers who were bitter, resentful, and susceptible to propaganda might become the "catalyst for American fascism."[141]

In this context, Gerald L. K. Smith presented the ACLU with simultaneous opportunities and difficulties. On the one hand, defense of Smith's constitutional rights made the organization look evenhanded instead of left-wing; on the other, many members balked at aiding someone whom they considered the country's foremost fascist. For his part, Smith sometimes listed the ACLU among the nation's "dangerous enemies" but regularly sought its help. Suspicious of Jewish lawyers at the national office, however, he dealt directly with Roger Baldwin, whom he credited with rare integrity. Baldwin, in turn, offered legal advice, recommended attorneys, and urged local chapters to protect Smith's right to speak. Furthermore, until Smith endorsed *The Protocols* in 1946, Baldwin believed that his anti-Semitism was "greatly exaggerated," and even thereafter regarded him as a "pet reactionary."[142]

The ACLU helped Smith to secure meeting halls in Minneapolis, Milwaukee, Cleveland, and elsewhere, yet the decision to do so often divided chapters. In 1943, the chairman of the Erie County, New York, Civil Liberties Union resigned in protest when the group supported Smith's appearance in Buffalo. Similarly, though Carey McWilliams held office in both the Southern California Civil Liberties Union and the national organization, he actively opposed Smith's use of Los Angeles school auditoriums in 1946.[143]

The beneficiary of previous ACLU assistance, Smith telephoned Baldwin the day after he and Terminiello were arrested in February 1946. After considerable internal debate, the organization remained aloof from their respective trials for contempt and disturbing the peace. The Chicago affiliate, facing opposition from members and staff lawyers, declined also to participate in Terminiello's appeals. General Counsel Osmond Fraenkel, believing that the priest's speech came "very close to the borderline of incitement," recommended that the national office also confine itself to "less doubtful and less malodorous cases."[144]

Nevertheless, in May 1948 the board of directors voted unanimously to assist Terminiello's appeal to the United States Supreme Court (they had to petition to be an amicus curiae because the appellant's lawyer Albert Dilling considered the ACLU subversive). No reason was given for the ACLU's turnabout in *Terminiello*, but the directors were apparently moved by the general decline in civil liberties accompanying the Cold War. The House Committee on Un-American Activities had resumed sustained pursuit of the left in 1946, and the Justice Department was currently preparing to indict Communist leaders under the Smith Act. The briefs for *Terminiello* v. *Chicago*, which was argued before the United States Supreme Court on 1 February 1949, encapsulated prevailing disputes concerning freedom of speech and assembly.[145]

In this case, as in *McWilliams*, Albert Dilling combined legal skill and flamboyance. The lower court rulings against Terminiello, he said "would operate as a 'previous restraint' " on all future speakers. Furthermore, the discriminatory application of the Chicago ordinance conflicted with recent Supreme Court rulings. Dilling conceded that utterances producing a "clear and present danger" of disorder were unprotected by the Constitution. Yet nothing in Terminiello's speech "even tended to cause any breach of the peace inside the hall." If Jesse Cantwell had not created a clear and present danger of an illegal disturbance, then it was "childish" to accuse Terminiello of doing so. *Chaplinsky* was not relevant because the priest had uttered "no 'face-to-face' words" to specific persons and had used "no epithets whatsoever." His speech, addressed to a general audience, might have been "colored" by the turmoil inside and outside the hall. Still, he showed remarkable restraint in not recommending direct action against the "real lawbreakers" among the demonstrators. The appellant brief contained copious allusions to such defenders of free speech as Voltaire, Zechariah Chafee, Jr., and Justice Louis Brandeis, "perhaps the most distinguished American of Jewish faith." With the supposition that First Amendment freedoms finally stood in a "preferred place," Dilling asked the court to give his client the "benefit of any doubt."[146]

Lawyers for Chicago, quickly disposing of Dilling's claim that Terminiello's conviction imposed a previous restraint on speech, then challenged his reading of recent precedents. In *Cantwell*, they said, the Supreme Court had "manifestly recognized" a state's right to punish breaches of the peace. Furthermore, resembling Walter Chaplinsky instead of Jesse Cantwell, Terminiello had directed "personal abuse" at persons in the audience, choosing language "clearly calculated" to disturb the peace. Thus provoked, a man had breached the peace by yelling, "You're a God-damned liar."[147]

Even in normal times, the Chicago corporation counsel argued, Terminiello's epithets "scum" and "slimy scum" qualified as "classical 'fighting words.'" But the Supreme Court should take "judicial notice that these are not normal times." Describing the social context, city attorneys inadvertently undermined their own claim that the ordinance had been narrowly framed and construed. Not only had utterances like Terminiello's promoted genocide in Europe but, before World War II, they had produced American disunity. Since passions had not yet cooled, the mere act of scheduling the meeting was provocative. The corporation counsel wondered, "What greater incitement to disturbance of the peace . . . could be conceived of by the most diabolically ingenious mind" than a session sponsored by Gerald L. K. Smith featuring the "Father Coughlin of the South?" When Terminiello faced his ethnically mixed audience, he deliberately stirred anti-Semitic rage among non-Jews and made Jews fear for their safety.[148]

More sensitive than the Chicago corporation counsel to the Bill of Rights, the American Jewish Congress (AJC) prepared an impressive amicus curiae brief. According to the AJC, the critical issue was that Terminiello's "fighting words" had indeed incited immediate violence. In characterizing the priest's language, the AJC considered a "totality" of factors: his demeanor, his status as a "professional agitator," and the probability that, five months after World War II, his remarks sounded to Jews like a revival of Nazism.[149]

In a reply brief, Dilling reasserted his client's peaceful intent on 7 February 1946, recalling that Smith, not Terminiello, had been called a "God-damned liar" and suggesting that the term "slimy scum," though intemperate, aptly described the "lawless mob" seeking to deny free speech and assembly. If the respondent's position were accepted, then a protester might, simply by calling any speaker a "God-damned liar," render him subject to arrest.[150]

This objection to the "heckler's veto," raised in passing by Dilling, was central to the ACLU lawyers. In their view, Terminiello could not be charged with provoking violence by demonstrators who had gathered before his arrival and never heard his talk. According to the Illinois decisions, moreover, Terminiello might have been subject to prosecution even if he had never shown up. At least, the ACLU brief warned, affirmantion of the courts below would sanction "advance censorship by opponents."[151]

The United States Supreme Court was no more able than contending witnesses and attorneys to agree on the facts or the law. Speaking for a bare majority on 16 May 1949, Justice William O. Douglas reversed the Illinois verdict. Douglas's opinion formally turned on the procedural point that Judge McCormick in his charge to the jury had defined breach of the peace as any statement that "stirs the public to anger, invites dispute, or creates a disturbance." Without deciding whether or not Terminiello had uttered "derisive, fighting words," Douglas reminded his brethren—and a nation increasingly committed to Cold War conformity—of the value of dispute and disturbance. Free speech, he wrote, was "protected against censorship and punishment, unless shown likely to produce a clear and present danger of serious substantive evil" rising "far above inconvenience, annoyance, or unrest." Unmoved by Douglas's admonition, Justice Fred M. Vinson and Justice Felix Frankfurter questioned the wisdom of reversing the conviction on grounds not urged by the appellant. Justice Robert H. Jackson held Terminiello responsible for fueling a riot, accused the Supreme Court majority of forsaking the "wholesome principles" of clear and present danger, and warned that Douglas's "dogma of absolute freedom" might convert the Bill of Rights "into a suicide pact."[152]

Jackson's famous dissent, though best known for his warning against constitutional self-immolation, also incorporated Brown Scare motifs that had circulated since the early 1930s. Formerly chief prosecutor at the War Crimes Tribunal in Nuremberg, Jackson was especially sensitive to the horrors of Nazism. He quoted long passages from Terminiello's speech and detected a "fidelity that is more than coincidental" to Adolf Hitler's agitation. Jackson shared the prevailing fear that American fascism-in-disguise might triumph through a combination of cunning demagogy and mass ignorance; Terminiello, who "of course" denied his own fascism, had mastered subtle means to manipulate "herd opinion."[153]

Furthermore, Jackson combined memories of the recent hot war against Nazism with concern about the Cold War currently in progress. He assumed that Communists had joined the demonstration against Terminiello and Smith, compared the resulting clash to the "battle for the streets" during the Weimar Republic, and ascribed the "same terror tactics" to "fanatics" on both fringes of the political spectrum. Thus, by repudiating Chicago's mild punishment of Terminiello, the Supreme Court had fulfilled the "most extravagant hopes of right and left totalitarian groups."[154]

Terminiello attracted widespread attention, with the most revealing reactions coming from the left. As congealing Cold War orthodoxy narrowed the range of acceptable opinion, some liberals and radicals rediscovered the tactical value of supporting civil liberties for all sides. "In these anxious times," the *New Republic* commented, "there can be no error in a reaffirmation of freedom of speech." Similarly, I. F. Stone, who had applauded the *McWilliams* prosecution, now criticized the four dissenting justices who "would have permitted some measure of suppression in my protection." "In too many recent cases," Stone said, "current anti-Red hysteria has kept them from doing the humane, the just and rightful thing." Even the Communist *People's Daily World*, while lamenting a "fascist's" legal victory, hoped that *Terminiello* might serve as a basis to challenge the "persecution" of the twelve Communists indicted under the Smith Act. During the next decade, however, judicial affirmations of the First Amendment would be rare.[155]

6. Far Right, Divided Left, and Vital Center

Second Red Scare

Justice Jackson spoke for a minority of the Supreme Court in *Terminiello* v. *Chicago,* but his fear of complementary dangers on the far right and far left already dominated discourse in the nation at large. As Soviet-American relations deteriorated after World War II, President Harry S. Truman concluded that there was not "any difference" between fascists and Communists; in 1947, Attorney General Tom Clark released the first official list of allegedly Communist, fascist, and totalitarian organizations. Scholars, too, increasingly stressed similarities between Nazi and Soviet "totalitarianism." This emerging orthodoxy affected both the far right and the chief theories purporting to explain it.[1]

While fighting the Cold War, national leaders restored stability to a political spectrum that had been in flux since the early 1930s. The turning point for the left was the 1948 election, when Truman deflated Henry A. Wallace's challenge by exaggerating his connection with the Communist party. Thereafter, liberal reputability required rejection of Communist "extremists," fellow travelers, and "anti-anti-Communists." Erstwhile advocates of Popular Front unity either converted to ostentatious moderation or followed Wallace into ostracism. The Americans for Democratic Action policed liberalism's left flank, and an ADA founder, Arthur M. Schlesinger, Jr., provided a catch-phrase for the left's reorientation; the "politics of freedom," Schlesinger wrote in 1949, was confined to the "vital center."[2]

Meanwhile, a widely publicized "new conservatism" was constructed by diverse traditionalists, rhetoricians of laissez faire, old progressive foes of New Deal domestic or foreign policy, and militant anti-Communists (many of whom were former radicals). Practicing their own brand of vital centrism, they repudiated unpopular ideological inheritances and guarded a vulnerable flank (the right flank, in this instance) against disreputable supporters. For example, though some erstwhile isolationists within conservative ranks remained skeptical of United States commitments abroad, most favored containment of Communism or the liberation of eastern Europe. Furthermore, much as centrist liberals advertised their respectability by ostracizing domestic Communists, prominent conservatives advertised their respectability by ostracizing conspiratorial anti-Semites.[3]

The exaggerated fear of Communism that accompanied the nation's ideological consolidation reflected not only venerable antiradical sentiments, but also more recent Brown Scare legacies. The specific legacies varied, of course, among pursuers of alleged subversion, their victims, and prospective quarry who managed to cover their tracks. When President Truman ordered a crackdown on American Communists in 1947, he was able to use the internal security apparatus created by his predecessor partly to crack down on the far right. When FBI Director J. Edgar Hoover thereafter exercised wide latitude in ordering surveillance and infiltration, he was exercising habits acquired during the late 1930s and World War II. Head of the Justice Department Criminal Division during *United States* v. *McWilliams*, Attorney General Clark was well-prepared in 1948 to initiate *United States* v. *Dennis*, an analogous conspiracy prosecution of leading Communists.[4]

Dennis echoed the wartime sedition case in other ways. The presiding judge, Harold R. Medina, prepared for his duties by studying the *McWilliams* record and conferring with former Assistant Prosecutor William Burns. Recalling Chief Justice Eicher's death in midtrial, and convinced that the Communists, like their fascist predecessors, had decided on a strategy of disruption, Medina was sterner with his defendants and less impartial than Eicher had been. After a raucous trial lasting seven months, eleven Communists were convicted of violating the Smith Act; in 1951, the verdict was upheld by the United States Supreme Court. Also in 1951, the Supreme Court's endorsement of noisy dispute contained in *Terminiello* v. *Chicago* was repudiated in *Feiner* v. *New York*, a case containing reminders of the wartime sedition trial as well as *Terminiello*. During 1949, Irving Feiner had been arrested for disturbing the peace while urging a small crowd in Syracuse to attend a speech by O. John Rogge, the chief prosecutor in *McWilliams*, who remained active in the Progressive Party. Feiner's speech was more temperate than Terminiello's and his audience far less agitated, but the Supreme Court nevertheless upheld his conviction. Voting with the majority in both *Dennis* and *Feiner*, Justice Jackson no longer worried that the Constitution might become a suicide pact.[5]

Whether or not the accused in *Dennis* deliberately emulated the disrupters in *McWilliams*, most Communists did view Cold War suppression through lenses ground during the Brown Scare. The triumph of American fascism, feared since the early 1930s, appeared imminent in the late 1940s. Hence the party decided to send key members underground. Implementation of this disastrous strategy apparently began after O. John Rogge, discerning "incipient fascism" in the second Red Scare, predicted in 1947 that the Justice Department was planning a dramatic round-up of Communists and their allies.[6]

Among conservatives, the second Red Scare was primarily a continuation of the first, an opportunity to reassert, in a more hospitable climate, that left subversion menaced the United States. In addition, however, conservatives who believed that the respectable right had been "smeared" since the 1930s took special pleasure in the Cold War turnabout. Eugene Lyons, for example, felt scant sympathy for stigmatized Popular Fronters who had themselves perpetuated an "intellectual red terror." The old isolationists Robert E. Wood, Hamilton Fish, and John T. Flynn supported Senator Joseph R. McCarthy. Furthermore, the conservative version of lessons of the 1930s was passed to the younger generation. Defending McCarthy's tactics—including press agentry and sweeping charges of disloyalty—William F. Buckley, Jr., and L. Brent Bozell asked in 1954, "Where were the Liberals when the weapons they now forbid us to use against the Communists were being used, fifteen years ago, against American fascists and against a number of Americans who were *not* fascists?"[7]

The liberal record was more complex than Buckley and Bozell implied. Many centrist liberals, having denounced extremism for more than a decade, adapted to the mood of the late 1940s by focusing increased attention on the left extreme. In *The Plotters*, a sequel to *Under Cover* published in 1946, Avedis Derounian warned against Communism as well as the "nationalism symbolized by Gerald Smith's America First party." Derounian's associate L. M. Birkhead welcomed the attorney general's list and urged Americans to win the Cold War. A record of symmetrical hostility to the far left and the far right provided some security to liberals in suspicious times. Frequently, however, it was coupled with symmetrical disregard for the civil liberties of extremists. The American Civil Liberties Union, which had declined to participate in *McWilliams*, also declined to assist the defendants in *Dennis*. Senator Hubert H. Humphrey (Dem.-Minn.), who had fought Gerald L. K. Smith's access to the Minneapolis municipal auditorium in 1944, ten years later introduced legislation outlawing the Communist party.[8]

Apostate Popular Front liberals who tacked rightward out of conviction or convenience often retained a proclivity for invective polished during the Brown Scare. In the early 1940s, Walter Winchell had accused isolationist Senator Burton K. Wheeler of supporting Nazism, printed leaks from President Roosevelt and Special Prosecutor William Power Maloney, and urged his friend J. Edgar Hoover to pursue the far right; in the early 1950s, Winchell accused *New York Post* editor James Wechsler of supporting Communism, printed leaks from Senator McCarthy and Roy Cohn, and urged his friend J. Edgar Hoover to pursue the far left.[9]

The transition from Brown Scare to second Red Scare by unrepentant Popular Front liberals revealed the greatest ironies. To their credit, they opposed Smith Act prosecutions, irresponsible congressional investigations, loyalty oaths, and bans on books and speakers. Often, they suffered personally from these measures. Carey McWilliams, who in 1944 had tried to prevent Gerald L. K. Smith from speaking in Los Angeles public schools, found the *Nation*, which he edited, banned from public schools. O. John Rogge, who had prosecuted thirty alleged conspirators in 1944, later advised defendants in *Dennis*, served as defense counsel in lesser Smith Act cases, and astutely criticized conspiracy indictments. Yet neither Carey McWilliams, O. John Rogge, nor most other Popular Front liberals recognized that their own endorsement of "'Liberty for Our Side' only" had helped to diminish civil liberties for everyone.[10]

Pelley, Winrod, and Smith in the Cold War Era

The Cold War was a mixed blessing to far right veterans of the 1930s. As believers in an international Jewish conspiracy, they were usually shunned, at least in public, by conservative intellectuals, congressional promoters of the second Red Scare, and even avid segregationists. Although unable to recapture their prewar prominence, they nonetheless felt vindicated by the national attack on Communism abroad and at home.

Indeed, the Cold War ethos helped Pelley to get out of prison. As early as 1946, his daughter and son-in-law, Adelaide and Melford Pearson, lobbied Congress and circulated pamphlets purporting to show that he was being persecuted for exposing the "Communist menace." The conservative *Chicago Tribune* and *New York Daily News* argued that Pelley deserved his freedom. Still, federal courts refused to reopen his case, and the parole board twice spurned his entreaties. During February 1950, however, Pelley was paroled on the condition that he abstain from politics.[11]

The restriction was almost unnecessary. Pelley felt "no such animus" toward Truman as he had toward Roosevelt. Fresh editions of *Behold Life* and *Nations-in-Law*, published by Pelley's new enterprise, Soulcraft Press, eschewed hostile references to "oriental" Jews (through unreconstructed Silver Shirts could still find translucent allusions to "alien cartels"). In *Something Better*, a "corollary" to *No More Hunger*, Pelley confessed in 1952 that he, like the New Dealers, had overemphasized centralization. According to his revised version of the Christian Commonwealth, "States Right Cooperatives" would share authority with the federal corporation. Sounding more than ever like Edward Bellamy, he expected the new order to emerge "without totalitarianism in any form."[12]

Pelley concentrated on metaphysics during his last years. Sometimes working eighteen hours daily, he transcribed clairaudient messages, conducted seances, composed another sentimental novel, and published magazines for Soulcraft subscribers. During 1956–57, Indiana tax officials reported, Pelley received $142,000 in contributions and royalties. Clearly, Americans continued during the 1950s to hunger after "things of the spirit."[13]

In 1953, Pelley made his "climactic" otherworldly contact—with Mary Baker Eddy. His belief that she had chosen him to disseminate theological advances beyond Christian Science brought solace to Pelley's old age; Christian mysticism had been, after all, his "life's true brevet." The voice attributed to Eddy, a skeptical reporter wrote, sounded "less like Boston" than any he had ever heard. Even if Pelley's seances were deliberate frauds, his choice of Eddy underscores his place in the harmonial religious tradition. When Pelley "made the passing" on 1 July 1965, some local residents recalled his contributions to disharmony. They burned a cross in front of the funeral parlor.[14]

Gerald B. Winrod returned to Wichita after the sedition trial, exhausted but unshaken in his faith. The use of nuclear weapons in 1945, for example, reinforced his belief in the biblical chart and compass, and also provided added evidence of Armageddon's approach. Prefiguring modern physics, Ezekiel 28:14 had treated matter as a mass of electrical charges—"stones of fire." During the "last days," Satan would teach the deadly secret of nuclear power to the

Antichrist. In the shorter run, however, Winrod, like Pelley, was encouraged by postwar assaults on Communism at home and abroad. The House Committee on Un-American Activities, Winrod wrote in 1948, was fighting subversion "exactly" as he had done until "men of the Alger Hiss, Henry Wallace type" almost destroyed his organization. O. John Rogge's participation in Wallace's Progressive party proved that *United States* v. *McWilliams* had been a Communist plot all along, according to Winrod and fellow indictees who now wrote for the *Defender.* The evangelist also renewed feuds with Walter Winchell, Avedis Derounian, and L. M. Birkhead.[15]

The Defenders of the Christian Faith prospered again during the Cold War era. The organization acquired a larger headquarters in 1947, magazine subscriptions climbed to 100,000 during the next decade, and though Winrod was unable to buy radio time in the United States, he broadcast to the Midwest from powerful Mexican stations. In print and on the air, he fit emerging issues into familiar frameworks. For instance, violent television programs provided new evidence of the national moral sag. Riding the wave of "positive thinking," Winrod endorsed "Christian psychology," which he defined as cultivation of originality, concentration, and piety. Civil rights legislation looked like the latest tactic of the "red underground." More convinced than ever that effective anti-Communism required a "united religious front," Winrod included a Roman Catholic among *Defender* columnists and urged "respect" for Moslems who fought Soviet expansion in the Middle East. He still judged presidential aspirants on their private faith as well as their public policies. In 1948, the "good Christian" Harry S. Truman seemed no worse than Thomas E. Dewey, the latest Republican "me too" candidate. Endorsing Dwight D. Eisenhower for re-election in 1956, Winrod recalled that the President's "sainted mother" had attended his services in Abilene, Kansas. God, not the White House, would ultimately decide America's fate, the *Defender* insisted. Flying saucers, the World Council of Churches, and the Korean War were fresh signs that the last days approached. Winrod reiterated his plea for a nationwide revival and inferred from young Billy Graham's success in 1951 that one might be at hand.[16]

Retaining the relatively subdued tone adopted during World War II, the *Defender* no longer cited *The Protocols* but it still discerned a satanic Jewish conspiracy against Christian civilization. These plotters destroyed Senator Joseph R. McCarthy and prevented President Truman, whom Winrod belatedly repudiated, from uprooting Communist subversion. In 1956, Winrod surmised that "some demon" had induced British Prime Minister Anthony Eden to assist Israel's attack on Egypt. When the Eisenhower administration condemned this invasion, Winrod asked prayers for the President, whom he considered a likely target of Jewish assassins, and called John Foster Dulles the greatest secretary of state in history. While continuing to preach anti-Semitism, Winrod still worked with Hebrew Christians to convert Jews.[17]

Increasingly Winrod identified with Old Testament prophets, especially Jeremiah, who had been "accused of sedition." Though Winrod's faith never faltered, his health declined steadily after World War II. The "multiple infirmities," noted but unspecified by his authorized biographer, contributed to his last crusade—in behalf of unconventional physicians and outright quacks. He was especially vulnerable to those whom medical historian James Harvey Young designates "cancer irregulars." Remembering his mother's suffering at the hands of cancer regulars, he feared that the disease ran in his family. Some decades earlier, Winrod recalled in the 1950s, his own "tumors" has been cured by William Frederick Koch (whose "cattle shots" were indistinguishable from distilled water), and more recently Koch's treatments had eased his fatigue.[18]

Yet ill health alone does not explain Winrod's championship of such irregulars as Koch and Harry M. Hoxsey, who inherited anticancer potions from his veterinatian father. As early as 1936, the evangelist had published a tract on healing in the Bible, and fifteen years later he still linked medicine to fundamentalism. Koch, he noted, appreciated the "supernatural" aspects of health care. In addition, Koch and Hoxsey shared Winrod's disdain for scientific orthodoxy and regulation by Washington's "health dictatorship." Starting in the late 1940s Winrod sent patients to them, lobbied in their behalf with Senator William Langer, and mobilized prayers, petitions, and lawsuits against the Food and Drug Administration.[19]

In late 1957, Winrod came down with influenza. He refused to stop working or consult a physician; according to his authorized biographer, his suspicion of the medical profession had become a "phobia." Too late, an osteopath, an old family friend, was summoned. Winrod died of pneumonia on 11 November 1957. In his last years, this prophet in politics had become a prophet in medicine. Thus the tenacious commitment to fundamentalism that had shaped Winrod's life also hastened his death.[20]

Gerald L. K. Smith, who outlived Winrod by nineteen years, recaptured modest notoriety before his own death in 1976. Through the late 1940s, however, his prospects continued to decline. Immediately after World War II, a broadly based "nationalist" alliance that Smith attempted to organize with former Senator Robert R. Reynolds was stillborn. In 1948, the States Rights party repudiated his support of its presidential nominee, J. Strom Thurmond. Spurned by the Dixiecrats, Smith made a second symbolic run for the White House that year, attracting even less attention than in 1944.[21]

Repeating the pattern of 1937–38, Gerald and Elna Smith campaigned across country seeking constituents, living out of suitcases and feeling, he later remembered, "like gypsies for America." This time, too, he got an audience. The Christian Nationalist Crusade, as Smith renamed his organization in 1946, was receiving $140,000 annually in contributions by 1950. Yet his audience was not nearly so large as before World War II, radio and television stations refused to sell him air time (yielding to a Jewish "quarantine," Smith said), and even hostile media coverage was rare. By 1948, many opponents had come to agree with the American Jewish Committee that the dean of American anti-Semitism deserved silent contempt instead of the free publicity provided by picket lines.[22]

Smith tried but usually failed to believe that this "silent treatment" gave him valuable "quiet and calm." In the early 1950s, a *Cross and the Flag* series looked back wistfully on the "dramatic incidents" in his life, including the tumultuous protests against his speeches. Depressed by his exclusion from the mainstream, Smith wondered whether anyone "working alone in history ever got any place?" A supporter told him about the Revolutionary-era pamphleteer Samuel Adams, and he found solace in the parallel. The strain of isolation eased after Smith bought a house in Tulsa, Oklahoma, following his determination that no Jews lived on the street. From the late 1940s until 1964, he divided his time between Los Angeles, California, where the Christian Nationalist Crusade published the *Cross and the Flag*, and Tulsa, where he pursued his favorite hobbies, the collection of antiques, Bibles, and portrayals of Jesus in any medium from oil paint to carved walnuts.[23]

Insofar as Smith retained some miniscule influence during the last thirty years of his life, it had to be exercised behind the scenes. In 1950, for example, he worked with radio commentator Fulton Lewis, Jr., and members of Senator Joseph R. McCarthy's staff to fight the nomination of Anna Rosenberg as Assistant Secretary of Defense. When this news broke, however, Lewis denied any connection with Smith. Among elite conservatives, Merwin K. Hart stood out in openly welcoming him to "our side." More typically, William F. Buckley, Jr., cited Smith to define the limits of political respectability. Pleased that Smith on the far right had been "effectively isolated," Buckley recommended the same treatment in 1970 for Black Panthers on the far left.[24]

Living in relative obscurity, Smith magnified his past association with world-famous "friends," including Charles A. Lindbergh, Henry Ford, and Huey Long. Ford's picture decorated his living room, and one of Smith's paper organizations, called the Henry Ford Memorial Commission, presented patriotism awards to such "nationalists" as Merwin K. Hart. After eulogizing Long for almost forty years, Smith decided in 1973 to build a monument to him. This statue of the late senator, located in Winn parish, inspired scant enthusiasm within Long's family or among Louisianans generally. The postwar era also brought Smith a new hero comparable in eminence to Long and Ford: General Douglas MacArthur. The Christian Nationalist Party, along with several other far right groups, nominated MacArthur for president in 1952. Smith unhesitatingly listed MacArthur among his personal friends even though they met only once, for a three-hour social call in 1954.[25]

Religion as well as nostalgia eased Smith's transition into obscurity. Convivial places of worship were sometimes hard to find, however, both because Smith's deepening theological conservativism ran counter to a liberalizing trend within the Disciples of Christ, and because many Disciples disliked praying alongside a notorious bigot. While in Michigan, he attended the Pontiac Christian Church, sometimes making guest appearances in the pulpit; the pastor, Leland Marion, was a life-long friend who had nominated Smith with anti-Semitic panache at the 1944 American First party convention. Later, Smith was welcomed to the First Christian Church in Tulsa by his old mentor Rev. Claude Hill, but the congregation prevented him from teaching a Bible study class. From the mid-1960s until his death, Smith attended services at the Eureka Springs, Arkansas, Christian Church. The minister there was affiliated with the North American Christian Convention (or Disciples of Christ Number Two), and Smith remained a theological conservative in the distinctive mode of the Disciples. He continued to reject the "sectarian" label "fundamentalist," professed belief in a simple gospel untainted by human additions, and generally scorned "doctrinal apocalyptic theories" and "date-setters."[26]

Even in obscurity, moreover, Smith found dangerous enemies to assail. He revised an old pamphlet to damn "too much and too many Roosevelts" when FDR's sons sought office; a later edition savored revelations that Roosevelt had been a "libertine." Although Harry S. Truman seemed a "good man" whom Smith tried to warn about "organized Jewry," the *Cross and the Flag* denounced him for removing MacArthur as commanding general in Korea. President Dwight D. Eisenhower was not a Communist, as Robert Welch of the John

Birch Society contended, but a "knave" or a "blind fool." Only knavery or foolishness, Smith wrote, could explain Eisenhower's opposition to Senator McCarthy, appointment of Earl Warren to the Supreme Court, and conciliation with the Soviet Union.[27]

After the relatively lean Eisenhower years, the turmoil of the 1960s brought Smith fresh recruits and increased contributions. Donations to the Christian Nationalist Crusade rose from $209,000 in 1959 to $325,000 in 1967. Bequests from admirers and a legal settlement from former Attorney General Francis Biddle, whose memoirs had mistakenly listed Smith among defendants in *United States* v. *McWilliams*, helped the Smiths to live amid their antiques in cluttered affluence. In 1964, they moved their summer residence from Tulsa to Eureka Springs, Arkansas, a faded Ozarks resort.[28]

Whether in Arkansas or California, Smith still rose at 5:30 A.M. to write most of the *Cross and the Flag* (circulation: 21,000 in 1968). Residual qualms about capitalists occasionally moved him to criticize Federal Reserve Board "money changers." More frequently he demanded victory in the Indochina war, denounced the civil rights movement, and expressed revulsion over changing American mores. Smith retained his belief that blacks should stay in their place, a separate but "not necessarily unequal place." His major concession to their quest for equality was to substitute "black" for "Negro" in the *Cross and the Flag*. At the same time, he provided pamphlets to White Citizens Councils, quietly befriended segregationist Governor Orval Faubus (Dem.-Ark.), and applauded Governor George C. Wallace of Alabama until Wallace showed signs of compromising his racism. Martin Luther King, on the other hand, qualified as a "Moscow-trained revolutionist."[29]

During the 1960s, Smith's concern for civil liberties sank to a new low, while his belief in conspiracies and ambivalent interest in "sex perversion" rose to new heights. He charged the Jewish "hidden hand" with hiding Communist responsibility for President John F. Kennedy's assassination. According to Smith, welfare "loafers" deserved incarceration in work camps, the press needed to be disciplined for harsh criticism of public officials, and obnoxious demonstrators must be handled with the kind of "masculinity" he had used on hecklers during the 1930s. Still mixing prudery with prurience, he attacked homosexuality, abortion, and "libertine" magazines, but told tales about Senator Gerald P. Nye's love life, pronounced Eleanor Roosevelt a "bull dyke," and assailed "whore-mongers" who nominated Lyndon B. Johnson—one of their own—for President in 1964.[30]

The 1964 presidential campaign, in which Republican candidate

Barry M. Goldwater defended "extremism in the defense of liberty," prompted some press notice of Smith, whom the *New York Times* called the "epitome of the really extremist forces." The newspaper expressed equal surprise that Smith was "still in business" and that he had endorsed Senator Goldwater. Although Goldwater fell short of perfection, the *Cross and the Flag* explained, he was the first major party candidate within Smith's mature lifetime "worthy of respect." The senator's virtues included his vote against the Civil Rights Act of 1964, his refusal to repudiate Joseph R. McCarthy, and the enemies he had made among Communists, Jews, and the Republican "Eastern Establishment." In Smith's eyes, his endorsement of Goldwater, an Episcopalian fathered by a Jew, demonstrated his own moderation.[31]

Smith's support of Goldwater was hardly an indication of ebbing interest in the "Jewish question." On the contrary, his belief in Zionist conspiracy grew sturdier and more comprehensive during the last thirty years of his life. In the early 1950s he speculated that Presidents Roosevelt and Eisenhower might have had Jewish ancestors. Similarly, he came around to the position adopted by Pelley decades earlier that Jesus Christ was "not a Jew as we now know Jews." When Pelley left prison in 1950, Smith called him a contemporary "saint" who had been persecuted for discovering the truth about Jewish conspiracy "sooner than the rest of us." In addition, Smith printed anti-Semitic jokes in the *Cross and the Flag*, decorated Christian Nationalist Crusade pamphlets with ugly caricatures of Jews, and detected Jewish physical traits in various Christian enemies—including Senator Estes Kefauver (Dem.-Tenn.). During the early 1970s Smith tried to authenticate *The Protocals*, and, when pressed about their reliability, he paraphrased Henry Ford's remark that they fit the world situation. Reflecting his life-long individualist ethic, Smith continued to concede that Jews, like other Americans, held basic constitutional rights, including the right to worship as they wished; he became convinced, however, that their worship required rejection of Jesus as a "fraud" and derision of the Virgin Mary as a "harlot."[32]

Ironically, anti-Semitism, which had offered Smith a framework to explain the red menace in the 1940s, ultimately transcended anti-Communism as an issue. Convinced by the early 1970s that Jews no longer ruled the Kremlin, he endorsed détente, encouraged trade with the Soviet Union, and chided those on the right who disagreed. The "enigmatic" Secretary of State, Henry A. Kissinger, sometimes made Smith's list of "responsible" Jews. Not only did Kissinger stand by President Richard M. Nixon during the Watergate hearings (a "plot" reminiscent of conspiracies against Lincoln, Smith said), but his Middle East mediation outraged the "international Jewish political machine." Then, too, because their criticism of the "counterfeit" Israeli state counted for more than their wrongheaded opposition to the Indochina war, Smith praised left liberal Senator James Abourezk (Dem.-S.D.) and in 1974 endorsed Senator J. William Fulbright (Dem.-Ark.) for reelection. The *Cross and the Flag* regularly scorned one of the Senate's leading cold warriors, "Rabbi" Henry M. Jackson.[33]

While continuing in Los Angeles to publish militantly anti-Semitic pamphlets, Smith devoted almost equal time after 1964 to a series of "sacred projects" in Eureka Springs. The projects were a grandiose version of Smith's enthusiam for collecting things. A seven-story high "Christ of the Ozarks," completed in 1966, was followed by a Bible museum, the "Christ Only Art Gallery," a massive amphitheatre, and a Passion Play. The dramatic rendition of Jesus's final days, though much less blatantly anti-Semitic than the *Cross and the Flag*, nonetheless held Jews responsible for His crucifixion. All of these enterprises, formally entrusted to the Elna N. Smith Foundation, annually attracted hundreds of thousands of visitors, most of whom knew nothing of Smith's background and sordid projects elsewhere. Indeed, Smith arranged a personal détente with local artisans who, despite bohemian contempt for his politics and aesthetics, profitted from the the local economic revival. In lonely moments, the journalist John Fergus Ryan suggested in 1968, Smith could find comfort in being "Le Grand Seigneur" of Eureka Springs.[34]

As the sacred projects attracted attention beyond northwestern Arkansas, Smith again became a center of controversy. In 1969, labeling him a "native fascist," the *Arkansas Gazette* successfully opposed federal financing of a road to the Christ of the Ozarks. Four years later, syndicated columnist Jack Anderson chastized Armed Forces Radio for interviewing "America's most notorious hate-monger" about his Eureka Springs ventures. Enjoying national notoriety after a generation in obscurity, Smith defended the Passion Play on the grounds that he could not "alter Scripture." Furthermore, he planned the grandest project of all, a lifesize replica of the Holy Land as it had existed during Jesus's time.[35]

Construction on the New Holy Land had barely begun when Smith died in Eureka Springs on 15 April 1976. He was buried near the base of the Christ of the Ozarks. In September 1977, Smith's widow and aides closed the California office of the Christian Nationalist Crusade and terminated the *Cross and the Flag. The Protocols* and *The International Jew* remained available from the Elna M. Smith Foundation, faithful subscribers were assured.[36]

Brown Scare Revisited: From Native "Fascism" to the "Radical Right"

When, during the 1948 campaign, both President Truman and Henry A. Wallace warned against incipient fascism (which both associated with bigotry and economic concentration), their phraseology already sounded anachronistic. At home, the economy absorbed the returning soldiers whom many observers had considered a potential *Freikorps*. Abroad, with the exception of Spain, there were no fascist regimes, let alone a fascist threat in the bipolar world. Furthermore, to militant centrists now politically dominant, the term fascist, long favored as an epithet by Communists and Popular Front liberals, was suspect by association.[37]

Yet diminished allusions to native fascism during the twenty years after World War II should not obscure the survival of concerns that the term had expressed. Whereas social critics during the 1930s and early 1940s had feared domestic fascism, their intellectual descendants during the 1950s and early 1960s worried about the "radical right," which, along with the radical left, constituted the two deadly branches of "extremism." The concept of "extremism," one of several used to sort out the volatile politics during the Depression, rose to preeminence via three trends: the growing use of social science to combat bigotry; the reevaluation by centrist scholars of old progressive and Popular Front ideologies; and the rise to notoriety of Senator Joseph R. McCarthy.[38]

Even before the Depression, anthropologists, sociologists, and psychologists had launched what John Higham calls a "massive assault on racial thinking and ethnocentrism." Revulsion against Nazism lent support to this trend, and refugee social scientists helped to shape it. Possibly the most significant of these was Max Horkheimer, the former director of the Institute for Social Research at Frankfurt who became chief of research for the American Jewish Committee in 1944. Horkheimer guided a remarkable series of "studies in prejudice" by able and imaginative scholars. According to their common preface, each work attempted "to answer the question: What is there in the psychology of an individual that makes him more or less likely to respond favorably to the agitation of a Goebbels or a Gerald L. K. Smith?"[39]

The most important contribution to the series, *The Authoritarian Personality*, tried to explain "potentially fascistic" men and women whom the authors, led by Horkheimer's friend Theodor Adorno, considered a grave threat to the United States. Combining Freudian analysis, interviews, and questionaires, they concluded that children raised in hierarchical, exploitative families grew into "authoritarian" adults. These authoritarians, clinging to "what appears to be strong" while disdaining "whatever is relegated to the bottom," were probable anti-Semites and likely fascists. The research team contained liberals and radicals, émigrés and native-born scholars, empiricists and adherents to the Frankfurt school's "critical theory." Hence *The Authoritarian Personality*, which was rushed to publication in 1950, contained internal contradictions and anomalies. But the authors, by and large avoiding psychological reductionism, expected the "most powerful economic groups" to have a decisive impact on American fascism. They also agreed that prejudice was "irrational in its essential nature." Indeed, the authoritarian was an "'anthropological species'" qualitatively different from the "reasonable man" possessing a "mature" personality.[40]

Since 1950, students of "extremism" have cited *The Authoritarian Personality* (or, more often, referred to "authoritarian personalities") but, for ideological as well as methodological reasons, rarely accepted the book's full argument. Conservatives accused the authors of reducing their traditionalist views to mental aberrations. Among centrist liberals dominant in the academy, Edward Shils in 1954 expressed the primary objection. Many of the survey questions in *The Authoritarian Personality*, Shils complained, were Henry "Wallaceite clichés" that Communists could answer affirmatively and appear tolerant. The book was flawed, therefore, because an authoritarian temperament was one of the "important features" common to fascism and Communism.[41]

The New American Right, edited by Daniel Bell in 1955, appropriated *The Authoritarian Personality*'s insights for the "vital center." The "novel" essays in his anthology, Bell explained in the preface, were written by scholars who, working independently, discovered striking similarities in their approaches to "McCarthyism." Even former radicals among them had come to appreciate the "exhaustion of liberal and leftwing ideology." According to Richard Hofstadter's elaboration in *The Radical Right*, an expanded version of Bell's anthology published in 1963, the economic interpretation of politics was often "inadequate or misleading or altogether irrelevant." Hence, applying to one such problem "recent thought" in sociology and social psychology, the authors roughly agreed that McCarthy's constituency revealed "status anxiety" instead of class conflict, betrayed a conspiratorial worldview akin to mental illness, and descended from "populist" antecedents. In a word—a word Hofstadter borrowed from *The Authoritarian Personality*—McCarthyites were "pseudo-conservatives."[42]

Bell's collection of essays, though ostensibly focused on the radical right, devoted almost equal attention to the divided left and the vital center. For example, contributors discussed the relative redness of the "Red Decade," "The Intellectuals and the Discontented Classes" (as David Riesman and Nathan Glazer called their piece), and Henry A. Wallace's presidential race (to show, according to Allen F. Westin, that the radical right of the early 1960s replicated the "ideologies, programs, strategies and tactics" of the "extreme left" of 1945–48.) Like earlier commentators on native fascism, these students of the far right used their subject as a vehicle to study the whole society.[43]

The continuity in perspective is hardly surprising, since three of the original seven contributors to Bell's book had participated in the Brown Scare. In 1942, David Riesman had presented the most learned case for prosecuting native fascists who defamed racial or ethnic minorities. Peter Viereck, son of George Sylvester Viereck, the Nazi propagandist tried in *United States* v. *McWilliams*, had repudiated his father's views, called for a "new conservatism" as early as 1940, and denounced "communazis" on the left and right. Bell himself, anticipating a "groundswell of American fascism" in 1944, had outlined the arguments later placed at the core of *The Radical Right*. In particular, he had written that the "populist tradition," distorted "into reactionary form" by the likes of Father Coughlin, Huey Long, and Senator Gerald P. Nye, would probably breed "America's Fuehrer (Midwest product no doubt)"; a decade later, though shunning the archaic phrase "American fascism," Bell found in McCarthy the midwestern "populist" demagogue he had been looking for.[44]

The Radical Right demonstrates that postwar centrists owed more debts than they realized to "exhausted" liberal and left-wing ideology. Specifically, unlike liberals and radicals who had to fashion explanations of native fascism almost from scratch during the early 1930s, they could rely during the 1950s on firmly established conventions. Hence, slighting primary research, contributors to *The Radical Right* translated into social science idiom Brown Scare themes concerning both the far right and the country's vulnerability to it.[45]

The "novel" ideas in *The Radical Right* served as the basis for a sweeping interpretation of American life now so commonplace that it barely needs review. Numerous centrist scholars argued that the genius of our politics was, as Bell said, a capacity for "pragmatic give and take." Rather than fighting "wars-to-the-death," most groups shared power and traded economic concessions. But extremists behaved differently. Eschewing tangible economic gains, agitators on the far right and far left sought psychological relief from "status anxiety." Thus, instead of creating positive programs to build a better future, John H. Bunzel wrote, they retreated into an "ideal past." Habitually rejecting compromise, Seymour Martin Lipset and Earl Raab explained, they preferred to shut down the "open marketplace of ideas."[46]

Within this framework, "populism" was widely regarded as the proximate source of the radical right; Lipset and Raab, in their search for extremists, reached back to the Federalist pamphleteer Jedidiah Morse. Centrist scholars emphasized that far right activists also derived their "Manichean and apocalyptic" conceptions of politics from "fundamentalist" religion. This conspiratorial frame of mind—what Hofstadter called the "paranoid style"—was shared by adherents to the surrogate religion of Communism. According to Ralph Lord Roy, a "curious *de facto* alliance" between Communists and far right "apostles of discord" undermined "legitimate social concern and protest." Furthermore, though systematic comparison of the United States and Europe was rare, centrist scholars occasionally alluded to affinities between the radical right and followers of Hitler and Mussolini.[47]

The Depression emerged as a critical period in chronicles of extremism. In Peter Viereck's view, Father Charles E. Coughlin represented the "missing link" between "idealistic Populist-Progressives" and bigoted followers of McCarthy. Victor C. Ferkiss argued that a coherent worldview, a degenerate form of "Populism," underlay the intellectual fascism of Lawrence Dennis and Ezra Pound, and "fascism as a popular movement from its emergence under Senator Long and Father Coughlin in 1930 to its demise under Gerald L. K. Smith in 1946." This "American fascist movement" also included Senator Burton K. Wheeler, Senator Gerald P. Nye, Representative William Lemke, as well as Pelley and Winrod. Their neo-Populist ideology, though "basically indigenous" to the United States, was nonetheless virtually congruent with those of European Nazis and Fascists. According to Ferkiss, the common features included nationalism, economic appeals to middle class merchants and farmers, despair of liberal democratic institutions, and a conspiratorial approach to history. Among American fascists, however, nationalism took the form of isolationism instead of imperialism, and there was almost "no pseudo-mystical exaltation of the state."[48]

Far right activists—along with their supposed counterparts on the far left—attracted sustained scholarly attention in part because the concept of extremism was ideologically useful to liberal intellectuals. The continuous balancing that rendered liberalism synonymous with moderation not only provided "protective coloration" during the Cold War, Riesman and Glazer noted in *The Radical Right,* but it made "clear to ourselves that we are not fools or dupes of fellow-traveler rhetoric." Moreover, among social scientists sharing Bell's pluralist assumption that power was "hard to locate" in the United States, the theory of extremism had the advantage of associating any contrary view with paranoia; at least implicitly and often explicitly, Gerald L. K. Smith's belief in *The Protocols* and C. Wright Mills's dissection of a "power elite" were deemed comparably "conspiratorial." In addition, the concept of extremism was almost a logical necessity for centrists who, while applauding a system of "give and take," still found some countrymen too despicable to deal with, let alone to compromise with. If extremists differed tactically, psychologically, and perhaps "anthropologically" from "rational men," then, without apparent contradiction, liberals could bar them from the "open marketplace of ideas."[49]

Unfortunately, polemical convenience conflicted with historical accuracy. Grafting Brown Scare themes onto Cold War premises, authorities on extremism assumed that their political *prescription,* a center untainted by far right and far left, was also an accurate *description* of past politics. Speaking for conservatives excluded from the sensible center, William F. Buckley, Jr., dismissed *The Radical Right* as an anti-McCarthy "period piece"; Michael Paul Rogin, a representative left liberal in the late 1960s, inferred that the authors and their fellow pluralists had been "traumatized" by Senator McCarthy and the Cold War. Yet few critics, and none of the numerous authors who referred in monographs to far right extremists, recognized that this "non-ideological" concept was itself a legacy from the ideological conflicts of the 1930s.[50]

Ideas are not necessarily invalid because they were conceived in controversy, but an understanding of the intellectual origins of the theory of extremism guards against its routine application. Therefore, instead of squeezing Pelley, Winrod, and Smith into this familiar framework, I shall examine the ways in which their lives call it into question. In the process, we must appreciate that the reevaluation of American social thought conducted by centrist intellectuals, though flawed, was often insightful.

Any attempt to disentangle their insights from their errors inevitably intersects with the debate over "populism," which, with varying sophistication, they regarded as the fount of far right prejudice and incivility. Centrists typically used "Populist" as a shorthand designation for agrarian protest, extending from the People's Party at least to such western progressives as Senators Robert M. LaFollette, Gerald P. Nye, and Burton K. Wheeler. Historian Norman Pollack, on the other hand, reserved the term for the People's Party, which he found largely devoid of prejudice and rancor. Some students of the far right subsumed under Populism virtually any admirer of William Jennings Bryan, while some defenders of Populist sagacity considered Bryan unworthy of both the People's Party nomination in 1896 and the retrospective accolade. Straddling these positions, Michael Paul Rogin conceded a connection between agrarian radicalism and the "neo-fascist" Union Party of 1936, but minimized the tie to McCarthy and saw the "Populist tradition" flowering in Senator George McGovern's "humanitarian" liberalism.[51]

On all sides, this debate has been marked by methodological imprecision. Tradition lies in the eye of the beholder, and politicians across the spectrum claim posthumous endorsements from departed statesmen. During the 1930s, a time when such "usable pasts" were especially valued, Winrod recalled Bryan as an enemy of evolution instead of corporations, administration Democrats insisted that Bryan would have preferred President Roosevelt to the Union Party, and Communist William Z. Foster traced his own progression "from Bryan to Stalin." Even granting that Bryan represented Populism incarnate, we cannot know (unless we share Pelley's access to higher octaves) whether he would have joined the Defenders, the New Deal, or the Popular Front.[52]

Still, issues can be clarified. Centrist intellectuals, rejecting the old progressive and Popular Front tendency to envision a virtuous left combating an oppressive right, showed that economic reform and nativism often coexisted in the same person. Applying these valuable insights to the turn-of-the-century reformers, however, they exaggerated bigotry among Populists—whether the term embraced the People's Party or a wider range of agrarian rebels—while understating prejudice among more prosperous reformers (usually called progressives) and conservatives. They compounded this error by presuming, instead of proving, that later far right agitators acquired their ideas from Populists.[53]

The major premise, that intolerance bubbled up from the untutored masses, reveals again the complex continuity between formerly radical centrists and the ideology they sought to repudiate. As we have seen, suspicion of common men had circulated during the American celebration of the 1930s, but on the left it remained submerged beneath paeans to "the people." As intellectuals embraced the center and contemplated atrocities committed during World War

II, their latent suspicion surfaced. They continued the American celebration, however, by transferring applause from "the people" to the pluralist social order. Further compensating for lost faith in common men, they celebrated elites (including "true" as opposed to "pseudo-conservatives") whom they expected to preserve decorum; as Talcott Parsons wrote in *The Radical Right*, the United States needed a social stratum in which a "traditional political responsibility is ingrained."[54]

Ironically mirroring the left's earlier misjudgment of "the people," these postwar centrists suffered from inflated expectations regarding elites. While repeating the truism that persons threatened economically and psychologically were more likely than their comfortable neighbors to assail scapegoats, leading students of extremism missed the connection between far right activists and irresponsible, intolerant elites.

For example, Pelley, Winrod, and Smith borrowed their anti-radical rhetoric from presidents, senators, attorneys general, corporate executives, and labor leaders. Recognizing his own debt to the mainstream, Smith was perplexed by the pro-Soviet vogue during World War II:

> For twenty-five years all good Americans have been taught in Church, in school and in public meetings that Russia was bad, wrong, Communistic, and atheistic. Over night we are expected to assume that Russia is a democracy, that Stalin is Sir Gallahad, and that everything is lovely in the land of the Big Brown Bear.

Initially, Smith conceded that Stalin would acquire some wartime "loot"; as national leaders escalated the Cold War in 1946–47, he, too, became increasingly belligerent.[55]

With respect to anti-Semitism, the chief prejudice shared by Pelley, Winrod, and Smith, Carey McWilliams was correct to urge investigation "from the top down and not from the bottom up." As centrist intellectuals contended, Ignatius Donnelly's novels, Mary Elizabeth Lease's speeches, and Tom Watson's magazines undoubtedly encouraged some Americans to dislike Jews. It was misleading, however, to subsume these anti-Semitic expressions under Hofstadter's rubric, the "folklore of Populism"; the dominant symbols of Jewish iniquity in these works, Shylock and Judas Iscariot, belong rather to the folklore of western civilization. Furthermore, except for Watson's diatribes in the 1910s, the anti-Semitic views of present or former People's Party leaders were commonplace in an overwhelmingly nativist nation. Indeed, by the mid-1920s they were overshadowed by the harsher Anglo-Saxon cult, "scientific" racism, and quotas imposed by genteel anti-Semites.[56]

Significantly, though historians debate the anti-Semitic impact of Donnelly, Lease, and Watson, neither Pelley, Winrod, nor Smith cited them as influences. If Pelley read books by Donnelly, a fellow aficionado of Atlantis, they had less impact on his development than contact with prejudiced Red Cross volunteers, White Russians, and Justice Department officials. The chief document in Smith's conversion to conspiratorial anti-Semitism, *The International Jew*, was characterized by progressive motifs and sources, and sponsored by a billionaire who qualifies as a Populist only under the most far-fetched definition. In short, instead of postulating an extremist current flowing from Populism to McCarthy and beyond, we must recognize the far right debt to the economic elite and the cultural mainstream.[57]

If far right activists built their worldviews out of material from the dominant culture, to what extent did their political style diverge from New Deal "pragmatism"? As outs aspiring to get in, they naturally associated the incumbent administration with regression instead of regeneration, and attacked federal patronage instead of dispensing it. Looking beyond these differences, centrist scholars correctly saw the need, as Hofstadter wrote, for "some such concept" as "status politics" to encompass conflicts over "faith and morals" unexplained by the kind of economic interpretation his generation had encountered during the 1930s. But their specific formulation drew an unduly sharp distinction between "interest politics," the supposed realm of pragmatic moderates, and "status politics," the eccentric specialty of far right activists. Status politics, a concept popularized by the erstwhile radicals Hofstadter and Lipset, was the pluralist offspring of Marxist "false consciousness," a "luxurious" form of protest (as Hofstadter emphasized) that obscured basic issues. Inadvertently loyal to old left ideology, these authorities on extremism failed to appreciate that shrewd politicans across the spectrum practiced both sorts of appeal. Postulating the dominance of interest politics during periods of high unemployment, moreover, they misread the 1930s.[58]

The Depression *was* a crisis of faith and morals, and no one understood the situation better than President Roosevelt. Raising national morale at the expense of literal accuracy, he assured Americans that they needed to fear only fear itself. Indeed, because Roosevelt eased fears of apocalypse without repairing the economy, we might accord him greater success as a status politician than as a pragmatic reformer. On the other hand, while Pelley and Smith assured constituents that Christian values would prevail, they also promoted economic redistribution. Their particular economic programs, Share Our Wealth and the Christian Commonwealth, were utopian, but, along with more appealing activists on the left, they contributed indirectly to pragmatic reform by pushing the Roosevelt administration toward the welfare state.[59]

Although Pelley's presidential campaign consisted primarily of fantasy, Winrod and Smith, outs with serious prospects of getting into the Senate, followed the customary practices of wheeling, dealing, hedging, and bargaining. During his senatorial race in 1938, Winrod barely mentioned Jews and minimized his animosity to the Roman Catholic Church. Until the early 1940s, Smith received assistance from Governor Martin Davey of Ohio, Representative Hamilton Fish, and House Republican leader Joseph W. Martin; the contributions he received from Henry Ford, W. C. Durant, Ransom Olds, and the Dodge family show that far right organizations continued to appeal, as Norman Hapgood had observed in 1922, to the "property class." Above all, Smith's cordial alliance with Senator Arthur Vandenberg, later a hero to "vital center" liberals, suggests that the realm of shifting political coalitions is more complex than authorities on extremism have supposed.[60]

Winrod, Smith, and even Pelley spoke what Clinton Rossiter called our common "political language." Certainly their political dialects differed from those of President Roosevelt or Senator Robert A. Taft. Yet the label *radical* rightist, applied by centrists like John H. Bunzel, who viewed "radicalism" as a synonym for "incivility," obscures the far right's relationship with the wider culture. Pelley, Winrod, and Smith were noisy and nasty. With the significant exception of Pelley's plan to ghettoize Jews, however, they were not radical in the sense of seeking basic social change. Share Our Wealth and the Christian Commonwealth were intended to fulfill, not destroy, the American dream of success through hard work. And the agitation practiced by Pelley, Winrod, and Smith broke with convention less than sitdown strikes by the CIO.[61]

Several figures of speech adopted by these far right activists also highlight ties to the dominant culture. Winrod, a reputed fascist himself, came to denounce "Red fascism" during the Cold War; Pelley attacked "totalitarianism" in labor unions. The dean of paranoids to many scholars, Smith assailed "paranoid" Jews who failed to understand him. During the 1970s, he presented himself as the occupant of the real vital center, between backsliders like George C. Wallace on the left and "paranoids" on the right who stocked arms, rejected détente, or shunned Barry Goldwater. Propounding a far right version of pluralism, moreover, Smith emphasized that the "child-minded" masses must be guided by responsible leaders—like himself.[62]

In the final analysis, the assumption that extremist minds functioned in a "paranoid" fashion is critical to the prevailing theory. Paranoid stylists were not distinguished by contempt for evidence, Hofstadter said, but by peculiar use of it; a "curious leap of imagination" was "always made at some critical point in the recital of events." Accordingly, even if far right activists allied with mainstream politicians or appropriated countersubversive, anti-Semitic imagery from the dominant culture, they qualified as a separate "anthropological species" because they made peculiar use of that imagery.[63]

This interpretation moved beyond the "excessive rationalism" in old progressive historiography that Hofstadter cogently criticized, but the advance was limited both by intellectual baggage from the prewar period and by a kind of psychological vital centrism. Since Harold Lasswell's early efforts in the 1920s, psychoanalytical aproaches to politics had gone hand-in-hand with debunking. Yet unlike the pioneer social scientists and legal realists who had plumbed the hidden motives of congressmen and judges, centrist intellectuals during the 1950s, newly enamored of such insiders, minimized their unconscious drives and pronounced their behavior pragmatic. These writers largely confined the search for unconscious motives to far right and far left figures who seemed, in Hofstadter's phrase, "psychologically outside the frame of normal democratic politics." Thus, much as they arbitrarily separated status politics from interest politics, most students of extremism drew a crude distinction between rational and irrational behavior. Despite their ritual bows to *The Authoritarian Personality*, which retained Freud's understanding that rationality and irrationality intertwined, they were closer to the neo-Freudians who had argued since the cultural retrenchment of the 1930s that social deviance bred neurosis.[64]

Yet, in the historical as well as the psychoanalytical context, historian David Brion Davis properly emphasizes, a thin line often separates the views of rational persons from the "ravings of screwballs and nuts." During the crises of the 1930s and 1940s, for example, liberal leaders of the Brown Scare revealed traits that, using Hofstadter's framework, we could consider symptomatic of the paranoid style. L. M. Birkhead, Avedis Derounian, and their fellows believed that history was "at the turning point," lacked "sensible judgment about what can make a revolution," and badly exaggerated far right power; their documentary exposés, later cited as reliable sources by students of the far right, showed a "heroic striving for evidence to prove that the unbelievable is the only thing that can be believed."[65]

Rather than widening the scope of the paranoid style label, however, we should declare a moratorium on its use. The term itself, coined by Hofstadter as part of a worthy effort to examine the "nonrational side of politics," now discourages that very enterprise. Instead of exploring the complex relationship between ideology and personality, scholars less sophisticated than Hofstadter merely apply his catchy phrase. Ending analysis where it ought to begin, they typically assume that far right agitators who promote simplistic social remedies must also possess simpler personalities than mainstream politicians. Yet the opposite presumption may be warranted. Pelley, Winrod, and Smith were more complex than their foes, Harold L. Ickes and William Allen White, because, within the limits of biological constraint, each was "twice-born."[66]

Winrod's career highlights the difficulty of drawing the fine line between normality and abnormality. Postulating a homogeneous society, broken only by vestigial, "backward-looking" groups, centrist scholars logically ascribed extreme—or simply odd—views to personal idiosyncrasy. In fact, however, the American consensus had always been broken by more-or-less distinct subcultures, both admirable and appalling, in which our common political or religious "language" acquired strange accents. Among the fundamentalists who raised Winrod, for instance, "twice-born" men and women were commonplace. His life, viewed from the perspective of theologically conservative Protestantism, unfolds with remarkable symmetry. Indeed, Winrod would have been abnormal—and harder to interpret—if he had grown up to be a psychoanalyst or a skeptical historian.[67]

Smith's life undersocres the importance of tracing the development of prejudice instead of alluding to a static "style." His conversion to conspiratorial anti-Semitism, marked by his republication of *The International Jew* in 1946, grew out of a personal crisis and helped to resolve it. As late as 1941, though Smith accepted derogatory stereotypes about Jews that circulated widely in American culture, his views survived the scrutiny of the midwestern director of the B'nai B'rith Anti-Defamation League. Increasingly scorned by liberals and radicals, repudiated by conservatives, and feeling like a "lonely person walking through the woods," he retreated into a world of far right agitators who, in turn, fanned his suspicion of Jews. Smith's demagogy deserved condemnation even before he endorsed

The Protocols and *The International Jew,* but the presence of vigorous opposition shows that he did not concoct feelings of persecution out of thin air.[68]

A decisive factor in Smith's conversion to conspiratorial anti-Semitism was his need to identify with prominent men, surrogates for his father, whom he called the "best Christian man I ever knew." The need grew stronger as his isolation increased. During the early 1930s, facing the loss of his pulpit, Smith joined Huey Long's entourage and copied the Kingfish's dramatic demeanor. A decade later, on the verge of losing the last shreds of respectability, Smith cultivated Henry Ford and paid close attention to *The International Jew* because it bore Ford's imprimatur. Still, he wavered for a half decade before convincing himself that Jewish plotters controlled Communism and capitalism. Instead of saying that Smith made a "characteristic paranoid leap" avoided by genteel anti-Semites, a better metaphor pictures his slide down a grade to a more comprehensive form of prejudice.[69]

Nor was the slide inevitable. Even in cases of clinical paranoia, Freud recognized, the presence, absence, or form of symptoms often depended on chance encounters with external stimuli. Yet scholars who alluded to a paranoid style, prone to postulating an authoritarian childhood and a linear decline from there, underestimated the role of chance in the making of far right agitators. If Smith, for instance, had encountered Senator George Norris instead of Huey Long during the early 1930s, he could have become—while retaining the same aggressive personality, anxiety about his status, and craving for "high toned" company—dean of the social gospel instead of the dean of American anti-Semitism. And pluralists might now cite his rise from a Wisconsin farm to demonstrate the genius of American mobility.[70]

Pelley, who most closely resembled the classic authoritarian personality, shows that private delusions intersect with public issues. The insecure son of rigid, unsuccessful parents, he tried to demonstrate his toughness by degrading Jews and came to dwell largely in a world of apocalyptic expectation. Nonetheless, it is misleading to conclude—recalling Hofstadter's phrase—that he projected onto politics "utterly irrelevant fantasies and disorders of a *purely personal kind.*" On the contrary, his obsessions with sex, success, and life's meaning were shared by millions of men in his generation; his fantastic Christian Commonwealth was a refuge from the harsh realities of striving for affluence and love in New England, New York, and Hollywood.[71]

The texture of fears felt by Pelley, Winrod, and Smith, as well as the broader psychological impact of the Depression, are lost amid catch-phrases like status anxiety and paranoid style. Far right agitators look less like a distinct arthropological species if, substituting comparable concepts with different connotations, we say that social, intellectual, and political changes threatened their "identity" (a neo-Freudian term) or their "self-esteem" (a term favored by orthodox Freudian Otto Fenichel). The need for self-esteem, like unconscious motives generally, is not confined to extremists. Harold L. Ickes's admirable public career contrasts with Smith's appalling record, but Ickes, no less than Smith, sought surrogate fathers in politics—and found them in Theodore and Franklin Roosevelt. It is ironic that postwar centrist scholars, though fond of irony, rarely appreciated that good causes as well as bad attracted adherents for "personal" reasons.[72]

Attempts to explore the unconscious of political actors must complement, not replace, analyses of their worldviews. Studies of the far right rarely achieved this symbiosis because most authors agreed with Hofstadter that extremist opinions were "only marginally related" to manifest issues. Adapting a Brown Scare motif, centrist scholars did consider fundamentalism a bulwark of the far right; unfortunately, their understanding of these theological conservatives advanced little beyond that of the debunkers of the 1920s or the Popular Front of the 1930s. Lipset and Raab, for example, used "fundamentalist" as a timeless synonym for "Protestant moralism."[73]

Specialists in religious history might have countered the tendency toward glib generalization and psychological reductionism, but, often devout Christians, they tended to sacrifice analytical precision in order to promote tolerance. Ralph Lord Roy and Franklin H. Littell, for instance, maintained that proper understanding of Christianity precluded anti-Semitism. Accordingly, absolving mainstream Protestants and Catholics, they joined more secular scholars in blaming a fundamentalist fringe for far right extremism. Committing their own version of the centrist error noted earlier, Roy and Littell assumed that their *religious* prescription, a tolerant faith rooted in liberal theology, was also an accurate description of the religious past. Yet anti-Semitic expressions by Thomas Aquinas, Martin Luther, and other church fathers provided a usable past for Winrod and Smith. Within the United States during the 1930s, moreover, not all bigots were fundamentalists, and not all fundamentalists were bigots.[74]

Examining those cases where Christian belief directly nurtured bigotry, scholars must be sensitive to personal, denominational, and doctrinal variations. Differences among Pelley, Winrod, and Smith are instructive. Winrod supposed that the Jewish conspirators revealed in *The Protocols* would ally with a flesh-and-blood Antichrist whom he, as a dispensationalist, expected imminently to appear.

Smith, like evangelical Protestants since the origin of the republic, assumed that Americanism and Christianity went hand in hand. Unlike Winrod, however, he did not deduce his opinions about Jews from theological premises. Rather, declining the label fundamentalist, he seems to have recognized that his anti-Semitism was, in Disciples of Christ terminology, a matter of opinion rather than faith. Winrod was less vicious than Smith, with whom he is usually paired as an "apostle of discord," because he adhered consistently to dispensational theology. According to Smith, Jews sponsored subversion of their own free will; Winrod conceded that they were "simply being poured into molds of prophesy," and expected some to embrace Jesus before the final battle foretold in Revelation. Thus, without any sense of contradiction, the Defenders simultaneously distributed *The Protocols* and sought Jewish converts. Pelley, furthest from conventional Protestantism in his denial of Jesus's Jewishness, was the cruelest anti-Semite of the three.[75]

Finally, what was the relationship between the American far right—represented here by Pelley, Winrod, and Smith—and such European movements as German Nazism, Italian Fascism, Action Française, the Spanish Falange, and the British Union of Fascists? The definitive answer would require another book as long as this one. Yet tentative hypotheses are inescapable because this question influenced polemicists against American fascism during the Depression, federal prosecutors during World War II, and postwar scholarship on the radical right. Their diverse answers highlight the problem's difficulty. Along with the issue at the core of *United States v. McWilliams*—to what extent did the domestic far right receive support from abroad?—we must consider not whether but in what ways the United States is unique.

The "common issues of the West" take "strange and singular shape" in the United States, Louis Hartz has observed, and thus scholars need to recognize both parallels and singular adaptations. During the late nineteenth century, class tensions, rising ethnocentrism, pressures toward secularization, and upper middle-class malaise characterized industrializing nations on both sides of the Atlantic. Yet these strains in the United States produced neither a strong socialist party nor a distinctive far right. While American historians must stretch to find the roots of the radical right in Populism, colleagues studying Europe easily discern direct antecedents of Hitler and Mussolini.[76]

Far right groups like the Christian Social Party in Germany, the Pan German party in Austria, and the League of Patriots in France grew by borrowing ideas and soliciting members from rival camps. They promoted loyalty to God, the home, and their respective countries but, unlike conservatives who shared these views, rejected the economic status quo. They joined liberals in favoring expanded suffrage, yet feared that liberalism itself fostered social decay. They deplored Marxist internationalism, and nonetheless favored "socialist" measures ranging from graduated taxation to nationalization of railroads. Often, too, they recommended disfranchisement of Jews or restoration of the ghetto.[77]

The European far right, briefly thwarted by reformist governments roughly parallel to American progressivism, revived following World War I and the Russian Revolution. Hitler barely stood out among numerous German agitators during the 1920s. Emerging from an Italian far right crowd, Mussolini marched to the prime ministry in 1922. The Depression not only brought the Nazis to power in 1933, but added recruits to far right movements throughout Europe. Several paramilitary leagues, as well as the venerable Action Française, threatened the French Third Republic. In 1932, Sir Oswald Mosley organized the British Union of Fascists. A year later, Jose Antonio Primo de Rivera founded the Falange in Spain.[78]

The far right movements created after World War I added little to the conglomeration of notions developed a generation earlier. Pledging fealty to various fatherlands, they drew inspiration from past national triumphs and promised new ones, usually in the form of colonial expansion. In countries where racism and anti-Semitism had appealed during the 1880s, prejudice flourished again. Eclectic platforms still promised alternatives to exploitative capitalism on the one hand and materialistic socialism on the other. Above all, European far right leaders preached "heroic" action. Heroism, supposedly an ancestral virtue abandoned by economic man, had been rediscovered in World War I. Looking to the trenches for inspiration, Hitler, Mussolini, and Mosley, more than their nineteenth-century predecessors, favored uniforms and paramilitary organization.[79]

After Mussolini and Hitler seized power, their admirers attempted to graft aspects of Fascism and National Socialism onto far right movements elsewhere in Europe. In the "age of fascism," Oswald Mosley later recalled, "it was clearly jejune and probably dishonest to deny that we were fascist." Even established regimes were affected. Antonio Salazar organized "green-shirt" troopers and invited Heinrich Himmler, head of the Nazi SS (*Schutzstaffel*), to reorganize the Portuguese secret police. Rome and Berlin, in turn, offered much moral support and occasional material aid to other right-wing groups.

Nevertheless, ideological grafts affected style more than substance, sometimes producing what historian H. R. Trevor-Roper calls "fascitious fascisms."[80]

Most European far right movements were not offspring of Fascism or Nazism, but more or less distant ideological cousins. Pilgrims to Rome or Berlin returned with little more than corporate or racist rhetoric, inclinations to clad their followers in uniform, and memories of audiences with Hitler or Mussolini. These memories were not always pleasant. Primo de Rivera was unimpressed by the Nazis and disappointed in Mussolini. Although both Hitler and Il Duce charmed Mosley, his Keynesian economics owed more to the United States Federal Reserve System than to Fascism or Nazism.[81]

Divergent attitudes toward both Christianity and Judaism illustrate the impact of national contexts on the European far right. Mussolini made his peace with the Vatican. The Falange sought a Roman Catholic "reconstruction" in Spain. Hitler, though obliged to compromise with practitioners of the "Jewish-Christ creed," called himself a "heathen," longed for a "true religion rooted in . . . blood," and built Teutonic castles in which "knights" learned to combat racial decay. Most important, devoted to *völkisch* assumptions and *The Protocols,* he disrupted Germany's war effort to annihilate Jews. Far right parties attracted bigots throughout Europe, but his Nazi zeal was absent from countries lacking strong anti-Semitic backgrounds. Mussolini's belated persecution of Jews reflected Germany's power within the Axis, not indigenous Italian sentiments, and his edicts fell short of the rigorously racist Nuremberg laws. Though allied with Jew-baiting thugs, Mosley, unlike Hitler, thought *The Protocols* "complete nonsense."[82]

Extending these comparisons across the Atlantic, we can see that the left during the 1930s and 1940s exaggerated the connection between American far right agitators and the Axis. The prosecution in *United States* v. *McWilliams* failed to produce evidence of Nazi payments to such organizations as the Silver Shirts and the Defenders of the Christian Faith. Except for shared anti-Semitism, the case for ideological ties is only slightly stronger. Nor is their absence surprising. Far right agitators everywhere drew on favored nationalist axioms, and in the United States these included belief in American exceptionalism. To Winrod, all mankind was sinful, but Americans in the aggregate were less sinful than foreigners; finding biblical support in Isaiah, he expected the United States to avoid the worst terrors of earth's last days. To Smith, unconstrained by a doctrine of human depravity, the United States was unambigously God's country, a perfect land threatened only by alien "isms."[83]

Hence, in ideology as well as geography, American far right groups stood farther from Berlin or Rome than did the Action Française, the Falange, or the British Union of Fascists. Smith occasionally denounced the "pagan Nazis" and their disciples in the German-American Bund. While approving of Hitler's anti-Semitism, Winrod considered Nazi dictatorship inappropriate for the United States. Any dictator seizing power here, he predicted, would probably be killed by a "rugged individualist." Among the three figures central to this book, only Pelley adopted the trappings of "fascitious fascism," and even he claimed to be a Yankee constitutionalist. Significantly, too, Pelley's Silver Shirts attracted much less support than either Winrod's Defenders or Smith's Committee of One Million.[84]

Although the American far right was not spawned by the European, it did represent a parallel response to common issues framed in a particular national context, much as the progressivism of Theodore Roosevelt and Woodrow Wilson roughly paralleled the nonsocialist, reform governments in London, Paris, Berlin, and Rome at the turn of the century. Like German Nazis or Italian Fascists, Pelley, Winrod, and Smith responded to economic and cultural crisis by advocating a patriotic revival combined with calls, more or less zealous, to redistribute wealth. Along with leaders of European far right movements, they attacted primarily middle class support and applauded characteristically middle-class values: piety, propriety, family, and hard work. Along with their Europeans counterparts, they had mixed feelings about established conservatives, who were sources of funds and reputability but also devotees of caution and stability. The fact that conservatives in the United States were not Junkers but, in Smith's words, "short-sighted magnates" serves as a reminder that trans-Atlantic parallels must account for singular adaptations. This admonition, obvious to scholars comparing, for example, President Wilson with his contemporary, German Chancellor Theobald von Bethmann-Hollweg, is often lost on colleagues presenting Smith as an American Hitler.[85]

In their conceptions of the good society, Pelley, Winrod, and Smith stood apart from Hitler's Führer principle, Mussolini's "apotheosis of Rome," or even Mosley's mixture of "science and caesarism." Rather, devoted to the gospel of success by individual effort, all three believed that the best government governed least; Pelley and Smith promoted versions of a guaranteed annual income in order to reduce regulation from Washington. In the mid-1930s, when Mussolini regarded the National Recovery Administration as a pale imitation of his own corporate state and the Nazi *Völkischer Beobachter* hailed similarities between Roosevelt's "absolute" control and Hitler's,

Pelley, Winrod, and Smith were charging the president with usurpation of power.[86]

Unlike Nazi stormtroopers, Fascist squads, Mosley's BUF, and the Falangists, aspirants to what Primo de Rivera called a "military conception of life," the American far right was affected by this country's venerable suspicion of standing armies. Smith gloried in his brief encounter with General Douglas MacArthur, but also retained a conscientious objector on his staff during World War II. Winrod, influenced by Kansas Mennonites, sympathized with pacifism. Accordingly, their tactics diverged from the violent norm of the European far right. Hitler and Mussolini led successful coups; the Falange joined an insurrection; and French far right bands, historian Robert O. Paxton has noted, precipitated a "virtual civil war" during the 1930s. Winrod and Smith, on the other hand, shunned extralegal means to overthrow the New Deal.[87]

Again Pelley emerges as the exception to test the generalization. He yearned for valor, dreamed of a Silver Legion Protectorate, and openly encouraged thugs. Yet we should not necessarily infer from their gray shirts that the Chief's small following craved military discipline, violence, or a seizure of power. Often cowardly in street fights or abstracted on higher octaves, Silver Shirts (as Geoffrey Sutton Smith suggests) had more in common with the Odd Fellows than with the SS.[88]

In different countries, identical stereotypes were placed within substantially different worldviews. Nazi anti-Semitism rested on the proposition, expressed by Hitler in *Mein Kampf*, that all Jews possessed "definite racial characteristics." During World War II, this premise was translated into genocide with remarkable consistency. Pelley's version of anti-Semitism was fully congruent with Nazi racism, but Winrod and Smith were more complex in their prejudices. Winrod sometimes ascribed Roosevelt's actions to his "Jewish" ancestry and speculated that "Jewish" Soviet commissars carried hatred of Christ "in their blood." Most often, however, he thought "race" less significant than religion, reminded Defenders of Jesus's Jewish birth, and preached to "Hebrew Christians." Smith frequently recalled his Christian mother's admonition to shun prejudice, and, with typical hyperbole, declared in 1969 that he would "fight and bleed" to protect religious liberty for Jews.[89]

The temptation is strong to dismiss these protestations of tolerance, along with corollary distinctions between "good" and "bad" Jews, as "double talk" (the Illinois Supreme Court's view in *Terminiello* v. *Chicago*). Winrod undoubtedly received votes from fellow anti-Semites lacking any concern about converting some Jews;

Smith, though less vicious than Pelley, nevertheless made Jews the target of fierce invective. Yet this double talk must be taken seriously, because, like much else in their vocabularies, it was part of what Clinton Rossiter called our common political language.[90]

From Josiah Strong through Theodore Roosevelt to Henry Ford, American nativists typically maintained that white men and women, including those burdened by regressive cultural or "racial" traits, must be judged according to their individual behavior. Despite the impact of Madison Grant, Lothrop Stoddard, and other Anglo-Saxon cultists who insisted that inferior "races" could never become "100% American," the emphasis on assimilation remained dominant. Reflecting this prevailing attitude, Winrod in his evangelism and Smith in his invective hesitated to treat Jews as an undifferentiated mass. Neither did they propose disfranchisement, deportation, ghettoization, or legislation modeled on the Nuremberg laws forbidding sexual relations beteen gentiles and Jews.[91]

Would Winrod and Smith have joined Pelley in supporting harsher measures if they had had the power? In language recalling Smith's, after all, Nazi mass murderer Adolf Eichmann denied "hatred for Jews, for my whole education through my mother and my father had been strictly Christian." Obviously, we can only speculate about the tenacity of liberal individualist values among American bigots. Regarding anti-Semitic practices, however, Sinclair Lewis's portrait of a far right dictatorship was probably close to the mark. The Corpo regime in *It Can't Happen Here* considered *The Protocols* "bunk" but useful as propaganda, and harassed poor Jews while letting affluent Jews prosper if they paid graft and praised the United States as a sanctuary from European prejudice.[92]

But it didn't happen here. Although the United States suffered longer from the Depression than any other industrial nation, it produced no sustained far right movement. The Silver Shirts, Defenders, and Committee of One Million look puny, not only in comparison to Nazi and Fascist regimes, but also in comparison to the French far right that unsettled the Third Republic. Indeed, no far right group in the United States was as politically potent during the 1930s as the Ku Klux Klan had been during the 1920s. Share Our Wealth clubs may have attracted as many members as the Klan, but affiliation required little more than access to a radio and a postcard. Father Coughlin was strongest when he preached "Roosevelt or ruin," weakest when he tried to pull his radio audience rightward from the New Deal.[93]

Why was there no fascism in the United States? No simple answer suffices either to Werner Sombart's famous question concerning the relative weakness of socialism or to this complementary inquiry into the failure of the far right. Without collapsing the "extremes" into each other, we can note that Socialists and Communists on the one hand, and leaders of the far right on the other, faced common strategic problems. In both cases, moreover, lack of success was less due to sectarianism or eccentricity than to the nature of American society, which, long before Arthur Schlesinger, Jr., coined the term, cherished the vital center.[94]

Certainly the far right produced leaders of lower caliber than any other portion of the political spectrum. After the death of Huey Long (whose identification with the far right remains problematical in any case), none possessed the ability of a Eugene Debs or a Norman Thomas, and many shared Pelley's managerial ineptitude. Furthermore, though rank-and-file Protestants on the right were not necessarily unintelligent, they were less educated and cosmopolitan than contemporaries who passed through Socialist and Communist ranks. In different social circumstances, however, mediocre leadership might not have prevented the far right from exerting substantial influence. Despite his limitations, Smith was as capable and, until his conversion to conspiratorial anti-Semitism, no more prejudiced than congressmen elected by remnants of the Long machine. Winrod, devoid of Norman Thomas's wisdom, nevertheless exuded comparable charisma in his own circle.

Far right groups might have compensated for weak leadership by better exploiting the relative absence of government harassment. The Socialist and Communist parties were permanently damaged by suppression from 1917 to 1920; the far right, though placed under FBI surveillance and badgered locally, avoided federal prosecution until the outbreak of World War II. Throughout the 1930s, however, they lost the contest on the national level to define the American way of life. Radicals failed to convince the country that Communism or Socialism was "twentieth-century Americanism," but they, along with centrist politicians and social scientists, inoculated many citizens against far right bigotry. The war against Nazism further spread the view that ethnic and racial prejudice, long time American habits, were now un-American.

Much as Socialists and Communists were hampered by scant support from organized labor, far right activists received skimpy, usually covert, aid from big business. As in western Europe, far right ambivalence toward established conservatives was reciprocated. Yet the corporate elite Smith derided as "short-sighted" were wiser than he. While Smith launched uncompromising attacks on New Deal "subversion," Pierre S. Dupont, for instance, both financed Liberty League assaults on the Roosevelt administration and, recognizing that some form of welfare state was inevitable, consulted with New Dealers on the specific provisions of social security. Though less appealing than the New Era of the 1920s, the New Deal was, like the progressive presidencies a generation earlier, sufficiently moderate to be tolerated. For the most part, therefore, big business preferred to ride the latest wave of reform instead of backing erratic figures like Pelley, Winrod, and Smith. Radicals and liberals correctly inferred from European precedents that a far right triumph could not happen here without substantial aid from established conservatives, but they misread the specific situation in the United States.[95]

The failure of the far right, aborted rebirth of radicalism, New Deal moderation, and big business acquiescence in reform all depended on the general population's restrained response to the Great Depression. The crisis moved some men and women to militancy. But militancy—right, left, or center—was not synonymous with commitment to basic social change. Most factory workers who cooperated with radicals to build the CIO finally settled for the traditional trade union goal: "more." Posturing Silver Shirts who called the CIO a Jewish conspiracy asked in the next breath, Pelley lamented, to give the Roosevelt administration a chance to prove itself. The belief that success derived from individual effort, the gospel that had perplexed Pelley and driven Winrod and Smith to prosperity, survived nationally despite 25 percent unemployment. In the middle class particularly, anger was directed inward. Ultimately, the 1930s was neither a "red" nor a "brown" decade because so many Americans sought so little, sank into apathy, or blamed themselves for their suffering.[96]

Epilogue

FROM THE "RADICAL RIGHT" TO THE "NEW CHRISTIAN RIGHT"

Since 1955, when Daniel Bell's anthology, *The New American Right*, placed an academic imprimatur on the concept of extremism, several successor new rights have been proclaimed by adherents, denounced by opponents, and discovered by pundits. Between such periods of proclamation, denunciation, and discovery, the same opponents and pundits have announced the imminent demise of both conservatism and the far right. Hence, ill prepared for the next new right when it came along, they have persistently fallen back on formulas popularized by Bell and his associates. Discussion of fundamentalism, a persuasion still poorly defined but still considered the handmaiden of reaction, followed a parallel course. Prevailing opinion has oscillated between predictions that this supposedly vestigial faith verged on extinction and warnings that it seriously threatened liberty and progress. Since the late 1970s, a "New Christian Right," represented most articulately by Rev. Jerry Falwell of the Moral Majority, has been wooed by conservative politicians, discovered by news media, and assailed by the left. In this epilogue, I use the careers of Pelley, Winrod, and Smith as benchmarks for measuring change, not only within the Protestant far right, but also among its critics.

The proximate religious origins of the New Christian Right lie in the many-sided revival that began during World War II and continued into the 1950s. Heirs to the classic fundamentalism of the 1920s stood at the center of this awakening. In the two decades after the Scopes trial, fundamentalists continued to write books, tracts, and sermons; founded colleges, magazines, and missions; and trained leaders at Bible institutes and summer camps. The National Religious Broadcasters, organized in 1944, competed with theological liberals for radio and television time. The most popular of these broadcasters, Rev. Charles Fuller of the "Old-Time Revival Hour," reached a weekly audience of 15 million by the late 1940s. The fate of the next generation remained a major fundamentalist concern. Christian academies provided alternatives to public schools, the Inter-Varsity Christian Fellowship was imported from Britain, and the evangelistic Youth for Christ, "geared to the times but anchored to the Rock," was started in 1942. Hence, while theological liberals were recanting their lapses into innocence and the Popular Front, their conservative rivals were ready to win souls.[1]

Conservatives continued to disagree among themselves, however, and institutionalized their differences in the American Council of Christian Churches (ACCC), founded in 1941, and the National Association of Evangelicals (NAE), created a year later. Affiliates of both groups believed in Biblical inerrancy, the Trinity, and Jesus's personal return, but they differed occasionally about doctrine and often about strategy. While Rev. Carl McIntire, the ACCC's first president and dominant figure for twenty years, attacked the "apostate" Federal Council of Churches, scorned Pentecostalism, and warned against the "Roman Catholic terror," the National Association of Evangelicals tried to avoid intolerance and improve conservative Protestantism's image. Accordingly, NAE leaders welcomed Pentecostal churches and congregations whose parent denominations retained ties to the Federal Council, criticized Catholics and Protestant liberals politely if frequently, and sometimes compromised with Darwinism and higher criticism. Increasingly, too, they distinguished their "evangelical" position from fundamentalism.[2]

Much as McIntire symbolized strident separatism, Billy Graham personified the transition to a softened conservative gospel. Trained at several fundamentalist strongholds, he became field secretary of Youth for Christ and then, in 1947, succeeded the aged militant, William Bell Riley, as head of Riley's combined religious schools. Consistent with this heritage, Graham, as late as 1955, chided *Life* magazine for endorsing evolution. Already, however, the demands of mass evangelism, combined with Graham's prominence in a pluralist era, had begun to alter his message. He welcomed liberal Protestant sponsorship of his "crusades," and appreciated praise from Catholics and Jews; his frequent predictions of God's judgment rarely included dispensationalist exegeses. In this shift from fundamentalism to evangelicalism, Graham wrestled with doubts and elicited charges of apostasy from Carl McIntire. Ultimately, he claimed the theological vital center, opposed, Graham noted proudly, by "extreme fundamentalists from the right and extreme liberals from the left."[3]

In the 1950s, as in the 1930s, adherents to conservative Protestant doctrine did not necessarily vote for political conservatives. Some of them, seeking separation from a sinful world, abstained from politics. Most not only voted, but disproportionately supported liberal Democrat Adlai Stevenson in 1952 and 1956. By and large, fundamentalist and evangelical clergy still stood to the right of vital center. For example, Billy Graham not only alluded to Communism's satanic character and urged Congress to pursue "Fifth Columnists," but criticized the diplomatic "betrayal" at Yalta, obliquely praised Senator Joseph R. McCarthy, and recommended "semi-military" work camps for juvenile delinquents. In 1959, urging Christians to "get into politics," he added that Richard M. Nixon was the "best trained" presidential contender. Such partisan *obiter dicta* were camouflaged by Graham's professed "neutrality," frequent retractions, and general amiability.[4]

Disdaining camouflage, Carl McIntire, leader of the Twentieth Century Reformation, and Billy James Hargis, head of the Christian Crusade, emerged as the foremost Protestants on the far right during the 1950s. Because the Bible prescribed capitalism as the "very foundation" of society, McIntire doubly damned the Federal Council of Churches for disguising "Marxian philosophy" as Christianity. Hargis discerned flesh-and-blood demons behind a Communist threat stretching from the Kremlin to the AFL-CIO. Jew-baiters sometimes joined their respective organizations, and Hargis early in his career had sought Winrod's advice, but neither supposed that Zionist Elders ran international Communism (an error in judgment by good men, Gerald L. K. Smith lamented). Thus McIntire retained enough reputability to advise the Buckleyite Young Americans for Freedom and Hargis conferred occasionally with conservative members of Congress. Still, neither was much more visible than the ostracized editor of the *Cross and the Flag.*[5]

The proximate political origins of the New Christian Right lie in the collapse of consensus that began during the late 1950s. By that time, many conservatives had repudiated the Eisenhower administration for pursuing détente with the Soviet Union, and farther right, the Ku Klux Klan and White Citizens Councils fought civil rights demonstrators with epithets, economic sanctions, and violence. John F. Kennedy's paradoxical presidency furthered polarization. On the one hand, Kennedy's hesitant liberalism, like Roosevelt's in the 1930s, bulked large on the narrow political spectrum; on the other, his cold warrior rhetoric, like Truman's in the late 1940s, created a mood congenial to his adversaries. Soon after his inauguration, fresh contributions enlivened the political sects led by Hargis and McIntire as well as Gerald L. K. Smith. In addition, the American Nazi Party became the most prominent paramilitary band since the Silver Shirts, and the John Birch Society, a fount of ungrounded conspiracy theories, attracted many conservatives while discomfiting others.[6]

This right-of-center renewal produced a quick liberal response. Like the earlier attacks on native fascism, the numerous books, articles, and speeches treating the radical right in the early 1960s mixed useful information with exaggeration. Even the most lurid of these exposés served to document the far right role in restricting dissent locally, and the best of them related far right zeal to the broader quest for Cold War orthodoxy. On the whole, however, authors damned symmetrical extremes, assumed that intolerance bubbled up from a populist mass, and cited Daniel Bell's anthology—conveniently reissued as *The Radical Right* in 1963—for scholarly support. Thus themes born in the polemics of the 1930s were recycled through the academy to fuel polemics in the 1960s. Muckrakers of the radical right took more care than such wartime sleuths as Avedis Derounian to distinguish reputable conservatives from far right agitators. Accounts of the "Christian fright peddlers" sometimes separated "ultra fundamentalists" from prudent evangelicals. Yet critics of the radical right had difficulty resisting rhetorical flourishes or presumptions of guilt on the basis of slender association. And during 1964, the peak year of this latter-day Brown Scare, AFL-CIO President George Meany, Martin Luther King, Jr., and other foes saw signs of "Hitlerism" in Senator Barry Goldwater's presidential campaign.[7]

The next decade produced the fiercest battle since the Great Depression to define a normative American way of life. Unearthing issues that had lain dormant beneath years of national celebration, radicals, black nationalists, and feminists faced equally fervent defenders of capitalism, white supremacy, true womanhood, and the masculine mystique. Amid apocalyptic politics unparalleled since the 1930s, strange alliances again flourished. Trying to incorporate dissident Democrats into a "new Republican majority," President Richard M. Nixon launched this century's third red scare, a program of harassment and calumny that led to the Watergate scandal and his own resignation. Much as the scares of 1917–20 contributed to the tribal Twenties, Nixon's rallying of the "silent majority" against traitors and libertines left a rich legacy of intolerance to the 1980s.[8]

The collapse of consensus created religious as well as social unrest. Modernists contemplated the death of God, social gospelers led civil rights marches and draft resistance, and Roman Catholics ran for president after 1960 without having to broadcast their independence from Rome. There was a proliferation of non-Christian beliefs ranging from Oriental pantheism to Satan worship. The United States Supreme Court banned prayer in public schools, struck down bans on birth control, abortion, and pornography, and exempted devout humanists from military service. Billy Graham spoke for many conservative Protestants when he repudiated civil disobedience, demanded restoration of school prayer, endorsed the Vietnam War, and stepped up predictions of apocalypse. At the same time, self-proclaimed "worldly evangelicals" moved toward the theological and political left.[9]

Conservative Protestantism survived to face the subtler threat of success in the late 1970s. Graham remained our national pastor, evangelical congregations grew, and fundamentalism reached a mass market; Hal Lindsey's *The Late Great Planet Earth*, an incongruously breezy dispensationalist tract published in 1970, sold almost nine million copies. Evangelicals boasted that their brothers-in-Christ occupied seats of power in Washington, Wall Street, and Hollywood. Yet inclusion in this brotherhood typically required no more than personal testimony that one had been "born again." Former Black Panther Eldridge Cleaver, Watergate henchman Charles Colson, pornographer Larry Flynt, and President Gerald R. Ford were welcomed into the born again fold by evangelists who, impressed by their fame, left unexamined their views on Biblical inerrancy or the quality of their conversions.[10]

Jimmy Carter capitalized on recent social turmoil and the fashionableness of born again Christianity to become President. In 1976, Carter presented himself as the alternative to both Watergate corruption and counterculture immorality, and as a "populist" opposed to both special interests and Washington insiders. When his post-inauguration economic preferences revealed the values of a middle level businessman, some pundits finally learned that more than a drawl is required to make a populist. Remaining perplexed by born again religion, however, they barely distinguished between Hal Lindsey, who believed that the Antichrist was alive in Europe, and Jimmy Carter, who did not. Given this lack of thoughtful media coverage, vagueness of the term born again, and Carter's propensity for murkiness, it is difficult to locate him on the theological spectrum. Apparently a liberal influenced by neo-orthodoxy, he was religiously more sophisticated than Franklin D. Roosevelt and psychologically less stirred by rebirth than John Foster Dulles, neither of whom was ballyhooed as born again. By the late 1970s, many politically conservative evangelicals and fundamentalists had repudiated him. In short, Carter helped to discredit political liberalism even though he was indifferently liberal, and furthered politicization among evangelical Protestants even though he barely qualified as an evangelical.[11]

Carter's fractured presidency provided opportunities for a "New Right," the label adopted in the mid-1970s by Richard Viguerie, Paul Weyrich, Howard Phillips, John Terry Dolan, and other technicians dissociating themselves from old right failures and opprobrium. Yet Viguerie himself doubted the existence of "many new conservative ideas," and his own favorites, the threats of Soviet expansion, big government, and sexual license, were hardly fresh. Most New Right strategists had been active at least since the Goldwater campaign; Viguerie had also worked for George Wallace and Billy James Hargis. Thus the New Right's novelty was primarily tactical. Aided by wealthy contributors, these savvy organizers founded political action committees and mastered direct mail advertising. Unlike Goldwater, who had shunned what he called "organ-tone" rhetoric, they made special appeals to theologically conservative Protestants and arranged alliances with such television evangelists as James Robison, Pat Robertson, and Jerry Falwell. In 1979, Falwell founded the Moral Majority, a formally non-sectarian lobby dominated by fundamentalist clergy. The next year, after conducting an impressive voter registration drive and embracing Republican presidential nominee Ronald Reagan, he claimed credit, on behalf of the New Right's Christian component, for a conservative "avalanche at the polls." Agreeing in a way, opponents quickly adopted "moral majoritarian" as a synonym for the New Christian Right.[12]

Three years later, Falwell remains the movement's representative minister. He is difficult to interpret partly because he tailors his message to his diverse audiences, which include his devoted congregation, viewers of his televised "Old-Time Gospel Hour," and cosmopolitan critics whom he (like Gerald L. K. Smith a generation earler) enjoys debating. But his inconsistent assertions, retractions, and clarifications also reflect a personality that contains, as Falwell admits, "lots of paradoxes." The first paradox is that he became a clergyman at all. The ambitious son of a hard-drinking businessman, Falwell grew up in Lynchburg, Virginia, was converted at seventeen, abandoned engineering school for a Baptist Bible Fellowship seminary, and, two months before his twenty-third birthday founded the Thomas Road Baptist Church in his home town.[13]

A self-described "fundamentalist—big F, "Falwell identifies with William Bell Riley, J. Frank Norris, and other militants from the 1920s. He believes in an "inerrant" Bible, as well as Jesus's virgin birth, atoning death, bodily resurrection, and imminent return. An "independent, separatist Baptist," Farwell seeks separation, not only from immorality but also from "denominational mediocrity" and false doctrines preached by Protestant liberals, worldly evangelicals, and Pentecostals. Throughout the 1960s, he shunned politics too. Even then, however, his version of separatism left room for Cold War chauvinism, criticism of Martin Luther King, Jr., scriptural defenses of segregation, and denunciation of personal vices.[14]

Like Winrod two generations earlier, Falwell moved from moral issues to practical politics. He took these steps for roughly the same reason—opposition to cultural and religious change—and he took them reluctantly. For many years, Falwell recalled in 1982, he had waited for some religious leader to guide America "out of the wilderness," yet mainline denominations remained captives of social gospelers, most conservative churches wallowed in "dead orthodoxy," and energetic evangelicals continued to slide leftward. When candidate Jimmy Carter granted an interview to *Playboy,* Falwell endorsed President Ford for re-election. Also in 1976, he sponsored a series of Love America rallies; campaigns against homosexuality and the Equal Rights Amendment soon followed. By 1979, Falwell had decided that his abstention from politics had been "false prophecy."[15]

Falwell's politicization, like Winrod's, remains subordinate to his conviction that the great national issues are "spiritual." His discussions of foreign policy or domestic economics consist of staple New Right arguments supplemented by Biblical quotations. Not deficit spending or nuclear vulnerability but the apparent spread of personal vices stirs Falwell from routine indignation to passion. His defense of the patriarchal family could have been delivered by his far right forebears forty-five years earlier. To be sure, his list of threats to this "basic" social unit is modernized to include the "cult of the playboy," rock music, pornography, and abortion. Although Falwell avoids the prurience characteristic of Gerald L. K. Smith's prudery, his frequent discussions of sexual issues are just as forceful. He equates abortion with murder, and attributes the "abomination" of homosexuality to women's rejection of their divinely ordained roles as "weaker vessels."[16]

Falwell's identification with earlier militants should not obscure cultural retreats by fundamentalism since the 1930s. Concentrating on homosexuality and abortion instead of birth control, divorce, and teenage temptations, he almost concedes that premarital sex is here to stay (Richard Viguerie, a Roman Catholic, regrets this lapse by the New Christian Right, and Rev. James Robison still luridly describes adolescent kisses). Falwell writes wistfully about Prohibition and, unlike Billy Graham, abstains from alcohol, but attends meetings where strong drink is served. Whereas Winrod, Riley, and Norris attemped to ban Darwinism from the classroom, their doctrinal descendants compromise on equal time for "scientific creationism"; speaking in his capacity as chancellor, Falwell grudgingly said that graduates of Liberty Baptist College would present evolution "fairly" if certified to teach in Virginia schools. Similarly, while fond of remembering the de facto Protestant prayers that opened public school in his youth, he will accept a non-sectarian allusion to God in the 1980s. Elsewhere, he recognizes that fundamentalists were "woefully deficient" during the civil rights struggle and thanks God for purging his segregationist beliefs.[17]

Nor is Falwell's "old-time" gospel the same theology preached by most conservative Protestants before World War II. In 1981, Falwell noted that fundamentalists, including himself, had been "growing up" during the previous twenty years. It remains unclear where his own growth will take him. Falwell insists that salvation requires a "personal relationship with Christ," but neither elaborates on the mechanics of rebirth nor explicitly limits it to fundamentalists and evangelicals. Declining to hold joint services—"fellowship"—with liberal Protestants, Pentecostals, and other adherents to false doctrine, he nonetheless offers them "friendship." If Falwell equates the papacy with the whore of Revelation, he nowhere presses the point in print; at least one Catholic, Phyllis Schlafly of Stop-ERA, has addressed his congregation. Traditional religious rivals, Catholics and liberal Protestants, worry him less than his evangelical "cousins." Urging them to join fundamentalists in a crusade to Christianize the world "in our lifetime," Falwell—like Arthur M. Schlesinger, Jr., Gerald L. K. Smith, and Billy Graham—claims the center. According to his version of this rhetorical device, truth lies between "radical evangelicals" drifting toward liberalism and paranoid "hyper-fundamentalists" who quibble over trivia.[18]

No change is more significant than the rejection of overt anti-Semitism by most contemporary Protestants on the far right. According to Falwell, Christians must be "pro-Jewish" because Jesus was born a Jew, because creation of modern Israel fulfilled prophecy, and because, as Hitler could testify from Hell, individuals or nations persecuting Jews come to "tragic ends." Nazi Germany ended in rubble, but God blessed the United States "because America has always blessed the Jew."[19]

These theological premises merge with Cold War foreign policy in Falwell's dispensationalist scenario for mankind's last days. In the midst of the tribulation, after Israel allies with the Antichrist's European confederacy, Russia will invade the Middle East and suffer defeat, thus ending the Communist threat "forever." But the Antichrist will capture Jerusalem, demand to be worshipped, and slaughter all Jews except a remnant supernaturally hidden by God. After three and one half years, Jesus will return and defeat this monster at Armageddon. To Falwell, who thinks that the Antichrist may arise within his own lifetime, Soviet pressure on the Middle East and Israel's miraculous survival prove that the "pieces are falling together." Consistent with his belief that Christians must be Israel's "best friends" while awaiting these grand events, Falwell conferred with Prime Minister Menachem Begin in 1981 and defended the Israeli invasion of Lebanon a year later.[20]

Falwell's philo-Semitic interpretation of Bible prophecy, like that of most prominent postwar dispensationalists, represents a reaction to Nazi atrocities and an adaptation to American cultural pluralism. Yet fundamentalism still entails, perhaps inevitably, an ambivalence toward Jews. For example, though Falwell neither blames them for Jesus's crucifixion nor recruits "Hebrew Christians," he describes non-Christians as inherent "failures," expects some Jews to convert before the Second Coming, and surmises that God ignores prayers from "unredeemed gentiles or Jews." Furthermore, he quipped, apparently without malice, that Jews make more money "accidentally" than Christians can on purpose. Reacting to such remarks in late 1980, Rabbi Alexander Schindler, president of the Union of Hebrew Congregations, held Falwell indirectly responsible for increasing anti-Semitic incidents. Falwell called Schindler's charge groundless, but retreated to the position that God heard the "heart cry of any sincere person."[21]

Falwell's pronouncements and retractions began to receive national attention in 1980 because he seemed to command a vast following. His Thomas Road congregation was one of the country's largest, his "Old-Time Gospel Hour" raised $25 million annually, and Moral Majority mailings reached 72,000 clergy and two million lay persons. Yet this pious conglomerate was—and is—less impressive than appearances suggest. Falwell's weekly television audience is not 30 million, as he claims, but closer to two million; Moral Majority membership, like affiliation with Share Our Wealth Clubs in the 1930s, requires little more than a post card. Furthermore, if Falwell combines, so to speak, Winrod's theology with Smith's complex personality and dramatic invective, he also reveals managerial ineptitude worthy of Pelley. Though the Moral Majority raised $5.77 million for fiscal year 1981–82, it remained $500,000 in debt, and the situation apparently deteriorated thereafter. Occasionally Falwell admits to financial "bad judgment." In frequent fund appeals, however, he attributes his money problems to opposition from "homosexuals, Nazis, liberal clergymen, abortionists, pornographers, politicians, bureaucrats, humanists, Communists, etc."[22]

Although Falwell viewed the 1980 elections as a prelude to other national victories, he won none during the next two years. Ruling that "scientific creationism" was religion, not science, courts barred it from the public schools. The Coalition for Better Television, launched by Falwell and other foes of titilating programs, had scant impact on the networks. Local chapters of the Moral Majority managed to ban books, fire teachers, and intimidate politicians, but their zeal often embarassed Falwell. The Maryland contingent assailed "pornographic" cookies baked in Baltimore, and New York leader Rev. Daniel Fore charged that Jews controlled the mass media. While conceding in 1981 that his organization has been hurt by "loose cannons," Falwell himself careened alarmingly around Moral Majority decks. He invented conversations with Presidents Ford and Carter, adding that Carter had endorsed homosexuality during their tête a tête. Such outright lies are less frequent than conflicting pronouncements on major issues. Sometimes Falwell favors "superior rights" for women, legal equality for homosexuals, and a "pluralistic" America; elsewhere, he urges women to stay home, relegates homosexuality to the "gutter," and accuses Satan of keeping "Christians from running their own country."[23]

Falwell's contradictory declarations, reminiscent of Gerald L. K. Smith's forty years earlier, reveal less conscious duplicity than unconscious ambivalence. A year after founding the Moral Majority, this provincial pastor became a national figure. Falwell enjoyed the attention and (as Smith might have said) opportunized on all forums, even a televised confrontation with *Penthouse* publisher Bob Guccione. By early 1983, his forays into cosmopolitan culture had changed him more than he had changed it. While continuing on the "Old-Time Gospel Hour" to connect theological and political liberals with the devil, Falwell himself enjoys their company. Probably no more than Smith in 1943 can Falwell in 1983 unravel his amalgam of beliefs.[24]

Like Smith, Falwell may resolve his ambivalence by sliding from ordinary far right demagoguery into advocacy of some extraordinary conspiracy theory, or he may, like Billy Graham, drift instead to theological and political moderation. Indeed, involvement in the Moral Majority might undermine his Baptist separatism; certainly he must wonder whether the group's Catholic, Mormon and Jewish members, adherents to sound politics but false doctrine, are actually doomed to Hell. Signs of Falwell's latitudinarianism appear even as he denounces backsliding evangelicals. He accepts Ronald Reagan as a born again Christian though Reagan genially muses that "everyone can make his own interpretation of the Bible, and many individuals have been making different interpretations for a long time." Perhaps Falwell's denunciations of homosexuality will someday follow his defense of segregation into the realm of "false prophecy."[25]

The future of Falwell as well as lesser leaders of the New Christian Right depends largely on the course of the Reagan administration, the quality of left opposition, and the country's economic prospects. In 1980, candidate Reagan told Falwell, Robison, and 18,000 cheering Protestants that he favored "what you are doing"; New Christian Right efforts contributed to his plurality among fundamentalist and evangelical voters—though not as much as Falwell initially claimed. During his first two years in office, President Reagan treated the New Christian Right gingerly, much as President Roosevelt had kept Father Coughlin and Senator Long at arms length. Calling several cabinet appointees "Nixon-Ford retreads," Richard Viguerie realized in November 1980 that businessmen, not purity crusaders, would dominate the Reagan coalition. For two years thereafter, New Right clergy and political technicians hesitated to attack Reagan personally but chided his administration for failing to escalate the Cold War and restore American morality. In July 1981, Falwell criticized the nomination of Judge Sandra Day O'Connor to the Supreme Court because she had supported abortion and the Equal Rights Amendment. If Reagan was as disgusted with his New Right allies by 1982 as FDR had become with Long and Coughlin by 1934, he gave no public sign. But Senator Barry Goldwater scorned "political preachers," distinguished between the Moral Majority's "fascist line" and "old fashioned" conservatism, and urged good Christians "to kick Falwell in the ass."[26]

The second session of the ninety-seventh Congress showed that personal vices concerned Reagan less than inflation. Measures to facilitate prayer in public schools and restrict abortion stalled in the Senate, with Senator Goldwater helping to deliver the *coup de grâce* in September 1982. The President spent little political capital on either measure, though he promised in a post mortem to preach morality from the White House "bully pulpit." Appealing for Republican votes in 1982, however, he stressed declining interest rates, not rising national virtue.[27]

When school prayer and anti-abortion bills lost, Daniel Patrick Moynihan, senator and social scientist, exclaimed, "We've broken the radical right." Moynihan's exultation was echoed by few other leading pluralists from his generation. Many of these formerly self-conscious centrists had become self-conscious neo-conservatives and thus members of the Reagan coalition along with Jerry Falwell. Accordingly, they turned their polemical fire leftward and found few enemies on the right. Among surviving contributors to *The Radical Right,* only Seymour Martin Lipset continued regularly to analyze extremism. Uneasy about being on the same side as the far right in 1980, Lipset composed his most astute piece on the subject since his essay in the first edition of Bell's anthology. He and Earl Raab assured readers of *Commentary* that extremists alone had not elected Reagan, denied that fundamentalists followed their pastors like "robots," and noted that Jerry Falwell, unlike Gerald Winrod, shunned anti-Semitism. Ironically, Lipset's transition to neo-conservatism shows that politics makes stranger bed fellows than most of his writing on extremism would lead us to expect.[28]

Ironically, too, while Lipset and other neo-conservatives consider the latest far right at least marginally respectable, the concept of extremism popularized during their centrist phase still guides opponents of the New Christian Right. During the 1980 campaign, Secretary of Health and Human Services Patricia Roberts Harris accused moral majoritarians of threatening the American "consensus orientation," and columnist Anthony Lewis feared for the fate of "political safety in a pluralist society." After the election, the American Civil Liberties Union, Abortion Rights Action League, and Southern Poverty Law Center reiterated this position in newspaper advertisements and mass mailings. Defeated Senator George McGovern, philosopher Daniel Maguire, and television producer Norman Lear planned organizations specifically to fight what McGovern called the "new radical Right." The most successful of these groups, Lear's People for the American Way, persistently traded printed and filmed epithets with the Moral Majority during the next two years. At the same time, publishers issued book-length exposés of "God's bullies," "holy terror," and right-wing "new subversives."[29]

Like its predecessors, the Brown Scare that began in 1980 involved, on one level, a struggle among Protestants to define the political implications of their faith, and, on another, a mobilization by secular liberals. For modernist as well as conservative Protestants, the fundamentalist controversy had never ended. Sixty years after *Christian Century* had accused dispensationalists of serving big business, it condemned televised presentations of "right-wing views couched in biblical prophecy language." Continuity also characterized the University of Chicago Divinity School, where Martin E. Marty inherited Shirley Jackson Case's mantle as premier critic of fundamentalism. Across the theological spectrum, Bob Jones, Jr., spoke for conservatives still convinced that social activism aided Satan when he suggested that the Moral Majority prefigured the Antichrist's ecumenical church. In between, moderate liberals and evangelicals mixed criticism of far right politics with pleas—usually lost in the polemical din—for courtesy within the "Christian family." The foremost evangelical, Billy Graham, declared that the "hard right" was trying to "manipulate" fundamentalists. Most Roman Catholics merely observed this Protestant family feud, but several advised their flocks to shun the Moral Majority.[30]

Unlike these contenders for the faith, the secular left was stunned that fundamentalism had survived to become a political force. Paradoxically, most liberals explained this phenomenon by applying scholarship from the 1950s that had predicted fundamentalism's imminent demise. Hence, the New Christian Right was said to consist of resentful populists who, along with Communists and Nazis, rejected compromise and exhibited the paranoid style. Radicals were wary of this sort of interpretation, which had recently been used to discredit the New Left, but, consistent with Brown Scare habits, they, too, treated conservative theology as a social symptom. Alan Crawford's popular *Thunder on the Right* provided a special sense of déjà vu. Much as his mentor Peter Viereck had distinguished between "true conservatism" and Barry Goldwater's "pseudo-conservatism" in *The Radical Right,* Crawford repudiated Jerry Falwell in the name of "true conservatism." Simultaneously, Goldwater was promoted from extremist to true conservative by Crawford and several liberals who appreciated his criticism of the Moral Majority.[31]

Once again, attacks on the far right revealed as much about the attackers as their targets. Mechanically applying interpretive conventions from *The Radical Right* and *The Paranoid Style in American Politics,* they slighted subsequent scholarship that explored fundamentalist beliefs, questioned connections between mental instability and political deviance, and warned against glib use of the fascist label. In the aggregate, exposés of the New Christian Right were even worse than comparable polemics in the early 1960s. Confident of centrist ascendancy and censensus, liberals then had viewed McIntire, Hargis, and the Birch Society with some detachment. The Brown Scare of the early 1980s followed an era of intense cultural conflict, including fratricide on the left. Among liberal and radical survivors, fear of the far right—fear that inhibited analysis—was stronger than at any time since the Great Depression and World War II.[32]

Indeed, embattled centrists in the early 1980s explicitly extracted lessons from the 1930s. When Jimmy Carter distinguished his faith from "that of the Jerry Falwells or the Gerald L. K. Smiths," he joined a procession of observers who cited Smith, Winrod, or Pelley as precursors of the New Christian Right. Former Senator Thomas J. McIntyre learned about this earlier generation of "fear brokers" from his aide Kenneth M. Birkhead (L. M. Birkhead's son and successor at Friends of Democracy), used the countersubversive classic *Under Cover* to weigh the threat of a "new native fascism," and repeated Sinclair Lewis's warning that "it can happen here."[33]

Equally evocative of the 1930s was growing sympathy for what Roger Baldwin had called "'Liberty for Our Side' only." Anthony Lewis spoke for many liberals when he charged the New Christian Right with violating Article Six of the Constitution, which forbids religious tests for office, and the First Amendment, which separates church and state. To fight political manipulation "under cover of religion," communications theorists Flo Conway and Jim Siegelman favored an agency similar to the Securities and Exchange Commission for ideas Max Lerner had suggested forty years earlier. Increased activity by the Ku Klux Klan, paramilitary Nazi bands, and other groups farther right than the Moral Majority moved some liberals—and radicals—to endorse prior restraint on defamatory speech and laws against group libel.[34]

Although the Brown Scare begun in 1980 continues at this writing, it became less intense after Democrats, many of them liberals, made significant gains in the 1982 elections. Eminent commentators then agreed that issues like school prayer and abortion had become less significant than unemployment, that the New Right had therefore lost its clout, and that the power of politicized preachers had been overstated all along. These judgments, often issued from the same sources that had predicted an era of triumphant conservatism two years earlier, replaced one set of exaggerations with another. Much as the cultural conflicts of the 1920s affected the ways in which Americans reacted to the Great Depression, recent cultural conflicts influence their responses to the lesser Depression of the 1980s.[35]

In early 1983, the Reagan administration faces the perennial dilemma of modern Republican presidencies: whether to straddle the center in the fashion of Eisenhower or, like Nixon, to move right in search of a new majority. If Reagan chooses the latter course, he will embrace such groups as the Moral Majority, blame hard times on loose living, and perhaps embark on this century's fourth red scare. Convinced that the "old center [is] no longer 'vital,'" New Right analyst Kevin P. Phillips recommends a version of this "populist" strategy. Apparently experimenting with it, the President, in late 1982, accused congressional "big spenders" of excluding prayer from public schools and surmised that the Nuclear Weapons Freeze Campaign was being used by the Soviet Union. It is at least as likely, however, that Reagan, prodded by conservative devotees of order, will continue to stress economic retrenchment rather than social regeneration. In that case, some New Right technicians and evangelists may break with him completely. No longer susceptible to White House restraint, a few fundamentalists in search of scapegoats might even revive *The Protocols* and the anti-Semitic interpretation of Bible prophecy.[36]

Whatever strategy the Reagan administration adopts, the New Christian Right will retain influence in some communities, self-styled Nazis and Ku Klux Klansmen will parade for publicity, and the left must devise programs to deal with them all. The uproar in 1977–78 over a proposed march by the tiny National Socialist Party of America in Skokie, Illinois, shows that application of the Bill of Rights to cultural conflict remains controversial. Sometimes citing *Terminiello* v. *Chicago*, state and federal judges correctly refused to prohibit the demonstration, but 4,000 members quit the American Civil Liberties Union, which represented the Nazis in court. Although political activity by the New Christian Right has not yet provoked a comparable confrontation, it involves harder constitutional questions. The First Amendment not only forbids an establishment of religion but also guarantees free exercise thereof, and neither jurists nor philosophers agree on the proper relationship between these two clauses.[37]

Opponents of various far rights groups should avoid the temptation to litigate their enemies into silence or to apply constitutional double standards. Challenges to "scientific creationism" in public schools are appropriate; as the United States District Court for the Eastern District of Arkansas ruled in 1982, this product of a sectarian "crusade" clearly violates the First Amendment. But Article Six of the Constitution no more bars Rev. Jerry Falwell from political advocacy than it barred Rev. Martin Luther King, Jr. twenty-five years ago. Furthermore, King's group, the Southern Christian Leadership Conference, gained from Internal Revenue regulations much as Falwell's organizations do in the 1980s. Attempts to fight the New Christian Right with legal sleight-of-hand and clever use of the tax code will probably boomerang the next time social gospelers take the offensive. Conversely, short term legal victories by far right activists may serve good causes in the long run. The precedent set in *Terminiello* v. *Chicago* protected civil rights demonstrators in the 1960s as well as Nazis in the 1970s.[38]

My argument assumes that maximum freedom of expression benefits not only foes of the far right but society in general. At least in their rhetorical flourishes, proponents of this position typically declare that truth triumphs in the "open marketplace of ideas," while skeptics ranging from conservative Walter F. Berns to radical Herbert Marcuse contend that the intellectual market guarantees neither free access nor quality goods. Berns and Marcuse respectively propose explicit restrictions on "bad" or "regressive" expressions in order to build "virtuous" or "just" societies. Even granting the "curious proposition" that truth emerges from ideological competition, conservative Hadley Arkes commented on the Skokie imbroglio that Nazi ideas had been adequately tested and found pernicious.[39]

These skeptics show that it is easier to provide a "critique of pure tolerance" than an alternative to it: Berns and Marcuse would certainly disagree on definitions of "virtue" and "reason," and possibly proscribe each other's ideas. Moreover, the path from virtuous to ignoble suppression is a slippery slope. Civil libertarians must recognize that risks accompany a broad conception of freedom of expression, but in modern America graver problems have arisen because tolerance was not pure enough. For example, the Roosevelt administration's prosecution of far right bigots also discredited perceptive noninterventionists. Even if, as Arkes supposes, curbs could be confined to such widely discredited notions as the conspiratorial anti-Semitism of Pelley, Winrod, Smith, and the National Socialist Party of America, there would still be a social cost. Misdirected protests by villains signal flaws in a society eager to celebrate itself. Hence, the intellectual marketplace must trade in cries of pain as well as the higher currency of social thought.

In addition to flirtation with liberty for the left only, the latest Brown Scare is noteworthy for simplistic publicity campaigns promoting tolerance as the "American way." On the whole, both radicals and centrists have been too dispirited to organize grassroots resistance to the New Christian Right, let alone to address the cultural tensions it exploits. Rather, while promoting tolerance in the abstract, they often practice civility for their side only. Journalist Perry Deane Young denounced "God's bullies" for slurring liberals, yet speculated at length that a major New Right tactician was homosexual. "Life and Liberty . . . For All Who Believe," produced for television by People for the American Way, portrayed fundamentalists as rustic zealots controlled by authoritarian clergy. These caricatures reveal a failure of thought as well as a failure of nerve.[40]

Far right activists are made, not born, and to a certain point they can be unmade. In early 1983, the New Christian Right hardly commands a firm constituency. As Lipset and Raab observed, most evangelicals and fundamentalists who voted for Reagan were political "shoppers" seeking an alternative to Carter's inept, half-hearted liberalism. Some have already dropped back into political apathy, and others can be won over by the left. Perhaps the New Christian Right's greatest weakness is an economic program consisting of strained Scriptural endorsements of laissez faire. Whereas Gerald L. K. Smith both built the self esteem of his followers and promised to share the country's wealth with them, Jerry Falwell blandly says that private charity should "fill the vacuum" when the welfare state is dismantled. Indeed, Falwell's foes may steal his favorite issue by showing that titillating television programs threaten the family less than proverty, unemployment, dreary and dangerous working conditions, and declining real income.[41]

Appeals to economic self-interest will move few fundamentalists or evangelicals leftward, however, if the left persists in condescending to them. The tradition of ridicule stretching from *Elmer Gantry* to "Life and Liberty . . . For All Who Believe" has fueled a counter tradition of militancy stretching from the Defenders of the Christian Faith to the Moral Majority. Facing potential constituents with unconventional worldviews, liberals and radicals need to cultivate the tolerance that they demand from fundamentalists in the name of pluralism. The Genesis account of creation, for example, may be a social symptom but it is also an article of faith to millions of Americans; anyone tempted to ridicule them should pause to ask with sociologists Charles Y. Glock and Rodney Start: "Who can ask a man to surrender what he considers to be the ground for his being?" It is necessary to prevent men and women from translating such grounds for being into social policy, but this defense must not be conducted so smugly. By substituting civility for condescension, the political left can remove barriers to coalitions with the theological right, and also raise discussion of cultural pluralism above the level of slogans.[42]

Notes

Introduction: "Extremism" and Empathy

1. Leslie A. Fiedler, "The Two Memories: Reflections on Writers and Writing in the Thirties," in Morton J. Frisch and Martin Diamond, eds., *The Thirties: A Reconsideration in Light of the American Political Tradition* (DeKalb: Northern Illinois University Press, 1968), p. 51.

2. T. W. Adorno et al., *The Authoritarian Personality* ([1950]; rpt. New York: Wiley, 1969); Richard Hofstadter, *The Paranoid Style in American Politics and Other Essays* (New York: Vintage Books, 1967), pp. 1, 4.

3. Philip Rieff, *Freud: The Mind of the Moralist* (Garden City, N.Y.: Doubleday, 1961), pp. 248, 65.

4. Sigmund Freud and William C. Bullitt, *Thomas Woodrow Wilson* (Boston: Houghton Mifflin, 1966). For astute comments on the problem of applying psychology to history, see Saul Friedlander, *History and Psychoanalysis: An Inquiry Into the Possibilities and Limitations of Psychohistory*, trans. Susan Suleiman (New York: Holmes & Meier, 1978), and Cushing Strout, "The Uses and Abuses of Psychology in American History," *American Quarterly* 28 (Bibliography Issue, 1976): 324–42.

5. Anna Freud, *The Ego and the Mechanisms of Defense*, rev. ed. (New York: International Universities Press, 1966); Otto Fenichel, *The Psychoanalytic Theory of Neurosis* (New York: Norton, 1972); Erik H. Erikson, *Childhood and Society*, 2d ed. (New York: Norton, 1963) and *Insight and Responsibility* (New York: Norton, 1964); Thomas S. Szasz, *The Myth of Mental Illness: Foundations of a Theory of Personal Conduct* (New York: Hoeber-Harper, 1961), *Ideology and Insanity: Essays on the Psychiatric Dehumanization of Man* (Garden City, N.Y.: Anchor Books, 1970), and *The Manufacture of Madness: A Comparative Study of the Inquisition and the Mental Health Movement* (New York: Harper Colophon, 1970); R. D. Laing, *The Divided Self: An Existential Study in Sanity and Madness* (Baltimore: Penguin Books, 1965) and *The Politics of Experience* (New York: Ballantine Books, 1967); William James, *The Varieties of Religious Experience: A Study in Human Nature* (rpt. New York: Modern Library, 1929); Erving Goffman, *Stigma: Notes on the Management of Spoiled Identity* (Englewood Cliffs, N.J.: Prentice-Hall, 1963); Karl Mannheim, *Ideology and Utopia: An Introduction to the Sociology of Knowledge*, trans. Louis Wirth and Edward Shils (New York: Harcourt, Brace, 1936); Peter L. Berger, *The Sacred Canopy: Elements of a Sociological Theory of Religion* (Garden City, N.Y.: Anchor Books, 1969) and *A Rumor of Angels: Modern Society and the Rediscovery of the Supernatural*

(Garden City, N.Y.: Anchor Books, 1970); Peter L. Berger and Thomas Luckmann, *The Social Construction of Reality: A Treatise in the Sociology of Knowledge* (Garden City, N.Y.: Anchor Books, 1967).

6. Sigmund Freud, *The Future of an Illusion*, trans. James Strachey (New York: Norton, 1961), p. 43, and *Civilization and Its Discontents* (New York: Norton, 1962), p. 21; Paul Roazen, *Freud: Political and Social Thought* (New York: Knopf, 1968), chap. 3. For a sophisticated example of the rapprochement between liberal religion and neo-Freudian psychology, see Erich Fromm, *Psychoanalysis and Religion* (New York: Bantam Books, 1967).

7. Sigmund Freud, "Notes Upon a Case of Obsessional Neurosis," in *The Standard Edition of the Complete Psychological Works of Sigmund Freud*, trans. James Strachey (London: Hogarth Press, 1978), Vol. 10, p. 229; William James, "Final Impressions of a Psychical Researcher," in John J. McDermott, ed., *The Writings of William James: A Comprehensive Edition* (New York: Modern Library, 1968), p. 797; O. Mannoni, *Freud*, trans. Renaud Bruce (New York: Pantheon Books, 1971), p. 34.

8. Sigmund Freud, "Psychoanalytical Notes on an Autobiographical Account of a Case of Paranoia (Dementia Paranoides)," in Strachey, *Standard Edition*, Vol. 12, pp. 17–18.

9. For perceptive criticism of this pluralist conception of American society, see T. B. Bottomore, *Classes in Modern Society* (New York: Vintage Books, 1966), and Richard Parker, *The Myth of the Middle Class* (New York: Harper Colophon Books, 1972).

10. As examples of this double standard, see Daniel Bell, *The End of Ideology: On the Exhaustion of Political Ideas in the Fifties* (New York: Free Press, 1962), chaps. 3, 6, 12, and Daniel Bell, ed., *The Radical Right: The New American Right, Expanded and Updated* (Garden City, N.Y.: Doubleday, 1963).

11. Christopher Lasch, *The World of Nations: Reflections on American History, Politics, and Culture* (New York: Vintage Books, 1974), p. 341.

12. My own idea of the class context in which Pelley, Winrod, and Smith came of age has been influenced especially by Bottomore, *Classes in Modern Society*; Lasch, *World of Nations*, chap. 7; Parker, *Myth of the Middle Class*, chap. 5; Herbert G. Gutman, *Work, Culture, and Society in Industrializing America: Essays in American Working-Class and Social History* (New York: Vintage Books, 1977); Gabriel Kolko, *The Triumph of Conservatism: A Reinterpretation of American History, 1900–1916* (Chicago: Quadrangle Books, 1967); Richard P. Coleman and Lee Rainwater, with Kent A. McClelland, *Social Standing in America: New Dimensions of Class* (New York: Basic Books, 1978); C. Wright Mills, *The Power Elite* (New York: Oxford University Press, 1959); and C. Wright Mills, *White Collar: The American Middle Classes* (New York: Oxford University Press, 1953).

13. Berger, *Rumor of Angels*, p. 6.

14. Henry L. Feingold, *The Politics of Rescue: The Roosevelt Administration and the Holocaust, 1938–1945* (New Brunswick, N.J.: Rutgers University Press, 1970), pp. 302–3; David S. Wyman, *Paper Walls: America and the*

Refugee Crisis, 1938–1941 (Amherst: University of Massachusetts, 1968), pp. 210–11.

15. J. Glenn Gray, *The Warriors: Reflections on Men in Battle* (New York: Harper Torchbooks, 1970), p. 154.

16. Peter Stansky, "Thinking About Biography," *New Republic* 171 (19 April 1975): 21.

1. The Politics of Apocalypse: From the Twenties to the Thirties

1. Edmund Wilson, *The Shores of Light* (New York: Noonday Press, 1967), p. 496; George Soule, *The Coming American Revolution* (New York: Macmillan, 1935); John L. Spivak, *America Faces the Barricades* (New York: Covici, Friede, 1935); Reinhold Niebuhr, *Reflections on the End of an Era* (New York: Scribner's Sons, 1934); William G. McLoughlin, Jr., *Billy Sunday Was His Real Name* (Chicago: University of Chicago Press, 1955), p. 289.

2. Warren I. Susman, *Culture and Commitment, 1929–1945* (New York: George Braziller, 1973), p. 7; Warren I. Susman, "The Thirties," in Stanley Coben and Lorman Ratner, eds., *The Development of an American Culture* (Englewood Cliffs, N.J.: Prentice-Hall, 1970), pp. 179–218; Caroline Bird, *The Invisible Scar* (New York: McKay, 1969), chap. 3.

3. Francis P. Weisenberger, *Ordeal of Faith: The Crisis of Church-Going America* (New York: Philosophical Library, 1959); Robert T. Handy, *The American Religious Depression 1925–1935* (rpt. Philadelphia: Fortress Press, 1968), pp. 3–22.

4. Robert Moats Miller, *American Protestantism and Social Issues, 1919–1939* (Chapel Hill: University of North Carolina Press, 1958), pp. 17–18, 45, chap. 4; Paul Carter, *Decline and Revival of the Social Gospel* (Ithaca, N.Y.: Cornell University Press, 1954); Donald B. Meyer, *The Protestant Search for Political Realism, 1919–1941* (Westport, Conn.: Greenwood Press, 1973), chap. 6; Leo P. Ribuffo, "Jesus Christ as Business Statesman: Bruce Barton and the Selling of Corporate Capitalism," *American Quarterly* 33 (Summer 1981): 206–31; Charles W. Ferguson, *The New Book of Revelations* (Garden City, N.Y.: Doubleday, Doran, 1929), pp. 3, 7, 9.

5. Susman, "The Thirties," pp. 207–8; Handy, *Depression*, p. 14; Richard H. Pells, *Radical Visions and American Dreams: Culture and Social Thought in the Depression Years* (New York: Harper Torchbooks, 1974), p. 172; Miller, *American Protestantism*, pp. 42, 342; Peter G. Filene, *Americans and the Soviet Experiment, 1917–1933* (Cambridge, Mass.: Harvard University Press, 1967), pp. 84–86, 247–51; Meyer, *Protestant Search*, chaps. 10–11.

6. David Brion Davis, ed., *The Fear of Conspiracy: Images of Un-American Subversion from the Revolution to the Present* (Ithaca, N.Y.: Cornell University Press, 1971); Roderick Nash, *The Nervous Generation: American Thought, 1917–1930* (Chicago: Rand McNally, 1970), pp. 51–57; Walter Lippmann, *Public Opinion* (rpt. New York: Macmillan, 1961), p. 29; Stuart

Chase, *The Tyranny of Words* ([1938] rpt. New York: Harcourt Brace, n.d.); Harold D. Lasswell, *Propaganda Technique in World War I* (rpt. Cambridge, Mass.: MIT Press, 1971), pp.2–3.

7. John Higham, *Strangers in the Land: Patterns of American Nativism 1960–1925* (New York: Atheneum, 1966), chaps. 1–5; William Preston, *Aliens and Dissenters: Federal Suppression of Radicals, 1903–1933* (New York: Harper Torchbooks, 1966), chaps. 1–3.

8. Theodore Roosevelt, "Where We Cannot Work with Socialists," *Outlook* 91 (29 March 1909), excerpted in William H. Harbaugh, ed., *The Writings of Theodore Roosevelt* (Indianapolis: Bobbs-Merrill, 1967), pp. 303–9.

9. Higham, *Strangers*, chap. 8; Preston, *Aliens and Dissenters*, chaps. 4–7; George Creel, *How We Advertised America: The First Telling of the Amazing Story of the Committee on Public Information That Carried the Gospel of Americanism to Every Corner of the Globe* (New York: Harper and Brothers, 1920), especially chaps. 1–2, 12–13; Robert K. Murray, *Red Scare: A Study of National Hysteria, 1919–1920* (New York: McGraw-Hill, 1964); Paul L. Murphy, "Sources and Nature of Intolerance in the 1920s," *Journal of American History* 51 (June 1964): 60–76, rpt. in Milton Plesur, ed., *The 1920s: Problems and Paradoxes* (Boston: Allyn and Bacon, 1969), p. 168; Stanley Coben, "A Study in Nativism: The American Red Scare of 1919–20," *Political Science Quarterly* 79 (March 1964), rpt. in Richard M. Abrams and Lawrence W. Levine, eds., *The Shaping of Twentieth-Century America: Interpretive Essays* (Boston: Little, Brown, 1971), p. 299.

10. Ole Hanson, *Americanism versus Bolshevism* (Garden City, N.Y.: Doubleday, Page, 1920), pp. 6, 293–94; "Lee Overman," *Dictionary of American Biography*, vol. 14, (New York: Scribner's Sons, 1934), pp. 114–15.

11. Stanley Coben, *A. Mitchell Palmer, Politician* (New York: Columbia University Press, 1963), chaps. 11–13; Murray, *Red Scare*, chaps. 12–13; Palmer, "The Case Against the 'Reds,'" *Forum* 63 (Feb. 1920), excerpted in Loren Baritz, ed., *The Culture of the Twenties* (Indianapolis: Bobbs-Merrill, 1970), pp. 75–85.

12. Murphy, "Sources of Intolerance," p. 170; Coben, "A Study in Nativism," pp. 302–4, 289–90; David M. Chalmers, *Hooded Americanism: The History of the Klu Klux Klan* (New York: New Viewpoints, 1981), chaps. 4–41; Kenneth T. Jackson, *The Klu Klux Klan in the City* (New York: Oxford University Press, 1967), pp. 235–36; Norman Hapgood, ed., *Professional Patriots* (New York: Boni, 1927), pp. 4, 13, 24; Richard Merrill Whitney, *Back to Barbarism* (New York: American Defense Society, n.d.), pp. 2, 24; [Richard Merrill Whitney], *Reds in America* (New York: Beckwith Press, 1924), pp. 189–205; Ralph M. Easley, *The Youth Movement: Do We Want It Here?* (n.p.: [National Civic Federation], n.d.), pp. 3, 11; James Weinstein, *The Corporate Ideal in the Liberal State, 1900–1918* (Boston: Beacon Press, 1969), chap. 1; Marguerite Green, *The National Civic Federation and the American Labor Movement* (Washington, D.C.: Catholic University Press, 1956), chap. 7.

13. Russell B. Nye, *Midwestern Progressive Politics: A Historical Study of Its Origins and Development, 1870–1958* (New York: Harper Torchbooks,

1965), p. 313; "Peace Time Need for the League's Work," *National Security League Quarterly* 1 (March, 1927): 1; Hapgood, *Professional Patriots*, pp. 162–65; Murphy, "Sources of Intolerance," p. 172; Donald S. Strong, *Organized Anti-Semitism in America: The Rise of Group Prejudice During the Decade 1930–1940* (Washington, D.C.: American Council on Public Affairs, 1941), chap. 8.

14. Hapgood, *Professional Patriots*, pp. 13–14, 48, 191–204; Whitney, *Reds*, pp. 55–69, 117–26, 141–54, 189–205; Easley, *Youth Movement*, p. 15; "Bolshevism and the Methodist Church," *Current Opinion* 66 (June 1919): 380–81.

15. Leonard Dinnerstein, *The Leo Frank Case* (New York: Columbia University Press, 1968), pp. 66–67; John Higham, "Social Discrimination Against Jews in America, 1830–1930," rpt. in Abraham J. Karp, ed., *Jewish Experience in America: Selected Studies from the Publications of the American Jewish Historical Society*, vol. 5 (New York: KATV, 1969), pp. 351–55; Louis Harap, *The Image of the Jew in American Literature: From Early Republic to Mass Immigration* (Philadelphia: Jewish Publication Society of America, 1974), chap. 2; Irving Katz, *August Belmont: A Political Biography* (New York: Columbia University Press, 1968), pp. 144, 39, 82.

16. Michael N. Dobkowski, *The Tarnished Dream: The Basis of American Anti-Semitism* (Westport, Conn.: Greenwood Press, 1979), chaps. 1–6; Moses Rischin, *The Promised City: New York's Jews, 1870–1914* (New York: Harper Torchbooks, 1970), p. 259; Oscar Handlin, *Adventure in Freedom: Three Hundred Years of Jewish Life in America* (rpt. Port Washington, N.Y.: Kennikat Press, 1971), pp. 170–84; Richard Hofstadter, *The Age of Reform: From Bryan to FDR* (New York: Vintage Books, 1955), pp. 77–81; Harap, *Image of the Jew* chaps. 7–10, 13–17; John Higham, "Anti-Semitism in the Gilded Age: A Reinterpretation," *Mississippi Valley Historical Review* 43 (March 1957): 570, 565–66; Dinnerstein, *Leo Frank*, p. 68; Glenn C. Altschuler, *Race, Ethnicity, and Class in American Social Thought, 1865–1919* (Arlington Heights, Ill.: Harlan Davidson, 1982), pp. 43, 50; Frederic Cople Jaher, *Doubters and Dissenters: Cataclysmic Thought in America, 1885–1918* (New York: Crowell-Collier, 1964), pp. 131–40, 151–57, 165–66, 171; Josiah Strong, *Our Country* (rpt. Cambridge, Mass.: Harvard University Press, 1963).

17. Dinnerstein, *Leo Frank*, p. 65; Higham, "Gilded Age," pp. 559–78; Handlin, *Adventure in Freedom*, pp. 174–80, 184; Oscar Handlin, "American Views of the Jew at the Opening of the Twentieth Century," in Karp, ed., *Jewish Experience*, vol. 5, pp. 1–22; Harap, *Image of the Jew*, pp. 3–6, 424–33; Robert A. Rockaway, "Anti-Semitism in an American City: Detroit, 1850–1914," *American Jewish Historical Quarterly* 64 (Sept. 1974): 42–54; William F. Holmes, "White Capping: Anti-Semitism in the Populist Era," *American Jewish Historical Quarterly* 63 (Mar. 1974): 244–61; Norman Pollack, "The Myth of Populist Anti-Semitism," *American Historical Review*, 68 (Oct. 1962): 76–80; Walter T. K. Nugent, *The Tolerant Populists: Kansas Populism and Nativism* (Chicago: University of Chicago Press, 1963), pp. 109–15; David A. Gerber, "Cutting Out Shylock: Elite Anti-Semitism

and the Quest for Moral Order in the Mid-Nineteenth-Century American Market Place," *Journal of American History* 69 (December 1982): 615–637.

18. Dinnerstein, *Leo Frank*, chaps. 5–8; George M. Frederickson, *The Black Image in the White Mind: The Debate on Afro-American Character and Destiny, 1817–1914* (New York: Harper Torchbooks, 1971), p. xiii; Higham, *Strangers*, pp. 271, 155–57; Thomas F. Gossett, *Race: The History of an Idea in America* (Dallas, Tex.: Southern Methodist University Press, 1963), chaps. 12–15; Madison Grant, *The Passing of the Great Race* (1916; rpt. New York: Arno Press, 1970), pp. 167, 12, 16, 91, 77.

19. Jacob Riis, *How the Other Half Lives: Studies Among the Tenements of New York* (rpt. New York: Sagamore Press, 1957), pp. 78–79; Burton J. Hendrick, "The Jewish Invasion of America," *McClure's Magazine* 40 (March 1913): 140, 147, 150, 154–57, 163; Hendrick, "The Great Jewish Invasion," *McClure's Magazine* 28 (Jan. 1907): 307–21; Edward Alsworth Ross, *The Old World in the New* (New York: Century, 1914), pp. 146–47, 149, 150, 153–54, 156–60, 163–65, 143–44; Thomas G. Dyer, *Theodore Roosevelt and the Idea of Race* (Baton Rouge, La.: Louisiana State University Press, 1980), pp. 124–25.

20. John Spargo, *The Jew and American Ideals* (New York: Harper and Brothers, 1922), p. 7; Edward H. Flannery, *The Anguish of the Jews: Twenty-three Centuries of Anti-Semitism* (New York: Macmillan, 1965), p. 248; Higham, "Social Discrimination," p. 369; Carey E. McWilliams, *A Mask for Privilege: Anti-Semitism in America* (Boston: Little, Brown, 1948), p. 232; Robert D. Schulzinger, *The Making of the Diplomatic Mind: The Training, Outlook, and Style of United States Foreign Service Officers, 1908–1931* (Middletown, Conn.: Wesleyan University Press, 1975), pp. 131–32; Martha Graham Synnott, *The Half-Opened Door: Discrimination and Admissions at Harvard, Yale, and Princeton, 1900–1970* (Westport, Conn.: Greenwood Press, 1979).

21. Theodore Lothrop Stoddard, *The Rising Tide of Color: Against White World Supremacy* (New York: Scribner's Sons, 1920), p. 163; Kenneth Roberts, *Why Europe Leaves Home* (Brooklyn, N.Y.: Bobbs-Merrill, 1922), pp. 118, 115, 114; Paul A. Carter, *The Twenties in America* (New York: Crowell, 1968), pp. 89–90.

22. Filene, *Americans and the Soviet Experiment*, pp. 104–5; United States Congress, Senate, *Hearings Before a Subcommittee of the Committee on the Judiciary, Bolshevik Propaganda*, 65th Cong., 3d sess., 11 Feb.–10 March 1919, pp. 12, 114–15, 123, 141–42, 178–79, 194, 200, 309, 269, 355, 262.

23. Schulzinger, *Making of the Diplomatic Mind*, p. 131; Stoddard, *The Revolt Against Civilization: The Menace of the Under-Man* (New York: Scribner's Sons, 1922), pp. 151–52; Spargo, *Jew and American Ideals*, chaps. 5–6; Arthur Liebman, *Jews and the Left* (New York: Wiley and Sons, 1979), pp. 57–64.

24. Norman Cohn, *Warrant for Genocide: The Myth of the World-Conspiracy and the Protocols of the Elders of Zion* (New York: Harper

Torchbooks, 1969), chaps. 1–4. In this book I use a "standard" edition, Victor E. Marsden, trans., *The Protocols of the Learned Elders of Zion* (Los Angeles: Christian Nationalist Crusade, n.d.).

25. U.S. Senate, *Hearings on Bolshevik Propaganda*, pp. 138, 135.

26. The remainder of this section is condensed from Leo P. Ribuffo, "Henry Ford and *The International Jew*," *American Jewish History* 69 (June 1980): 437–77.

27. Clinton Rossiter, *Conservatism in America: The Thankless Persuasion* (New York: Vintage Books, 1962), p. 147; William H. Harbaugh, ed., *The Writings of Theodore Roosevelt* (Indianapolis: Bobbs-Merrill, 1967), p. 19.

28. Rossiter, *Conservatism in America*, p. 153. On the search for American conservatives, see, for example, Allen Guttmann, *The Conservative Tradition in America* (New York: Oxford University Press, 1967); Ronald Lora, *Conservative Minds in America* (Chicago: Rand McNally, 1971); and Robert Green McClosky, *American Conservatism in the Age of Enterprise, 1865–1910* (New York: Harper Torchbooks, 1964).

29. Chalmers, *Hooded Americanism*, chap. 2; Richard Maxwell Brown, ed., *American Violence* (Englewood Cliffs, N.J.: Prentice-Hall, 1970), pp. 96–99.

30. Albert U. Romasco, *The Poverty of Abundance: Hoover, the Nation, the Depression* (New York: Oxford University Press, 1965), p. 15; Allan J. Lichtman, *Prejudice and the Old Politics: The Presidential Election of 1928* (Chapel Hill: University of North Carolina Press, 1979), chap. 1; Ellis W. Hawley, *The Great War and the Search for a Modern Order: A History of the American People and Their Institutions, 1917–1933* (New York: St. Martin's, 1979), pp. 126–29; David Burner, *The Politics of Provincialism: The Democratic Party in Transition, 1918–1932* (New York: Knopf, 1968), p. 86.

31. William E. Leuchtenburg, *Franklin D. Roosevelt and the New Deal* (New York: Harper Torchbooks, 1963), pp. 10–11.

32. Irving Howe and Lewis Coser, *The American Communist Party: A Critical History (1919–1957)* (Boston: Beacon Press, 1957) chap. 5; David A. Shannon, *The Socialist Party of America: A History* (Chicago: Quadrangle, 1967), chaps. 9–10; Frank A. Warren, III, *Liberals and Communism: The 'Red Decade' Revisited* (Bloomington: Indiana University Press, 1966), chaps. 1–2; R. Alan Lawson, *The Failure of Independent Liberalism, 1930–1941* (New York: Putnam's Sons, 1971), pp. 219–50.

33. Otis L. Graham, Jr., *An Encore of Reform: The Old Progressives and the New Deal* (New York: Oxford University Press, 1967), chaps. 2, 5; Joan Hoff Wilson, *Herbert Hoover: Forgotten Progressive* (Boston: Little, Brown, 1975), chap. 7; Herbert Hoover, *The Challenge to Liberty* (New York: Harper & Brothers, 1934), p. 2; George Wolfskill, *The Revolt of the Conservatives* (Boston: Houghton Mifflin, 1962); Frederick Rudolph, "The American Liberty League, 1934–1940," *American Historical Review*, 56 (Oct. 1950): 19–33.

34. James T. Patterson, *Congressional Conservatism and the New Deal: The Growth of the Conservative Coalition in Congress, 1933–1939* (Lexing-

ton: University of Kentucky Press, 1967), p. 13; Arthur M. Schlesinger, Jr., *The Coming of the New Deal* (Boston: Houghton Mifflin, 1960), pp. 44, 48; Leuchtenburg, *Roosevelt and the New Deal,* p. 55.

35. Arthur M. Schlesinger, Jr., *The Politics of Upheaval* (Boston: Houghton Mifflin, 1960), pp. 625, 619, 518, 624, 606, 636.

36. Strong, *Organized Anti-Semitism in America,* pp. 24–31, 124, 128–29, chap. 7; Neil R. McMillen, "Pro-Nazi Sentiment in the United States, March 1933–March 1934," *Southern Quarterly* 2 (Oct. 1963): 62–64; Dilling, *The Red Network: A "Who's Who" and Handbook of Radicalism for Patriots* (Kenilworth, Ill.: priv. pub. 1935), pp. 34, 51–53, 86, 89, 74; T. Harry Williams, *Huey Long* (New York: Knopf, 1969), chaps. 22, 24; Sheldon Marcus, *Father Coughlin: The Tumultuous Life of the Priest of the Little Flower* (Boston: Little, Brown, 1973), chap. 5.

37. Marcus, *Father Coughlin,* pp. 72, 31, 87–88; Williams, *Huey Long,* p. 800.

38. Dilling, *Red Network,* pp. 340–62.

39. Paul K. Conkin, *The New Deal* (Arlington Heights, Ill.: AHM, 1975), chap. 1.

40. Leuchtenburg, *Roosevelt and the New Deal,* p. 331.

41. Wolfskill, *Revolt of the Conservatives,* p. 121.

42. Leuchtenburg, *Roosevelt and the New Deal,* p. 9; Patterson, *Congressional Conservatism,* p. 142; Schlesinger, *Politics of Upheaval,* p. 606.

43. John M. Allswang, *The New Deal and American Politics: A Study in Political Change* (New York: Wiley and Sons, 1978), pp. 39, 52–62; Harvard Sitkoff, *A New Deal for Blacks: The Emergence of Civil Rights as a National Issue* (New York: Oxford University Press, 1978), chaps. 4–5.

44. Schlesinger, *Coming of the New Deal,* pp. 583–84, 575, 569; Schlesinger, *Politics of Upheaval,* pp. 602, 612; Patterson, *Congressional Conservatism,* p. 73.

45. Williams, *Huey Long,* pp. 681–82; Patterson, *Congressional Conservatism,* pp. 147, 166–67.

46. John P. Diggins, *Mussolini and Fascism: The View from America* (Princeton, N.J.: Princeton University Press, 1972), pp. 42–73, 111–203; Alan Cassels, "Fascism for Export: Italy and the United States in the Twenties," *American Historical Review* 69 (April 1964): 707–12; Wolfgang Sauer, "National Socialism: Totalitarianism or Fascism?" *American Historical Review* 73 (Dec. 1967): 404–6; Raymond Gram Swing, *Forerunners of American Fascism* (New York: Messner, 1935), p. 13.

47. Roberta Sigel, "Opinions of Nazi Germany: A Study of Three Popular American Magazines, 1933–1941" (unpub. Ph.D. diss., Clark University, 1950), especially chap. 3; F. K. Wentz, "American Catholic Periodicals React to Nazism," *Church History* 31 (Dec. 1962): 400–20; F. K. Wentz, "American Protestant Journals and the Nazi Religious Assault," *Church History* 23 (Dec. 1954): 400–20; Sander A. Diamond, *The Nazi Movement in the United States, 1924–1941* (Ithaca, N.Y., Cornell University Press, 1974), pp. 161–62; Leland V. Bell, *In Hitler's Shadow: The Anatomy of American Nazism* (Port Washington, N.Y.: Kennikat Press, 1973), p. 14; Arnold A. Offner, *American*

Appeasement: United States Foreign Policy and Germany, 1933–1938 (Cambridge, Mass.: Harvard University Press, 1959), pp. 60, 82; Pierre Van Passen and James Waterman Wise, eds., *Nazism: An Assault on Civilization* (New York: Smith & Haas, 1934), pp. 1–38.

48. John M. Cammett, "Communist Theories of Fascism, 1920–1935," *Science and Society* 31 (Spring, 1967): 149–63; R. Palme Dutt, *Fascism and Social Revolution: A Study of the Economics and Politics of the Last Stages of Capitalism in Decay* (London: Martin Lawrence, 1935), p. vii; Pierre Ayçoberry, *The Nazi Question: An Essay on The Interpretation of National Socialism (1922–1975)*, trans. Robert Hurly (New York: Pantheon, 1981), pp. 47–57.

49. Alfred M. Bingham, *Insurgent America: Revolt of the Middle Classes* (New York: Harper & Brothers, 1935), pp. 105, 126, 145, 125, 138, 171; Warren, *Liberals and Communism*, p. 92.

50. George Seldes, *Sawdust Caesar: The Untold Story of Mussolini and Fascism* (New York: Harper & Brothers, 1935), p. xiii; Swing, *Forerunners of American Fascism*, p. 168; Bingham, *Insurgent America*, pp. 97, 185–89.

51. Harold Loeb and Selden Rodman, "American Fascism in Embryo," *New Republic* 77 (27 Dec. 1933): 185–87.

52. "Tinder for the Fascist Fires," *Nation* 146 (4 June 1938): 633; Benjamin Stolberg, "Vigilantism, 1937," *Nation* 145 (14 Aug. 1937): 166; Amy Schecter, "Fascism in Pennsylvania," *Nation* 140 (19 June 1935): 713; Raymond Gram Swing, "Patriotism Dons the Black Shirt," *Nation* 140 (10 April 1935): 409–11; Anna Wallace, "Fascism Comes to Campus," *New Republic* 81 (9 Jan. 1935): 239; Dale Kramer, "The American Fascists," *Harper's Magazine* 180 (Sept. 1940): 392; Hamilton Basso, "The Little Hitlers of Asheville," *New Republic* 88 (2 Sept. 1936): 101; Mike Gold, "Out of the Fascist Unconscious," *New Republic* 75 (26 July 1933): 295; Daniel Aaron, *Writers on the Left* (New York: Avon Books, 1965), p. 283.

53. Albert Brandt, "The Invasion of America," in Van Passen and Wise, *Nazism*, pp. 227–49; Diamond, *Nazi Movement*, p. 146; Bell, *In Hitler's Shadow*, pp. 17, 22; Charles Angoff, "Nazi Jew-Baiting in America," pt. 1, *Nation* 140 (1 May 1935): 501–03, and "Nazi Jew-Baiting in America," pt. 2, *Nation* 140 (8 May 1935): 531–35; Ludwig Lore, "Nazi Politics in America," *Nation* 137 (29 Nov. 1933): 615; Frederick L. Schuman, "The Nazi International," *New Republic* 87 (8 July 1936): 275; Albert Grzesinski and Charles E. Hewitt, Jr., "Hitler's Branch Office, USA," *Current History and Forum* 52 (26 Nov. 1940): 11–12; Niel M. Johnson, *George Sylvester Viereck: German-American Propagandist* (Urbana: University of Illinois Press, 1972).

54. Brandt, "Invasion of America," p. 245; Stanley High, "Star-Spangled Fascists," pp. 338–53; John J. Smertenko, "Hitlerism Comes to America," *Harper's Magazine* 167 (Nov. 1933): 660–70; Loeb and Rodman, "Fascism in Embryo," pp. 185–87; Harry F. Ward, "The Development of Fascism in the United States," *Annals of the American Academy of Political and Social Science* 180 (1 July 1935); Harold Lavine, "Fifth Column 'Literature,'" *Saturday Review of Literature* 122 (14 Sept. 1940): 3–4, 14–15; Kramer, "The American Fascists," pp. 380–93; Swing, *Forerunners of American Fascism*,

of *American Fascism*, p. 49; "The Nazis Are Here," *Nation* 148 (4 March 1939): 253; Bingham, *Insurgent America*, pp. 186–88.

55. Sigel, "Opinions of Nazi Germany," p. 42; Shannon, *Socialist Party of America*, p. 229; Schlesinger, *The Politics of Upheaval*, p. 518; Soule, *Coming American Revolution*, p. 295.

56. Howe and Coser, *American Communist Party*, chap. 5; Warren, *Liberals and Communism*, pp. 37–38; Leuchtenburg, *Roosevelt and the New Deal*, p. 247; Norman Thomas, *The Choice Before Us: Mankind at the Crossroads* (New York: Macmillan, 1934), pp. 7, 43–61, 185–99.

57. Sinclair Lewis, *It Can't Happen Here* (Garden City, N.Y.: Doubleday, Doran, 1935).

58. Vincent Sheehan, *Dorothy and Red* (Boston: Houghton Mifflin, 1963), pp. 132, 56–57, 260, 262, 270–71; Mark Schorer, *Sinclair Lewis: An American Life* (New York: McGraw-Hill, 1961), pp. 608–9; Marion K. Sanders, *Dorothy Thompson: A Legend in Her Time* (Boston: Houghton Mifflin, 1973), pp. 135–36, 211.

59. Lewis, *It Can't Happen Here*, pp. 127, 120, 102–3, 100, 157, 80, 20, 39, 2, 169, 360, 173, 265, 249–52, 343, 260–63.

60. Ibid., pp. 57, 25, 354, 410–11, 418, 427, 450, 458.

61. Ibid., pp. 204, 412, 190, 318, 344.

62. Ibid., pp. 9, 189, 107.

63. Ibid., pp. 87, 100; Sinclair Lewis, *Main Street* (1920: rpt. New York: Signet Books, 1961).

64. Schorer, *Sinclair Lewis*, pp. 609–10, 523–24, 614, 678, 690, 697–98; Sinclair Lewis, "Statement" (n.d.), Lewis Collection, Yale University; Jane DeHart Mathews, *The Federal Theatre, 1935–1939: Plays, Relief, and Politics* (Princeton, N.J.: Princeton University Press, 1967), pp. 95–101.

2. William Dudley Pelley: Spiritualist in Politics

1. Sinclair Lewis, *It Can't Happen Here* (Garden City, N.Y.: Doubleday, Doran, 1935), p. 74.

2. U.S. Congress, House of Representatives, Special Committee on Un-American Activities, *Hearings on Investigation of Un-American Propaganda Activities in the United States* (cited hereafter as *HUAC*), 67th Cong., 3d sess., 1939–40, vol. 12, p. 7202; William Dudley Pelley, *The Door to Revelation: An Autobiography* (Asheville, N.C.: Pelley Publishers, 1939), pp. 4, 6, 10, 22; William Dudley Pelley, *Why I Believe the Dead Are Alive* (Noblesville, Ind.: Soulcraft Chapels, 1954), pp. 36–37; "Paste-Pot Pelley," *Philosopher* 1 (June 1909): 12; United States Census, 1900, Massachusetts, vol. 87, E. D. 1628, Sheet 3, line 66, Worcester; "William Dudley Pelley," *Who's Who in America, 1924–25* (Chicago: Marquis, 1924), p. 2528. *Who's Who* puts his birth date five years earlier, but I have accepted the date Pelley gave under oath to the House Committee on Un-American Activities.

3. *Door to Relevation*, pp. 11, 13; "Pa and the Chickens," *Philosopher* 1

(Aug. 1909): 14–15; William Dudley Pelley, *My Seven Minutes in Eternity with Their Aftermath* (Noblesville, Ind.: Soulcraft Press, 1952), pp. 36–38; John S. Haller and Robin M. Haller, *The Physician and Sexuality in Victorian America* (New York: Norton, 1977), chaps. 3, 5; Nathan G. Hale, Jr., *Freud and the Americans: The Beginnings of Psychoanalysis in the United States* (New York: Oxford University Press, 1971), chap. 2.

4. *Door to Revelation*, pp. 36–38; Advertisement for Fulton Toilet Paper Company, *Philosopher* 1 (June, 1909), n.p.

5. *Door to Revelation*, pp. 31–34; Elbert Hubbard II, ed., *The Philosophy of Elbert Hubbard* (New York: Wise, 1941), pp. 54, 63, 65, 71, 89, 96, 141, 146, 148; "Fool Socialism and the Other Kind," *Philosopher* 1 (July 1909): 1; Freeman Champney, *Art and Glory: The Story of Elbert Hubbard* (New York: Crown Publishers, 1968), pp. 55–58, 112.

6. Cover, *Philosopher* 1 (Oct. 1909); "What Is the Matter with Our Churches?" *Philosopher* 2 (Nov. 1909): 5–6.

7. "Ma's Hairbrush and a Little Bear Behind" [sic] *Philosopher* 1 (June 1909): 4; "Pa and the Chickens," pp. 14–15; Peter Gabriel Filene, *Him/Her Self: Sex Roles in Modern America* (New York: New American Library, 1976), pp. 95–96; Joe L. Dubbert, *Man's Place: Masculinity in Transition* (Englewood Cliffs, N.J.: Prentice-Hall, 1979), pp. 148–53; Charles Larsen, *The Good Fight: The Life and Times of Ben B. Lindsey* (Chicago: Quadrangle Books, 1972), chap. 2; Anthony Platt, *The Child Savers: The Invention of Delinquency* (Chicago: University of Chicago Press, 1977).

8. Cover, *Philosopher* 1 (June 1909); "Proclamation," *Philosopher* 1 (June 1909), n.p.; "500 Years Hence!" *Philosopher* 1 (Oct. 1909): 6–7; untitled epigrams, *Philosopher* 1 (Sept. 1909): 14.

9. "The Heart of Norene: A Story," *Philosopher* 1 (July 1909): 11; "Proclamation," n.p.; "500 Years Hence!" p. 8.

10. "Punk Pastors and Pious Priests," *Philosopher* 1 (Sept. 1909): 9; "500 Years Hence!" p. 3; "The New Declaration of Independence," *Philosopher* 1 (Sept. 1909): 3; "What Is the Matter?" p. 6; "The Model Church," *Philosopher* 1 (Oct. 1909): 10; "A Letter and a Reply," *Philosopher* 1 (Sept. 1909): 13.

11. "What Is the Matter?" p. 4; "A Remedy, " *Philosopher* 1 (Sept. 1909): 10; "Punk Pastors," pp. 7–9; Back cover, *Philosopher* 1 (Aug. 1909); "Model Church," p. 11.

12. "Letter and Reply," p. 13; "Punk Pastors," pp. 6–9; Dubbert, *Man's Place*, pp. 136–40.

13. "The New Christianity," *Philosopher* 1 (Aug. 1909): 5; "Punk Pastors," p. 9; "Remedy," p. 10; "Model Church," pp. 12–13; "Wanted: A Religion of Laughter," *Philosopher* 2 (Nov. 1909): 10–11; Edward Bellamy, *Looking Backward* (1888; rpt. New York: New American Library, 1960).

14. "500 Years Hence!" p. 6; "Remedy," p. 11; "August 1st, 1959," *Philosopher* 1 (Aug. 1909): 2; Champney, *Art and Glory*, pp. 115–16.

15. "Editorial," *Philosopher* 1 (Oct. 1909): 2; "What Is the Matter?" p. 7; *Door to Revelation*, p. 20.

16. Untitled article, *Philosopher* 1 (June 1909): 15.

17. "New Christianity," p. 5; "What Is the Matter?" p. 8; "New Declaration of Independence," p. 2; "Religion of Laughter," p. 10; "Ma's Hairbrush," p. 6; "Letter and Reply," p. 14. "Letter and Reply," p. 14.

18. "Punk Pastors," p. 8; "Fool Socialism," p. 3; "Announcement," *Philosopher* 1 (June 1909): 11; "Letter and Reply," p. 14; Daniel Bell, *Marxian Socialism in the United States* (Princeton, N.J.: Princeton University Press, 1967), pp. 86–87.

19. "Editorial," *Philosopher* 2 (Nov. 1909): 2; "One Man's Advice: Written for Boys Who Want to Get Rich Quick," *Philosopher* 1 (July 1909): 6; "Count Boni De Castellene Bought Seat in French Chamber of Deputies," *Philosopher* 1 (June 1909): 13–14; "500 Years Hence!" p. 4; untitled article, *Philosopher* 1 (June 1909): 15; Felix Shay, *Elbert Hubbard of East Aurora* (New York: Wise, 1926), pp. 163–67.

20. "Fool Socialism," p. 2; "Common-Sense Government," *Philosopher* 1 (July 1909): 9, 11; "August 1st, 1959," p. 3; "Remedy," p. 10.

21. "Common-Sense Government," pp. 8–9.

22. "Common-Sense Government," pp. 9–10; "New Christianity," pp. 5–6; "A Common-Sense Education," *Philosopher* 1 (Aug. 1909): 7–8.

23. "Common-Sense Education," p. 10; untitled epigrams, *Philosopher* 1 (June 1909): 16.

24. "Paste-Pot Pelley," *Philosopher* 1 (June 1909): 12; "Letter and Reply," p. 13; "Count Boni De Castellene," p. 13; "New Declaration of Independence," p. 4.

25. "New Christianity," p. 6; "Andrew Carnegie vs. Orville Wright," *Philosopher* 1 (July 1909): 12–14.

26. "August 1st, 1959," pp. 3–4; "Letter and Reply," p. 14.

27. *Door to Revelation*, pp. 31, 56; *Seven Minutes*, pp. 6–7; "Why I Am Glad I Married a Suffragist," *American Magazine* 89 (April 1920): 48.

28. *Door to Revelation*, pp. 56–61, 65; *Seven Minutes*, p. 7; *St. Johnsbury (Vermont) Caledonian*, 13 March 1918.

29. *Door to Revelation*, pp. 70–75; *St. Johnsbury Caledonian*, 13 March 1918; *Why I Believe*, p. 256; *Bennington (Vermont) Banner*, 3 Nov. 1916.

30. "I Married a Suffragist," p. 48; *Door to Revelation*, pp. 76–77, 80–83; "Their Mother," *American Magazine* 84 (Aug. 1917): 15–18.

31. Dubbert, *Man's Place*, pp. 17–19, 133–36; Filene, *Him/Her Self*, pp. 3–43; James R. McGovern, "The American Woman's Pre-World War I Freedom in Manners and Morals," *Journal of American History* 55 (Sept. 1968): 315–33.

32. Thoedore Peterson, *Magazines in the Twentieth Century* (Urbana: University of Illinois Press, 1964), pp. 142–43; *St. Johnsbury Caledonian*, 13 March 1918.

33. *St. Johnsbury Caledonian*, 13 March, 18 Sept. 1918; 15 March 1919.

34. *Door to Revelation*, pp. 92–96; *Seven Minutes*, p. 7; "Siberia, with the Lid Off," *Sunset* 43 (July 1919): 17; "Siberia Back of the Whiskers," *Sunset* 43 (Nov. 1919): 17; *St. Johnsbury Caledonian*, 10, 11, 12 Oct., 12 Dec. 1918.

35. *Door to Revelation*, pp. 123–24; "Lid Off," p. 17; "Whiskers," p. 17; *St. Johnsbury Caledonian*, 26 Aug., 12 Dec. 1918; Young Men's Christian

Association, *Service With Fighting Men: An Account of the Work of the American Young Men's Christian Association in the World War,* vol. 2 (New York: Association Press, 1922), p. 441.

36. *Door to Revelation,* pp. 123, 152; *St. Johnsbury Caledonian,* 12 Dec. 1918.

37. *St. Johnsbury Caledonian,* 22 March 1919; *Door to Revelation,* pp. 162–63; *The Greater Glory* (Boston: Little, Brown and Co., 1919).

38. "Hustling the Far East," *Sunset* 42 (March 1919): 13–14; "The Dollar in Service on the Missionary Firing-Line," *World Outlook* 5 (April 1919): 10–11, 30; "Korea and Japan's Boot," *Sunset* 43 (Oct. 1919): 22–23; "Whiskers," p. 84; *St. Johnsbury Caledonian,* 24, 30 Jan., 3 Feb. 1919.

39. *St. Johnsbury Caledonian,* 14 April, 16 June, 21 Feb., 1919; "Korea and Japan's Boot," p. 23.

40. *St. Johnsbury Caledonian,* 4, 7 Feb., 6, 11 March, 18 April, 1919.

41. *St. Johnsbury Caledonian,* 16, 26 May, 16 June, 1 Feb., 25 Jan. 1919; 27 Dec. 1918; "Lid Off," pp. 17, 85–87; "Whiskers," pp. 18–19, 54; Thomas J. McCormick, *China Market: America's Quest for Informal Empire, 1893–1901* (Chicago: Quadrangle Books, 1967), p. 162.

42. *St. Johnsbury Caledonian,* 6, 19, 23 June, 5, 21 April, 15, 3, 4 March, 28 Jan., 6 Feb. 1919; 20 Dec. 1918.

43. *Door to Revelation,* pp. 111, 117–21, 136; *St. Johnsbury Caledonian,* 4, 9 Oct., 4 Nov., 1918; 8 April 1919.

44. *St. Johnsbury Caledonian,* 24 Jan., 8, 12 May, 14 April, 16 June 1919; Thomas G. Dyer, *Theodore Roosevelt and the Idea of Race* (Baton Rouge: Louisiana State University Press, 1980), p. 30.

45. *St. Johnsbury Caledonian,* 13 March, 10 June 1919.

46. Ibid., 13 Feb. 1919; "I Married a Suffragist," pp. 48–49, 122, 125–26.

47. "I Married a Suffragist," pp. 48–49, 126; *St. Johnsbury Caledonian,* 16 April 1919.

48. "I Married a Suffragist," pp. 48, 126; *Door to Revelation,* p. 70; *St. Johnsbury Caledonian,* 20 Feb., 29, 19 April, 9 June, 8 July 1919.

49. *Door to Revelation,* pp. 162–73.

50. Ibid., pp. 177–84.

51. Ibid., pp. 184–85, 61.

52. Ibid., pp. 218–19; "Human Nature, as the Country Editor Knows It," *American Magazine* 88 (Nov. 1919): 213; Malcolm Cowley, *Exile's Return: A Literary Odyssey of the 1920s* (New York: Viking Compass Edition, 1973), pp. 1–7, 9, 38; Henry F. May, *The End of American Innocence: A Study of the First Years of Our Own Time, 1912–1917* (Chicago: Quadrangle Books, 1964).

53. *Greater Glory,* p. 304; *Drag* ([1925]; rpt. Indianapolis: Fellowship Press, 1942), pp. 167, 78, 80; "Wanted: A Younger and More Practical Man," *American Magazine* 85 (March 1918): 10–15; "Through Thick and Thin," *American Magazine* 85 (May 1918): 41–44; "Why the Judge Felt Safe," *American Magazine* 86 (Oct. 1918): 40–43; "What Put 'Pep' Into John Stevens," *American Magazine* 86 (July 1918): 23.

54. *Greater Glory,* pp. 290–91; "Wanted," p. 14.

55. "The Face in the Window," *Current Opinion* 69 (Nov. 1920): 639; "Through Thick and Thin," p. 41; *Greater Glory*, pp. 9, 31, 124; "Birds of Passage," *Sunset* 48 (April 1922): 52; "Russet and Gold," *American Magazine* 84 (Dec. 1917): 33–34; "Bud Jones—Small Advertiser," *American Magazine* 85 (Feb. 1918): 23.

56. "Russet and Gold," pp. 119–20; "Bud Jones," p. 23, 89; "Third-Speed Tarring," *Everybody's* 43 (Dec. 1920): 59; "Their Mother," pp. 16–17; "Wanted," p. 14; *Greater Glory*, pp. 9–10; "Aunt Julia," *American Magazine* 85 (Jan. 1918): 91–92; "Face in the Window," p. 647; "What Put 'Pep' Into John Stevens," p. 90.

57. *Greater Glory*, pp. 11, 19, 23, 27, 31, 41, 43, 69, 110, 124, 203, 220–23, 274–75.

58. Ibid., pp. 106, 109–10, 163, 210, 262.

59. Ibid., pp. 144, 349, 347, 316, 306, 309, 311–12.

60. Ibid., pp. 291, 343, 296–97, 340, 359, 369.

61. *The Fog* (1921; repub. Indianapolis: Fellowship Press, 1941), pp. 443–44; *Door to Revelation*, pp. 176–77; Sinclair Lewis, *Main Street* (1920: rpt. New York: New American Library, 1961).

62. *Fog*, pp. 7, 19, 68, 92–93, 104, 106, 150, 154, 156, 174, 179, 216, 239.

63. Ibid., pp. 79, 85, 88, 122, 163, 165, 168, 183, 257, 310, 407.

64. Ibid., pp. 263, 287, 382, 385, 387, 417, 422, 441, 436.

65. Ibid., pp. 417, 480, 456–57.

66. Ibid., pp. 258, 144, 288, 332; "The New Books," *Literary Review* (10 Dec. 1921), p. 263.

67. Pelley, *The Fog*, pp. 225, 279, 255.

68. Ibid., pp. 455, 342, 304, 320.

69. Ibid., pp. 289, 387, 362–63.

70. *St. Johnsbury Caledonian*, 18 Sept., 10 Oct. 1917.

71. *Door to Revelation*, pp. 182–84; Kenneth W. Munden, *The American Film Institute Catalog of Motion Pictures Produced in the United States: Feature Films, 1921–1930*, vol. F2 (New York: Bowker, 1970), p. 433.

72. *Door to Revelation*, pp. 182–83, 196, 188–89, 193, 231; *Seven Minutes*, p. 8; John McIntyre Werly, "The Millenarian Right: William Dudley Pelley and the Silver Legion of America," (unpub. Ph.D. diss., Syracuse University, 1972), p. 19.

73. *Door to Revelation*, p. 184; Munden, *Feature Films, 1921–1930*, pp. 27, 340, 417, 11, 2, 33, 257–58, 710; trailer for *The Shock*, Division of Motion Pictures, Broadcasting and Recorded Sound, Library of Congress.

74. Robert Sklar, *Movie-Made America: A Cultural History of American Movies* (New York: Vintage Books, 1976), pp. 76–78, 81–82; Garth Jowett, *Film: The Democratic Art* (Boston: Little, Brown, 1976), pp. 69, 135, 161; Richard Schickel, *Movies: The History of an Art and an Institution* (New York: Basic Books, 1964), pp. 60–61; Molly Haskell, *From Reverence to Rape: The Treatment of Women in the Movies* (New York: Holt, Rinehart and Winston, 1975), pp. 45, 49–50, 54, 76–78.

75. *St. Johnsbury Caledonian*, 14 April, 1 July 1919; *Door to Revelation*, pp. 196–98, 225.

76. *Door to Revelation*, pp. 183, 196, 193, 231.

77. Sklar, *Movie-Made America*, pp. 87, 97–100, 228; *Door to Revelation*, pp. 196–98.

78. Pelley to Will Irwin, 2 Feb. 1925, Irwin Collection, Bancroft Library, University of California, Berkeley; *Door to Revelation*, pp. 196–97; Munden, *Feature Films, 1921–1930*, pp. 433, 257–58.

79. Pelley to Irwin, 2 Feb. 1925.

80. Ibid.; Jowett, *Film*, pp. 87–88; Sklar, *Movie-Made America*, pp. 42–47; *The International Jew: Jewish Activities in the United States*, vol. 2 [(Dearborn, Mich.: *Dearborn Independent*, 1921)], chaps. 31–32.

81. *The Fog*, p. 474; Pelley to Irwin, 2 Feb. 1925; F. Scott Fitzgerald, *The Great Gatsby* (New York: Scribner's Sons, 1925), pp. 68–74, 171–73.

82. *Door to Revelation*, pp. 209–16, 288; *Seven Minutes*, pp. 14–15.

83. *Door to Revelation*, pp. 190–98, 216–18, 224–25, 263–70; *Who's Who, 1924–25*, p. 2528; *Seven Minutes*, pp. 8–10.

84. *Drag*, pp. 3, 10, 19, 49, 62–63, 71, 77, 97, 170, 175, 151–52, 192–216.

85. Ibid., 169, 236–37, 251, 273, 276, 289, 304–5, 338–39, 349, 354.

86. Ibid., pp. 355, 351, 356, 256, 237, 272–73, 246, 243, 259.

87. *Door to Revelation*, pp. 194, 208, 218–19; "The Higher Summons," *American Magazine*, 107 (May 1929): 149–50.

88. *Door to Revelation*, pp. 217, 226, 272; *Seven Minutes*, pp. 8–10.

89. *Door to Revelation*, pp. 272, 290–92; *Seven Minutes*, p. 18, 23; *Why I Believe*, p. 19; *Door to Revelation*, pp. 52, 297, 302, 307.

90. *Seven Minutes*, pp. 47–49, 44; *Door to Revelation*, pp. 310, 316; "My Seven Minutes in Eternity," *American Magazine* 107 (March 1929): 7, 141–42.

91. *Seven Minutes*, pp. 47–48, 43; *Door to Revelation*, pp. 314–17; "My Seven Minutes," p. 142.

92. *Why I Believe*, pp. 93–94, 51; *Seven Minutes*, p. 14; "My Seven Minutes," p. 141.

93. "My Seven Minutes," p. 141; *Seven Minutes*, p. 41; William James, *The Varieties of Religious Experience: A Study in Human Nature* (rpt. New York: Modern Library, n.d.), pp. 202, 208–9, 232, 251–52.

94. Hubbard, *Philosophy of Elbert Hubbard*, pp. 77–91; *Drag*, p. 249; *Fog*, p. 444; *Why I Believe*, p. 22; Sylvia E. Bowman, *The Year 2000: A Critical Biography of Edward Bellamy* (New York: Bookman Associates, 1958), pp. 60–62; Champney, *Art and Glory*, pp. 144–50; Mary Derieux, "Starting a New Era," *Psychic Research* 22 (Jan. 1928): 1–5.

95. *Door to Revelation*, pp. 304–5, 309, 292; *Seven Minutes*, pp. 29, 27, 23.

96. *Door to Revelation*, pp. 302, 295, 46, 333; *Seven Minutes*, pp. 13, 38; "People Have Queer Notions About the Psychic Senses," *New Liberator*, 1 (June–Oct. 1930): 60–61; "If We Have Lived Other Earthly Lives Why Do We Not Consciously Remember Them?" *New Liberator* 1 (March 1930): 192; "A Great Flood of Supernal Wisdom Awaits Those Who Now Walk in Error," *Liberation* 3 (March 1932): 8.

97. *Door to Revelation*, pp. 299–301, 164, 42.

98. *Door to Revelation*, pp. 333–36; *Why I Believe*, pp. 32, 121, 123; *Seven*

Minutes, pp. 62, 64–66; [Fred Bligh Bond], "Subjective Evidence for Survival or Continuity," *Journal of the American Society for Psychical Research* 24 (Jan. 1930): 35–38.

99. *Why I Believe*, p. 32; *London Times Literary Supplement*, 30 July 1925; *The Blue Lamp* (New York: Fiction League, 1921) and *Golden Rubbish* (New York: Putnam's Sons, 1929).

100. "What Is the Mystery in Liberation Work?" *Liberation Weekly* 3 (March 4, 1933): 10.

101. *Why I Believe*, p. 63; Charles W. Ferguson, *The New Book of Revelations* (Garden City, N.Y.: Doubleday, Doran, 1929), p. 7; Paul A. Carter, *The Twenties in America* (New York: Crowell, 1968), p. 13; Kahlil Gibran, *The Prophet* ([1923]; rpt. New York: Knopf, 1966), p. 79; Bruce F. Campbell, *Ancient Wisdom Revived: A History of the Theosophical Movement* (Berkeley: University of California Press, 1980), pp. 128–37, 161–63; R. Laurence Moore, *In Search of White Crows: Spiritualism, Parapsychology, and American Culture* (New York: Oxford University Press, 1977), pp. 175–79, 185–203; Hale, *Freud and the Americans*, chap. 9; J. B. Rhine, *New Frontiers of the Mind: The Story of the Duke Experiments* (New York: Farrar and Rinehart, 1937), pp. 4, 23, 35, 41, 51–55, 272; Upton Sinclair, *Mental Radio* (Pasadena, Calif.: priv. pub., 1930).

102. Sydney E. Ahlstrom, *A Religious History of the American People* (New Haven: Yale University Press, 1972), chaps. 60–61; Gail Thain Parker, *Mind Cure in New England: From the Civil War to World War I* (Hanover, N.H.: University Press of New England, 1973), p. 10; Donald Meyer, *The Positive Thinkers: A Study of the American Quest for Health, Wealth, and Personal Power from Mary Baker Eddy to Norman Vincent Peale* (Garden City, N.Y.: Anchor Books, 1966), chaps. 1–7; John G. Cawelti, *Apostles of the Self-Made Man: Changing Concepts of Success in America* (Chicago: University of Chicago Press, 1968), chap. 6; Charles S. Braden, *Spirits in Rebellion: The Rise and Development of New Thought* (Dallas, Tex.: Southern Methodist University Press, 1963); Lawrence Chenoweth, *The American Dream of Success: The Search for the Self in the Twentieth Century* (North Scituate, Mass.: Duxbury Press, 1974), chaps. 1–2; Irvin G. Wyle, *The Self-Made Man in America: The Myth of Rags to Riches*, chap. 4.

103. "Why I Have No Quarrel with Any Existent Creed," *New Liberator* 1 (May 1930): 16–18.

104. "The Dead Are Alive and Organized!" *New Liberator* 1 (Dec. 1930–March 1931): 148; "The True Meaning of College Atheism," *New Liberator* 1 (Nov. 1930): 139; "Strange Knowledge Awaits Learning by Those Who Resent the Ban on Truth," *Liberation* 3 (March 1932): 14–21; "You Came Into Life on a Vibration That Is the Basis of Numerology," *New Liberator* 1 (June–Oct. 1930): 67; "Science is Proving What Religion Has Guessed At," *New Liberator* 1 (April 1931): 202–7; "Why We Can't See the 'Dead,'" *New Liberator* 1 (Dec.–March 1931): 162–65; "Great Flood of Supernal Wisdom," p. 13; "Every Clergyman Should Be a Psychic," *Liberation* 2 (Feb. 1932): 396; Alvin Boyd Kuhn, *Theosophy: A Modern Revival of Ancient Wisdom* (New York: Holt, 1930), pp. 2, 87–88, 147, 212, 216, 249, 292–93, 343. On pyrami-

dology, see Martin Gardner, *Fads and Fallacies in the Name of Science* (New York: Dover, 1957), chap. 15; and Braden, *Spirits in Rebellion*, p. 214.

105. "Does Your Pastor Fear to Make the Details of Heaven Too Realistic?" *New Liberator* 1 (April 1931): 214; "Are You Terrified at the Prospect of the 'Theological Day of Judgment?'" *New Liberation* 1 (Dec. 1930–March 1931): 168–78; "Have You the Poise to Take Up Psychics?" *Liberation* 3 (March 1932): 40, 43; "You Were Given a Mind for Fearless Thinking," *New Liberation* 1 (April 1931): 242.

106. "Have You the Poise?" pp. 42–43; "Details of Heaven," pp. 215–16; "Are You Terrified?" pp. 170–71; *Why I Believe*, pp. 210, 10; "Why Confusion Prevails in Reporting Details of After-Life Conditions," *New Liberator* 2 (June 1931): 36; "The Supreme Mystery," *New Liberator* 1 (June–Oct. 1930): 53; "Do You Know How to Put a Protective Armor About Your Mental Self?" *New Liberator* 2 (June 1931): 46; Moore, *In Search of White Crows*, pp. 9–10; Campbell, *Ancient Wisdom Revived*, pp. 53–56, 68.

107. "Supreme Mystery," p. 53; "Behold the Man!" *New Liberator* 1 (May 1930): 1, cover; "Protective Armor," p. 46.

108. "Suppose You Saw Men's Naked Souls," *Liberation* 3 (March 1932): 1–7, 22; "Why Do Not Those in the Higher Life Help Us Suppress Crime?" *New Liberation* 2 (July 1931): 83–84; "You Can Remember Before You Were Born!" *New Liberator* 1 (May 1930): 10; "Why You Feel Sorrow in the Face of Change," *New Liberator Weekly* 2 (21 Nov. 1931): 216; *Why I Believe*, p. 52; "If We Have Lived Other Earthly Lives Why Do We Not Consciously Remember Them?" p. 191; "You Can Remember," pp. 10–11; "Not for One Moment of Life Are You Strictly Alone!" *New Liberator Weekly* 2 (7 Nov. 1931): 162–64; "Do You Know What Your Conscience Is?" *Liberation* 3 (Mar. 1932): 32; "Who Are Your True Friends and Foes?" *Liberation* 2 (Feb. 1932): 404–7; "What Metaphysics Can Mean to You," *New Liberator* 1 (Nov. 1930): 106–11; Campbell, *Ancient Wisdom Revived*, pp. 55–56.

109. "This Magazine," *New Liberation* 1 (Dec. 1930–Mar. 1931): 183; "If You Know, You Avoid Catastrophe!" *New Liberator* 2 (June 1931): 4.

110. "You Will Alter Your Attitude Toward Morals When You Find Yourself in the Higher Life," *New Liberator* 2 (Aug.–Sept. 1931): 140–43; "Why Do Women Have 'No Use' for Women?" *Liberation* 2 (Feb. 1932), p. 388; "Does Christ Sanction Divorce?" *New Liberator* 1 (June–Oct. 1930): 90–94; "How You Will Look Upon Earthly Marriage from the After Life," *New Liberator* 1 (Aug.–Sept. 1930): 129–33; "Those in the Afterlife Have Changed Ideas On Earthly Marriage," *New Liberator* 1 (Apr. 1931): 231–36; Campbell, *Ancient Wisdom Revived*, pp. 47, 55.

111. "How to Use Money Vibration," *Liberation* 3 (Mar. 1932): 36; "Why Gross Men Acquire Great Riches," *New Liberator* 1)June–Oct. 1930): 79–81; "Do You Confuse Your Guardian Angels," *New Liberator* 1 (June–Oct. 1930): p. 73; Champney, *Art and Glory* pp. 87–91; "Silent Contact," *New Liberator* 2 (Aug.–Sept. 1931): ii; "Have You Troubles on Which You Need Help?" *New Liberator Weekly* 2 (7 Nov. 1931): iii; "Silent Contact Is the Medium for a Higher Help," *Liberation* 2 (Feb. 1932): 402–3; "Suicide Cases Receive Helpful Enlightenment," and "How This Woman Saved Her Brother

from Suicide," *Liberation* 3 (19 Feb. 1933): 11; "You Were Given a Mind for Fearless Thinking," p. 241; "Do You Know You May Have Left a Record of Great Works Behind You in Previous Lives?" *New Liberator* 1 (May 1931): 254–58; "Why Do Not Those in Higher Life Help Us Suppress Crime?" pp. 84–86; "Why the Lindbergh Crime Was Shunned by Psychics," *Liberation* 3 (8 Apr. 1933): 6–7; "Why Little Children Die in Childhood," *New Liberator* 1 (Dec. 1930–March 1931): 179–82.

112. "Do You Confuse Your Guardian Angels," p. 74; "How You Can Master the Process of Producing Thought Materializations," *Liberation* 2 (June 1931): 39–42; "How Right Contacts Are Made in Psychics," *Liberation* 3 (March 1932): 47–48; "Making Contact with the 'Dead,'" *New Liberation* 1 (June–Oct. 1930): 104–5.

113. *Door to Revelation*, pp. 354–59, 370–71, 374–75, 388–89; "Make Public Stewardship Your Profession," *Liberation* 3 (Oct. 1932): i–vi. On James Edgerton, see Braden, *Spirits in Rebellion*, pp. 211–17.

114. "People Have Queer Notions About the Psychic Senses," *New Liberator* 1 (June–Oct. 1930): 61–62; "People Hold Queer Ideas About a Spiritual Movement," *Liberation* 4 (22 July 1933): 1–3.

115. *Door to Revelation*, pp. 336–41; "This Is Not a New Religious Movement!" *New Liberator* 2 (June 1931): iii; "Are Europe's Great Money Banks Planning to Make the World a Debasing Proposal?" *New Liberator* 2 (Aug.–Sept. 1931): 104–5; "The *Liberator* Is Published Weekly from Washington," *New Liberator Weekly* 2 (7 Nov. 1931): 165–68.

116. "Supreme Mystery," p. 3; "Do You Want to Know the Future?" *New Liberator Weekly* 2 (7 Nov. 1931): 147; "The Wild Hoardes of Ghengis Khan May Swoop Again Out of Riotous Asia," *New Liberator* 1 (April 1931): 210–12; "Why the Human Race Is Allowed to Suffer Great Natural or Social Catastrophes," *New Liberator* 2 (June 1931): 6–11; "Great Flood of Supernal Wisdom," p. 12; "You Can Leap Upon the Mighty Juggernaut of World Events If You Know What Impends" (psychic reception), *New Liberator* 1 (May 1931): 288–90; "Great Souls On the 'Other Side' Have Much to Say About the Present Depression," *New Liberation* 1 (Dec. 1930–March 1931): 150–58; "A Pall Remains on the Nations Till Mankind Alters Its Thinking!" (psychic reception), *Liberation* 2 (July 1931): 56; "Why Do You Have a Money Problem?" (psychic reception), *Liberation* 3 (March 1932): 33–35; "What Great Souls on the 'Other Side' Have to Say About Tomorrow's Business," (psychic reception), *New Liberator Weekly* 2 (28 Nov. 1930): 232–34; "Great Souls on Higher Levels of the World Counsel the American Businessman," *New Liberator* 1 (April 1931): 220–26; "The Brevet," *New Liberation* 2 (June 1931): inside front cover; "What Definite Program of Change Lies Ahead for the Human Race in the Present Generation" (psychic reception), *New Liberator* 1 (April 1931): 198–200, 210; "The Immortals Are Appearing Among Us to Alter the Form of World Governments!" *New Liberator* 1 (Dec.–March 1931): 172–78; "Supreme Mystery," *New Liberator* 1 (June–Oct. 1930): 53; "You Can Be Wise Beyond Your Generation!" *New Liberator* 2 (July 1931): 50; "Strange Mutterings and Rumblings Are Heard in the East," *New Libera-*

tion 1 (May 1930): 6; "A Great Soul Appears in Japan," *New Liberation* 1 (Nov. 1930): 137; "Strange Stories Come of Christ Being Seen," *New Liberation* 2 (April 1931): 195–97; "Photograph" of Jesus in *New Liberation* 1 (June–Oct. 1930): viii; "The Riddle of the Cosmos Summed Up After Three Years of Higher Contact" (including Pelley's reply), *New Liberation* 2 (Feb. 1932): 370–75.

117. *Why I Believe,* pp. 54–56; "What Definite Program of Change Lies Ahead?" pp. 198–200; "—And This Is America!" *Liberation* 4 (24 June 1933): 12; *Door to Revelation,* pp. 322–23.

118. "What Great Souls on the 'Other Side' Have to Say About the Trend in Russia and Italy," *New Liberator Weekly* 2 (14 Nov. 1931): 176–79, iii; "The Marplots Are Slated for Disaster," *New Liberator Weekly* 2 (14 Nov. 1931): 169–72; "Hoover's Super-Bank Plan," *New Liberator Weekly* 2 (28 Nov. 1931): 230; "What Can Be Done by the Individual to Save Civilization?" *New Liberator Weekly* 2 (5 Dec. 1931): 252–53; "Is a Divine Miracle Around the Corner?" *New Liberator Weekly* 2 (28 Nov. 1931): 224; "The Strange Conduct of President Hoover," *New Liberator Weekly* 2 (21 Nov. 1931): 193–97; "Why Has This Book Wierdly Disappeared?" *New Liberator Weekly* 2 (12 Dec. 1931): 269–73; "To Whom Were You Referring, Mr. Hoover?" *New Liberator Weekly* 2 (14 Nov. 1931): 173–75; "Is Mr. Hearst Dumb or Has He Acquired a Bullet-Proof Vest?" *New Liberator Weekly* 2 (5 Dec. 1931): 249; "Does This Mean Riot in Washington Soon?" *New Liberator Weekly* 2 (28 Nov. 1931): 217–22; "Does Your Pastor Dare Make Reply?" *New Liberator Weekly* 2 (12 Dec. 1931): 274–77; "Suppose Money Vanishes from American Life," *Liberation* 3 (Oct. 1932): 85–90; "You Are Threatened by World Plotting for Revolution," *New Liberator Weekly* 2 (28 Nov. 1931): 226–29; "The Marplots Are Slated for Disaster," pp. 169–72; "The Most Eventful Year in Human History May Lie Ahead," *New Liberator Weekly* 2 (19 Dec. 1931): 311; "The Marplots Reply on Your Ignorance!" *New Liberator Weekly* 2 (12 Dec. 1931): 265–68; "What Will Follow the Depression?" *Liberation* 3 (Oct. 1932): 94; Ernest M. Palmer, "Did You Know That Christ Was Not a Jew?" *New Liberator Weekly* 2 (19 Dec. 1931): 298–301; Pelley, *Door to Revelation,* pp. 337, 358.

119. "The Block and the Wedge," *Pelley's—The Silver Shirt Weekly* (cited hereafter as *Pelley's Weekly*) 1 (15 Jan. 1936): 4.

120. Pelley, *Door to Revelation,* pp. 197–98, 288–89; Pelley, *Seven Minutes,* pp. 14–15; *Why I Believe,* pp. 16–17; "Silver Shirts Mean to Fight Universal Vulgarization," *Liberation* 4 (8 July 1933): 4–5.

121. Khun, *Theosophy,* pp. 22–25; Norman Cohn, *Warrant for Genocide: The Myth of the Jewish World-Conspiracy and the Protocols of the Elders of Zion* (New York: Harper Torchbooks, 1969), pp. 100–101; Jean-Michael Angebert, *The Occult and the Third Reich: The Mystical Origins Of Nazism and the Search for the Holy Grail,* trans. Lewis A. M. Sumberg (New York: Macmillan, 1974), pp. 62–64.

122. *HUAC,* p. 7329; "What Is a White Man?" *Pelley's Weekly* 2 (5 Aug. 1936): 4; *Door to Revelation,* pp. 358–68; "Why German-Americans Should

Support the Commonwealth," *Pelley's Weekly* 1 (4 March 1936): 4; Percy W. Birdwell, "Louis T. McFadden," *Dictionary of American Biography* (New York: Scribner's Sons, 1958), p. 410.

123. William Dudley Pelley, *Forty-five Questions Most Frequently Asked About the Jews with the Answers* (Asheville, N.C.: Pelley Publishers, 1939), pp. 8, 15–16, 35; "What Is a White Man?" p. 4; "Great Pyramid Prophecy Comes True on the Dot," *Liberation* 3 (18 Feb. 1933): 3.

124. *Forty-five Questions*, pp. 36, 40, 14, 17, 21, 24, 27, 30, 33, 36–37; *No More Hunger: An Exposition of Christian Democracy* (Asheville, N.C.: Foundation for Christian Economics, 1933), pp. 137–42.

125. *No More Hunger*, p. 142; "The Real Inside Story of the Rise of Rothschild," *Liberation* 5 (27 Jan. 1934): 4–6; "The Dead Bodies of Colonials Began International Banking," *Liberation* 4 (13 May 1933): 5–6; "What Farmers Should Know About Farm Foreclosures," *Liberation* 4 (20 May 1933): 1–4; "Jewish Persecutions Have Nothing to Do with Religion," *Liberation* 5 (11 Nov. 1933): 8; "More Hoaxing to Bedevil the Dizzied Gentile," *Liberation* 4 (19 Aug. 1933): 5; *Door to Revelation*, pp. 136–39; *Forty-five Questions*, pp. 45–46; *There Is a Jewish World Plot—Jews Say So* (Asheville, N.C.: Pelly Publishers, n.d.), pp. 15–16; "She Sobbed in Midnight with No One to See," *Liberation* 5 (29 Oct. 1933): 7–8; "The Mystery of the Civil War and Lincoln's Death," *Liberation* 5 (10 Feb. 1934): 1–4; "Shall Gullible Gentiles Spill All Their Business Secrets?" *Liberation* 5 (2 Sept. 1933): 2; "What Silver Shirts Must Know About Our Federal Reserve," *Liberation* 4 (27 May 1933): 1–2; "Don't Be Fooled by Startling Propaganda," *Liberation* 6 (17 March 1934): 1; "Americans, Get Ready to Save Your Country from Chaos!" *Liberation* 4 (3 June 1933): 2; "Our Ship of State Sails Away to Meet Mr. Finkelstein," *Liberation* 5 (26 Aug. 1933): 1.

126. "Did Benjamin Franklin Say This About the Hebrews?" *Liberation* (3 Feb. 1934): 5; Charles A. Beard, "Exposing the Anti-Semitic Forgery about Benjamin Franklin," *Jewish Frontier* 2 (March 1935): 10–13.

127. "Will You Help Regain Control of Runaway Officialdom?" *Liberation* 4 (15 May 1933): 1–3; "Facts You Should Know About Political 'Remedies,'" *Liberation* 4 (6 May 1933): 1–3, 11; *No More Hunger*, pp. 148–49; *Door to Revelation*, pp. 429–30; "The Battle Score of Futile Barucheracy," *Liberation* 5 (2 Sept. 1933): 8; "This Nation Must Come to Christian Democracy," *Liberation* 4 (20 May 1933): 5; "Exactly Where Roosevelt Stands," *Liberation* 5 (11 Nov. 1933): 1; "Don't Be Fooled by Startling Propaganda," *Liberation* 6 (17 March 1934): 3; *There Is a Jewish World Plot*, pp. 2–3, 75; "Not State Socialization, But Protocolism!" *Liberation* 6 (14 April 1934): 1.

128. Germany's Jews Give the Lie to Scheming American Zionists," *Liberation* 4 (12 Aug. 1933): 1; "Dead Bodies of Colonials," pp. 5–6; "Futile Barucheracy," p. 8; *What Every Congressman Should Know* (Asheville, N.C.: Pelley Publishers, n.d.), p. 48; Pelley, *There Is a Jewish World Plot*, p. 77; "The American Civil Liberties Union Is Ugly Communism!" *Liberation* 5 (21 Oct. 1933): 1–4, 11; "Judaized Chief Executive," *Liberation* 5 (27 Jan. 1934): 8; "Jews Use Christian Science," *Pelley's Weekly* 1 (13 May 1936): 1–2; "All I

"All I Know Is What I Don't Read in the Papers," *Pelley's Weekly* 1 (26 Feb. 1936): 6.

129. *Door to Revelation*, pp. 25, 36; "The Silver Shirts Rewrite the Declaration of Independence," *Liberation* 5 (17 Feb. 1934): 1–3. See also *Little Visits*, Pelley's occasional magazine containing "sublime" biographies of "souls showing courage," including Christopher Columbus, Benjamin Franklin, Tom Paine, and John Cotton. The model for this series was Elbert Hubbard's *Little Journeys*.

130. "Will the Silver Shirts Decide American Affairs in 1934?" *Liberation* 5 (30 Dec. 1933): 1–2; "Fair Play to All Jews Commands Frank Statement of Facts," *Liberation* 4 (8 July 1933): 2; *Forty-five Questions*, p. 43; "Water-Bars and Pot Holes on the Road to Ruin," *Liberation* 5 (27 Jan. 1934): 7; "What Life's Higher Mentors Think About Russia" (psychic reception), *Liberation* 3 (15 April 1933): 8; "Pyramid Prophecy Comes True on the Dot!" p. 4; "Walter Winchell Gets Excited Over the Silver Shirts," *Liberation* 4 (6 May 1933): 4; "Meet Stephen S. Wise of the Jewish Rabbinate!" *Liberation* 5 (6 Jan. 1934): 5–6; "Silvershirts Gain Suddenly," *Pelley's Weekly* 2 (8 July 1936): 2; "Cogitations," *New Liberation* 7 (Feb. 1937): 11.

131. "Cogitations," *New Liberation* 7 (Jan. 1937): 11; *Forty-five Questions*, p. 43.

132. "Are You Revolutionary-Minded Through Jewish Entertainment?" *Liberation* 4 (14 Oct. 1933): 5–6, 11; "Hollywood in Government but Suppose Something Snaps," *Liberation* 4 (13 Aug. 1933): 4; "The World, the Flesh, and Withal the Devil" (psychic reception), *Liberation* 5 (13 Jan. 1934): 7–8; "The Mask is Now Stripped from the Movie Monopoly!" *Liberation* 5 (13 Jan. 1934): 1–2; "Not Passed by the National Board of Censors," *Liberation* 5 (13 Jan. 1934): 5–6; "Poor Old George Arliss Becomes a Jewish Propagandist," *Liberation* 5 (27 Jan. 1934): 1–3; "Has Your Child Learned to Applaud Murder Yet?" *Liberation* 4 (15 July 1933): 6; "Behind the Silver Screen," *Pelley's Weekly* 1 (22 Jan. 1936): 4.

133. "Sugar Coated Communism for American Movie Audiences," p. 11.

134. "Has Your Child Learned?" p. 5; "Mask Now Stripped," p. 2; *Door to Revelation*, pp. 188–89, 197–98.

135. *Door to Revelation*, pp. 188, 197–98; "Don't Be Bamboozled by This Syphilis Tommyrot," *Liberation* 9 (14 June 1938): 11; "More About Syphilis," *Liberation* 9 (21 July 1938): 9.

136. *United States* v. *McWilliams*, 54 F.Supp. 791, *Transcript*, Acc. 64-A-379, Loc. 16/79-31-1, p. 16,901; Washington National Records Center, Suitland, Maryland; "Leadership in this Crisis Must Be Utterly Sincere," *Liberation* 4 (22 July 1933): 4–5; "Many a Man Has Lost His Job by Taking a Vacation," *Liberation* 4 (15 July 1933): 2, 9; "A Nation Burns as Little Souls Squabble Over Fire Helmets," *Liberation* 5 (18 Nov. 1933): 1–3, 10; *Door to Revelation*, pp. 414–15; "Split Society by Ideas," *Pelley's Weekly* 2 (1 July 1936): 8; "All I Know," p. 6.

137. "What Higher Mentors Say of 'The Emptiness of Israel,'" *Liberation* 4 (6 May 1933): 8–9; "'The Emptiness of Israel' Seen from Higher Levels," *Liberation* 4 (13 May 1933): 8–9.

138. "We Go with Sure Purpose Undaunted by Deceits," *Liberation* 5 (16 Sept. 1933): 2.

139. "People Hold Queer Ideas," p. 1; "Pitfalls are Fallacies," *Liberation* 4 (5 Aug. 1933): 12; *HUAC*, p. 7330; *Door to Revelation*, p. 400.

140. "Know the Stairs of Your Turret and the Majesty of Stars!" *Liberation* 3 (4 March 1933): cover; "Men Fighting for Public Order Are Not Revolutionaries," *Liberation* 3 (25 Feb. 1933): cover; "Why the Human Race Lauds Personal Chivalry" (psychic reception), *Liberation* 3 (12 March 1933): 8–9; "We Must Recast Ourselves in a More Heroic Mold!" *Liberation* 3 (18 March 1933): 2–3; "Whence This Sound of Marching in Morning Mystic Gray?" and "Chamberlains of Valor," *Liberation* 3 (18 Feb. 1933): 1–2; *Door to Revelation*, pp. 396, 436.

141. "Pelley Arrest Called for in Sheriff's Circular," *The Hour*, no. 20 (18 Nov. 1939): 4; John Roy Carlson (pseud. for Avedis Derounian), *Under Cover: My Four Years in the Nazi Underworld of America* (New York: Dutton, 1943), pp. 398–99; *HUAC*, p. 7264; Robert Carlyle Summerville, "Chief," in *Door to Revelation: An Intimate Biography* (Asheville, N.C.: Foundation Fellowship, 1936), n.p.

142. *HUAC*, pp. 7224–25, 7234, 7212, 7285, 7226; "Money Is Secondary," *Liberation* 5 (30 Sept. 1933): 12; Robert Summerville, "Just What Is the Silver Legion?" *Liberation* 5 (14 Oct. 1933): 10–11.

143. "Battle Hymn of the Silver Shirts," *Liberation* 3 (18 Feb. 1933): 4; "Boots and Saddles," *Liberation* 5 (14 Oct. 1933): 12; "Dispatch Number One," quoted in *HUAC*, pp. 7227–34; Robert Summerville, "Just What Is the Silver Legion?" pp. 10–11; Robert Summerville "What Silver Shirts Think of Race Prejudice," *Liberation* 5 (3 Feb. 1934): 9; Donnell B. Portzline, "William Dudley Pelley and the Silver Shirt Legion of America," (unpub. Ph.D. diss., Ball State University, 1965), pp. 36–37.

144. "Cogitations," *Pelley's Weekly* 2 (26 Aug. 1936): 5; "Walter Winchell Gets Excited," pp. 4–5; "The Challenge of This Crisis," *Liberation* 4 (19 Aug. 1933): 12; "The Silver Juggernaut?" *Liberation* 5 (10 Feb. 1934): 12; *HUAC*, p. 7263; Summerville, "Just What Is the Silver Legion?" pp. 10–11.

145. *HUAC*, pp. 7211–12; Werly, "Millenarian Right," chap. 8.

146. *HUAC*, pp. 7209, 7274; "The Liberation Scribe," *Liberation* 5 (2 Sept. 1933): 10; "Consolation for the Squeamish Regarding Our Program," *Liberation* 5 (16 Sept. 1933): 7–8; "Should Not Free Men Criticize?" *New Liberator Weekly* 2 (28 Nov. 1931): 230; "Facts You Should Know About Political 'Remedies,'" pp. 1–3, 11; *Door to Revelation*, pp. 429–30; "The Coming Class War," *Liberation* 6 (31 March 1934): 12; "Cogitations," *Pelley's Weekly* 2 (26 Aug. 1936): 5; "C. Oliver Dean," *Liberation* 6 (31 March 1934): 11; "Chief Pelley Repudiates Maverick Silver Shirts," *Liberation* 6 (14 April 1934): 10–11; "People Hold Queer Ideas," pp. 1–3.

147. Werly, "Milleniarian Right," pp. 221–22, 236, 243, 253–54, 259–61.

148. "All the World Is Waiting for the Son Rise," *Liberation* 4 (8 July 1933): 8; "Christ or Chaos," *Pelley's Weekly* 1 (29 Jan. 1936): 1; *HUAC*, pp. 7218, 7272; *Door to Revelation*, pp. 429–30.

149. *Door to Revelation*, p. 430; "Cogitations," *Pelley's Weekly* 2 (26 Aug.

1936): 5–6; "Undaunted by Deceits," p. 2; "The Judan Mountains Labor and Bring Forth Mice," *Liberation* 5 (10 Feb. 1934): 10; "Action That Scours," *Liberation* 5 (13 Jan. 1934): 12; "The Silver Shirts Are Gathering!" *Liberation* 3 (18 Feb. 1933): 2.

150. Werly, "Milleniarian Right," pp. 228, 239–40, 261–63, 275–76, 292; U.S. Congress, House of Representatives, Special Committee on Un-American Activities, *Investigation of Nazi Propaganda and Investigation of Certain Other Propaganda Activities.* 73d Cong., 2d sess., 1934–35, *Hearings,* 7 Aug. 1934, pp. 4–11; "Zachary Counsels Silvershirts," *Liberation* 11 (21 Oct. 1939): 3; "Behold Democracy in Chicago!" *Liberation* 12 (28 Jan. 1940): 1–2, 10; *New York Herald-Tribune* 31 March 1934; *New York Times,* 25 Oct. 1939; *New York Post,* 24 Oct. 1939; Werly, "Millenarian Right," pp. 227–28, 239–41, 275–76, 287, 292.

151. "Action That Scours," p. 12; "Get the Name of Every Jew Who Intimidates a Gentile," *Liberation* 5 (10 Feb. 1934): 6.

152. "Our Ship of State," pp. 1, 4; "Will France Go Nazi?" *Pelley's Weekly* 2 (29 July 1936): 8; "Made-to-Order Turmoil Overseas," *Pelley's Weekly* 1 (29 Jan. 1936): 7; *What Every Congressman Should Know,* p. 57; "Winchell Gets Excited," p. 4; "Pelley Refused the Air!" *Liberation* 4 (27 May 1933): 10–11; "Why German-Americans Should Support," p. 4; "Dead Bodies of Colonials," pp. 5–6; "The Judan Swarm Is Coming and Americans Must Like It!" *Liberation* 5 (11 Nov. 1933): 1–3, 11; "Pyramid Prophecy Comes True on the Dot," p. 3; "The Fight Grows Dangerous as Judah Becomes Desparate," *Liberation* 5 (3 Feb. 1934): 1–2; *Door to Revelation,* p. 310; *HUAC,* pp. 7216–17, 7237–39, 7268; *United States* v. *McWilliams, Transcript,* pp. 16,026, 16,818; Sander A. Diamond, *The Nazi Movement in the United States 1924–1941* (Ithaca, N.Y.: Cornell University Press, 1974), pp. 244, 318.

153. "Know America After Collapse," *Pelley's Weekly* 1 (1 April 1935): 1; "What Farmers Should Know," p. 3; "Nations Await Jewish Coup," *Pelley's Weekly* 2 (10 June 1936): 1; "Our Ship of State," p. 4; "Silver Shirts Are Marching," *Liberation* 5 (26 Aug. 1933): 12; "Who Says I Can't Stop Communism?" *Pelley's Weekly* 1 (29 Jan. 1936): 2; *Door to Revelation,* p. 400.

154. *No More Hunger,* pp. 14, 60–61.

155. Ibid., pp. 30, 37–39, 118–33, 67, 18–19, 12, 79, 6–7, 97–98, 7, 171–74, 20–22; "Remember Edward Bellamy's Parable of the Water Tank?" *Liberation* 3 (25 March 1933): 5; *Something Better: How to Bring the Christian Commonwealth* (Noblesville, Ind.: Soulcraft Chapels, 1952), pp. 62, 158; "Your Child Worth $750 Year," *Pelley's Weekly* 1 (4 March 1936): 1. Bellamy was curious about parapsychological phenomena but not a committed spiritualist, let alone an "adept psychic."

156. *No More Hunger,* pp. 100, 73, 10, 116, 47, 79; "General Electric Swope Now Offers a Plan," *Liberation* 5 (18 Nov. 1933): 4–6, 11; "Clean Your Institutions, Don't Overthrow Them," *Liberation* 3 (4 March 1933): 3; "This Is Not a Contest Between Labor and Capital!" *Liberation* 3 (31 March 1934): 6–7; R. Alan Lawson, *The Failure of Independent Liberalism, 1930–1941* (New York: Putnam's Sons, 1971), pp. 44–45, 210.

157. *No More Hunger,* pp. 10, 83–86, 65, 117.

158. Ibid., pp. 12, 30, 10.

159. Ibid., pp. 79, 89–93, 11; "Silver Shirts Mean to Fight Universal Vulgarization," *Liberation* 4 (8 July 1934): 4.

160. "Cogitations," *Pelley's Weekly* 2 (1 July 1936): 6, 8.

161. Ibid., p. 1; *No More Hunger,* pp. 69, 64, 70, 76; "Liberate Wives Financially," *Pelley's Weekly* 1 (26 Feb. 1936): 1.

162. "Reds Coax Blacks to Race Equality," *Pelley's Weekly* 2 (15 July 1936): 2; "Americans Face Menace of Negro Revolution," *Pelley's Weekly* 1 (12 Feb. 1936): 3; "Cogitations," *Pelley's Weekly* 2 (22 July 1936): 2; *St. Johnsbury Caledonian,* 21 Feb. 1919.

163. *No More Hunger,* pp. 19, 24–25; *HUAC,* p. 7260; "How I Would Treat the Jews," *Pelley's Weekly* 1 (6 May 1936): 1; "Why German-Americans Should Support," p. 4.

164. *No More Hunger,* pp. 23–24, 48; "Suppose a Mystical Adept Should Head This Nation," *Liberation* 3 (25 Feb. 1933): 5.

165. *HUAC,* pp. 7305, 7301, 7312–16; *Door to Revelation,* pp. 252–54; "Put Your Money Under the Auspices of a Militant Christian Institution!" *Liberation* 3 (March 1932): ii; *New York Times,* 30 April 1934.

166. *HUAC,* pp. 7330, 7309, 7312, 7331; *New York Times,* 29 Aug. 1939.

167. John J. Smertenko, "Hitlerism Comes to America," *Harper's Magazine* 167 (Nov. 1933): 663; Harold Lavine, "Fifth Column 'Literature,'" *Saturday Review of Literature* 22 (14 Sept. 1940): 2; Samuel Levenson, "Pelley's Kampf," *Christian Century* 57 (10 April 1940): 4; Arthur Graham, "Carzy Like a Fox: Pelley of the Silver Shirts," *New Republic* 78 (18 April 1934): 264–65; Nathanael West, *A Cool Million,* in *Two Novels by Nathanael West* (New York: Noonday Press, 1969); Walter Goodman, *The Committee: The Extraordinary Career of the House Committee on Un-American Activities* (Baltimore: Penguin Books, 1969), pp. 9–11.

168. *HUAC* pp. 7314–15, 7323; *New York Times,* 23, 25 April, 2, 24, 27 May 1934; Pelley to All Loyal Silver Shirts, 27 June 1934, William Wirt Collection, Lilly Library, Indiana University; Werly, "Millenarian Right," p. 43; Geoffrey S. Smith, *To Save A Nation: American Countersubversives, the New Deal, and the Coming of World War II* (New York: Basic Books, 1973), pp. 64–65.

169. Pelley to All Loyal Silver Shirts; *Door to Revelation,* pp. 454, 467; *New York Times,* 22 Nov. 1934; 23 Jan. 1935; *HUAC,* pp. 7206–7, 7238; Floyd Hatfield, "The Case of William Dudley Pelley," *Liberation* 12 (14 March 1940): 1–2, 11; Werly, "Millenarian Right," pp. 45–46.

170. Pelley to All Loyal Silver Shirts; *HUAC,* pp. 72–73, 7325, 7207, 7204.

171. *Seven Minutes,* p. 8; *Door to Revelation,* pp. 424, 403; *HUAC,* pp. 7319, 7321, 7295–7333; "Live in the Land of the Sky!" *Liberation* 3 (Oct. 1932): v.

172. *Door to Revelation,* pp. 455–58; *HUAC,* pp. 7252–53; "Christian Party Is Autumn Dark Horse," *Pelley's Weekly* 1 (15 Jan. 1936): 1; "Minnesota Close to Red Abyss," *Pelley's Weekly* 1 (22 Jan. 1936): 1; "Get Ready to Save Your Country," pp. 1–4; "Split Society by Ideas," p. 8; "Huey Long Isn't

Dead, Jews Keep Rulership," *Pelley's Weekly* 1 (5 Feb. 1936): 3; "Christian Party's Great Aim, Recreate Happier Family Life," *Pelley's Weekly* 1 (26 Feb. 1936): 1; "Chief Answers Townsendite Who Bemoans Party Stand," *Pelley's Weekly* 1 (12 Feb. 1936): 5; "The Quick and the Dead," from *Editorials in Pelley's Weekly* (Asheville, N.C.: Pelley's Weekly, 1936), n.p.

173. "Chief Answers Townsendite," p. 5; "Enter King's Chamber Today," *Pelley's Weekly* 2 (16 Sept. 1936): 1; Werly, "Millenarian Right," pp. 206–7.

174. "The Cart with Silver Wheels Rolls Forward," *New Liberation* 7 (Jan. 1937): 1–2; "Why You Should Keep Your Faith in Pyramid Prophecy," *New Liberation* 2 (Jan. 1937): 7, 15; "How God's Plan Was Served by Roosevelt's Re-Election," *New Liberation* 7 (Jan. 1937): 9; Leon Festinger et al., *When Prophecy Fails: A Social and Psychological Study of a Modern Group That Predicted the Destruction of the World* (New York: Harper Torchbooks, 1964).

175. "Why You Should Keep Your Faith," p. 7; "Cogitations," *New Liberation* 7 (Jan. 1937): 13–14; "Not for Publication," *New Liberation* 7 (Jan. 1937): 15; "Not for Publication," *New Liberation* 7 (June 1937): 15; *Earth Comes: Design for Materialization* (n.p., 1939); *Behold Life: Design for Liberation* (1939; 3rd ed., Noblesville, Ind.: Soulcraft Chapels, 1950).

176. "Why German-Americans Should Support," p. 4; "Heavy Meetings in Washington State," *Pelley's Weekly* 2 (4 Oct. 1936): 7; "What Chief Pelley Would Do for America's Indians!" *New Liberation* 7 (Feb. 1937): 9–10; "The Great Spirit Still Speaking," *New Liberation* 7 (Feb. 1937): 15; "Pelley Sues Ickes for Fraud and Thievery," *Liberation* 8 (28 May 1938): 1; "The Suit That Means the Peak of New Deal Radicalism," *Liberation* 8 (28 May 1938): 2–6; Jacob Thorkelson, *Who Are the Communists?* (Asheville, N.C.: Pelley Publishers, n.d.); George Van Horn Moseley, *"Thank God, the Constitution Still Gives Us the Right to Bear Arms"* (Asheville, N.C.: Pelley Publishers, 1939).

177. "Napoleon and the Jews," *Liberation* 9 (21 July 1938): 4; "The Red Stars of Hollywood," *Liberation* 12 (7 March 1940): 5, 8; "Holiday Movies, Propaganda Style," *Liberation* 12 (14 Jan. 1940): 6, 9; "Sick Movies," *Liberation* 13 (14 July 1940): 5; "Oh Say Can You See?" *Liberation* 13 (28 July 1940): 5; "Revolutionary Tactics in Detroit Challenge to Silvershirts," *New Liberation* 7 (May 1937): 2; "The Moment Is at Hand to Impeach Roosevelt," *Liberation* 10 (28 Jan. 1939): 1–2; "'True Confessions About My Daze' by Eleanor Glide Rossocampo," *Liberation* 10 (7 Jan. 1939): 6–8; "Make John Garner U.S. President," *New Liberation* 7 (21 Aug. 1937): 1; "Aren't We All?" *Liberation Weekly* 8 (28 Feb. 1939): 2; "More Details You Have Been Awaiting About Franklin D. Roosevelt's Ancestry," *Liberation* 9 (28 Oct. 1938): 6–8; "Rothschilds Need Help S-O-S World's Jews," *Liberation* 9 (7 June 1938): 3.

178. "Why the Silvershirts Oppose the Jew Religiously," *Liberation* 9 (28 Sept. 1938): 8; "Seriously, What Is to Become of the Jew?" *Liberation* 9 (14 Oct. 1938): 1–2, 10–11; "What Every Gentile Should Know About the Talmud and the Protocols," *New Liberation* 8 (7 Nov. 1937): 6; "Rothschilds Need Help," pp. 2–4; "We Don't Want Pogroms for Reasons of Our Own," *Liberation Weekly* 8 (28 April 1938): 4–5.

179. "Israel's Darkest Hour," *New Liberation* 8 (28 Dec. 1937): 2–3; "Business Clubs Begin Discussions of Disfranchising Jews," *Liberation* 9 (14 May 1939): 3–4; "'The Times of the Gentiles' Gleam Brighter for 1938," *Liberation Weekly* 8 (14 Jan. 1938): 6; "The Nation Now Seeks Brain," *Liberation* 8 (7 March 1938): 1; "Is the Iceberg About to Melt?" *Liberation* 9 (28 May 1939): 12; "Terminating a Cycle," *Liberation* 9 (7 Nov. 1938): 11.

180. "Does Roosevelt Get All Proceeds of Birthday Paralysis Balls?" *Liberation* 10 (28 March 1939): 3; FDR, Memorandum for the Attorney General, 21 April 1938; Stephen Early to J. Edgar Hoover, 26 Oct. 1937; TOI to Marguerite LeHand, 15 Dec. 1938; FDR, Memorandum for Mr. McIntyre, December 1938, both in OF 3205; Stephen Early, Memorandum for the Attorney General, 17 May 1939; Frank Murphy to Early, 15 Aug. 1939, both in PPF 1, Whispering Campaigns file, Franklin D. Roosevelt Library (FDRL).

181. "Dies Probe of Silvershirts Postponed for Present," *Liberation* 9 (7 Nov. 1938): 3–4; "Dickstein in Ash-Can as Probe Bill Backfires," *Liberation* 9 (14 June 1938): 1–2; "Fake, Fiction, and Flub-dub That the Dies Committee Makes No Attempt to Refute or Deny," *Liberation* 11 (14 Nov. 1938): 6–8; "By Their Deeds Are They Known," *Liberation* 10 (21 May 1939): 12; "The Dies Committee Is Illegal and Operating Unlawfully," *Liberation* 11 (28 June 1939): 3–4; "The Dies Committee Goes Fascist," *New Liberation* 9 (7 Oct. 1939): 3; "Jordan Road Sho Am Hard!" *Liberation* 11 (21 Sept. 1939): 12; "Representative Dies Strikes Back at Silvershirt Chief," *Liberation* 11 (28 Aug. 1939): 6; "Three Million Dollars!" *Liberation* 11 (28 Aug. 1939): 2; "The Dies-Pelley Lawsuit May Shape Current History," *Liberation* 11 (28 Aug. 1939): 9.

182. "Why I Gave the Dies Probers My Blessing," *Liberation* 12 (21 Feb. 1940): 2–4; "The Probers," *Liberation* 11 (28 Sept. 1939): 8–9; "What the Liberation Movement Must Fight to a Show-Down," *Liberation* 12 (21 March 1940): 5; August Raymond Ogden, *The Dies Committee: A Study of the Special House Committee for the Investigation of Un-American Activities, 1938–1943* (Washington, D.C.: Catholic University Press, 1943), p. 127; "The Weapon Used in the Present Crack-Down," *Liberation* 11 (14 Oct. 1939): 3; "American Jurisprudence, 1939!" *Liberation* 11 (14 Oct. 1939): 5; "Judge Nettles' Denunciation Backfires Nationally," *Liberation* 11 (21 Nov. 1939): 12.

183. "Why I Gave the Dies Probers My Blessing," pp. 2–4; Goodman, *The Committee*, pp. 90–95; Smith, *To Save a Nation*, p. 146; Werly, "Millenarian Right," pp. 56–57.

184. "Why I Gave the Dies Probers My Blessing," p. 4; *HUAC*, pp. 7218, 7216, 7237–8, 7247, 7290, 7295; Ogden, *Dies Committee*, p. 189.

185. "The Pelley Appeal Verdict," *Roll-Call*, 1 (28 April 1941): 13–14; "New Pelley Fight Looms as Appeal Is Denied," *Roll-Call* 1 (21 April 1941): 5–6; "Why I Gave the Dies Probers My Blessing," pp. 3–4; *Indianapolis Star*, 21 Jan. 1942.

186. *No More Hunger*, pp. 158–59, 163–65; *Door to Revelation*, pp. 101, 103; "Japan Merits Friends, Not Vicious Critics!" *New Liberation* 8 (7 Oct. 1937): 2.

187. "German Jews Get What They Asked For," *Liberation* 9 (7 Nov. 1938): 1–2; "Jewish Atrocity Fables," *Liberation* 10 (14 Feb. 1939): 2; "Hitler's Beth-Haven Programs Brings Jewish Screech," *Liberation* 12 (7 Dec. 1939): 3; "Baron Von Steuben," *Liberation* 12 (7 Dec. 1939): 3; "The Coming World Axis," *Liberation* 9 (7 July 1938): 3; "How Czechoslovakia Was Created by Fraud," *Liberation* 9 (7 Aug. 1938): 4–5; "Behind Bunk and Funk in Czechoslovakia," *Liberation* 9 (14 Sept. 1938): 1–3, 11; "American Jews on Hotter Spot as Hitler Absorbs Czechs," *Liberation* 10 (21 March 1939): 3; "History Was Made in 1938," *Liberation* 10 (21 Jan. 1939): 10; "Need More Be Said at the Present Moment?" *Liberation* 11 (21 Aug. 1939): 5; "Berlin-Moscow Pact Gives Reds First Inkling of Their Duping," *Liberation* 11 (21 Aug. 1939): 8–9; "Let Us Clean Our Own Household Before Essaying to Clean Europe's," *Liberation* 11 (7 Oct. 1939): 6–7; "The Chief of the Silvershirts Won't Be Stampeded," *Liberation* 11 (21 Aug. 1939): 3–4; "What You Should Know About the 'British' Government," *Liberation* 11 (7 Sept. 1939): 3–4; "Millions Are Sensing What Is Wrong About This War," *Liberation* 11 (14 Sept. 1939): 3–4; "Winston Churchill," *Liberation* 11 (14 Sept. 1939): 9; "France Eats Crow!" *Liberation* 13 (14 June 1940): 2; *After Dictators, What?* (Asheville, N.C.: Pelley Publishers, n.d.), p. 49.

188. "Catch Your Spies!" *Liberation* 11 (7 Oct. 1939): 2; "Drastic Change Ordered," *Liberation* 12 (14 Feb. 1940): 1–2; "To My National Compatriots," *Liberation* 12 (14 Feb. 1940): 2–5; "Behind the Propaganda," p. 2; "And Now, a Higher Octave," *Liberation* 13 (28 Nov. 1940): 1–4; "We Are Pro-Christian and Pro-American," *Liberation* 12 (7 April 1940): 1; *Indianapolis Star*, 28 Dec. 1940; *Indianapolis News*, 25 Dec. 1940.

189. "Where Do We Go From Here?" *Liberation* 12 (14 May 1940): 12; "Courage That Is Quiet," *Liberation* 13 (21 June 1940): 9.

190. "Shall We Let 'Them' Regiment Our Daughters?" *Roll-Call* 1 (5 May 1941): 5–6; "What Nation Is the Real Aggressor?" *Roll-Call* 1 (24 March 1941): 10; "Stripping United States Army to 'Aid' Britain Is Not a Joke," *Roll-Call* 1 (24 March 1941): 4; "Pelley's Book in Japan," *Roll-Call* 1 (26 May 1941): 15; "When Americans Grasp Loss of Liberties, What Then?" *Roll-Call* 1 (24 Feb. 1941): 1; "If Hitler Had Every Ship on Earth, He Could Not Invade United States," *Roll-Call* 1 (28 April 1941): 7; "Why International Bankers Have Financed Bolshevism," *Roll-Call* 1 (7 April 1941): 3–4; "Are We in the United States of Lehman Brothers?" *Roll-Call* 1 (14 April 1941): 1–2, 10; "Krazy Kosher Entertainment Racket," *Roll-Call* 2 (22 Sept. 1941): 11; "Shoot 'Em on Sight," *Roll-Call* 2 (22 Sept. 1941): 16; "Kosher Yeast," *Roll-Call* 2 (21 Sept. 1941): 3; "America First, Last," *Roll-Call* 2 (1 Dec. 1941): 5–6.

191. Pelley to Dear Colleague, 12 Dec. 1941, Miscellaneous Pelley File, Hoover Institution; *After Dictators, What?* pp. 5, 12, 14, 16, 19, 22–23, 26, 29, 31, 42, 7, 51; "War Is the Expedient Used by the Mentors," *Galilean* 1 (5 Jan. 1942): 12; "Why Britain, as a Piscean Empire, Confronts Defeat," *Galilean* 1 (2 Feb. 1941): 5; *Nations-in-Law: An Unconventional Interpretation* ([1935]; 3rd ed., Noblesville, Ind.: Soulcraft Fellowship, 1956), pp. 384–465.

192. Pelley to Dear Colleague, 12 Dec. 1941; *New York Times*, 4 Aug.

1942; "Enlisted Winchell Smears Superiors," *Galilean* 1 (12 Jan. 1942): 12; "Gale Over Galilee," *Galilean* 1 (22 Dec. 1941): 3; "The Resplendent Order on Its Way," *Galilean* 1 (5 Jan. 1942): 1; "The Role the Almighty Decrees America to Play," *Galilean* 1 (22 Dec. 1941): 10; "Nippon Grabs the Lead," *Galilean* 1 (29 Dec. 1941): 12; "America Concurs in No Scheme to Regulate Earth," *Galilean* 1 (19 Jan. 1942): 4.

193. FDR, Memorandum for Hoover, 21 Jan. 1942, PSF 76, FDRL; *Door to Revelation*, pp. 405–6; *Indianapolis Star*, 1 April, 1, 10 June, 20 July 1942; "Tarnished Silver Shirt," *Newsweek* 19 (13 April 1942): 29–30; *An Exact Copy of the Pelley Indictment for Sedition* ([Noblesville, Ind.: Pelley Publishers, 1942]).

194. *Indianapolis Star*, 29, 30 July 1942.

195. *New York Times*, 21 July 1942; *Indianapolis Star*, 1 Aug. 1942; "The Pelleyponesian War," *New Republic* 107 (10 Aug. 1942): 157.

196. *Indianapolis Star*, 1, 3, 4, 5 Aug. 1942; *New York Times*, 29 July 1942; Charles A. Lindbergh, *The Wartime Journals of Charles A. Lindbergh* (New York: Harcourt, Brace, Jovanovich, 1970), pp. 683, 688–89.

197. *New York Times*, 4 Aug. 1942; *Indianapolis Star*, 4 Aug. 1942; *Indianapolis News*, 4 Aug. 1942.

198. *Indianapolis Star*, 5, 6 Aug. 1942.

199. *New York Times*, 28 July, 6 Aug. 1942; *Indianapolis Star*, 5, 15 Aug. 1942; *Indianapolis News*, 6 Aug. 1942; [Melford Pearson], *The Price of Truth* (Noblesville, Ind.: Aquila Press, n.d.), pp. 2, 26; Werly, "Millenarian Right," pp. 76–78.

3. Gerald B. Winrod: Prophet in Politics

1. *Philadelphia Record*, 24 July 1938; "The Key-Note Address," *Defender*, 2 (Dec. 1927): 1; G. H. Montgomery, *Gerald Burton Winrod: Defender of the Faith* (Wichita: Mertmont, 1965), p. 14; John Waltner, "Gerald B. Winrod, Deluded Defender of the Faith," *Mennonite Life*, 34 (Jan. 1969): 30.

2. J. W. Winrod, *Redeeming the Years the Locust Hath Eaten* (Wichita: Defender Publishers, [1932]), pp. 5–7, 9–13, 18–26; United States Census, 1900, Kansas, Vol. 48, E. D. 290, Sheet 9, line 45; Ann Mari Buitrago, "A Study of the Political Ideas of Gerald B. Winrod: 1926–1938 (unpub. M.A. thesis, Kansas University, 1955), p. 161; "Father Winrod—'Absent From The Body . . . Present With The Lord,'" *Defender* 20 (May 1945): 2, 21–22.

3. J. W. Winrod, *Redeeming the Years*, pp. 28–30; Montgomery, *Winrod*, pp. 10–11; Buitrago, "Political Ideas," p. 186.

4. J. W. Winrod, *Redeeming the Years*, pp. 30–31; *Wichita City Directory 1925* (Wichita: R. L. Polk and Co., 1925), p. 656.

5. J. W. Winrod, *Redeeming the Years*, p. 31; Montgomery, *Winrod*, pp. 10, 4; Buitrago, "Political Ideas," p. 186; Waltner, "Deluded Defender," p. 30; Geraldine Winrod Korrell, "Last Moments with My Father," *Defender* 32 (Dec. 1957): 24; Gail Ann Sindell, "Gerald B. Winrod and the 'Defender': A Case Study of the Radical Right" (unpub. Ph.D. diss., Case Western Reserve University, 1973), p. 10; Author's interview with Winrod's secretary, M. L.

Flowers, 4 Jan. 1973; *Wichita City Directory 1917* (Wichita: R. L. Polk and Co., 1917), p. 478.

6. Montgomery, *Winrod*, pp. 13–15; "The Way It Was . . . ." *Defender* 50 (Nov. 1975): 20–23.

7. Ray Ginger, *Six Days or Forever:* Tennessee *v.* John T. Scopes (Chicago: Quadrangle Books, 1969); Willard B. Gatewood, ed., *Controversy in the Twenties: Fundamentalism, Modernism, and Evolution* (Nashville, Tenn.: Vanderbilt University Press, 1969).

8. Sydney E. Ahlstrom, *A Religious History of the American People* (New Haven, Conn.: Yale University Press, 1972), chaps. 44–47; Robert D. Cross, ed., *The Church and the City, 1865–1910* (Indianapolis: Bobbs-Merrill, 1976); Francis P. Weisenberger, *Ordeal of Faith: The Crisis of Church-Going America* (New York: Philosophical Library, 1959); Kenneth Cauthen, *The Impact of American Religious Liberalism* (New York: Harper & Row, 1962); William B. Hutchison, *The Modernist Impulse in American Protestantism* (Cambridge, Mass.: Harvard University Press, 1976), chaps. 1–6; Arthur M. Schlesinger, Sr., *A Critical Period in American Religion* (rpt. Philadelphia: Fortress Press, 1967); Paul A. Carter, *The Spiritual Crisis of the Gilded Age* (DeKalb: Northern Illinois University Press, 1971); William G. McLoughlin, *Revivals, Awakenings, and Religion: An Essay on Religion and Social Change in America* (Chicago: University of Chicago Press, 1978), pp. 141–78.

9. Ibid.; C. Howard Hopkins, *The Rise of the Social Gospel in American Protestantism, 1865–1915* (New Haven, Conn.: Yale University Press, 1967); Henry F. May, *Protestant Churches and Industrial America* (New York: Harper Torchbooks, 1967).

10. Ahlstrom, *Religious History*, chap. 48; Bernard A. Weisberger, *They Gathered at the River: The Story of the Great Revivalists and Their Impact Upon Religion in America* (Chicago: Quadrangle Books, 1966), chaps. 7–8; Ernest R. Sandeen, *The Roots of Fundamentalism: British and American Millenarianism, 1800–1930* (Chicago: University of Chicago Press, 1970), chap. 5; William G. McLoughlin, Jr., *Modern Revivalism: Charles Grandison Finney to Billy Graham* (New York: Ronald Press, 1959), pp. 347–445; George M. Marsden, *Fundamentalism and American Culture: The Shaping of Twentieth-Century Evangelicalism, 1870–1925* (New York: Oxford University Press, 1980), chaps. 3–13.

11. Sandeen, *Roots of Fundamentalism*, chaps 6–7; Timothy P. Weber, *Living in the Shadow of the Second Coming: American Premillenialism, 1875–1925* (New York: Oxford University Press, 1979), pp. 17–22, 50–55, 67.

12. Weber, *Living in the Shadow*, pp. 33–41; James F. Findlay, Jr., *Dwight L. Moody: American Evangelist, 1839–1899* (Chicago: University of Chicago Press, 1969), pp. 249–55, 406–9; William G. McLoughlin, Jr., *Billy Sunday Was His Real Name* (Chicago: University of Chicago Press, 1955), pp. 121–27.

13. Sandeen, *Roots of Fundamentalism*, chaps. 8–9; Marsden, *Fundamentalism and American Culture*, pp. 43, 106–23.

14. Weber, *Living in the Shadow*, pp. 105, 124; Marsden, *Fundamentalism and American Culture*, pp. 91, 161, 142, 163; Ray H. Abrams, *Preachers Present Arms* (New York: Round Table Press, 1933); Hutchison, *Modernist Impulse*, chap. 7.

15. Weber, *Living in the Shadow*, pp. 129–30, 161–62; Marsden, *Fundamentalism and American Culture*, p. 152; Gatewood, *Controversy in the Twenties*, pp. 4, 21.

16. Marsden, *Fundamentalism and American Culture*, pp. 147–48; Weber, *Living in the Shadow*, pp. 120–21.

17. Norman F. Furniss, *The Fundamentalist Controversy, 1918–1931* (Hamden, Conn.: Archon Books, 1963), chaps. 6, 8, 10–11; Marsden, *Fundamentalism and American Culture*, chaps. 18–20; Hutchison, *Modernist Impulse*, chap. 8.

18. Karen Gullen, ed., *Billy Sunday Speaks* (New York: Chelsea House, 1970), p. 15; C. Allyn Russell, *Voices of American Fundamentalism: Seven Biographical Studies* (Philadelphia: Westminster Press, 1976), p. 30; L. M. Birkhead, *The Religion of a Free Man* (Girard, Kansas: Haldeman-Julius, 1929), pp. 22–23, 30; Gatewood, *Controversy in the Twenties*, p. 24; Obadiah Holmes, "The Threat of Millenialism," *Christian Century*, 39 (28 April 1921): 10, (5 May 1921): 16–17; "The Capitalists and the Premillenarians," *Christian Century* 38 (14 April 1921): 3.

19. Marsden, *Fundamentalism and American Culture*, pp. 102–3, 179; Kenneth K. Bailey, *Southern White Protestantism in the Twentieth Century* (New York: Harper & Row, 1964), pp. 49, 74, 80–81; *New York Times*, 9 May 1927.

20. Vernon Louis Parrington, *Main Currents in American Thought: The Colonial Mind* (1927; rpt. New York: Harcourt, Brace, 1954), p. 110; H. L. Mencken, "The Hills of Zion," in Alistair Cooke, ed., *The Vintage Mencken* (New York: Vintage Books, 1955), p. 161; Leon Harris, *Upton Sinclair: American Rebel* (New York: Crowell, 1975), pp. 168–69; Sinclair Lewis, *Elmer Gantry* (1927; rpt. New York: New American Library, 1970); Mark Schorer, *Sinclair Lewis: An American Life* (New York: McGraw-Hill, 1961), pp. 447–48.

21. Richard Hofstadter, *Anti-Intellectualism in American Life* (New York: Vintage Books, 1963), chaps. 4–5; Russell, *Voices of American Fundamentalism*, pp. 54–55, 30, 89, 192; Marsden, *Fundamentalism and American Culture*, pp. 131, 128.

22. Russell, *Voices of American Fundamentalism*, pp. 112, 142, 171–73; Marsden, *Fundamentalism and American Culture*, p. 93; "Higher Fundamentalism," *Defender* 3 (June 1928): 15.

23. Weber, *Living in the Shadow*, p. 94; Russell, *Voices of American Fundamentalism*, pp. 87, 76.

24. Gatewood, *Controversy in the Twenties*, p. 21; Marsden, *Fundamentalism and American Culture*, pp. 94, 96; Russell, *Voices of American Fundamentalism*, p. 62.

25. Bailey, *Southern White Protestantism*, chap. 5; Allan J. Lichtman,

Prejudice and the Old Politics: The Presidential Election of 1928 (Chapel Hill: University of North Carolina, 1979).

26. Montgomery, *Winrod*, pp. 2, 22; Defenders staff, *Fire by Night and Cloud by Day: A History of Defenders of the Christian Faith* (Wichita: Mertmont, 1966), pp. 9, 11, 26, 83; Stewart G. Cole, *The History of Fundamentalism* (New York: Richard R. Smith, 1931), pp. 267, 312, 316; "The Incomparable Book," *Defender* 2 (Feb. 1928): 5; Donald S. Strong, *Organized Anti-Semitism in America* (Washington, D.C.: American Council on Public Affairs, 1941), chap. 6; "Gerald B. Winrod, Our Next U.S. Senator," 1938 flyer in Kansas Historical Society, (KHS).

27. Korell, "Last Moments," p. 24; Gordon Winrod, "My Father Is Away," and Mrs. Gerald B. [Frances] Winrod, "Work for the Night Is Coming," *Defender* 32 (Dec. 1957): 9, 21; Defenders staff, *Fire by Night*, p. 49.

28. "Now I Know —," *Defender* 3 (June 1928): 12; William Allen White to Franklin D. Roosevelt, 10 June 1938, PSF 194, Franklin D. Roosevelt Library (FDRL); *New York Herald-Tribune*, 13 Nov. 1957; "The Majesty of God, A Lecture," Defender Records, #102, and "The Broken Hearted Christ," Defender Records, #103, State University of Iowa Library.

29. "In the Name of God We Shall Take Up Our Banners," *Defender* 3 (Feb. 1929): 5; "Items of Interest to Defenders" (a regular feature cited hereafter as "Items"), *Defender* 3 (Nov. 1928): 2; "My Reply," *Defender* 2 (Feb. 1928): 5; Montgomery, *Winrod*, chap. 5.

30. "Revising Denominationalism," *Defender* 4 (July 1929): 6; *Wichita Beacon*, 11 Nov. 1957; James C. Juhnke, "Gerald B. Winrod and the Kansas Mennonites," *Mennonite Quarterly Review* 43 (Oct. 1969): 293–98.

31. Defenders staff, *Fire by Night*, p. 11; Ferenc M. Szasz, "William Bell Riley and the Fight Against Teaching of Evolution in Minnesota," *Minnesota History* 41 (Spring 1969): 211–12; *New York Times*, 9 May 1927.

32. Gerald B. Winrod, *Christ Within* (New York: Fleming H. Revell, 1932), pp. 90–91, 96, 98–99, 104; "The Textbook Problem," *Defender* 1 (June 1926): 5; "An Amazing Flip-Flop," *Defender* 4 (Feb. 1930): 3; "Intellectual Colic," *Defender* 1 (June 1926): 11; "The Key-Note Address," p. 1; Gerald B. Winrod, *Science, Christ, and the Bible* (New York: Fleming H. Revell, 1929), p. 33.

33. *Science, Christ, and the Bible*, pp. 29–31, 28–49, 42; *Christ Within*, p. 31.

34. *Christ Within*, pp. 5, 39; *Science, Christ, and the Bible*, p. 31.

35. *Christ Within*, pp. 5, 39, 109, 113, 35; *Science, Christ, and the Bible*, pp. 31, 19, 28, 23, 20; "Damned Souls," *Defender* 1 (June 1926): 1; "How a Wichita Father and Mother Protected Their Son," *Defender* 2 (Nov. 1927): 4; Russell, *Voices of American Fundamentalism*, p. 70; Lawrence W. Levine, *Defender of the Faith: William Jennings Bryan, the Last Decade, 1915–1925* (New York: Oxford University Press, 1965), p. 262.

36. "Wichita Father," p. 1; *Christ Within*, p. 34; "Companionate Marriage," *Defender* 2 (Jan. 1928): 3.

37. *Christ Within*, pp. 130, 34; "Items," *Defender* 6 (Jan 1932): 2; "He Talked with the 'Messiah,'" *Defender* 3 (July 1928): 9; "The Jew First,"

Defender 3 (March 1928): 9; "Filthy Dreamers," *Defender* 3 (June 1928): 6; "Items," *Defender* 2 (Nov. 1927): 2; 3 (May 1928): 2; 3 (July 1928): 2; "Babbitt Wins," *Defender* 5 (Feb. 1931): 4.

38. Gerald B. Winrod, *The Great American Home* (Wichita: Defender Publishers, 1935), pp. 9–01.

39. *Great American Home*, pp. 8, 5, 7; "Companionate Marriage," p. 3; "Wichita Father," p. 4.

40. "Companionate Marriage," p. 3; *Christ Within*, p. 37; Gerald B. Winrod, *Three Modern Evils* (Wichita: Defender Publishers, 1932), pp. 9–10.

41. *Three Modern Evils*, p. 17.

42. Ibid., pp. 17, 19, 30–31; *Christ Within*, pp. 6, 74, 86, 63.

43. "Key-Note Address," p. 1; "Items," *Defender* 2 (Nov. 1927): 2; *Christ Within*, p. 68; *Three Modern Evils*, pp. 17, 19; *Science, Christ, and the Bible*, pp. 123–24; "Missions," *Defender* 3 (Sept. 1928): 10.

44. *Christ Within*, pp. 19, 14, 67, 75; Gerald B. Winrod, *The Great Religions of the World* (Wichita: Defender Publishers, 1943), p. 29; "Will Evangelism Die?" *Defender* 2 (Nov. 1927): 5.

45. *Science, Christ, and the Bible*, p. 54; "Hid with Christ," *Defender* 3 (Sept. 1928): 11; "Foreign Missions Are Slipping," *Defender* 4 (Feb. 1930): 10; "Will Evangelism Die?" p. 5; *Three Modern Evils*, pp. 8–9; *Christ Within*, pp. 27, 16, 14, 46, 44; "Berkeley Pastor Assailed," *Defender* 2 (March 1928): 5.

46. *Christ Within*, pp. 24–28; *Three Modern Evils*, p. 7; *Great Religions*, pp. 39, 45; "Satan and Demons," *Defender* 3 (Oct. 1928): 16.

47. *Christ Within*, pp. 6, 17, 75; *Science, Christ, and the Bible*, pp. 17–18, 46.

48. "Christ in the Old Testament," *Defender* 4 (March 1930): 7; Frances Winrod, "The Seven Dispensations," *Defender* 3 (July 1928): 11.

49. Frances Winrod, "Seven Dispensations," p. 11; "Perilous Times," *Defender* 3 (Oct. 1928): 16.

50. Ibid.

51. For summaries of dispensationalist premises and interpretive options, see Sandeen, *Roots of Fundamentalism*, pp. 139–43, 210–12, and Weber, *Living in the Shadow*, pp. 21–24, 63–64; Gerald B. Winrod, *The NRA in Prophecy and a Discussion of Beast Worship* (Wichita: Defender Publishers, 1933), p. 7; "Is Armageddon Near?" *Defender* 6 (March 1932): 1.

52. Weber, *Living in the Shadow*, pp. 36–37, 17; Sandeen, *Roots of Fundamentalism*, pp. 103–31.

53. Weber, *Living in the Shadow*, pp. 18–20.

54. Sandeen, *Roots of Fundamentalism*, p. 60.

55. Ibid., pp. 214–16, 221–22; Weber, *Living in the Shadow*, chap. 6; David A. Rausch, "Arno C. Gaebelein (1861–1945): Fundamentalist Protestant Zionist," *American Jewish History* 68 (Sept. 1978): 43–46; David A. Rausch, *Zionism Within Early American Fundamentalism, 1878–1918: A Convergence of Two Traditions* (New York: Edwin Mellen, 1979), chaps. 3–7.

56. Hertzel Fishman, *American Protestantism and a Jewish State* (Detroit: Wayne State University Press, 1973), pp. 21, 31–32; Yona Malachy,

American Fundamentalism and Israel: The Relation of American Fundamentalist Churches to Zionism and the State of Israel (Jerusalem: Institute of Contemporary Jewry, 1978), chap. 4.

57. Leonard Dinnerstein, *The Leo Frank Case* (New York: Columbia University Press, 1968), p. 65; "Aspects of Jewish Power in the United States," *Our Hope* 29 (Aug. 1922): 103; Weber, *Living in the Shadow*, pp. 154–56.

58. "A Review of Philip Maruo's New Book," *Defender* 3 (Oct. 1928): 10; "Date Fixers," *Defender* 6 (Dec. 1931): 9; Philip Mauro, *The Gospel of the Kingdom: With an Examination of Modern Dispensationalism* (Boston: Hamilton Brothers, 1928), p. 8.

59. "Filthy Dreamers," p. 6. "In like manner also these filthy dreamers defile the flesh, despise dominion, and speak evil of dignities" (Jude 8, New Schofield Reference Bible [NSR]).

60. "The Jew First," p. 9.

61. "Items," *Defender* 2 (April 1928): 2; "Esther and the Feast of Purim," *Defender* 4 (March 1930): 1; "Old Legend About Jews Using Human Blood in Sacrifice Revived," *Defender* 3 (Nov. 1928): 17.

62. "Date Fixers," p. 9; "The Seven Churches of Revelation," *Defender* 3 (Feb. 1929): 11, 14; "The World Calendar," *Defender* 5 (June 1930): 11; *NRA in Prophecy*, pp. 9–10; "Europe's Proposed United States," *Defender* 5 (Sept. 1930): 1.

63. "World Problems," *Defender* 6 (Sept. 1931): 4.

64. Gerald B. Winrod, *Mussolini's Place in Prophecy* (Wichita: Defender Publishers, 1933), p. 6.

65. "Religious Jazz," *Defender* 4 (Jan. 1930): 1; "Russian Propaganda in Our Schools," *Defender* 5 (Aug. 1930): 3; "Wichita Father," p. 4; "Items," *Defender* 2 (Feb. 1928): 3.

66. *Mussolini's Place*, p. 8; "Fascism—A World Menace," *Defender* 2 (Dec. 1927): 4–5; "That Man Mussolini," *Defender* 4 (Feb. 1930): 12; "Europe's Proposed United States," p. 1; "Items," *Defender* 2 (April 1928): 3; "Watch Mussolini," *Defender* 2 (April 1928): 6.

67. Ibid.

68. "Congressman Ayers," *Defender* 3 (Nov. 1928): 21; "Letters and Notes," *Defender* 2 (Nov. 1927): 6; *Christ Within*, pp. 118, 114; Flowers interview.

69. "Congressman Ayers," p. 21; "Will Al Smith Be the Next President?" *Defender* 2 (April 1928): 5; "Items," *Defender* 3 (Sept. 1928): 2; 3 (Oct. 1928): 2; 3 (Nov. 1928): 2; Frances Winrod, "Women's Department," *Defender* 3 (Nov. 1928): 14.

70. "Babson Speaks," *Defender* 5 (Jan. 1931): 1.

71. "Revival or Ruin," *Defender* 5 (Dec. 1930): 21.

72. "Items," *Defender* 6 (Jan. 1932): 2, and 7 (June 1932): 2.

73. J. W. Winrod, "Carry Nation Smashed My Saloon," *Defender* 7 (July 1932) 11; "The Saloon Must Never Come Back," *Defender* 7 (Nov. 1932): 1; "Three Lines of Defense," *Defender* 7 (Oct. 1932): 1, 15; " 'Vote Sober'—November 8th," *Defender* 7 (Sept. 1932): 5.

74. "Facing Our International Foe," *Revealer* 2 (15 July 1935): 4; "Three Lines of Defense," p. 1; "Red Menace," *Defender* 7 (March 1933): 1; "Roosevelt, Hitler, and the Present Economic Collapse Considered in Light of Prophecy," *Defender* 8 (May 1933): 5.

75. "Roosevelt, Hitler," p. 5; "The Coming Golden Calf," *Defender* 7 (April 1933): 10; *NRA in Prophecy*, p. 36.

76. "Joseph of Egypt and Wallace of Iowa," *Revealer* 2 (15 Aug. 1935): 2; "Supreme Court Kills the Soviet AAA," *Revealer* 2 (15 Jan. 1936): 2; "Sinister Forces in Washington," *Revealer* 3 (15 June 1936): 2; "Roosevelt's Jewish Appointments," *Defender* 8 (Feb. 1934): 10.

77. "Swat the Rich," *Revealer* 2 (15 July 1935): 1; Gerald B. Winrod, *The United States at the Crossroads* (Wichita: [Defender Publishers], n.d.), p. 22.

78. *United States at the Crossroads*, pp. 16–17, 22; "Swat the Rich," p. 1.

79. Gerald B. Winrod, *Adam Weishaupt, Human Devil* (Wichita: Defender Publishers, 1935), p. 50; "Senator Borah a Dangerous Man," *Revealer* 3 (15 April 1936): 2; "Items," *Defender* 10 (Sept. 1935): 4; "'Subterfuge,'" *Revealer* 2 (15 Nov. 1935): 5; "Will There Be a Political Crack-Up?" *Revealer* 1 (Nov. 1934): 4; "Hoover Throws Down the Gauntlet," *Revealer* 1 (Nov. 1934): 8; "Hoover's Slashing Attacks," *Revealer* 3 (June 1936): 7; "Roosevelt, the Autocrat," *Revealer* 2 (15 Jan. 1936): 2; "The Present Political Situation," *Revealer* 1 (15 Nov. 1934): 4.

80. Gerald B. Winrod, *Communism and the Roosevelt Brain Trust* (Wichita: Defender Publishers, 1933), pp. 8, 6; "Present Political Situations," pp. 3–4; "Sinister Forces in Washington," *Revealer* 3 (June 1936): 1; "The Coming Golden Calf," p. 10; "Collectivism versus Free Society," *Revealer* 3 (Nov. 1936): 1; "The Tie That Binds," *Revealer* 2 (15 Dec. 1935): 6.

81. *Roosevelt Brain Trust*, pp. 8, 13, 14, 11, 20, 5; "Antichrist, Liberalism, Socialiam, Fascism, and Communism," *Defender* 8 (Feb. 1934): 19.

82. *Roosevelt Brain Trust*, p. 6; "Christians Are Not Inferior People," *Defender* 8 (Feb. 1934): 3–4.

83. "Will There Be a Political Crack-Up?" p. 4; *Roosevelt Brain Trust*, p. 24; "Antichrist, Liberalism," p. 19; Gerald B. Winrod, *The United States and Russia in Prophecy and the Red Horse of the Apocalypse* (Wichita: Defender Publishers, 1933), p. 13.

84. Gerald B. Winrod, *The Hidden Hand—The Protocols and the Coming Superman* (Wichita: Defender Publishers, 1932), p. 19; "The Roosevelt Hot-Dog Boys," *Defender* 9 (May 1934): 16; "Gutter Language," *Revealer* 2 (Nov. 1935): 1; *Roosevelt Brain Trust*, pp. 9, 23; "Welles Learns a Lesson," *Revealer* 1 (15 Nov. 1934): 2; "The Highway Massacre," *Revealer* 2 (15 Sept. 1935): 2.

85. *Red Horse*, p. 7; *United States at the Crossroads*, p. 5; "What Is Behind Communism?" *Defender* 8 (Jan. 1934): 7; *Brain Trust*, p. 14.

86. "What Is Behind Communism?" p. 6; "Collectivism," pp. 1–2; *Red Horse*, p. 12; "Antichrist, Liberalism," p. 19.

87. "Will There Be a Political Crack-Up?" p. 4; *United States at the Crossroads*, p. 8; "Sinister Forces," p. 1.

88. "The Present Political Situation," p. 4; *United States at the Crossroads*, p. 8; "Sinister Forces," p. 1.

89. "Roosevelt, Hitler," p. 5; *NRA in Prophecy*, pp. 41, 44.

90. "Roosevelt, Hitler," pp. 5–6; *Red Horse*, p. 24; *Mussolini's Place*, pp. 7, 17; *Hidden Hand*, p. 9; Gerald B. Winrod, *Hitler in Prophecy* (Wichita: Defender Publishers, 1933), p. 9.

91. *Hidden Hand*, pp. 31–32; *Red Horse*, pp. 29, 37; *Hitler in Prophecy*, pp. 16–17; *Mussolini's Place* p. 18.

92. Gerald B. Winrod, *Antichrist and the Tribe of Dan* (Wichita: Defender Publishers, 1936), p. 7; *Red Horse*, pp. 37, 29; *Mussolini's Place*, p. 33; *Hidden Hand*, pp. 33, 28–29.

93. "Roosevelt, Hitler," pp. 5–6; *Mussolini's Place*, pp. 6, 13–16, 28–31, 20, 25; *Red Horse*, pp. 16–19, 29, 37; *Tribe of Dan*, p. 25.

94. "The Reds Are Coming," *Revealer* 2 (15 Oct. 1935): 2; *Hitler in Prophecy*, p. 8; *Red Horse*, pp. 30–31.

95. *Hitler in Prophecy*, pp. 10–12.

96. Ibid; "Roosevelt, Hitler," p. 10; "War Is Hell," *Defender* 8 (Nov. 1933): 17; "1934 in Prophecy," *Defender* 8 (Jan. 1934): 20; *Red Horse*, p. 25.

97. "Antichrist, Liberalism," p. 22; *Hidden Hand*, p. 22; *Red Horse*, pp. 20–24.

98. "Antichrist, Liberalism," p. 22; *NRA in Prophecy*, p. 38; *Roosevelt Brain Trust*, pp. 24–25.

99. *Hidden Hand*, p. 11; *Adam Weishaupt*, pp. 10, 35.

100. "Defender Book Department," *Defender* 7 (June 1932): 12; Colnel E. N. Sanctuary, "Why I Wrote 'Tainted Contacts,'" *Defender* 7 (July 1932): 13, 18.

101. Gerald B. Winrod, *The Jewish Assault on Christianity* (Wichita: Defender Publishers, 1935), p. 48; Gerald B. Winrod, *The Truth About the Protocols* (Wichita: Defender Publishers, 1935), pp. 24–25, 27; Norman Cohn, *Warrant for Genocide: The Myth of the Jewish World-Conspiracy and the Protocols of the Elders of Zion* (New York: Harper Torchbooks, 1969), pp. 71–76, 275–79.

102. "Hidden Control of News," *Defender* 13 (Jan. 1940): 2; *Truth About the Protocols*, pp. 17–18.

103. *Christ Within*, pp. 68, 109; "Will There Be a Political Crack-Up?" p. 4; "The Tie That Binds," p. 6.

104. Hofstadter, *Anti-Intellectualism in American Life*, pp. 132–36; Malachy, *American Fundamentalism and Israel*, pp. 142–46; Rausch, *Zionism Within Early American Fundamentalism*, pp. 327–33; McLoughlin, *Billy Sunday*, pp. 148–50.

105. For a contrary interpretation of Winrod's psychological state during the 1930s, see, Sindell, "Gerald B. Winrod," pp. 203–05.

106. Joel A. Carpenter, "Fundamentalist Institutions and the Rise of Evangelical Protestantism, 1929–1942," *Church History* 49 (March 1980): 63–75; Louis Gaspar, *The Fundamentalist Movement* (The Hague: Mouton, 1963), pp. 77–78, 93–97; Juhnke, "Winrod and Kansas Mennonites," pp. 295–96.

107. *Red Horse*, p. 28; *Hidden Hand*, p. 13; *Truth About the Protocols*, p. 10; *Jewish Assault*, pp. 6, 9.

108. *Jewish Assault*, pp. 9, 14, 23–31; *Hidden Hand*, p. 15; Gerald B. Winrod, *The Conflict of the Christ* (Wichita: Defender Publishers, 1955), pp. 8–18; Gerald B. Winrod, *Martin Luther and the Reformation* (Wichita: Defender Publishers, 1935), p. 15; Gerald B. Winrod, *With Paul in Macedonia* (Wichita: Defender Publishers, 1935), p. 7; *Truth About the Protocols*, pp. 12–13, 15–16.

109. *Truth About the Protocols*, pp. 13–15; *Mussolini's Place*, p. 27; David Brion Davis, ed., *The Fear of Conspiracy: Images of Un-American Subversion from the Revolution to the Present* (Ithaca, N.Y.: Cornell University Press, 1971), pp. 36–47.

110. *Adam Weishaupt*, pp. 15, 19, 31, 8, 23, 18, 43, 11, 18, 15, 9, 34, 36.

111. Ibid., pp. 23, 43, 45, 47; "Secret Societies Unveiled," *Revealer* 2 (March 1936): 1–2; *Truth About the Protocols*, p. 20; "Jews Colonize in Russia," *Revealer* 2 (March 1936): 8; *Tribe of Dan*, p. 35; "War Is Hell," p. 19; Gerald B. Winrod, *Jewish Communism, the International Foe of Christianity* (Wichita: Defender Publishers, n.d.), p. 9.

112. *Jewish Assault*, p. 42; "Jews Colonize in Russia," p. 8; *Jewish Communism*, p. 5; *Hitler in Prophecy*, p. 18.

113. *Hitler in Prophecy*, p. 18; "Secret Societies," p. 2; *Jewish Communism*, p. 4; *Tribe of Dan*, p. 33.

114. *United States at the Crossroads*, pp. 17–18, 22; *Mussolini's Place*, p. 25; *Truth About the Protocols*, pp. 31–32, 35; *Hidden Hand*, p. 22; "The Coming Golden Calf," p. 22.

115. *Hidden Hand*, p. 26; *Adam Weishaupt*, pp. 47, 49; *Red Horse*, p. 36; *Tribe of Dan*, p. 27; *Jewish Assault*, p. 42; *Truth About the Protocols*, pp. 38–53.

116. *Roosevelt Brain Trust*, pp. 13, 17–20; "Roosevelt's Jewish Ancestry," *Revealer* 3 (15 Oct. 1936): 2.

117. *Hidden Hand*, pp. 10, 29–30; *Red Horse*, pp. 37–38.

118. *Red Horse*, p. 28; *Hitler in Prophecy*, p. 15; "Roosevelt, Hitler," p. 6; "Anti-Semitism in Prophecy," *Defender* 8 (Dec. 1933): 6; "Editor Winrod Answers Editor Cohen," *Defender* 8 (June 1933): 6. Joseph Cohen, editor of *Chosen People* magazine, was a Jewish convert to Christianity.

119. *Hitler in Prophecy*, p. 15; *Hidden Hand*, pp. 7–8; *Tribe of Dan*, p. 33.

120. *Hidden Hand*, pp. 7, 33; *Mussolini's Place*, pp. 21–23; "Destruction of Jewish Capitalistic Control Clearly Prophesied," *Defender* 13 (Jan. 1939): 3; *Jewish Assault*, p. 48; "Anti-Semitism," p. 6.

121. "Is There an International Conspiracy?" *Defender* 7 (June 1933): 6; *Hidden Hand*, pp. 13–14; *Tribe of Dan*, pp. 19–20; "The Fruit of Jewish Communism," *Defender* 9 (May 1934): 5; "Roosevelt's Jewish Appointments," *Defender* 8 (Feb. 1934): 11; "What Is Behind Communism?" p. 8; "Jewish Lies an Incentive to Anti-Semitism," *Revealer* 2 (15 March 1936): 2.

122. "Editor Cohen," p. 6; "Stigmatize Winrod," *Defender* 8 (Dec. 1933): 13.

123. *Tribe of Dan*, pp. 17, 22, 16, 24–25; Joshua Trachtenberg, *The Devil*

and the Jews: The Medieval Conception of the Jew and Its Relation to Modern Anti-Semitism (New York: Harper Torchbooks, 1966), p. 34.

124. "Propaganda and Prophecy," *Defender* 13 (Dec. 1938): 31; "A Talk with the Editor," *Defender* 13 (Dec. 1938): 1; "Offer Unto God Thanksgiving," *Defender* 13 (Dec. 1938): 1, 5–6; "God's Hand in American History," *Defender* 14 (July 1939): 3, 5; "The Unholy Alliance," *Defender* 12 (Aug. 1937): 1; "The Tie That Binds," p. 6; "Bolshevik Professors Exposed," *Revealer* 3 (15 May 1936): 2; "Communism and the CIO," *Defender* 12 (Dec. 1937): 5; "Items," *Defender* 12 (Aug. 1937): 2; "Destruction of Jewish Capitalistic Control," p. 5.

125. Gerald B. Winrod, *The Harlot Woman and the Scarlet Beast* (Wichita: Defender Publishers, 1936), pp. 12, 16, 27–30; "Mussolini," *Defender* 6 (Sept. 1931): 9; "Items," *Defender* 10 (Nov. 1935): 4; "Jews and Jesuits," *Defender* 10 (Aug. 1935): 3; *Adam Weishaupt*, pp. 29–30; "Terror in Spain," *Revealer* 3 (15 Oct. 1936): 11; "Answering Communist Falsehoods," flyer in KHS.

126. "Philip Dru: Administrator," ([Wichita: Defender Publishers, 1938]), n.p., flyer in KHS.

127. Edward M. House, *Philip Dru: Administrator* (New York: Huebsch, 1912).

128. "Philip Dru," n.p.

129. *Hitler in Prophecy*, pp. 13–15, "Defender Book Department," *Defender* 6 (April 1932): 12; Dorothy Thompson, *I Saw Hitler* (New York: Farrar and Winston, 1932); Robert W. Ross, *So It Was True: The American Protestant Press and the Nazi Persecution of the Jews* (Minneapolis: University of Minnesota Press, 1980), pp. 38, 44–48, 101–2.

130. "Jewish Hooligans Crushed in Berlin," *Revealer* 2 (15 Sept. 1935): 7; "Hiterism and Bolshevism," *Revealer* 2 (15 Dec. 1935): 8; "The Reds Are Coming," p. 1.

131. "Hitler Opposes Pagans," *Revealer* 2 (Nov. 1935): 6; "Protestantism in Germany," *Defender* 13 (Feb. 1939): 5–7. Melle's three sermons are in "Bishop Otto Melle Speaks in Kansas," "Modern Chapters in Apostolic Work," and "A Power Went Out from Jesus," *Defender* 13 (June 1939): 3; (July 1939): 9; and (Aug. 1939): 7.

132. Ernst Christian Helmreich, *The German Churches Under Hitler* (Detroit: Wayne State University Press, 1979), pp. 224–27, 372–74.

133. "Olympics in Snow and Ice," *Revealer* 2 (March 1936): 7; "Hitlerism and Bolshevism," p. 8; "Items," *Defender* 14 (July 1939): 4; Karl Schleunes, *The Twisted Road to Auschwitz* (Urbana: University of Illinois, 1970), chap. 7.

134. "Protestantism in Germany," p. 3.

135. Montgomery, *Winrod*, p. 39.

136. Francis W. Schruben, *Kansas in Turmoil, 1930–1936* (Columbia: University of Missouri Press, 1969), pp. 13–18, 21, 99; Kenneth T. Jackson, *The Ku Klux Klan in the City 1915–1930* (New York: Oxford University Press, 1967), p. 237; Charles William Sloan, Jr., "Kansas Battles the Invisible Empire: The Legal Ouster of the KKK From Kansas, 1922–1927," *Kansas*

Historical Quarterly 57 (Autumn 1974): 393–409; Jack Wayne Traylor, "William Allen White's 1924 Gubernatorial Campaign," *Kansas Historical Quarterly* 59 (Summer 1976): 180–91; *New York Times* 3 March 1937; Flowers interview.

137. Schruben, *Kansas in Turmoil*, chap. 3.

138. Ibid., pp. 28–46, 79–96; Donald R. McCoy, *Landon of Kansas* (Lincoln: University of Nebraska Press, 1966), pp. 92, 103, 108; Gerald Carson, *The Roguish World of Doctor Brinkley* (New York: Rinehart, 1960), chap. 10.

139. Schruben, *Kansas in Turmoil*, p. 89; "Tempting Wichita's School Children," *Revealer* 2 (15 Oct. 1935): 1; "Capper in Reverse," *Revealer* 3 (15 April 1936): 2; "Capper Disgraces Kansas," *Revealer* 2 (15 Aug. 1935): 1–2; "Capper Compromises with Communism," *Revealer* 2 (15 July 1935): 2; "An Open Letter to Mr. Landon," *Defender* 11 (Oct. 1936): 3, 5–7.

140. "The Crisis Hour Is Here," "A Frank Statement," and "Complete Text of an Address by Dr. Gerald B. Winrod" (2 March 1937), flyers in KHS; *New York Times*, 2, 3 March 1937; "A Furor on the Senate Floor," *Defender* 11 (April 1937): 2; Gerald B. Winrod, *Terse Talks* (Wichita: Defender Publishers, 1938), p. 12.

141. Buitrago, "Political Ideas," p. 121; Schruben, *Kansas in Turmoil*, pp. 20–27, 147; McCoy, *Landon*, pp. 25–63.

142. *Topeka State Journal* 28 July 1938; FDR to William Allen White, 8 June 1938, PSF 194, FDRL; *Philadelphia Record*, 24 July 1938; "Wilderness Voice," *Time* 32 (1 Aug. 1938): 12.

143. Schruben, *Kansas in Turmoil*, pp. 79, 31, 43; *Kansas City Star*, 21 Jan. 1938; Clifford R. Hope, Jr., "Strident Voices in Kansas Between the Wars," *Kansas History* 2 (Spring 1979): 54–64.

144. "Dangerous Trends Toward Dictatorship" (radio speech, 27 Jan. 1938), pp. 1, 6; "What Ails the Men in Washington?" (radio speech, 28 April 1938), p. 1; "Immigration and the Unemployment Problem" (radio speech, 31 March 1938), p. 1; "Enemies of Labor" (radio speech, 12 May 1938), p. 3; *Terse Talks*, pp. 3–5, 9; Gerald B. Winrod, *The New Federalist* (Wichita: Defender Publishers, [1938]). Transcripts of the radio speeches, which were delivered over WIBW and KCKN, are available at the Kansas Historical Society.

145. *Terse Talks*, pp. 12, 16–21, 30–36; "Government by Bureaus" (radio speech, 1 May 1938), p. 1; "Remove Not the Landmark" (radio speech, 5 May 1938), p. 1; "What's Blocking Recovery" (radio speech, 21 July 1938), p. 1; "Pump Priming" (radio speech, 2 June 1938), p. 1; "The Farm Problem" (radio speech, 9 June 1938), pp. 1–3; "Money and the Farm Question" (radio speech, 23 June 1938), pp. 1–3; "The Occult Pattern" (radio speech, 14 April 1938), p. 3; "Immigration," p. 1; "Enemies of Labor," p. 1.

146. "Pump Priming," p. 3.

147. White to FDR, 10 June 1938, PSF 194, FDRL; *Emporia Gazette*, 20, 23, 25, 26, 27, 29 July, 3 Aug. 1938.

148. Buitrago, "Political Ideas," p. 134; *New York Times*, 23 July 1938; *Philadelphia Record*, 24 July 1938; *Emporia Gazette*, 20 July 1938; McCoy, *Landon*, pp. 394–98; "Drive Fascist Ideas from Kansas" ([1938], flyer in KSH), n.p.

149. E. J. Kahn, Jr., "Democracy's Friend," pt. 1, *New Yorker* 23 (26 July 1947): 28–34 ff.; pt. 2, *New Yorker* 23 (2 Aug. 1947): 28–32 ff.; pt. 3, *New Yorker* 23 (9 Aug. 1947): 28–32, 36–37 ff.

150. *Philadelphia Record*, 24 July 1938; Birkhead to Lucille B. Milner, 8 Feb. 1938, bk. 2038, American Civil Liberties Union Collection, Princeton University; *What's Wrong with Winrod?* (Kansas City, Kansas: Friends of Democracy, 1938); "Grandma Birkhead Has Another Spasm." *Revealer* 2 (15 Aug. 1936): 1–2.

151. "Viewing the Facts," flyer in KHS, pp. 2, 4–6.

152. Ibid., pp. 2, 4–6, 7; *Terse Talks*, pp. 7–9; "Answering Communist Falsehoods," flyer in KHS.

153. "Viewing the Facts," pp. 7, 3; *Terse Talks*, p. 41; Preston Dunn, "Where Is All This Money Coming from That Is Being Spent Against Winrod?" flyer in KHS.

154. *Topeka State Journal*, 1 Aug. 1938; *Emporia Gazette*, 3 Aug. 1938; Juhnke, "Winrod and Kansas Mennonites," pp. 293–98. Final returns were Reed, 104,918 (42.3%); Knapp, 64, 068 (25.8%), Winrod, 53,149 (21.4%); and Fisher, 26,034 (10.5%); untitled Winrod circular letters, 8 Sept. 1938 and 4 Nove. 1938, in KHS.

155. "A Factual Analysis," *Defender* 15 (June 1941): 16; "Another Example of Lying Propaganda," *Defender* 14 (June 1939): 16; "*The Saturday Evening Post* Engages in Yellow Journalism," flyer at Hoover Institution, Stanford University; open letter in *Defender* 14 (June 1939): 2; Montgomery, *Winrod*, pp. 56, 61; Birkhead to Gardner Jackson, 30 Dec. 1938, bk. 2078, ACLU Collection; "*Saturday Evening Post* Not Interested in Truth," *Defender* 14 (Oct. 1939): 19; "Liars I Have Known," flyer in KHS; Flowers interview.

156. Gerald B. Winrod, *The Present International Crisis* (Wichita: Defender Publishers, 1939), pp. 19–22; "Europe's Crisis in Prophecy," *Defender* 14 (Oct. 1939): 1, 7; "Items," *Defender* 14 (July 1939): 4; "Prophetic Trends for 1940," *Defender* 14 (Jan. 1940): 5–6.

157. "Prophetic Trends," p. 10; "Rome in Prophecy," *Defender* 14 (Dec. 1939): 6; Gerald B. Winrod, *The Prophetic Destiny of the United States* (Wichita: Defender Publishers, 1939), pp. 21–22; *Present International Crisis*, p. 45.

158. Defenders staff, *Fire by Night*, pp. 67–68; "Petitions Against War," *Defender* 16 (June 1941): 2; "War Is Hell," p. 3; "The Fundamental Cause of War," *Revealer* 2 (15 Oct. 1935): 3; Gerald B. Winrod, *Radio Speeches on War and Peace* (Wichita: Defender Publishers, 1939), pp. 23–28.

159. *Radio Speeches*, pp. 23–24, 9; *Present International Crisis*, pp. 18, 22–24; "War Propaganda in America," *Defender* 14 (Oct. 1939): 2, 28–31; "Deception and War Hysteria," *Defender* 14 (Nov. 1939): 2.

160. *Present International Crisis*, p. 14; *Radio Speeches*, pp. 7, 11–13, 18–21, 45–57.

161. "A Book of War Miracles," *Defender* 19 (Sept. 1944): 2; Defenders staff, *Fire by Night*, p. 72.

162. "Will You Send Us a Picture of Your Soldier Son?" advertisement for

the National Spiritual Defense Crusade, *Defender* 19 (Nov. 1944): 38; "A Prophecy Regarding Poland," and "War Situation Demands More New Testaments," *Defender* 19 (Feb. 1945): 2, 8, 22–23; "MacArthur—Fighter for Freedom," *Defender* 19 (Aug. 1944): 23; "Kaj Monk—Denmark's Niemoller," *Defender* 19 (Aug. 1944): 1; "God's Hand in American History," *Defender* 19 (Nov. 1944): 3–6; "God's Hand in the South Pacific," *Defender* 19 (Dec. 1944): 2, 22–27.

163. Defenders staff, *Fire by Night*, p. 72; Office of the Chief of Staff, cross reference card, Record Group 165, 15W3, Row 6, Compartment S, Shelf B, Box 368, National Archives; *Wichita Beacon*, 14 April, 28 July 1942; *United States* v. *Winrod*, box 1350, Acc. 64-A-379, Loc. 16/79-32-1, Washington National Records Center, Suitland, Maryland.

164. *Prophetic Destiny*, pp. 23, 29–34; *Wichita Beacon*, 18 Aug. 1942.

4. Gerald L. K. Smith: Dramatist in Politics

1. "France Lost Christ—and Then the People Lost Their Liberty," *Cross and the Flag*, 1 (June 1942): 6–7; "If America Loses Christ—The People Will Lose America," *Cross and the Flag*, 1 (Aug. 1942): 12; Ralph Lord Roy, *Apostles of Discord: A Study of Organized Bigotry and Disruption on the Fringes of Protestantism* (Boston: Beacon Press, 1953), chap. 4.

2. Elna M. Smith and Charles F. Robertson, eds., *Besieged Patriot: Autobiographical Episodes Exposing Communism, Traitorism and Zionism from the Life of Gerald L. K. Smith* (Eureka Springs, Ark.: Smith Foundation, 1978), p. 291; author's interview with Smith, 25 August 1969 (cited hereafter as Interview I); interview with Smith by Glen Jeansonne, 10 August 1974, transcript provided by Professor Jeansonne (cited hereafter as Jeansonne I).

3. Smith and Robertson, *Besieged Patriot*, pp. 4, 141; Interview I; Jeansonne I.

4. Smith and Robertson, *Besieged Patriot*, pp. 4, 141; Interview I; Jeansonne I.

5. Smith and Robertson, *Besieged Patriot*, pp. 5, 37, 74, 96, 225, 236, 255, 258; Interview I; Jeansonne I.

6. Interview I; Smith and Robertson, *Besieged Patriot*, p. 5; Jeansonne I; Glen Jeansonne, "Preacher, Populist, Propagandist: The Early Career of Gerald L. K. Smith," *Biography* 2 (Fall 1979): 305.

7. Alfred T. DeGroot, *The Disciples of Christ: A History* (St. Louis: Christian Board of Publication, 1948); William E. Tucker, *J. H. Garrison and Disciples of Christ* (St. Louis: Bethany Press, 1964); David Edwin Harrell, Jr., *Quest of a Christian America: The Disciples of Christ and American Society to 1866* (Nashville: Disciples of Christ Historical Society, 1966).

8. Tucker, *Garrison*, pp. 186–201; David Edwin Harrell, Jr., "The Sectional Origins of the Churches of Christ," *Journal of Southern History* 30 (Aug. 1964): 261–75; Interview I; author's interview with Smith, 8 January 1973 (cited hereafter as Interview II); Interview I; Jeansonne I.

9. Interview I; Jeansonne I.

10. Smith and Robertson, *Besieged Patriot*, pp. 143–45; Interview I; Jeansonne I; John Strietelmeier, *Valparaiso's First Century: A Centennial History of Valparaiso University* (Valparaiso, Ind.: Valparaiso University, 1959), chap. 3.

11. Gerald L. K. Smith, "Wisconsin Notes," *Christian Standard* 55 (6 March 1920): 594; "More About the Home-Coming at Soldier's Grove," *Christian Standard* 53 (29 June 1918): 1233; "Five Modern 'Timothys,'" *Christian Standard* 56 (15 Jan. 1921): 1702–03; "Constructive Program of the Rural Church," *Christian Standard* 56 (26 March 1921): 2053, 2067; Smith and Robertson, *Besieged Patriot*, n.p.; Interview I; Jeansonne I; Jeansonne, "Preacher, Populist, Propagandist," p. 310.

12. Gerald L. K. Smith, "Fields White Unto the Harvest," *Christian Standard* 58 (28 Oct. 1922): 105–6; "Program of the Rural Church," p. 2053.

13. Gerald L. K. Smith, "Wisconsin's Policy of Aggression," *Christian Standard* 57 (18 March 1922): 3327; "White Unto the Harvest," pp. 105–6; "A Crop of Specialists," *Christian Standard* 57 (9 Sept. 1922): 3933; Jeansonne, "Preacher, Populist, Propagandist," p. 310.

14. Gerald L. K. Smith, "From the Field," *Christian Standard* 57 (15 April 1922): 3450; "Acts of the Brethren," *Christian Standard* 57 (11 Feb. 1922): 3209; Smith and Robertson, *Besieged Patriot*, pp. 93–94, 131, 145–46, 233, 311; Interview I; Jeansonne, "Preacher, Populist, Propagandist," pp. 311–12.

15. "Acts of the Brethren," *Christian Standard* 59 (15 Dec. 1923): 266; "Called to Capitol Avenue," *Christian-Evangelist* 63 (30 Sept. 1926): 1235; L. Peres Buroker, "Two and One-Half Years of Fruitful Service," *Christian-Evangelist* 63 (8 July 1926): 857; Frederick D. Kershner, "University Place Church, Indianapolis," *Christian-Evangelist* 66 (27 June 1929): 851; *Indianapolis Star*, 19 Nov. 1928.

16. Tucker, *Garrison*, pp. 81–104; DeGroot, *The Grounds for Division Among the Disciples of Christ* (Chicago: priv. pub., 1940), pp. 183–215; Norman Furniss, *The Fundamentalist Controversy* (rpt. Hamden, Conn.: Archon Books, 1963), pp. 170–76; James Brownlee North, "The Fundamentalist Controversy Among the Disciples of Christ, 1890–1930" (unpub. Ph.D. diss., University of Illinois, 1973).

17. Gerald L. K. Smith, "The Boy and Girl Go to College," *Christian-Evangelist* 65 (23 Aug. 1928): 1073; "White Unto the Harvest," p. 106; Interviews I and II; Claude E. Hill, *Keeping the Faith: A Book of Sermons* (St. Louis: Bethany Press, [1929]), pp. 20, 26, 166.

18. Hill, *Keeping the Faith*, p. 269; Interview I; Smith and Robertson, *Besieged Patriot*, p. 197; U.S. Congress, House of Representatives, Committee on Un-American Activities, *Investigation of Un-American Propaganda Activities in the United States: Gerald L. K. Smith* (cited hereafter as *HUAC*), 79th Cong., 2d Sess., 30 Jan. 1946, p. 7; "Gerald L. K. Smith," *Current Biography 1943*, p. 707; "News and Comment from the National Capital," *Literary Digest* 119 (16 March 1935): 12.

19. Smith and Robertson, *Besieged Patriot*, p. 131; Interview I; Kenneth T. Jackson, *The Ku Klux Klan in the City, 1915–1930* (New York: Oxford University Press, 1967), p. 150; "Memo on Gerald L. K. Smith," 24 June 1942,

Material File, Midwest Fact Finding Reports, 1941–52, Microfilm Roll 50, B'nai B'rith Anti-Defamation League, Chicago, Illinois (hereafter cited as ADL). The scant surviving evidence from the church, now called the University Park Christian Church, supports Smith's view of his career there and his reasons for leaving. Unspecified trustee and elder to Charles S. Medbury, 18 Dec. 1929 (copy provided by the current pastor, Reverand Tom Martin).

20. Smith and Robertson, *Besieged Patriot*, p. 197; Interview I; Jeansonne I; Jeansonne, "Preacher, Populist, Propagandist," pp. 313–14, 325; Isabel B. Price, "Gerald L. K. Smith and Anti-Semitism," (unpub. M.A. thesis, University of New Mexico, 1965), pp. 32–33, *New Orleans Times-Picayune*, 4 Feb. 1932.

21. *American Progress*, 22 Feb. 1934; Interview I; Frederick D. Kershner, "As I Think On These Things," *Christian-Evangelist* 69 (23 June 1932): 811; "Honor for 'Social Gospel' Preacher," *Christian Century* 50 (9 Aug. 1933): 1019; Jeansonne, "Preacher, Populist, Propagandist," pp. 313–14.

22. Interview I.

23. Alan P. Sindler, *Huey Long's Louisiana* (Baltimore: Johns Hopkins University Press, 1956), pp. 68–97; T. Harry Williams, *Huey Long* (New York: Knopf, 1969) is the standard biography, but Carleton Beals, *The Story of Huey P. Long* (Philadelphia: Lippincott, 1935), is in some respects more perceptive.

24. Alan Brinkley, *Voices of Protest: Huey Long, Father Coughlin, and the Great Depression* (New York: Knopf, 1982), pp. 174–75; Williams, *Huey Long*, pp. 588, 620, 708, 639–813; Sindler, *Long's Louisiana*, p. 99; Forrest Davis, *Huey Long, A Candid Biography* (New York: Dodge, 1935), pp. 37, 39; Raymond Gram Swing, *Forerunners of American Fascism* (New York: Messner, 1935), p. 107.

25. *American Progress*, 22 Feb. 1934; "Mr. Hopkins' Engagements 1934," Container 102, Harry L. Hopkins Collection, Franklin D. Roosevelt Library (FDRL); *New Orleans Times-Picayune*, 3 Feb. 1934.

26. *American Progress*, 22 Feb. 1934; New Orleans *Times-Picayune*, 4 Feb. 1934; Jeansonne, "Preacher, Populist, Propagandist," pp. 315–16.

27. "How Come Huey Long? Or Superman," *New Republic* 82 (13 Feb. 1935): 14–15; Gerald L, K. Smith, "The Huey Long Movement," in Rita James Simon, ed., *As We Saw the Thirties* (Urbana: University of Illinois Press, 1967), p. 56; Studs Terkel, *Hard Times* (New York: Avon Books, 1970), p. 370.

28. Interview I; Simon, *Thirties*, pp. 72–73; Jeansonne, "Preacher, Populist, Propagandist," pp. 316–17.

29. Interview I; Terkel, *Hard Times*, p. 370; Simon, *Thirties*, pp. 67–68, 60–61, 64.

30. Davis, *Long: A Candid Biography*, pp. 299–307; *American Progress*, 8 Feb., 22 March 1934; Williams, *Huey Long*, pp. 692–702; Beals, *Story of Long*, p. 314; Brinkley, *Voices of Protest*, pp. 71–74.

31. Swing, *Forerunners*, pp. 101–2, 98; Davis, *Long: A Candid Biography*, p. 43; Beals, *Story of Long*, p. 312.

32. Williams, *Huey Long*, p. 699; David H. Bennett, *Demogogues in the*

Depression: American Radicals and the Union Party, 1932–1936 (New Brunswick, N.J.: Rutgers University Press, 1969), p. 19; *New York Times*, 16 Aug. 1936; F. Raymond Daniell, "Land of the Free," in Hanson W. Baldwin and Shepherd Stone, *We Saw It Happen: The News Behind the News That's Fit to Print* (New York: Simon and Schuster, 1939), pp. 96–99; *American Progress*, 22 Feb., 29 May 1934; *National Townsend Weekly*, 27 July 1936.

33. Hodding Carter, "How Come Huey Long? Bogeyman—," *New Republic* 82 (13 Feb. 1935): 11; Harnett T. Kane, *Louisiana Hayride: The American Rehearsal for Dictatorship, 1928–1940* (New York: Morrow, 1941), p. 152; *Detroit News*, 3 May 1942; William Bradford Huie, "Gerald Smith's Bid for Power," *American Mercury* 55 (Aug. 1942): 149; Heywood Broun, "Broun's Page," *Nation* 143 (22 Aug. 1936): 213.

34. *American Progress*, 29 March, 5 April 1934; Brinkley, *Voices of Protest*, pp. 173–75, 180–86, 203–9; Alan Brinkley, "Huey Long, The Share Our Wealth Movement, and the Limits of Depression Dissidence," *Louisiana History* 22 (Spring 1981): 117–34; Glen Jeansonne, "Challenge to the New Deal: Huey P. Long and the Redistribution of National Wealth," *Louisiana History* 21 (Fall 1980): 331–40; Robert E. Snyder, "Huey Long and the Presidential Election of 1936," *Louisiana History* 19 (Spring 1975): 117–43.

35. Beals, *Story of Long*, p. 291; Swing, *Forerunners*, p. 100; Kane, *Louisiana Hayride*, pp. 148–49; Interviews I and II.

36. Williams, *Huey Long*, pp. 865–76; *New York Times*, 12 Sept. 1935; Terkel, *Hard Times*, p. 372; Interview I.

37. Terkel, *Hard Times*, p. 272; Smith and Robertson, *Besieged Patriot*, pp. 120–25.

38. *New York Times*, 12, 17, 22 Sept. 1935, 22 June 1936; "The Spirit and Purpose of Huey Long Shall Never Die," flyer in the George Kernion Collection, Louisiana Room, Louisiana State University (hereafter cited as LSU); Sindler, *Long's Louisiana*, pp. 121–22.

39. Kane, *Louisiana Hayride*, pp. 148–57; Sindler, *Long's Louisiana*, pp. 117–27; *New York Times*, 18, 22 Sept. 1934; Interview I; Elmer L. Irey, *The Tax Dodgers: The Inside Story of the T-Men's War with America's Political and Underworld Hoodlums* (New York: Greenberg, 1948), chap. 4; "Share Our Wealth—the Slogan of the Hour," flyer in the Maury Simmons Collection, Louisiana Room, LSU.

40. Kane, *Louisiana Hayride*, pp. 157–62, 181–87; Sindler, *Long's Louisiana*, pp. 120–26.

41. Interview I; *New York Times*, 29 Aug., 22 Sept. 1936; Terkel, *Hard Times*, p. 376.

42. Williams, *Huey Long*, pp. 633, 562–63, 808; *American Progress*, 5 Oct. 1933, 14 Sept. 1933, 22 Feb. 1934, April 1935.

43. *American Progress*, June 1935; Smith to H. L. Mencken, 14 Aug. 1939 and 25 Feb. 1944, Mencken Collection, New York Public Library.

44. *New York Times*, 22 June 1936.

45. Smith and Robertson, *Besieged Patriot*, p. 96; Smith to Mencken, 14 Aug. 1939; *New York Times*, 25, 27, 29, 30, 31 Jan., 2, 4 Feb. 1936; William Anderson, *The Wild Man From Sugar Creek: The Political Career of Eugene*

Talmadge (Baton Rouge: Louisiana State University Press, 1975), pp. 95, 117–19.

46. Francis E. Townsend, *New Horizons (An Autobiography)*, ed. Jesse George Murray (Chicago: Stewart, 1943), p. 189; Abraham Holtzman, *The Townsend Movement: A Political Study* (New York: Bookman Associates, 1963); Richard L. Neuberger and Kelley Loe, *An Army of the Aged* (Caldwell, Idaho: Caxton, 1936); Bennett, *Demagogues*, especially chaps. 10–13.

47. Gerald L. K. Smith, "Contempt of Congress," *Plain Talk* 13 (July 1936): 24–27; *National Townsend Weekly*, 15 June 1936; Townsend, *New Horizons*, pp. 165, 197, 156, 204; Terkel, *Hard Times*, p. 374; Interview I.

48. Holtzman, *Townsend Movement*, pp. 63, 170, 44, 36–40, 218 n.; *National Townsend Weekly*, 18 Sept., 29 June, 6, 13, 20, 27 July, 7, 10 Aug., 2 Nov. 1936; *New York Times*, 31 May, 1 June 1936; Holtzman, *Townsend Movement*, pp. 167–72.

49. Sheldon Marcus, *Father Coughlin: The Tumultuous Life of the Priest of the Little Flower* (New York: Little, Brown, 1973), chaps. 3, 5–6; Charles J. Tull, *Father Coughlin and the New Deal* (Syracuse, N.Y.: Syracuse University Press, 1965), chaps. 3–4; David J. O'Brien, *American Catholics and Social Reform: The New Deal Years* (New York: Oxford University Press, 1968), chap. 3; Brinkley, *Voices of Protest*, chap. 8.

50. Interview I; Gerold Frank, "Huey Long the Second," *Nation* 143 (25 July 1936): 93–94. For accounts of the Union party campaign, see Bennett, *Demagogues*, especially chaps. 14–22; Marcus, *Father Coughlin*, chap. 6; Edward C. Blockorby, *Prarie Rebel: The Public Life of William Lemke* (Lincoln: University of Nebraska Press, 1963), chap. 10; and Brinkley, *Voices of Protest*, pp. 252–61.

51. *New York Times*, 16 July 1936; *National Townsend Weekly*, 27 July 1936. Mencken's comments appeared in the *Baltimore Evening Sun* under the title, "Why Not Gerald?" and a copy was supplied to me by Smith.

52. *National Townsend Weekly*, 27 July 1936; *New York Times*, 16 July 1936.

53. *National Townsend Weekly*, 27 July 1936; *New York Times*, 20 July 1936.

54. *New York Times*, 14, 15, 16 Aug. 1936; *National Townsend Weekly*, 27 July 1936.

55. *New York Times*, 21 July, 12, 16, 25 Aug. 1936; Herbert Harris, "That Third Party," *Current History* 45 (Oct. 1936): 83–84; "Four Preachers in Political Arena," *Literary Digest* 122 (1 Aug. 1936): 5–6; Frederick D. Kershner, "As I Think On These Things," *Christian-Evangelist* 74 (3 Sept. 1936): 1142.

56. *National Townsend Weekly*, 27 July 1936; Heywood Broun, "Broun's Page," *Nation* 143 (22 Aug. 1936): 213.

57. Earle Christenberry, "Tearing the Mask of Hypocrisy from Gerald L. K. Smith," flyer in Louisiana Room, LSU; Clinton Wunder, "Awaken Louisiana," flyer in Louisiana State Library, Baton Rouge; *New York Times*, 24 June, 21, 24 July, 3, 5, 6 Nov. 1936; *New Orleans Times-Picayune*, 3, 5 Nov. 1936; Simon, *Thirties*, p. 72.

58. Harris, "That Third Party," p. 82; Broun, "Broun's Page," p. 213; Kane, *Louisiana Hayride*, p. 153; *National Townsend Weekly*, 28 Sept. 1936.

59. *New York Times*, 20, 21, 25 Oct. 1936; Wunder, "Awaken Louisiana"; *National Townsend Weekly*, 2 Nov. 1936; *Detroit News*, 3 May 1942.

60. March of Time, "The 'Lunatic Fringe,'" Motion Picture, Sound, and Video Branch, National Archives; Raymond Fielding, *The March of Time, 1935–1951* (New York: Oxford University Press, 1978), pp. 159–61.

61. Smith and Robertson, *Besieged Patriot*, pp. 74–75; Fielding, *March of Time*, p. 161; *New York Times*, 19 March 1939.

62. Broun, "Broun's Page," p. 213; *American Progress*, 22 Feb. 1934; Smith to Mencken, 14 Aug. 1939; Interview I; Gutstadt to Samuel Sievers, 2 Dec. 1936; Julius Feist to Gutstadt, 7 Dec. 1935, both in Material File, G. L. K. Smith, 1935–1946, ADL.

63. *National Townsend Weekly*, 17 July 1936; Smith to Richard Gutstadt, 9 Dec. 1940, Material File, G. L. K. Smith, 1935–1946, ADL; Beals, *Story of Long*, pp. 292–93; "White Unto the Harvest," p. 105.

64. *New York Times*, 2 March, 23 Aug., 30, 31 Oct. 1937.

65. Smith and Robertson, *Besieged Patriot*, p. 36; Interview I; Morris L. Ernst, "Gerald L. K. Smith," PSF 146, FDRL; *New York Times*, 23 Aug. 1937; Smith to Mencken, 10 April 1937, 14 Aug. 1939, and 13 March 1944, all in Mencken Collection.

66. William Bradford Huie, "Gerald Smith's Bid for Power," *American Mercury* 55 (Aug. 1942): 141, 150–51; U.S. Congress, House of Representatives, Committee to Investigate Campaign Expenditures, *America First Party* (cited hereafter as *Expenditures*), 78th Cong., 2d Sess, 3 Oct. 1944, p. 255; Smith and Robertson, *Besieged Patriot*, pp. 72–73; Interview I.

67. Smith to Mencken, 14 Aug. 1939; Huie, "Smith's Bid," pp. 151–52; Smith and Robertson, *Besieged Patriot*, pp. 107–8; *New York Times*, 13 Jan. 1939; Merwin K. Hart to George Washington Robnett, 21 April 1959, Addenda, Hart Collection, University of Oregon; Interview I.

68. Gerald L. K. Smith, *Too Much Roosevelt* (Detroit: Committee of One Million, 1940), pp. 50–51; Huie, "Smith's Bid," pp. 151–52; Walter Davenport, "The Mysterious Gerald Smith," *Collier's* 113 (4 March 1944): 15; *HUAC*, pp. 9–10, 21; *Expenditures*, pp. 349–53; Smith and Robertson, *Besieged Patriot*, pp. 36, 136, 59; Interview I; interview with Smith by Glen Jeansonne, 21 Jan. 1975 (cited hereafter as Jeansonne II).

69. Smith to Mencken, 20 July, 14 Aug. 1939; Interview I; author's interview with O. John Rogge, 1 Feb. 1980; Sindler, *Long's Louisiana*, pp. 137–53.

70. Smith to Mencken, 14 Aug. 1939.

71. Frank, "Huey Long the Second," p. 93; Broun, "Broun's Page," p. 213; Lloyd Ray Henderson, "The Political Activities of Gerald L. K. Smith" (unpub. M.A. thesis, University of California, Berkeley, 1955), p. 133A; Bennett, *Demagogues*, pp. 117, 138, 145.

72. Smith, *Roosevelt*, pp. 7–10, 12, 55, 53, 73.

73. Smith, *Roosevelt*, pp. 13, 18, 21, 30–34.

74. Ibid., p. 53; *HUAC*, pp. 8, 19; Gerald L. K. Smith, *Dangerous Enemies: A Warning and an Appeal to All Americans* (Detroit: Committee of One

Million, 1939), pp. 4, 86, 11–14; Interview I; Smith, *Dangerous Enemies*, pp. 83, 97; "Laboratory for Revolution," undated radio speech, WJR, in Michigan Historical Collections, University of Michigan (items from this file, which apparently date from 1939–1940, are cited hereafter as WJR).

75. Davenport, "Mysterious Gerald Smith," p. 15; "Red Terror" (WJR).

76. "The Next President of the United States" (WJR); "Civil War" (WJR); Smith, *Dangerous Enemies*, p. 63.

77. "The Next President of the United States" (WJR); "Vermin in the Dark" (WJR); "No Third Term" (WJR); *Dangerous Enemies*, pp. 63, 15; Smith, *Roosevelt*, pp. 2, 80–81, 35–41, 11.

78. Smith, *Dangerous Enemies*, pp. 6–7, 17, 15, 42, 23, 73, 50–51, 27–28, 74; "Red Terror" (WJR); *New York Times*, 3 May 1937.

79. Smith, *Dangerous Enemies*, pp. 20, 66–69, 81; *Expenditures*, pp. 359–70; Huie, "Smith's Bid," p. 155. For a sympathetic treatment of the Communist role in the CIO, see Harvey Levenstein, *Communism, Anti-Communism, and the CIO* (Westport, Conn.: Greenwood Press, 1981), chaps. 2–6.

80. Smith to Mencken, 14 Aug. 1939, and to Mencken, n.d., both in Mencken Collection; *New York Times*, 5 Aug. 1938; *New York Daily Worker*, 27 April 1938.

81. Smith, *Dangerous Enemies*, pp. 66–69, 8, 22–23; *New York Times*, 10 July 1939; Interview I; Irving Bernstein, *Turbulent Years: A History of the American Worker, 1933–1941* (Boston: Houghton Mifflin, 1971), pp. 555–69, surveys the complex struggle within the UAW.

82. "Laboratory for Revolution" (WJR); "CIO Communism" (WJR); "Red Terror" (WJR); "15 Issues for 1940" (WJR).

83. "15 Issues for 1940" (WJR); "The Next President of the United States" (WJR); "Red Terror" (WJR).

84. "Red Terror" (WJR); "Civil War" (WJR); "Vicious Enemies" (WJR); Smith, *Dangerous Enemies*, pp. 43, 85, 64–65, 10, 30.

85. "The Next President of the United States" (WJR); "Fifteen Issues for 1940" (WJR); *HUAC*, p. 29; "America Awake," undated radio address, in OF 5286, FDRL.

86. Smith, "Contempt of Congress," pp. 26–27; Morris L. Ernst, "Gerald L. K. Smith"; *Congressional Record*, 29 April 1941, pp. 1987–1988, 25 July 1940, pp. 9596–9598; January 30, 1941, pp. A350–352; Smith and Robertson, *Besieged Patriot*, pp. 294, 59–60.

87. Harry Bennett, as told to Paul Marcus, *We Never Called Him Henry* (New York: Gold Medal Books, 1951), p. 128; Interview I; Smith and Robertson, *Besieged Patriot*, p. 160; Smith to Liebold, 2 May, 9 Sept., 11 Sept., 18 Sept., 3, 5 Oct. 1941; 12, 22 Jan 1942; Smith to Ford, 18 June 1941; Liebold to Smith, 7 April, 7 May, 5, 11 Sept. 1941, all in Office File, 1943–44, box 2582, File 1068, Ford Archives, Henry Ford Museum; Ernest Liebold, *Reminiscences*, pp. 1272–73, Ford Archives.

88. Smith and Robertson, *Besieged Patriot*, pp. 44, 42, 162; Liebold, *Reminiscences*, pp. 1272–74; Interview I; Bennett, *We Never Called Him Henry*, pp. 128–29; Smith to Liebold, 2 May 1941 and Liebold to Smith, 7 May 1941, both in File 1068, Ford Archives.

89. Smith radio address, "Henry Ford—By Labor Voted Labor's Friend—Those Who Would Destroy Him," *Congressional Record*, 29 April 1941, p. A1987; Smith and Robertson, *Besieged Patriot*, pp. 43, 45, 258; Interview I.

90. Leo P. Ribuffo, "Henry Ford and The International Jews," *American Jewish History* 69 (June 1980): 469–70.

91. Smith to Mencken, 14 Aug. 1939 and Smith to Butzel, 1 Oct. 1941, both in File 1068, Ford Archives; Gudstadt to Smith, 4 Dec. 1940, Material File, G. L. K. Smith, 1935–1947, microfilm roll 50, ADL.

92. Gutstadt to Smith, 4 Dec. 1940; Harold Saks and Robert Ochs, "T and T," 14 Sept. 1940; Smith to Gutstadt, 9 Dec. 1940, all in Matrial File, G. L. K. Smith, 1935–1947.

93. Smith to Gutstadt, 9 Dec. 1940.

94. Ibid.; Gutstadt to Smith, 12 Dec. 1940, Material File, G. L. K. Smith, 1935–1947.

95. Huie, "Smith's Bid," p. 153; *Christian Science Monitor*, 20 Aug. 1942; [L. M. Birkhead], "Gerald L. K. Smith Doesn't Go to Washington," *Propaganda Battlefront* 2 (Dec. 1942): 2.

96. Smith to Liebold, 9 Sept, 1941; Liebold, *Reminiscences*, p. 1396; Interviews I and II; Smith and Robertson, *Besieged Patriot*, pp. 160–62; "Editorial Comment," *Cross and the Flag* 4 (Feb. 1946): 702.

97. "Gerald L. K. Smith and the Jews: A Significant Summary" and "Quarantined by the Anti-Christ," undated flyers in author's possession; Interviews I and II; Smith and Robertson, *Besieged Patriot*, p. 161.

98. "Quarantined by the Anti-Christ"; Interview II.

99. "15 Issues for 1940" (WJR); "America Awake" (WJR); "Wars and Rumors of Wars" (WJR); "Winchell, You Naughty Pervaricator!" *Cross and the Flag* 4 (Feb. 1945): 522; Smith, *Roosevelt*, pp. 73, 49, 83; Smith to Arthur Vandenberg, rpt. in *Congressional Record*, 25 July 1940, p. 9597; "All for America; Nothing for Russia," undated radio speech (but apparently from late 1941) in OF 5286, FDRL.

100. Wayne S. Cole, *America First: The Battle Against Intervention, 1940–41* (Madison: University of Wisconsin Press, 1953), pp. 134, 139; Wayne S. Cole, *Charles A. Lindbergh and the Battle Against Intervention in World War II* (New York: Harcourt Brace Jovanovich, 1974), p. 177; *New York Herald-Tribune*, 23 April 1943; Will Chasen and Victor Riesel, "'Keep them Out!' The Reverend Gerald L. K. Smith." *Nation* 154 (16 May 1942): 567; Jeansonne II; John T. Flynn to Mrs. John J. Theobold, 24 Sept. 1947, box 20, Flynn Collection, University of Oregon.

101. *Congressional Record*, 25 July 1940, pp. 9596–98; Smith telegram to Arthur Vandenberg, 18 Jan. 1941, box 1, Vandenberg Collection, Michigan Historical Collection.

102. *Congressional Record*, 30 Jan. 1941, pp. A350–52 (cited hereafter as *Foreign Affairs*); U.S. Congress, Senate Committee on Foreign Relations, *To Promote the Defense of the United States* (cited hereafter as *Foreign Relations*), 77th Cong., 1st sess., 4–10 Feb. 1941, pp. 467–73.

103. *Foreign Relations*, pp. 467–73.

104. *New York Herald-Tribune*, 23 April 1943; Interview I.

105. "Victory—A Definition," *Cross and the Flag* 1 (April 1942): 10–11,

15; "We, the People, Are Still Here," *Cross and the Flag* 1 (June 1942): 7–9, 14; "The Little Businessman Faces the Breadline," *Cross and the Flag* 1 (Aug. 1942): 10; "Seven Issues Worth Fighting For," *Cross and the Flag* 2 (Feb. 1944): 338; "Maintain the American Standard of Living (After the War)," *Cross and the Flag* 1 (Sept. 1942): 14; "A New Spirit for Youth" and "The Family Altar," *Cross and the Flag* 1 (Sept. 1942): 7; "Pin-Up Girl," *Cross and the Flag* 3 (May 1944): 392; "If America Loses Christ" and "Crucifixion Cannot Kill," *Cross and the Flag* 1 (July 1942): 5; "$1,000 for Each War Veteran," *Cross and the Flag* 2 (Jan. 1944): 336; "A Crusader's Platform," *Cross and the Flag* 1 (July 1942): 8–12.

106. "A Statement by the Editor," *Cross and the Flag* 1 (June 1942): 16; "Campaign Address," *Cross and the Flag* 1 (Sept. 1942): 3; "My Hat's in the Ring," *Cross and the Flag* 1 (May 1942): 8–9, 15; "Automobile Tires for Everybody," *Cross and the Flag* 1 (Aug. 1942): 8–9, 15; "Nomination Lost—Victory Won," *Cross and the Flag* 1 (Sept. 1942), pp. 8–10; Smith to Mencken, 27 April 1943, Mencken Collection.

107. "Crusader's Platform," p. 9; "Automobile Tires," p. 9; *Detroit Free Press*, 13 Sept. 1942; Richard Polenberg, *War and Society: The United States, 1941–1945* (New York: Lippincott, 1942), pp. 14–18; Richard R. Lingeman, *Don't You Know There's a War On?: The American Home Front, 1941–1945* (New York: Putnam's Sons, 1970): 235–39.

108. *Expenditures*, p. 319; Smith to Mencken, 27 April 1943.

109. "Homer Ferguson," *Current Biography 1943*, pp. 202–4; "One-Man Law Wave" *Time* 39, pt. 2 (1 June 1942): 14–15; *Lansing State Journal*, 11, 12 Sept. 1942; *Detroit News*, 13 Sept. 1942.

110. Smith to Butzel, 1 Oct. 1944.

111. Huie, "Smith's Bid," p. 154.

112. Smith spent $10,612.21; Ferguson, $6,037.22. *Detroit News*, 16 Sept. 1942, reported the following returns from 3,542 of 3,751 precincts: Ferguson, 192,177; Smith, 106,676; Eaton, 42,152; "Winchell's Man Loses," *Cross and the Flag* 1 (Sept. 1942): 14; *Lansing State Journal*, 16, 29 Sept. 1942; *Detroit News* 25, 26, 28, 30 Sept. 1942; *New Orleans Times-Picayune*, 22 Oct. 1942; John H. Hunter, "Gerald L. K. Smith for United States Senator" (unpub. paper, Michigan Historical Collection); E. Eastman Irvine, ed., *World Almanac for 1943* (New York: World Telegram, 1943), p. 731.

113. *Detroit Free Press*, 17 Sept. 1942; *New Orleans State Times*, 16 Sept. 1942; Walter Winchell, "Americans We Could Do Without," *Liberty* (1 Aug. 1942): 9–10; Chasen and Riesel, "Keep Them Out," pp. 566–68; "Enemies at Home," *New Republic* 155 (13 July 1942): 55; Vandenberg to Smith, 27 Aug. 1943, box 2, Vandenberg Collection; Liebold, *Reminiscences*, p. 1275; Smith and Robertson, *Besieged Patriot*, p. 154; *New York Herald-Tribune*, 23 April 1943; *New York Times*, 23 April 1944.

114. FDR, Memorandum for J. Edgar Hoover, 25 March 1943; J. Edgar Hoover to Marvin H. McIntyre, 31 March 1943, OF 10-b, FDRL.

115. Francis Biddle, Memorandum for the President, 2 June 1943 and "Gerald L. K. Smith: Personal History and Background," both in OF 10-b, FDRL; J. Edgar Hoover to Edwin H. Watson, 29 Sept. 1943, PSF 77, FDRL.

116. Smith to Liebold, 3 Oct. 1941; *Cleveland Plain Dealer,* 25 June 1942; Bernard A. Doman, "Cleveland Mayor," *Cross and the Flag* 1 (July 1942): 7, 12–14.

117. *Buffalo Evening News,* 17 Nov. 1943; *Minneapolis Morning Tribune,* 24 March 1944; *Minneapolis Star-Journal,* 25 March, 1 April 1944; "Minneapolis Court Room Scene," *Cross and the Flag* 3 (April 1944): 381; "Minneapolis Does It Again," *Cross and the Flag* 3 (May 1944): 398.

118. *Los Angeles Times,* 21 July 1945; *San Francisco Chronicle,* 18, 20 Oct., 9 Nov. 1945; James P. McLoughlin to Carey McWilliams, 16 Oct. 1945; McWilliams to McLoughlin, 19 Oct. 1945, McWilliams Collection, Bancroft Library, University of California, Berkeley; *Payroll Guarantee Association, Inc., et al.* v. *The Board of Education of the San Francisco Unified School District et al., Pacific Reporter,* Vol. 164, 2d Series, pp. 1–7. On the Payroll Guarantee Association, see Jackson P. Putnam, *Old Age Politics in California: From Richardson to Reagan* (Stanford, Calif.: Stanford University Press, 1970), pp. 94–114. "The City of Angels," *Cross and the Flag* 4 (July 1945): 592, 602; *HUAC,* pp. 37–38; Jonathan E. Perkins and Rev. Wesley A. Swift, "Moscow versus Gerald L. K. Smith," *Cross and the Flag* 4 (Aug. 1945): 614–17.

119. Los Angeles Council for Civil Unity, "America's Number One Fascist—Gerald L. K. Smith," flyer in McWilliams Collection; *Los Angeles Times,* 21 July 1945; Perkins and Swift, "Moscow," pp. 614–17; "Olivia DeHavilland and GLKS," *Cross and the Flag* 4 (Aug. 1945): 617; *HUAC,* pp. 38–39.

120. *Los Angeles Times,* 16 Oct. 1945; "'Mobilization for Democracy' Presentation at L.A. Board of Education Hearing," 15 Oct. 1945, flyer in McWilliams Collection.

121. *Los Angeles Times,* 18 Oct., 2, 3, 4 Nov. 1945.

122. "666 Slave Act Says . . . ," *Cross and the Flag* 2 (Feb. 1944): 344–47; Polenberg, *War and Society,* pp. 175–83.

123. Alfred McClung Lee and Norman D. Humphrey, *Race Riot* (New York: Dryden Press, 1943), pp. 6, 25; "Race Riots! An Interpretation," *Cross and the Flag* 2 (July 1943): 232–34.

124. "Race Riots," pp. 232–34; "Is It a Sin to Be White and Stay White?" *Cross and the Flag* 4 (Feb. 1946): 12.

125. Ibid.; "Pointed Comments," *Cross and the Flag* 2 (Aug. 1943): 246; "Joe Louis vs. Paul Robeson," *Cross and the Flag* 5 (Nov. 1946): 852; "FEPC," *Cross and the Flag* 2 (Oct. 1944): 450 (this is the first article to spell Negro with a capital). See also "Half-Breeds in England" and "Bad Stuff," (on intermarriage), *Cross and the Flag* 5 (April 1946): 741, 743; "FEPC Dead," *Cross and the Flag* 8 (May 1946): 729; and "Theodore Bilbo—The Man," *Cross and the Flag* 5 (June 1946): 774.

126. "What About the Negroes?" *Cross and the Flag* 3 (Sept. 1944): 437.

127. "Maintain the American Standard of Living," p. 14; "Postwar Recovery Commission," *Cross and the Flag* 4 (Sept. 1945): 630–32, 637.

128. "Limit Immigration," *Cross and the Flag* 2 (Dec. 1943): 314; "We the People," pp. 8–9; "Who Gets Hong Kong?" *Cross and the Flag* 3 (March

1945): 528; "Trade Hitler for Stalin?" *Cross and the Flag* 3 (Dec. 1944): 492; "What About India?" *Cross and the Flag* 2 (Aug. 1943): 252; "Ghandi and the Four Freedoms," *Cross and the Flag* 3 (May 1944): 389; "Christians and Traitors," *Cross and the Flag* 3 (Dec. 1944): 487.

129. "We the People," p. 8; "The New Congress," *Cross and the Flag* 1 (Oct.–Nov. 1942): 8–9; "An Open Letter," *Cross and the Flag* 1 (Dec. 1942): 8–10; "Pittsburgh Debate," *Cross and the Flag* 1 (March 1943): 171–74; "Henry Wallace—Super Internationalist," *Cross and the Flag* 1 (Oct.–Nov. 1942): 11–13; "Bretton Woods," *Cross and the Flag* 4 (Oct. 1945): 642; "A Challenge to Debate," *Cross and the Flag* 3 (May 1944): 390; Smith to Mencken, 4 March 1943, Mencken Collection.

130. "About San Francisco" and "An Open Letter to Secretary Stettinius," *Cross and the Flag* 4 (June 1945): 576–77, 590; Smith telegram to Truman, Harry S. Truman Library; "Statement," 25 May 1945, and "An Appraisal," 23 May 1945, in McWilliams Collection.

131. Huie, "Smith's Bid," p. 154; Seymour Martin Lipset and Earl Raab, *The Politics of Unreason: Right-Wing Extremism in America, 1790–1970* (New York: Harper & Row, 1970), p. 244.

132. "Walter Winchell: The Pop-Gun Patriot," *Cross and the Flag* 1 (Dec. 1942): 3; "Winchell Swears on Radio—Condemns American Voters," *Cross and the Flag* 1 (Feb. 1943): 158; "Gestapo Method," *Cross and the Flag* 2 (March 1944): 367–68; *HUAC*, pp. 11, 40–41; "Witch Hunters," *Cross and the Flag* 2 (July 1943): 229; "Libel and Smear Campaign Well Organized," *Cross and the Flag* 2 (Oct. 1943): 278; *Expenditures*, p. 324; Doman, "Cleveland Mayor," pp. 7, 12–14; Bernard A. Doman, "25 Lies About Gerald L. K. Smith," *Cross and the Flag* 3 (Nov. 1944): 473; Smith to Harold Lavine, 9 Dec. 1940, ADL.

133. *Cleveland Plain Dealer*, 25 June 1942; "The Reverend Gerald B. Winrod Persecuted," *Cross and the Flag* 2 (Nov. 1943): 303; "Elizabeth Dilling—The Frances Willard of Nationalism," *Cross and the Flag* 3 (Aug. 1944): 419–20; J. Edgar Hoover to Harry L. Hopkins, 18 Feb. 1943, OF 10-b, FDRL.

134. "The Church and Politics" and "I Confess," *Cross and the Flag* 2 (March 1944): 354; "Pointed Comments," *Cross and the Flag* 2 (May 1943): 203; "Editorial Comment," *Cross and the Flag* 2 (Sept. 1943): 270; "666" and "Russia and Bible Prophecy," *Cross and the Flag* 2 (Oct. 1943): 287; Interview I.

135. "Editorial Comment," *Cross and the Flag* 2 (April 1943): 185; Gerald L. K. Smith, *The Roosevelt Death: A Super Mystery* (1947, rpt. with new epilogue, Los Angeles: Christian Nationalist Crusade, n.d.), passim.

136. *Detroit Free Press*, 13 Sept. 1942; Smith and Robertson, *Besieged Patriot*, p. 225.

137. Erving Goffman, *Stigma: Notes on the Management of Spoiled Identity* (Englewood Cliffs, N.J.: Prentice-Hall, 1963), pp. 10, 17, 24–25, 106, 111.

138. Smith to Gutstadt, 9 Dec. 1941, Material File, G. L. K. Smith, 1935–1947.

139. "Pointed Comments," *Cross and the Flag* 2 (June 1943): 222; "Gentiles Threatened," *Cross and the Flag* 4 (April 1945): 556; "10 Years in Jail for Criticizing a Jew," *Cross and the Flag* 2 (Feb. 1944): 349; "Russia and the Jews," *Cross and the Flag* 4 (May 1945): 562.

140. Smith to Butzel, 1 Oct. 1941, File 1068, Ford Archives; "Pointed Comments," *Cross and the Flag* 2 (June 1943): 222; "Gentiles Threatened," p. 556.

141. Smith to Gutstadt, 9 Dec. 1940, Material File, G. L. K. Smith, 1935–1947; Smith to Mencken, 4 March 1943, Mencken Collection.

142. Smith to Butzel, 1 October 1941, File 1068, Ford Archives; William James, "Final Impressions of a Psychical Researcher," in John J. McDermott, ed., *The Writings of William James: A Comprehensive Edition* (New York: Modern Library, 1968), p. 797.

143. "The Cross and the Flag," undated flyer in McWilliams Collection.

144. "Libel and Smear Campaign," p. 278; "Limit Immigration," p. 314; "Rabbi Wise Has a Plan," *Cross and the Flag* 1 (March 1943): 170; "How to Watch the Sedition Trial," *Cross and the Flag* 3 (June–July, 1944): 412; "Race Riots," p. 234.

145. "An Open Letter," *Cross and the Flag* 3 (Aug. 1944): 418; "The Indiscreet Rabbi," *Cross and the Flag* 2 (Dec. 1943): 313; "Detroit Mob," *Cross and the Flag* 4 (Nov. 1945): 646; "St. Louis Episode," *Cross and the Flag* 5 (May 1946): 763.

146. "Low-Down on Democratic Convention," *Cross and the Flag* 3 (Aug. 1944): 431; "10 Years in Jail," p. 349 (italics added).

147. "Preachers(?) Ashamed of the Name of Christ," *Cross and the Flag* 2 (Nov. 1943): 290; "Russia and the Jews," p. 252.

148. "Why Are the Jews Against America First?" *Cross and the Flag* 3 (June–July 1944): 411; Goffman, *Stigma*, pp. 120–21.

149. "Libel and Smear Campaign," p. 278; "Gentiles Threatened," p. 556; "Baltimore Smear," *Cross and the Flag* 4 (April 1945): 558; "Gestapo Method," pp. 367–68; Smith to Butzel, 1 Oct. 1941, File 1068, Ford Archives; "Wanted—A Jewish Leader with Some Common Sense," *Cross and the Flag* 2 (Nov. 1943): 299.

150. "PM = Promoting Malice, An Open Letter," *Cross and the Flag* 2 (Nov. 1943): 296–97; "Dangerous Business," *Cross and the Flag* 3 (April 1944): 380; Smith to Mencken, 14 Aug. 1939, Mencken Collection.

151. "PM," p. 297; *Expenditures*, passim; Smith to Butzel, 1 Oct. 1941, File 1068, Ford Archives; "Gentiles Threatened," p. 556.

152. *New York Times*, 22, 23 March, 1 April 1944; Elsworth Barnard, *Wendell Willkie: Fighter for Freedom* (Marquette: Northern Michigan University Press, 1966), chap. 21; "Willkie—Ex-Candidate," *Cross and the Flag* 3 (April 1944): 375.

153. *New York Times*, 1, 6 April, 2, 16, 22, 27 May 1944; "Whose Man Is Dewey?" *Cross and the Flag* 3 (May 1944): 390; "An Open Letter," *Cross and the Flag* 3 (Aug. 1944): 418, 423.

154. "The America First Party," *Cross and the Flag* 1 (Jan. 1943): 8; *HUAC*, p. 27; *Expenditures*, p. 326; *Detroit Free Press*, 3, 30 Aug. 1944;

Detroit News, 1 Aug. 1944; *New York Times*, 27 July, 2, 3 Aug. 1944; "Dewey Condemns America First," *Cross and the Flag* 3 (Sept. 1944): 443; John T. Flynn telegram to Smith, 22 Jan. 1946, box 29, Flynn Collection.

155. *Detroit News*, 1, 31 Aug. 1944; *Detroit Free Press*, 30, 31 Aug. 1944; *Expenditures*, p. 335.

156. Ibid.; Smith to Justice Frank Murphy, 6 Sept. 1944, Murphy Collection, Michigan Historical Collection.

157. America First Party platform, bound in *Cross and the Flag* 3 (Sept. 1944): n.p. On growing anti-Semitism in the general population, see John Morton Blum, *V Was for Victory: Politics and American Culture During World War II* (New York: Harcourt Brace Jovanovich, 1976), pp. 172–81.

158. *New York Times*, 17 Aug., 30 Sept., 2, 11 Oct. 1944; *Detroit Free Press*, 17 Aug. 1944; *Expenditures*, p. 333; E. Eastman Irvine, ed., *The World Almanac and Book of Facts for 1946* (New York: World Telegram, 1946), p. 521; "Dewey Learned a Lesson," *Cross and the Flag* 3 (Nov. 1944): 478; "Bricker Could Have Won," *Cross and the Flag* 3 (Dec. 1944): 484.

159. *New York Times*, 17 Aug. 1944. *HUAC*, pp. 11–12.

160. *HUAC*, pp. 21, 24; *Expenditures*, p. 360; "City of Angels," p. 604; "Rallies! Riots!—Forbidden Manuscript Resurrected!" Sept. 1946, flyer in McWilliams Collection.

161. "Rabbi Exposes Zionist Racket," *Cross and the Flag* 6 (April 1947): 13; "Morgenthau's Bloody Deed," *Cross and the Flag* 3 (Nov. 1944): 475; "Lt. Gen. Morgan," *Cross and the Flag* 5 (Feb. 1947): 902; "Jewish Nationalism," *Cross and the Flag* 3 (Nov. 1944): 476; "Palestine First," *Cross and the Flag* 5 (Jan. 1946): 696; "Terror Mobs in Jerusalem and Chicago," *Cross and the Flag* 5 (Sept. 1946): 821.

162. "Martin Luther and the Jews," *Cross and the Flag* 6 (Jan. 1948): 7; "The Popes and the Jews," *Cross and the Flag* 6 (March 1948): 8–9; Gerald L. K. Smith, *Jesus vs. the Jews* (St. Louis: Christian Nationalist Crusade, [1948]), pp. 3–4, rpt. from *Cross and the Flag* 6 (Jan. 1948).

163. William James, *The Varieties of Religious Experience: A Study in Human Nature* (New York: Modern Library, n.d.), pp. 202, 186.

5. Brown Scare

1. Morris Schonbach, "Native Fascism During the 1930's and 1940's: A Study of Its Roots, Its Growth, and Its Decline" (unpub. Ph.D. diss., University of California, Los Angeles, 1958), pp. 232, 435–37; "Father Coughlin a Nazi Hero," *Anti-Nazi Forum* (April 1939), pp. 48–49; "The Nazi Fifth Column—USA," *Anti-Nazi Bulletin* 7 (Nov. 1940): 6–7, 10; *First Annual Report of the Council for Democracy* (New York: Council for Democracy, 1942), pp. 6–7, 10; "Silver Shirts Come East," *The Hour*, no. 6 (15 July 1939): 3 (published by the American Council Against Nazi Propaganda); "Gerald Smith's Fascist Star on the Rise," *The Hour*, no. 20 (18 Nov. 1939): 5; "The Council Against Intolerance in America: What and Why?" *American Unity: A Monthly Manual of Education* 1 (Nov. 1942): 22–23.

2. E. J. Kahn, Jr., "Democracy's Friend," pt. 1, *New Yorker* 23 (26 July 1947): 29, 38; pt. 2, *New Yorker* 23 (2 Aug. 1947): 29; "Friends of Democracy, Inc.," *Propaganda Battlefront* 1 (24 July 1943): 1–4; "An Explanation," *Propaganda Battlefront* 3 (30 April 1945): supplement; "Statement to Members and Prospective Members of the National Committee of Friends of Democracy," H. L. Mencken Collection, New York Public Library; Roy Tozier, "Confidential Report," carton 10, America First Committee Collection, Hoover Institution, Stanford University; John McAleer, *Rex Stout: A Biography* (Boston: Little, Brown, 1977), p. 316.

3. Clinton Rossiter, *Conservatism in America: The Thankless Persuasion* (New York: Vintage Books, 1962), p. 128.

4. T. Harry Williams, *Huey Long* (New York: Knopf, 1969), p. 760; Alfred M. Bingham, *Insurgent America: Revolt of the Middle Classes* (New York: Harper & Brothers, 1935), p. 186; A. B. Magil and Henry Stevens, *The Peril of Fascism: The Crisis of American Democracy* (New York: International Publishers, 1938), pp. 11–12; Norman Thomas, *After the New Deal, What?* (New York: Macmillan, 1936), p. 43; Sinclair Lewis, *It Can't Happen Here* (Garden City, N.Y.: Doubleday, Doran, 1935), pp. 249–52, 343, 68, 88; Harold Lavine, *Fifth Column in America* (New York: Doubleday, Doran, 1940); "Propaganda Is a Weapon," *Propaganda Battlefront 1* (27 Sept. 1943): 4; Harold D. Lasswell et al., *Language and Politics: Studies in Quantitative Semantics* (New York: Stewart, 1949), chap. 9; "The Attack on Democracy," *Propaganda Analysis* 2 (1 Jan. 1939): 1–8; "The Fifth Column," *Propaganda Analysis* 3 (8 July 1940): 1–8.

5. Warren Susman, "The Thirties," in Stanley Coben and Lorman Ratner, eds., *The Development of an American Culture* (Englewood Cliffs, N.J.: Prentice-Hall, 1970), pp. 184–85, 189; Harry F. Ward, "The Development of Fascism in the United States," *Annals of the American Academy of Political and Social Science* 180 (1 July 1935): 55.

6. Susman, "Thirties," pp. 213–14; Richard J. Walton, *Henry Wallace, Harry Truman, and the Cold War* (New York: Viking Press, 1976), pp. 10–15; "Fascism in America," *Life* 6 (6 March 1939): 57–63.

7. Heinz H. F. Eulau, "False Prophets in the Bible Belt," *New Republic* 110 (7 Feb. 1944): 171; Hamilton Basso, "The Little Hitlers at Asheville," *New Republic* 88 (2 Sept. 1936): 100–101; "Gerald L. K. Smith," *Current Biography, 1943* p. 707.

8. "The Capitalists and the Premillenarians," *Christian Century* 38 (14 April 1921): 3; L. M. Birkhead, *The Sins of Good People* ([Girard, Kan.]: Haldeman-Julius, n.d.), pp. 19, 25; C. Allyn Russell, *Voices of American Fundamentalism: Seven Biographical Studies* (Philadelphia: Westminister Press, 1976), p. 242.

9. Joel A. Carpenter, "Fundamentalist Institutions and the Rise of Evangelical Protestatism," *Church History* 47 (March 1980): 62–75; Robert Moats Miller, *American Protestantism and Social Issues, 1919–1939* (Chapel Hill: University of North Carolina Press, 1958), chap. 8.

10. Max Lerner, *It Is Later Than You Think: The Need for a Militant Democracy* (New York: Viking Press, 1939), p. 196; *A Confidential State-*

ment Concerning Pro-Nazi and Anti-Semitic Organizations (n.p.: Friends of Democracy, n.d.), n.p.; Les K. Adler and Thomas G. Paterson, "Red Fascism: The Merger of Nazi Germany and Soviet Russia in the American Image of Totalitarianism, 1930s–1950s," *American Historical Review* 75 (April 1970): 1046–64; "Red Fascism, Brown Bolshevism: The American Image of Totalitarianism in the 1930s," *Historian* 40 (Nov. 1977): 85–103.

11. "It Can Happen Here" and "Fascism in America," *Life* 6 (6 March 1939): 22–23, 57–63; Raymond Fielding, *The March of Time, 1935–1951* (New York: Oxford University Press, 1978), pp. 49–53, 159–61; Herman Klurfeld, *Winchell: His Life and Times* (New York: Praeger, 1976), pp. 81, 90–91, 146; Bob Thomas, *Winchell* (Garden City, N.Y.: Doubleday, 1971), pp. 98–101; Andrew Bergman, *We're in the Money: Depression America and Its Films* (New York: Harper & Row, 1972), pp. 107–9.

12. William Stott, *Documentary Expression and Thirties America (New York: Oxford University Press, 1973), pp. ix, 22, 276;* Richard Rollins, *I Find Treason: The Story of an American Anti-Nazi Agent* (New York: William Morrow, 1941), p. 63.

13. Schonbach, "Native Fascism," pp. 372, 367, 383; Edward L. Barrett, Jr., *The Tenney Committee: Legislative Investigation of Subversive Activities in California* (Ithaca, N.Y.: Cornell University Press, 1951), pp. 1–30; Walter Goodman, *The Committee: The Extraordinary Career of the House Committee on Un-American Activities* (Baltimore: Penguin Books, 1968), pp. 18–22, 59–64, 90–95, 154–159; August Raymond Ogden, *The Dies Committee: A Study of the Special House Committee for the Investigation of Un-American Activities, 1938–1943* (Washington, D.C.: Catholic University of America Press, 1943), chap. 3–7; Dov Fisch, "The Libel Trial of Robert Edward Edmondson: 1936–1938," *American Jewish History* 71 (Sept. 1981): 79–102.

14. Martin Dies, *The Trojan Horse in America* (New York: Dodd, Mead, 1940), pp. 9, 11, 146; Frank J. Donner, *The Un-Americans* (New York: Ballantine Books, 1961), pp. 25–31.

15. Jerry Voorhis, *Confessions of a Congressman (Garden City, N.Y.: Doubleday, 1947), p. 211;* Zechariah Chafee, Jr., *Free Speech in the United States* (Cambridge, Mass.: Harvard University Press, 1941), pp. 440–90.

16. "The Nazis Are Here," *Nation* 128 (4 March 1939): 253; "More About Free Speech," *New Republic* 96 (31 Aug. 1938): 105.

17. Ludwig Lore, "Nazi Politics in America," *Nation* 137 (29 Nov. 1933): 617; Heywood Broun, "Is There a *Nation*?" *Nation* 144 (17 April 1937): 437; "Free Speech, With Reservations," *New Republic* 95 (13 July 1938): 278; "Free Speech Again," *New Republic* 95 (3 Aug. 1938): 347; "Words Leading to Words," *New Republic* 95 (27 July 1938): 337.

18. Schonbach, "Native Fascism," p. 377; Birkhead to H. L. Mencken, 30 Jan. 1941, Mencken Collection, New York Public Library; Max Lerner, *Ideas Are Weapons: The History and Uses of Ideas* (New York: Viking Press, 1939), pp. 22–24; Lewis Mumford, *Faith for Living* (New York: Harcourt, Brace, 1940), pp. 106–7; Richard H. Pells, *Radical Visions and American Dreams: Culture and Social Thought in the Depression Years* (New York: Harper Torchbooks, 1974), p. 36.

19. Don Whitehead, *The FBI Story: A Report to the People* (New York: Random House, 1956), pp. 161–62; Louis Howe to Stephen Early, 27 Feb. 1934, OF 3206; Howe, Memorandum for the Attorney General, 27 March 1934, OF 950; FDR to Attorney General, 2 March 1934, OF 950; Howe, Memorandum for the Attorney General, 12 April 1938, PSF 77; [FBI] Memorandum Re: George W. Christians, 11 Oct. 1941, OF 950; FDR, Memorandum for McIntyre, 6 Feb. 1936, PPF 1632; Paul M. Hart, Memorandum for Mr. Jervis, 16 June 1934, PPF 1632, Franklin D. Roosevelt Library (hereafter cited as FDRL).

20. Sanford J. Ungar, *FBI* (Boston: Atlantic-Little, Brown, 1976), pp. 54–55, 59–61; Whitehead, *FBI Story*, chaps. 8–17; Ovid Demaris, *The Director: An Oral Biography of J. Edgar Hoover* (New York: Harper's Magazine Press, 1975), p. 56; Fred J. Cook, *The FBI Nobody Knows* (New York: Macmillan, 1964), pp. 138–39, 146–254; Max Lowenthal, *The Federal Bureau of Investigation* (New York: William Sloane Associates, 1950), chaps. 24–26; Francis Biddle, *In Brief Authority* (Garden City, N.Y.: Doubleday, 1962), p. 165; United States Senate, *Final Report of the Select Committee to Study Governmental Operations with Respect to Intelligence Activities* (cited hereafter as *Church Committee*), 94th Cong., 2d sess., bk. 3, pp. 382–91; Kenneth O'Reilly, "A New Deal for the FBI: The Roosevelt Administration, Crime Control, and National Security," *Journal of American History* 69 (Dec. 1982): 638–58.

21. *Church Committee*, bk. 3, pp. 394–405, 413–15; bk. 2, p. 31; Whitehead, *FBI Story*, p. 166; Ungar, *FBI*, p. 102; FDR, Memorandum, 26 June 1939, box 20, OF 10-b, FDRL.

22. Manfred Jonas, *Isolationism in America, 1933–1941* (Ithaca, N.Y.: Cornell University Press, 1966); R. Alan Lawson, *The Failure of Independent Liberalism, 1930–1941* (New York: Putnam's Sons, 1971), pp. 233–55; Frank A. Warren, *An Alternative Vision: The Socialist Party in the 1930s* (Bloomington: Indiana University Press, 1974), chap. 9; Irving Howe and Lewis Coser, with Julius Jacobson, *The American Communist Party: A Critical History (1919–1957)* (Boston: Beacon Press, 1957), chap. 9; Pells, *Radical Visions*, chap. 8; Geoffrey S. Smith, "Isolationism, the Devil and the Advent of World War II: Variations on a Theme," *International History Review* 4 (Feb. 1982): 55–89.

23. Franklin D. Roosevelt, "Fireside Chat on National Defense," 26 May 1940, in Samuel I. Rosenman, ed., *The Public Papers and Addresses of Franklin D. Roosevelt*, Vol. 9 (New York: Macmillan, 1941), pp. 238–39, "We Choose Human Freedom," 27 May 1941, in Samuel I. Rosenman, ed., *The Public Papers and Addresses of Franklin D. Roosevelt*, Vol. 10 (New York: Harper & Brothers, 1942), p. 191; Geoffrey S. Smith, *To Save a Nation: American Countersubversives, the New Deal, and the Coming of World War II* (New York: Basic Books, 1973), p. 172; Wayne S. Cole, *America First: The Battle Against Intervention, 1940–41* (Madison: University of Wisconsin Press, 1953), p. 107; Michele Flynn Stenehjem, *An American First: John T. Flynn and the America First Committee* (New Rochelle, N.Y.: Arlington House, 1976), pp. 131, 154; Thomas, *Winchell*, pp. 164–68; Richard W.

Steele, "Franklin D. Roosevelt and His Foreign Policy Critics," *Political Science Quarterly* 94 (Spring 1979): 15–24.

24. Wayne S. Cole, *Charles A. Lindbergh and the Battle Against Intervention in World War II* (New York: Harcourt Brace Jovanovich, 1974), chaps. 19–21; "Kosher Yeast," *Roll Call* 2 (29 Sept. 1941): 3.

25. Friends of Democracy, *The America First Committee: The Nazi Transmission Belt* (Kansas City: Friends of Democracy, n.d.); Cole, *America First*, chap. 7; Cole, *Charles A. Lindbergh*, chaps. 17–18; Mark Lincoln Chadwin, *The Warhawks: American Interventionists Before Pearl Harbor* (New York: Norton, 1970), pp. 157, 168, 162, 209, 246; L. M. Birkhead to Peter F. H. Cusick, 24 April 1941, box 31; Ulric Bell to Birkhead, 22 Oct. 1941, box 11, Fight for Freedom Committee Collection, Princeton University; *Cincinnati Post*, 3 May 1941.

26. *Church Committee*, bk. 3, pp. 404–6, 413–15, 421–22; bk. 2, pp. 6, 27, 31; Cook, *FBI Nobody Knows*, pp. 253–57.

27. [FBI], "Gerald L. K. Smith," PSF 76; Hoover to Edwin M. Watson, 15 Jan. 1942 and Hoover to Watson, 22 July 1943, box 2, OF 10-b, FDRL.

28. FDR to Hoover, 14 June 1940; FDR, Memorandum for the Attorney General, 10 June 1940, box 20; Hoover to Watson, 11 Dec. 1940, enclosing "James True Associates," box 24; "Joseph P. Kamp," box 25; FDR to Watson, 29 April 1941; Watson to Hoover, 30 April 1941; "Lawrence Dennis," box 26; FDR, Memorandum for the Attorney General, 26 Jan. 1940, all in OF 3892, FDRL; Winchell to FDR, 15 Sept. 1939, OF 5547, FDRL.

29. Hoover, Memorandum, 18 Jan. 1941; Hoover to Watson, 27 Feb. 1941, box 25; Hoover to Watson, 14 August 1941, and 13 Oct. 1941, box 28; Watson, Memorandum for the President, FBI, Report #400 (22 Oct. 1941), Report #533 (13 Dec. 1940), box 24, all in OF 10-b, FDRL; Leonard Mosley, *Lindbergh: A Biography* (Garden City, N.Y.: Doubleday, 1976), pp. 286–89; Cole, *Charles A. Lindbergh*, p. 129.

30. *Church Committee*, bk. 2, pp. 9, 32; Vol. 6, pp. 452–54; Marvin McIntyre, Memorandum for the Attorney General, 26 Dec. 1940; FDR, Memorandum for the Attorney General, 11 May 1942, box 21; Early, Memorandum to Hoover, 27, 29 May 1940; FDR to Early, 21 Feb. 1941, box 20, all in OF 10-b, FDRL.

31. Biddle, *In Brief Authority*, p. 258; James Rowe, Jr., Memorandum for the Attorney General, 25 February 1943, PSF 76, FDRL; Neil M. Johnson, *George Sylvester Viereck: German-American Propagandist* (Urbana: University of Illinois Press, 1972), pp. 221–35.

32. Biddle, *In Brief Authority*, pp. 234–35, 237–38; *Washington Post*, 30 April, 3 May, 7 May, 22 July 1942; Wendell Berge to Attorney General, 1 May 1942; Berge to J. Edgar Hoover, 23 April 1942, box 24, Berge Collection, Library of Congress; Sheldon Marcus, *Father Coughlin: The Tumultuous Life of the Priest of the Little Flower* (Boston: Little, Brown, 1973), pp. 208–17; Sander A. Diamond, *The Nazi Movement in the United States, 1924–1941* (Ithaca, N.Y.: Cornell University Press, 1974), pp. 345–49; Leland V. Bell, *In Hitler's Shadow: The Anatomy of American Nazism* (Port Washington, N.Y.: Kennikat Press, 1973), p. 106; Paul L. Murphy, *The*

Constitution in Crisis Times, 1918–1969 (New York: Harper Torchbooks, 1972), pp. 224–26.

33. FDR to Hoover, 21 Jan. 1942, PSF 76, FDRL; Biddle, *In Brief Authority*, pp. 234–35, 237–38; FDR to Frank Knox, 19 Feb. 1942, OF 4811, FDRL; FDR, Memorandum for the Attorney General, 16 April 1942, PSF 10, FDRL.

34. *Washington Post*, 22 July, 20, 22, 24 March, 12 April, 7 May 1942; Rowe, Memorandum for the Attorney General, 25 February 1943.

35. Biddle, *In Brief Authority*, p. 238.

36. *New York Times*, 28 May 1942; "The 'Ism' of Appeasement," *Life* 10 (20 Jan. 1941): 26–27; "Enemies at Home," *New Republic* 106 (20 April 1942): 541–42; George Seldes, with Helen Seldes, *Facts and Fascism* (New York: In Fact, 1943); Michael Sayers and Albert E. Kahn, *Sabotage! The Secret War Against America* (New York: Harper & Brothers, 1942) and *The Plot Against the Peace: A Warning to the Nation* (New York: Dial Press, 1945); Henry Hoke, *Blackmail* (New York: Reader's Book Service, 1944), p. 2; Walter Winchell, "Americans We Could Do Without," *Liberty*, 1 Aug. 1942, pp. 9–11, 44–46.

37. "The Psychological Onslaught Against Us," *Propaganda Battlefront* 1 (27 Sept. 1943): 1; "The Coming American Menace," *Propaganda Battlefront* 1 (14 Feb. 1943): 1; "The Battle for the Mind of America," *Propaganda Battlefront* 1 (3 Nov. 1943): 1; Kahn and Sayers, *Sabotage!* p. 245; Seldes, *Facts and Fascism*, pp. 275, 12, 96–97, 151; Kahn and Sayers, *Plot Against the Peace*, p. 192; Radio Reports, Inc., Manuscript Service, Special for Committee on Constitutional Government (cited hereafter as *Radio Reports*), 1 Dec. 1943, box 23, John T. Flynn Collection, University of Oregon.

38. John Roy Carlson (pseud. for Avedis Derounian), *Under Cover: My Four Years in the Nazi Underground of America* (New York: Dutton, 1943), pp. 70, 72, 266, 278; Avedis Derounian, "An Immigrant American Speaks Out," *Forum* 102 (Nov. 1939): 195–99.

39. Carlson, *Under Cover*, pp. 283, 238, 480; E. J. Kahn, Jr., "Democracy's Friend," pt. 2, *New Yorker* 23 (2 Aug. 1947): 35; "John Roy Carlson," *Current Biography 1943*, p. 102; "Under Cover," *Propaganda Battlefront* 1 (27 Sept. 1943), p. 1; *Radio Reports*, 18 Aug. 1943, p. 2.

40. Carlson, *Under Cover*, pp. 293, 399–400, 167; *Radio Reports*, 18 Aug. 1943.

41. Carlson, *Under Cover*, pp. 294, 318, 73, 122, 303.

42. Ibid., pp. 241, 249; *St. Louis Post-Dispatch*, 7 May 1944.

43. *New York Journal-American*, 26 Sept. 1946; *St. Louis Post-Dispatch*, 7 May 1944; *New York Times*, 7 Aug. 1943; McAleer, *Rex Stout*, p. 329; "Dutton and Winchell Sued for 'Under Cover,'" *Publisher's Weekly* 144 (6 Nov. 1943): 1791; "Council 'Under Cover' Movie Short Released in Twenty Theaters," *Publisher's Weekly* 144 (13 Nov. 1944): 1871; *Radio Reports*, 8, 5, 2 Sept., 14, 4 Nov., 13 Oct. 1943.

44. Carlson, *Under Cover*, pp. 245, 250; Norman Thomas to Burton K. Wheeler, 29 Dec. 1943; General Lewis Hershey to Wheeler, 9 Dec. 1943; Senate Resolution 201, box 24, Flynn Collection; *New York Times*, 30 Sept. 1944, 6 Aug. 1943, 26 Sept. 1946; *Washington Times-Herald*, 28 Sept. 1946;

New York Journal-American, 26 Sept. 1946; St. Louis Post-Dispatch, 7 May 1944; "Dutton and Winchell Sued," p. 1791; John T. Flynn, *The Smear Terror* (New York: privately pub., 1947) pp. 23–24.

45. Flynn, *Smear Terror,* pp. 11, 17, 21; *Chicago Tribune,* 12 Jan. 1947; *Washington Times-Herald,* 20 Feb., 23 April 1945; Flynn to Robert E. Wood, 3 January 1944, box 24, Flynn Collection; John T. Flynn, "The Smear Offensive: A Report," p. 2, box 29, Flynn Collection; Stenehjem, *An American First,* pp. 168, 170; Richard Clark Frey, Jr., "John T. Flynn and the United States in Crisis, 1928–1950" (unpub. Ph.D. diss., University of Oregon, 1969), pp. 271–84.

46. *Radio Reports,* 1 Dec. 1943.

47. Flynn, *Smear Terror,* pp. 10–11, 14, 20, 24, 29; Carlson, *Under Cover,* p. 520; *New York Times,* 31 March 1944.

48. Wheeler to Flynn, 31 Dec. 1943, box 24, Flynn Collection.

49. *United States* v. *Winrod,* box 1350, Acc. 64-A-379, Loc. 16/79-32-1, Washington National Records Center, Suitland, Md.; *New York Times,* 5 Jan. 1943; Heinz H. F. Eulau, "Sedition Trials: 1944," *New Republic* 110 (13 March 1944): 337–38.

50. "Sherlock Stokes," *Time* 43 (11 Jan. 1943): 69; *New York Times,* 24 July 1942; Francis B. Sayre, "Criminal Conspiracy," *Harvard Law Review* 35 (Feb. 1922): 393–427; "Developments in the Law—Criminal Conspiracy," *Harvard Law Review* 72 (March 1959): 922–1008; "Connecting Defendants to Conspiracies: The Slight Evidence Rule and the Federal Courts," *Virginia Law Review* 64 (Oct. 1978): 881–95; Memorandum on Conspiracy Cases, 21 April 1944, bk. 2686, ACLU Collection, Princeton University.

51. Zechariah Chafee to A. L. Wirin, 13 October 1942, box 9; Chafee to Burton K. Wheeler, 12 March 1942, box 31, both in Chafee Collection, Harvard Law School; Roger N. Baldwin to John W. Jackson, 13 Oct. 1942, bk. 2497; "Minutes of the Committee on Sedition Prosecutions," 2 Dec. 1942; Morris L. Ernst to Baldwin, 13 May 1942, bk. 2605; [Arthur Garfield Hays et al.] to Biddle, 9 Oct. 1942; Statement on behalf of the majority of the board, 28 Jan. 1943, bk. 2686, all in ACLU Collection; Ernst to FDR, 8 April 1941, 23 May 1942, PSF 146, FDRL.

52. *Washington Post,* 9, 23 Nov. 1941, 22, 23, 24 July 1942, 4 Jan. 1943; *PM,* 6 April, 24 July 1942; *New York Times,* 4 Jan. 1943; *New York Daily Worker,* 16 Jan. 1942; "Small-Shot Conspiracy," *New Republic* 107 (3 Aug. 1942): 135; Kahn, "Democracy's Friend," pt. 1, p. 30; Carlson, *Under Cover,* pp. 409–15, 485–97; "Behind Fascist Dennis: Senators, GOP Big-Shots," *In Fact* 8 (17 Jan. 1944): 1–4; Kahn and Sayers, *Sabotage!* pp. 251–52.

53. *Chicago Tribune,* 25 July 1942, 12 Feb. 1943; Defenders staff, *The Sedition Case* (rpt. Hollywood, Calif.: Sons of Liberty, n.d.), pp. 20–24; *New York Times,* 15 Jan. 1943; *New York Post,* 23 April 1943; *New York Journal-American,* 24 March 1943; *New York Daily Worker,* 16 Jan. 1943; *Washington Post,* 20 Dec. 1942; author's interview with Burton K. Wheeler, 17 April 1970.

54. Berge to Rowe, 15 April 1942, box 24, Berge Collection, Rowe, "Memorandum"; *Washington Post,* 20 Dec. 1942; Dillard Stokes to Zecha-

riah Chafee, 4 Feb. 1943, box 31, Chafee Collection; author's interview with James Rowe, Jr., 5 Feb. 1980; *New York Times,* 7 Feb. 1943.

55. *New York Post,* 1, 3, 8 Feb 1943; *Washington Times-Herald,* 29 Jan. 1943; "The Shape of Things," *Nation* 156 (20 Feb. 1943); 254–55; Rowe, Memorandum; "O[etje] John Rogge," *Current Biography 1948,* pp. 533–34; author's interview with O. John Rogge, 1 Feb. 1980; O. John Rogge, *The Official German Report: Nazi Penetration, 1928–1942, Pan-Arabism, 1939–Today* (New York: Yoseloff, 1961), p. 173; Rowe interview.

56. *Wichita Beacon,* 6 March 1943; *Washington Post,* 6 March 1943; Rogge, *Official German Report,* p. 174; Rogge interview; Roger N. Baldwin, "Memorandum on Seditious Conspiracy Trial," 28 Dec. 1944, bk. 2686, and Baldwin to Committee on War Cases, 15 Dec. 1944, bk. 2605, both in ACLU Collection.

57. The indictment is reprinted in Maximilian St.-George and Lawrence Dennis, *A Trial on Trial: The Great Sedition Trial of 1944* (n.p.: National Civil Rights Committee, 1946), pp. 114–21.

58. *New York Herald-Tribune,* 4 Jan. 1944; *PM,* 4 Jan. 1944; *New York Times,* 4 Jan. 1944; Biddle to FDR, June 2, 1943, PSF 76, FDRL.

59. Ronald Radosh, *Prophets on the Right: Profiles of Conservative Critics of American Globalism* (New York: Simon and Schuster, 1975), p. 276; Jones to William Langer, 2 Sept. 1944, Langer Collection, University of North Dakota; [FBI], Memorandum, 8 March 1942; [FBI], Re: Detroit Riots, 20–22 June 1943, OF 10-b; J. Edgar Hoover to Attorney General, 18 April 1938, PSF 77, FDRL; Deatherage to William Langer, 3 March 1943, box 31, Chafee Collection; Flynn, "Smear Offensive," p. 4; *New York Herald-Tribune,* 4 Jan. 1944; *PM,* 4 Jan. 1944; *New York Times,* 4 Jan. 1944; Robert Lewis Taylor, "The Kampf of Joe McWilliams," *New Yorker* 16 (24 Aug. 1940): 34–44; Milton S. Mayer, "Mrs. Dilling: Lady of *The Red Network,*" *American Mercury* 47 (July 1939): 293–99.

60. Klein to William Langer, 16 Sept. 1944, box 145-A, Langer Collection; *Chicago Daily Times,* 23 July 1942; E. Hilton Jackson to Chafee, 17 March 1944, box 31, Chafee Collection; St.-George and Dennis, *Trial on Trial,* pp. 324, 342; author's interview with Elizabeth R. Young (court-appointed attorney for William R. Lyman), 15 Feb. 1980.

61. Dennis to Chafee, 21 Dec. 1943, encl. "Brief: In re Lawrence Dennis," pp. 3, 8, box 31, Chafee Collection. St.-George and Dennis, *Trial on Trial,* pp. 305–6; Radosh, *Prophets on the Right,* pp. 275–322; Justus D. Doenecke, "The Isolationist as Collectivist: Lawrence Dennis and the Coming of World War II," *Journal of Libertarian Studies* 3 (Summer 1979): 191–207.

62. Eicher to FDR, 2 March 1942, PPF 2681, FDRL; "Edward C(layton) Eicher," *Current Biography 1941,* p. 256; Rogge interview; *United States* v. *McWilliams,* 54 F.Supp. 791–95; "The Sedition Trial: A Study in Delay and Obstruction," *University of Chicago Law Review* 15 (Spring 1948): 691–94.

63. "Sedition Trial," pp. 691–94.

64. "Defendants in War Sedition Trial Enliven Opening by Circus Antics," *Newsweek* 23 (1 May 1944): 34; *Chicago Tribune,* 18 April 1944; James Wechsler, "Sedition and Circuses," *Nation* 158 (6 May 1944): 530–31.

65. *United States* v. *McWilliams*, transcript (cited hereafter as *Transcript*), boxes 1371–78, Acc. 64-A-379, Loc. 16/79-32-1, pp. 5, 83, 100–8, 15; *New York Post*, 24 April 1944; *Chicago Tribune*, 18 April 1944; *New York Times*, 18 April 1944.

66. *Transcript*, pp. 277, 266, 13, 420; *New York Times*, 19, 20 April 1944.

67. *Transcript*, pp. 1108–55, 5789, 499–500, 1429–30; *PM*, 23 April 1944; *New York Times*, 25, 27 April 1944; *Transcript*, pp. 710–37, 534, 710, 717–18, 727, 819, 959–60, 1391; *New York Times*, 26, 27 April 1944.

68. *Transcript*, p. 1651; *PM*, 24 April 1944; *New York Times*, 4 May 1944, 27 April 1944.

69. Robert Noble to Langer, 20 Sept. 1944, box 128, Langer Collection; *Transcript*, pp. 1124–38; *New York Times*, 25 April, 2, 3, 6, 9, 11 May 1944; *PM*, 23, 24, 27 April, 2 May 1944; *New York Herald-Tribune*, 27 April 1944; *Washington Post*, 11 May 1944; *Laughlin* v. *United States*, 151 F.2d 282–83.

70. *Transcript*, pp. 1152, 2271; *New York Times*, 2, 16 May 1944; St.-George and Dennis, *Trial on Trial*, p. 346; Lawrence Dennis, "Notes on the Mass Sedition Trial," 18 Aug. 1944, box 17, Bruce Barton Collection, State Historical Society of Wisconsin.

71. *Transcript*, pp. 1802–1900, contains Rogge's opening.

72. *Transcript*, pp. 1901, 1903, 1942, 1970, 1979; *New York Times*, 18 May 1944; *PM*, 18 May 1944; *New York Herald-Tribune*, 18 May 1944.

73. *Transcript*, pp. 1895, 2147, 2183, 2553, 2301, 2051–52, 2100; *PM*, 19 May 1944.

74. *Transcript*, pp. 2177, 2169, 2074–80; *New York Herald-Tribune*, 23 May 1944; *New York Times*, 23 May 1944; *Jones* v. *United States*, 151 F.2d 289.

75. *Transcript*, pp. 11,400, 12,435, 2627, 1822, 12,529; St.-George and Dennis, *Trial on Trial*, p. 323.

76. *Transcript*, pp. 6395, 15,647, 17,718, 3751.

77. Ibid., pp. 3478, 6507, 10,424–25, 10,562, 3114, 5571, 9517, 9429, 9554–56.

78. Ibid., pp. 11,374, 5901, 11,248, 16,816, 5494, 8426, 16,223, 8744, 16,433–44, 16,497, 9927, 17,784.

79. Ibid., pp. 16,518, 16,601, 8609–12, 8612–19, 8628, 9339, 17,759, 17,764, 17,778, 9482.

80. Ibid., pp. 7901, 8284, 8252, 7896, 17,844, 2453, 2458–59, 16,444, 2301, 4165, 16,818, 10,308, 16,440.

81. Ibid., pp. 8324, 9339, 12,192–93, 12,580, 17,790–91, 11,065, 11,076, 11,227–28.

82. Ibid., pp. 13,088, 5835, 10,408, 10,304, 3497, 11,745, 12,577; Rogge interview.

83. *Transcript*, pp. 15,965, 5748, 3733, 13,387, 14,567, 8285, 17,047–48, 13,599–601, 17,402–44, 15,041, 15,006, 13,376–77, 959, 8201, 3460, 13,346, 6150, 10,578, 15,417, 14,373. Anti-Semitism among lawyers is treated in Jerold S. Auerbach, *Unequal Justice: Lawyers and Social Change in Modern America* (New York: Oxford University Press, 1976), especially pp. 99–129, 184–88.

84. *Transcript*, pp. 3955, 3760, 3794–95, 3768, 2675, 2546, 17,568, 17,617, 2717–18, 16,418, 10,424–25, 16,418, 8783, 9198, 10,980.

85. Ibid., 9536, 9542, 4567, 10,367, 7861, 13,861.

86. *Transcript*, pp. 10,816, 8775–76, 10,218, 13,111–12, 4251, 12,569, 4567, 13,573, 10,282; St.-George and Dennis, *Trial on Trial*, pp. 314, 338–39.

87. *Transcript*, pp. 9611–13, 9856, 7590, 10,084, 5819, 3412, 11,666, 11,669; St.-George and Dennis, *Trial on Trial*, p. 343.

88. *Transcript*, p. 323, 469–70, 8571–72; "Sedition," *Time* 44 (11 Dec. 1944): 24.

89. *Hartzel* v. *United States*, 322 U.S. 683, 685; *PM*, 19 June 1944.

90. *Transcript*, pp. 4434, 4444, 4440, 4448–49, 4456–57.

91. Ibid., 4491, 4459, 4460, 4474, 4463, 4488; *Hartzel* v. *United States*, 322 U.S. 687.

92. *Transcript*, pp. 4469, 4493, 4501, 12,500, 7867; *New York Herald-Tribune*, 21 June 1944.

93. *Transcript*, pp. 1129, 5777, 5779; *New York Times*, 11 June 1944; *PM*, 6 July 1944; Ickes to Eicher, 23 May 1944, Eicher Collection, State University of Iowa; author's interview with John W. Jackson, 2 Nov. 1982.

94. *Transcript*, pp. 5754–56, 5775–76, 5768–69, 5778, 5779–85, 5765; *Laughlin* v. *Eicher*, 145 F.2d 700; *Klein* v. *United States*, 151 F.2d 286; St.-George and Dennis, *Trial on Trial*, pp. 403–4.

95. *Transcript*, pp. 5478, 9520, 17,422–27, 15,971, 11,132, 11,551, 15,435; Young interview.

96. *Transcript*, pp. 10,204, 10,822, 13,642, 10,216, 13,642–43, 12,606, 11,490, 11,133, 11,489, 11,382, 10,414, 5790, 5792, 11,578, 11,583–84; *Noble* v. *Eicher*, 143 F.2d 1001; *New York World-Telegram*, 16 May 1944; *New York Post*, 29 Sept. 1944.

97. St.-George and Dennis, *Trial on Trial*, pp. 314–15, 345; *PM*, 22 April 1944; Winrod to Viereck, 21 Nov. 1945, box 2, Viereck Collection, State University of Iowa; Dennis, "Notes on the Mass Sedition Trial"; telephone interview with Prescott Freese Dennett, 1 Nov. 1982.

98. St.-George and Dennis, *Trial on Trial*, p. 313; "Trial by Exhaustion," *Newsweek* 24 (13 Nov. 1944): 33; *PM*, 14 June 1944; *New York Daily Worker*, 9 Jan., 20 April, 9 March, 17 July, 30, 26 April, 23 July 1944; *Washington Post*, 15, 16 July, 21 Aug. 1944; Baldwin to Max Lerner, 25 July 1944, box 1, Lerner Collection, Yale University; Arthur Garfield Hays, "Three Months in a Brawlroom," *Pathfinder*, 24 July 1944, pp. 22–23; Defenders staff, *Sedition Trial*, pp. 105–6; M. L. Flowers to Langer, 23 Sept. 1944, box 128, Langer Collection.

99. "Sedition," 44 *Time* (28 Aug. 1944): 15; "Trial by Exhaustion," p. 33; *New York Post*, 29 Sept. 1944; Rogge interview.

100. Dennis to Zechariah Chafee, Jr., 14 Aug. 1944, box 31, Chafee Collection; St.-George and Dennis, *Trial on Trial*, p. 403; Samuel I. Rosenman, ed., *Public Papers and Addresses of Franklin D. Roosevelt*, Vol. 13 (New York: Harper & Brothers, 1950), p. 323; *Transcript*, pp. 12,457, 12,461, 12,473.

101. *Transcript*, pp. 12,977, 13,183, 13,025, 12,960, 12,839; Herman Rauschning, *The Revolution of Nihilism: Warning to the West*, trans. E. W.

Dickes (New York: Longmans, Green, 1934; "Herman Rauschning," *Current Biography 1941*, pp. 696–98.

102. *Transcript*, pp. 14,475, 12,946, 12,977, 12,966, 13,005, 13,241, 13,177–78, 13,020, 13,022, 13,025.

103. Ibid., pp. 13,104, 13,088, 13,207, 12,996, 13,001, 13,031, 13,102–3, 13,106, 13,107.

104. Ibid., pp. 14,271, 13,838, 14,219–60, 13,651–70, 13,744–816, 14,141–200, 14,063–64.

105. Ibid., pp. 16,065, 16,316, 16,338, 16,376, 16,458, 16,327, 17,701.

106. Ibid., pp. 16,590, 16,136–63, 16,180, 16,418, 16,189, 16,571, 16,409, 16,318, 16,458.

107. Ibid., pp. 16,660, 16,793, 16,667, 16,662, 16,704, 16,844, 16,821, 16,884; St.-George and Dennis, *Trial on Trial*, pp. 322–33.

108. *Transcript*, pp. 16,050, 16,066–67, 17,231–32, 16,007, 16,588, 17,706–7, 17,232, 17,139, 17,022, 17,025, 17,256, 17,232.

109. Ibid., p. 16,588; St.-George and Dennis, *Trial on Trial*, p. 322.

110. *Transcript*, pp. 16,590, 16,652, 17,703, 17,628, 17,598, 17,432, 17,434, 17,675–76, 17,678, 16,291, 16,870, 16, 568, 17,667; St.-George and Dennis, *Trial on Trial*, p. 332.

111. "Death Stops a Trial," *Newsweek* 24 (11 Dec. 1944): 44; Defenders Staff, *Sedition Trial*, p. 115; Henry D. Allen to William Langer, 7 Dec. 1944, box 599, Langer Collection; *New York World-Telegram*, 1 Dec. 1944; *Transcript*, pp. 17,906–11; Jackson interview; Dennett interview.

112. *PM*, 8 Sept. 1945; *CIO News*, 25 Dec. 1944; Roger N. Baldwin, Memorandum on Seditious Conspiracy Trial; *United States* v. *McWilliams*, 163 F.2d 695, 692, 698; *United States* v. *McWilliams*, 69 F.Supp. 813; *Keegan* v. *United States*, 325 U.S. 495, decided with *Kunze* v. *United States*; Rogge interview.

113. *Keegan* v. *United States*, 325 U.S. 492, 480, 481, 488.

114. Rogge interview; *New York Times*, 23, 26, 27 Oct. 1946; "Bureaus: Talk Trouble," *Newsweek* 28 (4 Nov. 1946), pp. 26–27; Burton K. Wheeler, with Paul F. Healy, *Yankee From the West: The Candid, Turbulent Life Story of the Yankee-born U.S. Senator from Montana* (Garden City, N.Y.: Doubleday, 1962), pp. 372, 376.

115. *PM*, 28 Oct. 1946; *New York Daily Worker*, 27 Oct. 1946.

116. Curtis MacDougall, *Gideon's Army* (New York: Marzani and Munsell, 1965), Vol. 3, pp. 730, 740, 841–42; Rogge interview; *New York Times*, 26 Oct. 1947; "Rogge," p. 534.

117. *United States* v. *McWilliams*, 69 F.Supp. 814, 815; 163 F.2d 695.

118. "Death Stops a Trial," p. 44; *New York Herald-Tribune*, 1 Dec. 1944; *New York Post*, 1 Dec. 1944; *PM*, 1 Dec. 1944; *Freedom Digest*, (Nov. 1944); St.-George and Dennis, *Trial on Trial*, pp. 350–71.

119. Diamond, *Nazi Movement*, chap. 11; *Schenck* v. *United States*, 249 U.S. 47; *Gitlow* v. *New York*, 268 U.S. 652.

120. Dennis, "Notes on the Mass Sedition Trial"; Chafee, *Free Speech*, pp. 51–97, on World War I cases; St.-George and Dennis, *Trial on Trial*, pp. 123,

321–22; Young interview; author's interviews with jurors Leo F. Diegelmann (6 Feb. 1980) and Frederick A. Raulin (11 Feb. 1980).

121. *Transcript*, p. 2807. For typical evaluations of the trial, see "Sedition Trial," p. 700; Norman Dorsen et al., *Disorder in the Court: Report of the Association of the Bar of the City of New York, Special Committee on Courtroom Conduct* (New York: Pantheon, 1973), p. 45; Richard Polenberg, *War and Society: The United States, 1941–1945* (Philadelphia: Lippincott, 1972), p. 48; and Geoffrey Perret, *Days of Sadness, Years of Triumph: The American People, 1939–1945* (New York: Coward, McCann, and Geoghegan, 1973), pp. 360–61. An atypical, critical account appears in William Preston, Jr., "Shadows of War and Fear," in Alan Reitman, ed., *The Pulse of Freedom: American Liberties, 1920–1970s* (New York: New American Library, 1976), pp. 85–86.

122. *United States* v. *Pelley*, 132 F.2d 170; *Harzel* v. *United States*, 322 U.S. 686, 691; *Keegan* v. *United States*, 324 U.S. 500.

123. Biddle, *In Brief Authority*, p. 232; Edwin S. Corwin, *Total War and the Constitution* (New York: Knopf, 1947), p. 115.

124. For favorable evaluations of Roosevelt's civil liberties record, consult Alan F. Westin and Trudy Hayden, "Presidents and Civil Liberties from FDR to Ford: A Rating by 60 Experts," *Civil Liberties Review* 3 (Oct.–Nov. 1976): 27–30 and Arthur M. Schlesinger, Jr., "A Comment on 'Roosevelt and His Foreign Policy Critics,'" *Political Science Quarterly* 94 (Spring 1979): 33–35.

125. Barton J. Bernstein, "The Road to Watergate and Beyond: The Growth and Abuse of Executive Authority Since 1940," *Law and Contemporary Problems* 40 (Spring 1976): 58–86. Athan Theoharis, *Spying on Americans: Political Surveillance from Hoover to the Huston Plan* (Philadelphia: Temple University Press, 1978) contains much valuable information on this issue, but Theoharis understates the connection between Roosevelt's actions and later abuses.

126. *Terminiello* v. *Chicago*, 337 U.S. 1.

127. Chicago Council Against Racial and Religious Discrimination, "Gerald L. K. Smith Comes to Chicago," Labadie Collection, University of Michigan, pp. 3–4; author's interview with Smith, 25 Aug. 1969 (cited hereafter as Interview I).

128. *Chicago Daily News*, 8 Feb. 1946; "Smith Comes to Chicago," pp. 4–7; R. E. Legant, "Red Mobsters Attack America First Rally," *Cross and the Flag* 4 (March 1946): 724–26, 731; Smith to Roger N. Baldwin, 14 Feb. 1946, bk. 2752; Baldwin to Adolph Sabath, 3 April 1947, bk. 4, ACLU Collection; *City of Chicago* v. *Terminiello*, 332 Ill. App. 17, 74 N.E.2d 50 (cited hereafter as *Appellate Court*); *Terminiello* v. *Chicago*, 337 U.S. 20.

129. *Terminiello* v. *Chicago*, 337 U.S. 20–21, 17; Smith to Baldwin, 14 Feb. 1946; Albert W. Dilling, *Petition for a Writ of Certiorari to the Supreme Court of the State of Illinois and Brief in Support Thereof*, p. 2, in *Transcript of Record*, Supreme Court of the United States, Oct. 1948, no. 272, *Arthur Terminiello, Petitioner* v. *City of Chicago.*

130. *Chicago Daily News*, 27, 28, 29 March, 4, 9 April 1946; *Appellate Court*, p. 51; "Prison for Gerald L. K. Smith," *Cross and the Flag* 5 (May 1946): 765–69; "Saved from Prison by Justice," *Cross and the Flag* 5 (Oct. 1946), p. 846; "Chicago Christians Victorious," *Cross and the Flag* 4 (April 1945): 544; Roger N. Baldwin, "Memo for the Files," 4 April 1946; Smith to Baldwin, 12 April 1946, bk. 2752, both in ACLU Collection.

131. Albert W. Dilling, *On Writ of Certiorari to the Supreme Court of Illinois, Petitioner's Reply Brief*, pp. 1, 25, in *Transcript of Record*, Supreme Court of the United States, Oct. 1948, no. 272; Murphy, *Constitution in Crisis Times*, pp. 120, 138, 181–82, 196, 203.

132. *Cantwell* v. *Connecticut*, 310 U.S. 296; *Chaplinsky* v. *New Hampshire*, 315 U.S. 568.

133. *Appellate Court*, pp. 45, 53; *City of Chicago* v. *Terminiello*, 400 Ill. 23, 79 N.D.2d 91 (cited hereafter as *Illinois Supreme Court*).

134. Interview I; Dora Pollack to Clifford Forster, 28 April 1946, box 31, ACLU Collection.

135. "More About Free Speech," p. 105; Council for Democracy, *Freedom of Assembly and Anti-Democratic Groups: A Memorandum of the Council for Democracy* (Washington, D.C.: American Council on Public Affairs, [1941]), pp. 22, 24; David Riesman, "Democracy and Defamation: Control of Group Libel," *Columbia Law Review* 42 (May 1942): 771, 733. See also David Riesman, "Democracy and Defamation: Fair Game and Fair Comment," pts. 1 and 2, *Columbia Law Review* 42 (Sept. 1942): 1085–1123 and (Nov. 1942): 1282–1318.

136. "Why We Defend Free Speech for Nazis, Fascists and Communists," in Corliss Lamont, *The Trial of Elizabeth Gurley Flynn by the American Civil Liberties Union* (New York: Horizon Press, 1968), pp. 181–84.

137. Jerold S. Auerbach, "The Depression Decade," in Reitman, *Pulse of Freedom*, pp. 56–61; Charles Lamm Markmann, *The Noblest Cry: A History of the American Civil Liberties Union* (New York: St. Martin's Press, 1965), p. 158; Peggy Lamson, *Roger Baldwin: Founder of the American Civil Liberties Union* (Boston: Houghton Mifflin, 1976), pp. 196–204; William H. McIlhany II, *The ACLU on Trial* (New Rochelle, N.Y.: Arlington House, 1976), p. 140.

138. Lamont, *Trial of Elizabeth Gurley Flynn*, pp. 42–43.

139. Ibid., pp. 187–89; Auerbach, "Depression Decade," pp. 66–76; Markmann, *Noblest Cry*, pp. 94–97.

140. Auerbach, "Depression Decade," pp. 61–64; ACLU, *From War to Peace: American Civil Liberties, 1945–46* (New York: American Civil Liberties Union, 1946), p. 59; Markmann, *Noblest Cry*, p. 194.

141. Council for Democracy, *Freedom of Assembly*, p. 13; Daniel Bell, "The Face of Tomorrow," *Jewish Frontier* 11 (June 1944): 18–19.

142. Smith to Baldwin, 28 April 1944, bk. 2619; Baldwin, Memorandum on Gerald L. K. Smith, 9 Feb. 1946 and Smith to Baldwin, 14 Feb. 1946, bk. 2752; Baldwin to Clinton J. Taft, 1 Feb. 1945, bk. 2749, all in ACLU Collection; Lamson, *Roger Baldwin*, pp. 215–16.

143. Baldwin to Samuel Warren, 30 Jan. 1946, bk. 2734; A. A. Heist to

Baldwin, 1, 7 Feb. 1946, bk. 2734; both in ACLU Collection; *Buffalo Evening News*, 17 Nov. 1943.

144. Baldwin, Memorandum on Gerald L. K. Smith; Chicago Division, ACLU, "Statement on the Terminiello Case—November 21, 1946"; Chicago Division, ACLU, "Executive Committee Minutes," 20 May 1948; Osmond Fraenkel to Clifford Forster, 5 May 1948, box 31, all in ACLU Collection.

145. Forster telegram to Dora Pollack, 19 May 1948; Baldwin to John Lapp, 11 May 1948; William W. Rodriguez to Baldwin, 25 May 1948; Rodriguez to Gentlemen, 4 Oct. 1948, all in file 154, box 31, ACLU Collection; Michal R. Belknap, *Cold War Political Justice: The Smith Act, the Communist Party, and American Civil Liberties* (Westport, Conn.: Greenwood Press, 1977), pp. 45–53.

146. Dilling, *Petition and Brief*, pp. 9, 11, 20, 10, 22, 16, 30, 36, 39; Dilling, *Reply Brief*, pp. 15, 6.

147. Benjamin S. Adamowski et al., *Brief in Opposition to Petition for Certiorari*, pp. 5, 9–10; Benjamin S. Adamowski et al., *Brief and Argument for Appellee*, pp. 8, 15, 7, 24, 26–27, in *Transcript of Record*, Supreme Court of the United States, Oct. 1948, no. 272.

148. Adamowski, *Brief and Argument*, pp. 15, 18–20, 8, 17, 22–23, 29.

149. William Maslow et al., *Brief of the American Jewish Congress as Amicus Curiae and Motion*, pp. 7, 14, 1, 9, in *Transcript of Record*, Supreme Court of the United States, Oct. 1948, no. 272.

150. Dilling, *Reply Brief*, pp. 18–20, 15, 21.

151. American Civil Liberties Union, *Motion for Leave to File Brief as Amicus Curiae and Brief in Support Thereof*, pp. 13–16, in *Transcript of Record*, Supreme Court of the United States, Oct. 1948, no. 272.

152. *Terminiello* v. *Chicago*, 337 U.S. 3–4, 7, 11, 12, 13, 28, 37.

153. Ibid., pp. 22, 23, 33; Glendon Schubert, *Dispassionate Justice: A Synthesis of the Judicial Opinions of Robert H. Jackson* (Indianapolis: Bobbs-Merrill, 1969), pp. 88, 90.

154. *Terminiello* v. *Chicago*, 337 U.S. 30, 23–24, 14.

155. "Free Speech Reaffirmed," *New Republic* 120 (30 May 1949): 7; I. F. Stone, *The Truman Era* (New York: Vintage Books, 1972), pp. 109, 111; *San Francisco People's Daily World*, 18 May 1949.

6. Far Right, Divided Left, and Vital Center

1. Alonzo L. Hamby, *Beyond the New Deal: Harry S. Truman and American Liberalism* (New York: Columbia University Press, 1973), chaps. 1, 6, 12; Richard M. Freeland, *The Truman Doctrine and the Origins of McCarthyism: Foreign Policy, Domestic Politics, and Internal Security, 1946–1948* (New York: Knopf, 1972), chaps. 5, 7; Les K. Adler and Thomas G. Paterson, "Red Fascism: The Merger of Nazi Germany and Soviet Russia in the American Image of Totalitarianism, 1930s–1950s," *American Historical Review* 85 (April 1970): 1046; Mary Sperling McAuliffe, *Crisis on the Left: Cold War Politics and American Liberals, 1947–1954* (Amherst, Mass.: University of

Massachusetts Press, 1978), chaps. 1–5; Pierre Ayçonberry, *The Nazi Question: An Essay on The Interpretation of National Socialism (1922–1975)*, trans. Robert Hurley (New York: Pantheon, 1981), pp. 127–137.

2. Norman D. Markowitz, *The Rise and Fall of the People's Century: Henry Wallace and American Liberalism, 1941–1948* (New York: Free Press, 1973), chaps. 6–8; Arthur M. Schlesinger, Jr., *The Vital Center: The Politics of Freedom* (Boston: Houghton Mifflin, 1949); Richard J. Walton, *Henry Wallace, Harry Truman, and the Cold War* (New York: Viking Press, 1976).

3. George H. Nash, *The Conservative Intellectual Movement in America: Since 1945* (New York: Basic Books, 1976), chaps. 5–6; Justus D. Doenecke, *Not to the Swift: The Old Isolationists in the Cold War Era* (Lewisburg, Pa.: Bucknell University Press, 1979), chaps. 3–9.

4. Athan Theoharis, *Spying on Americans: Political Surveillance from Hoover to the Huston Plan* (Philadelphia: Temple University Press, 1978), pp. 44–48, 76–78, 99–102, 160, 199–207; Freeland, *Truman Doctine*, pp. 122–25, 142–44, 148–49, 208–19, 233–34, 294–98.

5. Michal R. Belknap, *Cold War Political Justice: The Smith Act, the Communist Party, and American Civil Liberties* (Westport, Conn.: Greenwood Press, 1977), pp. 68–69, 77–151; author's interview with Joseph W. Burns, 2 June 1980; *Dennis* v. *United States* 341 U.S. 494; *Feiner* v. *New York* 340 U.S. 315; Glendon Schubert, *Dispassionate Justice: A Synthesis of the Judicial Opinions of Robert H. Jackson* (Indianapolis: Bobbs-Merrill, 1969), pp. 97–99.

6. Joseph R. Starobin, *American Communism in Crisis, 1943–1957* (Cambridge, Mass.: Harvard University Press, 1972), pp. 15–16, 172–73, 220; *New York Times*, 26 Oct. 1947; Irving Howe and Lewis Coser, with Julius Jacobson, *The American Communist Party: A Critical History (1919–1957)* (Boston: Beacon Press, 1957), pp. 454–57; David A. Shannon, *The Decline of American Communism: A History of the Communist Party of the United States Since 1945* (New York: Harcourt, Brace, 1959), pp. 57, 191–95.

7. Doenecke, *Not to the Swift*, p. 233; Ronald Radosh, *Prophets on the Right: Profiles of Conservative Critics of American Globalism* (New York: Simon and Schuster, 1975), pp. 264–71; Eugene Lyons, *The Red Decade* (1941; rpt. New Rochelle, N.Y.: Arlington House, 1970), pp. 10–11, 324–41; William F. Buckley, Jr., and L. Brent Bozell, *McCarthy and His Enemies: The Record and Its Meaning* (Chicago: Regnery, 1954), p. 326.

8. John Roy Carlson (pseud. for Avedis Derounian), *The Plotters* (New York: Dutton, 1946), pp. vii, 210–57; E. J. Kahn, Jr., "Democracy's Friend," pt. 1, *New Yorker* 23 (26 July 1947): 28, 30–31; pt. 2 (2 Aug. 1947): 28–29; "Whose Front?" *Time* 53 (28 Feb. 1949): 58–59; McAuliffe, *Crisis on the Left*, pp. 95–96; Robert Griffith, *The Politics of Fear: Joseph R. McCarthy and the Senate* (Rochelle Park, N.J.: Hayden, 1971), pp. 292–94.

9. Bob Thomas, *Winchell* (Garden City, N.Y.: Doubleday, 1971), pp. 237, 242–43.

10. Charles Lamm Markmann, *The Noblest Cry: A History of the American Civil Liberties Union* (New York: St. Martin's, 1965), p. 248; Belknap,

Cold War Political Justice, pp. 96, 115; O. John Rogge, *The First and the Fifth: With Some Excursions Into Others* (New York: Nelson and Sons, 1960), pp. 88, 91–93, 97–100.

11. Melford Pearson, *Life Imprisonment for Exposing Communists* (Noblesville, Ind.: no pub., 1947), pp. 3, 12; John McIntyre Werly, "The Millenarian Right: William Dudley Pelley and the Silver Legion of America" (unpub. Ph.D. diss., Syracuse University, 1972), pp. 83–87.

12. Werly, "Millenarian Right," pp. 86–87; William Dudley Pelley, *My Seven Minutes in Eternity with Their Aftermath* (Noblesville, Ind.: Soulcraft Press, 1952), p. 77; *Nations-in-Law*, 2d ed. (Noblesville, Ind.: Fellowship Press, 1956), passim; *Behold Life: Design for Liberation* (Noblesville, Ind.: Soulcraft Chapels, 1950), passim; and *Something Better: How to Bring the Christian Commonwealth* (Noblesville, Ind.: Soulcraft Chapels, 1952), pp. 278, 292, 254–56, 288–98.

13. Pelley, *Seven Minutes*, p. 75; William Dudley Pelley, *Why I Believe the Dead Are Alive*, 2d ed. (Noblesville, Ind.: Soulcraft Chapels, 1954), p. 75; *Indianapolis News*, 9 Aug. 1955.

14. Pelley, *Why I Believe*, p. 297; *Indianapolis News*, 10 Aug. 1955; 2 July 1965; Werly, "Millenarian Right," p. 93.

15. Gerald B. Winrod, *The Antichrist and the Atomic Bomb* (Wichita: Defender Publishers, [1945], pp. 66, 72–73; "All Call to Prayer" and "Calling All Americans," 12 April 1946, flyers in Hoover Institution, Stanford University; "A Clarifying Statement," *Defender* 23 (Nov. 1948): 23; "The Sedition Case," *Defender* 24 (April 1950): 3–5; "Colonel Sanctuary Writes His Alma Mater," *Defender* 22 (April 1947): 21–22; "Winchell Spreads Hate," *Defender* 20 (Dec. 1945): 22; "Smear Book Proved Fraudulent," *Defender* 21 (Nov. 1946): 2; "Undermining the Church," *Defender* 20 (Nov. 1945): 16; Prescott Dennett, "The Sedition Trial," *Defender* 23 (July 1948): 2, 19; "A Report On Winrod (and the Fundamentalists)," *Democracy's Battle* 7 (1 June 1949): 4.

16. G. H. Montgomery, *Gerald B. Winrod: Defender of the Faith* (Wichita: Mertmont, 1965), p. 90; Defenders staff, *Fire by Night and Cloud by Day* (Wichita: Mertmont, 1966), pp. 83–96; *Wichita Beacon*, 7 Jan. 1951; Gerald B. Winrod, *Brain Building and Soul Growth* (Wichita: Defender Publishers, 1945), p. 6; "Editorials," *Defender* 26 (May 1951): 20; "Civil Rights," *Defender* 23 (Aug. 1948): 2; "United Religious Front Needed," *Defender* 32 (March 1952): 2; "The President's Plight," *Defender* 25 (Sept. 1950): 3–4; "The Westward Course," *Defender* 23 (Feb. 1949): 4; "Flying Saucers Considered Prophetically," *Defender* 25 (July 1950): 3–6; "World Church: The Bride of Antichrist," *Defender* 23 (Sept. 1948): 3–7; "The War Crisis," *Defender* 25 (July 1950): 20; "The Cure for National Ills," *Defender* 22 (Jan. 1948): 23–25; "Trinity College Has a New Home," *Defender* 25 (April 1951): 2; George E. Sullivan, "Sentinels of Liberty," *Defender* 21 (May 1946): 19–24.

17. "Americanism and Illuminism," *Defender* 24 (Oct. 1949): 3–5; "McCarthy's Death," *Defender* 32 (June 1957): 23; "The Terrible Truman,"

Defender 31 (June 1956): 25–26; "Defender Hour Election Broadcast," *Defender* 31 (Dec. 1956): 2; Winrod mimeograph letter to Anthony Eden and John Foster Dulles, 3 Nov. 1956, Hoover Institution.

18. "Prophetic Messages for Our Time," *Defender* 22 (Aug. 1947): 3–6; Montgomery, *Winrod*, p. 94; James Harvey Young, *The Medical Messiahs: A Social History of Health Quackery in Twentieth-Century America* (Princeton, N.J.: Princeton University Press, 1967), p. 372, chap. 17.

19. Gerald B. Winrod, *Healing in the Bible* (Wichita: Defender Publishers, 1936); *The Koch Treatment: A Record of Results* (Wichita: Winrod Publisher, 1951), and *The New Science in the Treatment of Disease: A Symposium* (Wichita: Winrod, Publisher, 1950); pp. 31–32, 15; Montgomery, *Winrod*, chap. 10; Winrod to Langer, 17 May 1948, Langer Collection, University of North Dakota; "Health Dictatorship," *Defender* 24 (Jan.–Feb. 1950): 11–13; "Prayer Crusade Organized," *Defender* 31 (Jan. 1957): 6; "Laughlin Files Another Court Action Against Food and Drug Administration," *Defender* 32 (Sept. 1957): 3–6.

20. Montgomery, *Winrod*, p. 100.

21. Lloyd Ray Henderson, "The Political Activities of Gerald L. K. Smith" (unpub. M.A. thesis, University of California, Berkeley, 1955), chap. 5; *New York Times*, 6, 9 July 1946; *New York World-Telegram*, 16–21 July 1945; Ellen H. Posner, "Anti-Jewish Activities," *American Jewish Yearbook* 48 (Philadelphia: Jewish Publication Society of America, 1946), p. 173.

22. Elna M. Smith and Charles F. Robertson, eds., *Besieged Patriot: Autobiographical Episodes Exposing Communism, Traitorism, and Zionism from the Life of Gerald L. K. Smith* (Eureka Springs, Ark.: Smith Foundation, 1978), pp. 88, 282–83, 285; Isabel N. Price, "Gerald L. K. Smith and Anti-Semitism" (unpub. M.A. thesis, University of New Mexico, 1965), pp. 143, 156; *New York Times*, 17 April 1976; David Riesman, *Individualism Reconsidered and other Essays* (New York: Free Press, 1964), chap. 8.

23. "The Beautiful Silent Treatment," *Cross and the Flag* 8 (Dec. 1949): 24; "Dramatic Incidents in the Life of Gerald L. K. Smith: Huey Long," *Cross and the Flag* 9 (Jan. 1951): 7, 28; "Dramatic Incidents in the Life of Gerald L. K. Smith: Minneapolis Riot," *Cross and the Flag* 9 (March 1951): 2; Smith and Robertson, *Besieged Patriot*, pp. 84–85, 88, 236–37; Isaiah M. Minkoff, "Intergroup Relations," *American Jewish Yearbook* 49 (1947), p. 192.

24. Smith and Robertson, *Besieged Patriot*, pp. 148–51; Jack Anderson and Ronald W. May, *McCarthy: The Man, the Senator, the "Ism"* (Boston: Beacon Press, 1952), pp. 309–12; Merwin K. Hart to George Washington Robnett, 21 April 1959, Addenda, Hart Collection, University of Oregon; William F. Buckley, Jr., *Inveighing We Will Go* (New York: Putnam's Sons, 1972), pp. 49–50.

25. Smith and Robertson, *Besieged Patriot*, pp. 3, 42, 205, 255, 199–201, 218–21; John Fergus Ryan, "Twilight Years of a Kindly Old Hatesmith," *Esquire* 70 (Aug. 1968): 90; Smith to Merwin K. Hart, 7 Jan. 1960, Addenda, Hart Collection; Gerald L. K. Smith, *A Tribute to Huey P. Long* (Green Forest, Ark.: Larimer Publications, [1973]).

26. Smith and Robertson, *Besieged Patriot*, pp. 136–40, 283–84; William Bradford Huie, "Gerald Smith's Bid for Power," *American Mercury* 55 (July

1942): 155; author's interview with Smith, 25 Aug. 1969 and 8 Jan. 1973 (cited hereafter as Interviews I and II respectively).

27. Gerald L. K. Smith, *Too Much and Too Many Roosevelts* (St. Louis: Christian Nationalist Crusade, 1950); Gerald L. K. Smith, *The Roosevelt Death: A Super Mystery* (1947; rpt. with a new epilogue, Los Angeles: Christian Nationalist Crusade, n.d.), pp. 4, 57–58; Interview I; Smith to Truman, 24 March 1948, Harry S. Truman Library; Gerald L. K. Smith, *Is Eisenhower a Communist? No! But—* (Los Angeles: Christian Nationalist Crusade, n.d.), p. 5; "We Don't Like Ike—and Why," *Cross and the Flag* 10 (Aug. 1952): 7; "Small Man," *Cross and the Flag* 30 (Oct. 1971): 34.

28. Ryan, "Twilight Years," p. 88; *New York Times*, 17 April 1976; Smith and Robertson, *Besieged Patriot*, pp. 225, 250, 80.

29. Interviews I and II; Ryan, "Twilight Years," p. 9; Smith and Robertson, *Besieged Patriot*, pp. 27, 288–89; Gerald L. K. Smith, *The Shades of Sodom and Gomorrah: A Devastating Document* (Los Angeles: Christian Nationalist Crusade, n.d.), n.p.; Gerald L. K. Smith, *Danger! Warning!* (St. Louis: Christian Nationalist Crusade, n.d.), p. 15; Gerald L. K. Smith, *Governor George C. Wallace: A New Star on the Horizon of Statesmanship* (Los Angeles: Christian Nationalist Crusade, n.d.), p. 1; "Formula for Solving the Negro Problem," *Cross and the Flag* 25 (Nov. 1966): 4, 21–22; "A Majority," *Cross and the Flag* 27 (Sept. 1968): 8–9; "Lyndon B. Johnson," *Cross and the Flag* 31 (March 1973): 28–29; "George Wallace," *Cross and the Flag* 32 (Jan. 1974): 35–36; Neil R. McMillen, *The Citizens Council: Organized Resistance to the Second Reconstruction, 1954–1964* (Urbana: University of Illinois Press, 1971), p. 22.

30. Smith and Robertson, *Besieged Patriot*, pp. 28, 24, 95; "The Assassination," undated flyer in author's possession; Interview I; *New York Times*, 11 Oct. 1964.

31. *New York Times*, 11 Oct. 1964; Theodore H. White, *The Making of the President, 1964* (New York: Atheneum, 1965), p. 228; "Barry Goldwater: An Appraisal," *Cross and the Flag* 23 (Sept. 1964): 5, 23–25.

32. Gerald L. K. Smith, *Too Many Roosevelts*, pp. 58–60; Smith and Robertson, *Besieged Patriot*, pp. 239, 317, 19, 22; "Welcome, Pelley," *Cross and the Flag* 8 (March 1950): 12; "Ike Eisenhower, the Mystery Man," *Cross and the Flag* 9 (Sept. 1950): 30; "Benjamin Franklin and the Jews" and "General Grant Bans Jew Traders," *Cross and the Flag* 8 (Sept. 1949): 3–5, 32; "Big Lie Challenged," *Cross and the Flag* 31 (Dec. 1972): 17–18; "People," *Cross and the Flag* 31 (Aug. 1972): 24; Gerald L. K. Smith, *Is Communism Jewish?* (Detroit: Christian Nationalist Crusade, n.d.); Gerald L. K. Smith, *Background Facts and Historical Documents Which Reveal the Origins of the Protocols of the Learned Elders of Zion* (Los Angeles: Christian Nationalist Crusade, n.d.); Interview I and II; *New York Times*, 11 Oct. 1964; George Thayer, *The Farther Shores of Politics: The American Political Fringe Today* (New York: Simon and Schuster, 1968), pp. 51–52.

33. "Ignorance, Cowardice, Treason" and "People," *Cross and the Flag* 32 (Feb. 1974): 9, 21; "Logical Summary," *Cross and the Flag* 33 (Aug. 1974): 14; "Smith Missiles" and "Difficult Choices," *Cross and the Flag* 32 (Oct. 1973): 30, 36; "New Letter Items" and "What About Russia and China?" *Cross and*

the Flag 33 (Sept. 1974): 13, 21; "Smith Missiles," *Cross and the Flag* 33 (Nov. 1974): 11; "People," *Cross and the Flag* 33 (Dec. 1974): 17; Smith to author, 5 June 1974.

34. Gerald L. K. Smith, ed., *The Story of the Statue: The Christ of the Ozarks* (Eureka Springs, Ark.: Smith Foundation, 1967), pp. 6–7, 56–70; Ryan, "Twilight Years," p. 91; Calvin Trillin, *U.S. Journal* (New York: Dutton, 1971), pp. 265–67, 272; *New York Times*, 27 July 1972; *Kansas City Star*, 18 Jan. 1970; *Arkansas Gazette*, 25 June 1970; 9 Dec. 1969. I attended the "Great Passion Play" with Gerald and Elna Smith after my first interview with him.

35. Smith and Robertson, *Besieged Patriot*, pp. 261–63; "Help Build the New Holy Land," *Cross and the Flag* 34 (March 1976): 4; *An Open Letter from Gerald L. K. Smith* (Eureka Springs, Ark.: Smith Foundation, 1973), pp. 6–11; *Washington Post*, 20 Jan. 1973; *New York Times*, 27 July 1972; *Arkansas Gazette*, 9 Dec. 1969; 25 June 1970; *Arkansas Democrat*, 2 Nov. 1969; *Kansas City Star*, 18 Jan. 1970; Arnold Forster and Benjamin Epstein, *The New Anti-Semitism* (New York: McGraw-Hill, 1974), chap. 2.

36. *New York Times*, 17 April 1976; "We Mourn the Loss of a Great Christian Patriot," *Cross and the Flag* 35 (May 1976): 6; Roland L. Morgan, Mrs. Gerald L. K. Smith, and Charles F. Robertson to Dear Friend, 25 Nov. 1977, circular letter in author's possession.

37. Robert J. Donovan, *Conflict and Crisis: The Presidency of Harry S. Truman, 1945–1948* (New York: Norton, 1977), chaps. 40–42; Hamby, *Beyond the New Deal*, chaps. 10–12; Markowitz, *Rise and Fall*, chap. 8.

38. Daniel Bell, ed., *The Radical Right: The New American Right, Expanded and Updated* (Garden City, N.Y.: Doubleday, 1963).

39. John Higham, "American Anti-Semitism Historically Reconsidered," in Charles Herbert Stember et al., *Jews in the Mind of America* (New York: Basic Books, 1966), p. 239; Theodor W. Adorno et al., *The Authoritarian Personality* (1950; rpt. New York: Science Editions, 1964), p. ix; Theodor W. Adorno, "Scientific Experiences of a European Scholar in America," in Donald Fleming and Bernard Bailyn, eds., *The Intellectual Migration: Europe and America, 1930–1960* (Cambridge, Mass.: Harvard University Press, 1969), pp. 355–57; H. Stuart Hughes, *The Sea Change: The Migration of Social Thought, 1930–1965* (New York: McGraw-Hill, 1977), pp. 148–51.

40. Adorno, *Authoritarian Personality*, pp. 1, 7, 9, 11, 968, 974–75; Adorno, "Scientific Experiences," pp. 357–58, 361, 369; Martin Jay, *The Dialectical Imagination: A History of the Frankfurt School and the Institute of Social Research 1923–1950* (Boston: Little, Brown, 1973), chaps. 5–7.

41. Nash, *Conservative Intellectual Movement*, pp. 138–39; Edward A. Shils, "Authoritarianism 'Right' and 'Left,'" in Richard Christie and Marie Jahoda, *Studies in the Scope and Method of the Authoritarian Personality* (Glencoe, Ill.: Free Press, 1954), pp. 27, 38.

42. Bell, *Radical Right*, pp. xii, 39, 63–86.

43. Ibid., pp. 53, 106, 185, 189, 87–134, 219.

44. David Riesman, "Democracy and Defamation: Control of Group

Libel." *Columbia Law Review* 42 (May 1942): 727–80; Peter Viereck, "But—I'm a Conservative," *Atlantic Monthly* 165 (April 1940): 538–43; Daniel Bell, "The Face of Tomorrow," *Jewish Frontier* 11 (June 1944): 17–18.

45. Bell, *Radical Right*, p. 39.

46. Ibid., pp. 57, 19, 48, 55, 137; John H. Bunzel, *Anti-Politics in America: Reflections on the Anti-Political Temper and Its Distortions of the Democratic Process* (New York: Vintage Books, 1967), p. 73; Seymour Martin Lipset and Earl Raab, *The Politics of Unreason: Right-Wing Extremism in America, 1790–1970* (New York: Harper & Row, 1970), pp. xv, xviii, 20.

47. Lipset and Raab, *Politics of Unreason*, pp. xx, 13, 168–69, 185, 195–98; Peter Viereck, *The Unadjusted Man: A New Hero for Americans* (New York: Capricorn, 1956), p. 163; Richard Hofstadter, *The Paranoid Style in American Politics and Other Essays* (New York: Vintage Books, 1967), pp. 9, 72; Ralph Lord Roy, *Communism and the Churches* (New York: Harcourt, Brace, 1960), p. 429, and *Apostles of Discord: A Study of Organized Bigotry and Disruption on the Fringes of Protestantism* (Boston: Beacon Press, 1963).

48. Viereck, *Unadjusted Man*, p. 163; Victor C. Ferkiss, "Populist Influences on American Fascism," *Western Political Quarterly* 10 (June 1957): 350–73; Victor C. Ferkiss, "The Political and Economic Philosophy of American Fascism" (unpub. Ph.D. diss., University of Chicago, 1954).

49. Bell, *Radical Right*, pp. 107, 45; Talcott Parsons, "The Distribution of Power in American Society," in Richard Gillam, ed., *Power in Postwar America: Interdisciplinary Perspectives on a Historical Problem* (Boston: Little, Brown, 1971), p. 67.

50. Michael Paul Rogin, *The Intellectuals and McCarthy* (Cambridge, Mass.: MIT Press, 1967), p. 2; William F. Buckley, Jr., *Up from Liberalism* (New York: Hillman Books, 1961), p. 28.

51. Michael Paul Rogin, *Intellectuals and McCarthy*, pp. 213–15, 267; Norman Pollack, "Fear of Man: Populism, Authoritarianism, and the Historian," *Agricultural History* 39 (April 1965): 59–67, and "The Myth of Populist Anti-Semitism," *American Historical Review* 68 (Oct. 1962): 76–80; Paul S. Holbo, "Wheat or What? Populism and American Fascism," *Western Political Quarterly* 14 (Sept. 1961): 727–36; Lawrence Goodwyn, *Democratic Promise: The Populist Movement in America* (New York: Oxford University Press, 1976), especially chaps. 13–15.

52. William Z. Foster, *From Bryan to Stalin* (New York: International Publishers, 1937).

53. Richard Hofstadter, *The Progressive Historians: Turner, Beard, Parrington* (New York: Vintage Books, 1970), pp. 437–44; John Higham, *History: Professional Scholarship in America* (New York: Harper Torchbooks, 1973), chaps. 5–6.

54. Bell, *Radical Right*, pp. 84, 191, 225, 265–66; Hofstadter, *Paranoid Style*, p. 65; Robert Booth Fowler, *Believing Skeptics: American Political Intellectuals, 1945–1964* (Westport, Conn.: Greenwood Press, 1978), pp. 156–65.

55. "Americans Fear Russia, Why?" *Cross and the Flag* 3 (May 1944): 398.

56. Carey McWilliams, *A Mask for Privilege* (Boston: Little, Brown, 1948), p. 124; Richard Hofstadter, *The Age of Reform: From Bryan to FDR* (New York: Vintage Books, 1955), chap. 2.

57. On "progressive" motifs in *The International Jew*, see Leo P. Ribuffo, "Henry Ford and *The International Jew*," *American Jewish History* 69 (June 1980): 471–72.

58. Bell, *Radical Right*, pp. 82–83, 280; Hofstadter, *Paranoid Style*, pp. 52–53.

59. On the New Deal as a psychological success, see Warren Susman, "The Thirties," in Stanley Coben and Lorman Ratner, eds., *The Search for an American Culture* (Englewood Cliffs, N.J.: Prentice-Hall, 1970), pp. 191–92.

60. Norman Hapgood, ed., *Professional Patriots* (New York: Boni, 1927), p. 4. Vandenberg emerges as a centrist hero in Schlesinger, *Vital Center*, pp. 30–31.

61. Clinton Rossiter, *Conservatism in America: The Thankless Persuasion* (New York: Vintage Books, 1962), p. 128; Bunzel, *Anti-Politics in America*, p. 37.

62. Winrod, "Calling All Americans," 12 April 1946, circular letter, Hoover Institution, Stanford University; Pelley, *Something Better*, p. 252; Interview I; Gerald L. K. Smith, "The Huey Long Movement," in Rita James Simon, ed., *As We Saw the Thirties* (Urbana: University of Illinois Press, 1967), pp. 60–61, 64, 67–68.

63. Hofstadter, *Paranoid Style*, p. 37.

64. Bell, *Radical Right*, p. 86; Hofstadter, *Paranoid Style*, p. 90. On the connection between neo-Freudian psychology and affirmation of the status quo, see Russell Jacoby, *Social Amnesia: A Critique of Conformist Psychology from Adler to Laing* (Boston: Beacon Press, 1975), chaps. 1–3.

65. David Brion Davis, *The Slave Power Conspiracy and the Paranoid Style* (Baton Rouge: Louisiana State University Press, 1969), p. 7; Hofstadter, *Paranoid Style*, pp. 3, 30, 36–37, 29, 110.

66. Hofstadter, *Paranoid Style*, p. ix; William James, *The Varieties of Religious Experience: A Study in Human Nature* (New York: Modern Library, n.d.), p. 163.

67. Bell, *Radical Right*, pp. 195, 197; Hofstadter, *Paranoid Style*, pp. 52–53, 118; Ferkiss, "Political and Economic Philosophy," p. 318; Rogin, *Intellectuals and McCarthy*, pp. 15–16, 30.

68. Richard E. Gutstadt to Smith, 4, 12 Dec. 1940, Material File, G. L. K. Smith, 1935–47, B'nai B'rith Anti-Defamation League, Chicago, Ill.; Smith to Leo Butzel, 1 Oct. 1941, Office File, 1943–44, box 2582, file 1068, Ford Archives, Henry Ford Museum.

69. Smith and Robertson, *Besieged Patriot*, p. 292.

70. Sigmund Freud, "Notes Upon a Case of Obsessional Neurosis," in *The Standard Edition of the Complete Psychological Works of Sigmund Freud*, trans. James Strachey (London: Hogarth Press, 1978), vol. 10, p. 210.

71. Bell, *Radical Right*, p. 83, italics added.

72. Otto Fenichel, *The Psychoanalytic Theory of Neurosis* (New York:

Norton, 1972), pp. 40–41, 456–57, 406; Linda J. Lear, *Harold L. Ickes: The Aggressive Progressive 1874–1933* (New York: Garland, 1981), pp. 396–99.

73. Bell, *Radical Right*, pp. 19–21; Lipset and Raab, *Politics of Unreason*, pp. 113–21, 160, 165, 198–99; Hofstadter, *Paranoid Style*, pp. 72–73.

74. Roy, *Apostles of Discord*, p. 5; Franklin H. Littell, *Wild Tongues: A Handbook of Social Pathology* (New York: Macmillan, 1969), pp. 9–10.

75. Smith Interview I; Roy, *Apostles of Discord*, pp. 62–65; Gerald B. Winrod, *The Hidden Hand—The Protocols and the Coming Superman* (Wichita: Defender Publishers, 1932), p. 7.

76. Louis Hartz, *The Liberal Tradition in America* (New York: Harcourt, Brace, 1955), p. 14.

77. Eugen Weber, "The Right: An Introduction" and "France," Ernst Nolte, "Germany," and Andrew Whiteside, "Austria", all in Hans Rogger and Eugen Weber, *The European Right: A Historical Profile* (Berkeley: University of California Press, 1966), pp. 1–28, 85–95, 287–93, 310–26; John Weiss, *The Fascist Tradition: Radical Right-Wing Extremism in Modern Europe* (New York: Harper & Row, 1967), pp. 4, 6, 48–49; F. L. Carsten, *The Rise of Fascism* (Berkeley: University of California Press, 1969), chap. 1; Robert F. Byrnes, *Antisemitism in Modern France: The Prologue to the Dreyfus Affair* (rpt. New York: Fertig, 1969), chaps. 3–6, 8; P. G. J. Pulzer, *The Rise of Political Anti-Semitism in Germany and Austria* (New York: Wiley and Sons, 1964), chaps. 10–13, 17–22; George L. Mosse, *The Crisis of German Ideology: Intellectual Origins of the Third Reich* (New York: Universal Library, 1964), chaps. 1–12; Edward R. Tannenbaum, *The Action Française: Die-Hard Reactionaries in Twentieth-Century France* (New York: Wiley, 1962); Eugen Weber, *Action Française: Royalism and Reaction in Twentieth-Century France* (Stanford, Calif.: Stanford University Press, 1962); Jacob Katz, *From Prejudice to Destruction: Anti-Semitism, 1700–1933* (Cambridge, Mass.: Harvard University Press, 1980), chaps. 20–24.

78. Weiss, *Fascist Tradition*, pp. 31–64, 66–82; Eugen Weber, *Varieties of Fascism: Doctrines of Revolution in the Twentieth-Century* (Princeton, N.J.: Van Nostrand, 1964), pp. 134–137; Alan Bullock, *Hitler: A Study in Tyranny* (New York: Harper Torchbooks, 1964), chap. 2; Karl-Dietrich Bracher, *The German Dictatorship: The Origins, Structure, and Effects of National Socialism* (New York: Praeger, 1970), chap. 4; Robert J. Soucy, "The Nature of Fascism in France" and Gilbert D. Allardyce, "The Political Transition of Jacques Doriot," both in Walter Laqueur and George L. Mosse, eds., *International Fascism: 1920–1945* (New York: Harper Torchbooks, 1966), pp. 27–74; G. Warner, "France," in S. J. Woolf, ed., *European Fascism* (New York: Vintage Books, 1969), pp. 263–65; Oswald Mosley, *My Life* (New Rochelle, N.Y.: Arlington House, 1972), chap. 16; Stanley G. Payne, *Falange: A History of Spanish Fascism* (Stanford, Calif.: Stanford University Press, 1961), chap. 4.

79. Bracher, *German Dictatorship*, chaps. 3–4; Edward R. Tannenbaum, *The Fascist Experience: Italian Society and Culture, 1922–1945* (New York: Basic Books, 1972), pp. 36–43; Henry Ashby Turner, Jr., "Fascism and Mod-

ernization," *World Politics* 24 (July 1972): 554–55; Juan J. Linz, "Some Notes Toward a Comparative Study of Fascism in Sociological Historical Perspective" and Zeev Sternhell, "Fascist Ideology," both in Walter Laquer, ed., *Fascism: A Reader's Guide* (Berkeley: University of California Press, 1978), pp. 33–40, 336–55.

80. Mosley, *My Life*, p. 291; Charles F. Delzell, ed., *Mediterranean Fascism, 1919–1945* (New York: Harper & Row, 1970), p. 246; H. R. Trevor-Roper, "The Phenomenon of Fascism," in S. J. Woolf, ed., *European Fascism* (New York: Vintage Books, 1969), p. 34; Carsten, *Rise of Fascism*, chaps. 5–6.

81. Ernst Nolte, *Three Faces of Fascism: Action Française, Italian Fascism, National Socialism*, trans. Leila Vennewitz (New York: Holt, Rinehart and Winston, 1966), pp. 365–70; Payne, *Falange*, p. 77; Stanley G. Payne, *Franco's Spain* (New York: Crowell, 1967), p. 22; Mosley, *My Life*, chap. 19; Robert Skidelsky, *Sir Oswald Mosley* (New York: Holt, Rinehart and Winston, 1975), pp. 284, 302, 299.

82. Delzell, *Mediterranean Fascism*, pp. 174–84, 331–50; Alan Cassels, *Fascist Italy* (New York: Crowell, 1968), pp. 69, 92; Tannenbaum, *Fascist Experience*, pp. 77–78, 241–43; Herman Rauschning, *The Voice of Destruction* (New York: Putnam's Sons, 1940), pp. 49, 56, 229; Robert Cecil, *The Myth of the Master Race: Alfred Rosenberg and Nazi Ideology* (New York: Dodd, Mead, 1972), pp. 94, 118; Robert Koehl, "Feudal Aspects of National Socialism," *American Political Science Review* 54 (Dec. 1960): 921–33; Nolte, *Three Faces of Fascism*, pp. 229–30; Michael R. Marrus and Robert O. Paxton, *Vichy France and the Jews* (New York: Basic Books, 1981), chap. 2; Mosley, *My Life*, p. 342; Skidelsky, *Mosley*, chaps. 20–21.

83. Gerald B. Winrod, *The United States and Russia in Prophecy and the Red Horse of the Apocalypse* (Wichita: Defender Publishers, 1933), pp. 20–22; Gerald L. K. Smith, *Dangerous Enemies: A Warning and an Appeal to All Americans* (Detroit: Committee of One Million, 1939), pp. 19, 35, 48–49; Gerald L. K. Smith, "The Next President of the United States," "Mice or Men?" and "Laboratory for Revolution," radio addresses, c. 1939–40, Michigan Historical Collection, University of Michigan.

84. Smith, *Dangerous Enemies*, pp. 78–79, 83–86, 91; "Race Riots! An Interpretation," *Cross and the Flag* 2 (July 1943): 232; "The Present Political Situation," *Revealer* 1 (15 Nov. 1934): 4.

85. Arno J. Mayer, *Dynamics of Counterrevolution in Europe, 1870–1956: An Analytical Framework* (New York: Harper Torchbooks, 1971), pp. 42–55; George E. Mowry, "Social Democracy, 1910–1918," in C. Vann Woodward, ed., *The Comparative Approach to American History* (New York: Basic Books, 1968), pp. 271–84.

86. Herman Finer, *Mussolini's Italy* (New York: Grosset & Dunlap, 1965), p. 190; John A. Garraty, "The New Deal, National Socialism, and the Great Depression," *American Historical Review* 78 (Oct. 1973): 934.

87. Delzell, *Mediterranean Fascism*, p. 280; Robert O. Paxton, *Vichy France: Old Guard and New Order, 1940–45* (New York: Alfred A. Knopf, 1972), p. 243.

88. Geoffrey S. Smith, *To Save a Nation: American Countersubversives, the New Deal, and the Coming of World War II* (New York: Basic Books, 1973), p. 86.

89. Adolf Hitler, *Mein Kampf*, trans. Ralph Manheim (Boston: Houghton Mifflin, 1943), p. 312; Winrod, *Hidden Hand*, p. 7; Lucy S. Dawidowicz, *The War Against the Jews, 1933–1945* (New York: Holt, Rinehart and Winston, 1975), pp. 3–22, 141–147; Gerald B. Winrod, *Antichrist and the Tribe of Dan* (Wichita: Defender Publishers, 1936), p. 33; "Roosevelt's Jewish Ancestry," *Revealer* 3 (15 Oct. 1936): 2; Smith interview I.

90. *City of Chicago* v. *Terminiello* 400 Ill. 23, 79 N. D. 2d, 44; Rossiter, *Conservatism in America*, p. 128.

91. John Higham, *Strangers in the Land: Patterns of American Nativism, 1860–1925* (New York: Atheneum, 1966), pp. 276–77.

92. Hannah Arendt, *Eichmann in Jerusalem: A Report on the Banality of Evil* (New York: Viking Press, 1970), p. 30; Sinclair Lewis, *It Can't Happen Here* (Garden City, N.Y.: Doubleday, Doran, 1935), pp. 190–91, 204–7.

93. John A. Garraty, *Unemployment in History: Economic Thought and Public Policy* (New York: Harper Colophon, 1979), pp. 164–65, 207; Alan Brinkley, *Voices of Protest: Huey Long, Father Coughlin, and the Great Depression* (New York: Knopf, 1982), chaps. 8–10.

94. Werner Sombart, *Why Is There No Socialism in the United States*, Patricia M. Hocking and C. T. Husbands, trans. (1906; rpt. White Plains, N.Y.: International Arts and Sciences Press, 1976).

95. Pierre S. DuPont to Robert F. Wagner, 7 March 1934, box 100, Wagner Collection, Georgetown University; Hans Mommsen, "National Socialism—Continuity and Change," Alan S. Milward, "Fascism and the Economy," and Francis L. Carsten, "Interpretations of Fascism," all in Laqueur, *Fascism*, pp. 185–87, 380–90, 429–30.

96. Caroline Bird, *The Invisible Scar* (New York: McKay, 1966), chaps. 3, 11; Garraty, *Unemployment in History*, pp. 181–87.

Epilogue

1. Sydney E. Ahlstrom, *A Religious History of the American People* (New Haven, Conn.: Yale University Press, 1972), chap. 56; Louis Gaspar, *The Fundamentalist Movement* (The Hague: Mouton, 1963), pp. 76–107, 120–21; William G. McLoughlin, Jr., *Billy Graham: Revivalist in a Secular Age* (New York: Ronald Press, 1960), p. 37; Joel A. Carpenter, "Fundamentalist Institutions and the Rise of Evangelical Protestantism, 1929–1942," *Church History* 49 (March 1980): 62–75.

2. Gaspar, *Fundamentalist Movement*, pp. 25–30, 54–59, 68, 115–24; Erling Jorstad, *The Politics of Doomsday: Fundamentalists of the Far Right* (Nashville: Abingdon Press, 1970), pp. 49–51, 130–34; James Morris, *The Preachers* (New York: St. Martin's Press, 1973), pp. 204–11.

3. McLoughlin, *Billy Graham*, p. 212; Morris, *Preachers*, pp. 202–4; Marshall Frady, *Billy Graham: A Parable of American Righteousness* (Boston: Little, Brown, 1979), pp. 51, 81–84, 96–104, 175, 375.

4. Frady, *Billy Graham*, pp. 198, 237–39, 420, 438; McLoughlin, *Billy Graham*, pp. 89, 93, 105; Seymour Martin Lipset and Earl Raab, "The Election and the Evangelicals," *Commentary* 71 (March 1981): 27.

5. Carl McIntire, *The Rise of the Tyrant: Controlled Economy vs. Private Enterprise* (Collingswood, N.J.: Christian Beacon Press, 1945), pp. xiii, 150; Billy James Hargis, *Why I Fight for a Christian America* (Nashville: Nelson, 1974), pp. 59, 138–43, 122, 73; Jorstad, *Politics of Doomsday*, chaps. 1–3; John Harold Redekop, *The American Far Right: A Case Study of Billy James Hargis and Christian Crusade* (Grand Rapids, Mich.: Eerdman's, 1968); Gary K. Claburgh, *Thunder on the Right: The Protestant Fundamentalists* (Chicago: Nelson-Hall, 1974), chaps. 6–7. "People," *Cross and the Flag* 32 (Jan. 1974): 7.

6. Michael W. Miles, *The Odyssey of the American Right* (New York: Oxford University Press, 1980), chap. 15; Neil R. McMillen, *The Citizens' Council: Organized Resistance to the Second Reconstruction, 1954–64* (Urbana: University of Illinois Press, 1971); David M. Chalmers, *Hooded Americanism: The History of the Ku Klux Klan* (New York: New Viewpoints, 1981), chaps. 46–49; Leland V. Bell, *In Hitler's Shadow: The Anatomy of American Nazism* (Port Washington, N.Y.: Kennikat Press, 1973), chap. 7.

7. Arnold Forster and Benjamim R. Epstein, *Danger on the Right* (New York: Random House, 1964); Mike Newberry, *The Yahoos* (New York: Marzani and Munsell, 1964); Donald Janson and Bernard Eismann, *The Far Right* (New York: McGraw-Hill, 1963); Irwin Suall, *The American Ultras: The Extreme Right and the Military-Industrial Complex* (New York: New America, 1962); Harry and Bonaro Overstreet, *The Strange Tactics of Extremism* (New York: Norton, 1964); Mark Sherwin, *The Extremists* (New York: St. Martin's Press, 1963); Brooks R. Walker, *The Christian Fright Peddlers* (Garden City, N.Y.: Doubleday, 1964); Robert A. Rosenstone, ed., *Protest from the Right* (Beverly Hills, Calif.: Glencoe Press, 1968), pp. 70–99, 110–29; Lionel Lokos, *Hysteria 1964: The Fear Campaign Against Barry Goldwater* (New Rochelle, N.Y.: Arlington House, 1967), pp. 129, 150, 153.

8. Miles, *Odyssey of American Right*, chap. 17.

9. Frady, *Billy Graham*, pp. 410–11, 422–37; Cushing Strout, *The New Heavens and New Earth: Political Religion in America* (New York: Harper Torchbooks, 1975), pp. 300–12; William G. McLoughlin, *Revivals, Awakenings, and Reform: An Essay on Religion and Social Change in America, 1607–1977* (Chicago: University of Chicago Press, 1978), pp. 193–211; Donald W. Dayton, *Discovering the Evangelical Heritage* (New York: Harper & Row, 1976), pp. 1–4, 127–41; Lowell D. Streiker and Gerald S. Strober, *Religion and the New Majority: Billy Graham, Middle America, and the Politics of the 70s* (New York: Association Press, 1972), chap. 2.

10. Erling Jorstad, *That New-Time Religion: The Jesus Revival in America* (Minneapolis: Augusburg, 1972), pp. 61–92; Dean M. Kelley, *Why Conservative Churches Are Growing: A Study in the Sociology of Religion* (New York: Harper & Row, 1962); Hal Lindsey, with C. C. Carlson, *The Late Great Planet Earth* (New York: Bantam Books, 1977); *Washington Post*, 26 Jan., 22 Nov. 1977.

11. William Lee Miller, *Yankee from Georgia: The Emergence of Jimmy Carter* (New York: *Times* Books, 1978), pp. 169–240; *New York Post*, 16 Oct.

1976; Hal Lindsey, *There's a New World Coming: A Prophetic Odyssey* (Santa Ana, Calif.: Vision House, 1973), p. 183.

12. Richard A. Viguerie, *The New Right: We're Ready to Lead* (Falls Church, Va.: Viguerie, 1981), pp. 12, 6–8, 51–59, 123–35; Hargis, *Why I Fight,* p. 113; Erling Jorstad, *The Politics of Moralism: The New Christian Right in American Life* (Minneapolis: Augsburg, 1981), pp. 27–68; Jorstad, *Politics of Doomsday,* p. 116; Allen Hunter, "In the Wings: New Right Ideology and Organization," *Radical America* 15 (Spring 1981): 115–27; Jeffrey K. Hadden and Charles E. Swann, *Prime Time Preachers: The Rising Power of Televangelism* (Reading, Mass.: Addison-Wesley, 1981), chap. 7; *Washington Post,* 5 Nov. 1980; A Bartlett Giamatti, "A Liberal Education and the New Coercion," *Yale Alumni Magazine and Journal* 45 (Oct. 1981): 27–30.

13. Frances FitzGerald, "A Disciplined, Charging Army," *New Yorker* 56 (18 May 1981): 80–82; Jerry Strober and Ruth Tomczak, *Jerry Falwell: Aflame for God* (Nashville: Nelson, 1979), pp. 20–32; "An Interview with the Lone Ranger of American Fundamentalism," *Christianity Today* 25 (4 Sept. 1981): 24.

14. Jerry Falwell, with Ed Dobson and Ed Henson, *The Fundamentalist Phenomenon: The Resurgence of Conservative Christianity* (Garden City, N.Y.: Doubleday, 1981), pp. 210–20, 224, 231, 136; "Jerry Falwell Comments," *Fundamentalist Journal* 1 (Oct. 1982): 6–7; FitzGerald, "Charging Army," pp. 62–63, 113; "Lone Ranger of Fundamentalism," p. 23; William R. Goodman and James T. H. Price, *Jerry Falwell: An Unauthorized Profile* (Lynchburg, Va.: Paris and Assoc., 1981), pp. 119–21.

15. Falwell, *Fundamentalist Phenomenon,* pp. 187, 218; "Charging Army," pp. 114, 122–24.

16. Falwell, *Fundamentalist Phenomenon,* p. 217; Jerry Falwell, *Listen, America!* (New York: Bantam Books, 1981), pp. 84, 61, 66, 44, 46, 82, 104–6, 200, 174, 143, 158–59; "Lone Ranger of Fundamentalism," p. 24; Jere Real, "What Jerry Falwell *Really* Wants," *Inquiry* 4 (3 and 24 Aug. 1981): 17.

17. Viguerie, *New Right,* p. 159; William Martin, "God's Angry Man," *Texas Monthly* 9 (April 1981): 223–24; FitzGerald, "Charging Army," p. 118; Falwell, *Fundamentalist Phenomenon,* pp. 231, 206; Falwell, *Listen, America,* p. 178; *Washington Post,* 3 June, 25 Sept. 1982; "Lone Ranger of Fundamentalism," p. 25.

18. "Lone Ranger of Fundamentalism," pp. 23–24; Falwell, *Listen, America,* pp. 131, 212–23; Falwell, *Fundamentalist Phenomenon,* pp. 160, 167, 182, 213–23.

19. Falwell, *Fundamentalist Phenomenon,* p. 215; Falwell, *Listen, America,* pp. 97–98; *New York Times,* 12 Sept. 1981.

20. Jerry Falwell, *Armageddon and the Coming War with Russia* ([Lynchburg, Va.: n.p., 1981]), pp. 18–36; Falwell, *Listen, America,* pp. 97–98; *New York Times,* 12 Sept. 1981; *Washington Post,* 9 Oct. 1982; Yona Malachy, *American Fundamentalism and Israel: The Relation of Fundamentalist Churches to Zionism and the State of Israel* (Jerusalem: Institute of Contemporary History, 1978), pp. 146–61.

21. FitzGerald, "Charging Army," p. 133; Falwell, *Listen, America*, pp. 53, 98; *Washington Post*, 13 Oct. 1980; *Washington Star*, 22 Nov. 1980; *New York Times*, 26 Nov. 1980.

22. FitzGerald, "Charging Army," pp. 89–90, 96; "Lone Ranger of Fundamentalism," pp. 22–23; Hadden and Swann, *Prime Time Preachers*, pp. 50–52; *Washington Post*, 28 June 1981; *New York Times* , 10 Dec. 1981; Falwell circular letter to author, 24 Dec. 1981.

23. "Lone Ranger of Fundamentalism," pp. 22–23; Goodman and Price, *Jerry Falwell*, pp. 152, 11–12, 133, 91; Real, "What Falwell Wants," p. 17; Ben Stein, "The War to Clean Up TV," *Saturday Review* 8 (Feb. 1981): 23–28; Donahue Transcript no. 10200 (Cincinnati: Multimedia Program Productions, 1982), pp. 1, 3; *New York Village Voice*, 19–25 Nov. 1980; *Washington Post*, 26 Jan. 1981.

24. FitzGerald, "Charging Army," p. 135; *Washington Post*, 3 Feb. 1981.

25. Jorstad, *Politics of Moralism*, p. 95.

26. Ibid., pp. 93–94; *Washington Post*, 19 Nov. 1980, 8, 9 July, 16 Sept. 1981, 22 Jan., 28 July, 28 Sept. 1982; *Washington Star*, 11 July 1981; Albert J. Menendez, "Religion at the Polls, 1980" *Church and State* 33 (Dec. 1980): 15–18.

27. *Washington Post*, 25, 28 Sept. 1982; *New York Times*, 25 Oct. 1982; Falwell circular letter to Dear Friend, 1 Oct. 1982.

28. *Washington Post*, 22 Sept. 1982; Lipset and Raab, "Election and Evangelicals," pp. 25–31; Peter Steinfels, *The Neoconservatives: The Men Who Are Changing America's Politics* (New York: Simon & Schuster, 1979).

29. *Washington Post*, 21 Oct. 1980, 25 July 1981, 5 Oct. 1982; *New York Times*, 25 Sept. 1980; *Washington Star*, 24 Sept. 1980; Kurt Vonnegut undated circular letter to Dear ACLU Member; Karen Mulhauser undated circular letter to Dear Friend; Julian Bond undated circular letter to Dear Friend; George McGovern undated circular letter to Dear Friend; L. J. Davis, "Conservatism in America," *Harper's* 261 (Oct. 1980): 22; Flo Conway and Jim Siegelman, *Holy Terror: The Fundamentalist War on America's Freedoms in Religion, Politics and Our Private Lives* (Garden City, N.Y.: Doubleday, 1982); Perry Deane Young, *God's Bullies: Native Reflections on Preachers and Politics* (New York: Holt, Rinehart & Winston, 1982); Daniel C. Maguire, *The New Subversives: Anti-Americanism of the Religious Right* (New York: Continuum, 1982); Jerry Falwell, "'Holy Terror' Is Wholly Error," *Fundamentalist Journal* 1 (Dec. 1982): 8–10.

30. James M. Wall, "God's Piece of Cheese," *Christian Century* 97 (27 Feb. 1980): 219; Martin E. Marty, "Inside the Second Coming Cocoon," *Christian Century* 97 (7 May 1980): 535, and "Precursors of the Moral Majority," *American Heritage* 33 (Feb.-March 1982): 98–99; Goodman and Price, *Jerry Falwell*, pp. 64–65; Peggy L. Shriver, "Conflict in the Christian Family: Can You Listen to Your Relatives?" *Christianity and Crisis* 41 (5 Oct. 1981): 264–66; Carl F. H. Henry, "The Fundamentalist Phenomenon: The Ricochet of Silver Bullets," *Christianity Today* 25 (4 Sept. 1981): 30–31; George G. Higgins, "The Prolife Movement and the New Right," *America*

143 (13 Sept. 1980): 107–10; *Washington Post,* 7 Oct. 1981; *Washington Post,* 1 Feb. 1981.

31. Conway and Siegelman, *Holy Terror,* pp. 74, 199, 276, 41; Young, *God's Bullies,* pp. 107, 59, 157, 267; Maguire, *New Subversives,* pp. 114, 10, 21, 27; Thomas J. McIntyre, with John C. Obert, *The Fear Brokers* (Boston: Beacon Press, 1979), pp. 13, 155, 88, 330–32; David Bollier, *Liberty and Justice for Some: Defending a Free Society from the Radical Right's Holy War on Democracy* (Washington, D.C.: People for the American Way, 1982), p. 49; Alan Crawford, *Thunder on the Right: The "New Right" and the Politics of Resentment* (New York: Pantheon Books, 1980), pp. 30, 165–66 290–308, 114–15; Gloria Steinem, "The Nazi Connection: If Hitler Were Alive, Whose Side Would He Be On?" *MS* 9 (Oct. 1980): 88–90, and "The Nazi Connection: Authoritarianism Begins at Home," *MS* 9 (Nov. 1980): 14–15, 20–24.

32. William E. Ellis, "Evolution, Fundamentalism, and the Historians: An Historiographical Review," *Historian* 44 (Nov. 1981): 25–30; Milton Rokeach et al., *The Open and Closed Mind: Investigations Into the Nature of Belief Systems and Personality Systems* (New York: Basic Books, 1960); Alan C. Elms, "Psychological Factors in Right-Wing Extremism," in Robert A. Schoenberger, ed., *The American Right Wing: Readings in Political Behavior* (New York: Holt, Rinehart & Winston, 1969), pp. 143–63.

33. Young, *God's Bullies,* p. 21; Conway and Siegelman, *Holy Terror,* p. 107; Crawford, *Thunder on the Right,* pp. 299–302; McIntyre, *Fear Brokers,* pp. xxi, xviii, 51–52, 108, 331.

34. *New York Times,* 25 Sept. 1980; *Washington Post,* 13 Oct. 1982; Dean M. Kelley, "How Much Freedom of Speech Is Allowed to the Churches?" *Christianity and Crisis* 41 (5 Oct. 1981): 260–64; Conway and Siegelman, *Holy Terror,* pp. 41, 341–42; Aryeh Neier, *Defending My Enemy: American Nazis, the Skokie Case, and the Risks of Freedom* (New York: Dutton, 1979), pp. 15, 30–31.

35. *Washington Post,* 4 Nov. 1982; *New York Times,* 1, 4 Nov. 1982; Morton Kondracke, "Hard Times for the Hard Right," *New Republic* 187 (20 Dec. 1982): 20–23.

36. *Washington Post,* 10 Dec. 1982; Kevin P. Phillips, *Post-Conservative America: People, Politics and Ideology in a Time of Crisis* (New York: Random House, 1982), pp. xiii, xx.

37. *Arkansas Gazette,* 10 Jan. 1982; Neier, *Defending My Enemy,* p. 79; David Hamlin, *The Nazi/Skokie Conflict: A Civil Liberties Battle* (Boston: Beacon Press, 1980), pp. 135–49, 158–60. Donald A. Gianella, "Religious Liberty, Nonestablishment, and Doctrinal Development: The Religious Liberty Guarantee," *Harvard Law Review* 80 (May 1967): 1381–1431 and "Religious Liberty, Nonestablishment, and Doctrinal Development: The Nonestablishment Principle," *Harvard Law Review* 81 (Jan. 1968): 513–90.

38. Neier, *Defending My Enemy,* pp. 119–22.

39. Walter F. Berns, *Freedom, Virtue and the First Amendment* (Chicago: Regnery, 1965); Herbert Marcuse, "Repressive Tolerance," in Robert Paul

Wolff et al., *A Critique of Pure Tolerance* (Boston: Beacon Press, 1970), pp. 81–123; Hadley Arkes, "Marching Through Skokie," *National Review* 30 (12 May 1978): 588–93.

40. Young, *God's Bullies*, pp. 139–53; *Washington Post* 30 (Oct. 1982); "Life and Liberty . . . for All Who Believe," WTTG-TV, Washington, D.C., 30 Oct. 1982.

41. Lipset and Raab, "Election and Evangelicals, p. 31; "Lone Ranger of Fundamentalism," p. 23; Jerry Falwell, *Listen, America*, pp. 61–67.

42. Leo P. Ribuffo, "Monkey Trials, Past and Present," *Dissent* 28 (Summer 1981): 358–61; Charles Y. Glock and Rodney Stark, *Christian Beliefs and Anti-Semitism* (New York: Harper Torchbooks, 1966), p. 209.

Index